asis

Volume
14
1979

Annual Review of
Information Science
and Technology

MARTHA E. WILLIAMS, Editor

Published by

KNOWLEDGE INDUSTRY PUBLICATIONS, INC.
for
AMERICAN SOCIETY FOR INFORMATION SCIENCE

ISSN: 0066-4200
CODEN: ARISBc

Knowledge Industry Publications, Inc.
2 Corporate Park Drive
White Plains, New York 10604

LC Catalog Card Number: 66-25096
ISBN: 0-914236-44-X
ISSN: 0066-4200
CODEN: ARISBc
Printed in the United States of America

ASIS Publications Staff

Linda (O'Brien) Holder, Graphic Compositor

Contents

Preface   v
Acknowledgments   vii
Advisory Committee for *ARIST*   ix
Contributors   xi
Chapter Reviewers   xiii

I
Planning Information Systems and Services   1

1   **System Design—Principles and Techniques**
Ronald E. Wyllys
3

2   **Cost Analysis of Systems and Services**
Colin K. Mick
37

II
Basic Techniques and Tools
65

3   **Empirical Foundations of Information Science**
Pranas Zunde and John Gehl
67

4   **Experimental Techniques of Information Retrieval**
Michael J. McGill and Jennifer Huitfeldt
93

5   **Unconventional Computer Architectures for Information Retrieval**
Lee A. Hollaar
129

6   **Database Management Systems**
Michael A. Huffenberger and Ronald L. Wigington
153

III
Applications
191

7   **Library Automation**
Mary Jane Pobst Reed and Hugh T. Vrooman
193

IV
The Profession 217

8 **Education and Training for Online Systems**
Judith Wanger 219

V
Special Topics 247

9 **Information Systems in Latin America**
Tefko Saracevic, Gilda Braga and Alvaro Quijano Solis 249

Introduction to Index 283

Index 285

Introduction to KWOC Index 333

KWOC Index of *ARIST* Titles for Volumes 1-14 335

Preface

This is the 14th volume of the *Annual Review of Information Science and Technology* (*ARIST*) produced by the American Society for Information Science (ASIS). ASIS (formerly American Documentation Institute) initiated the series in 1966 with the publication of Volume 1. ASIS is the owner of *ARIST*, maintains the editorial control, and has the sole rights to the series.

Through the years several organizations have been responsible for publishing and marketing *ARIST*. Volumes 1 and 2 were published by Interscience Publishers, a division of John Wiley & Sons. Volumes 3 through 6 were published by Encyclopaedia Britannica, Inc. Volumes 7 through 11 were published by ASIS itself and with Volume 12 Knowledge Industry Publications, Inc. assumed the role of publisher for *ARIST*.

Purpose. The purpose of *ARIST* is to describe and appraise the publications and trends in the field of information science and technology. Comprehensive coverage of the field is provided each year through the basic core material and various aspects of this many-faceted field are emphasized in individual volumes. *ARIST* provides an annual review of literature. One volume is produced each year. A master plan for the series encompasses the entire field in all its aspects and topics for a given volume are selected from the plan on the basis of timeliness and an assessment of reader interest. If a chapter topic has not appeared for several years the chapter author generally covers the significant material published in the intervening years. Thus, the time period covered in a given chapter may be one year or several years.

References cited in text and bibliography. The format for referring to bibliographic citations within the text involves use of the cited author's name instead of reference numbers. The cited author's surname is printed in upper case letters. The reader, wishing to find the bibliographic references, can readily locate the appropriate reference in the bibliography (alphabetically arranged by first author's last name); the author's last name again appears in upper case letters in the text. A single author appears as SMITH; coauthors as SMITH & JONES; and multiple authors as SMITH ET AL. If multiple papers by the same author are cited, the distinction is made by indicating the year of publication after the last name (e.g., SMITH, 1975), and if a further distinction is required, for multiple papers within the same year, a lower case alpha character follows the year (e.g., SMITH, 1975a). Except for the fact that all authors in multi-authored papers are included in bibliographic references, the same basic conventions are used in the chapter bibliographies. Thus, the reader can easily locate in the bibliography any references discussed in the text.

Because of the emphasis placed on the requirement for chapter authors to discuss the key papers and significant developments reported in the literature, and because *ARIST* readers have expressed their liking for comprehensive bibliographies associated with the chapters, there are more references listed in the bibliographies than are discussed in the text.

The format used for references in the bibliographies is based on the *American National Standard for Bibliographic References*, ANSI Z39.29. We have followed the ANSI guidelines with respect to the sequence of bibliographic data elements and the punctuation used to separate the elements. Adoption of this convention should facilitate conversion of the references to machine-readable form as need arises. Journal article references follow the ANSI guide as closely as possible. Conference papers and microform publications follow an *ARIST* adaptation of the format.

Structure of the volume. In accordance with the *ARIST* master plan, this volume's nine chapters fit within the basic framework: I. Planning Information Systems and Services; II. Basic Techniques and Tools; III. Applications; IV. The Profession; V. Special Topics. Chapter titles are provided in the Table of Contents and an Introduction to each section highlights the events, trends and evaluations given by the chapter authors. An Index to the entire volume is provided to help the user locate material relevant to the subject content, authors, and organizations cited in the book. An explanation of the guidelines employed in the Index is provided in the Introduction to the Index.

Acknowledgments. Appreciation should be expressed to many individuals and organizations for their roles in creation of this volume. First and foremost are the authors of the individual chapters who have generously contributed their time and efforts in searching, reviewing and evaluating the large body of literature upon which their chapters are based. The *ARIST* Advisory Committee Members and *ARIST* Reviewers provided valuable feedback and constructive criticism of the content. Major contributions toward the production of this publication were made by Mary W. Rakow, Copy Editor; Elaine Tisch Dunatov, Bibliographic Editor; and Laurence Lannom, Index Editor. Appreciation is expressed to all of the members of the *ARIST* technical support staff who are listed on the Acknowledgments page.

Martha E. Williams

Acknowledgments

The American Society for Information Science and the Editor wish to acknowledge the contributions of the three principals on the editorial staff and the technical support staff.

Elaine Tisch Dunatov, Bibliographic Editor

Laurence Lannom, Index Editor

Mary W. Rakow, Copy Editor

Technical Support Staff

Scott E. Preece, Technical Advisor
Dorothy Saxner, Technical Advisor
Laurel P. Preece, Proofreader and Data Input Technician
Margery Johnson, Editorial Assistant
Jill Edwards, Secretary

Advisory Committee for *ARIST*

Margaret T. Fischer

Charles M. Goldstein

Glynn Harmon

Laurence B. Heilprin

Donald W. King

Howard L. Resnikoff

Harold Wooster

Contributors

GILDA MARIA BRAGA
Instituto Brasileiro de
Informação em Ciência e
Technologia
Av. General Justo 171
40 Rio de Janeiro, BRAZIL

JOHN GEHL
School of Information and
Computer Science
Georgia Institute of Technology
Atlanta, Georgia 30332

LEE A. HOLLAAR
Computing Services Office
193 DCL
University of Illinois
Urbana, Illinois 61801

MICHAEL A. HUFFENBERGER
Chemical Abstracts Service
P.O. Box 3012
Columbus, Ohio 43210

JENNIFER HUITFELDT
School of Information Studies
113 Euclid Avenue
Syracuse University
Syracuse, New York 13210

MICHAEL J. MCGILL
School of Information Studies
113 Euclid Avenue
Syracuse University
Syracuse, New York 13210

COLIN K. MICK
Applied Communication Research, Inc.
P.O. Box 5849
Stanford, California 94305

ALVARO QUIJANO SOLIS
Biblioteca Daniel Cosio Villegos
El Colegio de México
Camino A1 Ajusco No. 20
Apartado Postal 20-671
Mexico 20, DF, MEXICO

MARY JANE POBST REED
Associate Director for Research
and Planning
Washington State Library
Olympia, Washington 98504

TEFKO SARACEVIC
School of Library Science
Case Western Reserve University
Cleveland, Ohio 44106

HUGH T. VROOMAN
Illinois State Library
Centennial Building
Springfield, Illinois 62706

JUDITH WANGER
Cuadra Associates, Inc.
1523 6th Street
Suite 12
Santa Monica, California 90401

RONALD L. WIGINGTON
Chemical Abstracts Service
P.O. Box 3012
Columbus, Ohio 43210

RONALD E. WYLLYS
Graduate School of Library Science
University of Texas at Austin
Austin, Texas 78712

PRANAS ZUNDE
School of Information and
Computer Science
Georgia Institute of Technology
Atlanta, Georgia 30332

Chapter Reviewers

Henriette D. Avram

Wesley T. Brandhorst

Walter Carlson

Carlos A. Cuadra

Margaret T. Fischer

Stephen E. Furth

Charles M. Goldstein

Glynn Harmon

Laurence B. Heilprin

Frederick G. Kilgour

Donald W. King

Joseph H. Kuney

Herbert B. Landau

Susan K. Martin

Thomas H. Martin

Richard H. Orr

Edwin B. Parker

Howard L. Resnikoff

Gerard Salton

Roger K. Summit

Herbert S. White

Harold Wooster

I

Planning Information Systems and Services

The two chapters in this section deal with "System Design—Principles and Techniques" and "Cost Analysis of Systems and Services." Ronald E. Wyllys of the University of Texas reviews system design, and Colin Mick of Applied Communication Research reviews cost analysis.

In his chapter, Wyllys reviews materials that deal with the design of systems for handling information. He begins by outlining a background for system design in general systems theory and then presents a structure for system design, embedding it within a system-development cycle. This cycle consists of the following phases: analysis, design, production, implementation, and operation. He views system analysis as intertwined with system design and stresses the iterative nature of the whole system-development cycle.

Techniques for system design are discussed under the headings of Cost Analysis, Flowcharting, Job Description and Analysis, Operations Research and Analysis, and Simulation.

Colin Mick's chapter focuses on the analysis process rather than on costs per se. It covers the literature roughly from 1975 to 1979. Cost analysis is discussed on four levels. The first deals with the cost analysis of individual functions or services, such as acquisitions, cataloging, or online searching. The second level is concerned with cost analysis across an entire information organization (e.g., a library). The third level concerns libraries or information services that operate under the umbrella of a larger organizational structure, such as a university, a city, or a company. The fourth level considers cost analysis that compares information services across structures—for example, in different companies, cities, or universities.

The literature shows an array of costing methodologies with varying levels of sophistication. Mick finds that there is no lack of methodologies but rather an unwillingness or inability to develop a common framework for applying them so that the results can be either generalized or compared across studies.

Mick notes that by and large little cost analysis has been done to assess the utility of emerging technologies, which are already having significant impact on the information community. In general, studies of new technologies seem to focus on problems (and/or benefits) of implementation and often fail to assess either the costs of operations to be automated (or changed or replaced) or the costs of the system or technology that will replace them.

1 System Design—Principles and Techniques

RONALD E. WYLLYS
University of Texas at Austin

He, who through vast immensity can pierce,
See[s] worlds on worlds compose one universe,
Observe[s] how system into system runs,
What other planets circle other suns. . . .

Alexander Pope, *An Essay on Man.*

INTRODUCTION

This chapter discusses the principles and techniques that are used to design systems for handling information. Although the emphasis is on the literature during 1975-1978, important earlier materials are also treated since the approach here is somewhat different from that in previous *ARIST* reviews of system design (BORKO; CLEVERDON; DEBONS & MONTGOMERY; KATTER; KING; LANCASTER & GILLESPIE; SWANSON). If one judges by frequency, design seems to be one of the topics covered best in the *ARIST* volumes.

This review begins by seeking a foundation for system design in general systems theory. It then places system design in the context of the system development cycle. Finally, techniques of system analysis and design are treated in the sections on Cost Analysis, Job Description and Analysis, Flowcharting, Operations Research and Analysis, and Simulation.

General Systems Theory

What is a system? *Webster's Third New International Dictionary* contains several dozen definitions, the first being, "A complex unity formed of many often diverse parts subject to a common plan or serving a common purpose."

In this definition the word "complex" deserves special notice. Indeed, one definition that is widely and by no means facetiously used among systems people is that a "system is a group of things that operates at a level of complexity higher than the highest level that we think we understand." On the other hand, sometimes the complexity one finds is the result of one's having noted too many scattered data instead of the right number of pertinent data.

The object of a system design effort is to define a grouping of diverse parts that will accomplish at least one purpose. In information systems, the parts are usually people, machines, procedures, and records; the purpose(s), typically to accomplish one or more of the tasks of acquiring, processing, storing, retrieving, and disseminating information.

A Foundation. One would expect that the ideas of system design could be derived from a theoretical foundation in "systems science" or "general system theory." In a book bearing the latter name (which the author claims to have originated), VON BERTALANFFY introduces this theory, treating its history, basic concepts, and applications in physical and biological systems. He defines his subject matter as the "formulation of principles that are valid for 'systems' in general, whatever the nature of their component elements and the relations or 'forces' between them." Pointing out that "concepts like those of organization, wholeness, directiveness, teleology, and differentiation are alien" to some sciences and difficult to define in others, he argues that general systems theory should and can provide exact definitions for them and, in suitable cases, it can analyze them quantitatively. A text in "general systems thinking" by WEINBERG gives an elementary and extremely readable introduction to general systems theory.

Living Systems. The usual meaning of information system includes living organisms—humans—only as part of a system of otherwise inanimate objects. However, in a very important sense all living organisms are systems that must process information about their environments or cease to live. Although almost all the information systems that *Living Systems* (MILLER) treats are those of live organisms, this book is so ambitious and such an important snythesis of systems concepts that it merits mention here. Miller applies ideas of systems theory to life and shows how a view of living organisms as systems that process energy and information supplies a relatively new, enlightening way to study them. Beginning at the level of the cell and moving through those of the organ and the organism to the level of systems that comprise more than one individual. Miller ends by discussing all of human society as a system. Throughout the book, he shows how system-theoretic concepts can illuminate the workings of any system. The result is a fascinating synthesis of biological activities that extends to psychological and sociological systems. STUDER discusses biological information systems in a similar manner.

Systems Theory and System Design

What can one learn from systems theory about system design? Much of the effort of workers such as Von Bertalanffy and J.G. Miller has been on systems analysis rather than design. Their work analyzes, at a rather high level, common features of an impressively wide array of systems.

The features of systems that general systems theory finds important are: the transmission of information, both directly and as feedback; similarities in functional groupings within different levels of organization; the tendency for systems, if they do attain equilibrium, to attain it dynamically rather than statically; and the presence of qualities such as adaptiveness and purposiveness. By implication, system designers should pay attention to these features. Other links between systems theory and design are more obscure. Most current practice in system design is still empirical, thus leaving a gap that system theorists, analysts, and designers should work to fill.

One might expect a review of system design principles to cite papers reporting on such efforts. Unfortunately, most accounts of system analysis and design are too specific to provide much general guidance. Hence, no effort was made to collect examples *per se.*

THE SYSTEM DEVELOPMENT CYCLE

What is known empirically about system design? First, it occurs as part of what is usually called the overall system development cycle. In discussing this cycle most writers distinguish five or more phases, beginning with an existing system to be analyzed and culminating in a new system that in turn may lead to the beginning of another new cycle. For example, ROSOVE (1967a) calls the phases: requirements, design, production, installation, and operation; HAYES & BECKER include a preliminary phase—feasibility—and follow it with specification, design, programming, test, implementation, and maintenance; HICE ET AL., concentrating on data-processing system development, call their phases: definition, preliminary design, detail design, program and human job development, testing, data conversion and system implementation, and system operation and maintenance. Here the phases will be called: analysis, design, production, implementation, and operation. These phases span an ongoing process that ordinarily, but not necessarily, begins with the analysis of an existing system for which a modification or improvement is proposed in the form of a new system. (Because of the iterativeness of most system development, KATTER speaks of the system "*re*development" cycle.) An interesting historical survey of system analysis techniques, together with a bibliography, is provided by COUGER.

The Phases of System Development

The analysis phase identifies the desired functions of the new system. In an article urging librarians to utilize system analysis, FASANA says that this body of techniques and doctrine is:

> concerned with systematically analyzing a total system in context and in identifying and describing the interrelatedness of all the

> component parts of operations of the overall system. [It deals not with a] single operation or a narrowly focussed set of operations, but [with] the system as a whole relative to the stated objectives and [constraints] of the parent organization.

When (as is usual) an antecedent system exists, an analysis of its functions can be expected to yield a better understanding of what is really being done and what this implies for the proposed system. This analysis often produces surprises.

The design phase follows the analysis phase, although the two phases can overlap. In the second phase the system design team (one-person design efforts are possible but less desirable) considers how the functions that are required in the proposed system could be carried out. This process of thinking is the essence of the design process. MINDER calls design "the inverse of analysis" and outlines design principles by saying:

> Whereas the analysis activity is an attempt to determine how an operation now works, design is the attempt to create the best possible operation from both existing and new pieces. Whereas analysis tends to be a straightforward dissection activity with little feedback or interaction between parts, design is very much a cybernetic activity.

The next phases in the system-development cycle—production, implementation, and operation—can be sketched briefly (BLACK gives a sample plan for these phases). In the production phase, the design is translated into reality. This process usually includes acquiring equipment, preparing programs for computers, and writing sets of procedures for people (WENDER). As these various components come into existence, they are tested and put into operation.

As sub-systems of the overall new system begin to evolve from the completed components, the cycle moves into the implementation phase. This phase concludes when each sub-system has been completed, tested, installed, and found to be acceptable and when those who will operate the system have been trained. There is usually a formal step of transferring responsibility from the organization that has been handling the system development to the organization that will operate the system in its completed, functional form.

The operational phase is considered by system theorists to belong to the cycle since here evaluation of the system continues, often leading to further improvements.

Legal and other purely administrative aspects of system development have received little attention in the literature. The proceedings edited by DIVIL-BISS (1978) help to fill this gap. They concentrate mostly on negotiation, with examples that can be used in role playing; they include a paper on contracts by DYER; and altogether they constitute a valuable survey of administrative aspects of system development.

SYSTEM ANALYSIS AS A PRELUDE TO SYSTEM DESIGN

In the analysis phase, the system design team begins by defining the over-all purpose of the existing system and of the desired changes. (In rare cases no antecedent system exists; in such a case, the system design process is simplified. However, this discussion assumes that an antecedent system does exist and hence omits qualifiers such as "existing and/or proposed systems.")

Once the purpose is defined, the system design team details the existing and desired capabilities, which should be formalized into statements of the requirements. In her brief and very readable introduction to the analysis of systems for information retrieval, TOWNLEY suggests that this process is "best tackled by creating a hierarchical listing of the requirements"; broad requirements should be refined into detailed statements by reviewing such matters as the "circumstances in which and frequency with which" the requirement arises, "the demand which it satisfies," "the records [that] must be maintained," the decisions that must be made, and the reports that must be generated to fulfill the requirement.

The determination of requirements for library systems is discussed by COREY & BELLOMY in some detail. CHAPMAN ET AL., as part of their text on systems analysis in libraries, devote special attention to the importance of distinguishing between requirements and demands. Requirements are those functions that are consonant with the purposes of the system and that the system therefore should perform. Although some demands may, after study, turn out to be requirements, "demand" usually connotes the performance of unnecessary or undesirable functions which, if added to the system, would degrade its performance of its primary purposes. For example, one might argue on the grounds of cost that some of the functions that LANCASTER (1978a; 1978b) suggests for his "electronic information system for the year 2000" represent demands rather than "realistic" requirements. A similar comment applies to the discussion by CAWKELL (1978b) of paperless information systems.

The identification of system requirements is accompanied by considerations of various constraints on the new system. Constraints typically include: cost; schedule (when the new system must be put into operation); state-of-the-art (limitations of currently or prospectively available equipment and software); system history (analysis of how the system came to have its present functions and modes of operation, which often clarifies the reason certain things are being done in the system); system context (the boundaries of the system and the aspects of the environment with which it must interface); and the present and proposed organizational structures pertinent to the system. ROSOVE (1967b) gives some examples of system constraints from a variety of fields. MILLER reviews constraints that stem from sources internal and external to an organization and considers how these constraints limit the possible designs of systems through which the organization can solve its problems.

This kind of careful and integrated analysis should eventually lead to a formal statement of what the new system is to do, often called the requirements analysis document. The system design team and the organization that will use the system—the sponsor—should formally acknowledge this statement as a detailed explanation of the requirements of the new system. This "concurrence" step marks the end of the analysis phase and the start of the design phase.

PRINCIPLES OF SYSTEM DESIGN

When the analysis phase has produced the requirements analysis document or some other form of report, the system design team can carry out its eponymous function. The first step is to generate a preliminary design concept—i.e., how to construct a system that will fulfill the requirements. Here it is especially important to use the creative and imaginative thinking that CHURCHMAN calls for in his now classic text, *The Systems Approach*. This work still constitutes one of the best introductions to the central theme of system analysis and design: thinking "about whole systems" and in terms of the functions that a system is to perform rather than its structure.

GILDERSLEEVE and LUCAS also present well-argued appeals for innovative solutions to system problems and suggest some ways to heighten one's creative thinking. GILCHRIST warns designers to include in their thinking the possibility of catastrophes. ZIMMERMAN offers three models for design, which she calls the "microanalytic, macroanalytic, and esoteric," and evaluates their underlying principles. KRAKOWIAK suggests that the intellectual techniques of the system designer are: "decomposition of a complex object into more manageable parts"; "abstraction" that retains "relevant properties and omits irrelevant ones"; "refinement" of simple objects into more complicated ones; and, last but by no means least, "iteration." HANSEN ET AL. survey several decision-oriented concepts of design and relate them to the design of information systems.

The next and major part of the design phase can be divided into four areas: 1) internal design, 2) environmental interface design, 3) component design, and 4) system-test design. Internal design concerns those parts of the system that will be solely controlled by the organization operating the system. Typical considerations are the allocation of functions between people and machines and the definition of flow of information and materials.

Environmental interface design deals with those parts of the system that are not under the control of the operating organization. The principal concern is how to define the interfaces—i.e., how to deal with the flow of information into the system from external sources and vice-versa. Typically this involves agreement on computer formats, document formats, materials standards, etc.

Component design deals with how the functions, equipment, and procedures of the system are to be grouped into sub-systems—e.g., groupings of people, equipment, procedures, and records.

System-test design concerns the evaluation of system performance and procedures for carrying out appropriate tests during the production and implementation phases. Although her focus is computer systems, SCHARER's discussion of system testing is also useful for system-test design in general.

Each of these four areas furnishes data for the others. The final result is the completed design of the new system. The design phase should conclude with a formal document that presents the final design. Again both the system design team and the sponsor should formally acknowledge their acceptance of this document.

TECHNIQUES OF SYSTEM ANALYSIS AND DESIGN

It would be difficult (and pointless) to try to separate the techniques of system analysis from those of system design; thus, in the following discussion these two terms are used together.

To carry out the various steps in designing a system, the system design team must use various tools. One of the arguments for team design efforts is that so many tools are needed that few people can master them all. An ideal analyst-designer would be skilled in computer programming, statistics, operations research, accounting, and personnel management. This person would also be very intelligent, mathematically skilled, articulate, have a photographic and phonographic memory, be able to analyze amorphous situations incisively, and be able to work well with many different kinds of people. (To this last point FEENEY & SLADEK and KEEN & GERSON direct some helpful comments on how a system analyst-designer works with managers in the sponsoring organization. BOLAND discusses the user's participation in the design process, the designer's typical reluctance to involve the user sufficiently, and how designer and user might be encouraged to cooperate more.) Because persons with all these skills and qualities are rare, teams are usually organized to provide the necessary combination.

Teams would be desirable in any case, simply to provide synergism. CHAPMAN mentions that even for a system study in a "relatively small library," it is important to have a team of at least two people "to furnish mutual stimulus"; in managing such a study he notes that "the guidance, direction and personal participation of the chief executive of the [sponsoring organization] are critical" to the success of the effort.

The techniques of system analysis and design are drawn principally from the areas and skills just mentioned, although potentially useful tools can come from any field. Among the helpful introductions to system analysis and design tools in general is an issue of *Library Trends* (edited by LANCASTER, 1973) in which such tools and the system approach itself are discussed in terms of libraries. A broad survey of the techniques can be found in a text by BOCCHINO. Another survey, by FITZGERALD & FITZGERALD, offers the reader sets of problems written as case studies, many of which are good stimuli to the thinking of an analyst-designer trainee. The book by KIRK, which pays more attention than most to human aspects of system analysis and design, remains useful. One of the most recent system analysis-design texts is chapter 8 in the handbook by LORD & STEINER; although it emphasizes analysis and design for data processing, this chapter provides good general coverage of the field. SAMUELSON ET AL. offer concise guidelines for designing information systems, with emphasis on the needs of designers in developing countries and on the role of networks.

The remainder of this chapter discusses various major tools used in system analysis and design. The order of treatment, necessarily arbitrary, is alphabetical.

Cost Analysis

Costs have, of course, been treated frequently over the years in the *ARIST* series. However, only in recent years have whole chapters in *ARIST* been devoted to costs in contrast to the halcyon days of the 1960s. H.S. WHITE (1976; 1977) compares attitudes toward costs in the 1960s and 1970s. Two *ARIST* chapters have appeared under the title, "Economics of Information": that by COOPER in 1973 and that by HINDLE & RAPER in 1976.

This section is confined to sources of actual cost figures, which system designers can use for guidance, and to the ideas of cost-benefit analysis, by which designers can weigh alternative system designs. (Here "cost-benefit" means both "cost-benefit" and "cost-effectiveness," even though strict definitions would distinguish them.)

The 1974 *ARIST* report by SPENCE presents his approach to information costs as an economist. His useful insights are an interesting contrast to the usual accounting approach to cost-benefit analysis. Both approaches are treated briefly by WILSON in *ARIST* Volume 7; published in 1972, this was the first chapter in the *ARIST* series (which started in 1966) to contain the word "cost" in its title. Although titled "The Economics of Library Automation," a volume of proceedings edited by DIVILBISS (1977) also discusses costs of publication and of computer output media. Included in the book are examples of both unit costs and cost-benefit analysis.

Unit Costs. COOPER & DEWATH (1976; 1977) investigate and provide detailed costs of online bibliographic searching; LEIMKUHLER & COOPER analyze costs and benefits in terms of relative numbers of uses in branch libraries at the University of California, Berkeley. In what the author calls "a personal overview," DAMMERS reviews costs of computer-based information systems and gives a bibliography that includes the European scene.

Examples of unit costs of operations in information systems (mainly libraries) are numerous in the literature and include articles by AXFORD (1971; 1973), BUTKOVICH & BRAUDE, CAMPEY, and MORITA & GAPEN.

Costs in technical services departments are covered in a short bibliography by WEST & BAXTER and are discussed in an article by WELCH that touches also on the problems of statistics and standards. Later, Welch, now writing as TUTTLE, offers a short history of studies of library costs that highlights the lack of standards for such studies and suggests ways to develop them.

Past examples of costs must be adjusted for inflation if one wishes to apply them to current costs, and WYLLYS (1978a) explains procedures for making such adjustments. A useful study, which is relevant to costs and is independent of the effects of inflation because it emphasizes time, is that by VOOS (1965) who analyzed times for clerical activities in technical processing in libraries. This same study was later published in a condensed version (VOOS, 1966). REVILL reports on a study of some unit times measured in academic libraries in Britain.

Cost-Benefit Analysis. It is often unclear just where cost-benefit analysis ends and performance evaluation begins. The present review has tended to mention those papers that speak explicitly of benefits but has not excluded all those that lack this term. For example, two papers dealing with performance measures in school and college libraries place considerable emphasis on measures related to benefits (DANIEL; WALDHART & MARCUM); SARACEVIC ET AL. treat a performance measure that might be called the inverse of benefit, viz., user frustration. Other recent works on performance measures include those by DIVILBISS (1977), GORE, KANTOR (1976), POWELL, SCHOFIELD ET AL., SINGLETON, and G.T. WHITE. A book by LANCASTER (1977) deals extensively with evaluating the performance of libraries.

Among the earliest published efforts to deal with cost-benefit analyses in libraries is that by RAFFEL & SHISHKO; they report on their application of cost-benefit analysis to the MIT libraries. Their book discusses various techniques and is a useful exposition of such analysis for libraries and other information systems; however, the actual dollars-and-cents figures they discuss are out of date because of inflation. Other early efforts are those of JOHNSON & KING, who discuss benefits from libraries in terms of the value of time saved by faculty and students, and GODDARD, who relates library benefits to the users (in various social groups) and to their purposes, candidly suggesting that certain groups and purposes should be ranked quite low in assessments of benefits. A later example is an article by BOMMER & FORD on determining the value of a library-security system relative to its benefits. In a brief note, LINE (1975) discusses a cost-benefit analysis of the use of biochemical journals, comparing subscription costs with numbers of citations. LANCASTER (1978a) uses cost-benefit analysis in arguing that his "electronic information system for the year 2000" will be economically realistic.

A book by HAMBURG ET AL. (1974) surveys planning and decision making in libraries, beginning with how to analyze the performance of libraries in terms of benefits, among other criteria; an earlier version of one chapter in the book appeared in *Library Quarterly* (HAMBURG ET AL., 1972) and concentrated on benefit analysis in terms of units of exposure of library materials to users. In his monograph on "dynamic" information processing, SALTON discusses the difficult problem of evaluating information systems, and he provides a concise treatment of cost-benefit analysis.

The book by LANCASTER & FAYEN deals with costs and benefits in several ways; pertinent chapters discuss the evaluation of performance, the evaluation of effectiveness, human factors, and cost-performance-benefit factors. An interesting argument against depending too heavily on cost-benefit analysis is offered by RAFFEL; he believes that the more critical the library decision is, the more important it is for the decision process to incorporate political as well as technical factors.

Other recent articles on the cost-benefit analysis of information systems are those by AXELROD, ECKELS & LYDERS, ELCHESEN, GREENBERG & KRAFT, MONTGOMERY, MOSLEY, OLSEN, PIERCE & TAYLOR, REGAZZI, and ROBERTSON & HENSMAN. Finally, commenting about the effects of Proposition 13 on California libraries, BLAKE gives an alarming view of the possible financial future of public information systems.

Flowcharting

In a typical system analysis and design effort, flowcharting is an indispensable tool. Best used in iterative interaction with the also indispensable tool of prose description, flowcharts lucidly and explicitly clarify relationships, movements of materials and data, and places where decisions are made.

Unfortunately for the analyst-designer, most standards for flowcharting have been developed for computer programming. Although the analysis and design of people-machine systems share some features with the writing of computer programs, systems that involve people often function in different and more complicated ways from systems of mere computers. For the more complicated kind of analysis and design needed for people-machine systems, one has to use flowcharting tools that are not yet standardized.

Standards for computer-program and computer-system flowcharting have been established by the American National Standards Institute (ANSI). A very helpful discourse on these standards is given by CHAPIN. BOCCHINO and FITZGERALD & FITZGERALD present the ANSI flowchart symbols and discuss the need for additional symbols and kinds of charts to handle the complexities of people-machine systems; their discussions cover organization, work-distribution, and process-flow charts, as well as decision tables (for which see also HEINRITZ, 1978). A book by BRANDEJS on Canadian health information systems provides excellent examples of how flowcharts can be used for purposes other than computer programs (and offers some interesting, but brief, comments on system analysis and design). THOMAS also gives instructive examples of flowcharts of several areas within a library; MORROW offers a "generalized" flowchart for online bibliographic searching; and KAZLAUSKAS discusses the teaching of flowcharting.

Although it is not strictly a flowchart technique, a little-known graphic technique, the Kiviat graph (ELLIOTT), which is a circular display of several performance parameters in close juxtaposition, deserves mention as a tool to measure performance, S.W. SMITH discusses the use of Venn diagrams to explain Boolean combinations of terms in online bibliographic searching.

Job Description and Analysis

Job descriptions are an important tool for the analysis and design of the human side of people-machine systems. In the usual case of an existing information system, it is likely that job descriptions for the people involved will be available at the time the system analysis-design effort starts. However, they are likely to be somewhat out of date, incomplete, and inaccurate with respect to the functions the people are currently performing, and they are also likely to contain some information that is more important to the personnel department than to the system analysts and designers. Thus, the system team must expect to conduct interviews with enough current workers in the system to cover all of the type of existing jobs but not necessarily all the individual workers (e.g., several workers might be performing the same type of job).

The technique of interviewing is fraught with underrecognized difficulties, and probably few system analyst-designers are adequately aware of them. A classic work by HYMAN ET AL., even though directed toward sociologists, provides a wealth of information about these difficulties and ways to minimize them, information of considerable usefulness in system analysis and design. One of the merits of the forthcoming text by BURCH ET AL. on the design of data-processing systems is its attention to the importance of good interviews.

As an introduction to job analysis and description, two pamphlets from the U.S. CIVIL SERVICE COMMISSION (1973a; 1973b) are helpful, although they tend toward the personnel-department approach. CHAPMAN ET AL. devote a chapter to job analysis, and an article by JAHNIG offers an innovative way to use matrices in analyzing the skills needed in various jobs.

Operations Research and Analysis

"Operations research" and "operations analysis" are contrasted and defined by SWANSON. She considers that the former is directed toward developing mathematical models whereas the latter "encompasses examinations of the structures and processes of systems, the flows of material and information through systems, and resource allocations." HEINRITZ (1972) classifies the problems of these fields into resource allocation (e.g., "optimal shelving of books by size"; see RADHAKRISHNAN & VENKATESH), sequencing (e.g., "determining the minimal time or cost order for searching a group of bibliographical tools"), queuing (e.g., analyzing the effects of "duplicate services, usage restrictions, and reserves"), inventory, replacement, and competitive strategies.

In this section the combined term operations research and analysis (OR&A) is used since the discussion treats items that do not necessarily fall neatly into either field. The topic has been dealt with meagerly in *ARIST*, although COOPER (1973), GROSCH, HARMON, and LEIMKUHLER & BILLINGSLEY (in addition to SWANSON) allot short portions of their reviews to it.

The classic work in library OR&A is the 1968 monograph by MORSE. This was the first book on the application of a wide range of standard OR&A techniques to library problems, and it discusses techniques that are equally useful to more general information systems. However, another early work, published in 1961 and revised in 1969 (FUSSLER & SIMON) is an example of library OR&A even though its authors do not use this term to describe their work.

A major impetus to librarians to start thinking about using OR&A techniques was the 35th Annual Conference of the Graduate Library School of the University of Chicago in 1971 (SWANSON & BOOKSTEIN). The proceedings include an excellent bibliography on library OR&A through 1970. Another bibliography, whose coverage extends into 1975, was prepared by BUCKLAND & KRAFT and was published as part of a useful anthology (BROPHY ET AL.). This anthology is an excellent starting place for anyone interested in OR&A in general and as applied to libraries and other information systems. ADEYEMI gives a brief introduction to OR&A. A recent text by THIERAUF covers OR&A broadly at an introductory level; it appears well suited to autodidactics.

Recent studies in library OR&A include a book by CHEN (this incorporates an earlier article she co-authored (MORSE & CHEN), on which BOOKSTEIN (1975a) has commented). Chen's book describes her experiences in using some of Morse's theoretical OR&A models to analyze the use of monographs in the medical library at Harvard University. BOOKSTEIN & COOPER suggest a general model for information retrieval systems. Other recent work in OR&A includes papers by BOMMER, BOOKSTEIN (1975b), BRUCE, BUCKLAND ET AL., BYRD & KOENIG, COOPER & WOLT-HAUSEN, DROTT, GOEHLERT, KRAFT ET AL., LEIMKUHLER, MC-CLURE, RADECKI, REGAZZI & HERSBERGER, ROUSE, SAMPSON, and TURNER.

Bibliometrics. Closely related to information system OR&A is bibliometrics (once known, according to WITTIG, as "statistical bibliography"). NICHOLAS & RITCHIE define bibliometrics as the "statistical or quantitative description of a literature . . . [i.e.,] a group of related documents . . . [providing] . . . methods by which significant features of a literature may be described and its working monitored." In an earlier survey of bibliometrics, with particular reference to the literature of the natural sciences, DONOHUE mentions several applications, including techniques for the "identification of a 'core' literature—that segment which is potentially most useful," for "tracing the spread of ideas, analogous to . . . the study of epidemics," and for "classifying segments of a literature by reference to the interconnections shown in the citations given by publications."

Bibliometrics, the subject of an *ARIST* review by NARIN & MOLL in 1977, can trace its beginnings to the work of Samuel C. Bradford in the 1930s and 1940s, which led to what is now called Bradford's law (which says that articles on a given topic decrease in frequency as one moves out from the core journals in a given field) (BOOKSTEIN, 1976; BOYCE & FUNK; BROOKES; BROOKES & GRIFFITHS; DROTT & GRIFFITH; GOSSET; HUBERT, 1976; HUBERT, 1978; URQUHART). PRICE (1976) (in a paper on which KANTOR (1978) and PRICE (1978) comment) offers a persuasive argument for having found the long-sought theoretical foundation for Bradford's law and other related phenomena—e.g., the laws of Lotka, Pareto, Willis, and Zipf. The monograph by NICHOLAS & RITCHIE surveys bibliometrics, with examples mainly from the social sciences.

Soviet information workers continue to show interest in the dynamics of information in scientific fields (BURBULYA & KOVARSKAYA; KAN; KLEMENT'EV; KRASHENINNIKOVA; KURENKOVA; LASTOVKA; LIFLYANDCHIK; YANOVSKII). A major area of international effort is the analysis of citation patterns (BRENNEN & DAVEY; CAWKELL, 1976; 1978a; CORTH; CRAWFORD; CULNAN; ELLIS ET AL.; GHOSH; HAFNER, 1976a; 1976b; KUCH; LABORIE & HALPERIN; MARTYN; MURUGESAN & MORAVCSIK; NARIN & CARPENTER; NELSON; OPPENHEIM & RENN; PINSKI & NARIN; SCALES; TOBIAS; VOOS & DAGAEV; WOODWARD & HENSMAN).

Other recent papers in bibliometrics, some of which touch on citation analysis, include those by AIYEPEKU (1976; 1977), ANDERSON, ANDERSON ET AL., ARMS & ARMS, BAKER, BOOKSTEIN (1975c; 1977), BRAGA, BULICK, CLARK, COILE (1977a; 1977b), HAFNER (1977), HASPERS, HEINE, HIRST, KING ET AL., LAWANI, LINE (1977), MORTON, NARIN ET AL., OROMANER, PALAIS, PAO, POPE, PRATT (1977), PRAUNLICH & KROLL, SCHORR, G.M. SMITH, VIRGO, and WORTHEN.

Statistics. Another area related to information system OR&A is statistics. As CHILDERS, PITERNICK, and PRATT (1975) report, descriptive statistics (statistics that do not emphasize interpretation) present managers of libraries and other information agencies with problems—e.g., they are not used enough and standards for them are lacking. An even more lamentable problem is the infrequent use of inferential statistics (which do emphasize interpretation); their potential has been recognized only slowly by information system workers, especially librarians. Nevertheless, many of the techniques of system analysis and design require from the outset statistically sound procedures for gathering and interpreting data.

The role of statistics in the analysis and design of information systems (e.g., as exemplified by WILLIAMS & SHEFNER) is so large that only a few suggestions can be given about where further details can be found. The best single book on statistical techniques and their applications in libraries is that by STOCK; unfortunately, it is in German. A short book by CARPENTER & VASU can serve as a refresher on statistics for librarians but is probably too concise to be used as an introductory text.

Information system articles that use inferential statistics include those by GOLDSTEIN & SEDRANSK and MILLER & SORUM on how to sample the collection of a library. CASPER, COOPER (1977), and RAOUF ET AL. explore the predictability of various aspects of information system performance; KHALAF & RUBEIZ discuss the prediction of increases in library costs; and HARTER & FIELDS treat the evaluation of public library service. TRAVIS discusses the use of citation statistics in designing retrieval systems. WYLLYS (1978b) examines the use of statistics in the library and information science literature and argues, as do HOUSER & LAZORICK, for increased emphasis on teaching not only descriptive but also inferential statistics to library school students.

Simulation

When the system analyst-designer encounters complex flow or scheduling problems, especially when these problems involve a random element (e.g., random arrivals of users or materials), then "system simulation" becomes very important. With simulation, computers can be programmed to imitate the movements of materials, people, or data; arrivals, departures, and choices of alternate paths or decisions can all occur with appropriate probabilities. In a computer these movements and choices can be made to occur hundreds or thousands of times in a few seconds, and the results can be recorded and analyzed.

With this technique the analyst-designer can observe the long-term consequences of various system designs without actually implementing them. To make the writing of simulation programs easier, special-purpose computer-programming languages have been developed; the best known are probably GPSS (General Purpose Simulation System), SIMSCRIPT, and SIMULA.

A new edition of a standard text on simulation by GORDON appeared in 1978. This book treats not only discrete-system simulation, the type that is appropriate to most information systems, but also the simulation of continuous systems, and it contrasts GPSS and SIMSCRIPT in some detail. Among the few examples of the use of simulation to analyze and to design information systems are articles by ARMS & WALTER, DELUTIS ET AL., REED (1976; 1977), SHAW (1975; 1976), THOMAS & ROBERTSON, and WILLIAMS.

CONCLUSION

This chapter has surveyed recent work in information system design, with emphasis on the literature during 1975-1978—i.e., since the previous *ARIST* review.

The chapter has emphasized that system design is inescapably intertwined with system analysis. The techniques of system analysis-design were examined in five categories: cost analysis, flowcharting, job description and analysis, operations research and analysis, and simulation.

The numbers of papers cited in these five categories are by no means equal. This inequality reflects the uneven effort in the literature of information system design. It is currently fashionable to study citation analysis and to use simulation models, while multiple-regression techniques are becoming popular. These techniques are worthwhile, but job analysis is apparently viewed as too prosaic to be worth writing about, and the subtleties of good interviewing tend to be ignored.

Little information that could be generalized was found. There were repeated disappointments when a paper would begin with a discussion of a general mathematical model for information system design, only to leap into an account of the design of a particular system with little visible linkage between the model and the design.

Information system design remains an art rather than a science—but an art that requires many skills and techniques. This review has tried to point out these techniques and to provide a guide to their current status.

BIBLIOGRAPHY

ADEYEMI, NAT M. 1977. Library Operations Research—Purpose, Tools, Utility, and Implications for Developing Libraries. Libri. 1977 March; 27(1): 22-30. ISSN: 0024-2667.

AIYEPEKU, WILSON O. 1976. The Productivity of Geographical Authors: A Case Study from Nigeria. Journal of Documentation (England). 1976 June; 32(2): 105-117. ISSN: 0022-0418.

AIYEPEKU, WILSON O. 1977. The Bradford Distribution Theory: The Compounding of Bradford Periodical Literatures in Geography. Journal of Documentation (England). 1977 September; 33(3):210-219. ISSN: 0022-0418.

ANDERSON, JAMES D. 1978. Across the Language Barrier: Translations of Scientific and Technical Journal Literature: A Test of Their Predictability on the Basis of Bibliometric Criteria. In: Brenner, Everett H., ed. The Information Age in Perspective: Proceedings of the 41st Annual Meeting of the American Society for Information Science (ASIS): Volume 15; 1978 November 13-17; New York, NY. White Plains, NY: Knowledge Industry Publications, Inc.; 1978. 9-12. ISSN: 0044-7870; ISBN: 0-914236-22-9; LC: 64-8303.

ANDERSON, RICHARD C.; NARIN, FRANCIS; MCALLISTER, PAUL. 1978. Publication Ratings versus Peer Ratings of Universities. Journal of the American Society for Information Science. 1978 March; 29(2): 91-103. ISSN: 0002-8231.

ARMS, W.Y.; ARMS, C.R. 1978. Cluster Analysis Used on Social Science Journal Citations. Journal of Documentation (England). 1978 March; 34(1): 1-11. ISSN: 0022-0418.

ARMS, W.Y.; WALTER, T.P. 1974. A Simulation Model for Purchasing Duplicate Copies in a Library. Journal of Library Automation. 1974 June; 7(2): 73-82. ISSN: 0022-2240.

AXELROD, C. WARREN. 1977. The Economic Evaluation of Information Storage and Retrieval Systems. Information Processing & Management. 1977; 13(2): 117-142. ISSN: 0306-4573.

AXFORD, H. WILLIAM. 1971. An Approach to Performance Budgeting at Florida Atlantic University. College & Research Libraries. 1971 March; 32(2): 87-104. ISSN: 0010-0870.

AXFORD, H. WILLIAM. 1973. Performance Measurement Revisited. College & Research Libraries. 1973 September; 34(5): 249-257. ISSN: 0010-0870.

BAKER, DAVID. 1978. Characteristics of the Literature Used by English Musicologists. Journal of Librarianship (England). 1978 July; 10(3): 182-200. ISSN: 0022-2232.

BLACK, DONALD VINCENT. 1975. Project AIMS [Automated Instructional Materials Handling System] Implementation Plan. Networks—International Communications in Library Automation. 1975 June; 2(6): 19-22 (England). ISSN: 0028-3037.

BLAKE, FAY M.   1978.   The Effect of Jarvis-Gann on Normal Life.   Journal of Library Automation.   1978 December; 11(4): 308-312.   ISSN: 0022-2240.

BOCCHINO, WILLIAM A.   1972.   Management Information Systems: Tools and Techniques.   Englewood Cliffs, NJ: Prentice-Hall, Inc.; 1972.   404p.   ISBN: 0-13-548693-9; LC: 73-38416.

BOLAND, RICHARD J., JR.   1978.   The Process and Product of System Design.   Management Science.   1978 May; 24(9): 887-898.   ISSN: 0025-1909.

BOMMER, MICHAEL R.W.   1975.   Operations Research in Libraries: A Critical Assessment.   Journal of the American Society for Information Science.   1975 May-June; 26(3): 137-139.   ISSN: 0002-8231.

BOMMER, MICHAEL R.W.; FORD, BERNARD.   1974.   A Cost-Benefit Analysis for Determining the Value of an Electronic Security System.   College & Research Libraries.   1974 July; 35(4): 270-279.   ISSN: 0010-0870.

BOOKSTEIN, ABRAHAM.   1975a.   Comments on the Morse-Chen Discussion of Noncirculating Books.   Library Quarterly.   1975 April; 45(2): 195-198.   ISSN: 0024-2519.

BOOKSTEIN, ABRAHAM.   1975b.   Effect of Uneven Card Distribution on a Card Catalog.   Library Resources & Technical Services.   1975 Winter; 19(1): 19-23.   ISSN: 0024-2527.

BOOKSTEIN, ABRAHAM.   1975c.   Optimal Loan Periods.   Information Processing & Management.   1975; 11(8/12): 235-242.   ISSN: 0020-0271.

BOOKSTEIN, ABRAHAM.   1976.   The Bibliometric Distributions.   Library Quarterly.   1976 October; 46(4): 416-423.   ISSN: 0024-2519.

BOOKSTEIN, ABRAHAM.   1977.   Patterns of Scientific Productivity and Social Change: A Discussion of Lotka's Law and Bibliometric Symmetry.   Journal of the American Society for Information Science.   1977 July; 28(4): 206-210.   ISSN: 0002-8231.

BOOKSTEIN, ABRAHAM; COOPER, WILLIAM S.   1976.   A General Mathematical Model for Information Retrieval Systems.   Library Quarterly.   1976 April; 46(2): 153-167.   ISSN: 0024-2519.

BORKO, HAROLD.   1967.   Design of Information Systems and Services.   In: Cuadra, Carlos A., ed.   Annual Review of Information Science and Technology: Volume 2.   New York, NY: Interscience Publishers; 1967.   35-61.   LC: 66-25096.   Available from American Society for Information Science, Washington, DC.

BOYCE, BERT R.; FUNK, MARK.   1978.   Bradford's Law and the Selection of High Quality Papers.   Library Resources & Technical Services.   1978 Fall; 22(4): 390-401.   ISSN: 0024-2527.

BRAGA, GILDA MARIA.   1978.   Some Aspects of the Bradford's Distribution.   In: Brenner, Everett H., ed.   The Information Age in Perspective: Proceedings of the 41st Annual Meeting of the American Society for Information Science (ASIS): Volume 15; 1978 November 13-17; New York, NY.   White Plains, NY: Knowledge Industry Publications, Inc.; 1978.   51-54.   ISSN: 0044-7870; ISBN: 0-914236-22-9; LC: 64-8303.

BRANDEJS, JAN FLICK.   1976.   Health Informatics: The Canadian Experience.   Amsterdam, The Netherlands: North-Holland Publishing Co.; 1976.   239p.   (Volume 2 of the IFIP [International Federation for Information Processing] Medical Informatics series).   ISBN: 0-7204-0409-6.

BRENNEN, PATRICK W.; DAVEY, W. PATRICK. 1978. Citation Analysis in the Literature of Tropical Medicine. Bulletin of the Medical Library Association. 1978 January; 66(1): 24-30. ISSN: 0025-7338.

BROOKES, BERTRAM C. 1977. Theory of the Bradford Distribution. Journal of Documentation (England). 1977 September; 33(3): 180-209. ISSN: 0022-0418.

BROOKES, BERTRAM C.; GRIFFITHS, JOSE M. 1978. Frequency-Rank Distributions. Journal of the American Society for Information Science. 1978 January; 29(1): 5-13. ISSN: 0002-8231.

BROPHY, PETER; BUCKLAND, MICHAEL K.; HINDLE, ANTHONY, eds. 1976. Reader in Operations Research for Libraries. Englewood, CO: Information Handling Services, Library and Education Division; 1976. 392p. ISBN: 0-910972-46-X; LC: 75-8053.

BRUCE, DANIEL R. 1975. A Markov Model to Study the Loan Dynamics at a Reserve-Loan Desk in a Lending Library. Library Quarterly. 1975 April; 45(2): 161-178. ISSN: 0024-2519.

BUCKLAND, MICHAEL K.; HINDLE, ANTHONY; WALKER, GREGORY P.M. 1975. Methodological Problems in Assessing the Overlap between Bibliographical Files and Library Holdings. Information Processing & Management. 1975 August; 11(3/4): 89-105. ISSN: 0020-0271.

BUCKLAND, MICHAEL K.; KRAFT, DONALD H. 1976. A Bibliography on Operations Research in Libraries. In: Brophy, Peter; Buckland, Michael K.; Hindle, Anthony, eds. Reader in Operations Research for Libraries. Englewood, CO: Information Handling Services, Library and Education Division; 1976. 355-392. ISBN: 0-910972-46-X; LC: 75-8053.

BULICK, STEPHEN. 1978. Book Use as a Bradford-Zipf Phenomenon. College & Research Libraries. 1978 May; 39(3): 215-219. ISSN: 0010-0870.

BURBULYA, YU. T.; KOVARSKAYA, B.P. 1975. The Structure of the Information Flow in the Field of Mechanics (Oscillations of Elastic Bodies). Scientific and Technical Information Processing. 1975; (4): 32-36.

BURCH, JOHN G., JR.; STRATER, FELIX R.; GRUDNITSKI, GARY. 1979. Information Systems: Theory and Practice. 2nd edition. New York, NY: John Wiley & Sons, Inc.; 1979 (In press). 571p. ISBN: 0-471-12322-6; LC: 78-17820.

BUTKOVICH, MARGARET; BRAUDE, ROBERT M. 1975. Cost-Performance Analysis of Cataloging and Card Production in a Medical Center Library. Bulletin of the Medical Library Association. 1975 January; 63(1): 29-34. ISSN: 0025-7338.

BYRD, GARY D.; KOENIG, MICHAEL E.D. 1978. Systematic Serials Selection Analysis in a Small Academic Health Sciences Library. Bulletin of the Medical Library Association. 1978 October; 66(4): 397-406. ISSN: 0025-7338.

CAMPEY, L.H. 1974. Costs of Producing KWIC/KWOC Indexes. Information Storage and Retrieval. 1974 September/October; 10(5): 293-307. ISSN: 0020-0271.

CARPENTER, RAY L.; VASU, ELLEN STOREY. 1978. Statistical Methods for Librarians. Chicago, IL: American Library Association; 1978. 119p. ISBN: 0-8389-0256-1; LC: 78-3476.

CASPER, CHERYL A. 1978. Estimating the Demand for Library Service: Theory and Practice. Journal of the American Society for Information Science. 1978 September; 29(5): 232-237. ISSN: 0002-8231.

CAWKELL, A.E. 1976. Citations, Obsolescence, Enduring Articles, and Multiple Authorships. Journal of Documentation (England). 1976 March; 32(1): 53-58. ISSN: 0022-0418.

CAWKELL, A.E. 1978a. Evaluating Scientific Journals with *Journal Citation Reports*—A Case Study in Acoustics. Journal of the American Society for Information Science. 1978 January; 29(1): 41-46. ISSN: 0002-8231.

CAWKELL, A.E. 1978b. The Paperless Revolution: Forces Controlling the Introduction of Electronic Information Systems. Wireless World. 1978 July; 84(1511): 38-42. 1978 August; 84(1512): 69-74. ISSN: 0043-6062.

CHAPIN, NED. 1970. Flowcharting with the ANSI Standard: A Tutorial. Computing Surveys. 1970 June; 2(2): 119-146. ISSN: 0010-4892.

CHAPMAN, EDWARD A. 1973. Planning for Systems Study and Systems Development. Library Trends. 1973 April; 21(4): 465-478. ISSN: 0024-2594.

CHAPMAN, EDWARD A.; ST. PIERRE, PAUL L.; LUBANS, JOHN, JR. 1970. Library Systems Analysis Guidelines. New York, NY: Wiley-Interscience; 1970. 226p. ISBN: 0-471-14610-2; LC: 75-109391.

CHEN, CHING-CHIH. 1976. Applications of Operations Research Models to Libraries: A Case Study of the Use of Monographs in the Francis A. Countway Library of Medicine, Harvard University. Cambridge, MA: The MIT Press; 1976. 212p. ISBN: 0-262-03056-X; LC: 75-28210.

CHILDERS, THOMAS. 1975. Statistics that Describe Libraries and Library Service. In: Voigt, Melvin J., ed. Advances in Librarianship: Volume 5. New York, NY: Academic Press, Inc.; 1975. 107-122. ISBN: 0-12-785005-8; LC: 79-88675.

CHURCHMAN, C. WEST. 1968. The Systems Approach. New York, NY: Dell Publishing Co., Inc.; 1968. 243p. LC: 68-20106.

CLARK, C.V. 1976. Obsolescence of the Patent Literature. Journal of Documentation (England). 1976 March; 32(1): 32-52. ISSN: 0022-0418.

CLEVERDON, CYRIL W. 1971. Design and Evaluation of Information Systems. In: Cuadra, Carlos A.; Luke, Ann W., eds. Annual Review of Information Science and Technology: Volume 6. Chicago, IL: Encyclopaedia Britannica, Inc.; 1971. 41-73. ISBN: 0-85229-166-3; LC: 66-25096. Available from: American Society for Information Science, 1010 16th Street, N.W., Washington, DC 20036.

COILE, RUSSELL G. 1977a. A Bibliometric Examination of the Square Root Theory of Scientific Publication Productivity. In: Fry, Bernard M.; Sheperd, Clayton A., eds. Information Management in the 1980's: Proceedings of the 40th Annual Meeting of the American Society for Information Science (ASIS): Volume 14, Part 2: Full Papers; 1977 September 26-October 1; Chicago, IL. White Plains, NY: Knowledge Industry Publications, Inc.; 1977. 2-F14; microfiche; 24X reduction. ISSN: 0044-7870; ISBN: 0-914236-12-1; LC: 64-8303.

COILE, RUSSELL G. 1977b. Lotka's Frequency Distribution of Scientific Productivity. Journal of the American Society for Information Science. 1977 November; 28(6): 366-370. ISSN: 0002-8231.

COOPER, MICHAEL D. 1973. The Economics of Information. In: Cuadra, Carlos A.; Luke, Ann W., eds. Annual Review of Information Science and Technology: Volume 8. Washington, DC: American Society for Information Science; 1973. 5-40. ISBN: 0-87715-208-X; LC: 66-25096.

COOPER, MICHAEL D. 1977. Input-Output Relationships in On-Line Bibliographic Searching. Journal of the American Society for Information Science. 1977 May; 28(3): 153-160. ISSN: 0002-8231.

COOPER, MICHAEL D.; DEWATH, NANCY A. 1976. The Cost of On-Line Bibliographic Searching. Journal of Library Automation. 1976 September; 9(3): 195-209. ISSN: 0022-2240.

COOPER, MICHAEL D.; DEWATH, NANCY A. 1977. The Effect of User Fees on the Cost of On-Line Searching in Libraries. Journal of Library Automation. 1977 December; 10(4): 304-319. ISSN: 0022-2240.

COOPER, MICHAEL D.; WOLTHAUSEN, JOHN. 1977. Misplacement of Books on Library Shelves: A Mathematical Model. Library Quarterly. 1977 January; 47(1): 43-57. ISSN: 0024-2519.

COREY, JAMES F.; BELLOMY, FRED L. 1973. Determining Requirements for a New System. Library Trends. 1973 April; 21(4): 533-552. ISSN: 0024-2594.

CORTH, ANNETTE. 1977. Coverage of Marine Biology Citations. Special Libraries. 1977 December; 68(12): 439-446. ISSN: 0038-6723.

COUGER, J. DANIEL. 1973. Evolution of Business System Analysis Techniques. Computing Surveys. 1973 September; 5(3): 167-198. ISSN: 0010-4892.

CRAWFORD, SUSAN G. 1977. Co-Citation Analysis: Recent Investigations of Relationships among Interacting Publications. In: Fry, Bernard M.; Sheperd, Clayton A., eds. Information Management in the 1980's: Proceedings of the 40th Annual Meeting of the American Society for Information Science (ASIS): Volume 14, Part 2: Full Papers; 1977 September 26-October 1; Chicago, IL. White Plains, NY: Knowledge Industry Publications, Inc.; 1977. 2-G5; microfiche; 24X reduction. ISSN: 0044-7870; ISBN: 0-914236-12-1; LC: 64-8303.

CULNAN, MARY J. 1978. Information Usage Patterns in the Computer Field: A Citation Analysis of a National Conference Proceedings and a Scientific Journal. In: Brenner, Everett H., ed. The Information Age in Perspective: Proceedings of the 41st Annual Meeting of the American Society for Information Science (ASIS): Volume 15; 1978 November 13-17; New York, NY. White Plains, NY: Knowledge Industry Publications, Inc.; 1978. 89-92. ISSN: 0044-7870; ISBN: 0-914236-22-9; LC: 64-8303.

DAMMERS, H.F. 1975. The Economics of Computer-Based Information Systems: A Review. Journal of Documentation (England). 1975 March; 31(1): 38-45. ISSN: 0022-0418.

DANIEL, EVELYN H. 1976. Performance Measures for School Librarians; Complexities and Potential. In: Voigt, Melvin J.; Harris, Michael H., eds. Advances in Librarianship: Volume 6. New York, NY: Academic Press, Inc.; 1976. 1-51. ISBN: 0-12-785006-6; LC: 79-88675.

DEBONS, ANTHONY; MONTGOMERY, K. LEON. 1974. Design and Evaluation of Information Systems. In: Cuadra, Carlos A.; Luke, Ann W., eds. Annual Review of Information Science and Technology:

Volume 9. Washington, DC: American Society for Information Science; 1974. 25-55. ISBN: 0-87715-209-8; LC: 66-25096.

DELUTIS, THOMAS G.; RUSH, JAMES E.; WONG, PATRICK. 1977. The Modeling of a Large On-Line, Real-Time Information System. In: Key, William G.; Kumar, Sudesh; May, Leroy; Morrow, John L., eds. Record of Proceedings of the 10th Annual Simulation Symposium; 1977; Tampa, FL. 353-370. Available from: Annual Simulation Symposium, P.O. Box 22621, Tampa, FL 33622; or from IEEE Computer Society, 5855 Naples Plaza, Suite 301, Long Beach, CA 90803. IEEE no. 77CH1177-5C.

DIVILBISS, JAMES L., ed. 1977. The Economics of Library Automation: Proceedings of the 1976 Clinic on Library Applications of Data Processing; 1976 April 25-28; Urbana-Champaign, IL. Urbana-Champaign, IL: University of Illinois, Graduate School of Library Science; 1977. 164p. ISBN: 0-87845-046-7; LC: 77-075153.

DIVILBISS, JAMES L., ed. 1978. Negotiating for Computer Services: Proceedings of the 1977 Clinic on Library Applications of Data Processing; 1977 April 24-27; Urbana-Champaign, IL. Urbana-Champaign, IL: University of Illinois, Graduate School of Library Science; 1978. 117p. ISBN: 0-87845-048-3; LC: 78-13693.

DONOHUE, JOSEPH C. 1973. Understanding Scientific Literatures: A Bibliometric Approach. Cambridge, MA: The MIT Press; 1973. 101p. ISBN: 0-262-04039-5; LC: 72-10334.

DROTT, M. CARL. 1978. Selecting Journals Based on Search Results: A Study of Variability. In: Brenner, Everett H., ed. The Information Age in Perspective: Proceedings of the 41st Annual Meeting of the American Society for Information Science (ASIS): Volume 15; 1978 November 13-17; New York, NY. White Plains, NY: Knowledge Industry Publications, Inc.; 1978. 112-114. ISSN: 0044-7870; ISBN: 0-914236-22-9; LC: 64-8303.

DROTT, M. CARL; GRIFFITH, BELVER C. 1978. An Empirical Examination of Bradford's Law and the Scattering of Scientific Literature. Journal of the American Society for Information Science. 1978 September; 29(5): 238-246. ISSN: 0002-8231.

DYER, CHARLES. 1978. Data Processing Contracts: A Tutorial. In: Divilbiss, James L., ed. Negotiating for Computer Services: Proceedings of the 1977 Clinic on Library Applications of Data Processing; 1977 April 24-27; Urbana-Champaign, IL. Urbana-Champaign, IL: University of Illinois, Graduate School of Library Science; 1978. 31-53. ISBN: 0-87845-048-3; LC: 78-13693.

ECKELS, DIANE COLE; LYDERS, RICHARD A. 1978. The Allocation of Operating Costs to Users of a Medical Library. In: Brenner, Everett H., ed. The Information Age in Perspective: Proceedings of the 41st Annual Meeting of the American Society for Information Science (ASIS): Volume 15; 1978 November 13-17; New York, NY. White Plains, NY: Knowledge Industry Publications, Inc.; 1978. 123-125. ISSN: 0044-7870; ISBN: 0-914236-22-9; LC: 64-8303.

ELCHESEN, DENNIS R. 1978. Cost-Effectiveness Comparison of Manual and On-Line Retrospective Bibliographic Searching. Journal of the American Society for Information Science. 1978 March; 29(2): 56-66. ISSN: 0002-8231.

ELLIOTT, ROGER W. 1976. Kiviat-Graphs as a Means for Displaying Performance Data for On-Line Retrieval Systems. Journal of the American Society for Information Science. 1976 May-June; 27(3): 178-182. ISSN: 0002-8231.

ELLIS, P.; HEPBURN, G.; OPPENHEIM, C. 1978. Studies on Patent Citation Networks. Journal of Documentation (England). 1978 March; 34(1): 12-20. ISSN: 0022-0418.

FASANA, PAUL J. 1973. Systems Analysis. Library Trends. 1973 April; 21(4): 465-478. ISSN: 0024-2594.

FEENEY, WILLIAM; SLADEK, FREA. 1977. The Systems Analyst as a Change Agent. Datamation. 1977 November; 23(11): 85-88. ISSN: 0011-6963.

FITZGERALD, JOHN M.; FITZGERALD, ARDRA F. 1973. Fundamentals of Systems Analysis. New York, NY: John Wiley & Sons, Inc.; 1973. 531p. ISBN: 0-471-26255-2; LC: 72-13160.

FUSSLER, HERMAN H.; SIMON, JULIAN L. 1969. Patterns in the Use of Books in Large Research Libraries. Chicago, IL: The University of Chicago Press; 1969. 210p. ISBN: 0-226-27556-6; LC: 72-79916.

GELLER, NANCY L. 1978. On the Citation Influence Methodology of Pinski and Narin. Information Processing & Management. 1978; 14(2): 93-95. ISSN: 0306-4573.

GHOSH, JATA S. 1975. Uncitedness of Articles in Nature, a Multidisciplinary Scientific Journal. Information Processing & Management. 1975; 11(5/7): 165-169. ISSN: 0020-0271.

GILCHRIST, BRUCE. 1978. Coping with Catastrophe: Implications to Information System Design. Journal of the American Society for Information Science. 1978 November; 29(6): 272-277. ISSN: 0002-8231.

GILDERSLEEVE, THOMAS R. 1976. Insight and Creativity. Datamation. 1976 July; 22(7): 89-96. ISSN: 0011-6963.

GODDARD, HAYNES C. 1971. An Economic Analysis of Library Benefits. Library Quarterly. 1971 July; 41(3): 244-255. ISSN: 0024-2519.

GOEHLERT, ROBERT. 1978. Periodical Use in an Academic Library: A Study of Economists and Political Scientists. Special Libraries. 1978 February; 69(2): 51-60. ISSN: 0038-6723.

GOLDSTEIN, MARIANNE; SEDRANSK, JOSEPH. 1977. Using a Sample Technique to Describe Characteristics of a Collection. College & Research Libraries. 1977 May; 38(3): 195-202. ISSN: 0010-0870.

GORDON, GEOFFREY. 1978. System Simulation. 2nd edition. Englewood Cliffs, NJ: Prentice-Hall, Inc.; 1978. 324p. ISBN: 0-13-881797; LC: 77-24579.

GORE, DANIEL. 1978. The Mischief in Measurement: A Caveat on the Hazards of Using Faulty Instruments to Measure Library Performance. Library Journal. 1978 May 1; 103(9): 933-937. ISSN: 0000-0027.

GOSSET, M. 1977. S.C. Bradford: Keeper of the Science Museum Library 1925-1937. Journal of Documentation (England). 1977 September; 33(3): 173-176. ISSN: 0022-0418.

GREENBERG, HARVEY J.; KRAFT, DONALD H. 1977. On Computing a Buy/Copy Policy Using the Pitt-Kraft Model. Information Processing & Management. 1977; 13(2): 125-134. ISSN: 0306-4573.

GROSCH, AUDREY N. 1976. Library Automation. In: Williams, Martha E., ed. Annual Review of Information Science and Technology: Volume

11. Washington, DC: American Society for Information Science; 1976. 225-266. ISSN: 0066-4200; ISBN: 0-87715-212-8; LC: 66-25096.

HAFNER, ARTHUR W. 1976a. Citation Characteristics of Physiology Literature, 1970-72. International Library Review. 1976 January; 8(1): 85-115. ISSN: 0020-7837.

HAFNER, ARTHUR W. 1976b. Primary Journal Selection Using Citations from an Indexing Service Journal: A Method and Example from Nursing Literature. Bulletin of the Medical Library Association. 1976 October; 64(4): 392-401. ISSN: 0025-7338.

HAFNER, ARTHUR W. 1977. Characteristics of Individual Physiology Source Journals, 1970-72. International Library Review. 1977 January; 9(1): 19-42. ISSN: 0020-7837.

HAMBURG, MORRIS; CLELLAND, RICHARD C.; BOMMER, MICHAEL R.W.; RAMIST, LEONARD E.; WHITFIELD, RONALD M. 1974. Library Planning and Decision-Making Systems. Cambridge, MA: The MIT Press; 1974. 274p. ISBN: 0-262-08065-6; LC: 73-16422.

HAMBURG, MORRIS; RAMIST, LEONARD E.; BOMMER, MICHAEL R.W. 1972. Library Objectives and Performance Measures and Their Use in Decision Making. Library Quarterly. 1972 January; 42(1): 107-128. ISSN: 0024-2519.

HANSEN, JAMES V.; MCKELL, LYNN J.; HEITGER, LESTER E. 1977. Decision-Oriented Frameworks for Management Information Systems Design. Information Processing & Management. 1977; 13(4): 215-225. ISSN: 0306-4573.

HARMON, GLYNN. 1976. Information Science Education and Training. In: Williams, Martha E., ed. Annual Review of Information Science and Technology: Volume 11. Washington, DC: American Society for Information Science; 1976. 347-380. ISSN: 0066-4200; ISBN: 0-87715-212-8; LC: 66-25096.

HARTER, STEPHEN P.; FIELDS, MARY ALICE S. 1978. Circulation, Reference, and the Evaluation of Public Library Service. RQ. 1978 Winter; 18(2): 147-152. ISSN: 0033-7072.

HASPERS, JAN H. 1976. The Yield Formula and Bradford's Law. Journal of the American Society for Information Science. 1976 September-October; 27(5/6): 281-287. ISSN: 0002-8231.

HAYES, ROBERT M.; BECKER, JOSEPH. 1974. Handbook of Data Processing for Libraries. 2nd edition. Los Angeles, CA: Melville Publishing Co.; 1974. 688p. ISBN: 0-471-36483-5; LC: 74-9690.

HEINE, M.H. 1978. Indices of Literature Dispersion Based on Qualitative Attributes. Journal of Documentation (England). 1978 September; 34(3): 175-188. ISSN: 0022-0418.

HEINRITZ, FRED J. 1972. Quantitative Management in Libraries. In: Hoadley, Irene Braden; Clark, Alice S., eds. Quantitative Methods in Librarianship: Standards, Research, Management. Westport, CT: Greenwood Press, Inc.; 1972. 157-169. ISBN: 0-8371-6061-8. LC: 73-149962.

HEINRITZ, FRED J. 1978. Decision Tables: A Tool for Librarians. Library Resources & Technical Services. 1978 Winter; 22(1): 42-46. ISSN: 0024-2527.

HICE, GERALD F.; TURNER, WILLIAM S.; CASHWELL, LESLIE F. 1978. System Development Methodology. Revised edition. Amsterdam, The

Netherlands: North-Holland Publishing Co.; 1978. 449p. ISBN: 0-444-85143-7; LC: 78-3784.

HINDLE, ANTHONY; RAPER, DIANE. 1976. The Economics of Information. In: Williams, Martha E., ed. Annual Review of Information Science and Technology: Volume 11. Washington, DC: American Society for Information Science; 1976. 27-54. ISSN: 0066-4200; ISBN: 0-87715-212-8; LC: 66-25096.

HIRST, GRAEME. 1978. Discipline Impact Factors: A Method for Determining Core Journal Lists. Journal of the American Society for Information Science. 1978 July; 29(4): 171-172. ISSN: 0002-8231.

HOUSER, LLOYD J.; LAZORICK, GERALD J. 1978. Introducing a Significant Statistics Component into a Library Science Research Methods Course. Journal of Education for Librarianship. 1978 Winter; 18(3): 175-192. ISSN: 0022-0604.

HUBERT, JOHN J. 1976. On the Naranan Interpretation of Bradford's Law. Journal of the American Society for Information Science. 1976 September-October; 27(5/6): 339-341. ISSN: 0002-8231.

HUBERT, JOHN J. 1978. A Relationship between Two Forms of Bradford's Law. Journal of the American Society for Information Science. 1978 May; 29(3): 159-161. ISSN: 0002-8231.

HURT, C.D. 1977. A Correlation Study of the Journal Article Productivity of Environmental Scientists. Information Processing & Management. 1977; 13(5): 305-309. ISSN: 0306-4573.

HYMAN, HERBERT H.; COBB, WILLIAM J.; FELDMAN, JACOB J.; HART, CLYDE W.; STEMBER, CHARLES HERBERT. 1954. Interviewing in Social Research. Chicago, IL: University of Chicago Press; 1954. 415p. LC: 54-11209.

JAFFE, JACK. 1967. The System Design Phase. In: Rosove, Perry E., ed. Developing Computer-Based Information Systems. New York, NY: John Wiley & Sons, Inc.; 1967. 94-137. ISBN: 0-471-73672-4; LC: 67-21331.

JAHNIG, FREDERICK F. 1975. Skills Matrixing. Datamation. 1975 September; 21(9): 71-76. ISSN: 0011-6963.

JOHNSON, HERBERT F.; KING, JACK B. 1969. Information Systems Management in the Small Liberal Arts College. College & Research Libraries. 1969 November; 30(6): 483-490. ISSN: 0010-0870.

KAN, M.I. 1978. The Structure of the Documentary Information Flow on the Topic of Potato Planting Machines. Scientific and Technical Information Processing. 1978; (1): 48-50.

KANTOR, PAUL B. 1976. The Library as an Information Utility in the University Context: Evolution and Measurement of Service. Journal of the American Society for Information Science. 1976 March-April; 27(2): 100-112. ISSN: 0002-8231.

KANTOR, PAUL B. 1978. A Note on Cumulative Advantage Distributions. Journal of the American Society for Information Science. 1978 July; 29(4): 202-204. ISSN: 0002-8231.

KATTER, ROBERT E. 1969. Design and Evaluation of Information Systems. In: Cuadra, Carlos A.; Luke, Ann W., eds. Annual Review of Information Science and Technology: Volume 4. Chicago, IL: Encyclopaedia Britannica, Inc.; 1969. 31-70. ISBN: 0-85229-147-7; LC: 66-25096. Available from: American Society for Information Science, 1010 16th Street, NW, Washington, DC 20036.

KAZLAUSKAS, EDWARD JOHN. 1976. The Application of the Instructional Development Process to a Module on Flowcharting. Journal of Library Automation. 1976 September; 9(3): 234-244. ISSN: 0022-2240.

KEEN, PETER G.W.; GERSON, ELIHU M. 1977. The Politics of Software Systems Design. Datamation. 1977 November; 23(11): 81-84. ISSN: 0011-6963.

KHALAF, NADIM; RUBEIZ, JOHN. 1978. Economics of American University of Beirut Library. Libri. 1978 March; 28(1): 58-83. ISSN: 0024-2667.

KING, DONALD W. 1968. Design and Evaluation of Information Systems. In: Cuadra, Carlos A., ed. Annual Review of Information Science and Technology: Volume 3. Chicago, IL: Encyclopaedia Britannica, Inc.; 1968. 61-103. LC: 66-25096. Available from: American Society for Information Science, 1010 16th Street, NW, Washington, DC 20036.

KING, DONALD W.; MCDONALD, DENNIS D.; RODERER, NANCY K.; SCHUELLER, CHARLES G.; WOOD, BARBARA L. 1978. Statistical Indicators of Scientific & Technical Communication Updated to 1975. In: Brenner, Everett H., ed. The Information Age in Perspective: Proceedings of the 41st Annual Meeting of the American Society for Information Science (ASIS): Volume 15; 1978 November 13-17; New York, NY. White Plains, NY: Knowledge Industry Publications, Inc.; 1978. 177-179. ISSN: 0044-7870; ISBN: 0-914236-22-9; LC: 64-8303.

KIRK, FRANK G. 1973. Total System Development for Information Systems. New York, NY: John Wiley & Sons, Inc.; 1973. 284p. ISBN: 0-471-48260-9; LC: 73-4359.

KLEMENT'EV, A.F. 1975. Some Citation Characteristics of Mathematics Publications (Based on Soviet Sources). Scientific and Technical Information Processing. 1975; (3): 20-22.

KRAFT, DONALD H.; POLACSEK, RICHARD A.; SOERGEL, LISSA; BURNS, KATHLEEN; KLAIR, ARLENE. 1976. Journal Selection Decisions: A Biomedical Library Operations Research Model; I. The Framework. Bulletin of the Medical Library Association. 1976 July; 64(3): 225-264. ISSN: 0025-7338.

KRAKOWIAK, S. 1978. Methods and Tools for Information Systems Design. In: Bracchi, Giampio; Lockemann, P.C., eds. Information Systems Methodology: Proceedings of the 2nd Conference of the European Cooperation in Informatics: 1978 October 10-12; Venice, Italy. Berlin, West Germany: Springer-Verlag; 1978. 193-210. (Goos, G.; Hartmanis, J., eds. Lecture Notes in Computer Science Series, no. 65). ISBN: 3-540-08934-9; ISBN: 0-387-08934-9; LC: 78-12358.

KRASHENINNIKOVA, N.L. 1976. Dynamics of the Development of the *Mechanics* Abstract Journal (The Mechanics of Deformable Solids; a Comparison with Other Abstracts Journals). Scientific and Technical Information Processing. 1976; (4): 53-60.

KUCH, T.D.C. 1978. Predicting the Citedness of Scientific Papers: Objective Correlates of Citedness in the *American Journal of Physiology*. In: Brenner, Everett H., ed. The Information Age in Perspective: Proceedings of the 41st Annual Meeting of the American Society for Information Science (ASIS): Volume 15; 1978 November 13-17; New York, NY. White Plains, NY: Knowledge Industry Publications, Inc.; 1978. 185-187. ISSN: 0044-7870; ISBN: 0-914236-22-9; LC: 64-8303.

KURENKOVA, M.G. 1976. Analysis of Information Flows in the VINITI Abstracts Journal *Tractors and Farm Machinery and Implements*. Scientific and Technical Information Processing. 1976;(3): 66-69.

LABORIE, TIM; HALPERIN, MICHAEL. 1976. Citation Patterns in Library Science Dissertations. Journal of Education for Librarianship. 1976 Spring;16(4): 271-283. ISSN: 0022-0604.

LANCASTER, F. WILFRID, ed. 1973. Systems Design and Analysis for Libraries. Library Trends. 1973 April; 21(4): 463-605. (Entire issue on title topic). ISSN: 0024-2594.

LANCASTER, F. WILFRID. 1977. The Measurement and Evaluation of Library Services. Washington, DC: Information Resources Press; 1977. 395p. ISBN: 0-87815-017-X; LC: 77-72081.

LANCASTER, F. WILFRID. 1978a. Toward Paperless Information Systems. New York, NY: Academic Press, Inc.; 1978. 179p. ISBN: 0-12-436050-5; LC: 78-51237.

LANCASTER, F. WILFRID. 1978b. Whither Libraries? or, Wither Libraries. College & Research Libraries. 1978 September; 39(5): 345-357. ISSN: 0010-0870.

LANCASTER, F. WILFRID; FAYEN, EMILY GALLUP. 1973. Information Retrieval On-Line. Los Angeles, CA: Melville Publishing Co.; 1973. 597p. ISBN: 0-471-51235-4; LC: 73-9697.

LANCASTER, F. WILFRID; GILLESPIE, CONSTANTINE J. 1970. Design and Evaluation of Information Systems. In: Cuadra, Carlos A.; Luke, Ann W., eds. Annual Review of Information Science and Technology: Volume 5. Chicago, IL: Encyclopaedia Britannica, Inc.; 1970. 33-70. ISBN: 0-85229-156-6; LC: 66-25096. Available from: American Society for Information Science, 1010 16th Street NW, Washington, DC 20036.

LASTOVKA, E.V. 1975. The Structure of the Information Flow in Biology. Scientific and Technical Information Processing. 1975;(4): 25-31.

LAWANI, S.M. 1975. Obsolescence of American and French Agronomic Literatures. Journal of Librarianship (England). 1975 January; 7(1): 12-30. ISSN: 0022-2232.

LEIMKUHLER, FERDINAND F. 1977. Operational Analysis of Library Systems. Information Processing & Management. 1977; 13(2): 79-93. ISSN: 0306-4573.

LEIMKUHLER, FERDINAND F.; BILLINGSLEY, ALICE. 1972. Library and Information Center Management. In: Cuadra, Carlos A.; Luke, Ann W., eds. Annual Review of Information Science and Technology: Volume 7. Washington, DC: American Society for Information Science; 1972. 499-533. ISBN: 0-87715-206-3; LC: 66-25096.

LEIMKUHLER, FERDINAND F.; COOPER, MICHAEL D. 1971. Cost Accounting and Analysis for University Libraries. College & Research Libraries. 1971 November; 32(6): 449-464. ISSN: 0010-0870.

LIFLYANDCHIK, B.I. 1975. A Study of the Characteristics of the Distribution of the Materials of Scientific and Technical Conferences. Scientific and Technical Information Processing. 1975;(3): 45-51.

LINE, M.B. 1975. Optimization of Library Expenditure on Biochemical Journals. Journal of Documentation (England). 1975 March; 31(1): 36-37. ISSN: 0022-0418.

LINE, M.B. 1977. Citation Analyses: A Note. International Library Review. 1977 October; 9(4): 429. ISSN: 0020-7837.

LORD, KENNISTON W., JR.; STEINER, JAMES B. 1978. CDP Review Manual: A Data Processing Handbook. 2nd edition. New York, NY: Van Nostrand Reinhold Co.; 1978. 510p. (See particularly 349-475). ISBN: 0-442-80523-3; LC: 78-9452.

LUCAS, HENRY C., JR. 1974. Toward Creative Systems Design. New York, NY: Columbia University Press; 1974. 147p. ISBN: 0-231-03791-0; LC: 74-4129.

MARTYN, BRUCE. 1975. Citation Analysis. Journal of Documentation (England). 1975 December; 31(4): 290-297. ISSN: 0022-0418.

MASON, ROBERT M.; SASSONE, PETER G. 1978. A Lower Bound Cost Benefit Model for Information Services. Information Processing & Management. 1978; 14(2): 71-83. ISSN: 0306-4573.

MCCLURE, CHARLES R. 1977. Linear Programming and Library Delivery Systems. Library Resources & Technical Services. 1977 Fall; 21(4): 333-344. ISSN: 0024-2527.

MILLER, BRUCE; SORUM, MARILYN. 1977. A Two Stage Sampling Procedure for Estimating the Proportion of Lost Books in a Library. Journal of Academic Librarianship. 1977 May; 3(2): 74-80. ISSN: 0099-1333.

MILLER, JAMES GRIER. 1978. Living Systems. New York, NY: McGraw-Hill Book Co.; 1978. 1102p. ISBN: 0-07-042015-7; LC: 77-23362.

MINDER, THOMAS. 1973. Application of Systems Analysis in Designing a New System. Library Trends. 1973 April; 21(4): 465-478. ISSN: 0024-2594.

MONTGOMERY, K. LEON. 1977. Use and Users: Major Criteria for Acquisition of Library Materials. In: Fry, Bernard M.; Sheperd, Clayton A., eds. Information Management in the 1980's: Proceedings of the 40th Annual Meeting of the American Society for Information Science (ASIS): Volume 14, Part 2: Full Papers; 1977 September 26-October 1; Chicago, IL. White Plains, NY: Knowledge Industry Publications, Inc.; 1977. 6-B12; microfiche; 24X reduction. ISSN: 0044-7870; ISBN: 0-914236-12-1; LC: 64-8303.

MORITA, ICHIKO T.; GAPEN, D. KAYE. 1977. A Cost Analysis of the Ohio College Library Center On-Line Shared Cataloging System in the Ohio State University Libraries. Library Resources & Technical Services. 1977 Summer; 21(3): 286-302. ISSN: 0024-2527.

MORROW, DEANNA I. 1976. A Generalized Flowchart for the Use of ORBIT and Other On-Line Interactive Bibliographic Search Systems. Journal of the American Society for Information Science. 1976 January-February; 27(1): 57-62. ISSN: 0002-8231.

MORSE, PHILIP M. 1968. Library Effectiveness: A Systems Approach. Cambridge, MA: The MIT Press; 1968. 207p. LC: 68-25379.

MORSE, PHILIP M.; CHEN, CHING-CHIH. 1975. Using Circulation Desk Data to Obtain Unbiased Estimates of Book Use. Library Quarterly. 1975 April; 45(2): 179-194. ISSN: 0024-2519.

MORTON, DONALD J. 1977. Analysis of Interlibrary Requests by Hospital Libraries for Photocopied Journal Articles. Bulletin of the Medical Library Association. 1977 October; 65(4): 425-432. ISSN: 0025-7338.

MOSLEY, ISOBEL JEAN. 1977. Cost-Effectiveness Analysis of the Automation of a Circulation System. Journal of Library Automation. 1977 September; 10(3): 240-254. ISSN: 0022-2240.

MURUGESAN, POOVANALINGAM; MORAVCSIK, MICHAEL J.   1978. Variation of the Nature of Citation Measures with Journals and Scientific Specialties.   Journal of the American Society for Information Science. 1978 May; 29(3): 141-147.   ISSN: 0002-8231.

NARIN, FRANCIS; CARPENTER, MARK P.   1975. National Publication and Citation Comparisons.   Journal of the American Society for Information Science. 1975 March-April; 26(2): 80-93. ISSN: 0002-8231.

NARIN, FRANCIS; MOLL, JOY K.   1977. Bibliometrics.   In: Williams, Martha E., ed.   Annual Review of Information Science and Technology: Volume 12.   Washington, DC: Knowledge Industry Publications, Inc.; 1977.   35-58.   ISSN: 0066-4200; ISBN: 0-914236-11-3; LC: 66-25096.

NARIN, FRANCIS; PINSKI, GABRIEL; GEE, HELEN HOFER. 1976. Structure of the Biomedical Literature.   Journal of the American Society for Information Science.   1976 January-February; 27(1): 25-45.   ISSN: 0002-8231.

NELSON, DIANE M.   1977.   Methods of Citation Analysis in the Fine Arts. Special Libraries.   1977 November; 68(11): 390-395.   ISSN: 0038-6723.

NICHOLAS, DAVID; RITCHIE, MAUREEN.   1978.   Literature and Bibliometrics.   Hamden, CT: Linnet Books; 1978.   183p.   ISBN: 0-208-01541-8; LC: 77-20135. (Also published in London, U.K., by Clive Bingley, Ltd., as ISBN: 0-85157-228-6).

OLSEN, PAUL E.   1976.   The Union Catalog—Its Cost versus Its Benefit to a Network.   Special Libraries. 1976 May/June; 67(5/6): 251-255.   ISSN: 0038-6723.

OPPENHEIM, CHARLES; RENN, SUSAN P.   1978.   Highly Cited Old Papers and the Reasons Why They Continue to be Cited.   Journal of the American Society for Information Science.   1978 September; 29(5): 225-231.   ISSN: 0002-8231.

OROMANER, MARK.   1977.   The Diffusion of Core Publications in American Sociology.   Journal of the American Society for Information Science. 1977 January; 28(1): 34-37.   ISSN: 0002-8231.

PALAIS, ELLIOT S.   1976.   The Significance of Subject Dispersion for the Indexing of Political Science Journals.   Journal of Academic Librarianship.   1976 May; 2(2): 72-76.   ISSN: 0099-1333.

PAO, MIRANDA LEE.   1978.   Dispersion of a Non-Scientific Literature. In: Brenner, Everett H., ed.   The Information Age in Perspective: Proceedings of the 41st Annual Meeting of the American Society for Information Science (ASIS): Volume 15; 1978 November 13-17; New York, NY.   White Plains, NY: Knowledge Industry Publications, Inc.; 1978. 260-263.   ISSN: 0044-7870; ISBN: 0-914236-22-9; LC: 64-8303.

PIERCE, ANTON R.; TAYLOR, JOE K.   1978.   A Model for Cost Comparison of Automated Cataloging Systems.   Journal of Library Automation. 1978 March; 11(1): 6-23.   ISSN: 0022-2240.

PINSKI, GABRIEL; NARIN, FRANCIS.   1976.   Citation Influence for Journal Aggregates of Scientific Publications: Theory, with Application to the Literature of Physics.   Information Processing & Management.   1976; 12(5): 297-312.   ISSN: 0020-0271.

PITERNICK, GEORGE.   1977.   ARL Statistics—Handle with Care.   College & Research Libraries.   1977 September; 38(5): 419-423.   ISSN: 0010-0870.

POPE, ANDREW. 1975. Bradford's Law and the Periodical Literature of Information Science. Journal of the American Society for Information Science. 1975 July-August; 26(4): 207-213. ISSN: 0002-8231.

POWELL, RONALD R. 1978. An Investigation of the Relationships between Quantifiable Reference Service Variables and Reference Performance in Public Libraries. Library Quarterly. 1978 January; 48(1): 1-19. ISSN: 0024-2519.

PRATT, ALLAN D. 1975. The Analysis of Library Statistics. Library Quarterly. 1975 July; 45(3): 275-286. ISSN: 0024-2519.

PRATT, ALLAN D. 1977. A Measure of Class Concentration in Bibliometrics. Journal of the American Society for Information Science. 1977 September; 28(5): 285-292. ISSN: 0002-8231.

PRAUNLICH, PETER; KROLL, MICHAEL. 1978. Bradford's Distribution: A New Formulation. Journal of the American Society for Information Science. 1978 March; 29(2): 51-55. ISSN: 0002-8231.

PRICE, DEREK J. DE SOLLA. 1976. A General Theory of Bibliometric and Other Cumulative Advantage Processes. Journal of the American Society for Information Science. 1976 September-October; 27(5/6): 292-306. ISSN: 0002-8231.

PRICE, DEREK J. DE SOLLA. 1978. Cumulative Advantage Urn Games Explained: A Reply to Kantor. Journal of the American Society for Information Science. 1978 July; 29(4): 204-206. ISSN: 0002-8231.

RADECKI, TADEUSZ. 1977. Mathematical Model of Time-Effective Information Retrieval System Based on the Theory of Fuzzy Sets. Information Processing & Management. 1977; 13(2): 109-116. ISSN: 0306-4573.

RADHAKRISHNAN, T.; VENKATESH, K. 1978. On Optimal Storage of Books by Size. Journal of the American Society for Information Science. 1978 September; 29(5): 253-254. ISSN: 0002-8231.

RAFFEL, JEFFREY A. 1974. From Economic to Political Analysis of Library Decision Making. College & Research Libraries. 1974 November; 35(6): 412-423. ISSN: 0010-0870.

RAFFEL, JEFFREY A.; SHISHKO, ROBERT. 1969. Systematic Analysis of University Libraries: An Application of Cost-Benefit Analysis to the M.I.T. Libraries. Cambridge, MA: The MIT Press; 1969. 107p. ISBN: 0-262-18037-5; LC: 74-90749.

RAOUF, ABDUL; AHMED, FEROZ; ASAD, SYED M. 1976. A Performance Prediction Model for Bibliographic Search for Monographs Using Multiple Regression Techniques. Journal of Library Automation. 1976 September; 9(3): 210-221. ISSN: 0022-2240.

REED, MARY JANE POBST. 1976. Computer Simulation: A Tool for Analysis of Library Service. Journal of Library Automation. 1976 June; 9(2): 117-136. ISSN: 0022-2240.

REED, MARY JANE POBST. 1977. Computer Simulation: A Tool for Library Network Managers. In: Fry, Bernard M.; Sheperd, Clayton A., eds. Information Management in the 1980's: Proceedings of the 40th Annual Meeting of the American Society for Information Science (ASIS): Volume 14, Part 2: Full Papers; 1977 September 26-October 1; Chicago, IL. White Plains, NY: Knowledge Industry Publications, Inc.; 1977. 7-A14; microfiche; 24X reduction. ISSN: 0044-7870; ISBN: 0-914236-12-1; LC: 64-8303.

REGAZZI, JOHN J. 1977. Performance Measures for Information Retrieval Systems. In: Fry, Bernard M.; Sheperd, Clayton A., eds. Information Management in the 1980's: Proceedings of the 40th Annual Meeting of the American Society for Information Science (ASIS): Volume 14, Part 2: Full Papers; 1977 September 26-October 1; Chicago, IL. White Plains, NY: Knowledge Industry Publications, Inc.; 1977. 7-C10; microfiche; 24X reduction. ISSN: 0044-7870; ISBN: 0-914236-12-1; LC: 64-8303.

REGAZZI, JOHN J.; HERSBERGER, RODNEY M. 1978. Queues and Reference Service: Some Implications for Staffing. College & Research Libraries. 1978 July; 39(4): 293-298. ISSN: 0010-0870.

REVILL, D.H. 1977. Unit Times in Studies of Academic Library Operations. Aslib Proceedings (England). 1977 October; 29(10): 363-380. ISSN: 0001-253X.

ROBERTSON, S.E.; HENSMAN, SANDY. 1975. Journal Acquisition by Libraries: Scatter and Cost-Effectiveness. Journal of Documentation (England). 1975 December; 31(4): 273-282. ISSN: 0022-0418.

ROSOVE, PERRY E. 1967a. Introduction. In: Rosove, Perry E., ed. Developing Computer-Based Information Systems. New York, NY: John Wiley & Sons, Inc.; 1967. 1-24. ISBN: 0-471-73672-4; LC: 67-21331.

ROSOVE, PERRY E. 1967b. The System Requirements Phase. In: Rosove, Perry E., ed. Developing Computer-Based Information Systems. New York, NY: John Wiley & Sons, Inc.; 1967. 67-93. ISBN: 0-471-73672-4; LC: 67-21331.

ROTHENBERG, D.H.; HO, D.Y. 1977. The Geometrical Location of Information Centers. Information Processing & Management. 1977; 13(6): 317-327. ISSN: 0306-4573.

ROUSE, WILLIAM B. 1975. Optimal Resource Allocation in Library Systems. Journal of the American Society for Information Science. 1975 May-June; 26(3): 157-165. ISSN: 0002-8231.

SALTON, GERARD. 1975. Dynamic Information and Library Processing. Englewood Cliffs, NJ: Prentice-Hall, Inc.; 1975. 523p. ISBN: 0-13-221325-7; LC: 74-31452.

SAMPSON, GARY S. 1978. A Staffing Model for Telephone Reference Operations. Special Libraries. 1978 May/June; 69(5/6): 220-222. ISSN: 0038-6723.

SAMUELSON, KJELL; BORKO, HAROLD; AMEY, GERALD X. 1977. Information Systems and Networks: Design and Planning Guidelines of Informatics for Managers, Decision Makers and Systems Analysts. Amsterdam, The Netherlands: North-Holland Publishing Co.; 1977. 148p. ISBN: 0-7204-0407-X; LC: 75-40169.

SARACEVIC, TEFKO; SHAW, WILLIAM M., JR.; KANTOR, PAUL B. 1977. Causes and Dynamics of User Frustration in an Academic Library. College & Research Libraries. 1977 January; 38(1): 7-18. ISSN: 0010-0870.

SATARIANO, WILLIAM A. 1978. Journal Use in Sociology: Citation Analysis versus Readership Patterns. Library Quarterly. 1978 July; 48(3): 293-300. ISSN: 0024-2519.

SCALES, PAULINE A. 1976. Citation Analyses as Indicators of the Use of Serials: A Comparison of Ranked Title Lists Produced by Citation

Counting and from Use Data. Journal of Documentation (England). 1976 March; 32(1): 17-25. ISSN: 0022-0418.

SCHARER, LAURA L. 1977. Improving System Testing Techniques. Datamation. 1977 September; 23(9): 115-132. ISSN: 0011-6963.

SCHOFIELD, J.L.; COOPER, A.; WATERS, D.H. 1975. Evaluation of an Academic Library's Stock Effectiveness. Journal of Librarianship. 1975 July; 7(3): 207-227. ISSN: 0022-2232.

SCHORR, ALAN EDWARD. 1975. Lotka's Law and Map Librarianship. Journal of the American Society for Information Science. 1975 May-June; 26(3): 189-190. ISSN: 0002-8231.

SCHWUCHOW, WERNER. 1977. The Economic Analysis and Evaluation of Information and Documentation Systems. Information Processing & Management. 1977; 13(5): 267-272. ISSN: 0306-4573.

SHAW, WILLIAM M., JR. 1975. Computer Simulation of the Circulation Subsystem of a Library. Journal of the American Society for Information Science. 1975 September-October; 26(5): 271-279. ISSN: 0002-8231.

SHAW, WILLIAM M., JR. 1976. Library-User Interface: A Simulation of the Circulation System. Information Processing & Management. 1976; 12(1): 77-91. ISSN: 0020-0271.

SINGLETON, ALAN. 1976. Journal Ranking and Selection: A Review in Physics. Journal of Documentation (England). 1976 December; 32(4): 258-289. ISSN: 0022-0418.

SMITH, GERRY M. 1977. Key Books in Business and Management Studies: A Bibliometric Analysis. Aslib Proceedings (England). 1977 May; 29(5): 174-188. ISSN: 0001-253X.

SMITH, SALLYE WRYE. 1976. Venn Diagramming for On-Line Searching. Special Libraries. 1976 November; 67(11): 510-517. ISSN: 0038-6723.

SPENCE, A. MICHAEL. 1974. An Economist's View of Information. In: Cuadra, Carlos A.; Luke, Ann W., eds. Annual Review of Information Science and Technology: Volume 9. Washington, DC: American Society for Information Science; 1974. 57-78. ISBN: 0-87715-209-8; LC: 66-25096.

STOCK, KARL FRANZ. 1974. Grundlagen und Praxis der Bibliotheksstatistik. Pullach bei München, West Germany: Verlag Dokumentation; 1974. 397p. ISBN: 3-7940-3205-5; LC: 74-341999.

STUDER, PAUL A. 1978. The "Age of Information" from the Viewpoint of Biology: A General Systemic Analysis. In: Brenner, Everett H., ed. The Information Age in Perspective: Proceedings of the 41st Annual Meeting of the American Society for Information Science (ASIS): Volume 15; 1978 November 13-17; New York, NY. White Plains, NY: Knowledge Industry Publications, Inc.; 1978. 333-336. ISSN: 0044-7870; ISBN: 0-914236-22-9; LC: 64-8303.

SWANSON, DON R.; BOOKSTEIN, ABRAHAM, eds. 1972. Operations Research: Implications for Libraries: Proceedings of the 35th Annual Conference of the Graduate Library School; 1971 August 2-4; Chicago, IL. Chicago, IL: University of Chicago Press; 1972. 160p. ISBN: 0-226-78466-5; LC: 73-185760. Also available in: Library Quarterly. 1972 January; 42(1): 1-160. (Entire issue devoted to title topic). ISSN: 0024-2519.

SWANSON, ROWENA W. 1975. Design and Evaluation of Information Systems. In: Cuadra, Carlos A.; Luke, Ann W., eds. Annual Review of Information Science and Technology: Volume 10. Washington, DC: American Society for Information Science; 1975. 43-101. ISBN: 0-87715-210-1; LC: 66-25096.

THIERAUF, ROBERT J. 1978. An Introductory Approach to Operations Research. New York, NY: John Wiley & Sons, Inc.; 1978. 412p. ISBN: 0-471-03125-9; LC: 77-23031.

THOMAS, PAULINE ANN. 1971. Task Analysis of Library Operations. London, U.K. Aslib; 1971. 68p. (Aslib Occasional Publication no. 8). ISBN: 0-85142-034-6; LC: 72-183423.

THOMAS, PAULINE ANN; ROBERTSON, STEPHEN E. 1975. A Computer Simulation Model of Library Operations. Journal of Documentation (England). 1975 March; 31(1): 1-18. ISSN: 0020-0418.

TOBIAS, AUDREY SILVIA. 1975. The Yule Curve Describing Periodical Citations by Freshmen: Essential Tool or Abstract Frill? Journal of Academic Librarianship. 1975 March; 1(1): 14-16. ISSN: 0099-1333.

TOWNLEY, HELEN M. 1978. Systems Analysis for Information Retrieval. London, U.K.: André Deutsch Limited; 1978. 121p. ISBN: 0-2-96920-9; LC: 78-317765.

TRAVIS, IRENE L. 1977. Design Equations for Citation Retrieval Systems: Their Role in Research and Analysis. Information Processing & Management. 1977; 13(1): 49-56. ISSN: 0306-4573.

TURNER, STEPHEN J. 1977. The Identifier Method of Measuring Use as Applied to Modeling the Circulation Use of Books from a University Library. Journal of the American Society for Information Science. 1977 March; 28(2): 96-100. ISSN: 0002-8231.

TUTTLE, HELEN WELCH. 1970. Standards for Technical Service Cost Studies. In: Voigt, Melvin J., ed. Advances in Librarianship: Volume 1. New York, NY: Academic Press, Inc.; 1970. 95-111. ISBN: 0-12-024601-5; LC: 79-88675.

U.S. CIVIL SERVICE COMMISSION. 1973a. Job Analysis: Developing and Documenting Data; A Guide for State and Local Governments. Washington, DC: U.S. Civil Service Commission, Bureau of Intergovernmental Personnel Programs; 1973. 27p. (Bureau of Intergovernmental Personnel Programs document BIPP 152-35).

U.S. CIVIL SERVICE COMMISSION. 1973b. Job Analysis: Key to Better Management. Washington, DC: Government Printing Office; 1973. 12p. (Bureau of Intergovernmental Personnel Programs document BIPP 152-32). (USGPO: 0600-00743).

URQUHART, D.J. 1977. S.C. Bradford. Journal of Documentation (England). 1977 September; 33(3): 177-179. ISSN: 0022-0418.

VIRGO, JULIE A. 1977. A Statistical Procedure for Evaluating the Importance of Scientific Papers. Library Quarterly. 1977 October; 47(4): 415-430. ISSN: 0024-2519.

VON BERTALANFFY, LUDWIG. 1969. General System Theory: Foundations, Development, Applications. New York, NY: George Braziller; c1968, 1969. 289p. ISBN: 0-8076-0452-6; LC: 68-25176.

VOOS, HENRY. 1965. Standard Times for Certain Clerical Activities in Technical Processing. New Brunswick, NJ: Rutgers—The State University; 1965. 141p. (Ph.D. dissertation). Available from: University Microfilms, Ann Arbor, MI.

VOOS, HENRY. 1966. Standard Times for Certain Clerical Activities in Technical Processing. Library Resources & Technical Services. 1966 Spring; 10(2): 223-227. ISSN: 0024-2527.

VOOS, HENRY; DAGAEV, KATHERINE S. 1976. Are All Citations Equal? Or, Did We *Op. Cit.* Your *Idem*? Journal of Academic Librarianship. 1976 January; 1(6); 19-21. ISSN: 0099-1333.

WALDHART, THOMAS J.; MARCUM, THOMAS P. 1976. Productivity Measurement in Academic Libraries. In: Voigt, Melvin J.; Harris, Michael H., eds. Advances in Librarianship, Volume 6. New York, NY: Academic Press, Inc.; 1976. 53-78. ISBN: 0-12-785006-6; LC: 79-88675.

WEINBERG, GERALD M. 1975. An Introduction to General Systems Thinking. New York, NY: Wiley-Interscience; 1975. 279p. ISBN: 0-471-92563-2; LC: 74-26689.

WELCH, HELEN M. 1967. Technical Service Costs, Statistics, and Standards. Library Resources & Technical Services. 1967 Fall; 11(4): 436-442. ISSN: 0024-2527.

WENDER, RUTH M. 1977. The Procedure Manual. Special Libraries. 1977 November; 68(11): 407-410. ISSN: 0038-6723.

WEST, MARTHA W.; BAXTER, BARBARA A. 1976. Unpublished Studies of Technical Service Time and Costs: A Supplement. Library Resources & Technical Services. 1976 Fall; 20(4): 326-333. ISSN: 0024-2527.

WHITE, G. TRAVIS. 1977. Quantitative Measures of Library Effectiveness. Journal of Academic Librarianship. 1977 July; 3(3): 128-136. ISSN: 0099-1333.

WHITE, HERBERT S. 1976. Publishers, Libraries, and Costs of Journal Subscriptions in Times of Funding Retrenchment. Library Quarterly. 1976 October; 46(4): 359-377. ISSN: 0024-2519.

WHITE, HERBERT S. 1977. Library Management in the Tight Budget Seventies: Problems, Challenges, and Opportunities. Bulletin of the Medical Library Association. 1977 January; 65(1): 6-12. ISSN: 0025-7338.

WILLIAMS, JAMES G. 1977. Simulation and Library Network Design. In: Fry, Bernard M.; Sheperd, Clayton A., eds. Information Management in the 1980's: Proceedings of the 40th Annual Meeting of the American Society for Information Science (ASIS): Volume 14, Part 2: Full Papers; 1977 September 26-October 1; Chicago, IL. White Plains, NY: Knowledge Industry Publications, Inc.; 1977. 10-A1; microfiche; 24X reduction. ISSN: 0044-7870; ISBN: 0-914236-12-1; LC: 64-8303.

WILLIAMS, MARTHA E.; SHEFNER, GORDON J. 1976. Data Element Statistics for the MARC II Data Base. Journal of Library Automation. 1976 June; 9(2): 89-100. ISSN: 0022-2240.

WILSON, JOHN H., JR. 1972. Costs, Budgeting, and Economics of Information Processing. In: Cuadra, Carlos A.; Luke, Ann W., eds. Annual Review of Information Science and Technology: Volume 7. Washington, DC: American Society for Information Science; 1972. 39-67. ISBN: 0-87715-206-3; LC: 66-25096.

WITTIG, GLENN R. 1978. Statistical Bibliography—A Historical Footnote. Journal of Documentation (England). 1978 September; 34(3): 240-241. ISSN: 0022-0418.

WOODWARD, A.M.; HENSMAN, SANDY.   1976.   Citations to Review
    Journals.   Journal of Documentation (England).   1976 December;
    32(4): 290-293. ISSN: 0022-0418.
WORTHEN, DENNIS B.   1975.   The Application of Bradford's Law to
    Monographs.   Journal of Documentation (England).   1975 March;
    31(1): 19-25. ISSN: 0020-0418.
WYLLYS, RONALD E.   1978a.   On the Analysis of Growth Rates of
    Library Collections and Expenditures.   Collection Management.   1978
    Summer; 2(2): 115-128. ISSN: 0146-2679.
WYLLYS, RONALD E.   1978b.   Teaching Descriptive and Inferential Sta-
    tistics in Library Schools.   Journal of Education for Librarianship.
    1978 Summer; 19(1): 3-20. ISSN: 0022-0604.
YANOVSKII, V.I.   1978.   Quantitative Analysis of Publications on Prob-
    lems in Materials Science.   Scientific and Technical Information Process-
    ing.   1978; (1): 42-47.
ZIMMERMAN, PATRICIA J.   1977.   Principles of Design for Information
    Systems.   Journal of the American Society for Information Science.
    1977 July; 28(4): 183-192. ISSN: 0002-8231.

2 Cost Analysis of Information Systems and Services

COLIN K. MICK
Applied Communication Research, Inc.

Unfortunately, the literature of information system costing has not, to date, been characterized by either rationality or usefulness.

—PRICE (1974)

INTRODUCTION

The information community is now in a time of dynamic change. Increasing sophistication in computer-based information systems is blurring the boundaries between documents and other types of information. Technology is changing the way we produce, publish, store, and retrieve all types of information. Information management is no longer the province of a small segment of society; it pervades all of society.

The information community is also faced with serious problems. The "taxpayers' revolt" is resulting in reduced revenues to public libraries. Declining R&D support is affecting industrial and special libraries, and academic libraries are feeling the pinch of falling enrollments. Copiers threaten to bury us all in a paper blizzard. Publishers protest that unrestricted copying is reducing their revenues, but revisions of the copyright law to ensure royalty payments seem to confuse issues more than they clarify them. Computer hardware and software vendors offer the seductive temptations of reduced labor costs and increased production through automation, but although system performance may improve, overall costs rarely go down. The challenge of sweeping technical change in a time of shrinking budgets calls for the careful analysis of the

The assistance of Fred Spielberg, Daniel Callahan, and Georg Lindsey is gratefully acknowledged.

costs of existing and proposed information systems and services. Unfortunately, the mechanics of costing information systems and services have not kept pace with technology, and Price's comments are as valid today as they were in 1974.

Consider the previous volumes of *ARIST*. The term "cost" does not even appear in the indexes of the first two volumes covering 1965 and 1966; the first cost study was reported in Volume 4 (covering 1968). The number of references to costs increased rapidly in the *ARIST* volumes of the late 1960s and peaked in 1972, although it remained fairly constant from 1969 to 1976. In the past two years, however, the indexes show a marked decline in cost studies. These observations may in part be an artifact of the indexing terms, but they seem indicative of the problem.

Previous Reviews

Four previous *ARIST* chapters have dealt with the economics of information. In the first, published in 1972, WILSON provided extensive coverage of the literature on costs to that date and concluded that although the methodologies for measuring costs were available, application of them was hampered by the lack of standards. The following year COOPER (1973) followed a more economics-oriented approach but provided some coverage of the literature on costs. In 1974 SPENCE took a more theoretical approach and did not focus on pragmatic issues such as costing. HINDLE & RAPER provided a broad look at the literature on costs and noted that "the dearth of reasonable, complete and comprehensive case studies detected by other reviewers" continues.

H.A. OLSEN developed a major bibliography on the economics of information and a set of categories to describe the field. His bibliography provided excellent coverage of much of the literature in 1971-1972. The paper by FLOWERDEW & WHITEHEAD (1974) provided a benchmark on the measurement of costs, effectiveness, and benefits in scientific and technical information.

A number of unpublished studies of technical service time and costs were covered by WEST & BAXTER in an update of an earlier annotated bibliography of the same area by TESOVNIK & DEHART. KOUNTZ offered a brief and whimsical annotated bibliography on costing methods as part of his article on library cost analysis. It covered 19 studies published between 1859 and 1971. REYNOLDS developed a selected bibliography of costing studies as the first stage in a cost analysis study of library operations. A 1975 review by TRESSEL & BROWN covered the economics of the scientific and technical information industry.

KLEIJNEN (1978b) developed a critical survey of theories and tools for quantifying the financial benefits of information. His paper dealt primarily with computer systems, but much of his work and the literature cited can also be applied to other types of information systems.

Scope of the Review

This review focuses primarily on the literature between 1975 and 1979. It is not intended to provide exhaustive coverage but rather to describe a representative sample of key studies. The bibliography contains some items that are not covered in the text, either because of space restrictions or because a complete copy of the paper could not be obtained for review. Some previous reviews and bibliographies are covered to aid those who wish to see what has gone before.

A CONCEPTUAL FRAMEWORK

A four-level conceptual framework was used to approach the literature. These levels were: 1) the *function* or *service*—an operation within an information organization; 2) the information *organization* itself; 3) the *structure* within which the organization is located (e.g., university, town, corporation); and 4) the *aggregate* level, which looks across similar types of organizations.

The literature generally failed to share our enthusiasm for this framework. Its distribution across these levels was at best uneven and left some large gaps, both in coverage of functions and at the structural level. Some articles overlapped levels, and it was necessary to add the *other studies* category. However, as PRICE (1974) notes, the literature on costing has not been characterized by rationality.

The Function/Service Level

This level contains the bulk of the literature on costing because most studies have focused on specific operations. The literature falls into four areas: acquisitions, cataloging, online searching, and production.

Acquisitions. A major external cost to libraries and information services is the acquisition of information products. There are two types of literature in this area. The first type reports prices of books and serials annually and is represented by articles such as that by CLASQUIN (1978) and by the BOWKER COMPANY annuals. The second type deals with the internal costs represented by acquisitions. Some of the recent literature in this category is described below.

PALMOUR ET AL. expanded on a model developed by WILLIAMS ET AL. to determine when, based on frequency of use, it is cheaper to own a periodical than to borrow it. The revised model updates the cost estimates of the original model and has been expanded to deal with the maintenance and discard of periodicals.

The cost of replacing current paper periodicals with commercially available microforms was explored by J.R. REED. Very general cost categories were used, and the data seem to have been drawn from other papers rather than from empirical study. As noted, cost data in the literature are extremely suspect, and Reed found that the lack of good data prevented any general conclusions. The data do, however, suggest that microforms can be an economic substitute for paper journals.

COHEN used an economic model to explore the costs and benefits of book use. He focuses on resource sharing and offers an equation for analyzing its cost. His paper includes a detailed breakdown of book costs for the Hillman Library for 1974-1975.

Two papers have explored the role of photocopying in resource sharing. PITT & KRAFT developed a library operations research model to assist in budget allocation for acquisitions and photocopying. KING RESEARCH INC. assessed the impact of the revised copyright law on library photocopying. Although this study was concerned primarily with photocopying volume, it is also very relevant to cost analysis. Other sources in this area include AXFORD, GOLD, LEONARD ET AL., and MATTAJ.

Cataloging. AULBACH developed a decision rule for adding drawer space to the card catalog. He describes methods for determining the cost of maintaining an existing catalog and for expanding it. The paper is theoretical, and no application of the methodology is presented. Applying his QUBMIS (quantitatively based management information system) approach to assessing the effectiveness of the card catalog, KANTOR collected detailed cost estimates and associated them with specific performance measures. He found that the cost of conducting such analysis was excessive and recommended overall performance measures (without cost data) for present planning.

The cost of purchasing monograph catalog cards rather than preparing them in-house was studied by BUTKOVICH & BRAUDE. BOCK ET AL. augmented the original study by providing comparable costs for producing the cards via the National Library of Medicine CATLINE database. Alternatives for building bibliographic files of monographs were examined by GROSCH in a study that planned a minicomputer-supported online data management system at the University of Minnesota. Detailed cost data are presented for the various alternatives, together with the methodology used to develop the costs. This is an excellent example of how cost analysis can be applied to a specific problem.

Among other things, networking represents a shared, computerized approach to cataloging. Because of the labor-intensive nature of manual cataloging and the results of studies such as that by BOCK ET AL., one would assume that the cost implications of networking would be a major topic of discussion. Apparently, however, networking has not reached the stage where it can be studied in this manner. MARTIN (1974; 1976) has produced two reports that cover the growth of networking but does not consider costs. LEVINE & LOGAN developed a detailed comparison of BALLOTS (now RLG RLIN) and OCLC, Inc. (two of the major online cataloging organizations), but their discussion of costs was limited to a tabulation of "list prices" for services. M.J.P. REED (1975) provided some cost data and cost projections for the Washington Library Network but did not include data on manual cataloging costs for comparison. Other studies in this area include JONES, MORITA & GAPEN, and P.E. OLSEN.

Online searching. Online bibliographic searching has become one of the most active areas in the costing arena because it is new, it requires specialized equipment, and it generates real costs (in the form of connect, telecommunications, and print charges), which must be absorbed or passed on to the user.

ELCHESEN compared the cost effectiveness of retrospective manual and online bibliographic searching in a carefully controlled study. He observed that failure to consider all the relevant costs as well as poor methodology have caused problems with many online cost studies. He provided a good methodological framework for his study and compared his costs with those reported by other studies in this area. Unfortunately, comparisons of this type can be quite deceiving since cost categories and data collection methodologies are seldom reported in detail and rarely match.

SHIRLEY focused on measuring all the costs associated with online searching, not just "out-of-pocket" costs, such as connect time, telecommunications, and offline prints. Her study gives a very detailed list of cost categories, including generally overlooked items, such as supplies, manuals and search aids, record keeping, and clerical support.

A three-year study of online searching in four California public libraries (the DIALIB project) generated several reports dealing with the cost of online searching in that setting. AHLGREN (1975; 1976) reported initial findings and noted that staff time was a significant cost factor. COOPER & DEWATH (1976; 1977) reported the results of two studies of staff time conducted in the participating libraries. They developed a good methodology for measuring search-related staff time but did not consider related staff-time costs, such as training and record keeping. FIRSCHEIN ET AL. (1978a; 1978b) offered some observations on the cost of online searching in public libraries and on the question of cost allocation. MICK & MILLER expanded on the Cooper and DeWath model to develop a detailed model for studying the direct costs of online searching.

Building on his cost studies with the DIALIB project, COOPER (1977) explored the relationship between input variables (search characteristics, searcher characteristics, and client characteristics) and output variables (measures of cost and cost effectiveness) in online searches. The approach was an interesting first step, but the sophistication of the methodology does not seem justified by the data.

BEMENT compared two different searches on the three commercial search services (BRS, DIALOG, and ORBIT). Although his topic is laudable, his paper has several weaknesses. The cost comparisons were apparently based strictly on connect time and number of citations. Preparation time was excluded as was the cost of obtaining offline listings of the output. What is interesting, however, is that supposedly comparable searches on different systems can produce such different results.

In a primer on online services, ATHERTON & CHRISTIAN noted that the "cost-per-search" data reported in many studies seldom include all the caveats that accompanied the data collection and can often be misleading. They described some of the costs involved in online searching but not in enough detail to provide guidance for accurate costing. Other worthwhile studies in this area are those by BIVANS, COOPER (1972), ELMAN, GILL, LANGLEY, LANTZ, ROBERTSON & DATA, SMETANA ET AL., and WANGER ET AL.

Although 1200-baud computer communication has been shown to produce much higher operator efficiency than slower rates, there has been little discussion of the cost effectiveness of 1200 baud in information science literature. MICK & MILLER offered a brief discussion of the theoretical advantages of 1200 baud for online searching (including printing online at that speed rather than requesting offline prints). WISH ET AL. proposed a methodology for comparing the costs of 110-, 300-, and 1200-baud terminals for online searching, but they failed to consider the potential cost and time savings of listing online at 1200 baud rather than listing offline at the search service (and having the printout mailed to the searcher).

Readily available auxiliary memory devices (e.g., floppy disk drives) offer the opportunity for both searching and listing results at high speed, with later offline editing of the searches. A discussion of the cost and copyright implications of this technology is sorely needed.

Production. The studies on costs reviewed so far have dealt with the post-production phase of information services. Although labor is probably the key ingredient in all these services, the cost of information products—books, journals, search services, online databases, etc.—is also a major factor. The costs involved in the production of information products and services and the complex relationships in vertically integrated organizations are seldom discussed in the literature. This is unfortunate because the forces acting on libraries and information services are also acting on the private, professional, and public organizations that produce information products and services.

Some data on production costs are provided by studies on statistical indicators by KING (1976). These data are valuable, but they are derived almost entirely from other publications and reports and do not represent a single, organized approach to data collection. SENDERS ET AL. report on a detailed analysis of scientific publishing systems. They describe in detail the current paper-based system and include an analysis of costs and factors that affect this system. They also discuss the potential of electronic media for scientific publishing, including cost projections.

In a study of the economic impact of page charges BRAUNSTEIN (1977) argues that such charges allow a more efficient allocation of resources by publishers and result in increased social good. His argument is based on the assumption that without page charges academic publishers cannot recover their production and distribution costs without raising subscriptions to a level that will create significant circulation losses.

The innovative use of computers and telecommunications in information processing has been explored in several studies sponsored by the National Science Foundation (NSF). CAPITAL SYSTEMS GROUP, INC. developed and produced a handbook describing some innovations for scientific and technical information (STI) dissemination. Some projected cost data are provided. A similar, but more technology-oriented guide was prepared by APPLIED COMMUNICATION RESEARCH, INC. Another study by King Research, Inc. and Applied Communication Research, Inc. analyzed current STI communications systems and conducted a detailed feasibility and cost analysis of technological alternatives. This study was reported in a series of volumes by KING ET AL. and by MILLER & MICK.

One key problem area in the costing of information products deals with the relationship between primary products (e.g., journals) and secondary products (e.g., machine-readable databases). Some publishers are already producing their primary products (or at least portions of them) via computer and generating databases as a spinoff product; others do not. Those who do must allocate costs between the primary and the spinoff products. In the past, the primary product has carried the brunt of the costing, but increasing use of online databases and copiers and increased resource sharing are beginning to change the cost allocations of all publishers. Although this area is crucial to the information community, there is little discussion of it in the literature. A recent paper by COLLIER presents some discussion, and the topic is appearing more frequently in professional conferences, but more discussion is needed.

The Organizational Level

At the organizational level the literature on costing falls into three areas: staff time, the academic library, and the industrial or technical library.

Staff time. Staff time is a key ingredient in cost analysis, and several studies have focused specifically on time variables. Staff time associated with online searching in public libraries was analyzed by COOPER & DEWATH (1976; 1977) as part of the DIALIB study in northern California. They developed a series of task categories and, using the search as unit of analysis, collected data on staff time via a short diary. Using the data they were able to calculate the probability that a particular task would be performed as part of a search and how much time each task took.

WEST & BAXTER provide a good annotated bibliography of unpublished time and cost studies of technical services. This is an update of an earlier bibliography by TESOVNIK & DEHART. The summaries focus on cost figures rather than on the methodologies used, but given the problems of comparing cost data across studies, more attention to the methodology used would have been helpful.

LEONARD ET AL. developed and implemented a time-based cost analysis methodology in their study of book-processing costs. Their study used a combination of time study methodologies: task-oriented diaries, direct observation, and flow process analysis. The diaries were highly structured and were kept by respondents for two five-day work periods. Data from all three time studies were used to calculate average times for various book-processing activities. A more focused approach with a simplified diary was used by SMITH & SCHOFIELD in a series of time studies conducted at several libraries. They note that variation over time may be a significant problem in analyzing staff time and suggest that studies using simpler reporting forms over a longer time are better than short, intensive studies.

The utility of random sampling coupled with self-reporting was demonstrated by SPENCER in a study of interlibrary loan and photocopying services in a regional medical library. Random alarm devices were issued to staff members working on the functions under study, together with a short recording form. Spencer included a detailed discussion of how the random alarm devices were used and noted that the methodology did provide low cost, reliable data with minimal interruption to library operations.

ROBERTSON ET AL. developed a set of task categories that were used to develop operation-oriented diaries. In a follow-up report, WILKIN ET AL. described the analysis of data collected via the diaries to identify those variables contributing to variations in staff time. Although this is methodologically interesting, a more fruitful approach would have been to focus on variables that could be manipulated by library management.

The academic library. Costing in complex organizations such as an academic library is a formidable task, and the literature indicates that it is discussed more than it is practiced.

BRAUNSTEIN (1979) looked at the library from an economics-oriented perspective and suggested that libraries are only one of several potential sources of information, each of which has a set of costs attached to any information transaction. The price a user must pay is quite different from the library's cost to provide the transaction. He suggests that libraries consider user costs in planning or allocating funds for library services.

DRAKE (1977) described four bases for cost allocation in academic libraries: faculty size, faculty salaries, intended use, and actual use. She compared the results from a Purdue study, which compared all four bases with results from earlier studies done at the Columbia University and Stanford University libraries. She suggested that allocation based on faculty size or salaries may be appropriate for small colleges, but methods based on usage will provide more accurate allocations in large institutions.

The complexities of allocating the costs of the Houston Academy of Medicine-Texas Medical Center Library are described by LYDERS ET AL. Since standard cost allocation techniques were too inaccurate, they developed a model based on three factors: 1) basic, capital cost; 2) head count; and 3) actual usage.

MONTGOMERY ET AL. studied the use of library materials at the University of Pittsburgh. The study was done to develop a cost-benefit model that could be used for decisions involving purchase, resource sharing, and weeding and retirement of materials. A later paper by KENT ET AL. provided a more detailed discussion of the model and the study.

MARCHANT explored the relationship between some cost variables and data collected from several academic libraries and developed two models; one determines professional staff size according to collection size and decentralization, and the other determines library expenditures according to professional staff size, subprofessional staff size, and annual acquisitions. LEIM-KUHLER & COOPER (1971a; 1971b) developed a generalized cost model for academic libraries and then a detailed cost accounting model for the library at the University of California, Berkeley. They used data from the library to illustrate the applicability of the Berkeley model in several areas, including acquisitions, circulation, labor, and space.

The industrial/technical library. Information services in the private sector have long been concerned with costing and cost-benefit analysis. Not surprisingly, this area has received considerable attention in the literature.

Cost-benefit analysis of information analysis centers (IACs) was studied by Mason and co-workers. MASON & SASSONE developed an economic modeling approach for analyzing and evaluating the costs and benefits associated with IACs. MASON (1977; 1978) described the application of that model to a number of IACs. Although his model provides a method for calculating benefits, he found that data describing benefits were scarce and that benefits were extremely difficult to measure.

A detailed study of the costs associated with information centers is being conducted by TALAVAGE ET AL. They surveyed 500 industrial information centers and collected detailed data that describe operations, costs and charging policies, budget, etc. Their data describe not only the services but also the costs associated with providing them. JACKSON & JACKSON conducted a baseline study of industrial technical libraries. Their study is a good point of departure for studies of industrial library costs; unfortunately, it is based almost exclusively on information obtained from secondary sources.

LINDQUIST explored the potential for information search services in a collection of papers. He presented a system dynamics model to simulate their performance. Although the model is concerned with overall operations, several cost variables were included. Using his model Lindquist concluded that the online search market has been overestimated and that the growth of searching may decline.

In what first seems to be a case study of information service costing in industry MOISSE described the methods used at Battelle-Geneva to account for both staff time and support costs. Unfortunately, he did not describe the costing of related STI services but presented a general discussion of the relationship between STI and R&D. Although this discussion is interesting, it failed to live up to the promise of its title. Other interesting papers include those by GEE, HELMKAMP, KABI, KLINTOE, KRAMER, VOLLHARDT, WILLS & CHRISTOPHER, WOLFE ET AL., and ZAAIMAN.

The Structural Level

At the structural level we sought studies that would look at the costing of information systems and services across an entire structure, such as a corporation or university. Unfortunately, this area seems to have received little attention. We were unable to find any studies of this type in the literature.

The Aggregate Level

The preceding sections have been concerned with costing studies and methodologies at the operational level or an organizational level. As previous reviewers have noted, one of the major deficiencies in the literature on information costing and economics is the lack of external validity—the results cannot be generalized to other settings. Most costing studies are idiosyncratic, either by design or by default. Thus, it is nearly impossible to compare cost data across studies or to aggregate these data in any meaningful way.

Other authors have explored this problem. PORAT and MACHLUP examined the role and impact of information at the national level. The series of reports on statistical indicators of scientific and technical communication by KING (1976) provides a good overview of the costs and economic factors involved in STI.

An NSF-funded systems analysis of scientific and technical communication in the United States has provided a wealth of cost and economic data as well as an exploration of technological alternatives to current practices (KING ET AL.). A set of working papers prepared by MILLER & MICK for this study provide a detailed cost analysis of present and future technologies for STI communication.

A few studies have attempted to explore the cost of technical information services in the private sector. One of the first—reported in a 1959 issue of INDUSTRIAL AND ENGINEERING CHEMISTRY—provides some of the first data on information group budgets and on internal information costs. A 1976 study by KEARNEY to explore the determinants of STI usage collected some data on information costs. Unfortunately, this study suffered from an extremely low response rate, and the results do not appear generalizable.

JACKSON & JACKSON studied characteristics of the industrial special library. Although they could obtain some idea of the scope and diversity of this area, they did not collect any cost or budget data. TALAVAGE ET AL. are also studying the industrial special library. A preliminary report indicates that they are collecting detailed cost data from approximately 500 industrial libraries via a survey. If the survey is successful, the resulting data should be invaluable for the managers of special libraries.

KING & RODERER report on a study of federal information pricing policies. They note that cost recovery, agency mission, type of information, and social value of that information affect federal pricing decisions. KING (1978) has extended this analysis to pricing policies in academic libraries. Both papers deal with pricing and costing from a theoretical and policy perspective rather than from an applied perspective and report little or no data.

Other Areas

Some issue-oriented papers cut across our framework: "how to" papers on costing, computer and telecommunications services, and allocation of costs to users (fee-for-service).

"How to" papers. An interesting subset of the literature deals with the "how to" of costing. Most of the articles reported here are somewhat old and have been covered in other reviews. One exception is a recent monograph prepared by ATHERTON for Unesco. She provides a good outline of the basics of cost analysis for information services. A second exception is the book by LANCASTER on evaluation of library services, which discusses costing of automated systems, reference services, storage, and technical services.

A paper by KOUNTZ provides a good introduction and a short annotated bibliography, which is now somewhat out of date. Much more detailed approaches are offered by PRICE (1971; 1973a; 1973b; 1974) and SHOFFNER. Price presented his ideas on continuing cost analysis in a number of papers. His "building-block" approach is objective and structured and provides a good methodological foundation for cost studies. Shoffner offered a personalized view of costing, which is more pragmatic and applied. Together the two authors balance the objective and subjective approaches to costing. DUCHESNE demonstrated a systems approach to cost analysis. His paper is essentially theoretical, and although he provides table headings to illustrate his concepts, there are no "real-life" examples.

A narrow view, dealing primarily with costing of secondary information services is provided by WOLFE ET AL. in their book on technical information services. Their discussion includes development of cost categories, data collection methodology, analysis, and reporting.

Some studies show how costing is applied in special situations. LEONARD ET AL. provide an interesting combination of theory, conceptualizing, data collection, and analysis in their description of a study of the Colorado Academic Libraries Book Processing Center. LEIMKUHLER & COOPER (1971a; 1971b) give a general cost analysis model and demonstrate its application. An older paper by HELMKAMP gives a good example of cost accounting in a technical information center. The paper describes Helmkamp's system, discusses how it was implemented, and gives the results from a trial operation.

Computers and telecommunications. The use of computers to replace and to augment human labor continues to increase in all areas, including the information field. Costing and cost-benefit analysis of computerization is a complex topic, but it has received much attention.

MILLER & MICK explored the feasibility and costs of an electronically based STI communication system. Some of this work is summarized by KING EL AL.

COTTON prepared a state-of-the-art assessment of cost-benefit analyses of interactive computer systems in general. He offered good theoretical discussion but did not apply his concepts. CONTI described a synthetic benchmark technique for estimating batch processing charges at service bureau sites. A detailed example of its application is presented. As with the Cotton paper, Conti is concerned with general computer costing techniques, but his methodology should be applicable to information groups that have their own computer.

ASHFORD developed a checklist for exploring the applications of minicomputers in the library environment. His approach is brief and has little actual cost methodology, but many of the issues he raised have cost implications. WAINWRIGHT compared the advantages and disadvantages of in-house mainframe and minicomputers for library housekeeping routines. She focused on the cost trade-offs involved in software decisions.

FIELDING & COCKRELL described their experiences in automating library procedures and some of the costs and impacts of automation. BAJEMA described the experience of the Marin County Free Library with dedicated minicomputers for acquisition and circulation. He provided detailed operating costs for both systems for 1974–1975 but did not give any breakdowns or comparisons with the costs of manual systems. Other computer cost pricing studies include those by DEI ROSSI, HAMILTON, HOOTMAN, PALMER, and the U.S. GENERAL ACCOUNTING OFFICE report.

Fee-for-service. Charging for services has become a highly visible issue in the past four to five years, primarily in the public library area. It has received considerable attention at national conventions and public meetings and has been hotly debated in the literature. Since it is directly related to cost allocation, a brief discussion of the literature is in order.

The literature on this topic can be arbitrarily divided into two categories. The first contains primarily rhetorical discussions of the issues and has, for the most part, been based primarily on emotional or theoretical abstractions. The second and smaller category is empirically based and reports on actual experiences in library settings.

The *LIBRARY JOURNAL* (1977a; 1977b; 1978) provides good coverage of the rhetorical discussion in this area. Reports on recent American Library Association conventions and the 1977 Pittsburgh Conference (The Online Revolution in Libraries) offer considerable discussion of the opposing views.

BLAKE & PERLMUTTER were among the first to sound the alarm in this conflict. In 1974 they warned that the fee-for-service movement might mean the demise of the tax-supported public library. A later article by DE GENNARO gives a detailed introduction to the issues. He describes many of the events leading to this conflict and identifies many of the participants.

LINDFORD focused on the fact that public libraries have been a repository for materials for patrons who have traditionally been expected to do their own work. He pointed out that fee services, such as copiers and online searching, save time for patrons, and one can reasonably expect them to pay for this. COOPER (1978) took a philosophical and economic approach to the issue but failed to integrate fully the empirical data from the studies on which his treatise is based.

GELL offered another philosophical discussion of the issues but did not provide the background of the earlier DE GENNARO article. It is also disappointing that she failed to draw on the empirical studies dealing with this issue.

CHESHIER described the experiences of the Cleveland Health Science Library in developing a fee-based institutional membership program in 1972. This is one of the better discussions of the fee-for-service issue. It includes a description of the background and factors involved, a description of the program, and a philosophical discussion of the issues. Unfortunately, it does not provide any operational data on the program. Another substantive discussion is given by VANTINE, who described the fee-for-service INFORM program at the Minneapolis Public Library. This paper provides a good subjective description of the development, evolution, and operations of a fee-for-service program of a public library.

The DIALIB study conducted by Lockheed Information Systems and Applied Communication Research, Inc. for NSF is the largest source of empirical data in this area. In the final evaluation report MICK (1977) reported that user fees did not seem to deter patrons. The major problem appeared to be the "hidden costs" of the search, primarily staff time, which were not recovered via user fees. A spinoff study (MICK, 1978) described the operation of a fee-for-service online search program by the New York Metropolitan Reference and Research Service. Again, fees did not seem to be a major deterrent to use.

BRAUNSTEIN (1979) proposed that the library consider itself one of many competing potential sources of information. Each user attaches a set of personal costs and benefits to each source and considers them in deciding where to obtain specific information. Braunstein suggests that libraries might do well to consider these "private" costs and benefits in determining policy issues such as budget allocations and fee-for-service.

The first expressions of concern over the "taxpayers' revolt," which started with the 1978 California primary election, began to surface in the literature in mid-1978. Falling property tax revenues will contribute significantly to the fee-for-service controversy, and we will see much more of this issue in the future. It is hoped that future discussions will consider empirical studies and the true cost to the user (and nonuser) of both free and fee services.

CONCLUSIONS

There is no paucity of methodological tools for costing information systems and services. Many have been around for years, although some techniques have been automated with the introduction of computers. Many good cost studies are available to guide those who are planning such studies. There is also a good "how to" literature to help those who are planning their first study.

The problem is the application of these tools. Most of the problems cited by earlier authors such as COOPER (1972), HINDLE & RAPER, PRICE (1974), and WILSON remain. There is virtually no standardization. Studies at the operational/functional levels have focused on individual situations, with little thought to reliability and external validity. Most cost data that are reported in the literature cannot be used for comparisons because of a lack of external validity and the failure of authors to document their methodology adequately.

The basic building blocks are there; what is needed is some kind of glue to hold them together: a standard methodology and set of definitions that can be applied to a variety of situations. The main problems lie in the area of staff costs and in the allocation of (or failure to consider) capital costs and overhead. This does not seem a particularly formidable task and, considering the pressures coming to bear on the information community, it should be undertaken posthaste.

The lack of aggregate data across institutions is a related problem. Nearly all cost studies have focused on either a single function or a single institution. We need cost studies that are conducted across a number of similar institutions (e.g., public, academic, or industrial libraries) using a common methodology.

The lack of movement toward standardization and improvement of methodologies and models is disappointing. LEIMKUHLER & COOPER (1971a; 1971b) developed a model for costing in academic libraries in 1971, but the literature shows little application or extension of it. ROBERTSON ET AL. proposed a standardized approach for studies of staff time, but nine years later we still do not have a standardized methodology. PRICE (1971; 1973a; 1974) developed an approach for continuous cost analysis of information services, but we see little indication that it is being used, much less improved.

During the next decade the information community will undergo major changes. Significant cost and economic data will be required to help guide these changes. It is hoped that many of these problems will be resolved so that the decision makers will have access to accurate and reliable cost data. Failure to deal with these issues may result in significant problems for many segments of our information community. Successful resolution of them may lead to much stronger information systems and services and a better integration of the public and private sectors.

BIBLIOGRAPHY

AHLGREN, ALICE E.   1975.   Factors Affecting the Adoption of On-Line Services by the Public Library.   In: Spigai, Frances G.; Graws, Theodore C.W.; Kawabata, Julie, eds.   Information Roundup: A Continuing Education Session on Microforms and Data Processing in the Library Information Center: Costs/Benefits/History/Trends; Proceedings of the 4th Mid-Year Meeting of the American Society for Information Science (ASIS); 1975 May 15-17; Portland, OR.   Washington, DC: ASIS; 1975.   123-132.   ISBN: 0-87715-112-1.

AHLGREN, ALICE E.   1976.   Cost/Utility Implications of Providing On-Line Searches through Public Libraries.   Stanford, CA: Stanford University, Department of Communications; 1976 March.   154 leaves.   (Ph.D. dissertation).   Available from: University Microfilms, Ann Arbor, MI. (UM order no. 76-18,743).

APPLIED COMMUNICATION RESEARCH, INCORPORATED.   1975. Planning Guide: Innovation in the Dissemination of Scientific and Technical Information.   Palo Alto, CA: Applied Communication Research, Inc.; 1975 April.   399p.   NTIS: PB 243438/AS.

ASHFORD, JOHN.   1976.   Software Cost: Making It or Buying It.   Program (England).   1976 January; 10(1): 1-6.   ISSN: 0033-0337.

ATHERTON, PAULINE.   1977.   Handbook for Information Systems and Services.   Paris, France: United Nations Educational, Scientific and Cultural Organization (Unesco); 1977.   259p.   Available from: Unesco.

ATHERTON, PAULINE; CHRISTIAN, ROGER W. 1977. Librarians and Online Services. White Plains, NY: Knowledge Industry Publications, Inc.; 1977. 124p. ISBN: 0-914236-13-Y.

AULBACH, LOUIS F. 1978. Decision Rules for Card Catalog Expansion. 1978. 9p. Available from: the author, Ashland Exploration, Inc., P.O. Box 1053, Houston, TX 77001.

AXFORD, H. WILLIAM. 1975. The Validity of Book Price Indexes for Budgetary Projections. Library Resources & Technical Services. 1975 Winter; 19(1): 5-12. ISSN: 0024-2527.

BAJEMA, BRUCE D. 1975. Marin County Free Library: Cost-Effectiveness of a Dedicated Mini-Computer. In: Spigai, Frances G.; Graws, Theodore C.W.; Kawabata, Julie, eds. Information Roundup: A Continuing Education Session on Microforms and Data Processing in the Library Information Center: Costs/Benefits/History/Trends; Proceedings of the 4th Mid-Year Meeting of the American Society for Information Science (ASIS); 1975 May 15-17; Portland, OR. Washington, DC: ASIS; 1975. 57-61. ISBN: 0-87715-112-1.

BAUMOL, W.J.; ORDOVER, J. 1976. Private Financing of Information Transfer: On the Theory and Execution. In: Martin, Susan K., comp. Information Politics: Proceedings of the 39th Annual Meeting of the American Society for Information Science (ASIS): Volume 13, Part I: Abstracts of Papers; 1976 October 4-9; San Francisco, CA. Washington, DC: ASIS; 1976. 88. (Abstract). ISSN: 0044-7870; ISBN: 0-87715-413-9; LC: 64-8303. Full text available from: the author.

BAUMOL, W.J.; BRAUNSTEIN, Y.; FISCHER, D.; ORDOVER, J. 1978. Manual of Pricing and Cost Determination for Organizations Engaged in Dissemination of Knowledge. New York, NY: New York University; 1978. 122p. Available from: the author.

BEMENT, JAMES H. 1977. The New Prices: Some Comparisons. Online. 1977 April; 9-20. ISSN: 0146-5422.

BIVANS, MARGARET M. 1974. A Comparison of Manual and Machine Literature Searches. Special Libraries. 1974; 65(5/6): 216-222. ISSN: 0038-6723.

BLAKE, FAY M.; PERLMUTTER, EDITH L. 1974. Libraries in the Marketplace: Information Emporium or People's University? Library Journal. 1974 January 15; 99(2): 108-111. ISSN: 0000-0027.

BOCK, ROCHELLE; BRAUDE, ROBERT M.; BUTKOVICH, MARGARET. 1975. Cataloging Costs with CATLINE: A Follow-Up Study. Bulletin of the Medical Library Association. 1975 October; 63(4): 414-415. ISSN: 0025-7338.

BOWKER COMPANY, R.R. The Bowker Annual of Library and Book Trade Information. New York, NY: R.R. Bowker Company. (Annual editions). (Surpassed by Ulrich's International Periodicals Directory, also a Bowker publication). ISSN: 0000-0094.

BRAUNSTEIN, YALE M. 1977. An Economic Rationale for Page and Submission Charges by Academic Journals. Journal of the American Society for Information Science. 1977 November; 28(6): 355-357. ISSN: 0002-8231.

BRAUNSTEIN, YALE M. 1979. Costs and Benefits of Library Information: The User Point of View. Library Trends. 1979 Summer; 28(1): 79-87. ISSN: 0024-2594.

BRES, E.S.; CHARNES, A.; ECKELS, DIANE COLE; HITT, S.; LYDERS, RICHARD; ROUSSEAU, J.; RUSSELL, K.; SHOEMAN, M. 1977. Costs and Their Assessment to Users of a Medical Library. Austin, TX: Center for Cybernetic Studies; 1977. 55p. (Research report no. CSS 303). Vol. 3 of 4 volumes. Available from: the authors.

BUTKOVICH, MARGARET; BRAUDE, ROBERT M. 1975. Cost-Performance Analysis of Cataloging and Card Production in a Medical Center Library. Bulletin of the Medical Library Association. 1975 January; 63(1): 29-34. ISSN: 0025-7338.

CALKINS, MARY L. 1977. On-Line Services and Operational Costs. Special Libraries. 1977; 68(1): 13-17. ISSN: 0038-6723.

CAPITAL SYSTEMS GROUP, INCORPORATED. 1975-78. Improving the Dissemination of Scientific and Technical Information. Rockville, MD: Capital Systems Group, Inc.; 1975-1978 (Continuous updating through 1978). Available from: Capital Systems Group, Inc., Rockville, MD.

CHESHIER, ROBERT G. 1972. Fee for Service in Medical Library Networks. Bulletin of the Medical Library Association. 1972 April; 60(2): 325-332. ISSN: 0025-7338.

CLASQUIN, F.F. 1975. Serials Costs and Budget Predictions. Drexel Library Quarterly. 1975 July; 11(3): 64-71. ISSN: 0012-6160.

CLASQUIN, F.F. 1978. Periodical Prices: A 1976-1978 Update. Library Journal. 1978 October 1; 103(17): 1924-1927. ISSN: 0000-0027.

CLEMENTS, D.W.G. 1975. The Costing of Library Systems. Aslib Proceedings (England). 1975 March; 27(3): 98-111. ISSN: 0001-253X.

COHEN, JACOB. 1977. Book Cost and Book Use: The Economics of a University Library. In: Kent, Allen; Galvin, Thomas J., eds. Library Resource Sharing: Proceedings of the Conference on Resource Sharing in Libraries; 1976 September 29-October 1; Pittsburgh, PA. New York, NY: Marcel Dekker, Inc.; 1977. 197-224. (Books in Library and Information Science, Volume 21). ISBN: 0-8247-6605-9. LC: 77-5399.

COLE, DIANE DAVIS. 1976. Mathematical Models in Library Management: Planning, Analysis and Cost Assessment. Austin, TX: University of Texas; 1976. 351p. Available from: University of Texas at Austin.

COLLIER, H.R. 1978. Long-Term Economics on On-Line Services and Their Relationships to Conventional Publishers Seen from the Data Base Producer's Viewpoint. Aslib Proceedings (England). 1978 January; 30(1): 16-24. ISSN: 0001-253X.

CONTI, DENNIS M. 1976. A Method for Estimating Service Bureau Processing Charges. In: Lindsay, Davis S., ed. Proceedings of the 7th International Conference of the Computer Measurement Group, Inc.; 1976 November 16-19; Atlanta, GA. Camp Springs, MD: Computer Measurement Group, Inc.; 1976. 34-60. Available from: Ian K. Roone, CMG Treasurer, MCAUTO-West, 3885 Lakewood Blvd., Long Beach, CA 90846.

COOPER, MICHAEL D. 1972. A Cost Model for Evaluating Information Retrieval Systems. Journal of the American Society for Information Science. 1972 September-October; 23(5): 306-312. ISSN: 0002-8231.

COOPER, MICHAEL D. 1973. The Economics of Information. In: Cuadra, Carlos A., ed. Annual Review of Information Science and Technology: Volume 8. Washington, DC: American Society for Information Science; 1973. 5-40. ISSN: 0066-4200; ISBN: 0-87715-212-8.

COOPER, MICHAEL D. 1977. Input-Output Relationships in On-Line Bibliographic Searching. Journal of the American Society for Information Science. 1977 May; 28(3): 153-160. ISSN: 0002-8231.

COOPER, MICHAEL D. 1978. Charging Users for Library Services. Information Processing & Management. 1978; 14(6): 419-427. ISSN: 0306-4573.

COOPER, MICHAEL D. 1979. The Economics of Library Size: A Preliminary Inquiry. Library Trends. 1979; Summer; 28(1): 63-78. ISSN: 0024-2594.

COOPER, MICHAEL D.; DEWATH, NANCY A. 1976. The Cost of On-Line Bibliographic Searching. Journal of Library Automation. 1976 September; 9(3): 195-209. ISSN: 0022-2712.

COOPER, MICHAEL D.; DEWATH, NANCY A. 1977. The Effect of Use Fees on the Cost of On-Line Searching in Libraries. Journal of Library Automation. 1977 December; 10(4):304-319. ISSN: 0022-2712.

COTTON, IRA. 1977. Cost-Benefit Analysis of Interactive Systems. Computer Networks. 1977 November; 1(1977): 311-324.

DAMMERS, H.F. 1975. Progress in Documentation: The Economics of Computer-Based Information Systems—a Review. Journal of Documentation (England). 1975 March; 31(1): 38-45. ISSN: 0022-0418.

DAVID, A. 1974a. [Report on the Work of the Pricing Group of the EEC]. Information et Documentation (France). 1974 May; (2): 3-13. (In French).

DAVID, A. 1974b. [Model for the Evaluation of Costs of Documentation Services and Pricing Policy]. Information et Documentation (France). 1974 May; (2): 14-29. (In French).

DAVID, A. 1975. [Cost of Information within a Company]. Information et Documentation (France). 1975 December; (9): 26-29. (In French).

DE GENNARO, RICHARD. 1975. Pay Libraries and User Charges. Library Journal. 1975 February 15; 100: 363-367. ISSN: 0000-0027.

DEI ROSSI, JAMES A. 1975. Cost Recovery in Pricing and Capacity Decisions for Automated Information Systems. Washington, DC: National Bureau of Standards (NBS); 1975 April. 63p. (NBS Technical note no. 864). LC: 75-600015; NTIS: COM-75-IQ616/IGA; GPO: C13.46:864.

DIEBOLD DEUTSCHLAND GMBH. 1975. The Economics of the European Information Network (EURONET); Study of the Cost of Alternative Network Configuration and Related Questions. Frankfurt, Germany: Diebold Deutschland GmbH; 1975. Available from: Diebold Deutschland GmbH, Feverbachstrasse 8, 6 Frankfurt/Main, West Germany.

DRAKE, MIRIAM A. 1976. Libraries and Audio-Visual Center Cost Allocation Study. West Lafayette, IN: Purdue University Libraries and Audio-Visual Center; 1976. 87p. ERIC: ED 125566.

DRAKE, MIRIAM A. 1977. Attribution of Library Costs. College and Research Libraries. 1977 November; 38(6): 514-519. ISSN: 0010-0870.

DUCHESNE, RODERICK M. 1973. Analysis of Costs and Performance. Library Trends. 1973 April; 21(4): 587-603. ISSN: 0024-2594.

ECKELS, DIANE COLE; LYDERS, RICHARD A. 1978. The Allocation of Operating Costs to Users of a Medical Library. In: Brenner, Everett H., comp. The Information Age in Perspective: Proceedings of the 41st Annual Meeting of the American Society for Information Science: Volume 15; 1978 November 13-17; New York, NY. White Plains, NY:

Knowledge Industry Publications, Inc.; 1978. 123-125. ISBN: 0-914236-22-9; ISSN: 0044-7870.

ELCHESEN, DENNIS R. 1978. Cost-Effectiveness Comparison of Manual and On-Line Retrospective Bibliographic Searching. Journal of the American Society for Information Science. 1978 March; 29(2): 56-66. ISSN: 0002-8231.

ELMAN, STANLEY A. 1975. Cost Comparison of Manual and On-Line Computerized Literature Searching. Special Libraries. 1975 January; 66(1): 12-18. ISSN: 0038-6723.

EUSTACHI, KUNO; FUNK, ROBERT. 1977. [Is Cost Accounting Replacing Public Finance Accounting Methods for Public Information and Documentation Services?]. Nachrichten für Dokumentation (West Germany). 1977 June; 28(3): 115-118. (Text in: German; Abstract in: English). ISSN: 0027-7436.

EUSTACHI, KUNO; SCHWUCHOW, WERNER. 1977. [The Economics of Information and Documentation Services]. Nachrichten für Dokumentation (West Germany). 1977 April; 28(2): 68-73. (Text in: German; Abstract in: English). ISSN: 0027-7436.

FIELDING, DEREK; COCKRELL, WENDELL. 1975. Considerations of Cost in Automating Library Procedures. LASIE (Australia). 1975 November/December; 6(3): 5-9. ISSN: 0047-3774.

FIRSCHEIN, OSCAR; SUMMIT, ROGER K.; MICK, COLIN K. 1978a. Planning for On-Line Search in the Public Library. Special Libraries. 1978 July; 69(7): 255-260. ISSN: 0038-6723.

FIRSCHEIN, OSCAR; SUMMIT, ROGER K.; MICK, COLIN K. 1978b. Use of On-Line Bibliographic Search in Public Libraries: A Retrospective Evaluation. On-Line Review. 1978 March; 2(1): 41-55. ISSN: 0309-314X.

FLOWERDEW, A.D.J.; WHITEHEAD, C.M.E. 1974. Cost-effectiveness and Cost Benefit Analysis in Information Science. London, England: London School of Economics and Political Science; 1974 October. 71p. (OSTI Report no. 5206).

FLOWERDEW, A.D.J.; WHITEHEAD, C.M.E. 1975. Problems in Measuring the Benefits of STI. In: Frielink, A.B., ed. Economics of Informatics. Amsterdam, The Netherlands: North Holland Publishing Co.; 1975. 119-128. ISBN: 0-444-108-483 (U.S.); ISBN: 0-7204-2831-9 (Holland).

FLOWERDEW, A.D.J.; THOMAS, J.J.; WHITEHEAD, C.M.E. 1978. Problems in Forecasting the Price and Demand for On-Line Information Services. In: Elton, Marton C.J.; Lucas, William A.; Conrath, David W.; eds. Evaluating New Telecommunications Services. New York, NY: Plenum Press; 1978. 285-302. ISBN: 0-306-40004-9.

FORD, JILL; FORD, GEOFFREY. 1975. The Costs and Supply Delays of Interlibrary Loans at the University of Lancaster Library. British Lending Library Review. 1975 April; 3(2): 51-54. ISSN: 0305-6503.

FRANCIS, D. PITT. 1976. Cost-Benefit Analysis and Public Library Budgets. Library Review (England). 1976 Spring/Summer; 25(5/6): 189-192. ISSN: 0024-2535.

FRY, BERNARD M.; WHITE, HERBERT S. 1975. Economics and Interaction of the Publisher-Library Relationship in the Production and Use of Scholarly and Research Journals. Bloomington, IN: Indiana University Graduate School of Library Science; 1975 November. 401p. (Final report, NSF Grant no. GN-41398). Available from: U.S. National Science Foundation (NSF), Office of Science Information Services, Washington, DC.

GEE, R.D. 1973. Justification of Information Services. Aslib Proceedings (England). 1973 October; 25(10): 354-363. ISSN: 0001-253X.

GELL, MARILYN KILLEBREW. 1979. User Fees I: The Economic Argument. Library Journal. 1979 January 1; 104(1): 19-23. User Fees II: The Library Response. Library Journal. 1979 January 15; 104(2): 170-173. ISSN: 0000-0027.

GILL, E.D. 1974. A Comparison of Manual and Computer Searches of the Chemical Evolution and Origin of Life Literature. San Jose, CA: San Jose State University, Department of Librarianship; 1974 January. 53p. ERIC: ED 092114.

GOLD, STEVEN D. 1975. Allocating the Book Budget: An Economic Model. College and Research Libraries. 1975 September; 36(5): 397-402. ISSN: 0010-0870.

GROSCH, AUDREY N. 1975. Current and Retrospective Sources of Machine Readable Monograph Cataloging Records: A Study of Their Potential Cost and Utility in Automated System Development at the University of Minnesota. Revised edition. Minneapolis, MN: University of Minnesota Library; 1975 August. 51p. ERIC: ED 112859.

HAMILTON, K.L. 1977. On Pricing of Computer Services: A Bibliography with Annotations and Categorical Listings. Atlanta, GA: Georgia Institute of Technology, College of Industrial Management; 1977 May. 61p. (Working paper no. MS-77-2). Available from: the author.

HAWGOOD, J.; MORRIS, W.E.M. 1976. Benefit Assessment for System Change in Libraries and Information Services: Report on Phase 1. Durham, NC: University of Durham, Department of Computing; 1976. 145p. (BLRD Report no. 5341). Available from: The British Library, Lending Division, Publications, Boston Spa, Wetherby, West Yorkshire LS237BQ.

HELMKAMP, JOHN G. 1969. Managerial Cost Accounting for a Technical Information Center. American Documentation. 1969 April; 20(2): 111-118.

HINDLE, ANTHONY; RAPER, DIANE. 1976. The Economics of Information. In: Williams, Martha E., ed. Annual Review of Information Science and Technology: Volume 11. Washington, DC: American Society for Information Science; 1976. 27-54. ISSN: 0066-4200; ISBN: 0-87715-212-11.

HOBROCK, BRICE G.; BIERMAN, J.; BEVERLY, H.W. 1975. Cost and Cost-Effective Studies in Libraries: 1. A Working Model. 2. Cost Analysis of the Preparations Division at VPI (Virginia Polytechnic Institute) and SU (State University). Blacksburg, VA: Virginia Polytechnic Institute and State University, University Libraries; 1975. 29p. ERIC: ED 108698.

HOOTMAN, J.T. 1977. Basic Considerations in Developing Computer Charging Mechanisms. Data Base. 1977 Spring; 8(4): 4-9. ISSN: 0095-0033.

HSU, JOHN H. 1975. Automated Cost System for an Automated Information Retrieval System. In: Spigai, Frances G.; Graws, Theodore C.W.; Kawabata, Julie, eds. Information Roundup: A Continuing Education Session on Microforms and Data Processing in the Library Information

Center: Costs/Benefits/History/Trends; Proceedings of the 4th Mid-Year Meeting of the American Society for Information Science (ASIS); 1975 May 15-17; Portland, OR. Washington, DC: ASIS; 1975. 159-170. ISBN: 0-87715-112-1.

HUMPHRIES, K.W. 1974. Costing in University Libraries. Library Bulletin. 1974 November/December; (5/6): 8-32. ISSN: 0140-170X.

INDUSTRIAL AND ENGINEERING CHEMISTRY. 1959. Administration of Technical Information Groups. Industrial and Engineering Chemistry. 1959 March; 51(3): 48A-61A.

JACKSON, EUGENE B.; JACKSON, RUTH L. 1977. The Industrial Special Library Universe—A "Base Line" Study of Its Extent and Characteristics. Journal of the American Society for Information Science. 1977 May; 28(3): 135-152. ISSN: 0002-8231.

JONES, JAMES F. 1977. Effort and Cost Analysis of the Cataloging Division. Tallahassee, FL: Florida State University Library; 1977 May. 16p. Available from: the author, Florida State University Library, Tallahassee, FL 32306.

KABI, A. 1972. Use, Efficiency, and Cost of External Information Services. Aslib Proceedings (England). 1972 June; 24(6): 356-362. ISSN: 0001-253X.

KANTOR, PAUL B. 1978. QUBMIS: A Quantitatively Based Management Information System for Libraries. In: Brenner, Everett H.; comp. The Information Age in Perspective: Proceedings of the 41st Annual Meeting of the American Society for Information Science: Volume 15; White Plains, NY: Knowledge Industry Publications, Inc.; 1978. 174-176. ISBN: 0-914236-22-9; ISSN: 0044-7870.

KEARNEY, A.T. 1976. Study of Determinants of Organizational Usage of Scientific and Technical Information. Washington, DC: A.T. Kearney, Inc.; 1976 August. 152p. Available from: A.T. Kearney, Inc., 1800 M Street NW, Washington, DC.

KENT, ALLEN; MONTGOMERY, K.L.; SHIREY D. 1978. A Cost-Benefit Model of Some Critical Library Operations in Terms of Use of Materials. Pittsburgh, PA: University of Pittsburgh: New York, NY: Marcel Dekker, Inc.; 1978 April. 272p. Available from: the author.

KING RESEARCH, INCORPORATED. 1977. Library Photocopying in the United States: With Implications for the Development of a Copyright Royalty Payment Mechanism. Washington, DC: National Commission on Libraries and Information Science; 1977 October. 251p. Available from: King Research Inc., 6000 Executive Blvd., Rockville, MD 20852.

KING, DONALD W. 1976. Statistical Indicators of Scientific and Technical Communication (1960-1980): Volume II. Rockville, MD: King Research, Inc.; 1976 January. 477p. (Also later volumes). Available from: King Research Inc., 6000 Executive Blvd., Rockville, MD 20852.

KING, DONALD W. 1978. Pricing Policies in Academic Libraries. Rockville, MD: King Research Inc.; 1978 December. 24p. Available from: King Research, Inc., 6000 Executive Blvd., Rockville, MD 20852.

KING, DONALD W. 1979. Pricing Policies in Academic Libraries. Library Trends. 1979 Summer; 28(1):47-62. ISSN: 0024-2594.

KING, DONALD W.; RODERER, N.K. 1978. A Study of Pricing Policies for Information Products and Services. Rockville, MD: King Research, Inc.; 1978 March. (Prepared for U.S. Geological Survey; National Cartographic Information Center). Available from: King Research, Inc., 6000 Executive Blvd., Rockville, MD 20852.

KING, DONALD W.; RODERER, N.K.; MICK, C.K.; MILLER, R.H. 1978. Systems Analysis of Scientific and Technical Communication in the United States. Rockville, MD: King Research, Inc.; 1978 May. Volumes 1-5. NTIS: PB 281847, PB 281848, PB 281849, PB 281850, PB 281851.

KLEIJNEN, JACK P.C. 1978a. Economic Framework for Information Systems. Tilburg, Netherlands: Tilburg University, Department of Economics; 1978 November. 23p. Available from: the author, Katholieke Hogeschool, Department of Business and Economics, P.O. Box 90153; 5000 LE Tilburg, Netherlands.

KLEIJNEN, JACK P.C. 1978b. Preliminary draft: Quantifying Financial Benefits of Information: A Critical Survey of Theories and Tools. 1978. 64p. Available from: the author, Katholieke Hogeschool, Department of Business and Economics, P.O. Box 90153; 5000 LE Tilburg, Netherlands.

KLEIJNEN, JACK P.C. 1979. Computers and Profits; Quantifying Financial Benefits of Information. Reading, MA: Addison-Wesley Publishing Co.; 1979. Available from: the author, Katholieke Hogeschool, Department of Business and Economics, P.O. Box 90153; 5000 LE Tilburg, Netherlands.

KLINTOE, KJELD. 1971. Cost Analysis of a Technical Information Center. Aslib Proceedings (England). 1971 July; 23(7): 362-371. ISSN: 0001-253X.

KOUNTZ, JOHN. 1972. Library Cost Analysis: A Recipe. Library Journal. 1972 February; 97(13): 459-464. ISSN: 0000-0027.

KRAMER, JOSEPH. 1971. How to Survive in Industry: Cost Justifying Library Services. Special Libraries. 1971 November; 62(11): 487-489. ISSN: 0038-6723.

LA ROCCO, AUGUST; FENG, CYRIL. 1977. Excerpta Medica Abstracting Journals: A Case Study of Costs to Medical School Libraries. Bulletin of the Medical Library Association. 1977 April; 65(2): 255-260. ISSN: 0025-7338.

LANCASTER, F. WILFRID. 1977. The Measurement and Evaluation of Library Services. Washington, DC: Information Resources Press; 1977. 395p. ISBN: 0-87815-017X.

LANGLEY, PHYLLIS R. 1976. A Comparison between Mail-Access Computer and Manual Searching. RQ: Reference Quarterly. 1976; 15(3): 229-232. ISSN: 0022-2232.

LANTZ, BRIAN E. 1978. Manual versus Computerized Retrospective Reference Retrieval in an Academic Library. Journal of Librarianship. 1978 April; 10(2): 119-130. ISSN: 0025-7338.

LEARMONT, CAROL L.; DARLING, RICHARD L. 1978. Placements and Salaries 1977: The Picture Brightens. Library Journal. 1978 July; 103(13): 1339-1345. ISSN: 0000-0027.

LEIMKUHLER, FERDINAND F.; COOPER, MICHAEL D. 1971a. Analytical Models for Library Planning. Journal of the American Society for Information Science. 1971 November-December; 22(6): 390-398. ISSN: 0002-8231.

LEIMKUHLER, FERDINAND F.; COOPER, MICHAEL D. 1971b. Cost of Accounting and Analysis for University Libraries. College and Research Libraries. 1971 November; 32(6): 449-464. ISSN: 0010-0870.

LEONARD, LAWRENCE E.; MAIER, JOAN M.; DOUGHERTY, RICHARD
M. 1969. Centralized Book Processing. Metuchen, NJ: Scarecrow
Press, 1969. 401p. ISBN: 8108-0263-5.

LEVINE, JAMIE J.; LOGAN, TIMOTHY. 1977. Online Resource Sharing,
a Comparison of Ballots and OCLC; A Guide for Library Administrators.
San Jose, CA: California Library Authority for Systems and Services;
1977. 171p. Available from: California Library Authority for Systems
and Services.

LIBRARY JOURNAL. 1977a. It All Boiled Down to Money. Library
Journal. 1977 March 15; 102(6): 682-691. ISSN: 0000-0027.

LIBRARY JOURNAL. 1977b. The Key Word Was Access. Library Journal. 1977 August; 102(14): 1555-1572. ISSN: 0000-0027.

LIBRARY JOURNAL. 1978. The Online Revolution in Libraries. Library
Journal. 1978 February 15; 103(3): 439-441. ISSN: 0000-0027.

LINDFORD, JOHN. 1977. To Charge or Not to Charge: A Rationale.
Library Journal. 1977 October 1: 2009-2010. ISSN: 0000-0027.

LINDQUIST, MATS G. 1978. The Dynamics of Information Search
Services. Stockholm, Sweden: The Royal Institute of Technology; 1978
February. 191p. (Report TRITA-LIB-6012). Available from: Royal
Institute of Technology Library, Publications Office, S-100 44 Stock-
holm 70, Sweden.

LYDERS, RICHARD; ECKELS, DIANE; LEATHERBURY, MAURICE C.
1978. Cost Allocation and Cost Generation. Paper presented at:
Annual Convention of the Association of College & Research Libraries;
1978 November 8-11; Boston, MA. 1978. 21p. Available from: R.
Lyders, Executive Director, Houston Academy of Medicine, Texas
Medical Center Library; Houston, TX 77030.

MACHLUP, FRITZ. 1979. The Production and Distribution of Knowledge in the United States. 2nd edition. Princeton, NJ: Princeton University Press; 1979. ISBN: 0-691-08608-7.

MARCHANT, MAURICE P. 1975. University Libraries as Economic Systems. College and Research Libraries. 1975 November; 36(6): 449-
457. ISSN: 0010-0870.

MARTIN, GORDON P.; WEST, MARTHA W. 1975. Basis for Resource
Allocation: Analysis of Operations in a Large Library System. Library
Trends. 1975 April; 3(4): 573-586. ISSN: 0024-2594.

MARTIN, SUSAN K. 1974. Library Networks 1974-1975. White Plains,
NY: Knowledge Industry Publications, Inc.; 1974. 110p. ISBN: 0-
914236-01-6.

MARTIN, SUSAN K. 1976. Library Networks 1976-1977. White Plains,
NY: Knowledge Industry Publications, Inc.; 1976. 131p. ISBN:
0-914236-06-7.

MASON, ROBERT M. 1977. Development of a Cost Benefit Methodology
for Scientific and Technical Information Communication and Application to Information Analysis Centers. Atlanta, GA: Metrics, Inc.; 1977.
223p. NTIS: PB 278566/AS.

MASON, ROBERT M. 1978. The Economics and Cost Benefit of Analysis
Services—The Case of Information Analysis Centers. In: Elton, Martin
C.J.; Lucas, William A.; Conrath, David W., eds. Evaluating New Telecommunications Services. New York, NY: Plenum Press; 1978. 303-
324. ISBN: 0-306-40004-9.

MASON, ROBERT M.; SASSONE, PETER G. 1978. A Lower Bound Cost Benefit Model for Information Services. Information Processing & Management. 1978;14(2):71-83. ISSN: 0306-4573.

MATTAJ, ALISA. 1977. Subscription Costs of Serials Held at the BLLD. British Lending Library Review. 1977 January; 5(1): 26-28. ISSN: 0305-6503.

MCQUISTON, MAKALA. 1975. A Comparison of Four Modes of Transmitting Inter-Library Loan Requests. RQ: Reference Quarterly. 1975 Winter; 15(2): 150-152. ISSN: 0033-7072.

MICK, COLIN K. 1977. Investigation of the Public Library as a Linking Agent to Major Scientific, Educational, Social and Environmental Data Bases: Final Evaluation Report. In: Summit, Roger; Firschein, Oscar. Investigation of the Public Library as a Linking Agent to Major Scientific, Educational, Social and Environmental Data Bases. Palo Alto, CA: Lockheed Missiles & Space Company; 1977 October. 120p. NTIS: PB 276727/5WL.

MICK, COLIN K. 1978. Evaluation of the METRO Online Search Program. Palo Alto, CA: Applied Communication Research, Inc.; 1978 February. 41p. NTIS: PB 278532/AS.

MICK, COLIN K.; MILLER, RICHARD. 1978. Developing a Methodology to Assess the "Health" of the STI Community in the U.S. Palo Alto, CA: Applied Communication Research, Inc.; 1978. 322p. NTIS: PB 278749/AS.

MILLER, RICHARD; MICK, COLIN K. 1978. A National Systems Analysis of Scientific and Technical Communication: Working Papers 1-14. Palo Alto, CA: Applied Communication Research, Inc. (ACR); 1978. Available from: ACR, P.O. Box 5849, Stanford, CA 94305.

MOISSE, E. 1976. Costing Information in an Independent Research Organization. Information Scientist (England). 1976 June; 10(7): 57-68. ISSN: 0020-0263.

MONTAGUE, ELEANOR; BROWN, MARYANN KEVIN; MCHUGH, ANITA; GLASSER, SCOTT; HAENSELMAN, MARY. 1976. Cost and Funding Studies of the Proposed Western Interstate Bibliographic Network. Boulder, CO: Western Interstate Commission for Higher Education (WICHE); 1976 November. 24p. Available from: the Author.

MONTGOMERY, K. LEON; BULICK, STEPHEN; FETTERMAN, JOHN; KENT, ALLEN. 1976. Cost-Benefit Model of Library Acquisitions in Terms of Use: Progress report. Journal of the American Society for Information Science. 1976 January-February; 27(1): 73-74. ISSN: 0002-8231.

MORITA, ICHIKI T.; GAPEN, D. KAYE. 1977. A Cost Analysis of the Ohio College Library Center On-Line Shared Cataloging System in the Ohio State University Libraries. Library Resources & Technical Services. 1977 Summer; 21(3): 286-302. ISSN: 0024-2527.

OLSEN, HAROLD A. 1972. The Economics of Information: Bibliography and Commentary on the Literature. 2nd edition. Information, Part 2: Reports-Bibliographies. 1972 March/April; 1(2): 1-40.

OLSEN, PAUL E. 1976. The Union Catalog—Its Costs versus Its Benefit to a Network. Special Libraries. 1976 May/June; 67(5/6): 251-255. ISSN: 0038-6723.

OWEN, J.L. 1977. Workshop Session II: Theme—Recording and Costing the Library's Activities. Australian Special Library News. 1977 March; 10(1): 29-41. ISSN: 0005-027X.

PALMER, C.R.; ed. 1975. Management Guidelines for Cost Accounting and Cost Control for Automatic Data Processing Activities and Systems. Washington, DC: U.S. General Accounting Office (GAO), Financial and General Management Studies Division; 1975 September 17. Available from: USGAO, Washington, DC 20548.

PALMOUR, VERNON; BELLASSAI, MARCIA C.; WIEDERKEHR, ROBERT R.V. 1977. Costs of Owning, Borrowing, and Disposing of Periodical Publications. Arlington, VA: Public Research Institute; 1977 October. 71p. NTIS: PB 274821/8WL.

PITT, WILLIAM BRUCE; KRAFT, DONALD H. 1974. Buy or Copy? A Library Operations Research Model. Information Storage and Retrieval. 1974 September/October; 10(9/10): 331-341. ISSN: 0020-0271.

PORAT, MARC URI. 1977. The Information Economy: Definition and Measurement. Washington, DC: U.S. Government Printing Office, Superintendent of Documents; 1977 May. 250p. (OT Special publication no. 77-12(1)). USGPO: SN 003-000-00512-7.

PRATT, GORDON, ed. 1976. Information Economics: Costs and Prices of Machine-Readable Information in Europe. London, England: Aslib and EUSIDIC; 1976. 115p. (European User Series, no. 2). ISBN: 85412-0788.

PRICE, DOUGLAS S. 1971. Collecting and Reporting Real Costs of Information Systems. Tutorial presented at the 34th Annual Meeting of the American Society for Information Science (ASIS); 1971 November 7-11; Washington, DC. 160p. ERIC: ED 055592.

PRICE, DOUGLAS S. 1973a. Real Costs for Information Managers. In: Slater, Frank, ed. Cost Reduction for Special Libraries and Information Centers: [Proceedings of] the National Library Week Symposium III; 1972 April 20-21; Minneapolis, MN. New York, NY: American Society for Information Science; 1973 June. 156-176. (Tutorial keynote address). ISBN: 0-87715-104-0.

PRICE, DOUGLAS S. 1973b. The Cost of Information: A Prerequisite for Other Analyses. In: Taylor, Robert S., ed. Economics of Information Dissemination: A Symposium; 1973; Syracuse, NY. Syracuse, NY: Syracuse University, School of Library Science; 1973. 21-48. Available from: Syracuse University, School of Library Science, Publications, 113 Euclid Avenue, Syracuse, NY 13210.

PRICE, DOUGLAS S. 1974. Rational Cost Information: Necessary and Obtainable. Special Libraries. 1974 February; 65(2): 49-57. ISSN: 0038-6723.

PROSSER, CAROLYN. 1975. Cost Analysis Without Tears: Some Hints for Librarians. New Library World (England). 1974 August; 75(890): 163-165.

RANDALL, G.E. 1975. Budgeting for Libraries. Special Libraries. 1975 January; 66(1): 6-11. ISSN: 0038-6723.

RANDALL, G.E. 1976. Randall's Rationalized Ratios. Special Libraries. 1976 January; 67(1): 8-12. ISSN: 0038-6723.

REED, JUTTA R. 1976. Cost Comparison of Periodicals in Hard Copy and on Microform. Microform Review. 1976 July; 5(3): 185-192. ISSN: 0002-6530.

REED, MARY JANE POBST. 1975. Cost Figures: Washington Library Network. In: Spigai, Frances G.; Graws, Theodore, C.W.; Kawabata, Julie, eds. Information Roundup: A Continuing Education Session on Microforms and Data Processing in the Library Information Center: Costs/Benefits/History/Trends; Proceedings of the 4th Mid-Year Meeting of the American Society for Information Science (ASIS); 1975 May 15-17; Portland, OR. Washington, DC: ASIS; 1975. 62-66. ISBN: 0-87715-112-1.

REGAZZI, JOHN J. 1977. Performance Measures for Information Retrieval Systems. In: Fry, Bernard M.; Shepherd, Clayton A., comp. Information Management in the 1980's: Proceedings of the 40th Annual Meeting of the American Society for Information Science (ASIS): Volume 14: 1977 September 26-October 1; Chicago, IL. White Plains, NY: Knowledge Industry Publications, Inc.; 1977. p13. ISSN: 0044-7870; ISBN: 0-914236.

REYNOLDS, ROSE. 1970. A Selective Bibliography on Measurement in Library and Information Services. London, England: Aslib; 1970. 19p. Available from: Aslib, 3 Belgrave Sq., London, England.

ROBERTSON, STEPHEN E.; DATTA, S. 1973. Analysis of On-Line Searching Costs. Information Scientist (England). 1973 January; 7(1): 9-13. ISSN: 0020-0263.

ROBERTSON, STEPHEN E.; REYNOLDS, ROSE; WILKIN, A.P. 1970. Standard Costing for Information Systems: Background to a Current Study. Aslib Proceedings (England). 1970 September; 22(9): 452-457. ISSN: 0001-253X.

ROWE, D. 1974. Application of the Theory of the Firm to Library Costing. Australian Library Journal. 1974 April; 23(3): 108-111. ISSN: 0004-9670.

SACHER, HANS JOACHIM; SCHULZE, ADELHEID. 1975. [Application of a Work Time Analysis for Cost Calculation in Libraries]. Zentralblatt für Bibliothekswesen (East Germany). 1975 March; 89(3): 116-126. (Text in German). ISSN: 0044-4081.

SENDERS, J.W.; ANDERSON, C.M.B.; HECHT, C.D. 1976. Scientific Publication Systems: An Analysis of Past, Present and Future Methods of Scientific Communication. Toronto, Canada: University of Toronto; 1976. 181p. (SIS74-12627 A01).

SHIRLEY, SHERRILYNNE. 1978. A Survey of Computer Search Service Costs in the Academic Health Sciences Library. Bulletin of the Medical Library Association. 1978 October; 66(4): 390-396. ISSN: 0025-7338.

SHOFFNER, RALPH M. 1975. Comparative Cost Analysis. In: Spigai, Frances G.; Graws, Theodore C.W.; Kawabata, Julie, eds. Information Roundup: A Continuing Education Session on Microforms and Data Processing in the Library Information Center: Costs/Benefits/History/Trends; Proceedings of the 4th Mid-Year Meeting of the American Society for Information Science (ASIS); 1975 May 15-17; Portland, OR. Washington, DC: ASIS; 1975. 1-32. ISBN: 0-87715-112-1.

SLATER, FRANK, ed. 1973. Cost Reduction for Special Libraries and Information Centers. New York, NY: American Society for Information Science; 1973 June. 187p. ISBN: 0-87715-104-0.

SMETANA, FREDERICK O.; FURNISS, MARY ANN; POTTER, T. ROBERT. 1974. A Study of the Relative Effectiveness and Costs of Computerized Information Retrieval in the Interactive Mode. Research Triangle Park,

NC: North Carolina Science and Technology Research Center; 1974 November. 99p. Available from: The Center.

SMITH, G.C.K.; SCHOFIELD, J.L. 1971. Administrative Effectiveness: Times and Costs of Library Operations. Journal of Librarianship. 1971 October; 3(4): 245-266. ISSN: 0022-2232.

SPENCE, A. MICHAEL. 1974. The Economics of Information. In: Cuadra, Carlos A.; Luke, Ann W.; Harris, Jessica L.; eds. Annual Review of Information Science and Technology: Volume 9. Washington, DC: American Society for Information Science; 1974. 57-78. ISSN: 0066-4200.

SPENCER, CAROL C. 1971. Random Time Sampling with Self-Observation for Library Cost Studies: Unit Costs of Interlibrary Loans and Photocopies at a Regional Medical Center. Journal of the American Society for Information Science. 1971 May-June; 22(3): 153-160. ISSN: 0002-8231.

TALAVAGE, J.; BARASH, H.; LEIMKUHLER, F.; LEVY, D. 1976. The Economic Characteristics of Information Analysis Centers. West Lafayette, IN: School of Industrial Engineering, Purdue University; 1976 August. 67p. (A Progress Report). Available from: the author.

TESOVNIK, MARY E.; DEHART, FLORENCE E. 1970. Unpublished Studies of Technical Service Time and Costs: A Selected Bibliography. Library Resources & Technical Services. 1970 Winter; 14(1): 56-67. ISSN: 0024-2527.

TRESSEL, GEORGE W.; BROWN, PATRICIA L. 1975. A Critical Review of Research Related to the Economics of the Scientific and Technical Information Industry. Washington, DC: National Science Foundation; 1975 March 25. 60p. NTIS: PB 245-665.

URQUHART, D.J. 1976. Economic Analysis of Information Services. Journal of Documentation (England). 1976; 32(2): 123-125. ISSN: 0022-0418.

U.S. GENERAL ACCOUNTING OFFICE (GAO). TASK GROUP ON MANAGEMENT GUIDELINES FOR COST ACCOUNTING. 1976. Selected Literature on Cost Accounting and Cost Control for Automatic Data Processing—a Bibliography. Washington, DC: USGAO, Division of Financial and General Management Studies; 1976 January 7.

VANTINE, CAROL. 1976. Fee-Based Information Services within the Public Library. In: Minor, Barbara B., ed. Proceedings of the Information Broker/Free Lance Librarian—New Careers—New Library Services Workshop; 1976; Syracuse, NY. Syracuse, NY: Syracuse University, School of Information Studies; 1976 August. 17-30. (Miscellaneous Studies no. 3). Available from: Syracuse University, School of Information Studies, Publications Office, 1133 Euclid Ave., Syracuse, NY 13210.

VICKERS, PETER H. 1976a. Extension and Revision of the Cost/Accounting Scheme to Interactive Systems of the Network. London, England: Aslib Consultancy Service; 1976 May. 90p. (Report no. EUR 5627e). Available from: EURONET.

VICKERS, PETER H. 1976b. Ground Rules for Cost-Effectiveness. Aslib Proceedings (England). 1976 June-July; 28(6-7): 224-229. ISSN: 0001-253X.

VICKERS, PETER H.; ROWAT, M. 1976. Development and Use of Models for the Prediction of Costs for Alternative Information Systems: Final Report. London, England: Aslib Consultancy Service; 1976 July. Available from: Aslib, 3 Belgrave Sq., London, England.

VOLLHARDT, CILLY. 1973. [Cost Structure in Industrial Libraries].
In: Kaegen, Paul, ed. [Library Cooperation: Aspects and Possibilities]:
Lectures Given at a Library Congress; 1973 June 12-16; Hamburg, West
Germany. 1974. 246-256.
WAINWRIGHT, JANE. 1976. Why Use a Mini-Computer? Some Factors
Affecting Their Selection. Program (England). 1976 January; 10(11):
7-13. ISSN: 0033-0307.
WANGER, JUDITH; CUADRA, CARLOS A.; FISHBURN, MARY. 1976.
Impact of On-line Retrieval Services: A Survey of Users, 1974-1975.
Santa Monica, CA: System Development Corporation; 1976. 294p.
ISBN: 0-916368-01-7.
WEST, MARTHA W.; BAXTER, BARBARA A. 1976. Unpublished Studies
of Technical Service Time and Costs: A Supplement. Library Resources
and Technical Services. 1976 Fall; 20(4): 326-333. ISSN: 0361-526X.
WESTERN INTERSTATE COMMISSION FOR HIGHER EDUCATION
(WICHE). 1976. Librarian's Handbook for Costing Network Services.
Boulder, CO: Western Interstate Commission for Higher Education; 1976
December 20. 31p. Available from: WICHE, Boulder, CO.
WHITE, HERBERT S. 1977. The Economic Interaction of Scholarly Jour-
nal Publishing and Libraries During the Present Period of Cost Increases
and Budget Reductions: Implications for Serials Librarians. Serials
Librarian. 1977 Spring; 1(3): 221-230. ISSN: 0361-526X.
WILDE, DANIEL W. 1976. Generation and Use of Machine-Readable Data
Bases. In: Williams, Martha E., ed. Annual Review of Information
Science and Technology: Volume 11. Washington, DC: American
Society for Information Science; 1976. 267-298. ISSN: 0066-4200;
ISBN: 0-87715-212-11.
WILKIN, A.P.; REYNOLDS, ROSE; ROBERTSON, STEPHEN E. 1972.
Standard Times for Information Systems: A Method for Data Collection
and Analysis. Journal of Documentation (England). 1972 June; 28(2):
131-150. ISSN: 0022-0418.
WILLIAMS, GORDON; BRYANT, EDWARD C.; WIEDEKEHR, ROBERT
P.V.; PALMOUR, VERNON E.; SIEHLER, CYNTHIA J. 1968. Library
Cost Models: Owning versus Borrowing Serial Publications. Bethesda,
MD: Westat Research, Inc.; 1968 November. 167p. ERIC: PB 182
304.
WILLS, GORDON; CHRISTOPHER, MARTIN. 1970. Cost/Benefit Analy-
sis of Company Information Needs. Unesco Bulletin for Libraries
(France). 1970 January/February; 24(1): 9-22. (English, Russian,
Spanish, French language editions available). ISSN: 0041-5243.
WILLS, GORDON; OLDMAN, CHRISTINE. 1977. The Beneficial Library:
A Methodological Investigation to Identify Ways of Measuring the
Benefits Provided by Libraries. Cranfield, England: Cranfield Institute
of Technology School of Management; 1977. 257p. (BLRD Report
no. 5389). Available from: Publications, The British Library Lending
Division, Boston Spa, Wetherby, West Yorkshire LS237BQ.
WILSON, JOHN H. 1972. Costs, Budgeting, and Economics of Informa-
tion Processing. In: Cuadra, Carlos A., ed. Annual Review of Informa-
tion Science and Technology: Volume 7. Washington, DC: American
Society for Information Science. 1972. 39-67. ISSN: 0066-4200;
ISBN: 0-87715-212-7.

WISH, JOHN R.; WISH, MARY ANN. 1975. Marketing and Pricing of On-Line Services. In: Spigai, Frances G.; Graws, Theodore C.W.; Kawabata, Julie, eds. Information Roundup: A Continuing Education Session on Microforms and Data Processing in the Library Information Center: Costs/Benefits/History/Trends; Proceedings of the 4th Mid-Year Meeting of the American Society for Information Science (ASIS); 1975 May 15-17; Portland, OR. Washington, DC: ASIS; 1975. 143-158. ISBN: 0-87715-112-1.

WISH, JOHN R.; COLLINS, CRAIG; JACOBSON, VANCE. 1977. Terminal Costs for On-Line Searching. College and Research Libraries. 1977 July; 38(4): 291-297. ISSN: 0010-0870.

WOLFE, J.N.; AITCHISON, THOMAS M.; BRYDON, DONALD H.; SCOTT, ALEXANDER; YOUNG, RALPH. 1974. The Economics of Technical Information Systems. New York, NY: Praeger Publishers; 1974. 167p. ISBN: 0-275-07520-6.

ZAAIMAN, R.B. 1972. A Breakdown of Manpower Costs in Relation to Tasks for an Industrial Information Service. In: Proceedings of the (ISLIC) International Conference on Information Science; 1972; Tel Aviv, Israel. 305-317.

ZAIS, HARRIET W. 1977. Economic Modeling: An Aid to the Pricing of Information Services. Journal of the American Society for Information Science. 1977 March; 28(2): 89-95. ISSN: 0002-8231.

II

Basic Techniques and Tools

The four chapters in this section include: "Empirical Foundations of Information Science" by Pranas Zunde and John Gehl of the Georgia Institute of Technology; "Experimental Techniques of Information Retrieval" by Michael McGill and Jennifer Huitfeldt of Syracuse University; "Unconventional Computer Architectures for Information Retrieval" by Lee Hollaar of the University of Illinois; and "Database Management Systems" by Michael Huffenberger and Ronald Wigington of Chemical Abstracts Service.

Zunde and Gehl treat the foundations of information science as an empirical discipline. They characterize empirical science and review the literature within the general framework of: core research problems; formal extensions—i.e., constructs, calculi, and measures; the search for empirical laws; and theories of information science. Among the core research problems they consider the aggregation of information, information decay, extension of Shannon's theory, development of new modeling methods, development of information measures and performance criteria, the relation between semiotic form and information content, the relation between information and knowledge, and the processes and mechanisms of cognition and learning.

Much of the research in information retrieval focuses on fundamental issues and theories. Since there is no single theory on which the field is based, McGill and Huitfeldt review papers on the various approaches researchers have studied, including set theory, fuzzy set theory, utility theory, and probabilistic theory. Probability theory provides a reasonable foundation for theoretical research in such areas as term clustering, frequency weighting, relevance weighting, and ranking. The field of artificial intelligence provides models for analysis and comparison, and short-term learning experiments and pattern recognition models provide insight into relevance judgment and feedback techniques. Much of this research on models and applications from models is experimental. Systems that use term weighting, clustered files, automatic feedback, and ranking algorithms seem to be practical, but they may not be commonly available for several years.

Natural language processing for text and fact retrieval is a complex and difficult research goal. There is some progress in this area, as well as in the understanding of the information needs of users. Research on improving indexing techniques and search strategies, as well as theoretical foundations and data organization, continues with substantial success. However, the evaluation of systems remains a concern, and many different performance criteria are used: access time, cost convenience to user, relevance of retrieved documents, etc.

Hollaar believes that the steadily increasing software costs and even more rapidly decreasing hardware costs are the rationale for seeking alternatives to the conventional, i.e., von Neumann, computer architecture, which has been the standard since it was first introduced more than 30 years ago. Recently, several projects have examined alternative internal structures for information retrieval computers. These have included the use of associative processors, rotating memory processors, full-text search machines, and computers that are optimized for handling structural information, such as inverted files.

Hollaar's chapter briefly describes a "conventional architecture" and its limitations and summarizes the proposed alternatives. Although most descriptions have been directed toward computer scientists, the potential impact of these proposed architectures make them of interest to anyone who is operating or is contemplating a large-scale information retrieval project.

The chapter by Huffenberger and Wigington marks the first review of database management systems (DBMS) in *ARIST*. After an initial development phase during the mid-1960s and early 1970s, the field has burgeoned; continued strong growth is confidently predicted. Thus, this review is timely.

Basic concepts and a definition of "database" lead off the chapter and provide a foundation for subsequent discussion. DBMS history is briefly recounted, with literature references to exhaustive accounts of early DBMS development.

The concepts of "logical" and "physical" are examined in the context of databases and database management systems. These concepts are used throughout to explain approaches to design and function of actual DBMS packages.

Technical and management views of DBMS software and administrative environments are presented. The chapter suggests that database management systems have enormous potential if the proper commitments and considerations are made.

Limitations and issues involved in database management systems are discussed. Referenced articles and the authors' experiences are summarized to provide insight into topics of interest for those who are committed (or about to be committed) to DBMS as a way of life.

The state-of-the-art and some predictions for database management systems are discussed. The chapter concludes with cautious optimism about the future of this field.

3 Empirical Foundations of Information Science

PRANAS ZUNDE
Georgia Institute of Technology

JOHN GEHL
Georgia Institute of Technology

INTRODUCTION

This chapter focuses on the foundations of information science as an *empirical discipline* and discusses research efforts that are attempting to strengthen and to expand the scientific foundations upon which all other work in this area is ultimately based. Essential in this respect is research on the nature of information aimed at discovering empirical laws that govern information phenomena. It includes, among other things, studies of information growth, aging and obsolescence of information, information diffusion and propagation, and effects of text structure on information content. Although some of these studies are often referred to as "bibliometrics" (which in *ARIST*, Volume 12, Chapter 2, was described as covering "all studies which seek to quantify the processes of written communication"), the coverage of this chapter is considerably broader since it is not limited to *written* communication processes.

ESSENTIAL CHARACTERISTICS OF AN EMPIRICAL SCIENCE

The main objective of any empirical science, beyond a mere *description* of empirical phenomena, is to establish, through laws and theories, *general principles* by which the phenomena can be explained and predicted. These underlying principles of an empirical discipline constitute its empirical foundations

Research by these authors on the empirical foundations of information science has been supported partly by the National Science Foundation; Grant DSI77-05297. This support is gratefully acknowledged.

(MARGENAU). Consequently, scientific activity entails data or empirical evidence, on the one hand, and theories, on the other, both in constant interplay.

If knowledge derived from observation and experimentation in a subject is to qualify as a scientific discipline, it should possess, in substance, the following characteristics:

- It must have identified and delimited its specific area of study and its fundamental (or "core") research problems;
- It must have developed its own characteristic constructs (concepts) and language for describing the subject matter scientifically and for deriving meaningful rules of correspondence (including operational definitions, measures, etc.) between the constructs and the empirical data;
- It must have discovered empirical laws that express certain continuing relationships among the phenomena observed; and
- It must have formulated, in terms of a theory or set of theories, a broad systematic structure that encompasses families of empirical laws and explains them in a scientifically rational manner.

Here we adopt the view that information science is the study of the nature of information as it manifests itself in various phenomena related to information generation, transmission, transformation, accumulation, storage, and other such processes. We do not limit the subject matter to a particular type of information, although there is a tendency, particularly in Europe, to restrict the domain of study to scientific and technical information. The history of information science as an intellectual discipline was covered in *ARIST*, Volume 12, by SHERA & CLEVELAND. Here we review only the contributions to the foundations of information science in the sense outlined above.

CORE RESEARCH PROBLEMS IN INFORMATION SCIENCE

A central problem in information science is the study of the nature of information. However, there is some confusion about "nature" as used in this context. Information science as an empirical discipline is *not* concerned with what information is in an ontological or metaphysical sense. (Likewise, physics and chemistry are not concerned with the question of whether or not things really exist.) Problems of this kind lie in the domain of philosophy, not science. The subject of concern to information science is the phenomena through which the nature of information is revealed and embodied.

Recently, the question of fundamental research problems in information science was discussed by BELKIN, BROOKES, RESNIKOFF, SLAMECKA, M.E. WILLIAMS, and ZUNDE (1978). Zunde and, in particular, Slamecka treat this topic at a rather abstract level, emphasizing the broad domain of research. The other authors, particularly Resnikoff, are primarily concerned with specific research problems. These problems are briefly described below.

The Problem of Aggregation of Information

As RESNIKOFF notes, the feature that dominates all practical considerations of information systems is *size* because real disorganization (or real organization) is possible only with large collections of information. For example, a "library" of only a few books cannot be disorganized in any interesting sense of that word. However, a substantial increase in the size of any kind of information collection not only brings up practical problems (e.g., access) but also raises vital theoretical questions about the effect of the size upon the nature, organization, and value of the information. Thus, the problem is to investigate how information collections are affected by and depend on their qualitative parameters.

Information Decay

In one sense, information decay is the converse of information growth—if we think of information as a valuable commodity and regard decay (aging, obsolescence) as a reduction of that value. Little is known about the different processes and the associated laws according to which different kinds of information lose their meaning, validity, relevance, or value. Work done so far has described only the aging of documents.

Extension of Shannon's Information Theory

Shannon's information theory is the best developed formal language (or calculus) in information science, but it is of limited interpretability. It found its most fruitful interpretation in the field of communication systems engineering. Straightforward attempts to interpret it in different contexts, particularly in information processes at semantic and pragmatic levels, have mostly failed to produce the expected results. Apparently the cause of the failure is not so much the language as the rules of interpretation used in applying it. When the rules of interpretation and the rules of correspondence between concepts of information theory and observables were chosen carefully, the results were encouraging (e.g., the extensions of information theory to certain semantic processes made by BAR-HILLEL & CARNAP). An overview of the limitations of Shannon's information theory relative to a general science of information has recently been given by SUPPE. However, a thorough analysis of possibilities of extending information theory to various information science problems and the eventual implementation of such extensions is a task still to be accomplished.

Development of New Modeling Methods

Specific suggestions for this kind of research have been made by RESNIKOFF. One is what the author calls "the problem of structure families." Here one is concerned with identification of an optimal information structure selected from a set of alternatives. The specification of families of structures that are reasonable candidates and their formal description in terms that are suitable for applying analytical processes is the problem of structure families. A second example is what Resnikoff calls the "problem of information homomorphism." This problem is to define mappings of some information store to an access collection (an index, collection of abstracts, etc.) preserving certain significant aspects of the information content of their domains and then to study their invariants. These mappings are called homomorphisms. Although some of their properties have been investigated by HEILPRIN (1972), the subject requires further research.

Development of Information Measures and Performance Criteria

ZUNDE (1978) has noted that:

> The order of advancement in the development of scientific tools for information systems design is, approximately, as follows: most advanced are methods and techniques which are primarily applicable to handle information systems design problems of a syntactic nature (e.g., communication system design); much less developed are methods and techniques to handle design problems of a semantic nature; and least developed are those required to handle design problems of a pragmatic nature. Indirectly, the above conclusions map out the most promising and prospective research areas in information systems design.

It is probably not a coincidence that the above order also reflects the state of development of information measures and performance criteria at the syntactic, semantic, and pragmatic levels, respectively. Development of quantitative measures, often a prerequisite for *optimization*, has been emphasized by RESNIKOFF as another fundamental problem of information science. The problem encompasses performance criteria relative to characteristics such as informativeness, relevance, timeliness, or utility. The problem of cost, suggested by Resnikoff, is in the same category.

Relation between Semiotic Form and Information Content

SLAMECKA identifies problems in this area as studies on: signs, symbol systems, language and information, and the formal properties of knowledge. ZUNDE (1978) adopts essentially the same viewpoint and emphasizes the need for identifying empirical laws associated with each of these research problems. Resnikoff characterizes this area as "the problem of form and content"; for linguistic communication the problem is the extent to which semantics is reducible to syntax. The question of whether or not there are formal substitutes for semantics, some of which may lie outside the usual realm of language studies, is still wide open.

The Problem of Relating Information to Knowledge

This problem is considered central to information science by both BROOKES and BELKIN. According to Brookes:

> In a rough and ready way we can say that *knowledge* is a summation of many bits of information which have been organized into some sort of coherent entity. This relationship can be expressed very simply in what I call the fundamental equation of information science: $\Delta I = (S + \Delta S) - (S)$, where (S) is a "knowledge structure" and $(S + \Delta S)$ is the modified knowledge structure caused by absorption of the increment of information I. The equation looks simple enough but in fact we do not know how to interpret any of its symbols or any of its signs. In effect, the equation merely defines information as that which changes a knowledge structure. But as we do not know what a knowledge structure is, the equation defines the unknown in terms of another unknown and is a process in a vicious circle of very small radius.

Brookes claims that the fundamental problem of information science is to interpret this equation and thereby to "explain" information processes.

Information Processes and Mechanisms of Cognition and Learning

SLAMECKA labels this area as work done on "the cognitive level" of fundamental research, and he identifies such subcategories as "sensory characteristics of human information processing," "human information processes," and "man/machine communication." RESNIKOFF characterizes the topic as "the problem of informational pattern recognition." A particularly important aspect of this research, which also attracts much attention in other disciplines, is the problem of information representation in animate and inanimate information processes (e.g., in human memory and in computers). M.E. WILLIAMS stresses the need to understand how the human converts both nonquantified and quantified knowledge information into retained knowledge. She is also in favor of fundamental research into how knowledge affects the human decision-making processes of individuals or groups.

FORMAL EXTENSIONS: CONSTRUCTS, CALCULI, AND MEASURES

Except for earlier work by SARACEVIC on the concept of relevance in information science, very little has been done to analyze systematically other theoretical constructs in information science and their operational definitions. This task merits more attention.

As to the development of formal languages or calculi of information science, we review here the efforts directed toward the interpretation and extensions of Shannon's information theory.

A general treatment is provided by GABIDULIN, who raises broad questions about the practical applications of information theory and suggests a tentative research program. Other authors concentrate on specific interpretations in many different areas: structural analysis and partitioning of large-scale systems (DUFOUR & GILLES), data analysis and classification (COMYN), image partitioning (FARAG), criminology (CHENG), and design of questionnaires (AGGARWAL & PICARD). KENNEDY explores problems in the quantum theory of communication and information theory. In a more general treatment, JUMARIE (1977b) surveys relativistic information and its applications, with a discussion of how fuzzy set theory relates to the study of information processes. Limitations of such extensions are investigated by BOURGEOIS.

Several contributions have been made to the development of operational definitions, specifically to measures of information and of various other fundamental quantities. For analysis, it is convenient to classify the field into: 1) syntactic or formal information measures, which are developed without any interpretation of meaning (semantic) or value, utility, or aesthetic, etc. (pragmatic) aspects; 2) semantic information measures, which measure meaning-related properties of information; and 3) pragmatic information measures, which measure the effects of information on its user. (For a brief explanation of these measures see ZUNDE (1971).) The general problem of information measurement in the semiotic context is discussed by PEARSON & SLAMECKA.

In his study of formal information measures, ACZÉL gives a concise but lucid review of essential properties of entropies and information measures of Shannon's type; the most important are boundedness on an interval, subadditivity, additivity, branching, and expansibility. He sees in the work by FORTE & SASTRI on entropies of mixed probabilistic and nonprobabilistic character a potential nucleus for a unified theory of information. He also discusses recent developments in the theory of measures of information gain, commonly known as divergence, and states some unsolved problems. KAZAKOS studied the maximization of divergence.

AGGARWAL & PICARD develop measures of information for events with preference or utility rankings; these measures are used in designing questionnaires. LEUNG-YAN-CHEONG & COVER identify some equivalences between Shannon entropy and Kolgomorov complexity measures. In the same area, GRAY pursues mathematical inquiries into the relation of information theory and ergodic theory, and BOEKEE examines the possibilities for generalizing the Fisher information measure, which found application in statistics.

On the semantic level, DOLBY proposes measures of ambiguity and information loss that closely resemble Shannon's measures. He shows that the proposed measures perform in intuitively reasonable ways in operations such as sorting, creation of search keys and sort keys, and the use of taxonomic numbers. STALKER proposes three measures of similarity among lines of text; they are based on: shared words, shared substrings of a given length, and a count of discontinuities observed in trying to match certain substrings, and their advantages and disadvantages are analyzed.

In an application to automatic indexing, PAO proposes quantitative criteria for selecting indexing terms directly from a word frequency list, and she investigates the semantic implications of these criteria.

A set of pragmatic information measures is developed by YOVITS & ROSE in the context of the proposed general theory of information flow and analysis. The development is based on the notion of information as data of value for decision making, with a hypothetical decision maker as the central construct of the theory. The proposed measures are direct correlates of the operational definitions of quantity of information, value of information, effectiveness of information and performance and effectiveness of the decision maker.

ROBERTSON & BELKIN conduct a thorough analysis of the ranking principles according to the degree of relevance of a document to a query and according to the probability of relevance. They discuss the implications of these principles for retrieval performance and utility measures.

In a paper that attempts to extend the decision-theory approach to information retrieval, KRAFT & BOOKSTEIN analyze various performance measures of document retrieval systems and their components such as precision, recall, specificity, concentration, resolution, elimination, noise, emission, distillation, and discrimination. Their relationships to "retrieval status values" are shown for normal and Poisson distributions. Decision-theoretical methods are also used by YU & SALTON to develop precision weighting of terms for automatic indexing and optimal query design applications. Terms that occur in user queries are weighted as a function of the balance between relevant and nonrelevant documents in which terms occur, so that these weights turn out to be somewhat equivalent to semantic measures of relevance. Relevance-based term weighting is developed further by HARPER & VAN RIJSBERGEN under conditions of relaxed term independence.

DUBOVNIKOV & SOL'C argue that the important information in a scientific or technical document is embodied in formulas, tables, and diagrams, which they call components of information. They define a measure of the (useful) amount of information that can be derived from these components and its complexity as a function of the quantity of these components.

SMITH investigates authorship, subject, nationality, publisher, and language and date of publication as indicators of quality of books in business and management studies and concludes that these characteristics are not yet good predictors of the quality of a new publication.

LAWANI uses citation analysis to derive measures for the quality of scientific publication productivity and discusses data that tend to show that scientists who publish the most also tend to be cited the most. Thus, there is a strong connection between the quantity and quality of scientific publications.

Several studies are done with library applications in mind. MARCUS ET AL. develop indicativity measures of catalog information and study their relation to relevance of documents. BROADUS uses the measurement techniques of citation analysis mentioned earlier to provide guidelines for building a library collection. POWELL develops measures for investigating quantifiable reference service variables and ultimately reference performance in public libraries. CAWKELL proposes impact factor (i.e., average number of citations received by an article) and immediacy index (i.e., average times an article was cited in the year of its publication) as effective derived measures for evaluating scientific journals. TRAVIS uses expected search length as a measure of system performance in developing design equations for citation retrieval systems.

LUNNEBORG proposes some information-processing correlates of measures of intelligence, and FREDERIKSEN & WARD suggest measures for studying creativity in solving scientific problems.

SEARCH FOR EMPIRICAL LAWS

Studies directed toward the generation of hypotheses and the discovery of empirical laws of information science are grouped into categories for this survey, but this grouping does not imply a systematic classification of this area.

Structures of Aggregate Information Sources

Bradford's law of information scatter expresses one of the important regularities reflecting the structure of aggregate information sources—namely, the distribution of the number of articles in a collection of journals on a certain subject. This law is still a topic of active research, and new formulations of it have been proposed (HAWKINS; PRAUNLICH & KROLL). HURT examines the publication patterns of environmental scientists and finds that they tend to remain within one subject area rather than to scatter their publications in journals across a broad subject range. SMOL'KOV proposed a different kind of law of information scatter, which gives a better fit to certain observed data than Bradford's law.

MCGRATH examines relationships between hard/soft, pure/applied, and life/nonlife descriptions and subject use in a university library but does not produce strong evidence of an empirical regularity. SMALL and then SULLIVAN ET AL. describe how certain regularities in citation patterns can be used to distinguish and to identify scientific specialties.

Relation between Semiotic Form of Texts and Their Information Content

This is one of the most active areas, possibly because results of such research find immediate applications in automatic processing, abstracting, information retrieval, and other practical problems. One of the major problems is to establish relationships between statistical properties of certain characteristics of semiotic forms in which information is encoded and information content (e.g., statistical properties of texts in some language and their meaning). A recent and fairly representative effort to explore the connection between information science, mathematical linguistics, and statistics is the study by EDMUNDSON. He also identifies several important areas in mathematical and computational linguistics of promising research interest for computer or information scientists.

A number of studies have been done recently on semantic implications of word frequencies. ANDRUKOVICH & KOROLEV studied the connection between statistical and lexicogrammatical properties of words: polysemy (i.e., semantic variations of a lexical unit), synonymy, number of derivatives of a word, number of compound words in which a particular word occurs, number of abbreviations of a word, and number of phrases in which a particular word is an argument of lexical function. The results may eventually be used in thesauri construction and updating. KRYLOV & IAKUBOVSKAIA conducted a statistical analysis of polysemy (multiple word meanings) in an attempt to examine the problem of the semantic identity of the word.

PEARSON (1976) compares various rank-frequency and type-token relationships (i.e., the relationship between the word type and its occurrence). He concludes that empirical studies of the type-token relation have several advantages over studies of the rank-frequency relation. First, since the type-token relation is an integral transform of the rank-frequency relation, it is not nearly as sensitive to experimental error. Second, certain type-token relations are all inherently independent of sample size. Third, several boundary value restrictions are known for the type-token relation and are easier to apply in this form.

GREENBLATT attempts to determine whether or not stylistic variation can be described in terms of the so-called "variable linguistic rules" (for an explanation see LABOV). TAGLIACOZZO examined stylistic variations in scientific writing by comparing two groups of articles dealing with the same subjects but differing in degree of specialization. The study was done to determine how syntactical and stylistic characteristics of scientific writing can be used to assess its degree of specialization. The texts of the more technical articles had a lower percentage of function words (articles, auxiliary verbs, conjunctions, demonstrative adjectives, possessive adjectives, prepositions, and pronouns) and a higher number of nouns than the texts of the more general articles, implying that the former texts are more concise. It appears that a gain in conciseness may result in a loss of precision; this suggests that some of the stylistic devices favored by scientific writers, such as function words, far from contributing to the effectiveness of communication, as they are presumed to do, may actually detract from it.

Several recent studies deal with empirical properties of artificial languages, in general, and computer software, in particular. ZWEBEN proposes a theory of the structural composition of algorithms, which allows the frequencies of occurrence of the individual operators and operands to be estimated, and derives certain functional relationships between properties of algorithms. The theory of operands is based partly on models of program construction by BAYER; the theory of operators is based on the work of ZIPF and MANDELBROT in natural language. A further relationship between the construction of algorithms and natural language text is indicated by demonstrating that the size of an algorithm as predicted by one of Bayer's programming models and the size of a section of text as predicted by Zipf's natural language model are identical. The results of the study indicate that there is much similarity in the way different algorithms are written; in fact, the way algorithms are written seems similar in some ways to the way natural language texts are written. This suggests that concepts such as dividing the basic entities of an algorithm into operators and operands may also be quite important and useful in studies of natural language texts.

Information Representation and Semantic Coding

In one effort (VERSTIGGEL & LE NY) pairs of sentences were presented to subjects who judged them as "same" or "different." In 25% of these pairs the sentences were formally identical. In another 25% the second sentence was derived from the first by semantic relations of synonymy or superordination among nouns; the subjects were then required to judge semantic identity and to respond "same." An equal number of pairs of sentences led to the response "different." Comparisons were done after an interval of zero or five seconds that was empty or spent in counting backwards. It was hypothesized that the processing of the information in the first sentence would produce two kinds of representations—a phono-articulatory one and a semantic one, which are developed differently. The interpolated activity would deteriorate the first but not the second. Analysis of judgment latencies shows a significant double interaction, corroborating this hypothesis: the interpolated activity lengthened the judgments of formal identity but not those of semantic identity.

BRACHMAN considers "semantic networks," which constitute one of the many attempts to capture human knowledge in an abstraction that is suitable for computer processing. He suggests that although semantic nets are popular, they never seem to live up to their authors' expectations of potency and ease of construction. He then examines the fundamentals of network representation to understand why the "formalism" has not been the panacea it was once regarded. He focuses on "concepts"—what authors think they are and how they might be represented in network nodes. The simplistic view of concept nodes as representing extensional sets is examined and found wanting. The author emphasizes the importance of considering an "epistemological foundation" on which to build representations for complex concepts. A level of representation above that of completely uniform nodes and links but below the level of conceptual knowledge itself is suggested as the key to using previously learned concepts to interpret and to structure new ones. A particular foundation is proposed, based on the notion of a set of functional roles bound by a structuring relationship.

Human Information Processing

Topics of interest to information science in this subject area are, among other things, information processes in perception and learning, data acquisition and organization, semantic encoding, and memory. The recent research discussed is limited to processing information contained in texts.

SHIFFRIN & SCHNEIDER and SCHNEIDER & SHIFFRIN, in comprehensive discussions of perceptual learning and of detection, search, and attention, set forth a general theory of human information processing that emphasizes the roles of automatic and controlled processing. In another general paper, FISHER ET AL. examine the human information processing aspects of complex communication systems. CHASTAIN studies feature analysis and analyzes the growth of a precept. RUBIN looks at human information processing from the viewpoint of impressions that are formed and emphasizes the role played by context.

Several researchers have focused on different aspects of verbal and visual human information processing. NUNNALLY ET AL. deal with psychometric issues that involve studies of voluntary visual attention; LOFTUS ET AL. consider the question of semantic integration of verbal information into a visual memory; ROSINSKI tests and confirms a hypothesis that asserts that picture-word interference is semantically based.

Several recent studies focus on the nature and role of human memory. SOWDER tests hypotheses that involve the effect of list length and organization on a person's ability to recall categorized lists. PRAWAT & CANCELLI suggest that semantic retrieval in young children is a function of type of meaning. ORTONY & ANDERSON indicate that semantic memory is a function of definite descriptions. CORNISH conducts a quantitative analysis of recall components as a way to explain the process of memorizing prose. HUNDAL & HORN examine the relationships between short-term learning and different kinds of intelligence.

The organization of data and information by humans is emphasized by CARROLL, who proposes ways to study individual differences in cognitive abilities, and by DURDING ET AL., who look at how people organize data. Information use is the subject of a study by PETTUS & DIENER, who consider factors affecting the effectiveness of abstract vs. concrete information.

The limitations of human information processing are the subject of several recent research efforts. SHWARTZ ET AL. conduct an additive factors analysis to determine state and process limitations in information processing. KISS & SAVAGE examine processing power and delay in an attempt to establish the limits of human performance.

Other researchers have focused on human information problem solving and decision making. CHAPANIS ET AL. examined the effects of four communication modes on the linguistic performance of teams during cooperative problem solving, and DONOHUE proposed an empirical framework for examining negotiation processes and results.

Miscellaneous Topics

An ideal model for the growth of knowledge in research programs that balances empirical growth vs. theoretical growth is proposed by KANTOROVICH but is not validated by empirical data. TURNER describes the so-called identifier method for selecting and determining objective criteria for weeding document collections and applies this method to measure use of books in a library. Requirements that "good" identifiers are expected to meet are discussed. However, the reliability of use data as criteria for retiring books is questioned by C. HARRIS.

Empirical properties of titles of articles in terms of their information content were investigated by GHOSH and by BUXTON & MEADOWS. Ghosh found that the use in document titles of terms that are good indicators of the content of the document has tended to increase over the past ten years and that, in the contraception literature, 92% of the titles contain at least one such term (i.e., a term that is a good content indicator). Results reported by Buxton & Meadows also support the finding that titles in scientific journals are becoming more informative. They also demonstrated that the proportion of good content indicators in titles varies across scientific disciplines, chemistry and botany having the highest percentage of such terms in titles.

Structures of scientific disciplines and their topical emphasis, growth, and so forth were studied by MEKHTIEV ET AL. and by ELLIS ET AL. using citation networks. The latter also demonstrate that under certain favorable conditions, citation networks can be used to identify key patents in a subject field.

THEORIES

We consider here only theories that explain empirical laws in a scientific, rational manner. This aspect of the foundation of information science is unfortunately the least developed—a circumstance that is often used to question the status of information science as a scientific discipline. However, it is not true that there are no theories of information science or that there is no prospect of new theories' being developed.

The "oldest" theories of information science are those that relate to the so-called "hyperbolic distribution model" that underlies various empirical laws, including the laws of Zipf, Bradford, and Lotka. A good survey of these laws, which conform to the hyperbolic distribution model, was done by FAIRTHORNE in 1969 but now needs updating.

PRICE proposed a new formulation of this theory that he calls the General Theory of Bibliometric and Other Cumulative Advantage Processes. It is derived from the premise that certain information processes can be explained adequately by assuming that "success breeds success." Thus, "a paper which has been cited many times is more likely to be cited again than one which has been seldom cited. An author of many papers is more likely to publish again than one who has been less prolific. A journal which has been frequently consulted for some purpose is more likely to be turned to again than one of previously infrequent use" (PRICE). Under these assumptions, he derives the Cumulative Advantage (CA) distribution in terms of the beta function, which is a generalized expression for hyperbolic distribution. He then shows that the mathematical formulations of the laws of Zipf, Lotka, and

Bradford are limiting cases of CA distribution and that most of the empirical results of citation frequency analysis are compatible with this theory. On the other hand, the general validity of some of the laws mentioned above is not yet demonstrated decisively. For example, COILE has shown that Lotka's law of scientific publication productivity does not hold for literature in the humanities and map librarianship.

More recently, a different theory leading to the same kind of distribution model was proposed by ARAPOV & SHREIDER. It is based on an analogy with the theories of statistical thermodynamics and interprets the closed system model of thermodynamics in terms of a system of signs (text) or a system of publications or a system of scientists or any other system with a finite number of elements and a fixed number of distinct classes into which these elements can be placed, every possible distribution of the elements by classes representing the state of the system. It is then shown that the most likely "state" of the system is that in which the distribution of elements by classes corresponds to hyperbolic distribution. This interesting result promises further extension and development of the theory.

YOVITS & ROSE are developing a "general theory of information flow." Their objectives are: 1) to identify and to quantify important variables and parameters in the information flow process; 2) to establish relationships among these variables; 3) to apply the theory to practical situations and to examine the resulting implications; and 4) to develop simulation and experimental models to utilize and to validate the theory. The theory is based on the premise that information is data of value in decision making, and the whole approach is strongly oriented to decision-making theory. Results have been reported on items (1) and (2) and some aspects of items (3) and (4), but the major work of validation and testing lies ahead.

CONCLUSION

In this chapter we briefly described the recent efforts by information scientists to develop the empirical foundations of the discipline. In reviewing the present status of these efforts, we offer the following conclusions:

- Many laws of information science have been proposed, but most are still hypotheses that need to be verified and validated under more diverse experimental conditions and on a more comprehensive collection of empirical data;
- In many of the proposed laws or hypotheses, constructs used in the theory are not the same as their operationally defined counterparts;
- Many constructs that appear in the proposed laws or hypotheses have little significance for information science;
- More general systems (methods) of information measurement, particularly more comprehensive measures of information in all its diversity, need to be developed; and

• No sufficiently general principles have been discovered, and theories of information science are in the early stage of development. Most of the proposed laws and hypotheses have limited applicability.

BIBLIOGRAPHY

ACZÉL, J. 1978. Some Recent Results on Characterizations of Measures of Information Related to Coding. IEEE Transactions on Information Theory. 1978 September; IT-24(5): 592-595. ISSN: 0018-9448.

AFANAS'EV, E.V.; NOVIKOV, IU.A. 1977. Psychological Features of the Informational Backup for Decision-making; a Survey of Soviet and Foreign Publications. Automatic Documentation and Mathematical Linguistics. 1977; 11(4): 1-6. ISSN: 0005-1055; UDC 65.012.122.

AGGARWAL, N.L.; PICARD, C.F. 1978. Functional Equations and Information Measures with Preference. Kybernetika (Czechoslovakia). 1978; 14(3): 175-181. (In English). ISSN: 0023-5954.

ALLEN, M.J. 1978. An Empirical Demonstration of the Factor Differentiation Hypothesis. Multivariate Behavioral Research. 1978 January; 13: 63-75. ISSN: 0027-3171.

ANDRUKOVICH, P.F.; KOROLEV, E.I. 1977. The Statistical and Lexicogrammatical Properties of Words. Automatic Documentation and Mathematical Linguistics. 1977; 11(1): 1-11. ISSN: 0005-1055; UDC 801.541.2.

ARAPOV, M.V.; LIBKIND, A.N. 1977. The Concept of Closed Information Flow. Automatic Documentation and Mathematical Linguistics. 1977; 11(2): 77-94. ISSN: 0005-1055; UDC 65.012.122.

ARAPOV, M.V.; SHREIDER, IU.A. 1978. Zipf's Law and the Principle of System Dissymmetry. Semiotika i informatika (USSR). 1978; 10: 74-95. (In Russian).

ATLAN, H. 1977. Sources of Information in Biological Systems. In: Dubuisson, B., ed. Information and Systems: Proceedings of the International Federation of Automatic Control (IFAC) Workshop; 1977 October 25-27; Compiegne, France. Oxford, England: New York, NY: Pergamon Press; 1977. 1-10. ISBN: 0-08-022440-7; LC: 78-40143.

BAR-HILLEL, Y.; CARNAP, R. 1953 Semantic Information. British Journal of the Philosophy of Science. 1953; 4: 147-157. ISSN: 0007-0882.

BAYER, R. 1972. A Theoretical Study of Halstead's Software Phenomenon. Lafayette, IN: Purdue University, Department of Computer Science; 1972 May. (Report CST-TR69).

BELKIN, N.J. 1974. Towards a Definition of Information for Informatics. In: Horsnell, Verina, ed. Informatics 2: Proceedings of a Conference sponsored by the Aslib Co-Ordinate Indexing Group; 1974 March 25-27; New College, Oxford, England. Chapel Hill, NC: University of North Carolina Press; 1974. 50-56.

BOEKEE, D.E. 1977. Generalized Fisher Information with Application to Estimation Problems. In: Dubuisson, B., ed. Information and Systems: Proceedings of the International Federation of Automatic Control (IFAC) Workshop; 1977 October 25-27; Compiegne, France. Oxford, England:

New York, NY: Pergamon Press; 1977. 75-82. ISBN: 0-08-022440-7; LC: 78-40143.

BOURGEOIS, MARCEL. 1977. Control and Power: Two Modes of Information. In: Dubuisson, B., ed. Information and Systems: Proceedings of the International Federation of Automatic Control (IFAC) Workshop; 1977 October 25-27; Compiegne, France. Oxford, England: New York, NY: Pergamon Press; 1977. 1-10. ISBN: 0-08-022440-7; LC: 78-40143.

BRACHMAN, RONALD J. 1977. What's in a Concept: Structural Foundations for Semantic Networks. International Journal of Man-Machine Studies. 1977; 9: 127-152. ISSN: 0020-7373.

BROADUS, ROBERT N. 1977. The Applications of Citation Analyses to Library Collection Building. In: Voigt, Melvin J.; Harris, M.H. Advances in Librarianship: Volume 7. New York, NY: Academic Press; 1977. 299-335. ISBN: 0-12-785007-4.

BROOKES, BERTRAM C. 1974. The Fundamental Problem of Information Science. In: Horsnell, Verina, ed. Informatics 2: Proceedings of a Conference sponsored by the Aslib Co-Ordinate Indexing Group; 1974 March 25-27; New College, Oxford, England. Chapel Hill, NC: University of North Carolina Press; 1974. 42-49.

BROOKES, BERTRAM, C.; GRIFFITHS, JOSE M. 1978. Frequency-Rank Distributions. Journal of the American Society for Information Science. 1978 January; 29(1): 5-13. ISSN: 0002-8231; CODEN: AISJB6.

BUSCHKE, HERMAN. 1977. Two-Dimensional Recall: Immediate Identification of Clusters in Episodic and Semantic Memory. Journal of Verbal Learning and Verbal Behavior. 1977; 16: 201-215. ISSN: 0022-5371.

BUXTON, A.B.; MEADOWS, A.J. 1977. The Variations in the Information Content of Titles of Research Papers with Time and Discipline. Journal of Documentation (England). 1977 March; 33(1): 46-52. ISSN: 0022-0418.

CARROLL, JOHN B. 1978. How Shall We Study Individual Differences in Cognitive Abilities? Methodological and Theoretical Perspectives. 1978 January. 57p. Available from: the author, University of North Carolina, L.L. Thurstone Psychometric Laboratory, Chapel Hill, NC 27514.

CASPI, P.; MILL, A.; ROBACH, C. 1977. An Information Measure on Nets—Application to the Testability of Digital Systems. In: Dubuisson, B., ed. Information and Systems: Proceedings of the International Federation of Automatic Control (IFAC) Workshop; 1977 October 25-27; Compiegne, France. Oxford, England: New York, NY: Pergamon Press; 1977. 35-40. LC: 78-40143.

CAWKWELL, A.E. 1978. Evaluating Scientific Journals with *Journal Citation Reports*—A Case Study in Acoustics. Journal of the American Society for Information Science. 1978 January; 29(1): 41-46. ISSN: 0002-8231; CODEN: AISJB6.

CHAPANIS, ALPHONSE; PARRISH, ROBERT N.; OCHSMAN, ROBERT B.; WEEKS, GERALD D. 1977. Studies in Interactive Communication: II, The Effects of Four Communication Modes on the Linguistic Performance of Teams During Cooperative Problem Solving. Human Factors. 1977; 19(2): 101-126.

CHASTAIN, GARVIN. 1977. Feature Analysis and the Growth of a Percept. Journal of Experimental Psychology: Human Perception and Performance. 1977; 3(2): 291-298.

CHENG, M.D. 1978. A Justification for Information Function as a Measure of Detective Performance. Kybernetes. 1978; 7: 153-158.

COILE, RUSSELL G. 1977. Lotka's Frequency Distribution of Scientific Productivity. Journal of the American Society for Information Science. 1977 November; 28(6): 366-370. ISSN: 0002-8231.

COMYN, GERARD. 1977. Generalized Information and Data Analysis. In: Dubuisson, B., ed. Information and Systems: Proceedings of the International Federation of Automatic Control (IFAC) Workshop; 1977 October 25-27; Compiegne, France. Oxford, England: New York, NY: Pergamon Press; 1977. 29-34. LC: 78-40143.

CORNISH, I.M. 1978. Memory for Prose: Quantitative Analysis of Recall Components. British Journal of Psychology. 1978; 69: 243-255.

COSERMANS, JEAN; DE LA VALLEE POUSSIN, CATHERINE. 1977. Les Effetes des liaisons associatives sur le temps de denomination verbale [The Effects of Associative Relation on Verbal Recall Times]. Annee Psychologie (France). 1977; 77: 15-18. (Text and abstract in French).

COVER, THOMAS, M. 1975. Open Problems in Information Theory. In: Proceedings of the 1975 Institute of Electrical and Electronics Engineers (IEEE)-USSR Joint Workshop on Information Theory; 1975 December 15-19; Moscow, USSR. New York, NY: IEEE; 1975. 35-36. Available from IEEE Service Center, 445 Hoes Lane, Piscataway, NJ 08854. (IEEE no. 75CH1167-6IT).

COVER, THOMAS, M. 1978. A Convergent Gambling Estimate of the Entropy of English. IEEE Transactions on Information Theory. 1978 July; IT-24(4): 413-421. ISSN: 0018-9948.

DAVIES, E.B. 1978. Information and Quantum Measurement. IEEE Transactions on Information Theory. 1978 September; IT-24(5): 596-599. ISSN: 0018-9448.

DOLBY, JAMES L. 1977. On the Notions of Ambiguity and Information Loss. Behavioral Science. 1977; 22: 290-298. (Appeared originally in Information Processing & Management. 1977; 13(1): 69-77).

DONOHUE, WILLIAM ANTHONY. 1978. An Empirical Framework for Examining Negotiation Processes and Outcomes. Communication Monographs. 1978 August; 45(3): 247-257. ISSN: 0363-7751.

DOW, JOHN T. 1977. A Metatheory for the Development of a Science of Information. Journal of the American Society for Information Science. 1977 November; 28: 323-331. ISSN: 002-8231; CODEN: AISJB6.

DUBOVNIKOV, M.S.; SOL'C, N.A. 1977. On the Quantitative Measure of Information Content of Scientific Documents. Nauchnaia informatsiia i dokumentatsii (USSR). Seriia 2. 1977; (3): 14-16. (In Russian).

DUFOUR, JACQUES; GILLES, GERARD. 1977. Application of Some Concepts of the Information Theory to Structural Analysis and Partition of Macroeconomic Large Scale Systems. In: Dubuisson, B., ed. Information and Systems: Proceedings of the International Federation of Automatic Control (IFAC) Workshop; 1977 October 25-27; Compiegne, France. Oxford, England: New York, NY: Pergamon Press; 1977. 19-28. ISBN: 0-08-022440-7; LC: 78-40143.

DURDING, BRUCE M.; BECKER, CURTIS A.; GOULD, JOHN D. 1977. Data Organization. Human Factors. 1977; 19(1): 1-14. ISSN: 0018-7208.

EDMUNDSON, H.P. 1977. Statistical Inference in Mathematical and Computational Linguistics. International Journal of Computer and Information Sciences. 1977; 6(2): 95-129. ISSN: 0091-7036.

EKATERINOSLAVSKII, IU. IU. 1977. Development of Research in Information Science, A Discussion. Automatic Documentation and Mathematical Linguistics. 1977; 1: 64-68. ISSN: 0005-1055; UDC 002.71.

ELLIS, P.; HEPBURN, G.; OPPENHEIM, C. 1977. Studies on Patent Citation Networks. Journal of Documentation (England). 1978 March; 34(1): 12-20. ISSN: 0022-0418.

EVANS, F.J. 1977. The Informational Content of System Structure—A Survey and Some Open Problems. In: Dubuisson, B., ed. Information and Systems: Proceedings of the International Federation of Automatic Control (IFAC) Workshop: 1977 October 25-27; Compiegne, France. Oxford, England: New York, NY: Pergamon Press; 1977. 51-64. ISBN: 0-08-022440-7; LC: 78-40143.

FAIRTHORNE, R.A. 1969. Empirical Hyperbolic Distributions (Bradford-Zipf-Mandlebrot) for Bibliometric Description and Prediction. Journal of Documentation (England). 1969; 25(4): 319-343. ISSN: 0022-0418.

FARAG, RAOUF F.H. 1978. An Information Theoretic Approach to Image Partitioning. IEEE Transactions on Systems, Man, and Cybernetics. 1978 November; SMC-8(11): 829-833. ISSN: 0018-9472.

FISHER, B. AUBREY; GLOVER, THOMAS W.; ELLIS, DONALD G. 1977. The Nature of Complex Communication Systems. Communication Monographs. 1977 August; 44(3): 231-240. ISSN: 0363-7751.

FORMAN, ERNEST H.; SINGPURWALLA, NOZER D. 1977. An Empirical Stopping Rule for Debugging and Testing Computer Software. Journal of the American Statistical Association. 1977 December; 72(360): 750-757. ISSN: 0162-1459.

FORTE, B.; SASTRI, C.C.A. 1975. Is Something Missing in Boltzmann's Entropy? Journal of Mathematical Physics. 1975; 16: 1453-1456. ISSN: 0022-2488.

FREDERIKSEN, NORMAN; WARD, WILLIAM C. 1978. Measures for the Study of Creativity in Scientific Problem-Solving. Applied Psychological Measurement. 1978 Winter; 2(1): 1-24. ISSN: 0146-6216.

GABIDULIN, E.M. 1975. Practical Applications of Information Theory. In: Proceedings of the 1975 Institute of Electrical and Electronics Engineers (IEEE)-USSR Joint Workshop on Information Theory; 1975 December 15-19; Moscow, USSR. New York, NY: IEEE; 1975. 57-58. Available from IEEE Service Center, 445 Hoes Lane, Piscataway, NJ 08854. (IEEE no. 75CH1167-6IT).

GHOSH, JATA S. 1977. The Information Content of Titles in Contraception Literature. Journal of Chemical Information and Computer Sciences. 1977; 17(1): 36-40. ISSN: 0095-2338; CODEN: JCISD8.

GILBERT, G. MIGEL. 1977. Referencing as Persuasion. Social Studies of Science. 1977; 7: 113-122. ISSN: 0306-3127.

GOTTINGER, HANS W. 1977. Lecture Notes on Concepts and Measures of Information. In: Longo, G. Information Theory: New Trends and Open Problems. 1977. 321p. (International Center for Mechanical Sciences Courses and Lectures no. 219). Available from: the author, University of Bielefeld, P.O.B. 8640, Bielefeld, West Germany.

GRAY, ROBERT M. 1975. Ergodic Theory and Information Theory. In: Proceedings of the 1975 Institute of Electrical and Electronics Engineers

(IEEE)-USSR Joint Workshop on Information Theory; 1975 December
15-19; Moscow, USSR. New York, NY: IEEE; 1975. 59-70. Available from IEEE Service Center, 445 Hoes Lane, Piscataway, NJ 08854.
(IEEE no. 75CH1167-6IT).

GREENBLATT, DANIEL L. 1978. Variable Rules and Literary Style.
Computers & the Humanities. 1978; 11: 193-197. ISSN: 0010-4817.

HALFF, HENRY M. 1977. The Role of Opportunities for Recall in Learning to Retrieve. American Journal of Psychology. 1977 September;
90(3): 383-406.

HALSTEAD, M.; BAYER, R. 1973. Algorithm Dynamics. In: Proceedings
of the 28th Annual Conference of the Association for Computing
Machinery (ACM); 1973; Atlanta, GA. 126-135. Available from: ACM,
P.O. Box 12105, Church Street Station, New York, NY 10249.

HAMMAD, PIERE. 1977. Shannon's Information and Fisher's Information
for Diffusion Processes. In: Dubuisson, B., ed. Information and Systems: Proceedings of the International Federation of Automatic Control
(IFAC) Workshop; 1977 October 25-27; Compiegne, France. Oxford,
England: New York, NY: Pergamon Press; 1977. 41-50. ISBN: 0-08-
022440-7; LC: 78-40143.

HARMAN, G.K. 1978. The Information Explosion and Its Consequences
for Data Acquisition, Documentation, and Processing. 1978 May. 36p.
(World Data Center A; Solid Earth Geophysics Report SE-11; Solar-
Terrestrial Physics Report UAG-65). Available from: National Oceanic
and Atmospheric Administration, National Geophysical and Solar-
Terrestrial Data Center, Boulder, CO 80302.

HARPER, D.J.; VAN RIJSBERGEN, C.J. 1978. An Evaluation of Feedback in Document Retrieval Using Co-occurrence Data. Journal of
Documentation (England). 1978 September; 34(3): 189-216. ISSN:
0022-0418.

HARRIS, C. 1977. A Comparison of Issues and In-Library Use of Books.
Aslib Proceedings (England). 1977 March; 29(3): 118-126. ISSN:
0001-253X.

HARRIS, DALE A. 1975. Information Theory in Neurophysiology. In:
Proceedings of the 1975 Institute of Electrical and Electronics Engineers
(IEEE)-USSR Joint Workshop on Information Theory; 1975 December
15-19; Moscow, USSR. New York, NY: IEEE; 1975. 71-82. Available
from IEEE Service Center, 445 Hoes Lane, Piscataway, NJ 08854.
(IEEE no 75CH1167-61T).

HAWKINS, DONALD T. 1976. Electrochemistry Journals. Journal of
Chemical Information and Computer Sciences. 1976; 17(1): 41-45.
ISSN: 0095-2338; CODEN: JCISD8.

HAYES-ROTH, BARBARA; HAYES-ROTH, FREDERICK. 1977. The
Prominence of Lexical Information in Memory Representations of Meaning. Journal of Verbal Learning and Verbal Behavior. 1977; 16: 119-
136. ISSN: 0022-5371.

HEILPRIN, L.B. 1972. On Access to Knowledge in the Social Sciences and
Humanities, from the Viewpoint of Cybernetics and Information Science.
In: Colby, R.A.; Gilfand, M.A., eds. Access to the Literature of the
Social Sciences and Humanities. Flushing, NY: Queen's College Press;
1974.

HEILPRIN, L.B. 1978. What Is Involved in the Demand for Empirical
Theories in System Science. Cybernetics Forum. 1978; (1-2).

HEINE, M.H. 1977. Incorporation of the Age of a Document into the Retrieval Process. Information Processing & Management. 1977; 13: 35-47. ISSN: 0306-4573.

HJERPPE, ROLAND. 1978. An Outline of Bibliometrics and Citation Analysis. 1978 October. 41p. (Stockholm Papers in Library and Information Science; Report TRITA-LIB-6014). Available from: The Royal Institute of Technology Library, S-100 44 Stockholm 70, Sweden.

HUBERT, JOHN J. 1978. A Relationship between Two Forms of Bradford's Law. Journal of the American Society for Information Science. 1978 May; 29(3): 159-162. ISSN: 0002-8231; CODEN: AISJB6.

HUNDAL, P.S.; HORN, JOHN L. 1977. On the Relationships between Short-Term Learning and Fluid and Crystallized Intelligence. Applied Psychological Measurement. 1977 Winter; 1(1): 11-21.

HURT, C.D. 1977. A Correlation Study of the Journal Article Productivity of Environmental Scientists. Information Processing & Management. 1977; 13: 305-309. ISSN: 0306-4573.

IBRAGIMOV, I.A.; KHAS'MINSKII, R.Z. 1975. Some Problems of Statistical Data Processing in Communications. In: Proceedings of the 1975 Institute of Electrical and Electronics Engineers (IEEE)-USSR Joint Workshop on Information Theory; 1975 December 15-19; Moscow, USSR. New York, NY: IEEE; 1975. 86-92. Available from: IEEE Service Center, 445 Hoes Lane, Piscataway, NJ 08854. (IEEE no. 75CH1167-6IT).

INHABER, HERBERT. 1977. Where Scientists Publish Social Studies of Science. Social Studies of Science. 1977; 7: 388-394. ISSN: 0306-3127.

JUMARIE, GUY. 1977a. Some Technical Applications of Relativistic Information, Shannon Information, Fuzzy Sets, Linguistics, Relativistic Sets, and Communication. Cybernetica. 1977; 20(2): 91-128. ISSN: 0011-4227.

JUMARIE, GUY. 1977b. A Survey of Relativistic Information and Its Applications. In: Dubuisson, B., ed. Information and Systems: Proceedings of the International Federation of Automatic Control (IFAC) Workshop; 1977 October 25-27; Compiegne, France. Oxford, England: New York, NY: Pergamon Press; 1977. 113-118. LC: 78-40143.

KANTOROVICH, AHARON. 1978. An Ideal Model for the Growth of Knowledge in Research Programs. Philosophy of Science. 1978; 45: 250-271. ISSN: 0031-8248.

KAZAKOS, DIMITRI, S. 1978. On the Maximization of Divergence. IEEE Transactions on Information Theory. 1978; 7: 509. ISSN: 0018-9948.

KENNEDY, ROBERT S. 1975. Problems in Quantum Communication and Information Theory. In: Proceedings of the 1975 Institute of Electrical and Electronics Engineers (IEEE)-USSR Joint Workshop on Information Theory; 1975 December 15-19; Moscow, USSR. New York, NY: IEEE; 1975. 105-110. Available from: IEEE Service Center, 445 Hoes Lane, Piscataway, NJ 08854. (IEEE no. 75CH1167-6IT).

KERVIN, JOHN B. 1977. An Information-Combining Model for Expectation States Theory: Derivation and Tests. Journal of Mathematical Sociology. 1977; 5: 199-214. ISSN: 0022-250X.

KIM, CHAI; KIM, SOON D. 1977. Consensus v. Frequency: An Empirical Investigation of the Theories for Identifying Descriptors in Designing Retrieval Thesauri. Information Processing & Management. 1977; 13: 253-258. ISSN: 0306-4573.

KISS, GEORGE R.; SAVAGE, JOHN E. 1977. Processing Power and Delay— Limits on Human Performance. Journal of Mathematical Psychology. 1977; 16: 68-90. ISSN: 0022-2496.

KOROLEV, E.I. 1977. The Use of the Distributive Statistical Method in the Language Apparatus of Automated Information Systems. Automatic Documentation and Mathematical Linguistics. 1977; 11(1): 31-37. ISSN: 0005-1055; UDC 025.4.036.001.

KRAFT, DONALD H.; BOOKSTEIN, ABRAHAM. 1978. Evaluation of Information Retrieval Systems: A Decision Theory Approach. Journal of the American Society for Information Science. 1978 January; 29(1): 31-40. ISSN: 0002-8231; CODEN: AISJB6.

KRYLOV, IU. K.; IAKUBOVSKAIA, M.D. 1977. Statistical Analysis of Polysemy as a Language Universal and the Problem of the Semantic Identity of the Word. Automatic Documentation and Mathematical Linguistics. 1977; 11(1): 80-87. ISSN: 0005-1055.

LABOV, W. 1972. Language in the Inner City. Philadelphia, PA: University of Pennsylvania Press; 1972.

LAWANI, S.M. 1977. Citation Analysis and the Quality of Scientific Productivity. BioScience. 1977 January; 27(1): 26-31. ISSN: 0006-3568.

LEGUYADER, H.; VALLET, C.L.; MOULIN, T.H.; LAFRENIERE, L.; APTER, H. 1977. Arithmetical Relators and Virtual Information. In: Dubuisson, B., ed. Information and Systems: Proceedings of the International Federation of Automatic Control (IFAC) Workshop; 1977 October 25-27; Compiegne, France. Oxford, England: New York, NY: Pergamon Press; 1977. 119-130. ISBN: 0-08-022440-7; LC: 78-40143.

LEUNG-YAN-CHEONG, SIK K.; COVER, THOMAS M. 1978. Some Equivalences between Shannon Entropy and Kolmogorov Complexity. IEEE Transactions on Information Theory. 1978 May; IT-24(3): 331-338. ISSN: 0018-9448.

LOFTUS, ELIZABETH F.; MILLER, DAVID G.; BURNS, HELEN J. 1978. Journal of Experimental Psychology: Human Learning and Memory. 1978; 4(1): 19-31. ISSN: 0096-1523.

LUNNEBORG, CLIFFORD E. 1978. Some Information-Processing Correlates of Measures of Intelligence. Multivariate Behavioral Research. 1978 April; 13: 153-161. ISSN: 0027-3171.

MAIRLOT, FERDINAND E.; JUMARIE, GUY; DU BOIS, DANIEL M.; LAFRENIERE, LISE; MOULIN, THEIRAUT. 1977. Symposium sur divers aspects du concept d'information [Symposium on Various Aspects of the Concept of Information]; held during the 8th International Cybernetics Congress; 1976 September 6-11; Namur, Belgium. Cybernetica. 1977; 20(1): 6-37. ISSN: 0011-4227.

MANDLEBROT, B. 1966. Information Theory and Psycholinguistics: A Theory of Word Frequencies. In: Lazarsfeld, P.F., ed. Readings in Theoretical Social Science. Cambridge, MA: MIT Press; 1966.

MARCUS, RICHARD S.; KUGEL, PETER; BENEFELD, ALAN R. 1978. Catalog Information and Text as Indicators of Relevance. Journal of the

American Society for Information Science. 1978 January; 29(1): 15-28. ISSN: 0002-8231; CODEN: AISJB6.

MARGENAU, H. 1950. The Nature of Physical Reality. New York, NY: McGraw Hill; 1950. LC: QC6.M3514.

MARSLEN-WILSON, WILLIAM D.; WELSH, ALAN. 1978. Processing Interactions and Lexical Access During Word Recognition in Continuous Speech. Cognitive Psychology. 1978; 10: 29-63. ISSN: 0010-0285.

MAYES, J. TERRY. 1977. Information and Memory. The Information Scientist (England). 1977 June; 11(2): 65-73. ISSN: 0020-0263.

MCGRATH, WILLIAM E. 1978. Relationships between Hard/Soft, Pure/Applied and Life/Nonlife Disciplines and Subject Book Use in a University Library. Information Processing & Management. 1978; 14: 17-28. ISSN: 0306-4573.

MEKHTIEV, A.M.; ARAKELOV, R.K.; MELLION, S.P.; KUL'GAVINA, O.E. 1977. Using an Index of Cited Literature to Analyze the Current State and Trends of Information Science. Automatic Documentation and Mathematical Linguistics. 1977; 11(2): 49-59. ISSN: 0005-1055; UDC 019.955.

MURUGESAN, POOVANALINGAM; MORAVCSIK, MICHAEL J. 1978. Variation of the Nature of the Citation Measures with Journals and Scientific Specialties. Journal of the American Society for Information Science. 1978 May; 29(3): 141-147. ISSN: 0002-8231; CODEN: AISJB6.

NAHVI, M.J. 1977. Human Visual Signal Detection by Simultaneous Observation through Multiple Channels: Experimental Study of Decision Behavior. Biological Cybernetics. 1977; 27: 99-106. ISSN: 0340-1200.

NUNNALLY, JUM C.; LEMOND, L. CHARLES; WILSON, WILLIAM H. 1977. Studies of Voluntary Visual Attention—Theory, Methods, and Psychometric Issues. Applied Psychological Measurement. 1977 Spring; 1(2): 203-218. ISSN: 0146-6216.

ODEN, GREGG C. 1977. Integration of Fuzzy Logical Information. Journal of Experimental Psychology: Human Perception and Performance. 1977; 3(4): 565-575. ISSN: 0096-1523.

OROMANER, MARK. 1977. The Career of Sociological Literature: A Diachronous Study. Social Studies of Science. 1977; 7: 126-132. ISSN: 0306-3127.

ORTONY, ANDREW; ANDERSON, RICHARD C. 1977. Definite Descriptions and Semantic Memory. Cognitive Science. 1977 June; 1(1): 74-83. ISSN: 0364-0213.

PAO, MIRANDA LEE. 1977. Automatic Text Analysis Based on Transition Phenomena of Word Occurrences. Journal of the American Society for Information Science. 1978 May; 29(3): 121-124. ISSN: 0002-8231; CODEN: AISJB6.

PEARSON, CHARLS. 1976. Quantitative Investigations into the Type-Token Relation for Symbolic Rhemes. In: Pearson, Charls; Hamilton-Faria, Hope, eds. Proceedings of the 1st Annual Conference of the Semiotic Society of America; 1976 September 24-25; Atlanta, Georgia. Atlanta, GA: Georgia Institute of Technology, School of Information and Computer Science; 1976. 312-328. Available from: the author, Georgia Institute of Technology, School of Information and Computer Science, Atlanta, GA 30332.

PEARSON, CHARLS. 1978. A New Law of Information; An Empirical Regularity between Word Shapes and Their Interpretation. Paper presented at the 41st Annual Meeting of the American Society for Information Science (ASIS); 1978 November; New York, NY. Available from: the author, Georgia Institute of Technology, School of Information and Computer Science, Atlanta, GA 30332.

PEARSON, CHARLS; SLAMECKA, VLADIMIR. 1977. A Theory of Sign Structure. Semiotic Scene: Bulletin of the Semiotic Society of America. 1977 April; 1(2): 1-22.

PENLAND, PATRICK R. 1977. Intrapersonal Information Processing. Library Science with a Slant to Documentation (India). 1977 March; 14(1): 17-24. ISSN: 0025-2423.

PETTUS, CLINTON; DIENER, EDWARD. 1977. Factors Affecting the Effectiveness of Abstract versus Concrete Information. The Journal of Social Psychology. 1977; 103: 233-242. ISSN: 0022-4545.

POLUSHKIV, V.A. 1977. The Concept of Information Aging. Automatic Documentation and Mathematical Linguistics. 1977; 11(4): 12-14. UDC 002.2.7129.

POTTER, MARY C.; VALIAN, VIRGINIA V.; FAULCONER, BARBARA A. 1977. Representations of a Sentence and Its Pragmatic Implications: Verbal, Imagistic, or Abstract? Journal of Verbal Learning and Verbal Behavior. 1977; 16: 1-12. ISSN: 0022-5371.

POWELL, RONALD R. 1978. An Investigation of the Relationships between Quantifiable Reference Service Variables and Reference Performance in Public Libraries. Library Quarterly. 1978 January; 48(1): 1-19. ISSN: 0024-2519.

PRAUNLICH, PETER; KROLL, MICHAEL. 1978. Bradford's Distribution: A New Formulation. Journal of the American Society for Information Science. 1978 March; 29(2): 51-55. ISSN: 0002-8231; CODEN: AISJB6.

PRAWAT, RICHARD S.; CANCELLI, ANTHONY A. 1977. Semantic Retrieval in Young Children as a Function of Type of Meaning. Developmental Psychology. 1977; 13(4): 354-358. ISSN: 0012-1649.

PRICE, DEREK DESOLLA. 1976. A General Theory of Bibliometric and Other Cumulative Advantage Processes. Journal of the American Society for Information Science. 1976 September; 27(5): 292-306. ISSN: 0002-8231; CODEN: AISJB6.

RADECKI, TADEUSZ. 1977. Fuzzy Sets Theoretical Approach to Document Retrieval. Komunikaty, Seria A: Automatyzacja Bibliotek (Poland). 1977; (66):33. (In English).

RESNIKOFF, HOWARD L. 1979. Working draft: On the Problems of Information Science. 1979. 44p. Available from: Dr. Howard L. Resnikoff, National Science Foundation, Washington, DC 20550.

ROBERTSON, S.E.; BELKIN, N.J. 1978. Ranking in Principle. Journal of Documentation (England). 1978 June; 34(2): 93-100. ISSN: 0002-0418.

RÖSING-SPIEGEL, INA. 1977. Science Studies: Bibliometric and Content Analysis. Social Studies of Science. 1977; 7(9): 7-13. ISSN: 0306-3127.

ROSINSKI, RICHARD R. 1977. Picture-Word Interference Is Semantically Based. Child Development. 1977; 48: 643-647. ISSN: 0009-3920.

RUBIN, REBECCA BORING. 1977. The Role of Context in Information Seeking and Impression Formation. Communication Monographs. 1977 March; 44(1): 81-90. ISSN: 0363-7751.

RUDD, ERNEST. 1977. The Effect of Alphabetical Order of Author Listing on the Careers of Scientists. Social Studies of Science. 1977; 7: 268-269. ISSN: 0306-3127.

SAMPSON, J.R. 1976. Adaptive Information Processing: An Introductory Survey. New York, NY: Springer-Verlag; 1976. 214p. ISBN: 0-387-07739-1.

SARACEVIC, TEFKO. 1970. The Concept of "Relevance" in Information Science: An Historical Review. In: Saracevic, Tefko, ed. Introduction to Information Science. New York, NY: R.R. Bowker Co.; 1970. 111-154. ISBN: 0-8352-03B-1.

SCARDAMALIA, MARLENE. 1977. Information Processing Capacity and the Problem of Horizontal Decalage: A Demonstration Using Combinatorial Reasoning Tasks. Child Development. 1977; 48: 28-37. ISSN: 0009-3920.

SCHNEIDER, WALTER; SHIFFRIN, RICHARD M. 1977. Controlled and Automatic Human Information Processing; I: Detection, Search, and Attention. Psychological Review. 1977 January; 84(1): 1-66. ISSN: 0033-295X.

SCHWARZ, JEAN-JACQUES. 1977. Some New Results about S-Shaped Curves and Life-Cycle Time-Series. In: Dubuisson, B., ed. Information and Systems: Proceedings of the International Federation of Automatic Control (IFAC) Workshop; 1977 October 25-27; Compiegne, France. Oxford, England: New York, NY: Pergamon Press; 1977. 93-100. ISBN: 0-08-02240-7; LC: 78-40143.

SHERA, JESSE H.; CLEVELAND, DONALD B. 1977. History and Foundations of Information Science. In: Williams, Martha E., ed. Annual Review of Information Science and Technology: Volume 12. White Plains, NY: Knowledge Industry Publications, Inc.; 1977. 249-275. ISSN: 0066-4200; CODEN: ARISBc.

SHIFFRIN, RICHARD M.; SCHNEIDER, WALTER. 1977. Controlled and Automatic Human Information Processing; II: Perceptual Learning, Automatic Attending, and a General Theory. Psychological Review. 1977 March; 84(2): 127-190. ISSN: 0033-295X.

SHWARTZ, STEPHEN P.; POMERANTZ, JAMES R.; EGETH, HOWARD E. 1977. State and Process Limitations in Information Processing: An Additive Factors Analysis. Journal of Experimental Psychology: Human Perception and Performance. 1977; 3(3): 402-410. ISSN: 0096-1523.

SLAMECKA, VLADIMIR. 1975. Long-Range Research Objectives in Information Science. 1975 October. 5p. (Contains 3 appendices). Available from: Georgia Institute of Technology, School of Information and Computer Science, Atlanta, GA 30332.

SLAMECKA, VLADIMIR; PEARSON, CHARLS. 1977. The Portent of Signs and Symbols. In: Weiss, Edward C., ed. The Many Faces of Information Science: American Association for the Advancement of Science (AAAS) Selected Symposium. Boulder, CO: Westview Press; 1977. 105-128. ISBN: 0-89158-430-7; LC: Z699.A136.

SMALL, HENRY C. 1977. A Co-Citation Model of a Scientific Specialty: A Longitudinal Study of Collagen Research. Social Studies of Science. 1977; 7: 139-166. ISSN: 0306-3127.

SMITH, GERRY M. 1977. Key Books in Business and Management Studies: A Bibliometric Analysis. Aslib Proceedings (England). 1977 May; 29(5): 174-188. ISSN: 0001-253X.

SMOL'KOV, N.A. 1977. An Equation for the Scattering of Publications in Periodicals. Automatic Documentation and Mathematical Linguistics. 1977; 11(1): 1-6. ISSN: 0005-1055; UDC 05.001.5.

SOWDER, CALVIN D. 1977. List Length and Organization in the Recall of Categorized Lists. Psychological Reports. 1977; 41: 839-842. ISSN: 0033-2941.

STALKER, GEORGE H. 1978. Some Notions of Similarity among Lines of Text. Computers & the Humanities. 1978; 11: 119-209. ISSN: 0010-4817.

STAMPER, R. 1973. Information in Business and Administrative Systems. London, England: B.T. Batsford; 1973. 362p.

STUPKIN, V.V.; SHECHKOV, B.N. 1977. The Documentary Information Flow in Hydrometerology. Automatic Documentation and Mathematical Linguistics. 1977; 11(4): 20-25. ISSN: 0005-1055; UDC 002.2.551. 579.

SULLIVAN, DANIEL; WHITE, D. HYWELL; BARBONI, EDWARD J. 1977. Co-Citation Analysis of Science: An Evaluation. Social Studies of Science. 1977; 7: 240. ISSN: 0306-3127.

SUPPE, F. 1978. Toward an Adequate Information Science. To be published; available from: the author, Committee on the History and Philosophy of Science, University of Maryland, College Park, MD 20742.

TAGLIACOZZO, RENATA. 1978. Some Stylistic Variations in Scientific Writing. Journal of the American Society for Information Science. 1978 May; 29(3): 136-140. ISSN: 0002-8231; CODEN: AISJB6.

TRAVIS, I.L. 1977. Design Equations for Citation Retrieval Systems: Their Role in Research Analysis. Information Processing & Management. 1977; 13: 49-56. ISSN: 0306-4573.

TREISMAN, MICHELL. 1978. Space or Lexicon? The Word Frequency Effect and the Error Response Frequency Effect. Journal of Verbal Learning and Verbal Behavior. 1978; 17: 37-59. ISSN: 0022-5371.

TURNER, STEPHEN J. 1977. The Identifier Method of Measuring Use as Applied to Modelling the Circulation Use of Books from a University Library. Journal of the American Society for Information Science. 1977 March; 28: 96-100. ISSN: 0002-8231; CODEN: AISJB6.

TZENG, OLIVER C.S. 1977. A Quantitative Method for Separation of Semantic Subspaces. Applied Psychological Measurement. 1977 Spring; 1(2): 171-184. ISSN: 0146-6216.

VAN RIJSBERGEN, C.J. 1977. A Theoretical Basis for the Use of Co-Occurrence Data in Information Retrieval. Journal of Documentation (England). 1977 June; 33(2): 106-119. ISSN: 0022-0418.

VERNIMB, CARLO. 1977. Automatic Query Adjustment in Document Retrieval. Information Processing & Management. 1977; 13: 339-353. ISSN: 0306-4573.

VERSTIGGEL, JEAN-CLAUDE; LE NY, JEAN-FRANCOIS. 1977. Information semantique et memoire a court terme: L'activite de comparaison de phrases [Semantic Information and Short Term Memory: The

Activity of Phrase Comparison]. Annee Psychologie (France). 1977; 77: 63-78. (Text in French; abstract in English).

VRISOU VAN ECK, W.F.V. 1977. Quality of Information. In: Dubuisson, B., ed. Information and Systems: Proceedings of the International Federation of Automatic Control (IFAC) Workshop; 1977 October 25-27; Compiegne, France. Oxford, England: New York, NY: Pergamon Press; 1977. 11-18. ISBN: 0-08-022440-7; LC: 78-40143.

WEISS, EDWARD C., ed. 1977. The Many Faces of Information Science. Boulder, CO: Westview Press; 1977. 128p. ISBN: 0-89158-430-7; LC: Z699.A136.

WHITELY, SUSAN E. 1977. Information-Processing on Intelligence Test Items: Some Response Components. Applied Psychological Measurement. 1977 Fall; 1(4): 465-476. ISSN: 0146-6216.

WILLIAMS, MARTHA E. 1978. Information Science and the Role of NSF in Information Science Research. Paper presented to the National Science Foundation Task Force on Science Information Activities, 1978 April 25; Washington, DC. Available from: the author, University of Illinois. 5-135 Coordinated Sciences Laboratory, Urbana, IL 61801.

WILLIAMS, TANNIS MAGBETH; AIKEN, LEONA, S. 1977. Development of Pattern Classification: Auditory-Visual Equivalence in the Use of Prototypes. Developmental Psychology. 1977; 13(3): 198-204. ISSN: 0009-3920.

WINDSOR, D.A. 1977. Adverse-Reactions Literature: A Bibliometric Analysis. Methodik der Information in der Medizin (West Germany). 1977; 16(1): 52-54. (Text in German; abstract in English). ISSN: 0026-1270.

WIPPICH, WERNER. 1977. Concrete and Abstract Information in Semantic and Episodic Memory. Psychological Reports. 1977; 41: 31-36. ISSN: 2033-2941.

WOLFENDALE, GARTH L. 1977. An Information-Processing Approach to Human Signal Detection. Perceptual and Motor Skills. 1977; 45: 319-331. ISSN: 0031-5125.

YOVITS, M.C.; ROSE, LAWRENCE L. 1978. Information Flow and Analysis: Theory, Simulation, and Examples. 1978 September. 99p. (Report no. OSU-CISRC-TR-78-5). Available from: the authors, The Ohio State University, Computer and Information Science Research Center, Columbus, OH 43210.

YOVITS, M.C.; ROSE, LAWRENCE L.; ABILOCK, J.G. 1977. Development of a Theory of Information Flow and Analysis. In: Weiss, Edward C., ed. The Many Faces of Information Science: American Association for the Advancement of Science (AAAS) Selected Symposium. Boulder, CO: Westview Press; 1977. 128p. ISBN: 0-89158-430-7.

YU, CLEMENT T.; SALTON, GERARD. 1976. Precision Weighting: An Effective Automatic Indexing Method. Journal of the Association for Computing Machinery. 1976 January; 23(1): 76-88. ISSN: 0004-5411.

ZIPF, GEORGE K. 1949. Human Behavior and the Principle of Least Effort. New York, NY: Hafner Publishing Co; 1972. 573p. LC: 65-20086.

ZUNDE, PRANAS. 1971. On Signs, Information and Information Measures. Instrumentation Society of America Transactions. 1971;10(2): 189-193. ISSN: 0019-0578.

ZUNDE, PRANAS. 1978. Empirical Laws for Information Systems Design. Paper presented at: NATO Advanced Study Institute in Information Science, 1978 August 1-11. (Research report). Available from: the author, Georgia Institute of Technology, School of Information and Computer Science, Atlanta, GA 30332.

ZUNDE, PRANAS; DEXTER, M.E. 1969. Indexing Consistency and Quality. American Documentation. 1969; 20: 259-267.

ZWEBEN, STUART H. 1977. A Study of the Physical Structure of Algorithms. IEEE Transactions on Software Engineering. 1977 May; SE-3(3): 250-258. ISSN: 0098-5589.

4 Experimental Techniques of Information Retrieval

MICHAEL J. MCGILL
School of Information Studies, Syracuse University

JENNIFER HUITFELDT
School of Information Studies, Syracuse University

INTRODUCTION

This review of recent research in information retrieval systems surveys several areas that may provide fruitful results. Many of the techniques, theories, and models covered are, at best, years away from practical implementation. In fact, the research emphasis seems to be increasingly on fundamental problems of information retrieval, thus shifting from the operational problems. (Perhaps this is a result of the state concern of the National Science Foundation and the National Library of Medicine (NLM) with fundamental problems in information systems.) Some of these studies may prove more fruitful than others. More analysis is required before their contribution to information retrieval can be realized.

The number of high quality and creative articles to review for this chapter was impressive. During the past few years established researchers, such as Bookstein, W.S. Cooper, Maron, Salton, Sparck Jones, and van Rijsbergen, have made substantial contributions. New researchers are also emerging, such as Yu, Croft, Noreault, Koll, and Harper. These fresh minds are bringing new perspectives, raising critical questions, and utilizing sophisticated methodologies to study long-standing problems. In preparing this review, we found that the number of studies dealing with information retrieval systems is increasing. However, if SUMMIT (1977) is accurate when he states that 90% of all current scientific and technical journal literature is available online, then we must face the challenge of bringing our knowledge up to the level of our capacities.

Survey Material

A comprehensive discussion of information retrieval requires more space than is available here. Fortunately there are related areas of study commonly distinguished from information retrieval, such as question-answering systems, database systems, and library systems, that need not be addressed in this review. The recent reviews by MINKER (1977) and PAICE examine these areas in more detail. Reviews of the mathematical foundations of information retrieval and related computational standards are also available (HEAPS; SALTON). In addition, new sources describing ongoing developments have emerged. Two new journals that deal specifically with information research and management are the *JOURNAL OF INFORMATICS* and *INFORMATION & MANAGEMENT*; bibliographies on this subject were published by BIBLIOSHARE and HAWKINS.

Chapter Organization

The scope of this chapter is limited to document or text retrieval. Models and theories of information retrieval are discussed first (e.g., fuzzy set theory, probabilistic retrieval, artificial intelligence). This discussion is followed by a section dealing with applications, such as indexing, term weighting, clustering, access methods, feedback, and ranking techniques. The next section reviews fact and natural language retrieval. Databases, design, and evaluation of systems are included as approaches to total systems in those cases that do not fit into the previous sections. Finally, trends in research that have and will affect the future of information retrieval are considered.

THEORIES AND MODELS OF INFORMATION RETRIEVAL

There is no generally accepted theory of information retrieval. Various approaches to fundamental concepts—e.g., set theoretic, fuzzy set theoretic, utility theoretic, probabilistic, and algebraic approaches—all address identical problems. This variety may encourage the development of ideas and the generation and testing of hypotheses. Effective arguments may be presented for each approach. Unfortunately, we are not equally conversant in the terminology of all disciplines, and we may be broadening our perspective instead of deepening our understanding. Our knowledge base, with few exceptions, is surprisingly shallow. Greater knowledge results when our analyses are based on well-established theory—e.g., probability theory and vector space interpretations.

Fuzzy Set Theory

Fuzzy set theory's appeal comes from the continuum of set membership in contrast to the dichotomous membership or nonmembership of an element to a set. That is, fuzzy set theory allows degrees of membership, whereas regular set theory does not. For example, an article on database management in a fuzzy set system would have some relationship to a group of articles on information retrieval. However, in a system based on regular set theory, these articles would either be included or not included in the same set. RADECKI (1977) used fuzzy set theory to propose a language for retrieval and subsequently developed a syntax and semantic structure for the proposed language (RADECKI, 1978). He formalized the retrieval process, including the similarity measure and the retrieval decision process in these terms.

ROBERTSON also examined fuzzy set theory as a model of information retrieval and found that the justification for its use was the ambiguity it allowed. He noted that fuzzy sets and probability theory can be used to examine search logic. However, Boolean operations performed on fuzzy sets lead to even "fuzzier" sets. For example, fuzzy set intersection requires that elements with two membership values be resolved to a single membership value for the newly defined set. The minimum membership value is used as the value for set intersection. There is no intuitive explanation for this procedure. On the other hand, the conditional probability of an element's being a member of a second set, given that it is included in the first, is intuitively well understood. Robertson indicated that in common situations probability theory provides a useful model. In these same situations fuzzy set theory has to be modified significantly to include random variables. The initial examination of fuzzy sets may provide reasonable analogies to information retrieval; however, closer examination shows its current inadequacies. Probability theory is a better developed and more precise mechanism for understanding retrieval systems.

Probability Theory

Probability theory is an intuitively pleasing model for describing and analyzing retrieval systems (VAN RIJSBERGEN, 1979). The central theme of this approach is that one can estimate the probability of the relevance of a given document. Van Rijsbergen proposed that a measure of the probability of the relevance of a given document to a particular theory be based on a vector representing that document. He assumed that the pattern of index terms in relevant documents will differ from their pattern in nonrelevant documents. Using a probability theory approach based on these patterns one can analyze a wide range of topics, including term clustering, frequency weighting, relevance weighting, and ranking.

BOOKSTEIN & KRAFT used probability theory to develop and to extend a model of indexing and retrieval based on word occurrences. A probability model based on the Poisson distribution was shown to be consistent with our intuitive belief that not all content-bearing words carry the content in the same manner; there is a more complex structure that must be considered. The particular Poisson model used (linked two-Poisson) takes into account the influence that the occurrence of one word has on another. Rules are formally derived for retrieval, which appear to conflict with retrieval methodologies established in algebraic or spatially oriented systems. For example, their evidence indicates that in order to determine the similarity between a query and a document, one should multiply values rather than add them and that terms that appear directly in the request should be treated differently from related terms.

Probability theory can also be used to rank order documents according to their probability of relevance (ROBERTSON). ROBERTSON shows that the order of documents can be based on term values and on an "optimal retrieval function." However, if one attempts to rank order documents in a Boolean environment, some difficulties arise, which are inherent in the Boolean logic (BOOKSTEIN, 1978). BOOKSTEIN suggested that the retrieved documents be ordered according to the number of Boolean expressions present in the document that are true.

One working application of probability theory is described by DOSZKOCS. Probabilistic associations are being used to find terms that are associated with other terms. The association procedures are based on term occurrences (in a set of items retrieved by a Boolean query) and the frequency of these terms in the database. The system is implemented on a database of 400,000 records at NLM.

Artificial Intelligence

The field of artificial intelligence (AI) has a number of research interests that parallel those of information retrieval (SMITH, 1976b). For example, the problem of pattern recognition is similar to that of determining relevant documents in response to a specific query. Query modification and feedback techniques in information retrieval resemble models of short-term learning in artificial intelligence.

SMITH (1976a) suggested that our understanding of the current state-of-the-art of artificial intelligence techniques may provide insights and techniques to enhance information retrieval. AI techniques developed in the study of pattern recognition, representation, problem solving, and learning may someday replace many human activities. Rather than suggesting that all intellectual activities be replaced, she proposed that those activities that cannot be represented as algorithms be learned by the user with computer-aided instruction.

Feature enhancement and pattern analysis are techniques that are used to isolate and to identify desired items. CAHN & HERR proposed the use of these techniques to map the contents of a database in one representation to a database in another representation. Their goal was to allow the user to view a system as though there were a single large database, even though several databases actually were being used. The user's query could be enhanced for each of the actual databases with no user effort.

The examination of AI techniques as applied to information retrieval systems has just begun. These techniques seem to have direct consequences for advancing the state-of-the-art, but their practical implementation is still many years away.

Vector Space Models

The vector model of an information environment, first described by Salton, is still being rediscovered (MCGILL). This model assumes that each information item can be placed in a vector space. The dimensionality of the space is determined by the number of terms or concepts in the database. MEINCKE & ATHERTON suggested a vector basis for organizing and visualizing information. They used vectors to represent a "concept" defined for a field of knowledge or a "state" vector for a person, based on the person's understanding of the concepts.

MCINROY used vectors for automatic extraction. He found that these extracts perform better than another automatic method but not as well as human-produced abstracts. As the extract sizes were reduced, performance in a retrieval environment decreased, but this depended on the database. A database of homogeneous documents on documentation was more severely affected by the size of the extract than a heterogeneous database of articles from a news magazine. The concept vector approach is not recommended as a substitute for the human-produced abstract.

One of the more interesting models is described by KOLL. His WEIRD system uses a vector space model to represent the relationships among terms and the relationships among documents. A concept is defined as a point in the space. The pragmatic meaning of a concept is derived from the position of the concept relative to all other concepts in the space. Both the terms and the documents are placed in the space by an iterative process, which ensures that each entity is located at the point that best indicates its pragmatic meaning. Retrieval is done by concept similarity—i.e., a similarity measure is used to establish the agreement of the query to the documents. Documents that lie above a specified threshold are retrieved, while those that lie below it are not.

CLEVELAND proposed a space whose dimensionality is maximally determined by the terms, journals, authors, and citations of the information systems. Relationships among documents were determined by calculating the distance between points representing the documents in the vector space. The tests showed that a best predictor of relationships between pairs of documents in this environment was achieved by using only author or author and journal in combination.

Other Models

The use of clusters in information retrieval remains a focus of interest. Clusters are groups of items (usually documents) that are identified as being related according to some measure of similarity that takes into account the characteristics used to represent the items.

CROFT (1978) reviewed the basic elements of cluster searching and models of predictors. The predictors were used to estimate the characteristics of any element of a cluster. He then reviewed the likelihood of errors across all clusters and mechanisms for reducing these errors, and he examined coefficients associating a new document with a cluster using a generalization of Dice's coefficient. Dice's coefficient is one measure of the similarity among items. Cluster searching will be useful for some applications. However, probabilistic retrieval is competitive with the cluster methods.

YU ET AL. (1978a) presented a generalized model of information retrieval using binary representations. The model was based on the assumption that a database can be divided into classes and that within a class each attribute is independent. They demonstrated the model's applicability in clustered searches, indexing strategies, and feedback systems. The model is mathematically pleasing because it is easily extended and tested. However, the independence assumptions are questionable (even if they are widely used). The "relaxation" of the assumptions presented by the authors showed that they shared this concern. Tests of the impact of the assumption or, better, the alteration of the model to remove the independence assumption would be a major stride forward.

A model of an information system must contain information elements and the relationships among the elements. If the information elements are ordered, assembled into a consistent format, and each ordered element is assigned an attribute, then one has the essential elements of a relational model. The formalization of this model permits mathematical analysis, such as determining the equivalence of representations; it may be used to ensure efficient file design or to establish an efficient syntactic structure for the information system.

CRAWFORD & MACLEOD note that new relationships can be calculated from predefined relationships. They used an example to show that a relational approach is a powerful mechanism for retrieving data. They conjectured that each relation table could represent an index, and new relation tables could be developed to represent various degrees of indexing sophistication. Relation tables could be dynamic and thus would provide an added flexibility that is not present in current systems. This brief paper presented the idea with an example of relational tables.

The application of probability theory to indexing allows one to determine which index terms should be applied to a document based on a preset threshold. The value of this threshold is currently arbitrary. W.S. COOPER suggested that utility theory should be the next step. If one uses expected utility as a criterion, then decision rules can be defined. On the other hand, one is left with the problem of determining the utilities of particular documents. This is a difficult task, requiring considerable user effort.

COOPER & MARON examined utility theoretic and probabilistic indexing. Utility theoretic indexing schemes assign terms to documents in a manner that reflects the probable value (utility) of the document to the user; probabilistic indexing schemes are shown to be subsets of utility theoretic approaches. Both can be analyzed using spatial representations, where each point in the space is considered as a future use. The space can then be partitioned according to the range of future uses relevant to an index term. In a binary indexing system, a goal is to determine the future uses for a request that includes a given index term. Each document will have a utility (probability of relevance) to each future use, where one can either retrieve the document or not retrieve the document. Based on these assumptions, one can establish decision rules for indexing. If the sum of the utilities with this specific document retrieved is greater than the sum of the utilities with this document not retrieved, the term should be used to index the document. Rules for other indexing schemes have been derived according to the same logic.

Approaches from probability theory, utility theory, and vector space all agree to some extent with our understanding of information retrieval systems. The vector space approaches include the assumption of term independence, which is difficult to relax. On the other hand, the impact of this assumption can be tested in models based on probability theory. Utility theory may be a generalization of probability theory. Certainly there are utility values (positive and negative) associated with the retrieval of a document, but the problems of assigning these values and adapting them to various users requires more examination. Perhaps probability theory will limit theoretical development, but it does provide a solid foundation for much research. The limits of probability theory may eventually become a constraint; for now they remain undefined and unconstraining.

APPLICATIONS FROM MODELS

The effective retrieval of information items is the focus of this section. Both theory and research in automatic retrieval methods are stressed. To improve the performance of retrieval systems, aids such as term weighting, clustered files, automatic feedback processing, and ranking algorithms have been developed. Most of the research here remains experimental. Systems that use these aids may now be practical, but users probably will not see these tools for several years. The reasons for this include conversion difficulties, costs, difficulty in evaluating these systems with our present performance measures, and a lack of communication among professionals and researchers.

Indexing

There has been much progress in our understanding of automatic indexing since it was first suggested by Luhn. Unfortunately, few operating systems attempt to index automatically. The operators and the users of current information systems seem to lack confidence in a system's ability to automatically characterize an information item for retrieval. However, research on computer applications in indexing indicates that automatic indexing gives results that are comparable with human indexing. A large-scale test at the University of Cambridge Computer Laboratory reported comparative tests on automatic indexing schemes that involved statistical weighting and classification (SPARCK JONES & BATES, 1977a). Results indicated that statistical weighting was effective and gave significantly improved indexing performance for retrieval. This finding agrees with Salton's SMART project results.

BARNES ET AL. described an experiment to test the feasibility of large-scale automatic indexing of scientific text abstracts using SLC-II, a language translator software package. The experiment consisted of two parts: 1) the comparison of automatic indexing with manual indexing, and 2) the comparison of the use of a preexisting thesaurus with an enriched thesaurus. No results were given in this report.

MARON examined the concept of "about" (e.g., is this term "about" this concept) as it relates to the effectiveness of an information retrieval system. He provided an operational definition of "about" based on probabilities. His examination indicates that "about" is only one of several factors that should be considered in representing a document. The purpose of retrieval is satisfaction of the user's information need, and this is partially satisfied by providing items "about" the user's need. Other considerations include comprehensibility, credibility, importance, timeliness, etc.

The importance of understanding the human process of indexing for those involved in natural language text manipulation was stressed by ARTANDI. Although much has been done, "the intellectual task of developing algorithms that will allow the machine to detect meaning through recognition of signs. . .has not yet been accomplished." BRINER saw a necessity to develop a mathematical theory of indexing by fusing information theory and language theory. He suggested the application of Shannon's information capacity to formula indexing. This capacity theorem states that a source of messages can be encoded so that information can be transmitted through a noisy channel with few errors, up to a limit known as the limiting capacity. Beyond this point, errors become more frequent.

SVENONIUS & SCHMIERER reviewed past and present issues in indexing and subject classification. They discussed the scientific approaches to subject control, such as natural language indexing, string index languages, indexing vocabulary convertibility, machine-aided indexing, and thesaurus generation.

Machine-aided indexing combines the speed and consistency of the computer and the intellectual power of the human indexer. CRAVEN described a program for the computer generation of permuted cross-references in a semiautomatic indexing system. NEPHIS (NEsted PHrase Indexing System) was developed to reduce the intellectual effort required to assign role indicators to index terms. Indicators, or grammatial tags, reflect contextual relationships among terms in an index string. KOENIG & VLADUTZ suggested that if the assignment of role indicators in PRECIS (PREserved Context Indexing System) were automated, the potential applications of PRECIS would increase. They argued that manual assignment of role indicators is time consuming, difficult to learn, and thus too expensive. The development of computer techniques for this purpose may be feasible, using automated language processing, parsing, and transformational analysis. As an example of such methods, the authors used the Linguistic String Project at New York University (described in the Natural Language Processing section of this chapter).

The use of the programming langauge APL for semiautomatic indexing of books was considered by PIERCE. He found that indexers with little computer experience could sort and format back-of-book indexes economically and quickly by using a system that he calls APLDEX.

Subject representation and subject access to book material are problems of wide interest. The final report of the project known as BOOKS, which tested improved access to books in online library catalogs, noted that BOOKS records, created by adding terms from the table of contents and index to the database in addition to the MARC-searchable fields (call number, main entry, title, and subject heading), could retrieve more relevant documents faster and cheaper than MARC records (ATHERTON, 1978a). Literature searches done by BOOKS and MARC were compared using the number of relevant books retrieved, the precision ratios, and computer connect time required for each search. Present operational systems, such as OCLC and LIBCON, could augment their files using words and phrases found within the book.

Interest has been rejuvenated in the study of machine-aided thesaurus generation. This research is concerned with the logical as well as physical grouping of terms and with determining relationships among the terms. SCHWARTZ & NOREAULT described their experiment on a portion of a physics database (INSPEC) of the SIRE (Syracuse Information Retrieval Experiment) system, and they suggested that machine-aided methods are becoming effective for thesaurus construction.

Term Weighting

ROBERTSON & SPARCK JONES showed that the use of relevance information to establish weights for search terms can be advantageous. Their theory was tested using binary document representations, schemes that use information about the occurrence of terms in relevant documents, and schemes that use information about the occurrence of terms in relevant and nonrelevant documents. Using a test collection, they demonstrated dramatic improvement in retrieval effectiveness, particularly when data indicated both the presence and absence of search terms in documents. Prediction of term weights from a sample of documents proved troublesome. The authors cited the need for a general method of estimation that takes advantage of prior information about the system, the questioner's prior expectations, the frequencies of terms, and available relevance data.

SPARCK JONES tested the robustness of relevance weighting—i.e., the ability of the scheme to withstand various alterations without affecting the validity of the results. She was concerned with the effects of the size of the document collection, poor matching conditions, heterogeneous data, and limited relevance information. A precision-recall analysis disclosed substantial improvement with the relevance weighting schemes over simple term matching, improvement over other statistical methods, and comparability with finely honed Boolean searches. The relevance weighting techniques were surprisingly sound even as the number of items considered for relevance judgment decreased significantly.

SALTON & WALDSTEIN reviewed term weighting schemes and tested their impact on ranking using fully automatic systems. Operational difficulties in using weights based on occurrence probabilities in relevant and nonrelevant documents were encountered. They concluded that it is feasible and effective to ask the user to judge the importance of terms, noting that informed users should perform this task better than uninformed users.

RAGHAVAN & YU (1978a) experimented with positive and negative relevance information. They proposed that relevance information be used to establish relationships between pairs of terms, using both positive and negative relationships. Results indicated that relationships among low-document frequency terms should be given greater significance.

The research projects described so far have assumed that terms are independent of one another. VAN RIJSBERGEN (1977) examined the possibility of removing this assumption. To determine the extent of the dependence among terms, one can construct a nonlinear weighting function based on occurrences and co-occurrences of terms. The abandonment of the independence assumption is reasonable and will allow a more realistic model of information retrieval.

In a dynamic environment it is difficult to calculate term values. CRAWFORD suggested that a term status map be used to record the document frequency, the total frequency, and the dynamic discrimination value of the term. Here the dynamic discrimination value measures the change in the compactness of the collection with and without the term. The average similarity among items will increase as the collection becomes more compact and will decrease as it becomes less compact. The proposed measure is based on the cosine correlation. Crawford concluded that use of the term status map makes dynamic dictionary updating feasible. In addition, the user can obtain information from the term status map to identify broader or narrower terms.

Clustering

A cluster is a group of items with similar characteristics that are gathered together. In clustered files documents are organized so that those with similar representations are grouped automatically. SALTON & WONG reviewed the file structures that can be adapted to information retrieval and postulated that clustered files would offer many advantages. A scheme for file clustering was developed along with searching schemes for the file. ENSER discussed a research project that uses a single-link clustering algorithm to classify a sample of 300 books automatically.

YU & LUK examined the effectiveness of clustered files. Using a system with several keys, they offered a probabilistic model that allows the number of relevant items in one cluster to be compared with those in another; this approach allows clusters to be rejected. Compared with other environments, the authors concluded that clustered file searching is effective in an online environment if a few records are desired. As the desired number of records increases, retrieval performance deteriorates.

Numerous techniques have been developed for generating and using clusters. CROFT (1978) investigated a method of developing clusters that uses an inverted file as input. The evaluation of his technique shows that clustered files can be generated in less than order n^2 time, where n is the number of items to be clustered. His method depends on the prior creation of the inverted file. Maximally connected clusters have been called cliques (GER-SON). They are developed by: 1) clustering using an algorithm that develops partitions of the items and optimizes these partitions within a subset of the database; and 2) enriching the clusters by adding to each one all items that cite an item originally in the cluster. This is said to increase the likelihood that all relevant documents will be obtained when a given clique is retrieved. KAR & WHITE used a "Bayesian distance" measure to determine nondiscriminating keywords as they were extracted from documents. The Bayesian distances are the *a posteriori* probability of clusters given the observation of keywords. The premise of Kar and White was that documents can be clustered by a sequential technique that extracts keywords and at each step uses a statistical prediction to determine whether or not the document can be classified using that term. The method was three to five times faster than nonsequential processes and sustained a "classification accuracy" of 80%. LAM & YU devised a procedure for estimating the number of close items in a cluster in response to a query, allowing for dependencies among items. Schemes that use dependencies were shown to be much more accurate than schemes that assume independence.

Clustered files are problematic in dynamic environments, primarily because the clusters can fluctuate as new items are entered. The stability of clustered files has been evaluated by RAGHAVAN & YU (1978b). The evaluation of a graph theoretic clustering method was based on the number of operations required to restore the set of clusters after it had been altered by new data. Clusters that are based on some connecting relationship (connected components) were more stable than those based on elements with specific relationships (e.g., maximally complete subgraphs).

Access Methods

Access methods, as defined here, are techniques for organizing and retrieving information regardless of the subject or content of that information. For example, SHNEIDERMAN & GOODMAN reexamined the batching of searches in disk-based online systems. They found that batched searches produced substantial savings over individual searches. Batching is feasible with storage structures other than sequential ones.

WILLIAMS & KHALLAGHI suggested that substrings of free text terms be used as search keys to ensure efficient search times. Their keys were limited in length, were grouped grammatically by stemming (through truncation), and frequency variations were limited creating a dictionary of manageable size. Their tests indicated that keys of this sort gave a precision level of about 80% while ensuring search efficiency.

Truncated search keys also help to ensure search efficiencies. RASTOGI examined two models of name/title-derived search keys. The model assumed that search keys are not independent of the number of postings for that key. He found that keys with many postings adversely affected the overall performance of a search and suggested that such keys be identified and placed in a separate file.

The design of derived search keys for a Superintendent of Documents Number was investigated by HICKEY ET AL. Bibliographic records for federal documents were retrieved from OCLC using these derived keys. Using measures of expected retrieval and relative entropy, a number of models were tested. After some frustration, a search key derived from the first 14 digits of the Superintendent of Documents Number was selected.

In another experiment using the OCLC system, SMITH & RUSH found that the use of truncated keys for corporate and personal authors was successful. They examined ten search key configurations using a database of 200,000 bibliographic records for personal authors and an equivalent database for computer authors. They determined that a 4, 3, 1, key structure was the most effective—i.e., a key is derived from the first four letters of the first word, the first three letters of the second word and the first letter of the third word. The fact that this particular key is effective is not surprising since it was also the most specific key structure tested. For practical use they suggested a key structure of 4, 2, 0, which retrieved one personal author 60.1% of the time and one corporate author 21.6% of the time. Derived search keys are an effective way to retrieve specific combinations of search terms. When subject searching is not required, they help to ensure an efficient search.

The hybrid access method requires that the user enter a search term that is expanded to include a "signature" (BOOKSTEIN, 1974). The signature is encoded information (a bit string) that allows the user to determine if a search term is of interest in a field of a particular document. For example, a signature is constructed of the title field for a given document by using a hashing scheme. Each three-letter sequence of characters in the title is encoded to a single item of information. The result is the signature of the title. When evaluated for retrieval, users had little difficulty in choosing terms that separated titles in their own minds. These terms were usually effective for searching. Often a single keyword is enough, and two keywords always worked. The procedure was effective, easily implemented, and efficient in its use of storage and CPU time.

In searching multiple attributes, the use of multiple indexes may be inefficient, especially if queries have a number of conjunctions. As an alternative, one may use combined indexes. Queries could then be handled without costly interactions. Unfortunately, the combining of indexes creates new indexes that are larger than either of the original indexes and thus are inefficient to store. SHNEIDERMAN (1977b) examined reduced combined indexes, which are more efficient to store. This technique seems appropriate when the ratio of retrieval to update is high, when many records have similar keys, when queries are complex, and when it is more important to minimize search time than storage.

Faced with the search of an ordered sequential file, one should consider the use of a "jump search algorithm" to decrease the number of comparisons and increase the search efficiency. These algorithms jump over a portion of the file. When a smaller block is updated, smaller jumps or sequential searches can be used. Variable jump searching is slightly better than fixed jump searching. In fact, substantial gains can be obtained by adjusting the jump size (SHNEIDERMAN, 1978b).

Research on access techniques is oriented toward ensuring search efficiency. The centers of interest are in the representation of the items, in the organization of the files, and in the specific techniques used to find the desired item. Truncated search keys are efficient, and in most instances, effective. However, in some cases ambiguities arise and search effectiveness is diminished. The particular techniques used to find an item depend on the file struture, and these are, in turn, dictated by the uses of the file.

Feedback

The development of a reasonable but suboptimal query immediately raises the question of how one can improve that query. Feedback in information retrieval is a process of attempting to improve the query by using relevance or nonrelevance information. It can be done manually (usually called query revision) or automatically (called automatic feedback or relevance feedback).

CHOW & YU constructed optimal feedback queries based on a rule that maximizes precision at any recall level and also ranks the documents. They also showed that terms of low weight can be deleted without seriously affecting retrieval performance.

Experiments that evaluate the impact of using the term-dependency model on feedback have also been conducted by HARPER & VAN RIJSBERGEN. Their model was tested with relevance information on a portion of the database. The test indicated that the use of term dependencies can significantly increase retrieval effectiveness when documents not previously seen by the user are sought. The initial model of strict dependence was replaced by one that uses weights based on a measure of the information among terms. A tree describing the relationships among terms (maximal spanning tree) was used to obtain an expanded set of terms. Using this feedback scheme, the authors demonstrated that over a broad range of test collections, the modified dependency feedback is more effective than feedback that is based on an assumption of independence among terms.

Clustering has also been used in feedback (ATTAR & FRAENKEL). Using a database of U.S. patents, the process of formulating a new search based on clustering terms from initially retrieved documents was explored. This process created a dynamic clustering environment that depended only on the user's initial query. When weighting was added to the feedback scheme, the overall performance of the system seemed to improve.

In a controlled vocabulary system VERNIMB used relevance judgments for query adjustment. Two or more relevant documents were initially required to begin the feedback. From these documents a list of descriptors was developed and partial queries were formed. Partial queries (descriptors from the initial query combined by the logical operator AND) were broadened to achieve a specific level of performance following specific logic modification rules; they were then combined to form the modified query. Comparisons with the traditional intellectual approach to developing queries indicated that the automatic procedure was as good as the traditional method, and the necessity of thesaurus reference, query development, and descriptor weighting was removed.

DAVIES described a project that used term frequencies combined with an appropriate matching scheme to enhance a system's performance. He proposed a scheme that used term frequency ranks within documents along with iterative matching. Document descriptions were compared with a pattern of terms from the user. The request pattern can be adjusted in response to the user's judgments in a feedback environment. According to the author, a "handful" of initial terms should lead rapidly to an effective pattern for retrieval.

Ranking

Ranking algorithms attempt to measure the degree of relevance of a document to a query and to rank the document according to this measure. SAGER & LOCKEMANN reviewed term weighting schemes and ranking algorithms. The algorithms were classified, and some of the classes were tested on a legal database. The authors found that ranking algorithms are of considerable help to inexperienced users, to users seeking a few highly relevant documents, and to users who need a "first impression." The cost of ranking was negligible.

NOREAULT ET AL. examined ranking algorithms in a Boolean environment using SIRE with a small physics database (from INSPEC). The coefficient of ranking effectiveness was developed to measure the relative improvement of ranking over the random order of retrieval of relevant documents. They found an average 30% improvement by using the cosine correlation as a ranking method over the unordered retrieval.

FACT AND NATURAL LANGUAGE SYSTEMS

The processing of natural language for information retrieval is a long-sought goal. The problems of relating syntactic structures, semantic structures, and user concepts are enormously complex. However, the potential benefits of methods for automatic processing are so significant that the considerable effort required should be encouraged. Retrieval of specific information without the need for full natural language processing is the goal of passage retrieval. Stimulus to work in this area has come from the advent of machine-readable natural language databases.

Natural Language Processing

An excellent review of research efforts to process English or other natural language documents was presented by SAGER. Her focus was the processing of documents to collect and to arrange the information so that it can be used in different ways. Inherent patterns of written language were used to recognize and to arrange the information. She described the procedures used to identify word classes and information structures. Automatic methods were used to convert an arbitrary text to a structured database. Potential applications include fact retrieval, data summarization, and exception condition reporting. Using a medical narrative as an example, it was shown that this process can represent the narrative information in tabular form (SAGER & LYMAN); this representation can then be processed for various needs.

A procedure has been developed (DUNHAM ET AL.) for analyzing pathology data. A structured nomenclature was used as both a point of analysis and the final representation, using medical diagnostic statements as entered data. These statements were analyzed using syntactic and comparative methods. Original statements were translated into a Systematized Nomenclature of Pathology (SNOP), which represented the narrative. The analysis was then extended to provide formal rules for translating participles to nominal forms, nominal forms to adjectival forms, and certain Greek and Latin terms to adjectival forms.

FORD & JOHNSON have developed a microprocessor-based system using full text and graphics. Using a hepatitis database, they combined low-cost mass storage devices with a microcomputer. The result is a self-contained information system, complete with line drawings.

Procedures for analyzing natural language so that it can be used in retrieval systems seem to be limited to medical environments, which are inherently structured. Unfortunately, they may not be extended easily to other less structured environments. CHERNIAVSKY attempted to show that the process of understanding or analyzing natural language is not algorithmic; his analysis was not mathematical. He concluded that algorithms to replicate the human intellectual process are not possible, based on a comparison of algorithms to humans. His comparisons did not take into account the considerable efforts of researchers in artificial intelligence or heuristic approaches.

Fact and Passage Retrieval

O'CONNOR (1978a) reviewed the use of passage retrieval in the legal field and concluded that it is effective, practical, and within economic constraints. In one experiment, recall was 67% with a minimal number of retrieved passages for each retrieved document. Passage or sentence retrieval has inherent advantages to the user. The entire document does not have to be reviewed either to find desired information or to reject the document as nonrelevant. In another experiment O'CONNOR (1978b) reported a recall of 80% and "high" precision using a cancer database. The selection of search terms is still a human process and apparently is critical to the effectiveness of this procedure.

In another test O'CONNOR (1977) reported on an analysis of searching when the texts being sought are data-bearing papers. The data portions of texts frequently cannot be referenced through a retrieval system. Use of the full text and words from figures and data in the text resulted in 60% recall.

Fifty percent of the recall was attributed to the searching of figures and data, and the additional ten percent came from the searching of the main text.

GRISHMAN & HIRSCHMAN described a system for answering questions about a collection of natural language medical records, based on schemes developed at the Linguistic String Project. The question-answering procedure is an extension of this process. The question undergoes the same initial processing as a medical narrative. It is then converted into a retrieval operation, and an answer is developed. The query was converted into a series of searches of the tabular columns that represented the medical narratives for the desired answer to a question (HIRSCHMAN & GRISHMAN).

MINKER (1978) analyzed the relationships among binary relations, directed graphs, and Boolean matrices. His formal treatment included a state space description of the process of deduction. Representation of the question-answering problem as a series of matrices is probably more useful for insight than for practical purposes. The matrices require considerable storage, and since they are inherently sparse, they waste a large portion of that space. Ordered matrices may be useful for small databases when questions of existence, binary relations, Boolean conditions, or quantification are involved.

APPROACHES TO TOTAL SYSTEMS

So far we have been concerned with either theoretic approaches or specific portions of an information retrieval system. Here we are concerned with a broader perspective: the system from the user's point of view, user access to the system and the information in the system. These complex topics are difficult to study independently. However, concerns such as understanding the needs of users are fundamental to the effective design and implementation of an information system.

User Interface

The information specialist is the key factor in the successful operation of online search services because this person knows the system conventions, understands the techniques and Boolean operations, and is familiar with the equipment (KRENTZ). The assumption that end users will remain unsophisticated in this regard was questioned by MEADOW. By drawing an analogy between computer programming and online searching, he views users as amateur programmers and foresees the role of the intermediary changing to that of a professional level analyst, where there would be "less time. . . devoted to hand-holding and more to problem solving."

Several research projects are examining the possibility of connecting interactive, commercial information retrieval systems through computer interfaces. At the MIT Electronic Systems Laboratory, a computer interface system of this type is under investigation (MARCUS & REINTJES). This system, known as CONIT (COnnector for Networked Information Transfer), implements an automatic call mechanism for connecting the interface to a remote computer system and a translation table mechanism for interpreting data from the system to the CONIT format. The report describes a neophyte's interaction with the system in detail and discusses the goals, problems, and results of the experiment.

GOLDSTEIN & FORD describe the concerns of user-oriented interaction. They point out that optimizing the interface for the end user and optimizing a single interface for a large, heterogeneous user population are often conflicting goals. They use an intelligent terminal environment to examine the interface problem. They conclude that the user interface is a matter of format of the command language and format of the display. These may be separated from the retrieval functions and adapted to a variety of users.

Along with improvements in standardization and user interface, W.S. COOPER stressed the need for improvements in indexing techniques, search strategies, theoretical foundations, and data retrieval systems. SHNEIDERMAN (1978a) discussed human-factor considerations, such as simplicity, elegance, and the pictorial representation of data model structures, as a starting point for research in this area. One of the specific research issues he addressed is an experiment on natural query language vs. relational query language.

Closely aligned with the user interface literature are descriptions of programs designed to train users. MEADOW & EPSTEIN described a program that is being developed for end users of scientific and technological information. The system—known as Individualized Instruction for Data Access (IIDA)—monitors the interaction between the user and the computer, providing general guidance on user technique. Another program, consisting of computer-assisted learning modules and practice modules (system emulators), was discussed by CARUSO (1978b). Her report described an online trainer that allowed end users (information professionals) to develop skills in using online search systems without computer charges.

Databases

One result of the expansion of database service is the importance of well-designed database management systems (WILLIAMS). SHNEIDERMAN (1977a) reviewed the historical development of database management systems and discussed two opposing ideologies—the network model and the relational model. The network model uses explicit representations of relationships among items. Items are thus connected and can be analyzed as if they were a network. The relational model assumes that relationships among entities can be viewed as mathematical relations. Tabular representations of the domain and ranges of specific relationships allow precise analyses to be performed. Data management techniques, standardization, and data integrity are still major research issues. MOHAN, in an extensive list of references on database research, stated that the greatest need of research is the evolution of new high-level data models that would enable designers to incorporate directly a major portion of the semantics of the database in the model.

An introduction to the concept of data organization, primarily in information retrieval but also in its application to library automation, is given by VAN RIJSBERGEN (1976). This is a review of data structure, file organization, and approaches to clustering. He describes the needs of data retrieval and information retrieval applications and relates them to organizations and structures.

The concept of a meta-database was described by COUSINS & DOMINICK. This "meta-base," useful in database management systems and in systems where there is user access to multiple databases, contains all the structural and semantic data of several databases. The use and size of document retrieval systems continue to grow and make work such as this important to those who are involved in the operation and the research of information retrieval systems.

BILLER & NEUHOLD (1978a) showed that it is not possible to give a completely formal description of a database system because one must consider the common understanding of natural language. They defined two languages, the logical data definition language (LDDL) and the logical data language (LDL) to distinguish between entities being modeled in different representations.

MACLEOD (1977) suggested that the relational database model be used as a basis for a query language than can interface several databases on different computer systems. In relational databases, every relation between terms is represented by a two-dimensional table that represents attributes of the database. SEQUEL is one language based on the relational model that is designed for use in database management systems. MACLEOD (1978) describes the use of this language for document retrieval in a straightforward way. The language is not always intuitive, which is a minor flaw. However, the inherent flexibility and the proposed extensions of the language make it increasingly attractive for user-based systems.

BIRD ET AL. compared inverted text files with inverted structured records. They concluded that inversion of the text files is useful but only in restricted situations. Inversion is practical when: 1) one has a specialized database; 2) the queries are limited to specific areas; 3) phrases, proximity, and partial string matches are not necessary; 4) the full text does not have to be inverted; 5) the language has few idiosyncracies or variations; and 6) the database is relatively small. ROBERTS described the design of a computer architecture for text retrieval. The device searches the entire text of a database for words, portions of words, or combinations of words. A simple state transition model (a universal finite state automaton) was developed into a sophisticated tool for full-text searching. The computer, which is now functional, features Boolean combinations, word proximity, and sentence, paragraph, and zone search restrictors. The key element of the specialized computer is a hardware searcher, which segmentally scans the database for matches with the query.

Design and Evaluation

The documentation on the evaluation and design of information systems and bibliographic databases has been reviewed extensively in previous *ARIST* chapters. The discussion here is limited to selected systems, concentrating on criteria assessment, techniques, and models. The initiation, planning, development, and testing of new systems is the task of an information system designer. Evaluators appraise and measure operational systems. The roles of the system designer and the evaluator are very closely interrelated, and attempts have been made to distinguish among models for design planning, formative evaluation, and performance measures (ARNOVICK & GEE). During the late 1960s and 1970s, new advances in computer and input-output capabilities and improvements in database design techniques contributed to the growth in online system use. Much of the current research in system design attempts to organize files more economically, using chained, inverted, and clustered file structures, as well as investigating new methods of data storage—e.g., virtual storage, text compression, and scatter storage. Ideally, primary files should be stored on devices with short access time. Since this is expensive, systems have been developed that use text compression techniques, thus reducing computer costs associated with file maintenance by 50% or more.

One experimental project of this type was conducted by the Royal Institute of Technology Library in Sweden (HJERPPE, 1976). The 3RIP system is an interactive search and editing system designed for large (up to four million records) textual files (LOFSTROM ET AL.). A text-compaction system compresses large files of data by using a 1:1 mapping of terms to codes by an iterative procedure (HULTGREN & LARSSON). The coder of the text-compaction module of 3RIP uses a scatter storage technique for sequential processing of files (LARSSON & HULTGREN). In a scatter storage system, input words are mapped into corresponding record addresses that are spread throughout the available storage area. This technique is useful for short queries, but problems arise with long queries.

A general consensus for evaluating the performance of information retrieval systems is still lacking, despite significant investigation into many proposed measures, including accuracy, cost, flexibility, quality, serviceability, simplicity, and utility, as well as the principle measures of precision and recall.

An economic modeling approach used to evaluate costs and benefits for information service providers was discussed by MASON & SASSONE. Using fundamental supply/demand principles to establish "time saved" by users, the authors calculated the lower boundary on benefits, noting problems jn distinguishing between the intrinsic value of information and that of the information service. M.D. COOPER developed statistical relationships between measures of output variables of a search (e.g., cost) and input variables (e.g., number of index terms, characteristics of searcher, etc.), using multiple linear regression analysis. The methodology described may be useful in the presearch estimate of costs based on characteristics of a query. ELCHESEN described a comparison between manual and online searching using a cost-effectiveness analysis technique. Measures of effectiveness included searcher-judged relevance, turnaround time, and cost per citation, as well as recall and precision ratios. COOPER & DEWATH, noting that efficiency is not only a function of cost, gave statistical evidence that search services are more efficient when user fees are assigned—i.e., search time at the terminal decreases. However, they also note that staff time devoted to search-related tasks increases by about 13%. Thus, the trade-off between system effort and user effort remains.

Serviceability is another cost-related measure used to evaluate an information retrieval system. HJERPPE (1974) outlined the process of modeling and designing an evaluation using serviceability criteria (convenience, accessibility, response time, document backup, etc.). DE LUTIS ET AL. (1978a) modeled the OCLC system using the Information Processing System Simulator (IPSS). Their approach was to identify problems and features of simulation languages that facilitate the examination of these problems. Although no specific results were provided, they concluded that building a model of an operational system is a valuable exercise. The process helps one to determine areas of misunderstanding, gaps in knowledge, and potentially troublesome areas. The authors extended the model-building process to allow for evaluation and planning (DE LUTIS ET AL., 1978b).

Research into the marketing and managerial decision making that is involved in information retrieval systems is beginning to appear in the literature. LINDQUIST (1978a; 1978b) analyzed the causes of growth and stagnation of information search services based on simulations using a systems dynamics model of a hypothetical service. Implications for marketing and managerial decision making were discussed.

The concept of relevance is central to retrieval evaluation. Goffman's indirect retrieval method uses conditional relevance of documents—i.e., if document A is relevant, there is a specifiable probability that document B is relevant. This method can define a chain of documents that can be retrieved in response to a query. CROFT & VAN RIJSBERGEN tested this method and found that the procedure is similar in performance to cluster-based retrieval. However, it was difficult to define a threshold probability and, more importantly, to determine the overhead required for system operation. KRAFT & BOOKSTEIN reviewed the Swets model of information retrieval based on decision theory. Under certain conditions, they determined that precision and recall may not be inversely related.

SWANSON is the latest in a series of authors who have argued that the inherent ambiguities in the concept of relevance make it a questionable measure for evaluation. He suggested that closer attention be paid to the trial-and-error nature of the retrieval process, which provides insights for improving services by enhancing both the user-system dialogue and citation searching. Because of past limitations in experimental test collections, such as inappropriate size and careless construction, an attempt has been made to provide researchers with a superior test collection for common use that meets a range of research requirements (SPARCK JONES & VAN RIJSBERGEN).

This "ideal" test collection would allow a variety of controlled experiments on indexing and retrieval to be conducted, thus inviting project comparisons and reducing data preparation. Although precision and recall are firmly entrenched measures of effectiveness, and indeed useful ones, additional efficiency criteria are clearly necessary, especially those involving human and machine effort and cost.

TRENDS AND CONCLUSIONS

In reviewing current information retrieval research projects, several trends can be identified. The foremost seems to be in the area of nonapplied research. Well-established and new researchers are concerned with the development of new formalisms and fundamental theories, but there is also an interest in user-effectiveness research. This can be seen in experimental systems that deal with the user interface, feedback, and pattern recognition. Artificial intelligence and psychology are giving us techniques and providing comparative models and standards. The growing interdisciplinary nature of information retrieval is evident.

Information retrieval is in a period of renewed interest. Our current methods are being questioned, and problems that have been lingering for years are receiving new attention. Fundamental assumptions are being tested. For instance, even though index terms are not independent of one another, we continue to use them as if they were. Two authors have questioned the performance of systems that use the independence assumption. Clusters are being tested for search efficiency and for performing enhancement, and dynamic (real-time) clustering may become practical. Results so far indicate competitive performance for clustered environments and for the traditional inverted file using Boolean logic. Thus, the basic design of operational systems is being questioned. Interest has been rejuvenated in automatic or machine-aided thesaurus construction, hardware designed for information retrieval, and evaluation techniques. There is a simultaneous effort to draw from other disciplines (such as artificial intelligence) and to eliminate those directions that do not add to our understanding (e.g., fuzzy sets).

Probability theory is emerging as the most promising paradigm for a more complete understanding of our discipline. Spatial models, network or graph theory, and utility theory have all been used to provide insights and will surely be drawn on whenever appropriate.

Experimental techniques are ready to be adopted by operational systems. It is evident that feedback using relevance information has been beneficial in every test environment. It is simple to implement and is efficient. Surely a relevance feedback system will be made available to searchers of the commercial systems. Ranked output is another feature that is a candidate for operational systems.

The next few years should be exciting, if unsettling. Many of our fundamental beliefs will be tested, such as the adequacy of our assumption about the inverse relationship between precision and recall. The outcomes of these tests may pit our economic concerns against our desire for better retrieval performance. There is a nontrivial investment in the operational systems, and changes to these systems will affect tens of thousands of people. It should not be surprising that change will come slowly.

Future research efforts will continue to be directed toward: 1) an understanding of the fundamental characteristics of the information system; 2) the integration of systems such as database management systems, information retrieval systems, and graphic systems—in fact, the decision support systems have already made significant advances in this area; and 3) the development of sophisticated hardware that is designed to meet the functional needs of the information system.

ACKNOWLEDGMENTS

A chapter is necessarily the result of the collective efforts of many people. M. Koll, T. Noreault, C. Schwartz, and J. Kuehn were significant in keeping the authors aware of the relevant literature. The *ARIST* reviewers and J. Katzer helped to make this chapter as readable as it is. M. Montgomery was our typing expert, confidant, and advisor. Many thanks to all.

BIBLIOGRAPHY

ALVEY, CELINE H.   1978.   Guide to DIALOG Databases—A Review. Online. 1978 July; 2(3): 21-23. ISSN: 0146-5422.

ARNOVICK, GEORGE N.; GEE, LARRY G.   1978.   Design and Evaluation of Information Systems. Information Processing & Management. 1978; 14(6): 369-380. ISSN: 0306-4573.

ARTANDI, SUSAN.   1976.   Machine Indexing: Linguistic and Semiotic Implications. Journal of the American Society for Information Science. 1976 July/August; 27(4): 235-239. ISSN: 0002-8231; CODEN: AISJB6.

ATHERTON, PAULINE A.   1977.   Improved Subject Access to Books in On-line Library Catalogs. In: On-Line Information: Proceedings of the 1st International On-Line Information Meeting; 1977 December 13-15; London, England.   Oxford, England; Learned Information (Europe) Ltd.; 1977.   131-138.   ISSN: 0-904933-10-5.

ATHERTON, PAULINE A.   1978a.   BOOKS Are for Use: Final Report of the Subject Access Project to the Council on Library Resources. 1978 February. 172p. Available from: Syracuse University, Printing Services, 125 College Place, Syracuse, NY 13210.

ATHERTON, PAULINE A.   1978b.   Standards for a User-System Interface Language in On-Line Retrieval Systems; The Challenge and the Responsibility.   Online Review (England).   1978; 2(1): 57-61.   ISSN: 0309-314X.

ATTAR, R.; FRAENKEL, S.   1977.   Local Feedback in Full-Text Retrieval Systems.   Journal of the Association for Computing Machinery.   1977 July; 24(3): 397-417.   ISSN: 0004-5411.

BARNES, C.I.; CONSTANTINI, L.; PERSCHKE, S.   1978.   Automatic Indexing Using the SLC-II System.   Information Processing & Management.   1978; 14(2): 107-119.   ISSN: 0306-4573.

BATH UNIVERSITY. LIBRARY. 1977. The Application of Clustering Techniques to Citation Data. 1977 October. 23p. (Design of Information Systems in the Social Sciences; Research Reports, Series B, no. 6). Available from: Bath University, Library, Claverton Down, Bath BA27AY England.

BIBLIOSHARE. 1977. Information Management. Dedham, MA: Docuprocessing Publications, 1977. 208p. Available from: Docuprocessing Publications, P.O. Box 1267, Dedham, MA 02026.

BILLER, HORST; NEUHOLD, ERICH J. 1978a. Semantics of Data Bases: The Semantics of Data Models. Information Systems. 1978; 3(1): 11-30. ISSN: 0306-4379; CODEN: INSYD6.

BILLER, HORST; NEUHOLD, ERICH J. 1978b. Remarks on the Comments of B. Langefors on Our Paper—Semantics of Data Bases: The Semantics of Data Models. Information Systems. 1978; 3(1): 35-36. ISSN: 0306-4379; CODEN: INSYD6.

BIRD, R.M.; NEWSBAUM, J.B.; TREFFTZS, J.L. 1978. Text File Inversion: An Evaluation. Paper presented at: 4th Workshop on Computer Architecture for Non-Numeric Processing; 1978 August 1-4; Syracuse University's Minnowbrook Conference Center, Blue Mountain Lake, NY. 1978. 42-50. Available from: Association for Computing Machinery, P.O. Box 12105, Church Street Station, New York, NY 10249.

BOOKSTEIN, ABRAHAM. 1974. A Hybrid Access Method for Bibliographic Records. Journal of Library Automation. 1974 June; 7(2): 97-104. ISSN: 0022-2240; CODEN: JLAUAY.

BOOKSTEIN, ABRAHAM. 1978. Brief Communications: On the Perils of Merging Boolean and Weighted Retrieval Systems. Journal of the American Society for Information Science. 1978 May: 29(3): 156-158. ISSN: 0002-8231; CODEN: AISJB6.

BOOKSTEIN, ABRAHAM; KRAFT, DONALD H. 1977. Operations Research Applied to Document Indexing and Retrieval Decisions. Journal of the Association for Computing Machinery. 1977 July; 24(3): 418-427. ISSN: 0004-5411.

BOOKSTEIN, ABRAHAM; RODRIGUEZ, C.E. 1978. Performance Test of Hybrid Access Method. Journal of Library Automation. 1978 March; 11: 41-46. ISSN: 0022-2240; CODEN: JLAUAY.

BRINER, L.L. 1978. A Mathematical Theory of Indexing. In: Brenner, Everett H., comp. The Information Age in Perspective: Proceedings of the 41st Annual Meeting of the American Society for Information Science: Volume 15; 1978 November 13-17; New York, NY. White Plains, NY: Knowledge Industry Publications, Inc.; 1978. 55-58. ISSN: 0044-7870; ISBN: 0-914236-22-9; CODEN: PAISDQ.

BROOKES, BERTRAM C.; GRIFFITHS, JOSE M. 1978. Frequency-Rank Distributions. Journal of the American Society for Information Science. 1978 Janaury; 29(1): 5-13. ISSN: 0002-8231; CODEN: AISJB6.

CAHN, D.F.; HERR, J.J. 1978. Automatic Database Mapping and Translation Methods. Paper presented at: 4th International Conference of Cybernetics and Systems; 1978 August 21-25: Amsterdam, The Netherlands. 1978 April. 13p. (Report LBL-6782). Available from: D.F. Cahn, Employee and Information Services Division, Lawrence Berkeley Laboratory, University of California, Berkeley, CA 94720.

CARROLL, JOHN M. 1976. Prospects for Parallelism and the Computer Crunch. Journal of the American Society for Information Science.

1976 January/February; 27(1): 63-69. ISSN: 0002-8231; CODEN: AISJB6.

CARUSO, ELAINE. 1978a. Hands on Online: Bringing it Home. Online Review (England). 1978 September; 2(3): 251-268. ISSN: 0309-314X.

CARUSO, ELAINE. 1978b. Training Modules for Use of Scientific and Technical Information Services. Work in Progress. 1978 June. 60p. Available from: the author, Department of Information Science, Graduate School of Library & Information Sciences, University of Pittsburgh, Pittsburgh, PA 15250.

CAWKELL, A.E. 1977a. Developments in Interactive On-line Television Systems and Teletext Information Services in the Home. Online Review (England). 1977 January; 1(1): 31-38. ISSN: 0309-314X.

CAWKELL, A.E. 1977b. Science Perceived through the Science Citation Index. Endeavor. 1977; New Series 1(2): 57-58. ISSN: 0013-7162.

CAWKELL, A.E. 1978. Evaluating Scientific Journals with Journal Citation Reports—A Case Study in Acoustics. Journal of the American Society for Information Science. 1978 January; 29(1): 41-46. ISSN: 0002-8231; CODEN: AISJB6.

CHERNIAVSKY, V. 1978. On Algorithmic Natural Language Analysis and Understanding. Information Systems. 1978; 3(1): 5-10. ISSN: 0306-4379; CODEN: INSYD6.

CHOW, D.; YU, CLEMENT T. 1978. On the Construction of Feedback Queries. 1978. 37p. Available from: C.T. Yu, University of Illinois at Chicago Circle, Department of Information Engineering, Box 4348, Chicago, IL 60680.

CLEVELAND, DONALD B. 1976. An n-Dimensional Retrieval Model. Journal of the American Society for Information Science. 1976 September/October; 27(5/6): 342-347. ISSN: 0002-8231; CODEN: AISJB6.

CLEVERDON, C.W.; KIDD, J.S. 1976. Redundancy, Relevance, and Value to the User in the Outputs of Information Retrieval Systems. Journal of Documentation (England). 1976 September; 32(3): 159-173. ISSN: 0022-0418.

COOPER, MICHAEL D. 1977. Input-Output Relationships in On-line Bibliographic Searching. Journal of the American Society for Information Science. 1977 May; 29(3): 153-160. ISSN: 0002-8231; CODEN: AISJB6.

COOPER, MICHAEL D.; DEWATH, NANCY A. 1977. The Effect of User Fees on the Cost of Online Searching in Libraries. Journal of Library Automation. 1977 December; 10(4): 304-319. ISSN: 0022-2240; CODEN: JLAUAY.

COOPER, WILLIAM S. 1978. The "Why Bother?" Theory of Information Usage. Journal of Informatics (England). 1978 April; 2(1): 2-5. ISSN: 0309-5657.

COOPER, WILLIAM S.; MARON, M.E. 1978. Foundations of Probabilistic and Utility-Theoretic Indexing. Journal of the Association for Computing Machinery. 1978 January; 25(1): 67-80. ISSN: 0004-5411.

COUSINS, THOMAS R.; DOMINICK, WAYNE D. 1978. The Management of Data Bases of Data Bases. In: Brenner, Everett H., comp. The Information Age in Perspective: Proceedings of the 41st Annual Meeting of the American Society for Information Science: Volume 15; 1978

November 13-17; New York, NY.   White Plains, NY: Knowledge Industry Publications, Inc.; 1978.   75-78.   ISSN: 0044-7870; ISBN: 0-914236-22-9; CODEN: PAISDQ.

CRAVEN, TIMOTHY C. 1978. A NEPHIS Thesaurus for Computer Generation of Permuted Cross References. In: Brenner, Everett H., comp. The Information Age in Perspective: Proceedings of the 41st Annual Meeting of the American Society for Information Science: Volume 15; 1978 November 13-17; New York, NY. White Plains, NY: Knowledge Industry Publications, Inc.; 1978.   79-82.   ISSN: 0044-7870; ISBN: 0-914236-22-9; CODEN: PAISDQ.

CRAWFORD, R.G. 1977. Dynamic Dictionary Updating. Information Processing & Management. 1977; 13(4): 235-245.   ISSN: 0306-4573.

CRAWFORD, R.G.; MACLEOD, IAN A. 1978. A Relational Approach to Modular Information Retrieval Systems. In: Brenner, Everett H., comp. The Information Age in Perspective: Proceedings of the 41st Annual Meeting of the American Society for Information Science: Volume 15; 1978 November 13-17; New York, NY. White Plains, NY: Knowledge Industry Publications, Inc.; 1978.   83-85.   ISSN: 0044-7870; ISBN: 0-914236-22-9; CODEN: PAISDQ.

CROFT, W.B. 1977. Clustering Large Files of Documents Using the Single-Link Method. Journal of the American Society for Information Science. 1977 November; 28(6): 341-344.   ISSN: 0002-8231; CODEN: AISJB6.

CROFT, W.B. 1978. Theoretical Models of Cluster Searching. Journal of Informatics (England). 1978 April; 2(1): 78-80.   ISSN: 0309-5657.

CROFT, W.B.; VAN RIJSBERGEN, C.J. 1976. An Evaluation of Goffman's Indirect Retrieval Method. Information Processing & Management. 1976; 12(5): 327-331.   ISSN: 0306-4573.

DAVIES, C.C. 1978. Reference Retrieval by User-Negotiated Term Frequency Ordering within a Dynamically Adjusted Notational "Document". Journal of Informatics (England). 1978 April; 2(1): 62-76.   ISSN: 0309-5657.

DELUTIS, T.G.; RUSH, JAMES E.; WONG, P. 1978a. The Modeling of a Large On-Line Real-Time Information System. 1978. 18p. Available from: the authors, Department of Computer and Information Science, The Ohio State University, Columbus, OH 43210.

DELUTIS, T.G.; RUSH, JAMES E.; WONG, P. 1978b. A Simulation Model for Information System Design, Evaluation and Planning. 1978. 9p. Available from: the authors, Department of Computer and Information Science, The Ohio State University, Columbus, OH 43210.

DONATI, ROBERT. 1977. Spanning the Social Sciences and Humanities through DIALOG. Online. Part I: 1977 October; 1(4): 48-54. Part II: 1978 January; 2(1): 41-52.   ISSN: 0146-5422.

DOSZKOCS, TAMAS E. 1978. AID: An Associative Interactive Dictionary for Online Searching. Online Review (England). 1978; 2(2): 163-173.   ISSN: 0309-314X.

DUNHAM, GEORGE S.; PACAK, MILOS G.; PRATT, ARNOLD W. 1978. Automatic Indexing of Pathology Data. Journal of the American Society for Information Science. 1978 March; 29(2): 81-90.   ISSN: 0002-8231; CODEN: AISJB6.

ELCHESEN, DENNIS R. 1978. Cost-Effectiveness Comparison of Manual and On-Line Retrospective Bibliographic Searching. Journal of the

American Society for Information Science. 1978 March; 29(2): 56-66. ISSN: 0002-8231; CODEN: AISJB6.

ENSER, P.G.B. 1978. An Investigation into the Automatic Classification of Book Material Represented by Back-of-the-Book Indexes. Journal of Informatics (England). 1978 April; 2(1): 18-23. ISSN: 0309-5657.

FIRSCHEIN, OSCAR; SUMMIT, ROGER K. 1978. Planning for Online Search in the Public Library. Special Libraries. 1978 July; 69(7): 255-260. ISSN: 0038-6723; CODEN: SPLBAN.

FIRSCHEIN, OSCAR; SUMMIT, ROGER K.; MICK, COLIN K. 1978. Use of Online Bibliographic Search in Public Libraries; A Retrospective Evaluation. Online Review (England). 1978 January; 2(1): 41-55. ISSN: 0309-314X.

FORD, WILLIAM H., JR.; JOHNSON, KRISTIN N. 1978. Microprocessor Implementation for Full Text Data Base with Graphics. In: Proceedings of the 1978 MUMPS Users' Group Meeting. St. Louis, MO; MUMPS Users' Group; 1978. Unpaged.

GEBHART, FRIEDRICH; STELLMACHER, IMART. 1978. Opinion Paper; Design Criteria for Documentation Retrieval Languages. Journal of the American Society for Information Science. 1978 July; 29(4): 187-199. ISSN: 0002-8231; CODEN: AISJB6.

GERSON, GORDON M. 1978. Cliqueing—A Technique for Producing Maximally Connected Clusters. Journal of the American Society for Information Science. 1978 May; 29(3): 125-129. ISSN: 0002-8231; CODEN: AISJB6.

GOLDSTEIN, CHARLES M.; FORD, WILLIAM H. JR. 1978. The User-Cordial Interface. Online Review (England). 1978 September; 2(3): 269-275. ISSN: 0309-314X.

GRAITSON, M. 1975. Identification et Transformation Automatique des Morphemes Terminaux dans le Lexique Medical Français. Cahiers de Lexicologie; Revue Internationale de Lexicologie et de Lexicographie (France). 1975-1; Volume XXVI. Available from: U.S. Department of Health, Education and Welfare, National Institutes of Health.

GRAITSON, M.; DUNHAM, G. 1977. Traitement automatique du Français medical. Cahiers de Lexicologie; Revue Internationale de Lexicologie et de Lexicographie (France). 1977-1; Volume XXX. Available from: U.S. Department of Health, Education and Welfare, National Institutes of Health.

GRISHMAN, RALPH; HIRSCHMAN, LYNETTE. 1978. Question Answering from Natural Language Medical Data Bases. Artificial Intelligence. 1978 August; 11(1/2): 25-43. (Special Issue). ISSN: 0004-3702; CODEN: AINTBB.

HARPER, D.J.; VAN RIJSBERGEN, C.J. 1978. An Evaluation of Feedback in Document Retrieval Using Co-Occurrence Data. Journal of Documentation (England). 1978 September; 34(3): 189-216. ISSN: 0022-0418.

HAWKINS, DONALD T. 1978. Online Information Retrieval Bibliography. Online Review (England). 1978 January; 2(1): 63-106. ISSN: 0309-314X.

HAWKINS, DONALD T.; MILLER, BETTY. 1977. On-line Data Base Coverage of the On-line Information Retrieval Literature. Online Review (England). 1977 January; 1(1): 59-64. ISSN: 0309-314X.

HEAPS, H.S. 1978. Information Retrieval: Computational and Theoretical Standards. New York, NY: Academic Press; 1978. 344p. ISBN: 0-12-335750-0.

HERLACH, GERTRUD. 1978. Can Retrieval of Information from Citation Indexes be Simplified? Journal of the American Society for Information Science. 1978 November; 29(6): 308-310. ISSN: 0002-8231; CODEN: AISJB6.

HICKEY, THOMAS B.; RYPKA, DAVID J.; GREENBERG, STEWART. 1978. Derived Search Keys for Government Documents. 1978. 30p. Available from: the authors, OCLC, Inc., 1125 Kinnear Rd., Columbus, OH 43212.

HIRSCHMAN, LYNETTE; GRISHMAN, RALPH. 1977. Fact Retrieval from Natural Language Medical Records. In: Shires, D.B.; Wolf, H., eds. MEDINFO-77: Proceedings of the 2nd World Conference on Medical Informatics; 1977 August 8-12; Toronto, Canada. Amsterdam, The Netherlands: North-Holland Publishing Co.; 1977. 247-251. (International Federation of Information Processing Societies (IFIPS) World Conference Series on Medical Informatics, Volume 1). ISBN: 0-7204-0754.

HIRSCHMAN, LYNETTE; GRISHMAN, RALPH; SAGER, NAOMI. 1976. From Text to Structured Information—Automatic Processing of Medical Reports. In: Winkler, Stanley, ed. Proceedings of the American Federation of Information Processing Societies (AFIPS) 1976 National Computer Conference (NCC): Volume 45; 1976 June 7-10; New York, NY. Montvale, NJ: AFIPS Press, 210 Summit Avenue; 1976. 267-275. LC: 55-44701.

HJERPPE, ROLAND. 1974. A Meta-Model for Evaluating Information Retrieval Serviceability. Stockholm, Sweden; The Royal Institute of Technology Library; 1974 November. 31p. (Stockholm Papers in Library and Information Science; Report TRITA-LIB-6002). Available from: Royal Institute of Technology Library, Publications Office, S-100 44 Stockholm 70, Sweden.

HJERPPE, ROLAND. 1976. Computerized Information Service—SDI: Annual Report 1974/75. Stockholm, Sweden: The Royal Institute of Technology Library; 1976 May. 27p. (Stockholm Papers in Library and Information Science; Report TRITA-LIB-4053). Available from: Royal Institute of Technology Library, Publications Office, S-100 44 Stockholm 70, Sweden.

HJERPPE, ROLAND; NORD, AKE; BJERRE, PER. 1976. The Utilization of the ESA-RECON System in Sweden during 1975. Stockholm, Sweden: The Royal Institute of Technology Library; 1976 November. 18p. (Stockholm Papers in Library and Information Science; Report TRITA-LIB-4058). Available from: Royal Institute of Technology Library, Publications Office, S-100 44 Stockholm 70, Sweden.

HULTGREN, JAN; LARSSON, ROLF. 1975. PASTIME—A System for File Compression. Stockholm, Sweden; The Royal Institute of Technology Library; 1975 April. 17p. (Stockholm Papers in Library and Information Science; Report TRITA-LIB-4043). Available from: Royal Institute of Technology Library, Publications Office, S-100 44 Stockholm 70, Sweden.

INFORMATION & MANAGEMENT. 1978-. Sibley, E.H., ed. Amsterdam, The Netherlands: North-Holland Publishing Co. (Issued six times a year;

available on subscription from North-Holland Publishing Co., 52 Vanderbilt Avenue, New York, NY 10017). ISSN: 0378-7206. CODEN: IMANDC.

JARDINE, N.; VAN RIJSBERGEN, C.J. 1971. The Use of Hierarchic Clustering in Information Retrieval. Information Storage and Retrieval. 1971 December; 7(5): 217-240. ISSN: 0020-0271.

JONES, WARREN T. 1976. A Fuzzy Set Characterization of Interaction in Scientific Research. Journal of the American Society for Information Science. 1976 September/October; 27(5/6): 307-310. ISSN: 0002-8231; CODEN: AISJB6.

JOURNAL OF INFORMATICS. 1977-. Brookes, B.C., ed. London, England: School of Library Archive and Information Studies, University College London, in association with the Aslib Co-ordinate Indexing Group. (Issued three times a year; available on subscription from School of Library, Archive and Information Studies, University College London, Gower Street, London WC1E 6BT England). ISSN: 0309-5657.

KANTOR, PAUL B. 1976. Availability Analysis. Journal of the American Society for Information Science. 1976 September/October; 27(5/6): 311-319. ISSN: 0002-8231; CODEN: AISJB6.

KAR, GAUTAM; WHITE, LEE J. 1978. A Distance Measure for Automatic Document Classification by Sequential Analysis. Information Processing & Management. 1978; 14(2): 57-69. ISSN: 0306-4573.

KOENIG, MICHAEL E.D.; VLADUTZ, GEORGE E. 1978. The Application of Automated Language Processing Techniques to PRECIS Indexing. 1978. 17p. Available from: the authors, Institute for Scientific Information, 325 Chestnut Street, Philadelphia, PA 19106.

KOLL, MATTHEW B. 1978. WEIRD: An Approach to Concept-Based Information Retrieval. In: Dattola, Robert T., ed. Association for Computing Machinery (ACM) Special Interest Group on Information Retrieval (SIGIR); International Conference on Information Storage and Retrieval; 1978 May 10-12; Rochester, NY. 1-19. (Supplement to Proceedings).

KRAFT, DONALD H. 1978. A Threshold Rule Applied to the Retrieval Decision Model. Journal of the American Society for Information Science. 1978 March; 29(2): 77-80. ISSN: 0002-8231; CODEN: AISJB6.

KRAFT, DONALD H.; BOOKSTEIN, ABRAHAM. 1978. Evaluation of Information Retrieval Systems: A Decision Theory Approach. Journal of the American Society for Information Science. 1978 Janaury; 29(1): 31-40. ISSN: 0002-8231; CODEN: AISJB6.

KRENTZ, DAVID M. 1978. On-line Searching—Specialist Required. Journal of Chemical Information and Computer Science. 1978 January; 18(1): 4-9. ISSN: 0095-2338; CODEN: JCISD8.

LAM, L.; YU, CLEMENT T. 1978. A Clustered Search Algorithm Incorporating Arbitrary Term Dependencies. 1978. 14p. Available from: C.T. Yu, University of Illinois at Chicago Circle, Department of Information Engineering, Box 4348, Chicago, IL 60680.

LANGEFORS, BORJE. 1978. Comments on a Paper by Biller and Neuhold. Semantics of Data Bases: The Semantics of Data Models. Information Systems. 1978; 3(1): 31-34. ISSN: 0306-4379; CODEN: INSYD6.

LARSSON, ROLF; HULTGREN, JAN. 1974. VIRA—A String-Oriented Information Retrieval System. Stockholm, Sweden: The Royal Institute of Technology Library; 1974 March. 16p. (Stockholm Papers in

Library and Information Science; Report TRITA-LIB-4036). Available from: Royal Institute of Technology Library, Publications Office, S-100 44 Stockholm 70, Sweden.

LINDQUIST, MATS G. 1978a. The Dynamics of Information Search Services. Stockholm, Sweden: The Royal Institute of Technology Library; 1978 February. 191p. (Stockholm Papers in Library and Information Science; Report TRITA-LIB-6012). Available from: Royal Institute of Technology Library, Publications Office, S-100 44 Stockholm 70, Sweden.

LINDQUIST, MATS G. 1978b. Growth Dynamics of Information Search Services. Journal of the American Society for Information Science. 1978 March; 29(2): 67-76. ISSN: 0002-8231; CODEN: AISJB6.

LOFSTROM, MATS; SUNNEBACK, JAN; BRYNTESSON, CHRISTER; JOHANSSON, BO; LARSSON, ROLF. 1977. 3RIP: Data Structures for Text Files. Stockholm, Sweden: The Royal Institute of Technology Library; 1977 June. 16p. (Stockholm Papers in Library and Information Science; Report TRITA-LIB-4061). Available from: Royal Institute of Technology Library, Publications Office, S-100 44 Stockholm 70, Sweden.

MACLEOD, IAN A. 1977. Towards an Information Retrieval Language Based on a Relational View of Data. Information Processing & Management. 1977; 13(3): 167-175. ISSN: 0306-4573.

MACLEOD, IAN A. 1978. SEQUEL as a Language for Document Retrieval. 1978 May. 18p. (Technical Report 78-62). Available from: the author, Department of Computing and Information Science, Queen's University, Kingston, Ontario, Canada.

MARCUS, RICHARD S.; KUGEL, PETER; BENENFELD, ALAN R. 1978. Catalog Information and Text as Indicators of Relevance. Journal of the American Society for Information Science. 1978 January; 29(1): 15-30. ISSN: 0002-8231; CODEN: AISJB6.

MARCUS, RICHARD S.; REINTJES, J. FRANCIS. 1977. Computer Interfaces for User Access to Heterogeneous Information-Retrieval Systems. 1977 April. 84p. (Report no: ESL-R-739). Available from: Electronic Systems Laboratory, Department of Electrical Engineering and Computer Science, Massachusetts Institute of Technology, Cambridge, MA 02139.

MARON, M.E. 1977. On Indexing, Retrieval and the Meaning of About. Journal of the American Society for Information Science. 1977 January; 28(1): 38-43. ISSN: 0002-8231; CODEN: AISJB6.

MASON, ROBERT M.; SASSONE, PETER G. 1978. A Lower Bound Cost Benefit Model for Information Services. Information Processing & Management. 1978; 14(2): 71-83. ISSN: 0306-4573.

MCGILL, MICHAEL J. 1976. Knowledge and Information Spaces: Implications for Retrieval Systems. Journal of the American Society for Information Science. 1976 July/August; 27(4): 205-210. ISSN: 0002-8231; CODEN: AISJB6.

MCINROY, JOHN WISE. 1978. A Concept-Vector Representation of the Paragraphs in a Document, Applied to Automatic Extracting. 118p. (PhD dissertation; Report TR-78-001). Available from: University of North Carolina, Department of Computer Science, Chapel Hill, NC 27514.

MEADOW, CHARLES T. 1979. Online Searching and Computer Programming: Some Behavioral Similarities (Or. . .Why End Users Will Eventually
Take Over the Terminal). Online. 1979 January; 3(1): 49-52. ISSN:
0146-5422.

MEADOW, CHARLES T.; EPSTEIN, B.E. 1977. Individualized Instruction
for Data Access. In: On-Line Information: Proceedings of the 1st International On-Line Meeting; 1977 December 13-15; London, England.
Oxford, England: Learned Information (Europe), Ltd.; 1977. 179-194.
ISBN: 0-904933-10-5.

MEADOW, CHARLES T.; TOLIVER, DAVID E.; EDELMANN, JANET V.
1978. A Technique for Machine Assistance to Online Searchers. In:
Brenner, Everett H., comp. The Information Age in Perspective: Proceedings of the 41st Annual Meeting of the American Society for Information Science: Volume 15; 1978 November 13-17; New York, NY.
White Plains, NY: Knowledge Industry Publications, Inc.: 1978. 222-
225. ISSN: 0004-7870; ISBN: 0-914236-22-9; CODEN: PAISDQ.

MEINCKE, PETER P.M.; ATHERTON, PAULINE A. 1976. Knowledge
Space: A Conceptual Basis for the Organization of Knowledge. Journal
of the American Society for Information Science. 1976 January/
February; 27(1): 18-24. ISSN: 0002-8231; CODEN: AISJB6.

MINKER, JACK. 1977. Information Storage and Retrieval—A Survey and
Functional Description. Forum: A Publication of the Association for
Computing Machinery (ACM) Special Interest Group on Information
Retrieval (SIGIR). 1977 Fall: XII (2):1-108.

MINKER, JACK. 1978. Binary Relations, Matrices and Inference Developments. Information Systems. 1978: 3(1): 37-47. ISSN: 0306-4379;
CODEN: INSYD6.

MOHAN, C. 1978. An Overview of Recent Data Base Research. Data Base:
Newsletter of the Association for Computing Machinery (ACM) Special
Interest Group on Business Data Processing. Fall 1978; 10(2): 3-24.
ISSN: 0095-0033.

NOREAULT, TERRY; KOLL, MATTHEW; MCGILL, MICHAEL J. 1977.
Automatic Ranked Output from Boolean Searches in SIRE. Journal of
the American Society for Information Science. 1977 November; 28(6):
333-339. ISSN: 0002-8231; CODEN: AISJB6.

O'CONNOR, JOHN. 1977. Data Retrieval by Text Searching. Journal of
Chemical Information and Computer Science. 1977; 17(3): 181-186.
ISSN: 0095-2338; CODEN: JCISD8.

O'CONNOR, JOHN. 1978a. Answer-Passage Retrieval by Text Searching.
1978. 47p. Available from: the author, Center for Information Science,
Lehigh University, Bethlehem, PA 18015.

O'CONNOR, JOHN. 1978b. Passage Retrieval for Cancer Questions. In:
Brenner, Everett H., comp. The Information Age in Perspective: Proceedings of the 41st Annual Meeting of the American Society for Information Science; Volume 15; 1978 November 13-17; New York, NY.
White Plains, NY: Knowledge Industry Publications, Inc.; 1978. 256-
259. ISSN: 0044-7870; ISBN: 0-914236-22-9; CODEN: PAISDQ.

PACAK, M.G.; PRATT, A.W. 1978. Identification and Transformation of
Terminal Morphemes in Medical English, Part II. Methodik der Information in der Medizin [Methods of Information in Medicine]. 1978 April;
17(2): 95-100. (Text in English). ISSN: 0026-1270.

PAICE, C.D.   1977.   Information Retrieval and the Computer.   London, England: MacDonald and Janes; 1977.   206p.   ISBN: 0-35-404095-2.

PAO, MIRANDA LEE.   1978.   Automatic Text Analysis Based on Transition Phenomena of Word Occurrences.   Journal of the American Society for Information Science.   1978 May; 29(3): 121-124.   ISSN: 0002-8231; CODEN: AISJB6.

PERSSON, OLLE; HOGLUND, LARS.   1975.   Evaluation of a Computer-Based Current Awareness Service for Swedish Social Scientists (Social Science Citation Index).   Stockholm, Sweden: The Royal Institute of Technology Library; 1975 March.   75p.   (Stockholm Papers in Library and Information Science; Report TRITA-LIB-6003).   Available from: Royal Institute of Technology Library, Publications Office, S-100 44 Stockholm 70, Sweden.

PIERCE, JOHN C.   1978.   Back-of-Book Subject Indexing with APL: Automated Indexing for Those without Computer Background.   Information Processing & Management.   1978: 14(2): 85-91.   ISSN: 0306-4573.

RADECKI, TADEUSZ.   1977.   Fuzzy Sets Theoretical Approach to Document Retrieval.   Paper presented at: 6th Cranfield International Conference on Mechanized Information Storage and Retrieval Systems: Cranfield, England.   33p.   1977.   Available from: the author, Wroclaw Technical University, Main Library and Scientific Information Centre, Wybrzeze Street, Wyspianskiego 27, 50-370 Wroclaw, Poland.

RADECKI, TADEUSZ.   1978.   A Model of Document Retrieval System Based on the Concept of Semantic Disjunctive Normal Form.   Paper presented at: International Congress of Cybernetics and Systems: 1978 August 21-25: Amsterdam, The Netherlands.   Available from: the author, Wroclaw Technical University, Main Library and Scientific Information Centre, Wybrzeze Street, Wyspianskiego 27, 50-370 Wroclaw, Poland.

RAGHAVAN, VIJAY V.; YU, CLEMENT T.   1978a.   Experiments on the Determination of the Relationships between Terms.   1978.   30p.   Available from: C.T. Yu, University of Illinois at Chicago Circle, Department of Information Engineering, Box 4348, Chicago, IL 60680.

RAGHAVAN, VIJAY V.; YU, CLEMENT T.   1978b.   Stability Analysis of Certain Graph Theoretic Clustering Methods.   1978.   44p.   Available from: C.T. Yu, University of Illinois at Chicago Circle, Department of Information Engineering, Box 4348, Chicago, IL 60680.

RASTOGI, KUNJ B.   1978.   Retrieval Behavior of Derived Truncated Search Keys for a Large On-Line Bibliographic File.   1978.   18p.   Available from: the author, OCLC, Inc., 1125 Kinnear Road, Columbus, OH 43212.

RICHMOND, PHYLLIS A.   1976.   Classification from PRECIS: Some Possibilities.   Journal of the American Society for Information Science.   1976 July/August; 27(4): 205-210.   ISSN: 0002-8231; CODEN: AISJB6.

ROBERTS, DAVID C.   1978.   A Specialized Computer Architecture for Text Retrieval.   Paper presented at: 4th Workshop on Computer Architecture for Non-Numeric Processing; 1978 August 1-4; Syracuse University's Minnowbrook Conference Center, Blue Mountain Lake, NY.   51-59.   Available from: Association for Computing Machinery, P.O. Box 12105, Church Street Station, New York, NY 10249.

ROBERTSON, STEPHEN E. 1978. On the Nature of Fuzz: A Diatribe. Journal of the American Society for Information Science. 1978 November; 29(6): 304-307. ISSN: 0002-8231; CODEN: AISJB6.

ROBERTSON, STEPHEN E.; SPARCK JONES, KAREN. 1976. Relevance Weighting of Search Terms. Journal of the American Society for Information Science. 1976 May/June; 27(3): 129-146. ISSN: 0002-8231; CODEN: AISJB6.

ROSENBERG, ARNOLD L.; STOCKMEYER, LARRY J. 1977. Hashing Schemes for Extendible Arrays. Journal of the Association for Computing Machinery. 1977 April; 24(2): 199-221. ISSN: 0004-5411.

SAGER, NAOMI. 1978. Natural Language Information Formatting: The Automatic Conversion of Texts to a Structured Data Base. In: Alt, F.L., ed. Advances in Computers: Volume 17. New York, NY: Academic Press; 1978. 89-162. ISBN: 0-12-012117-4.

SAGER, NAOMI; HIRSCHMAN, LYNETTE; GRISHMAN, RALPH; INSOLIO, CYNTHIA. 1977. Transforming Medical Records into a Structured Data Base. Association for Computing Machinery (ACM) Special Interest Group on Artificial Intelligence (SIGART) Newsletter. 1977 February; 61: 38-39.

SAGER, NAOMI; LYMAN, MARGARET. 1978. Computerized Language Processing: Implications for Health Care Evaluation. Medical Record News. 1978 June; 49(3): 20-30. ISSN: 0025-7486.

SAGER, WOLFGANG; LOCKEMANN, PETER. 1976. Classification of Ranking Algorithms. International Forum on Information and Documentation (The Netherlands). 1976; 1(4): 2-25. ISSN: 0304-9701.

SALTON, GERARD. 1978. Mathematics and Information Retrieval. Journal of Documentation (England). 1979 March. (In Press). ISSN: 0022-0418.

SALTON, GERARD; WALDSTEIN, ROBERT K. 1978. Term Relevance Weights in Online Information Retrieval. Information Processing & Management. 1978; 14(1): 29-35. ISSN: 0306-4573.

SALTON, GERARD; WONG, ANITA. 1978. Generation and Search of Clustered Files. ACM Transactions on Data Base Systems. 1978 December; 3(4): 321-346. ISSN: 0362-5915.

SALTON, GERARD; WONG, ANITA; YANG, C.S. 1974. A Vector Space Model for Automatic Indexing. 1974. 30p. Available from: the authors, Department of Computer Science, Cornell University, Ithaca, NY 14853.

SCHNEIDER, H.J. 1978. Are Intelligent Information Systems Ever Achievable? Inviting a Discussion. Information Systems. 1978; 3(1): 1-3. ISSN: 0306-4379; CODEN: INSYD6.

SCHWARTZ, CANDY; NOREAULT, TERRY. 1978. Human-Assisted Thesaurus Generation: A First Step. In: Brenner, Everett H., comp. The Information Age in Perspective: Proceedings of the 41st Annual Meeting of the American Society for Information Science: Volume 15; 1978 November 13-17; New York, NY. White Plains, NY: Knowledge Industry Publications, Inc.; 1978. 291-294. ISSN: 0044-7870; ISBN: 0-914236-22-9; CODEN: PAISDQ.

SCHWARZ, STEPHEN; CARLSSON, GUNNAR; FROBERG, GUDMUND. 1978. Library Services in Transition: A Presentation of Current Activities at the Royal Institute of Technology Library. Stockholm, Sweden:

Royal Institute of Technology Library; 1978. 242p. (Stockholm Papers in Library and Information Science; Report TRITA-LIB-1070).

SHARP, GEOFFREY. 1978. Online Business Information. Online. 1978 January; 2(1): 33-44. ISSN: 0146-5422.

SHNEIDERMAN, BEN. 1977a. Design, Development and Utilization Perspectives on Database Management Systems. Information Processing & Management. 1977; 13(1): 23-33. ISSN: 0306-4573.

SHNEIDERMAN, BEN. 1977b. Reduced Combined Indexes for Efficient Multiple Attribute Retrieval. Information Systems. 1977; 2(4): 149-154. ISSN: 0306-4379; CODEN: INSYD6.

SHNEIDERMAN, BEN. 1978a. Improving the Human Factors Aspect of Database Interactions. 1978. 39p. Available from: the author, University of Maryland, Department of Information Systems Management, College Park, MD 10742.

SHNEIDERMAN, BEN. 1978b. Jump Searching: A Fast Sequential Search Technique. Communications of the ACM. 1978 October; 21(10): 831-834. ISSN: 0001-0782.

SHNEIDERMAN, BEN; GOODMAN, VICTOR. 1976. Batched Searching of Sequential and Tree Structured Files. ACM Transactions on Database Systems. 1976 September; 1(3): 268-275. ISSN: 0900-0201.

SMITH, JOSEPH D.; RUSH, JAMES E. 1977. The Relationship between Author Names and Author Entries in a Large On-Line Union Catalog as Retrieved Using Truncated Keys. Journal of the American Society for Information Sciences. 1977 March; 28(2): 71-78. ISSN: 0002-8231; CODEN: AISJB6.

SMITH, L.C. 1976a. Artificial Intelligence in Information Retrieval Systems. Information Processing & Management. 1976; 12(3): 189-222. ISSN: 0306-4573.

SMITH, L.C. 1976b. Artificial Intelligence in Retrieval Systems as an Alternative to Human Intermediaries. 7p. Paper presented at: 5th ASIS Mid-Year Meeting; 1976 May 20-22: Vanderbilt University, Nashville, TN. Available from: the author, University of Illinois, Graduate School of Library Science, 329 Main Library, Urbana, IL 61801.

SPARCK JONES, KAREN. 1978. Experiments in Relevance Weighting of Search Terms. 1978. 15p. Available from: the author, University of Cambridge, Computer Laboratory, Corn Exchange Street, Cambridge CB2 3QB England.

SPARCK JONES, KAREN; BATES, R.G. 1977a. Research on Automatic Indexing 1974-1976. Volume 1: Text; Volume 2: Figures and Tables. Available from: the authors, University of Cambridge, Computer Laboratory, Corn Exchange Street, Cambridge CB2 3QB England.

SPARCK JONES, KAREN; BATES, R.G. 1977b. Report on a Design Study for the "Ideal" Information Retrieval Test Collection. 1977 October. 53p. Available from: the authors, University of Cambridge, Computer Laboratory, Corn Exchange Street, Cambridge CB2 3QB England.

SPARCK JONES, KAREN; VAN RIJSBERGEN, C.J. 1976. Information Retrieval Test Collections. Journal of Documentation (England). 1976 March; 32(1): 59-75. ISSN: 0022-0418.

STEVENS, B.A. 1978. Online Searching Techniques: Retrieving Every Metallic Element Using Registry Numbers. Online. 1978 July; 2(3): 67. ISSN: 0146-5422.

SUMMIT, ROGER K. 1977. The New Age of Computer Aided Information Access. Paper presented at: American Association for the Advancement of Science (AAAS) Meeting: 1977 February 23; Denver, CO. Available from: the author, Information Systems—52-08/201, Lockheed Palo Alto Research Laboratory, 3251 Hanover Street, Palo Alto, CA 94304.

SUMMIT, ROGER K. 1978. The New Era in Information. Paper presented at: Maruzen/Lockheed Information Retrieval Seminar; 1978 April 11: Tokyo, Japan. Available from: the author, Information Systems—52-08/201, Lockheed Palo Alto Research Laboratory, 3251 Hanover Street, Palo Alto, CA 94304.

SVENONIUS, ELAINE; SCHMIERER, HELEN F. 1977. Current Issues in the Subject Control of Information. Library Quarterly. 1977 July; 47(3): 326-346. ISSN: 0024-2519.

SWANSON, DON R. 1977. Information Retrieval as a Trial and Error Process. Library Quarterly. 1977; 47(2): 128-148. ISSN: 0024-2519.

TAGLIACOZZO, RENATA. 1977. Self-Citations in Scientific Literature. Journal of Documentation (England). 1977 December; 33(4): 251-265. ISSN: 0022-0418.

TAGLIACOZZO, RENATA. 1978. Some Stylistic Variations in Scientific Writing. Journal of the American Society for Information Science. 1978 May; 29(3): 136-140. ISSN: 0002-8231; CODEN: AISJB6.

TAGUE, JEAN; FARRADANE, JASON. 1978. Estimation and Reliability of Retrieval Effectiveness Measures. Information Processing & Management. 1978; 14(1): 1-16. ISSN: 0306-4573.

TEITELBAUM, HENRY H.; HAWKINS, DONALD T. 1978. Database Subject Index. Online. 1978 April; 2(2): 16-21. ISSN: 0416-5422.

VAN RIJSBERGEN, C.J. 1976. File Organization in Library Automation and Information Retrieval. Journal of Documentation (England). 1976 December; 32(4): 294-317. ISSN: 0022-0418.

VAN RIJSBERGEN, C.J. 1977. A Theoretic Basis for the Use of Co-Occurrence Data in Information Retrieval. Journal of Documentation (England). 1977 June; 33(2): 106-119. ISSN: 0022-0418.

VAN RIJSBERGEN, C.J. 1979. Probabilistic Retrieval. In: Van Rijsbergen, C.J. Information Retrieval. 2nd edition. London, England: Butterworths; 1979 (In Press).

VERNIMB, CARLO. 1977. Automatic Query Adjustment in Document Retrieval. Information Processing & Management. 1977; 13(6): 339-353. ISSN: 0306-4573.

WILLIAMS, MARTHA E. 1977. Opinion Paper: Data Bases—A History of Developments and Trends from 1966 through 1975. Journal of the American Society for Information Science. 1977 March; 28(2): 71-78. ISSN: 0002-8231; CODEN: AISJB6.

WILLIAMS, P.W.; KHALLAGHI, M.T. 1977. Document Retrieval Using a Substring Index. The Computer Journal (England). 1977 August; 20(3): 257-262. ISSN: 0010-4620.

YU, CLEMENT T. 1976. The Stability of Two Common Matching Functions in Classification with Respect to a Proposed Measure. Journal of the American Society for Information Science. 1976 July/August; 27(4): 248-255. ISSN: 0002-8231; CODEN: AISJB6.

YU, CLEMENT T.; LUK, W.S. 1977. Analysis of Effectiveness of Retrieval in Clustered Files. Journal of the Association for Computing Machinery. 1977 October; 24(2): 607-622. ISSN: 0004-5411.

YU, CLEMENT T.; RAGHAVAN, VIJAY V. 1977. Single-Pass Method for Determining the Semantic Relationships Between Terms. Journal of the American Society for Information Science. 1977 November; 28(6): 345-354. ISSN: 0002-8231; CODEN: AISJB6.

YU, CLEMENT T.; LUK, W.S.; SIU, M.K. 1978a. A Model for Information Retrieval Processes. Paper presented at: Canadian Classification Research Group Meeting; 1978 May 7-9. 46p. Available from: C.T. Yu, University of Illinois at Chicago Circle, Department of Information Engineering, Box 4348, Chicago, IL 60680.

YU, CLEMENT T.; LUK, W.S.; SIU, M.K. 1978b. On the Estimation of the Number of Desired Records with Respect to a Given Query. ACM Transactions on Data Base Systems. 1978 March: 3(1): 41-56. ISSN: 0900-0201.

YU, CLEMENT T.; SALTON, GERARD; SIU, M.K. 1978c. Effective Automatic Indexing Using Term Addition and Deletion. Journal of the Association for Computing Machinery. 1978 April; 25(2): 210-225. ISSN: 0004-5411.

ZIMMERMAN, PATRICIA J. 1977. Principles of Design for Information Systems. Journal of the American Society for Information Science. 1977 July; 28(4): 183-191. ISSN: 0002-8231; CODEN: AISJB6.

5 Unconventional Computer Architectures for Information Retrieval

LEE A. HOLLAAR
University of Illinois at Urbana-Champaign

INTRODUCTION

Architecture, *noun*, the art or practice of designing and building structures, and especially habitable ones.

Webster's Seventh New Collegiate Dictionary

Considerable interest has been shown recently in unconventional computer architectures to aid the efficient and flexible retrieval of information from structured (relational, hierarchical, or network modeled) or semi-structured (bibliographic or full-text) databases. This chapter discusses the major contributions and milestones in the development of unconventional computer architectures. Since most are still in the conceptual or development stage, several different approaches have been attempted; most promise to aid the efficient search and retrieval of information. The tutorial papers in a recent issue of *Computer* (BERRA & OLIVER; HOLLAAR, 1979a; KERR; SMITH & SMITH; SU, 1979) provide a good survey of current and past work on database computer architectures but were written primarily for those with some background in computer structures and design. This chapter gives the basic information regarding computer design and database computer architectures needed for one to appreciate and to understand better the more detailed material in tutorials and other papers.

The first questions regarding unconventional computer architectures for information retrieval are: what is a "computer architecture," and what is its conventional form. Unfortunately, there is no standard definition of computer architecture. In some cases, it means the view of the machine provided to the user or programmer, including the size of available memory and types of instructions available (BLAAUW). This definition does not include the internal organization of the computer, such as its data flow or controls, its logical design, or its implementation. A more common definition does consider the internal construction and closely parallels the dictionary definition of architecture. In this paper, computer architecture refers to the design or construction of computers ("structures," in the dictionary definition), including the internal portions not normally visible to the programmer or user. Just as building architectures can be classified according to style (Gothic, Baroque, etc.), computer architectures can be grouped by organizational similarity.

The style of computer architecture that is considered "conventional" today was proposed by John von Neumann in 1946 (BURKS ET AL.) and is commonly referred to as the von Neumann architecture. It was proposed as the design for one of the first digital computers, constructed for the U.S. government by the Institute for Advanced Study in Princeton. Its basic structure has two principal components. First, it has a hierarchy of memories. These range from slow, high-capacity peripheral devices (when proposed in 1946, generally loaded and unloaded with paper tape by the operator; today, magnetic tapes and disks), through a fast, limited capacity central memory (magnetic cores or semiconductors), to a few high-speed registers. The memory contents are addressed by their locations (number of words from the start for central memory; track and sector for disk memory); no inherent significance is assigned to any position, and no direct relationship is required of adjacent locations. All operations are performed in the high-speed registers, although some registers are used automatically, making it seem that certain operations such as data movement are performed in the central memory.

The second component is the central processing unit (CPU), which controls the memories and performs any data processing or checking specified by the programmer. Its two major sections are the arithmetic/logic unit, which takes the contents of the high-speed registers and adds, subtracts, or combines them according to some logical operation, and the control unit, which examines the programmer's instructions and starts and monitors the actions of the memories and the arithmetic/logic unit necessary to carry out the desired operation. The instructions are stored in the same memory as the data used by the instructions; in fact, there is no difference between instructions and other forms of data. Ordinary instructions can be used to modify other instructions in memory, although this practice is now discouraged.

Several extensions have been made to the conventional von Neumann architecture. Separate, outboard input/output controllers and channels, each a specialized digital computer, allow data to be transferred between central memory and peripheral memory while other data are being processed by the central processing unit. "Super" instructions have been provided to perform common data processing operations without the overhead of loop control. At first, these consisted of hardware multiply/divide and floating point instructions. Now, instructions that move or compare blocks of data or scan a character string for one of many specified characters (Translate And Test on the IBM System/360 or System/370) are common.

Obviously, considering the hundreds of thousands of processors based on it, the von Neumann-style of architecture is successful. It handles a wide variety of applications, including all current database management and information retrieval systems, with only minor inconvenience.

Problems for Information Retrieval

If the von Neumann-style architecture has been so successful, why should another, unconventional architecture be considered? Because, at least for information retrieval, a number of irreversible, generally beneficial trends combine to strain the conventional architecture to the breaking point.

The first and most important trend is the steadily diminishing cost of storing a quantum of data. Advances in both semiconductor and magnetic memories (primarily disk systems) have proceeded at a dramatic rate and will not abate in the near future. For example, about 15 years ago, the standard disk unit was the IBM 2311 or a similar unit, which could store 7.25 million characters on a single, removable disk pack. Now, for the same cost (and in actual dollars, not constant dollars), commonly available 3330-type disk spindles hold 300 million characters on a single removable pack, an increase by a factor of 40. Announced systems can hold more than one billion characters, and no end is in sight.

The same has been true for central memory, which, for the same cost, has doubled in capacity every year. New technologies, such as electron beam, optical, or holographic, although they are read-only technologies that are not directly usable for database management systems, promise to reduce further the cost of storing unchanging archival data (e.g., those for a legal retrieval system).

This increased storage capacity has been filled by the use of computers in other applications. Existing accounting and inventory control systems provide a natural source of data for a company's database management system. Computerized composition or typesetting systems form a low-cost input to document retrieval systems.

Viewed from the needs of information retrieval, two fundamental limitations exist in the von Neumann architecture. First, the arithmetic unit is structured primarily for computational tasks, such as computing scientific formulas, rather than for comparing data; comparisons are performed by treating the character strings as numbers and subtracting them, with a result of zero indicating equality. The overhead required to compare two character strings, each longer than the capacity of the registers, can be quite high, thus reducing the efficiency of the computer. Second, the computer can execute only a single instruction at any given time, and that instruction operates on only one unit of data (register, memory word, or character string). To repeat an operation, such as comparing one string against different sections of another string, additional loop control instructions must be used.

When only small amounts of data were stored in a computer system, satisfactory response times for search and retrieval were not hard to achieve. However, it is no longer reasonable to search an entire database for each query. For example, if the database contains 30 billion characters (the amount necessary in a legal retrieval system to hold most court decisions), it would take a computer more than eight hours to complete a single search at the rate of one character every microsecond; this is about ten times faster than a program currently run on an IBM System/370-158 (ROBERTS, 1978; HOLLAAR, 1979a) and would require an extremely fast computer. Obviously, this is not practical on machines that cost well over $1,000 per hour to operate. Even this processing rate may not be possible because of the bottleneck created by the von Neumann architecture's requirement that all data to be processed must be moved in the memory hierarchy from slower to faster memories before processing.

Several software techniques, primarily directory structured file organizations (e.g., inverted or indexed files) have been used to achieve satisfactory response times. Unfortunately, they have complicated both the structure of data and the resulting software needed for its management, thus increasing the occurrence of expensive and troublesome errors. Further, this additional software makes it harder to modify or to use the database for applications that were not anticipated when the system was developed.

Even without these difficulties, software techniques only delay the time when the von Neumann architecture will not be able to handle the amount of data online to a digital computer. Already, inverted file operations can place a severe burden on a conventional processor; in fact, the processor may spend more time on transferring and processing inverted file structures than on all other processing (HOLLAAR, 1978b; STELLHORN, 1974), indicating that even the software techniques used to avoid the breakdown of the conventional architecture are in danger of breaking down.

UNCONVENTIONAL ARCHITECTURES

Because the conventional, von Neumann architecture presents these difficulties, are there alternative architectures that are more "amenable" for information retrieval? Yes, although in the past severe problems existed that reduced their potential benefits. First, the development and construction of a limited number of special hardware systems are very expensive; government-funded research and advances in electronics are reducing these costs. Second, unlike a software-based system running on a conventional digital computer, a hardware-based solution cannot be modified readily to accommodate an oversight in its design; it must be complete and correct when first constructed. However, research on the structure and formal definitions of database systems have determined the effects of different structures and the actions required to allow all necessary operations.

Associative Memories

The obvious way to relieve much of the processing bottleneck caused by the conventional architecture's requirement that data first be transferred from slower memory to fast registers for processing is to place additional circuitry in the memory system to perform much of the required processing in the memory itself. Since most operations in information retrieval (and in many other applications) consist of searching for items that match a given criterion, the operation to provide is one that can search all items within the memory without moving them to the central processor. This is the basic concept behind the associative memory (BIRD ET AL., 1966; DAVIS; FULLER; RUDOLPH; THURBER & WALD; YAU & FUNG).

Instead of addressing memory words by their locations, as in the von Neumann architecture, an associative memory addresses the words by their contents. In addition to the memory array, which contains additional comparison circuitry for each word in the memory, the associative memory processor also has three special registers. The first is the comparand register, into which the data to be used in the next comparison operation are placed; the second—the mask register—indicates the portions of the comparand and memory words that are to participate in the comparison. The remaining special register is a flag register, which has one bit for each word in the associative memory and can be set, cleared, or read under program control. It can also be set or cleared according to a match operation, such as setting the mark bit for each word containing a match to the comparand register. Operations on individual words can be conditional on the state of their mark bit; for example, only those words already marked can take part in the next comparison operation.

The associative memory can also perform limited arithmetic operations, such as adding or subtracting a constant value from all marked words, arithmetically or logically combining marked words, or determining the minimum or maximum value for a field specified by the mask register for all marked words. Because there is a separate processor for each word of data in the memory, there is a high degree of parallelism, thus allowing extremely fast searching and processing (the search time is essentially constant for an arbitrary number of memory locations; it does not vary linearly as in the conventional von Neumann architecture).

Because an associative memory can perform high-speed searches, many people would find it a natural adjunct to a data retrieval system (ANDERSON & KAIN; BERRA, 1974; BERRA & OLIVER; DEFIORE; DEFIORE & BERRA, 1973; DEFIORE & BERRA, 1974; DEFIORE ET AL.; MOULDER). Most of the work in this regard has been conducted at Syracuse University, under the direction of P. Bruce Berra, because his students have access to one of the few associative memory systems in operation—the Goodyear STARAN processor located at the U.S. Air Force's Rome Air Development Center, Rome, NY.

Although it may seem trivial to implement a data retrieval system on an associative processor, this is not the case. Because of the high cost of each memory word, owing to the additional circuitry required, the size of the memory array is severely limited, and data must be moved to and from it for processing (much as in a conventional architecture, although at much higher speeds). Algorithms must be developed to process the data efficiently in small groups, deciding what to throw out of the associative memory and what to save for later processing. It is in this area that most papers on associative processing concentrate. A tutorial on the use of associative memories in database applications has been written by BERRA & OLIVER and discusses the features and difficulties of implementing database management systems on associative memories.

Because of the high cost (partly caused by limited production volumes, which are in turn caused by high costs), and the fixed-field nature of the associative memory's mask register mechanism, the use of associative memory technology remains limited to only selected aspects of retrieval, such as searching high-level directories (BERRA & SINGHANIA). This situation probably will not change until very low-cost associative memory arrays become available.

Rotating Associative Memories

In a conventional memory, each item is directly accessible at all times and remains in the same physical location. However, in a rotating memory the information is constantly circulating and can be accessed only when it passes the reading mechanism. The most obvious form of rotating memory is a disk storage unit, where information is recorded on a magnetic platter and can only be read or written when the desired location passes under a set of fixed mounted heads. Other forms of memory, generally classified as shift registers (and including delay lines, semiconductor and charge-coupled devices, and bubble memories) also behave as rotating memories if their outputs are returned to their inputs to form loops.

If special logic is attached to the rotating memory at its access point, every item in the memory will pass before the logic once per revolution. If it examines the passing information, comparing it against a specified pattern, it can search every item stored in the memory in a fixed time (the revolution period) without transferring the information from memory to a central processor. Many copies of the small search processor can be included in the total system, each executing the same search or processing command on a portion of the database (generally, one processor per track of data), further reducing the total time required to search the database exhaustively. Because of these similarities to an associative processor, this configuration is called a "rotating associative memory." One of the first suggestions for it came from SLOTNICK and his student, PARKER. Others (DEWITT; LEILICH ET AL.; LIN ET AL.; MINSKY, 1972a; MINSKY, 1972b; PARHAMI) in addition to those discussed below, have expanded on the idea for this associative memory, adding to its capability for high-level database operations. BABB has departed from using one processor per data track but uses search logic capable of concurrent searching based on more than one query. Tutorials on the use of rotating associative memories in database systems are given by SU (1979) and SMITH & SMITH.

Two major projects have concentrated on the design of a rotating associative memory architecture for database operations: CASSM, at the University of Florida at Gainesville (under the direction of G. Jack Lipovski and Stanley Su), and RAP, at the University of Toronto (under Stewart Schuster).

CASSM. CASSM, a content addressed segment sequential memory, was first described in detail by COPELAND ET AL. and has been described further by others (COPELAND, 1974; HEALY; HEALY ET AL.; LIPOVSKI, 1970; LIPOVSKI, 1977; LIPOVSKI, 1978; SU, 1977; SU & LIPOVSKI; SU ET AL., 1979). It behaves as a content addressed, or associative, memory, and the database has been divided into fixed-length segments, which are then stored sequentially in the individual processing cells of the machine. It is a back-end processor since it depends on another machine for much of its

supervisory control, the conversion of queries to internal CASSM instructions, and for formatting and writing the results of queries for the user. Unlike an associative memory and other rotating associative processors the instructions are also stored on the same rotating memory (the prototype used
a low-cost disk memory) and are retrieved by techniques similar to ordinary
associative searches.

The CASSM project produced a special data manipulation language for
writing its programs, called CASDAL (CASSM's Data Language), which can
support most views of data in a database (SU & EMAN). (Although CASSM
was designed for relational information structures, it can also handle
hierarchical or network models by simple format conversions so that it can
resemble the relational model more closely.)

Prototype versions of CASSM have been produced and demonstrated, and
an advanced implementation has been extensively simulated (LIPOVSKI,
1978; SU ET AL., 1979). Variants of CASSM to handle character operations
better have been suggested; HEALY proposed a modification that requires as
many revolutions as there are characters in the comparand string (which may
not be efficient for normal searches), and COPELAND (1974) produced
designs that handle much longer comparand strings during each revolution.
These designs form the basis for INDY, an experimental design for a retrieval computer being tested by Tektronix (COPELAND, 1978; OTIS &
COPELAND).

RAP. RAP, the relational associative processor, is also a back-end processor
for rapidly searching a relational-like database in parallel. It was first
described by OZKARAHAN ET AL. (1974; 1975). Both a prototype and
extensive simulations have verified its design and operation (OZKARAHAN &
SEVCIK). Although originally planned for a disk memory, such as CASSM, the
final two-cell prototype uses a charge-coupled shift register memory
(SCHUSTER ET AL., 1978). Unlike CASSM, which was designed to handle
only one user at a time, RAP can handle multiple users simultaneously.
(Actually, much like conventional computers, it can handle only a single user
at any given time, but its processing can be interrupted to handle another
user's short query.) The complete database does not need to be stored in the
RAP cells, as is required for CASSM; a virtual memory facility allows the data
to be stored on conventional disks that bring it rapidly into the actual RAP
rotating memories when needed (similar to virtual memories for a conventional computer) (SCHUSTER ET AL., 1976). Although the search time is
increased, if the amount of RAP memory is close to that needed by a single
user, little time is lost; while one user's queries are being processed, another
user's data are being brought into the backup set of RAP rotating memories.
SCHUSTER ET AL. (1978) describe the original organization of RAP, the
modifications made to produce the working prototype version (RAP.2), and
the expected direction for the next version (RAP.3).

Rotating associative memories will probably continue to have significant
cost and capacity advantages over true associative memories, with only
limited degradation of actual database system performance. Continued research will refine the design, and commercially produced back-end database
processors based on rotating associative memories will be introduced in the
foreseeable future.

Bubble Memories

In their simplest form, bubble memories are another form of rotating memory; the data are stored in a magnetic area, or "bubble." These bubbles keep their contents intact in the presence of a magnetic field, generally provided by a permanent magnet mounted next to the bubble memory; unlike other semiconductor memories, bubble memories do not forget their contents when power is removed (nonvolatile). They are organized in circulating loops and have special sections that can switch bubbles from one loop to another, create or annihilate bubbles, or detect the presence or absence of a bubble. Generally, bubble memories are arranged as a number of identical loops (minor loops), each of which can be switched onto or from another loop (the major loop). The minor loops correspond to the tracks of a conventional disk memory system, and the major loop represents the movable accessing mechanism (the rack with the read/write heads), which positions to a specific track and accesses its data. (For a more complete discussion of bubble memories, see CHEN & CHANG.) Like any other rotating memory device, bubble memories can be made to act as an associative memory by the addition of special logic outboard to the memory.

However, additional switching elements can be included within the bubble memory that will change the bubble paths according to whether or not the bubble currently by the switch is the same as a bit of data applied to the bubble memory. This allows a comparison to be performed without substantial logic, with the results setting a path switch or gate (much as an associative memory sets or clears bits in the mark register). This can allow simple insertion or deletion of data according to its contents or text editing (LEE & CHANG, 1974; LEE ET AL.).

With further modifications to the configuration of the bubble memory, possibly requiring the addition of transistorized digital logic to form a hybrid technology integrated circuit, operations such as arithmetic or finding the maximum of a number of values can be performed. This hybrid bubble memory provides the operations necessary to support a relational database management system (CHANG, 1978a; CHANG, 1978b; CHANG & NIGAN; JINO & LIU; LEE & CHANG, 1975). Unfortunately, the fabrication of a bubble/transistor hybrid integrated circuit is complex in comparison with single-technology integrated circuits and thus more expensive. However, it remains a strong competitor to other rotating memory associative processor designs, such as RAP or CASSM, especially for small databases.

Text Scanning Systems

The processors discussed above were designed primarily to operate on structured databases (e.g., relational or other data models). Although many are capable of, or can be easily modified for, scanning less structured data (e.g., bibliographic or full-text information), generally they do not perform satisfactorily because text retrieval is different from the retrieval of more structured information (HOLLAAR, 1978b; HOLLAAR, 1979a).

If the database contains a wide variety of items, the establishment of standard fields is difficult at best—a page from this book differs considerably from a page of a dictionary. Inconsistent spellings ("color" and "colour"), words with many different meanings ("will," "retort"), acronyms, and other anomalies complicate the formulation of successful search queries. The standard way to counter these problems is to use query constructs, such as "don't care" characters (which don't care what the actual character in the location is, only that there is a valid character there), word ordering, proximity (requiring two search terms to be within a given number of words of each other), or context (requiring terms to be in the same sentence or paragraph). These have a corresponding impact on the structure of the search processor.

Most processor architectures proposed to handle search and retrieval of full-text information consist of two distinct parts: 1) a term comparator, which searches for the occurrence of terms from the search expression, and 2) a query resolver, which determines whether or not the terms occur in the proper context or subset of the database. However, at least one machine (EL MASRI ET AL.) deviates from this, using instead a series of special processors, each of which examines its predecessor's results for a particular pattern. Three different approaches for the term comparator's implementation have been proposed.

Direct comparison. The most straightforward implementation—but also the most limited—of the term comparator was proposed by Stellhorn (HOLLAAR & STELLHORN). Like the rotating associative memory systems, it is based on the logic per track system of SLOTNICK. It consists of many fixed-length comparators, each of which looks for a particular search term. However, it cannot handle don't cares that are embedded within a search term although those at the beginning and end can be handled. It is only a paper design; there have been no prototypes or extensive simulations.

BIRD ET AL. (1977) discuss another direct comparison scheme, although in this case an associative memory device holds the search terms. As a word is received from the database memory, it is used as an input to the associative memory; if a match occurs, this fact is reported to the query resolver. The unit is produced and marketed by Operating Systems, Inc., of Woodland Hills, CA, and has been successful in retrieving textual information rapidly. However, like Stellhorn's system, it cannot process search terms with embedded don't cares.

Cellular comparators. Papers by MUKHOPADHYAY and by COPELAND (1974; 1978) describe an alternate implementation of the term comparator using cellular logic. Specialized units (cells), each capable of deciding whether or not the current character from the memory matches a single user-specified character, are connected to form larger networks. With appropriate connections, these networks can match long character strings, patterns with alternatives (e.g., matching the occurrence of any three different words), or don't care conditions. If enough cells are connected properly, the search can be for any arbitrary pattern.

Copeland's implementation is designed to match only a single term of maximum length and is considered to be an extension to the database matching facilities of processors such as CASSM. Mukhopadhyay's machine, which currently is only a preliminary proposal, is designed to handle all varieties of alternation and don't care conditions. In addition to implementing the primitive operations needed for search and retrieval, it is capable of complex matching and replacement operations, such as those in the programming language SNOBOL. However, the hardware necessary to dynamically produce the connections required by each different query may be much more expensive than the basic comparison hardware. Work is in progress to determine the cost and effect of this connection matrix and its practicality for actual systems.

Finite state automata. The final form of term comparator (HOLLAAR, 1979a; HOLLAAR & ROBERTS; ROBERTS, 1977; ROBERTS, 1978) involves the use of a finite state automaton. Finite state automata (FSA) are theoretical machines that can determine whether or not an input sequence matches a specified pattern. The pattern is specified as a state transition table, containing the next state for the FSA and its output as a function of the current state and input character. By appropriate changes to the table, any desired pattern can be recognized (the resulting implementation is called a universal FSA). This technique has been used in several software applications, particularly in compilers for higher-level languages.

However, when implemented in software on a conventional processor, the approach does not produce the desired performance (BULLEN & MILLEN). Special hardware is needed for the FSA to match the data transfer rate from the bulk memory that contains the desired database. Prototypes of this hardware have been constructed for the Central Intelligence Agency by Operating Systems, Inc. They seem to operate satisfactorily, providing the first high-speed text search system that uses specialized hardware capable of providing all desired query constructs, including embedded don't cares.

Structure or Directory Processors

All these specialized processors have been designed to search the entire database and do not require additional structural items, as with software approaches. However, for extremely large databases, even unconventional architectures may not provide adequate response times if the entire database must be searched repeatedly. It may be necessary to add structural items, processed by additional hardware, to enhance the response time of the retrieval system.

The most common form of database structure is the inverted, or indexed, file. For each index term (which may be a single word, a phrase, or a database attribute), a list of pointers or addresses is kept for all database items containing that term. Simple Boolean combining (the union or intersection) of a number of these lists gives a new list of documents that satisfies the desired criteria.

To minimize the size of the lists and to improve the performance of the list manipulation hardware, the pointers may not be to specific items but to groups of items. If more than one list entry pointed to the same group, only one would be included, thus reducing the length of the lists. Thus, the combining of the lists does not give a new list that contains only the items matching the query but only gives a list of groups for which there is some hope of satisfying the query during exhaustive searching.

The use of special hardware systems to process database structural information such as indexes is not new; modifications to early card collators were proposed and actually constructed to retrieve information "rapidly" (WOOSTER). However, as electronic digital computers became commonplace, interest in manipulating database structural information with special mechanical equipment died. An electronic version was developed for a special nonarithmetic extension to the IBM 7030 computer (CAMPBELL ET AL.). This extension, sometimes referred to as HARVEST, could combine or collate two lists stored in memory with a single instruction, following a series of instructions that were set up to indicate the merge or selection criteria. Unfortunately, again the concept of a special processor for indexes was abandoned, with only a handful of HARVEST systems constructed. Recently two projects, one at The Ohio State University and the other at the University of Illinois, have resurrected the idea of special hardware systems' processing database structural information as a means of improving response times.

Hsiao's database computer (DBC). The Database Computer, being designed at The Ohio State University under the direction of David K. Hsiao, has two distinct parts: a group of special processors for handling database structural items (the structural loop), and a partially associative memory (the main memory loop). (For a basic introduction to DBC, see BANERJEE & HSIAO, 1979; BANERJEE ET AL.; BAUM & HSIAO; BAUM ET AL.; KERR.) The design of the actual hardware and the decisions used to select appropriate technologies are given by HSIAO & KANNAN, HSIAO ET AL. (1977a), and KANNAN (1978). The support software is described by BANERJEE & HSIAO (1978a) and by HSIAO ET AL. (1977b), while the performance simulations are covered by BANERJEE & HSIAO (1978b), HSIAO & KANNAN (1978), and KANNAN (1977).

Unlike the previous rotating associative memories where there was an access mechanism (read/write head) for each track or loop of data, DBC uses a conventional moving-head disk access mechanism, although it can process data from all heads on the access mechanism simultaneously. This allows it to position to any group, or cylinder, of the database and to search the data on that cylinder rapidly. However, compared with the search speed, moving the access mechanism to another, possibly adjacent cylinder is very slow. The advantage of this technique is a substantial reduction in the cost and amount of searching circuitry for an extremely large database.

To reduce the number of repositionings of the access mechanism, the structural loop of the system is used to find only those cylinders that have some chance of satisfying the query. Thus, the structural memory must contain an accurate map of the contents of the main memory and must be updated whenever changes to main memory occur. Associative memories, hash encodings, and other design techniques are used to provide rapid processing for these updates. In addition, the structural loop supplies database security by preventing unauthorized users from reading or modifying protected data.

The detailed system design of DBC has been completed, and a prototype will be constructed soon. Its performance will probably equal that of the rotating associative processors (CASSM and RAP) but with less hardware required for extremely large databases.

List merging processors. Much of the work in an inverted file information retrieval system consists of moving index lists to and from bulk memory (such as disk) and merging them to form other lists. This task can be performed efficiently in a separate back-end processor that is dedicated to list merging; it appears to the user as a strange form of disk memory that contains every possible combination of the index lists. This back-end system approach was suggested by STELLHORN (1974; 1977), and an alternative approach was proposed by HOLLAAR (1975; 1978b; 1979b), both of the University of Illinois. Stellhorn's technique is based on the use of an even-odd merge network (BATCHER) to combine the sorted lists in parallel, with an additional coordination network necessary to remove undesired and duplicate entries from the network's output. Hollaar proposed a much simpler merge processing element; it does not require any post-processing of its output but can operate only serially on the list entries. To increase the performance to match that of Stellhorn's approach, these elements can be connected to form a network that can directly process many lists, based on a complex Boolean expression.

Much as the structural loop of the DBC reduces the amount of exhaustive searching later required, inverted file techniques in full-text retrieval can be used to minimize text searching. Not only does the inverted file allow one to ignore those portions of the database that cannot satisfy the query, but it can provide the interactive user with immediate feedback about his query. If a query is too broad, the result of the inverted file operations will be an extremely long list; if too specific, the result will be short (or even null). The user can then refine his query until the approximate number of expected items survive the inverted file operations. At this time, the remaining items can be searched exhaustively for the items of interest. Although inverted files are primarily thought of as a software technique, special hardware may be required for good response times and reasonable costs as the size of the database increases.

FINAL REMARKS

Although the conventional computer architecture based on von Neumann's 1946 proposal has proven successful in a wide variety of applications, including information retrieval, it will not be able to cope with the increasingly larger databases that are the result of lower memory costs. Since the cost of hardware is decreasing as rapidly as the cost of software is increasing, a hardware-oriented approach has the most promise. Research into the formal structure of database systems has provided a catalog of necessary operations, further simplifying the development of special purpose hardware.

Unconventional architectures, such as rotating associative memories and special structural processors, are currently in the research and development stage. They will play a substantial role in future information retrieval systems, first appearing in new, smaller applications even though current large-scale systems have the most immediate need. This is because the new users have no investment in software or database formats and can use the new systems as soon as they become commercially available. (When this might occur is open to speculation, but based on the success of the current research projects, the latter 1980s is a conservative estimate. Prototypes are beginning to change from laboratory toys to production machines that support representative applications.) As the technology matures, unconventional computer architectures based on those discussed here will make substantial contributions to information retrieval. They offer the potential of high-speed, low-cost search and retrieval of the large volumes of data that expanding memory technology will accommodate.

BIBLIOGRAPHY

To conserve space, some addresses have not been repeated throughout the Bibliography. They are: IEEE Service Center, 445 Hoes Lane, Piscataway, NJ 08854; AFIPS Press, 210 Summit Avenue, Montvale, NJ; Association for Computing Machinery, 1133 Avenue of the Americas, New York, NY 10036; IEEE Computer Society, 5855 Naples Plaza, Suite 301, Long Beach, CA 90803; University Microfilms, Ann Arbor, MI.

ANDERSON, GEORGE A.; KAIN, RICHARD Y. 1976. A Content-Addressed Memory Designed for Data Base Applications. In: Proceedings of the International Conference on Parallel Processing; 1976 August 24-27. New York, NY: Institute of Electrical and Electronics Engineers (IEEE); 1976. 191-195. IEEE: 76CH1127-OC.

BABB, E. 1979. Implementing a Relational Database by Means of Specialized Hardware. ACM Transactions on Database Systems. 1979 March; 4(1): 1-29. ISSN: 0362-5915.

BANERJEE, JAYANTA; HSIAO, DAVID K. 1978a. The Use of a 'Non-Relational' Database Machine for Supporting Relational Databases. In: Papers of the 4th Workshop on Computer Architecture for Non-Numeric Processing; 1978 August 1-4; Blue Mountain Lake, NY. New York, NY: Association for Computing Machinery (ACM); 1978. 91-98. Also available in: ACM SIGIR Newsletter: XIII(2); ACM SIGARCH Newsletter: VII(2); and ACM SIGMOD Newsletter: X(1).

BANERJEE, JAYANTA; HSIAO, DAVID K. 1978b. Performance Study of a Database Machine in Supporting Relational Databases. In: Proceedings of the 4th International Conference on Very Large Data Bases; 1978 September 13-15; Berlin, West Germany. New York, NY: The Institute of Electrical and Electronics Engineers; 1978. 319-329. IEEE: 78CH1389-6C; LC: 78-67197.

BANERJEE, JAYANTA; HSIAO, DAVID K. 1979. DBC—A Database Computer for Very Large Databases. IEEE Transactions on Computers. 1979 June; C28(6): 414-429. ISSN: 0018-9340.

BANERJEE, JAYANTA; BAUM, R.I.; HSIAO, DAVID K. 1978. Concepts and Capabilities of a Database Computer. ACM Transactions on Database Systems. 1978 December; 3(4): 347-384. ISSN: 0362-5915.

BATCHER, KENNETH E. 1968. Sorting Networks and Their Applications. In: Proceedings of the American Federation of Information Processing Societies (AFIPS) Spring Joint Computer Conference: Volume 32; 1968 December 6-11; San Francisco, CA. New York, NY: Thompson; 1968. 307-314. LC: 55-44701.

BAUM, R.I.; HSIAO, DAVID K. 1976. Database Computers—A Step towards Data Utilities. IEEE Transactions on Computers. 1976 December: C25(12): 1254-1259. ISSN: 018-9340.

BAUM, R.I.; HSIAO, DAVID K.; KANNAN, KRISHNAMURTHI. 1976. The Architecture of a Database Computer—Part I: Concepts and Capabilities. Columbus, OH: The Ohio State University, Computer and Information Science Research Center; 1976 September. 47p. (OSU-CISRC-TR-67-1). Available from: the Center.

BERRA, P. BRUCE. 1974. Some Problems in Associative Processing Applications to Data Base Management. In: Proceedings of the American Federation of Information Processing Societies (AFIPS) National Computer Conference: Volume 43; 1974 May 6-10; Chicago, IL. Montvale, NJ: AFIPS Press; 1974. 1-5. LC: 55-44701.

BERRA, P. BRUCE. 1978. Recent Developments in Data Base and Information Retrieval Hardware Architecture. In: Proceedings of the 2nd International Conference on Computer Software and Applications (COMPSAC); 1978 November 14-16; Chicago, IL. New York, NY: Institute of Electrical and Electronics Engineers (IEEE); 1978. 698-703. IEEE: 78CH1338-3.

BERRA, P. BRUCE; OLIVER, ELLEN. 1978. Associative Array Processor Utilization in Data Base Management. Computer. 1979 March; 12(3): 53-61. ISSN: 0018-9162.

BERRA, P. BRUCE; SINGHANIA, A.K. 1976. A Multiple Associative Memory Organization for Pipelining a Directory to a Very Large Database. In: COMPCON 76: Proceedings of the 13th IEEE Computer Society International Conference. 1976 September 7-10; Washington, DC. New York, NY: Institute of Electrical and Electronics Engineers (IEEE); 1976. 109-112. IEEE: 76CH1069-4.

BIRD, RICHARD M.; TANNER, P.E.; CASS, J.L.; TU, J.C.; FULLER, R.H. 1966. Study of Associative Processing Techniques. Rome, NY: Rome Air Development Center; 1966 September. (RADC-TR-66-209). Available from: Defense Documentation Center.

BIRD, RICHARD M.; TU, J.C.; WORTHY, R.M. 1977. Associative/Parallel Processors for Searching Very Large Textual Data Bases. In: Papers of the 3rd Workshop on Computer Architecture for Non-Numeric Processing; 1977 May 17-18; Syracuse, NY. New York, NY: Association for Computing Machinery (ACM); 1977. 8-16. Also available in: ACM SIGIR Newsletter: XII(1); ACM SIGARCH Newsletter: VI(2); and ACM SIGMOD Newsletter: IX(2).

BLAAUW, GERRIT A. 1970. Hardware Requirements for the Fourth Generation. In: Gruenberger, Fred, ed. Fourth Generation Computers: User Requirements and Transition. Englewood Cliffs, NJ: Prentice-Hall; 1970. 155-168. LC: 76-114699.

BRAY, OLIN; THURBER, KENNETH J. 1979. What's Happening with Data Base Processors. Datamation. 1979 January; 25(1): 146-156. ISSN: 0011-6963.

BULLEN, R.H., JR.; MILLEN, J.K. 1972. Microtext—The Design of a Microprogrammed Finite State Search Machine for Full-text Retrieval.

In: Proceedings of the American Federation of Information Processing Societies (AFIPS) Fall Joint Computer Conference: Volume 41, Part I; 1972 December 5-7; Anaheim, CA. Montvale, NJ: AFIPS Press; 1972. 479-488. LC: 55-44701.

BURKS, ARTHUR W.; GOLDSTINE, HERMAN H.; VON NEUMANN, JOHN. 1946. Preliminary Discussion of the Logical Design of an Electronic Computing Instrument. In: Taub, A.H., ed. Collected Works of John von Neumann: Volume 5. New York, NY: Macmillan Company; 1963. 34-79. Also in: Bell, C. Gordon; Newell, Allen. Computer Structures: Readings and Examples. New York, NY: McGraw-Hill; 1971. 92-119. ISBN: 07-004357-4; LC: 75-109245.

BUSH, J.A.; LIPOVSKI, G. JACK; SU, STANLEY Y.W.; WATSON, J.K.; ACKERMAN, S.J. 1976. Some Implementations of Segment Sequential Functions. In: Proceedings of the 3rd Annual Symposium on Computer Architecture; 1976 January 19-21; Clearwater, FL. New York, NY: Association for Computing Machinery and IEEE Computer Society; 1976. 178-185. IEEE: 76CH1043-5C.

CAMPBELL, S.G.; HERWITZ, P.S.; POMERENE, J.H. 1962. A Nonarithmetic System Extension. In: Buchholz, Werner, ed. Planning a Computer System, Project Stretch. New York, NY: McGraw-Hill; 1962. 254-271. LC: 61-10466.

CAPRARO, GERALD T. 1978. A Data Base Management Modeling Technique and Special Function Hardware Architecture. Syracuse, NY: Syracuse University; 1978 February. 248p. (Ph.D. dissertation). Available from: University Microfilms.

CHAMPINE, GEORGE A. 1978. Four Approaches to a Data Base Computer. Datamation. 1978 December; 24(13): 101-106. ISSN: 0011-6963.

CHANG, HSU. 1978a. Bubbles for Relational Database. In: Papers of the 4th Workshop on Computer Architecture for Non-Numeric Processing; 1978 August 1-4; Blue Mountain Lake, NY. New York, NY: Association for Computing Machinery (ACM); 1978. 110-116. Also available in: ACM SIGIR Newsletter: XIII(2), ACM SIGARCH Newsletter: VII(2), and ACM SIGMOD Newsletter: X(1).

CHANG, HSU. 1978b. On Bubble Memories and Relational Data Base. In: Proceedings of the 4th International Conference on Very Large Data Bases; 1978 September 13-15; Berlin, West Germany. New York, NY: The Institute of Electrical and Electronics Engineers; 1978. 207-229. IEEE: 78CH1389-6C; LC: 78-67197.

CHANG, HSU; NIGAN, A. 1978. Major-Minor Loop Chips Adapted for Associative Search in Relational Data Base. IEEE Transactions on Magnetics. 1978 November; MAG14(6): 1123-1128. ISSN: 0018-9464.

CHEN, T.C.; CHANG, HSU. 1978. Magnetic Bubble Memory and Logic. In: Yovits, Marshall, ed. Advances in Computers: Volume 17. New York, NY: Academic Press; 1978. 223-282. ISBN: 0-12-012177-4; LC: 59-15761.

CHEN, T.C.; LUM, V.Y.; TUNG, C. 1978. The Rebound Sorter: An Efficient Sort Engine for Large Files. In: Proceedings of the 4th International Conference on Very Large Data Bases; 1978 September 13-15; Berlin, West Germany. New York, NY: The Institute of Electrical and Electronics Engineers; 1978. 312-315. IEEE: 78CH1389-6C; LC: 78-67197.

CHEN, W.F. 1976. A Performance Study of the CASSM System. Gainesville, FL: University of Florida, Department of Electrical Engineering; 1976. (M.S. thesis). Available from: University of Florida.

CODD, E.F. 1970. A Relational Model of Data for Large Shared Data Banks. Communications of the ACM. 1970 June: 13(6): 337-387. ISSN: 0558-8069.

COPELAND, GEORGE P. 1974. A Cellular System for Nonnumeric Processing. Gainesville, FL: University of Florida, Department of Electrical Engineering; 1974. 164p. (Ph.D. dissertation). Available from: University Microfilms. Order no. 75-19321.

COPELAND, GEORGE P. 1978. String Storage and Search for Data Base Applications: Implementation of the INDY Backend Kernel. In: Papers of the 4th Workshop on Computer Architecture for Non-Numeric Processing; 1978 August 1-4; Blue Mountain Lake, NY. New York, NY: Association for Computing Machinery (ACM); 1978. 8-17. Also available in: ACM SIGIR Newsletter: XIII(2), ACM SIGARCH Newsletter: VII(2), and ACM SIGMOD Newsletter: X(1).

COPELAND, GEORGE P.; LIPOVSKI, G. JACK; SU, STANLEY Y.W. 1973. The Architecture of CASSM: A Cellular System for Non-Numeric Processing. In: Proceedings of the 1st Annual Symposium on Computer Architecture; 1973 December 9-11; Gainesville, FL. New York, NY: The Institute of Electrical and Electronics Engineers (IEEE); 1973. 121-130. IEEE: 73CH0824-3C.

DAVIS, EDWARD W. 1974. STARAN Parallel Processor System Software. In: Proceedings of the American Federation of Information Processing Societies (AFIPS) National Computer Conference: Volume 43; 1974 May 6-10; Chicago, IL. Montvale, NJ: AFIPS Press; 1974. 17-22. LC: 55-44701.

DEFIORE, CASPER R. 1972. An Associative Approach to Data Management. Syracuse, NY: Syracuse University; 1972 May. 210p. (Ph.D. dissertation). Available from: University Microfilms, Order no. 73-00716.

DEFIORE, CASPER R.; BERRA, P. BRUCE. 1973. A Data Management System Utilizing an Associative Memory. In: Proceedings of the American Federation of Information Processing Societies (AFIPS) National Computer Conference: Volume 42; 1973 June 4-8; New York, NY. Montvale, NJ: AFIPS Press; 1974. 181-185. LC: 55-44701.

DEFIORE, CASPER R.; BERRA, P. BRUCE. 1974. A Quantitative Analysis of the Utilization of Associative Memories in Data Management. IEEE Transactions on Computers. 1974 February; C23(2): 121-132. ISSN: 0018-9340.

DEFIORE, CASPER R.; STILLMAN, NEIL; BERRA, P. BRUCE. 1971. Associative Techniques in the Solution of Data Management Problems. In: Proceedings of the Association for Computing Machinery (ACM) Annual Conference; 1971 August 3-5; Chicago, IL. New York, NY: ACM; 1971. 28-36. LC: 77-649466.

DEMARTINIS, MANLIO; LIPOVSKI, G. JACK; SU, STANLEY Y.W.; WATSON, J.K. 1976. A Self Managing Secondary Memory System. In: Proceedings of the 3rd Annual Symposium on Computer Architecture; 1976 January 19-21; Clearwater, FL. New York, NY: Association for Computing Machinery and IEEE Computer Society; 1976. 186-194. IEEE: 76CH1043-5C.

DEWITT, DAVID J. 1978. DIRECT—A Multiprocessor Organization for Supporting Relational Data Base Management Systems. In: Proceedings of the 5th Annual Symposium on Computer Architecture; 1978 April 3-5; Palo Alto, CA. New York, NY: Association for Computing Machinery and IEEE Computer Society; 1978. 182-189. IEEE: 78CH1284-9C.

EDELBERG, MURRAY; SCHISSLER, L.R. 1976. Intelligent Memory. In: Proceedings of the American Federation of Information Processing Societies (AFIPS) National Computer Conference: Volume 45; 1976 June 7-10; New York, NY. Montvale, NJ: AFIPS Press; 1976. 393-400. LC: 55-44701.

EL MASRI, A.; ROHMER, JEAN; TUSERA, D. 1978. A Machine for Information Retrieval. In: Papers of the 4th Workshop on Computer Architecture for Non-Numeric Processing; 1978 August 1-4; Blue Mountain Lake, NY. New York, NY: Association for Computing Machinery (ACM); 1978. 117-120. Also available in: ACM SIGIR Newsletter: XIII(2); ACM SIGARCH Newsletter: VII(2); and ACM SIGMOD Newsletter: X(1).

FULLER, R.H. 1967. Associative Parallel Processing. Computer Design. 1967 December; 6(12): 43-46.

HEALY, LEONARD D. 1976. A Character-Oriented Context-Addressed Segment-Sequential Storage. In: Proceedings of the 3rd Annual Symposium on Computer Architecture; 1976 January 19-21; Clearwater, FL. New York, NY: Association for Computing Machinery and IEEE Computer Society; 1976. 172-177. IEEE: 76CH1043-5C.

HEALY, LEONARD D.; DOTY, K.L.; LIPOVSKI, G. JACK. 1972. The Architecture of a Content Addressed Segment Sequential Storage. In: Proceedings of the American Federation of Information Processing Societies (AFIPS) Fall Joint Computer Conference: Volume 41, Part II; 1972 December 5-7; Anaheim, CA. Montvale, NJ: AFIPS Press: 1972. 691-701. LC: 55-44701.

HOLLAAR, LEE A. 1975. A List Merging Processor for Inverted File Information Retrieval Systems. Urbana, IL: University of Illinois, Department of Computer Science; 1975 October. 78p. (Ph.D. dissertation). Available from: University Microfilms, order no. 76-06801.

HOLLAAR, LEE A. 1978a. Rotating Memory Processors for the Matching of Complex Textual Patterns. In: Proceedings of the 5th Annual Symposium on Computer Architecture; 1978 April 3-5; Palo Alto, CA. New York, NY: Association for Computing Machinery and IEEE Computer Society; 1978. 39-43. IEEE: 78CH1284-9C.

HOLLAAR, LEE A. 1978b. Specialized Merge Processor Networks for Combining Sorted Lists. ACM Transactions on Database Systems. 1978 September; 3(3): 272-284. ISSN: 0362-5915.

HOLLAAR, LEE A. 1979a. Text Retrieval Computers. Computer. 1979 March; 12(3): 40-50. ISSN: 0018-9162.

HOLLAAR, LEE A. 1979b. A Design for a List Merging Network. IEEE Transactions on Computers. 1979 June; C28(6): 406-443. ISSN: 0018-9340.

HOLLAAR, LEE A.; ROBERTS, D.C. 1978. Current Research into Specialized Processors for Text Information Retrieval. In: Proceedings of the 4th International Conference on Very Large Data Bases; 1978 September 13-15; Berlin, West Germany. New York, NY: Institute of Electrical and Electronics Engineers; 1978. 270-279. IEEE: 78CH1389-6C; LC: 78-67197.

HOLLAAR, LEE A.; STELLHORN, WILLIAM H. 1977. A Specialized Architecture for Textual Information Retrieval. In: Proceedings of the American Federation of Information Processing Societies (AFIPS) National Computer Conference: Volume 46; 1977 June 13-16; Dallas, TX. Montvale, NJ: AFIPS Press; 1977. 697-702. LC: 55-44701.

HSIAO, DAVID K.; KANNAN, KRISHNAMURTHI. 1976a. The Architecture of a Database Computer—Part II: The Design of Structure Memory and Its Related Processors. Columbus, OH: The Ohio State University, Computer and Information Science Research Center; 1976 October. 106p. (OSU-CISRC-TR-76-2). Available from: the Center.

HSIAO, DAVID K.; KANNAN, KRISHNAMURTHI. 1976b. The Architecture of a Database Computer—Part III: The Design of Mass Memory and Its Related Components. Columbus, OH: The Ohio State University, Computer and Information Science Research Center; 1976 December. 138p. (OSU-CISRC-TR-76-3). Available from: the Center.

HSIAO, DAVID K.; KANNAN, KRISHNAMURTHI. 1977. The Architecture of a Database Computer A Summary. In: Papers of the 3rd Workshop on Computer Architecture for Non-Numeric Processing; 1977 May 17-18; Syracuse, NY. New York, NY: Association for Computing Machinery (ACM); 1977. 31-34. Also available in: ACM SIGIR Newsletter: XII(1); ACM SIGARCH Newsletter: VI(2); and ACM SIGMOD Newsletter: IX(2).

HSIAO, DAVID K.; KANNAN, KRISHNAMURTHI. 1978. Simulation Studies of the Database Computer (DBC). Columbus, OH: The Ohio State University, Computer and Information Science Research Center; 1978 February. 39p. (OSU-CISRC-TR-78-1). Available from: the Center.

HSIAO, DAVID K.; MADNICK, S.E. 1977. Database Machine Architecture in the Context of Information Technology Evolution. In: Proceedings of the 3rd International Conference on Very Large Databases; 1977 October 6-8; Tokyo, Japan. New York, NY: Institute of Electrical and Electronics Engineers; 1977. 63-84. IEEE: 77CH1268-2C.

HSIAO, DAVID K.; KANNAN, KRISHNAMURTHI; KERR, DOUGLAS S. 1977a. Structure Memory Designs for a Database Computer. In: Proceedings of the Annual Conference of the Association for Computing Machinery (ACM); 1977 October 16-19; Seattle, WA. New York, NY: ACM; 1977. 343-350. LC: 77-649466.

HSIAO, DAVID K.; KERR, DOUGLAS S.; NG, F.K. 1977b. DBC Software Requirements for Supporting Hierarchical Databases. Columbus, OH: The Ohio State University, Computer and Information Science Research Center; 1977 April. 98p. (OSU-CISRC-TR-77-1). Available from: the Center.

HUTCHINSON, J.S.; ROMAN, W.G. 1978. MADMAN Machine. In: Papers of the 4th Workshop on Computer Architecture for Non-Numeric Processing; 1978 August 1-4; Blue Mountain Lake, NY. New York, NY: Association for Computing Machinery (ACM); 1978. 85-90. Also available as ACM SIGIR Newsletter: XIII(2); ACM SIGARCH Newsletter: VII(2); and ACM SIGMOD Newsletter: X(1).

JINO, MARIO; LIU, JANE W-S. 1978. Intelligent Magnetic Bubble Memories. In: Proceedings of the 5th Annual Symposium on Computer Architecture; 1978 April 3-5; Palo Alto, CA. New York, NY: Association for Computing Machinery and IEEE Computer Society; 1978. 166-171. IEEE: 78CH1284-9C.

KANNAN, KRISHNAMURTHI. 1977. The Design and Performance of a Database Computer. Columbus, OH: The Ohio State University; 1977 December. 308p. (Ph.D. dissertation). Available from: University Microfilms, Order no. 78-05863.

KANNAN, KRISHNAMURTHI. 1978. The Design of the Mass Memory for a Database Computer. In: Proceedings of the 5th Annual Symposium on Computer Architecture; 1978 April 3-5; Palo Alto, CA. New York, NY: Association for Computing Machinery and IEEE Computer Society; 1978. 44-51. IEEE: 78CH1284-9C.

KERR, DOUGLAS S. 1979. Database Machines Utilizing Very Large Content Addressable Blocks and Special Structural Information Processors. Computer. 1979 March; 12(3): 64-79. ISSN: 0018-9162.

LANGDON, GLEN G., JR. 1978. A Note on Associative Processors for Data Management. ACM Transactions on Database Systems. 1978 June; 3(2): 148-158. ISSN: 0362-5915.

LEE, C.Y.; PAULL, M.C. 1963. A Content Addressable Distributed Logic Memory with Application to Information Retrieval. Proceedings of the IEEE. 1963 June; 51(6): 924-932. ISSN: 0018-9219.

LEE, S.Y.; CHANG, HSU. 1974. An All-Bubble Text-Editing System. IEEE Transactions on Magnetics. 1974 September; MAG10(3): 746-749. ISSN: 0018-9464.

LEE, S.Y.; CHANG, HSU. 1975. Associative Search Bubble Devices for Content Addressable Memories. In: COMPCON 75: Proceedings of the 11th Annual IEEE Computer Society International Conference; 1975 September 9-11; Washington, DC. New York, NY: Institute of Electrical and Electronics Engineers, 1975. 91-92. IEEE: 75CH0988-6C.

LEE, S.Y.; CHEN, T.C.; CHANG, HSU; TUNG, C. 1974. Text Editing with Magnetic Bubbles. In: COMPCON 74: Proceedings of the 9th Annual IEEE Computer Society International Conference; 1974 September 10-12; Washington, DC. New York; Institute of Electrical and Electronics Engineers (IEEE), 1974. 69-72. IEEE: 74CH0869-8C; LC: 68-1628.

LEILICH, H-O.; STIEGE, G.; ZEIDLER, H.CH. 1978. A Search Processor for Data Base Management Systems. In: Proceedings of the 4th International Conference on Very Large Data Bases; 1978 September 13-15; Berlin, West Germany. New York, NY: Institute of Electrical and Electronics Engineers; 1978. 280-287. IEEE: 78CH1389-6C; LC: 78-67197.

LIN, C.S. 1977. Sorting with Associative Secondary Storage Devices. In: Proceedings of the American Federation of Information Processing Societies (AFIPS) National Computer Conference: Volume 46; 1977 June 13-16; Dallas, TX. Montvale, NJ: AFIPS Press; 1977. 691-695. LC: 55-44701.

LIN, C.S.; SMITH, DIANE C.P.; SMITH, JOHN MYLES. 1976. The Design of a Rotating Associative Memory for Relational Database Applications. ACM Transactions on Database Systems. 1976 March; 1(1): 53-65. ISSN: 0362-5915.

LINDE, RICHARD R.; GATES, R.; PENG, T-F. 1973. Associative Processor Applications to Real-Time Data Management. In: Proceedings of the American Federation of Information Processing Societies (AFIPS) National Computer Conference: Volume 42; 1973 June 4-8; New York, NY. Montvale, NJ: AFIPS Press; 1973. 187-195. LC: 55-44701.

LIPOVSKI, G. JACK. 1970. The Architecture of a Large Associative Processor. In: Proceedings of the American Federation of Information Processing Societies (AFIPS) Spring Joint Computer Conference: Volume

36; 1970 May 5-7; Atlantic City, NJ. Montvale, NJ: AFIPS Press; 1970. 385-396. LC: 55-44701.

LIPOVSKI, G. JACK. 1977. On Imaginary Field, Token Transfers, and Floating Codes in Intelligent Secondary Memories. In: Papers of the 3rd Workshop on Computer Architecture for Non-Numeric Processing; 1977 May 17-18; Syracuse, NY. New York, NY: Association for Computing Machinery (ACM); 1977. 17-21. Also available as ACM SIGIR Newsletter: XII(1), ACM SIGARCH Newsletter: VI(2), and ACM SIGMOD Newsletter: IX(2).

LIPOVSKI, G. JACK. 1978. Architectural Features of CASSM: A Content Addressed Segment Sequential Memory. In: Proceedings of the 5th Annual Symposium on Computer Architecture; 1978 April 3-5; Palo Alto, CA. New York, NY: Association for Computing Machinery and IEEE Computer Society; 1978. 31-38. IEEE: 78CH1284-9C.

MINSKY, NAFTALY. 1972a. Rotating Storage Devices as Partial Associative Memories. In: Proceedings of the 1972 ACM-SIGFIDET Workshop on Data Description, Access and Control; 1972 November 29-December 1; Denver, CO. New York, NY: Association for Computing Machinery (ACM); 1972. 213-241.

MINSKY, NAFTALY. 1972b. Rotating Storage Devices as Partial Associative Memories. In: Proceedings of the American Federation of Information Processing Societies (AFIPS) Fall Joint Computer Conference: Volume 41, Part I; 1972 December 5-7; Anaheim, CA. Montvale, NJ: AFIPS Press; 1972. 587-596. LC: 55-44701.

MOULDER, RICHARD. 1973. An Implementation of a Data Management System on an Associative Processor. In: Proceedings of the American Federation of Information Processing Societies (AFIPS) National Computer Conference: Volume 42; 1974 June 4-8; New York, NY. Montvale, NJ: AFIPS Press; 1974. 171-176. LC: 55-44701.

MUKHOPADHYAY, AMAR. 1978. Hardware Algorithms for Nonnumeric Computation. In: Proceedings of the 5th Annual Symposium on Computer Architecture; 1978 April 3-5; Palo Alto, CA. New York, NY: Association for Computing Machinery and IEEE Computer Society: 1978. 8-16. IEEE: 78CH1284-9C. Also available in: IEEE Transactions on Computers. 1979 June; C28(6): 384-394. ISSN: 0018-9340.

OTIS, ALLEN J.; COPELAND, GEORGE P. 1978. Editing Requirements for Data Base Applications and Their Implementation on the INDY Backend Kernel. In: Papers of the 4th Workshop on Computer Architecture for Non-Numeric Processing; 1978 August 1-4; Blue Mountain Lake, NY. New York, NY: Association for Computing Machinery (ACM); 1978. 18-29. Also available in: ACM SIGIR Newsletter: XIII(2); ACM SIGARCH Newsletter: VII(2); and ACM SIGMOD Newsletter: X(1).

OZKARAHAN, ESEN A.; OFLAZER, KEMAL. 1978. Microprocessor Based Modular Database Processors. In: Proceedings of the 4th International Conference on Very Large Data Bases; 1978 September 13-15; Berlin, West Germany. New York, NY: Institute of Electrical and Electronics Engineers; 1978. 300-311. IEEE: 78CH1389-6C; LC: 78-67197.

OZKARAHAN, ESEN A.; SEVCIK, K.C. 1977. Analysis of Architectural Features for Enhancing the Performance of a Database Machine. ACM Transactions on Database Systems. 1977 December; 2(4): 297-316. ISSN: 0362-5915.

OZKARAHAN, ESEN A.; SCHUSTER, S.A.; SMITH, K.C. 1974. A Database Computer. Toronto, Canada: University of Toronto, Computer Science Research Group; 1974 September. (CSRG-TR-43). Available from: University of Toronto.

OZKARAHAN, ESEN A.; SCHUSTER, S.A.; SMITH, K.C. 1975. RAP—An Associative Processor for Data Base Management. In: Proceedings of the American Federation of Information Processing Societies (AFIPS) National Computer Conference: Volume 44; 1975 May 19-22; Anaheim, CA. Montvale, NJ: AFIPS Press; 1975. 379-387. LC: 55-44701.

OZKARAHAN, ESEN A.; SCHUSTER, S.A.; SMITH, K.C. 1977. Performance Evaluation of a Relational Associative Processor. ACM Transactions on Database Systems. 1977 June; 2(2): 175-195. ISSN: 0362-5915.

PARHAMI, BEHROOZ. 1972. A Highly Parallel Computer System for Information Retrieval. In: Proceedings of the American Federation of Information Processing Societies (AFIPS) Fall Joint Computer Conference: Volume 41, Part II; 1972 December 5-7; Anaheim, CA. Montvale, NJ: AFIPS Press; 1972. 681-690. LC: 55-44701.

PARKER, JAMES L. 1971. A Logic Per Track Retrieval System. In: Proceedings of the International Federation for Information Processing (IFIP) Congress; 1971 August 23-28; Ljubljana, Yugoslavia. Amsterdam, The Netherlands: North Holland Publishing Co.; 1972. 711-716. LC: 76-184997.

ROBERTS, DAVID C., ed. 1977. A Computer System for Text Retrieval: Design Concept Development. Washington, DC: Central Intelligence Agency, Office of Research and Development; 1977 October 15. 82p. (RD-77-10011). Available from: David C. Roberts, Central Intelligence Agency, Washington, DC 20505.

ROBERTS, DAVID C. 1978. A Specialized Computer Architecture for Text Retrieval. In: Papers of the 4th Workshop on Computer Architecture for Non-Numeric Processing; 1978 August 1-4; Blue Mountain Lake, NY. New York, NY: Association for Computing Machinery (ACM); 1978. 51-59. Also available in ACM SIGIR Newsletter: XIII(2); ACM SIGARCH Newsletter: VII(2); and ACM SIGMOD Newsletter: X(1).

RUDOLPH, JACK A. 1972. A Production Implementation of an Associative Processor: STARAN. In: Proceedings of the American Federation of Information Processing Societies (AFIPS) Fall Joint Computer Conference: Volume 41, Part I; 1972 December 5-7; Anaheim, CA. Montvale, NJ: AFIPS Press; 1972. 229-241. LC: 55-44701.

SADOWSKI, PAUL J.; SCHUSTER, STEWART A. 1978. Exploiting Parallelism in a Relational Associative Processor. In: Papers of the 4th Workshop on Computer Architecture for Non-Numeric Processing; 1978 August 1-4; Blue Mountain Lake, NY. New York, NY: Association for Computing Machinery (ACM); 1978. 99-109. Also available in: ACM SIGIR Newsletter: XIII(2); ACM SIGARCH Newsletter: VII(2); and ACM SIGMOD Newsletter: X(1).

SCHUSTER, STEWART A., OZKARAHAN, ESEN A.; SMITH, K.C. 1976. A Virtual Memory System for a Relational Associative Processor. In: Proceedings of the American Federation of Information Processing Societies (AFIPS) National Computer Conference: Volume 45; 1976 June 7-10; New York, NY. Montvale, NJ: AFIPS Press; 1976. 855-862. LC: 55-44701.

SCHUSTER, STEWART A.; NGUYEN, H.B.; OZKARAHAN, ESEN A.; SMITH, K.C. 1978. RAP.2—An Associative Processor for Data Bases. In: Proceedings of the 5th Annual Symposium on Computer Architecture; 1978 April 3-5; Palo Alto, CA. New York, NY: Association for Computing Machinery and IEEE Computer Society; 1978. 52-59. IEEE: 78CH1284-9C. Also available in: IEEE Transactions on Computers. 1979 June; C28(6): 446-458. ISSN: 0018-9340.

SLOTNICK, DANIEL L. 1970. Logic Per Track Devices. In: Alt, Franz L.; Rubinoff, Morris, eds. Advances in Computers: Volume 10. New York, NY: Academic Press; 1970. 291-296. LC: 59-15761.

SMITH, DIANE C.P.; SMITH, JOHN MYLES. 1979. Relational Database Machines. Computer. 1979 March; 12(3): 28-38. ISSN: 0018-9162.

STELLHORN, WILLIAM H. 1974. A Specialized Computer for Information Retrieval. Urbana, IL: University of Illinois, Department of Computer Science; 1974 October. 115p. (Ph.D. dissertation). Available from: University Microfilms, Order no. 75-11634.

STELLHORN, WILLIAM H. 1977. An Information File Processor for Information Retrieval. IEEE Transactions on Computers. 1977 December; C26(12): 1258-1267. ISSN: 0018-9340.

SU, STANLEY Y.W. 1977. Associative Programming in CASSM and Its Applications. In: Proceedings of the 3rd International Conference on Very Large Databases; 1977 October 6-8; Tokyo, Japan. New York, NY: Institute of Electrical and Electronics Engineers (IEEE); 1977. 213-228. IEEE: 77CH1268-2C.

SU, STANLEY Y.W. 1979. On Cellular Logic Devices: Concept and Applications. Computer. 1979 March; 12(3): 11-25. ISSN: 0018-9162.

SU, STANLEY Y.W.; EMAN, AHMED. 1978. CASDAL: CASSM's Data Language. ACM Transactions on Database Systems. 1978 March; 3(1): 57-91. ISSN: 0362-5915.

SU, STANLEY Y.W.; LIPOVSKI, G. JACK. 1975. CASSM: A Cellular System for Very Large Data Bases. In: Proceedings of the 1st International Conference on Very Large Databases; 1975 September; Framingham, MA. New York, NY: Association for Computing Machinery (ACM); 1975. 456-472.

SU, STANLEY Y.W.; LUPKIEWICZ, S.; LEE, C-J.; LO, D.H.; DOTY, K.L. 1978. Micronet: A Microcomputer Network System for Managing Distributed Relational Databases. In: Proceedings of the 4th International Conference on Very Large Data Bases; 1978 September 13-15; Berlin, West Germany. New York, NY: The Institute of Electrical and Electronics Engineers; 1978. 288-298. IEEE: 78CH1389-6C; LC: 78-67197.

SU, STANLEY Y.W.; EMAN, AHMED; NGUYEN, LE; LIPOVSKI, G. JACK. 1979. The Architectural Features and Implementation Techniques of the Multi-cell CASSM. IEEE Transactions on Computers. 1979 June; C28(6): 430-445. ISSN: 0018-9340.

THURBER, KENNETH J.; WALD, L.D. 1975. Associative and Parallel Processors. Computing Surveys. 1975 December; 7(4): 215-255. ISSN: 0010-4892.

TUNG, C.; CHEN, T.C.; CHANG, HSU. 1975. Bubble Ladder for Information Processing. IEEE Transactions on Magnetics. 1975 September; MAG11(5): 1163-1165. ISSN: 0018-9464.

WOOSTER, HAROLD. 1971. Current Research and Development in Scientific Documentation. In: Kent, Allen; Lancour, Harold, eds. Encyclopedia of Library and Information Science: Volume 6. New York, NY: Marcel Dekker, Inc.; 1971. 336-365. ISBN: 0-8247-2106-3; LC: 68-31232.

YAU, STEPHEN S.; FUNG, H.S. 1977. Associative Processor Architecture—A Survey. Computing Surveys. 1977 March; 9(1): 3-28. ISSN: 0010-4892.

6 Database Management Systems

MICHAEL A. HUFFENBERGER
Chemical Abstracts Service

RONALD L. WIGINGTON
Chemical Abstracts Service

INTRODUCTION

The 1970s and 1980s will be called the database decades. This rapid evolution of data processing is not a passing fad—a threshold is being crossed. Billions of marginally accessible paper records will become available online.

The 1970s and 1980s will be a time of breakthroughs, victories, defeats, and dismal failures with respect to successful computerization of information. At the close of this dynamic expansion period, databases will be integral to most organized activities in business, industry, education, government, and the home. Outstanding among the technological advances that will bring about this state of affairs will be the development of the software packages known as database management systems (DBMSs).

This chapter reviews the DBMS literature in terms of eight perspectives: 1) basic concepts and definitions; 2) historical perspectives; 3) logical and physical databases; 4) components and environment (a technical view); 5) operational and organizational impacts (a management view); 6) commercial offerings and reported activities; 7) limitations and issues; and 8) state-of-the-art and trends.

BASIC CONCEPTS AND DEFINITIONS

Data as a Resource

As information becomes computerized, stark reality confronts many organizations; the information necessary for proper functioning occupies a surprising volume and represents an enormous investment. Perhaps this revelation most often occurs when manual, paper-based systems are being converted to computer-supported systems. Conversion often implies large expenditures of keyboard hours and computer time. FRY & SIBLEY estimate that keyboard input costs about 50 cents per 1,000 characters. A medium-sized database of 50 million characters thus represents $25,000 in keyboard costs alone.

Management-oriented literature (MCFADDEN & SUVER; NOLAN) strongly suggests that corporate information be managed as a tangible resource. Failure to do so results in decisions that may not properly match costs and values in collecting, organizing, and using corporate information. Accounting methods for this purpose are not established; even the concept is difficult to grasp since it is a level of abstraction removed from the management of tangible property using inventory management and investment/payback analyses. However, when the acquisition and use of information can be better related to capital investment and dollar gain or loss, organizations will be able to make better strategic decisions with regard to their information support function.

Organizations are finding it imperative to find economical ways to store and to process their information; in many cases this imperative leads them to obtain a DBMS.

Databases and the Database Approach

Terminology is something of a problem in this field. "Data base," "database," and "database" all appear in the literature, with a variety of connotations (LEWIS). There is certainly no consensus about the spelling, although a trend toward "database" is apparent. For this volume of *ARIST*, the form "database" is used. Moreover, the more generic term "information," used above, is sometimes meant to imply something other than "data," the latter being restricted to numerical information. No such distinction is meant here. The term "information" is used when general context is being discussed, and the term "data" is used in its ordinary "data processing" context.

"Database" has been defined in many ways in the literature, but a particularly lucid definition is: "A *data base* may be defined as a collection of inter-related data stored together without harmful or unnecessary redundancy to serve multiple applications" (MARTIN, 1977). Martin's definition provides for the practical observation that most organizations have several databases, distinct in structure, storage, and content. It does not specify storage media or how many physical files or record types must be involved in a database. It has become common practice in the bibliographic information handling community to refer to any computer-readable information collection as a database. Usually these files do not qualify in the context of what is properly called a DBMS. Moreover, characteristics of the data within the bibliographic files and the size of those files were beyond that handled efficiently by early DBMSs, and specialized bibliographic systems were developed. As development continues, more bibliographic applications can be expected to use general purpose DBMS software.

The database approach is simply one that promotes the development and controlled use of databases in an organization (LEWIS). It has certain objectives:

- The data are stored in formats that are independent of the application programs to allow multiple uses and to support future changes;
- A controlled approach to accessing and updating is used to ensure privacy and integrity of stored data;
- Redundancy is avoided to conserve storage resources and to maintain consistency among multiple uses of the same information; and
- Data structures provide accurate, simplified models of the real world.

The database approach acknowledges the central role of information to the successful functioning of an organization. This approach should lead to cheaper, faster, and more flexible system development when the entire organization's needs are considered (KROENKE; MARTIN, 1977), but a DBMS by no means ensures that this goal will be reached.

Features and Benefits of Data Management Software

Early data-processing activities were function oriented. Each function had a set of input and a set of output data requirements; each set of requirements was fulfilled by creation of a new file. This practice led to the storage and manipulation of much redundant data (DATAPRO RESEARCH CORPORATION). Such systems tended to be batch oriented, tape oriented, and relatively unresponsive to ad hoc and varying user requirements. Problems in data consistency and program sequencing also occurred and still do (ROSS, 1978).

DASD-oriented databases—allowing complex data interrelationships, minimizing redundancy, and servicing multiple applications—seemed to provide an answer. In the late 1960s and early 1970s, capable organizations developed software packages to accommodate such databases. These packages were the forerunners of DBMSs. Development costs currently limit most DBMS development to hardware manufacturers and major independent software houses.

Although the databases and thus DBMS applications vary widely, a more-or-less consistent set of DBMS features can be identified (DATAPRO RESEARCH CORPORATION; FONG ET AL.; ROSS, 1978):

- Data definitions depicting various data relationships and content are entered by a user;
- Data are mapped from the structure defined by the user to physical storage (usually on DASD);
- Data manipulation, including retrieval and update, is supported through a user language or host language interface; host language support usually includes COBOL (Common Business-

Oriented Language), FORTRAN (Formula Translation), PL/1 (Programming Language/One), and Assembler;
- An interface for data communications is provided to support real-time processing through remote terminals;
- Data integrity, security, and privacy are controlled in a multi-user environment;
- Restart and recovery facilities are included;
- Utility programs to load, to reorganize, and to copy data are provided; and
- Reporting mechanisms for optimization and management are provided.

Such a collection of facilities comprises a powerful software package for data storage and processing. Somewhat distinct from DBMSs are the software packages known as data management systems (DMSs); their principal purpose is to permit retrieval from existing files, usually for a single application. These systems generally pass files sequentially to produce reports (although some have query capabilities). A full set of data storage and processing tools as defined above is missing from DMSs (DATAPRO RESEARCH CORPORATION).

Also distinct from DBMSs are search and retrieval systems (e.g., ORBIT from System Development Corp. and STAIRS from IBM). These systems usually do not provide a generalized mechanism for maintaining databases in an application environment; rather they provide economical reference to large, nonvolatile data collections. Thus, data definitions, recovery and restart, and update control facilities are absent. A few search and retrieval systems have been created that incorporate DBMS features. One example is NASIS, an information system constructed for the National Aeronautics and Space Administration (GOLDSTEIN), which was designed to combine both aspects.

Many benefits are cited for DBMSs, although their attainment may depend on each organization's approach to their use (CUOZZO & KURTZ; KROENKE; MARTIN, 1977):

- Data entry and storage costs are reduced because redundancy is limited;
- More timely and consistent data are the result of one-time, controlled updates;
- Data are more secure and exhibit higher quality;
- Programming tasks are simpler and cheaper, even when sophisticated functions are requested; and
- Flexible data structures accommodate change with little or no conversion costs.

Thorough planning and care are needed to ensure that these benefits are realized; even with planning, payoffs may not accrue until a database begins to support a variety of applications (CUOZZO & KURTZ). DBMSs also have disadvantages (CUOZZO & KURTZ; KOSS & NOONAN):

- A DBMS for a large mainframe is not cheap software. Prices (1979) generally run about $100,000 to $150,000 for a fully equipped system.
- DBMSs soak up computer system resources, including memory and processing cycles. This overhead can be far from negligible; new hardware may be required.
- DBMS software entails substantial training of programmers, systems analysts, and systems programmers. Applications developed for complex software and data structures may take longer; trial-and-error efforts may be expensive.
- Some full-time support of the software is needed; a new organizational function called database administration is required.
- Online data stored without redundancy can be vulnerable to failure. Database recoveries in a multi-user environment tend to be visible, complex, and hazardous.

Despite these potential problems, organizations of all sizes are converting to DBMS-oriented processing at a considerable rate. MCFADDEN & SUVER estimated 5,000 installed DBMS packages in 1978 and predicted DBMS software to be pervasive in the 1980s. At least one survey has found most users to be satisfied overall after shifting to a DBMS (WIORKOWSKI & WIORKOWSKI).

DBMSs and Today's Databases

Many different commercial DBMSs are available, and they have been used in myriad ways. Present DBMSs are powerful software packages with several components (supporting the features listed previously). They are available on minicomputers as well as mainframes, so that applications and hardware of all sizes are accommodated. Most DBMSs are purchased from hardware or software vendors rather than being developed in-house; the most well-known commercial packages have hundreds of customer installations each. DBMS vendors now number in the dozens; there were a handful in 1970.

DBMS applications include maintenance of data involving banking, insurance, manufacturing, science, engineering, and government. The software is generalized so that few applications cannot be supported directly. The bibliographic field has not been a major target for DBMS use so far. Bibliographic applications generally involve very large files, long records with many data fields, optional fields in records, variable length fields, and access routes utilizing a variety of "keys" or terms. These complex requirements are not handled well by DBMSs that evolved in primarily numeric, coded data environments (e.g., payroll). The limitations are gradually being lifted.

Databases range in size from perhaps a few thousand to billions of characters (although billion-character databases are still not common). The definition of "large database" is changing even as this is being written; substantial increases in DASD capacities are making it possible to store enormous data collections online for manipulation through DBMSs.

HISTORICAL PERSPECTIVES

Pioneering Ideas

Many individually significant projects and systems mark the development of DBMSs, the earliest extending into the late 1950s. At that time a major task for application developers was simply to accommodate computer limitations involving the structuring and addressing of data; this proved to be more difficult than application development (SENKO, 1977). Generalized support software, including the symbolic assembler, procedural language compiler, and operating system, lifted some of the burden. The housekeeping related to data storage and retrieval, however, remained a problem.

Most innovations in this area arose from military and intelligence projects rather than industry development (FRY & SIBLEY). Early systems made major advancements, including the following (SENKO, 1977): 1) data definitions were separated from program code so that data content and structure changes could occur independently of program changes; and 2) user nonprocedural statements for retrieval were translated into machine-compatible instructions.

With the arrival of DASD came the random access systems. A major advance in this area was the development of random access methods supplied by a resident operating system. In the mid-1960s real-time systems gained significance; generalized data communications software was developed, with interfaces to data storage and retrieval software.

For practical operation and management (and commercial viability) a number of utility functions (file loading and unloading, recovery, etc.) were required. They were developed and joined the growing collection of components that comprise the modern DBMS. The DBMSs of today reflect software that is much more powerful, reliable, and efficient than the early systems.

Ancestry of Current DBMSs

This section gives brief histories of several major current DBMSs. FRY & SIBLEY provide a more complete review.

One of the most well-known current DBMSs is IMS/VS (Information Management System/Virtual Storage), the latest version of a series of systems dating to the mid-1960s. IMS is an outgrowth of the Apollo program and was a joint venture of Rockwell International and IBM. The original batch-only system was known as Data Language/1 (DL/1). IMS/360 was released in

1969, followed by IMS/360 Version 2 and more recently, IMS/VS (MCGEE, 1977).

Integrated Data Store (IDS), a DBMS for use on Honeywell computers, originated at General Electric Co. in 1964. Developed under the guidance of Charles Bachman, the latest version is known as IDS/II. The principles of IDS had a profound effect on the development of standards for DBMSs that were proposed by the Data Base Task Group of the Conference on Data Systems Languages (CODASYL, 1974).

B.F. Goodrich Co. implemented a system in the early 1970s for the IBM System/360 called the Integrated Data Management System (IDMS). The marketing and development of IDMS, a CODASYL-oriented system, have since been successfully taken over by Cullinane Corp. IDMS has been extended to operate on the Digital Equipment Corp.'s PDP/11 series of computers.

The Remote File Management System (RFMS) was developed in 1966 at the University of Texas. It was preceded by the Time-Shared Data Management System (TDMS) of System Development Corp. In 1970 a commercial package known as System 2000, a descendant of RFMS, was offered by MRI Systems Corp. System 2000 has been enhanced further and represents one of the better known current DBMSs.

ADABAS (Adaptable Database System) originated in West Germany at Software AG. The system slowly developed a U.S. customer base after it was imported in the early 1970s and is very popular today.

One of the most widely implemented DBMSs currently is TOTAL, first introduced in 1969 by CINCOM Systems, Inc. Although not constructed along the precise lines of the proposed CODASYL standards, TOTAL can store and process the data structures named in the CODASYL specifications. It is available on more types of hardware than any other DBMS.

MUMPS is a less well-known system, but it is one of special importance because of its specialization in non-numeric, character string, manipulations required in textual databases. MUMPS is not only a DBMS but also a language, one of three ANSI standard languages. It was originally developed for a mini-computer environment.

These DBMSs represent a small cross-section of the available packages. Their selection for discussion here is not an endorsement, simply an acknowledgment of their considerable role in the current DBMS industry. More complete listings of commercially available software are contained in AUERBACH PUBLISHERS and DATAPRO RESEARCH CORPORATION.

LOGICAL AND PHYSICAL DATABASES

The Contrast between Logical and Physical

Essential to effective discussion about databases and DBMSs is a clear perspective of the terms logical and physical. These terms help to divide a wealth of database concepts into manageable chunks; mixing heterogeneous notions such as data independence, hierarchies, relations, inverted indexes, and others is a confounding exercise. Failure or rejection of DBMSs and database projects in many organizations may have resulted from the inability to simplify a frustratingly complicated subject.

Data can be described as logical or physical. Logical descriptions refer to the way data appear to the application programmer, systems analyst, or end user. Physical descriptions refer to the way the data appear to data management software and to hardware (MARTIN, 1977; PRYWES & SMITH). Thus, the perception of a record on the database as a box that contains fields such as accession number, title, etc. is a logical view. The view of that record stored in a certain way at a specific location on a disk device (DASD) is a physical view. Terms such as hierarchies, relations, and inverted indexes can be organized under the concepts "logical" and "physical" for clarity; succeeding discussions in this section do just that.

Several authors in the recent literature have analyzed the logical and physical aspects of data (CHEN; SCHEUERMANN; SENKO ET AL.). What has emerged is a multilevel framework that describes data as stored and manipulated by DBMS software. A straightforward view of this framework is given in Figure 1 (adapted from SCHEUERMANN).

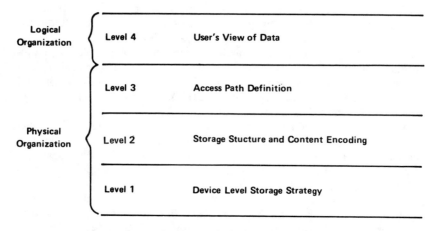

Figure 1. Multilevel framework for data

Level 4, the highest level of abstraction, is the logical view taken by a user of the DBMS (e.g., an application programmer). Such a logical view is often implicit in the data retrieval and storage statements coded in application programs. Lower levels show how one locates and stores data; these are physical considerations.

This framework offers a necessary and organized approach to database design. The approach asserts that design consists of two major stages. From specifications of the problem and services required, a logical organization is formulated; this logical view is then mapped to a physical one. The physical organization ensures operational tractability; in fact, service requirements (e.g., response time) may be so stringent as to demand a physical organization that complicates the logical view.

Logical and physical data organizations often show such trade-offs because the design objectives for each are different (MARTIN, 1977). For logical organizations, simplicity and stability are primary factors. For physical organizations, storage redundancy and access times are generally critical; simplicity can be neglected in physical organizations if performance is of paramount concern.

Implicit in the dual concepts of logical and physical organization is the notion that several different physical organizations can support the same logical view; how efficient these are depends on the DBMS, the hardware, and service requirements. The ability to separate the logical and physical views of data, permitting certain changes to one without having to change the other, is known as data independence. An example of data independence involves the ability to move a database physically from one DASD to another without changing the programs that normally use the database.

One certain aspect of database environments is that change will occur; the goal of data independence is to minimize the disruption when changes to logical or physical views are necessary. Different DBMSs protect against disruption to varying degrees (CURTICE, 1975). For some systems a simple change in logical view (e.g., allowing the insertion of a new type of data field to a record) precipitates an unload, redefinition, and reload of an entire database, which may be costly. Extending the allowable length of an existing field may be equally awkward. Insulating databases and programs to support stability of views and to provide for easy changes comes at a price in DBMS processing, but when the flexibility is needed, it can be crucial.

Logical Concepts: Data Models

Data models present a logical view of real entities and their relationships; it is about such things that a database is created.

An entity can be a person, place, event, or concept that we can identify. An entity identifier is called a key. A collection of similar entities forms an entity set. Entities can be described in terms of attributes (e.g., keys). Attributes assume specific values when they characterize a particular entity (KATZAN).

Attributes

	Accession Number	Title	Author	Publication Date
	2305	Database Systems	M. Moore	6/75
Entities	2306	Writing Style	R. T. Jones	2/78
	2307	Library Science	M. S. Peterson	1/79

Figure 2. Entity set example

A straightforward entity set is shown in Figure 2. Accession Number is a unique key. Author could be viewed as a key for some applications; if so, it is probably generic rather than unique. Entity sets can be represented figuratively by a labeled box (Figure 3). This notation is used in later examples.

Document

Figure 3. Entity set diagram for a collection of documents

Data models describe entity sets, entities, attributes, and their relationships; some of the popular models are hierarchical, network, and relational. Each is described more fully below, but remember that implementation (i.e., physical) details are not yet involved.

The hierarchical model, or tree, is a traditional mechanism for portraying relationships; organizational structures and outlines for written reports are commonly portrayed as hierarchies. Figure 4 shows a hierarchical structure.

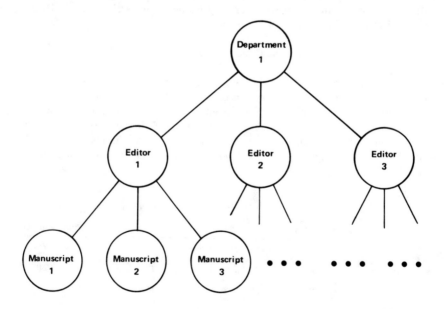

Figure 4. Typical hierarchy

Departments, Editors, and Manuscripts are identified as entity sets with hierarchical (one to many) relationships. Relationships between attributes and relationships between entities (e.g., Manuscripts 1 and 37 have the same author) are not modeled. If we define A↔B as "for one A there are many Bs, for one B there is one A," we can redraw this hierarchy in a more general way (Figure 5) (MARTIN, 1977).

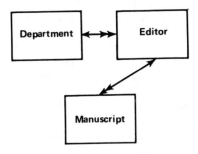

Figure 5. Typical hierarchy

Presumably a logical database could be described as having one logical record type for each entity set. The DBMS data definition language and supporting software would ultimately be required to accommodate such a logical view. Retrieval would be performed using keys defined for the entity sets (e.g., Manuscript Number).

One type of relationship between entity sets does not appear in the example above. This is the A↔B relationship: "for one A there are many Bs, for one B there are many As." In fact this relationship is forbidden in strict hierarchies (i.e., a node or leaf cannot reside on multiple branches of a tree).

Accommodating "many-to-many" relationships causes us to embrace network data models, of which hierarchical models are a subset. In Figure 6, Manuscripts and Authors have a many-to-many relationship. A relationship between Authors and Editors can be inferred but is not shown; it was not deemed necessary for this logical view.

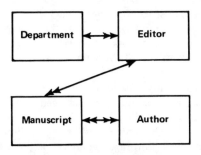

Figure 6. Network example

How such diagrams are derived depends on the logical database designer's view of what the entities are and how they relate. Beginning with the transactions an information system must support, the designer defines which entities and relationships exist. He must further determine the specific rules of correspondence (the A-to-B statements) for each relationship. This process produces a logical database design (or view) that must be supported by a DBMS later.

A logical view of data that is becoming prominent is that represented by the relational model. Relational concepts have been promoted by E.F. Codd of IBM (CODD) and have become the darling of database research in universities and industry. Some enthusiasm is warranted; simplicity and stability—goals of logical organization—are firmly supported by the relational approach. In addition, relational concepts can be described by rigorous mathematics; this basis promises to help make logical view construction (i.e., logical database design) much less intuitive and more algorithmic.

The relational model casts entities and their attributes in tabular form, similar to the entity set in Figure 2 (DATE, 1976). Relationships among attributes, entities, and entity sets are addressed by the relational model (attribute and entity relationships tend to be neglected in the others). The relational or tabular model avoids the logical pointers ($\leftrightarrow\rightarrow$) that are explicit in the other models by expressing them as relations (TSICHRITZIS & LOCHOVSKY, 1977).

Early debates were held on which of the data models is superior. It now appears that the relational model is a more formal, precise stage of modeling rather than a replacement for the hierarchical and network views (GERRITSEN; ROBINSON).

Physical Concepts

A DBMS provides storage and accessing support for data according to some logical view when it works with specific details of location and organization (the physical view). Physical aspects of storage and accessing differ markedly from logical aspects. Logical retrieval of a document record to a terminal screen is perceived as a single, simple action by the end user; the physical retrieval can be marked by index searching, pointer chain traversal, record key checking, and data translation. Other examples of physical considerations involving data storage and accessing follow.

It may be that data or messages regarding the data must traverse points of a geographically dispersed network of processing or storage sites; this property involves the concepts of distributed processing and distributed databases (discussed more fully later).

Data can be stored locally but on media from which they must be moved physically before use. For example, a record needed at a terminal might need to step from a mass storage device to a disk and from there to the main memory of the computer. In general, fast storage is limited in size, and large storage is limited in speed. "Storage hierarchy" is the term used to describe the cascade of memory devices needed to satisfy both capacity and response time demands.

The prospect of locating a record or records to service a data request is called record addressing, and it is a complex subject. One seeks techniques for locating records that provide acceptable service under various constraints. Four factors must be considered in determining a record-addressing scheme (SEVERANCE & CARLIS):

- The records to be stored—their size and volatility;
- The storage environment—its operating costs and access characteristics;
- The retrieval applications—their frequencies, priorities, criteria, and response requirements; and
- The design objective.

A simplified view suggests four major methods for locating records physically: the sequential, indexed, hashed, and pointer approaches.

Sequential record addressing is a tried-and-true method that originated in the earliest days of data processing. According to some key, records are placed physically in collated sequence (record A followed by record B, etc.).

Indexed addressing is done by creating a directory or index to the main body of records. The index can be viewed as a key value/record location table (Figure 7). The table is searched for the location of a given key (record surrogate), and the corresponding record is then accessed. This technique is also known as inverted indexing.

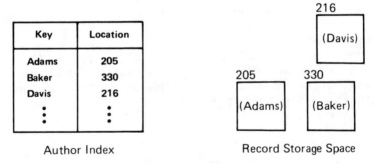

Figure 7. Indexed addressing

Hashing is a record-addressing technique that computes an appropriate location for a record from its key value according to some algorithm (Figure 8).

Pointers are physical address indicators that connect associated records. Starting from a head record, a chain of records can be traversed (Figure 9). Pointers can be set up to allow reverse as well as forward travel.

These physical addressing techniques can be combined to enhance retrieval performance; the selection of the best approach is not a trivial problem and has drawn some attention (AURDAL & SOLVBERG; CARDENAS,

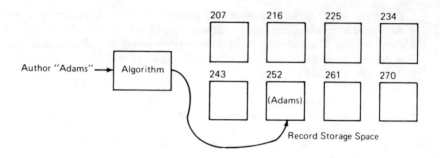

Figure 8. Hashed addressing

1975; SEVERANCE & CARLIS; SEVERANCE & DUHNE). Some authors have suggested that it would be valuable to automate the approach to this physical design problem (HAMMER, 1977). DBMSs differ in their techniques of record addressing; some utilize pointers, some indexing, others hashing. IMS/VS, for example, uses all of these (MCGEE, 1977).

Field addressing must be done by DBMSs when a desired record has been retrieved. For example, an application may require the publication date for the document whose accession number is 2305; this field is available somewhere in that document's record. Some DBMSs store fields in predefined locations (e.g., Publication Date begins in position 16 of the 500 characters comprising a document record). These DBMSs tend to lack data independence when fields are added or expanded, but locating a field is a trivial (and cheap) process.

Other DBMSs allow optional fields and variable length fields by not predefining field locations. The records must be searched internally at retrieval time to locate desired fields. These two field-addressing techniques exemplify the trade-off between economy and flexibility.

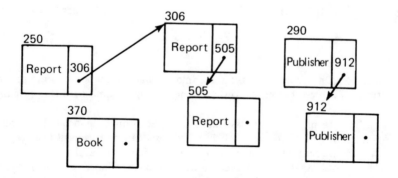

Figure 9. Pointer addressing

Other physical considerations remain. In storage, data fields are encoded according to some bit string convention (e.g., EBCDIC—Extended Binary Coded Decimal Interchange Code). Translation from one encoding to another may be needed to suit a logical view. Encrypting and decrypting of fields for security purposes is a similar effort. Fields also may need to be derived from existing fields (e.g., Priority Years from Publication Date).

Physical organizations of data differ greatly and apply to many levels. DBMSs vary considerably in their mechanisms for accommodating logical views by underlying physical representations (KROENKE; SENKO, 1977; TSICHRITZIS & LOCHOVSKY, 1977). Choice of a DBMS limits the techniques to be used, making DBMS selection an important process.

DBMS COMPONENTS AND ENVIRONMENT: A TECHNICAL VIEW

Components

The first section of this chapter described features that distinguish DBMSs from other software packages. These features are derived from a set of components common to most DBMSs (although details between systems may vary considerably). Figure 10 depicts these DBMS components in a general way (adapted from CURTICE, 1976).

Early DBMSs frequently lacked one or more of these components, but market pressures will cause commercial DBMSs to have them (CURTICE, 1976). Note how the components relate to an organization's staff. End users are generally preoccupied with the components and interfaces at the far left, application development staff with those in the middle, and database administrative staff (a new group) with those at the far right.

A key pair of components in the environment is represented by the data definition module and the set of database definitions ("1" in Figure 10). A language to provide definitions for the definition module is called the data definition language (DDL).

A proposed standard term for database definition is schema (CODASYL, 1976). The schema names all entities and attributes to appear in a database and describes relationships they may have (TSICHRITZIS & LOCHOVSKY, 1977). As such, it defines the logical database. The schema may also describe some aspects of the mapping to storage—e.g., block sizes for the files on DASD. In this regard, it doubles as a physical database definition. The logical specifications represent the database user; the physical specifications are required by the DBMS.

CODASYL has defined a logical view that represents a subset of the schema to be a "subschema" (CODASYL, 1976). One physical database may support many logical views if data independence is a strong feature of the DBMS. Subschemas can actually be defined and stored with the other database definitions; in most DBMSs however, specific logical views are implicit in the data manipulation statements of application programs (this practice somewhat obscures for an observer the logical view a program is actually taking).

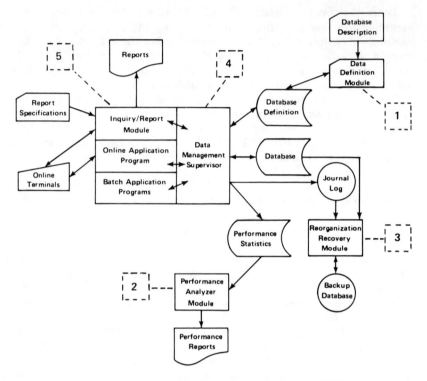

Figure 10. Generalized representation of a DBMS

The concept of data definitions that are external to application programs was vital to the evolution of DBMSs. A second step in this direction is the collection of all data definitions into a centralized library for reference and management. Many DBMS vendors are starting to provide data dictionary/ directories (DD/Ds) as part of their DBMS packages (SCHUSSEL).

Managing a complex software environment requires feedback on its activities. This need prompted DBMS users to ask vendors for performance reports on databases and database processing. Most commercial packages now offer some reporting facility, usually detailing online activities in the environment ("2" in Figure 10). This area of DBMS management is in its infancy; few systems provide adequate feedback to optimize their use, and self-optimizing features would be useful (HAMMER, 1977).

One critical function in the administration of databases is the ability to recover them in case of failures, such as program aborts, operating system crashes, and hardware failure. To this end, most DBMSs log images of changed database records to a special file (usually on a tape drive dedicated to the purpose) ("3" in Figure 10). Both "before" and "after" images of records can be logged, which, along with backup copies of the database, allow comprehensive failure recovery. The mere presence of these facilities does not guarantee adequate response to failure (CURTICE, 1977); a careful program must be established to ensure recovery (CANNING, 1976).

The data management supervisor is the central, memory-resident component of the DBMS ("4" in Figure 10). Memory requirements usually run about 300K bytes (much more in some cases); main memory committed to a DBMS has prompted more than one user to wonder where his once sufficient computer went (HINOMOTO; KOSS & NOONAN). This software interacts with applications and with the operating system access methods to store and to access data. It also controls multi-user concurrent access to databases. At the price of computer time, the DBMS data management supervisor greatly simplifies the interface between users and their data (i.e., by removing many details of the mapping between the physical organization and the logical organization).

Most DBMSs have a teleprocessing (TP) facility to allow online processing. It can be built in, or an interface can be provided to a popular TP monitor, such as IBM's CICS (Customer Information and Control System). In Figure 10 the TP monitor is subsumed into the data management supervisor ("4"). Critical factors involved with online processing through a DBMS include concurrent access control, memory use by online users, and response time. As stated, most DBMSs report on these factors in a limited way; tuning the online environment is still done mainly by trial and error—a potentially expensive approach.

The final component, the inquiry/report module ("5" in Figure 10), is an interface provided to end users and programmers. A straightforward language for batch reports and online queries is supplied, and the inquiry/report module translates these statements into actual program and data manipulation instructions. In general, more memory and computer time is expended for applications performed in the user-oriented languages than applications programmed in the traditional languages (COBOL, PL/1, Assembler). Nonetheless, staff time is conserved because the user-oriented languages are simpler and pack more punch per statement; less coding and debugging are involved. A definite trend will be to use inquiry/report facilities when computer resources are not critical (MCCRACKEN).

System Orientation

DBMSs are memory-resident software packages (at least the data management supervisor portion). Generally, only a single copy of the DBMS is present in memory, running as an application program. In another mode of operation, each application program uses its own copy of the DBMS, but considerable memory is expended and concurrent access control to databases is lost; the DBMS copies know nothing of each other.

The DBMS, as a special application program, is managed by the computer's operating system. The operating system access methods are the actual link to the physical databases for the DBMS (the DBMS is an intermediary to such system software and hardware functions for normal applications). Application programs invoke the DBMS through an interface language known as the data manipulation language (DML).

Operating Scenario

The inquiry/report module, online application programs, and batch application programs invoke the DBMS whenever data storage or access are needed. The requests are formulated in the data manipulation language (DML), which is specific to the DBMS. Figure 11 illustrates this activity using the PL/1 host language and the DML of IBM's IMS.

In step 1 the application asks for a record from the DBMS. Selection criteria in this example are implicit in the DML statement (CALL PLITDLI, etc.). The DBMS, using physical organization knowledge (access routes, location data), formulates specific retrieval requests for the operating system access methods (step 2). The access methods retrieve the data (step 3) and return them to the DBMS (step 4). The DBMS may have to manipulate the returned data into the logical view (subschema) needed by the application. Finally in step 5 the data are delivered to a work area in the application program.

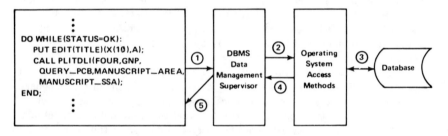

Figure 11. Batch application invoking a DBMS

Online applications and inquiry/report functions proceed in a similar fashion. Much checking and other details have been omitted from this example. Different DBMSs vary in the exact procedures followed and in their mapping capabilities; an argument for standardization is that DBMSs vary so widely in data definition and data manipulation interfaces (BERG).

DBMS OPERATIONAL AND ORGANIZATIONAL IMPACTS: A MANAGEMENT VIEW

Data Issues and Organizational Effects

The installation of a DBMS exerts a powerful effect on the data processing environment of an organization. A survey by MATTHEWS & SMITH rated DBMS installation second only to change of computer mainframe vendor as a disruptive influence. Those considering buying a DBMS or changing to a new one would do well to heed this ominous note. Other authors underline the reasons for a careful evaluation of prospective packages, of an organization's requirements, and of an organization's comprehension of and commitment to such a change (KOSS & NOONAN; PATTERSON; STERNBERG).

Earlier discussions have focused on advantages of DBMSs; they provide for data sharing, improved data quality, and management control of data (BENBASAT & GOLDSTEIN). Unfortunately, squabbles and confusion can arise on several fronts. Accountability for shared data is a complex organizational issue; data quality, when more data are being computerized and manipulated more often, becomes a serious problem (HAMMER, 1976). Ensuring the privacy and security of shared data must also be resolved; paradoxically, a DBMS that provides easy access to data must make an about-face in some cases and tenaciously refuse access (GUDES ET AL.).

User departments may find their data processing bills soaring for new DBMS applications (KOSS & NOONAN). A DBMS, as an extra layer of software, costs more than conventional access methods in computer time and input/output operations. More data are probably being processed through direct, simple interfaces to the system, but few users recognize that ease of use and increased volume offset higher data processing charges.

Other organizational effects are apparent. Because each DBMS has its own DDL and DML, considerable training may be needed for programmers and other processing staff to utilize these key languages effectively.

New organizational policies and standards will be necessary. One area that many organizations find in terrible disarray initially is that of data fields; data sharing requires discipline and control in this area (ROCKE). Instituting data field standards, however, may precipitate technical and political problems. Similar data fields may have had different names and formats in previously separate applications; these practices may be well entrenched (e.g., involving publications, policy manuals, and day-to-day procedures).

Creation of a DD/D involves standardizing data field definitions (and may also involve file, program, and other forms of documentation). The literature describes the virtues of DD/Ds at length (SCHUSSEL; UHROWCZIK; WALSH, 1978b). Although DD/Ds are critical in building a database environment, with few exceptions (EHRENSBERGER), little is made of the immense effort that may be required to populate them with standardized documentation.

One factor of DBMS commitment with vast implications is that a very expensive resource (data) is concentrated within a potentially vulnerable environment. After a time hard-copy backup may cease to exist. Recovery from program, operating system, hardware, and computer center failures is a paramount consideration (CANNING, 1976; CURTICE, 1977).

Finally, many organizations underestimate the inertia of existing systems and their data organizations and formats. Data conversion (from the physical organization now supported to that supported by the new DBMS) can be expensive (FRY ET AL.).

Database Administration

To ease the transitional problems in implementing a DBMS, many organizations have defined a new job function called database administration. One description of this responsibility is (LEONG-HONG & MARRON, 1978): "to optimize usage of data in a shared database environment; to incorporate a systematic methodology for the centralized management and control of data resources; and to balance conflicting objectives with respect to the organization's mission and the overall economy of data handling."

Several authors (LEONG-HONG & MARRON, 1978; ROSS, 1976) have compiled lists of functions for database administration, which include: database definition and standardization; selection and procurement of data management software; database design; database loading and testing; database security and integrity; database performance; liaison with users and systems staff; and training of users and systems staff. Early articles tended to describe the function as carried out by a single individual; it is now clear that the broad responsibilities call for a staff of database administrators (DBAs). Both technical and administrative tasks are involved. LYON suggests that a database administration unit might include the following: a manager; a DBMS expert; a database designer; a user/applications liaison; and a data definition and recovery expert.

The number of staff members and their assignments vary from one organization to another. Placement of the unit in the organizational hierarchy has been discussed in the literature. Generally, database administration is more successful the higher the level; if it reports only to the management of systems development or data processing operations, it cannot address organization-wide issues fairly (YASAKI).

Database administration finds itself in a sensitive position. New procedures and standards must be initiated, and disputes must be resolved; most of all, the organization's valuable data resources must be carefully protected. DBAs need a variety of skills that command the respect and backing of the organization.

Staff Perspectives

Data stored with one physical organization can be perceived as having various logical organizations (logical views) by different users (end users, programmers, DBAs, etc.). According to this concept, we consider appropriate "logical views" or perspectives on an installed DBMS below.

Systems programmers and operations staff can consider a DBMS as computer-resident software, similar to an operating system. Because most DBMSs are not delivered with program code, such software is a form of black box. This untouchable aspect is not all bad; it precludes introduction of subtle errors by customer changes to DBMS programs. Systems programmers and operations staff must observe vendor-supplied instructions for DBMS support and operation.

Systems analysts and applications programmers perceive a DBMS as a facility to simplify the development of applications with complex data storage and accessing requirements. Proper DBMS use at this level requires training and possibly a shift to more rigorous development and design procedures (FINNERAN & HENRY).

Database administration staff should consider the DBMS, along with a DD/D, as their major tool to promote effective use of data. It is incumbent on DBAs to play a major role during selection, installation, and operation of a DBMS.

End users should perceive a DBMS as a powerful data access and storage mechanism. The potential exists for vastly improved delivery of their data, with less lead time, with more variety in packaging, and with more retrieval options. These benefits come at a price in computer resources, but such costs are falling dramatically compared with personnel costs (PHISTER).

Management can look at a DBMS as an investment in overall control of an expensive, valuable resource—data, but several caveats are:

- A DBMS alone represents only part of a commitment to a database approach. A database administration function is needed. A DD/D should be built. An organizational understanding of database concepts and goals is necessary.
- DBMS introduction should proceed conservatively because a large-scale change in data processing to the organization will occur. Sound businesss decisions are needed.
- Although the potential for efficient, nonredundant, shared use of data exists, computer loads may not diminish. More data will be stored and used in more ways than ever before; most organizations have a latent need for the capabilities a DBMS can provide.

Management plays a critical role in the implementation of a database approach (thus, a DBMS) in an organization. DBMS installation is a step upward that needs to be made carefully and with deliberation (CUOZZO & KURTZ; MCFADDEN & SUVER), but it can usher in a new era for the organization (NOLAN).

COMMERCIAL OFFERINGS AND REPORTED ACTIVITIES

Commercial DBMS Packages

Organizations who move to a DBMS are confronted by a formidable array of commercial products. The alternative of building one's own DBMS is by now rarely viable; too many hours are required to produce a package that may well be inferior to a commercial offering. If a package that is less complex than a full DBMS seems appropriate, several good data management systems (e.g., MARK IV from Informatics and EASYTRIEVE from Pansophic Systems, Inc.) are available and probably represent a better investment than an in-house effort.

In this section describing commercial DBMSs, each package is characterized by the logical and physical terms explained earlier. The logical terms "hierarchy," "network," and "relation" are used to describe the data models supported by the packages. Physical terms such as "indexing," "hashing," and "pointers" describe how DBMSs retrieve records.

The packages have been selected because they are popular and used widely. Other packages exist, which are in no obvious way of lesser quality; however, the line must be drawn somewhere among the dozens of entries in the marketplace.

IMS/VS

IMS/VS is the latest offering from IBM in the DBMS arena. Various configurations are possible, including one with an integrated database/data communications (DB/DC) (teleprocessing) feature: IMS DB/DC. IMS supports COBOL, PL/1, and Assembler procedural languages, but query/report (user) language facilities must be obtained from an outside vendor.

IMS uses a hierarchical approach for data modeling, but networks can be implemented with "logical segments"—record types defined to relate separate hierarchies. Indexing, hashing, and pointers are all used for record retrieval; the design alternative is left to the analyst. IMS is often criticized for its complexity; training requirements for an installation's staff are usually substantial (WALSH, 1978a).

Security and recovery are considered excellent in IMS. Data independence extends only to the record level, not the field level as in other DBMSs, thereby rendering IMS-using programs somewhat sensitive to database changes. IMS is a powerful DBMS with relatively high operating and administrative costs (ROSS, 1978). It is available only for lease. The present user community has over 1,000 members.

IDS/II

IDS/II is the latest in a long line of DBMS software products from Honeywell. The package is designed around the CODASYL Data Base Task Group specifications and supports programming in COBOL. Query language facilities are offered. IDS/II as a CODASYL implementation supports network models of data. The system is primarily a pointer user, but indexing has been introduced. Overall, IDS/II is a well-established system for Honeywell machines. IDS/I, the previous version, had approximately 400 users (ROSS, 1978).

IDMS

IDMS is a package offered by Cullinane Corp. and represents the only major CODASYL implementation on IBM equipment. The package can be interfaced with commercial TP monitors for online work. FORTRAN, PL/1, COBOL, and Assembler procedural language support is included, as are query/report facilities. A data dictionary is integrated into the system. IDMS supports network data models and is a pointer user. Indexing has been added. IDMS is a vigorously developing package with several hundred users.

System 2000 (S2000)

S2000 is offered by MRI Systems Corp. and operates on IBM, Control Data Corp., and Sperry UNIVAC equipment. MRI offers its own TP monitor, but others can be used. Support for COBOL, FORTRAN, PL/1, and Assembler procedural languages is included, along with a query language feature. A data dictionary facility called Control 2000 is available. S2000 supports hierarchical data models and uses indexes for retrieval. Overall, the system seems well furnished, although some users have reported performance problems. The system has several hundred installations.

ADABAS

ADABAS is a DBMS for IBM systems marketed by Software AG. A TP monitor (Com-plete) is available, but others can be used. COBOL, FORTRAN, PL/1, and Assembler procedural languages are supported, and query/report facilities are included. Variable and optional fields are handled without wasted space, providing significant database compression for physical storage. ADABAS supports logical hierarchies and networks (but with restrictions on the implementation of hierarchies on a single physical file). Relations can be stored as ADABAS files and linked, providing a precursor relational database capability. ADABAS is an index-using system. Data independence at the field level is a high point. The system, aggressively marketed, has several hundred installations.

TOTAL

TOTAL is offered by CINCOM Systems, Inc. and is available on more varieties of hardware than any other DBMS. Online support is available through CINCOM's Environ/1 TP monitor or others. COBOL, FORTRAN, PL/1, and Assembler languages are supported.

TOTAL supports network data models similar to the CODASYL approach, although it is not defined according to CODASYL specifications. The system uses hashing and pointers for retrieval. It consumes fewer computer resources than other systems. The user community for TOTAL has more than 2,000 members, the largest among the popular DBMSs.

Other DBMS Packages

Many other packages are available. They accommodate computers of all sizes and makes. Prospective purchasers of minicomputer DBMSs should note that some of them lack features that are available on large system packages and may even dominate the lesser computer resources available with mini-computers (BOYLAN). Nonetheless, good minicomputer/DBMS systems are possible (GIBBONS).

Conspicuously absent from a list of widely recognized commercial DBMSs is a relational system (i.e., one that directly supports relations as data models). MAGNUM, available from Tymshare, Inc. via a communications network, is a relational facility, but no plans have been reported for in-house installations.

DBMS Selection

The proper selection of a DBMS package is not as simple as contacting vendors for sales presentations. At least two evaluation phases are necessary. The first involves a determination of needs, expected costs and benefits, and impact on the organization. The second phase is the technical evaluation of market packages.

In most organizations the evaluation begins with the selection of a team whose members represent a cross-section of affected departments (CODASYL, 1976)—e.g., a systems programmer, applications analyst, end user, and other hardware and software specialists (including a database administrator if that function exists).

The first evaluation phase should produce documents stating the need for a DBMS and the expected impacts (the degree of preparation and acceptance across the organization is important). Costs and benefits should be stated as accurately as possible (MCFADDEN & SUVER). Requirements and criteria for a DBMS should be formulated. This phase should not be done by vendors; their business is to sell packages (DATAPRO RESEARCH CORPORATION; ROSS, 1978). If an organization needs assistance, a consulting firm may be the answer.

The technical evaluation phase compares requirements with the capabilities of available packages. A number of excellent descriptions for this step are available (ADAM; AUERBACH PUBLISHERS; CODASYL, 1976; ROSS, 1978). A general outline of the recommended practice is:

- Weight each requirement based on an average value of say, 100;
- Rate competing packages on a scale of 1-10 with respect to the requirements; and
- Multiply each rating by the appropriate weighting factor and total over all requirements for each system.

An abbreviated example of this process is shown in Figure 12.

Requirement	Weight	Ratings		
		Ideal	DBMS A	DBMS B
Query Language	200	10	5	8
Memory Usage	50	10	3	5
Variable Records	150	10	0	5
Security	200	10	10	8
Recovery	250	10	10	10
Totals (Sum Weight x Rating)		8500	5650	6700

Figure 12. DBMS selection

Such a process must be used with considerable care and understanding. Despite its apparent objectivity, judgment goes into the selection of requirements, weights, and ratings. The evaluation team should ensure that the numeric results are intuitively reasonable. Universal acceptance of the requirements, weights, and ratings among an evaluation team is not necessary, but the team must have some confidence in its consensus judgments. The rating process may be hampered further by the hesitancy of vendors to reveal internal details of their proprietary software; most can be pressed into supplying the necessary facts, however. Finally, performance is often highly rated as a DBMS requirement. Benchmarking, simulation, and modeling can be used to compare systems (AUERBACH PUBLISHERS). In the author's experience, time and technical limitations preclude most performance comparisons except simple input/output analytical models; these are often revealing enough.

Reported Activities

The number and kinds of applications to which DBMSs have been subjected are too numerous to list. For example, the literature reports personnel, banking, real estate, insurance, production control, and others (AUERBACH PUBLISHERS; FONG ET AL.; GIBBONS: HINOMOTO; KOSS & NOONAN; SIMONSON & ALSBROOKS; STERNBERG). True horror stories about implementations are apparently seldom documented, although those who are most familiar with the field would agree that disasters occasionally happen. Some literature describing unhappy experiences is available and makes worthwhile reading (KOSS & NOONAN; STERNBERG). In essence these documents describe the disadvantages of a DBMS as cited earlier in this chapter. They underscore the observation that DBMS processing is often unsuccessful as a one-for-one replacement of traditional batch applications using system-provided sequential access methods. A different design approach is generally required with DBMSs; high-volume batch processing is often too costly. Whether or not an organization's needs can be met by other means may be the trickiest part of defining requirements in the DBMS selection process.

CURRENT LIMITATIONS AND ISSUES

An image of DBMSs has emerged in practice and in the literature. DBMSs represent powerful, generalized software packages that are capable of most facets of data management. Nonetheless, problems arise in this developing field that plague the wary and unwary alike. By no means is operation of a database-oriented shop as simple as vendor sales literature implies. This section of the chapter summarizes some of the current issues.

One problem with DBMSs involves data models. Although debate has raged over the relative values of hierarchical, network, and relational models, all have been used successfully. The newest entry (relational) simply represents a more formal way to define entities and relationships without injecting physical considerations into the logical model.

The major difficulty with data models is that the average systems analyst is not using any of them in a disciplined fashion—file design is being done primarily by intuition and tradition. This explains why some installed DBMSs are being used as high-priced access methods. Design is seldom separated into logical and physical phases; many logical database designs are shot through with program-accommodating features (e.g., special record types and pointers). These practices are still widespread despite the fact that good design approaches have appeared in the literature (FINNERAN & HENRY; KROENKE; MARTIN, 1977; SEVERANCE & CARLIS; TSICHRITZIS & LOCHOVSKY, 1978).

Prospective purchasers of DBMS software should look out for limitations in data structuring and handling. Some DBMSs support hierarchies on a single physical file only with severe restrictions. Others do not handle variable length, optional, or repeating fields well. These limitations can frustrate database designers.

Concurrent updating is a problem that many DBMSs themselves solve for the buyer. This issue arises, for example, when several online users wish to operate on the same data. The key requirement is to maintain data consistency—not to let one user make decisions based on out-of-date data or erase the effects of the other's processing. DBMSs will "lock" data during update to prevent such difficulties, but some systems lock at the record level, some at the file level. The level of locking is important because file accessibility is temporarily impaired.

Many DBMSs have limited capabilities for checking the validity of data being entered for storage. This problem has considerable significance (HAMMER, 1976). Application programs can edit data, but in large, complex, evolving application systems, the types and locations of data checking can become obscure. Inconsistent and even conflicting edits may result. Database definitions and DD/Ds should play an integral role with DBMSs in ensuring data quality by providing easy-to-reference validation criteria.

Privacy and security of data is another growing issue. Most DBMSs provide some facilities for protection and recovery. Devious humans however, usually can get what they seek. Organizations need to take a comprehensive approach; a few DBMS passwords provide only superficial protection (BERG; TSICHRITZIS & LOCHOVSKY, 1977).

Data independence is a serious concern. The need for change in data processing environments is strong; new record types, new fields, and changed field specifications should be integrated into a database with a minimum of disruption (MARTIN, 1976). Different DBMSs provide varying levels of data independence, some to only a limited degree (CURTICE, 1975).

A final problem involves the distribution or centralization of data. Because of decreasing hardware prices, significant computer power can be located at end user sites; whether this should be so and whether the concomitant data should also be so located is problematic. A distributed database can be viewed as a single logical database that is stored physically on devices that are not all attached to one computer (DAVENPORT). Many approaches are possible (CHAMPINE, 1977; CODASYL, 1978; ELAM & STUTZ). This environment can be very complex because of the myriad possible interactions (DAVENPORT; MARYANSKI & FISHER).

Performance and Costs

Most large-scale users of DBMSs confront performance and cost problems at some point. These problems stem from various sources:

- The technical staff may not be well trained in optimization techniques or in the basic physical strengths and weaknesses of the package available (CARDENAS, 1975; DUHNE & SEVERANCE; GHOSH & TUEL; SEVERANCE & CARLIS; SILER). Such cases lend credence to the claim that database designs should be reviewed carefully by specially trained database administration staff.
- Many DBMS packages do not report sufficient data on their performance to allow analysis of apparent problems.
- An application may press the limits of the hardware environment, especially with the overhead of DBMS software.

Standardization

The CODASYL Database Task Group (DBTG) has proposed standards for data manipulation and data definition languages (CODASYL, 1974). The American National Standards Institute (ANSI) could act on these proposals to set DBMS standards (this has not been done yet). Vigorous arguments have been made on both sides, with proponents making reasonable statements describing the benefits of standardization (AUERBACH PUBLISHERS; BERG).

Those opposed also have strong arguments, generally based on two ideas:

- Most installed DBMSs do not fit the proposed standards. The common sense of vendors and purchasers of these packages would be suspect, given their present investment, were they to support a massive changeover.
- By no means is there agreement among practitioners that the CODASYL DBTG proposals represent the best path for DBMSs. Backers of this point cite the danger that standardization that is too early will constrict technical development in a new field.

The controversy surrounding standardization somewhat confounds DBMS package selection. However, effective standardization clearly seems years away whether or not the CODASYL Data Base Task Group proposals are accepted by ANSI.

Organizational and Administrative Problems

One of the common problem situations at present involves the inability of database administration units to carry out appropriate functions because of staff limitations or lack of decision-making power. A frequent scenario is one in which database administration begins as a function that is tacked on at the end of DBMS installation; its main role is to provide technical support for database definitions and perhaps file recoveries. The unit may report to application system development management, which further limits its effectiveness. A survey of practicing database administrators (LEONG-HONG & MARRON, 1978) advises that database administration requires (among other things): management support, planning, skilled staff, and finally, patience. The proper organizational placement and role for database administration remain a problem in many organizations (DEBLASIS & JOHNSON).

Related to this problem is the determination of what actually comprises an organization's database (i.e., that which is to be administered). A narrow point of view includes only computer-readable data; a broad view includes all data that flow through the organization (BRYCE). With the ubiquitous appearance of online terminals and word processing systems it is somewhat amusing that these views are merging. Thus potentially to be managed are DBMS and non-DBMS accessed data, in both conventional and distributed applications.

A growing number of organizations face the DBMS/non-DBMS data problem because old applications are too expensive and involved to allow conversion all at once. Some organizations implement multiple DBMSs, compounding the issue further.

STATE-OF-THE-ART AND TRENDS

Proliferation

The first section of this chapter described the rapid growth in the DBMS field during the 1970s. Recent sources (FONG ET AL.; ROSS, 1978) suggest that the number of installations for the most popular DBMSs has grown on the average more than 20% per year. This rate will ultimately decrease, but at this point it attracts many new vendors. The availability of DBMSs for minicomputers adds fuel for a continuing growth phase. DBMS software will be pervasive in the coming decades.

DBMS Evolution

The major DBMSs have now been marketed for five or more years; drastic changes in their methods or capabilities probably should not be expected until the mid-1980s (CURTICE, 1976). Nonetheless, evolutionary improvements will be made (and are needed). Among the types of facilities and enhancements expected by BERG and by CURTICE (1976) in major systems are:

- Network data models will be supported;
- Sequential, indexed, and hashed access will be available;
- Variable length, repeating, and optional fields will be supported;
- Improved validity checking will be possible;
- Data independence at the field level will be supported;
- Recovery and backup will be more straightforward;
- Better statistics for performance tuning will be supplied; and
- Improved user-oriented language capabilities will appear.

Some current systems furnish most of these capabilities. However, in all cases enhancements are needed. DBMSs seem to be evolving to a more-or-less common set of capabilities (because of market pressures, not standards). Hardware improvements and DBMS software advances may mitigate some of the present performance difficulties, although our problem-solving scope will probably expand. Such expansion is likely to include more bibliographic applications, for which improved DBMSs will be more suited. Publishers, libraries, and information centers will commonly use DBMSs as tools for data storage, retrieval, and manipulation in a wide variety of applications.

Relational DBMSs

Of the advances in data management receiving attention, relational database systems probably reign supreme. CODD described relational concepts in a now classic paper. Other good descriptions have also appeared, which clarify the new terminology introduced (DATE, 1975; DATE, 1976; MARTIN, 1977).

The logical view of a relational database is a collection of simple tables, called relations. The relations are constructed according to rules for "normalization," which constitute a formal way to define entities, attributes, and relationships. The strength of relational concepts lies in the simplicity of the data model and its desirable properties of data independence, full retrieval, and database consistency.

At present the physical elements of relational systems are the familiar, mundane ones: relational systems use sequential scanning, hashing, pointers, and indexes to locate data. The retrieval power inherent in the logical organization is accomplished by considerable addressing and mapping efforts expended on the physical organization. As a result, present relational prototypes tend to give poor performance (CURTICE, 1976). The performance should improve greatly with new hardware technology—e.g., the content-addressability capability (discussed later). Nonrelational approaches would also benefit from immense strides in hardware.

Present efforts with relational systems are mostly experimental rather than commercial—e.g., IBM's System R development (ASTRAHAN). Nonetheless, some commercial offerings on a limited scale should be available in the early 1980s (CURTICE, 1976).

Distributed Databases

A volume of literature is available on distributed databases (CHAMPINE, 1977; CODASYL, 1978; DAVENPORT; HARDGRAVE; MARYANSKI). Most authors are cautiously optimistic, and CHAMPINE describes some successful implementations. It is clear that building an integrated network of databases is not yet for the inexperienced or those with limited development funds; the technology and management approaches for this complex environment are too new. Great numbers of distributed database applications are not expected soon (CURTICE, 1976); in fact, no commercial DBMS at present directly supports a logical database that is physically distributed.

Minicomputers and DBMSs

Minicomputers with considerable power are in the price range of many small organizations. DBMSs can aid such organizations in the data management problems brought by computerization. Resource limitations are among the difficulties involved in putting DBMSs on minicomputers (BENBASAT & GOLDSTEIN; FLOAM). Nonetheless, as the power and sophistication of these devices grow, DBMS usage will become prevalent. DBMS software cost for some minicomputer systems will probably exceed the price of the hardware.

Back-End Computers

In the area of back-end computers, data accessing and storage are removed from a mainframe and placed within a dedicated minicomputer (although mainframes can also be used as back-ends). Use of a back-end can have the following advantages (BAUM & HSIAO; MARYANSKI ET AL.):

- Mainframe memory and workload requirements are reduced;
- Database protection is handled by a machine that is out of the direct reach of application programs; and
- Database manipulation commands should be executed more efficiently, if they are not performed on the general-purpose hardware.

Experimental setups of back-end computers have been reported (CANADAY ET AL.), but no commercial products are available. Some believe that a future option from DBMS vendors will be a hardware box (i.e., back-end) with the DBMS functions built in (CHAMPINE, 1978).

Memory Developments

Main memory, disks (both fixed and movable head), and tapes have traditionally provided storage for data. Two kinds of changes are imminent with respect to memory components. First, new components such as IBM's 3850 mass storage, Memorex's 3770 disk cache, and STC's 4305 solid state disk will begin to be used widely (WITHINGTON, 1978). Thus, more of a continuum from slow, large-capacity memory to fast, small-capacity memory will be created. For database builders, physical storage and retrieval will gain speed at the expense of hardware complexity. System users, however, probably will be insulated from this physical complexity by software that manages the details of locating data (e.g., whether the data reside at the moment on mass storage, disk, disk cache, or in main memory).

A second notable change will be in available memory size in each category of memory device. Present single-disk devices have capacities of one-half billion bytes; billion-byte rotating devices should be forthcoming (WITH-INGTON, 1978). Main memory of five million bytes is used at many sites now. Computer systems with at least five times this much main memory should be delivered in the mid-1980s.

An interesting prediction for DBMSs can be made in view of the coming availability of larger, fast memory. Index-using DBMSs may hold a considerable advantage over pointer users. This is because pointer chain traversal in fast memory would require that much of a database be present (even 50 million bytes is not sufficient to hold a large database). However, indexes for databases often are much smaller than the database itself; whole indexes that reside in fast memory should make retrieval very rapid. The near-term growth in fast-memory capacity may provide sufficient space for index-using systems to stage database indexes for processing.

A final memory advancement is content-addressable storage. Instead of specifying a physical record address through indexes, hashing, or pointers, a DBMS will simply furnish a key to the operating system access method (e.g., Accession Number). The appropriate data will then be delivered. This process does not involve a "magic" record-addressing scheme. Proposed implementations call for numerous parallel search components to perform sequential scans on partitions of the stored data until the needed record is found (CHAMPINE, 1978; COULOURIS ET AL.). Large-capacity content-addressable memory implemented in this fashion is beginning to be commercially available.

CONCLUSION

The field of database management systems is growing rapidly. Improvements in management techniques, organizational perspectives, and computer software and hardware are needed because database practitioners now commonly experience the ambivalent feelings of delight and despair. Nonetheless, a sense of long-term confidence is inescapable.

As a result of the pressures to create and to manage databases, a reservoir of experience is building among hardware and software vendors, applications people, and managers. By the early 1980s the major packages will have been operating for a decade.

Some database failures are part of the future because the industry always insists on attempting implementations that stretch skills and technology. This is as it should be; with growing experience, steps once taken gingerly can be taken with assurance.

BIBLIOGRAPHY

ADAM, ROBERT G. 1978. Making the Move to Database Technology. ICP INTERFACE Data Processing Management. 1978 Summer: 6-17. Available from: International Computer Programs, Inc., 9000 Keystone Crossing, Indianapolis, IN.

ASTRAHAN, M.M. 1976. System R: Relational Approach to Data Base Management. ACM Transactions on Database Systems. 1976 June; 1(2): 621-628. ISSN: 0362-5915.

AUERBACH PUBLISHERS, INCORPORATED. 1978. Data Base Management. Pennsauken, NJ: Auerbach Publishers, Inc.; 1978. 1 volume (discontinuous paging). (Auerbach Information Management Series).

AURDAL, EIVIND; SOLVBERG, ARNE. 1977. A Multi-Level Procedure for Design of File Organizations. In: Korfhage, Robert R., ed. Proceedings of the American Federation of Information Processing Societies (AFIPS) 1977 National Computer Conference (NCC): Volume 46; 1977 June 13-16; Dallas, TX. Montvale, NJ: AFIPS Press, 210 Summit Grove Avenue; 1977. 509-521. LC: 55-44701.

BACHMAN, CHARLES W. 1972. The Evolution of Storage Structures. Communications of the ACM. 1972 July; 15(7): 628-634. ISSN: 0588-8069.

BACHMAN, CHARLES W. 1973. The Programmer as Navigator. Communications of the ACM. 1973 November; 16(11): 653-658. ISSN: 0588-8069.

BAUM, RICHARD I.; HSIAO, DAVID K. 1976. Database Computers—A Step toward Data Utilities. IEEE Transactions on Computers. 1976 December; C-25(12): 1254-1259. ISSN: 0018-9340.

BENBASAT, IZAK; GOLDSTEIN, ROBERT C. 1977. Data Base Systems for Small Business: Miracle or Mirage? Data Base. 1977 Summer; 9(1): 5-8. ISSN: 0095-0033.

BERG, JOHN L., ed. 1976. Data Base Directions—The Next Steps. Washington, DC: National Bureau of Standards (NBS); Association for Computing Machinery (ACM); 1976 September. 175p. (NBS Special Publication no. 451). CODEN: XNBSAV; LC: 76-608219.

BOYLAN, DAVID. 1977. Minicomputer DBMS: Less than Meets the Eye. Computer Decisions. 1977 January; 9(1): 50-54. ISSN: 0010-4558.

BRYCE, TIM. 1978. The DBMS in Data Management. ICP INTERFACE Data Processing Management. 1978 Summer: 18-19. Available from: International Computer Programs, Inc., 9000 Keystone Crossing, Indianapolis, IN.

CANADAY, R.H.; HARRISON, R.D.; IVIE, E.L.; RYDER, J.L.; WEHR, L.A. 1974. A Back-End Computer for Data Base Management. Communications of the ACM. 1974 October; 17(10): 575-582. ISSN: 0588-8069.

CANNING, RICHARD G. 1976. Recovery in Data Base Systems. EDP Analyzer. 1976 November; 14(11): 11p. ISSN: 0012-7523.

CANNING, RICHARD G. 1978. Installing a Data Dictionary. EDP Analyzer. 1978 January; 16(1): 13p. ISSN: 0012-7523.

CARDENAS, ALFONSO F. 1973. Evaluation and Selection of File Organization—A Model and System. Communications of the ACM. 1973 September; 16(9): 540-548. ISSN: 0588-8069.

CARDENAS, ALFONSO F. 1975. Analysis and Performance of Inverted Data Base Structures. Communications of the ACM. 1975 May; 18(5): 253-263. ISSN: 0588-8069.

CHAMPINE, GEORGE A. 1977. Six Approaches to Distributed Data Bases. Datamation. 1977 May; 23(5): 69-72. ISSN: 0011-6963.

CHAMPINE, GEORGE A. 1978. Four Approaches to a Data Base Computer. Datamation. 1978 December; 24(12): 101-106. ISSN: 0011-6963.

CHEN, PETER PIN-SHAN. 1976. The Entity-Relationship Model—Toward a Unified View of Data. ACM Transactions on Database Systems. 1976 March; 1(1): 9-36. ISSN: 0362-5915.

CODASYL. DATA DESCRIPTION LANGUAGE COMMITTEE. 1974. CODASYL Data Description Language. Washington, DC: US Department of Commerce, National Bureau of Standards (NBS); January 1974. 155p. (NBS Handbook 113). USGPO: C13.6/2:113.

CODASYL. SYSTEMS COMMITTEE. 1976. Selection and Acquisition of Data Base Management Systems. New York, NY: Association for Computing Machinery (ACM); 1976. 252p. Available from: ACM Order Dept., P.O. Box 12105, Church Street Station, New York, NY 10249.

CODASYL. SYSTEMS COMMITTEE. 1978. Distributed Data Base Technology—An Interim Report of the CODASYL Systems Committee. In: Ghosh, Sakti P.; Liu, Leonard Y., eds. Proceedings of the American Federation of Information Processing Societies (AFIPS) 1978 National Computer Conference: Volume 47; 1978 June 5-8; Anaheim, CA. Montvale, NJ: AFIPS Press, 210 Summit Avenue; 1978. 909-917. LC: 55-44701.

CODD, E.F. 1970. A Relational Model of Data for Large Shared Data Banks. Communications of the ACM. 1970 June; 13(6): 377-387. ISSN: 0588-8069.

COULOURIS, G.F.; EVANS, J.M.; MITCHELL, R.W. 1972. Towards Content-Addressing in Data Bases. The Computer Journal (England). 1972 May; 15(2): 95-98. ISSN: 0010-4620.

CUOZZO, D.E.; KURTZ, J.F. 1973. Building a Base for Data Base: A Management Perspective. Datamation. 1973 October; 19(10): 71-75. ISSN: 0011-6963.

CURTICE, ROBERT M. 1975. Data Independence in Data Base Systems. Datamation. 1975 April; 21(4): 65-71. ISSN: 0011-6963.

CURTICE, ROBERT M. 1976. The Outlook for Data Base Management. Datamation. 1976 April; 22(4): 46-49. ISSN: 0011-6963.

CURTICE, ROBERT M. 1977. Integrity in Data Base Systems. Datamation. 1977 May; 23(5): 64-68. ISSN: 0011-6963.

DATAPRO RESEARCH CORPORATION. 1977. A Buyer's Guide to Data Base Management Systems. In: DATAPRO 70—The EDP Buyer's Bible. Delran, NJ: Datapro Research Corp.; 1977 October. Volume 3 (Software). 70E-010-61a-70E-010-61e.

DATE, C.J. 1975. An Introduction to Database Systems. Reading, MA: Addison-Wesley Publishing Co.; 1975. 366p. ISBN: 0-201-14452-2.

DATE, C.J. 1976. Relational Data Base Concepts. Datamation. 1976 April; 22(4): 50-53. ISSN: 0011-6963.

DAVENPORT, R.A. 1978. Distributed or Centralized Data Base. The Computer Journal (England). 1978 February; 21(1): 7-14. ISSN: 0010-4620.

DEBLASIS, J-P.; JOHNSON, T.H. 1977. Data Base Administration— Classical Pattern, Some Experiences and Trends. In: Korfhage, Robert R., ed. Proceedings of the American Federation of Information Processing Societies (AFIPS) 1977 National Computer Conference (NCC):

Volume 46; 1977 June 13-16; Dallas, TX. Montvale, NJ: AFIPS Press, 210 Summit Avenue; 1977. 1-7. LC: 55-44701.

DODD, G.G. 1969. Elements of Data Management Systems. Computing Surveys. 1969 June; 1(2): 117-133. ISSN: 0010-4892.

DUHNE, RICARDO A.; SEVERANCE, DENNIS G. 1978. Selection of an Efficient Combination of Data Files for a Multiuser Database. In: Ghosh, Sakti P.; Liu, Leonard Y., eds. Proceedings of the American Federation of Information Processing Societies (AFIPS), National Computer Conference (NCC): Volume 47; 1978 June 5-8; Anaheim, CA. Montvale, NJ: AFIPS Press, 210 Summit Avenue; 1978. 843-847. LC: 55-44701.

EHRENSBERGER, MICHAEL. 1977. Data Dictionary—More on the Impossible Dream. In: Korfhage, Robert R., ed. Proceedings of the American Federation of Information Processing Societies (AFIPS) 1977 National Computer Conference (NCC): Volume 46; 1977 June 13-16; Dallas, TX. Montvale, NJ: AFIPS Press, 210 Summit Avenue; 1977. 9-11. LC: 55-44701.

ELAM, JOYCE; STUTZ, JOEL. 1977. Some Considerations for the Distribution of a Data Base. In: ACM—77: Proceedings of the Annual Conference of the Association for Computing Machinery (ACM); 1977 October 16-19; Seattle, WA. New York, NY: ACM; 1977. 23-27. Available from: ACM, P.O. Box 12105, Church Street Station, New York, NY 10249.

ENGLES, ROBERT W. 1970. A Tutorial on Data-Base Organization. Poughkeepsie, NY: International Business Machines (IBM); 1970. 87p. (IBM Technical Report TR.00.2004).

FINNERAN, THOMAS R. 1978. Data Base Systems Design Guidelines. Journal of Systems Management. 1978 March; 29(3): 26-30. ISSN: 0022-4839.

FINNERAN, THOMAS R.; HENRY, J. SHIRLEY. 1977. Structured Analysis for Data Base Design. Datamation. 1977 November; 23(11): 99-113. ISSN: 0011-6963.

FLOAM, GARY. 1976. Putting a Data Base on a Mini. Datamation. 1976 June; 22(6): 97-100. ISSN: 0011-6963.

FLORENTIN, J.J. 1973. Consistency Auditing of Databases. The Computer Journal (England). 1973 January; 17(1): 52-58. ISSN: 0010-4620.

FONG, ELIZABETH; COLLICA, JOSEPH; MARRON, BEATRICE A. 1975. Six Data Base Management Systems: Features Analysis and User Experiences. Washington, DC: National Bureau of Standards (NBS); 1975 November. 79p. (NBS Technical Note no. 887). CODEN: NBTNAE.

FRY, JAMES P.; SIBLEY, E.H. 1976. Evolution of Data Base Management Systems. Computing Surveys. 1976 March; 8(1): 8-42. ISSN: 0010-4892.

FRY, JAMES P.; BIRSS, EDWARD; DRESSEN, PETER; GOGUEN, NANCY; KAPLAN, MICHAEL; LOWENTHAL, EUGENE; LUM, VINCENT; MARION, ROBERT; NAVATHE, SHAMKANT; SCHINDLER, STEVEN; SHOSHANT, ARIE; SU, STANLEY; SWARTWOUT, DONALD; TAYLOR, ROBERT; YORMARK, BEATRICE. 1978. Distributed Data Base Technology—An Interim Report of the CODASYL Systems Committee. In: Ghosh, Sakti P.; Liu, Leonard Y., eds. Proceedings of the American Federation of Information Processing Societies (AFIPS)

National Computer Conference (NCC): Volume 47; 1978 June 5-8, Anaheim, CA. Montvale, NJ: AFIPS Press, 210 Summit Avenue; 1978. 887-907. LC: 55-44701.

GERRITSEN, ROB. 1976. The Relational and Network Models of Data Bases: Bridging the Gap. In: Shneiderman, Ben, ed. Database Management Systems. Montvale, NJ: AFIPS Press, 210 Summit Avenue; 1976. 127-131. (National Computer Conference Information Technology series, volume 1). LC: 76-41070.

GHOSH, SAKTI P.; TUEL, WILLIAM G., JR. 1976. A Design of an Experiment to Model Data Base System Performance. IEEE Transactions on Software Engineering. 1976 June; SE-2(2): 97-106.

GIBBONS, FRED M. 1976. The Mini's Impact on Data Base Management Systems. Mini-Micro Systems. 1976 November; 9(11): 26-29.

GOLDSTEIN, CHARLES M. 1972. A System Overview of the Aerospace Safety Research Data Institute Data Management Programs. 57p. (Prepared by: Neoterics, Inc., 2800 Euclid Avenue, Cleveland, OH). Available from: National Aeronautics and Space Administration (NASA), Washington, DC. (NASA CR-1976).

GUDES, EHUD; KOCH, HARVEY S.; STAHL, FRED A. 1976. The Application of Cryptography for Data Base Security. In: Winkler, Stanley, ed. Proceedings of the American Federation of Information Processing Societies (AFIPS) National Computer Conference (NCC): Volume 45; 1976 June 7-10; New York, NY. Montvale, NJ: AFIPS Press, 210 Summit Avenue; 1976. 97-107. LC: 55-44701.

GUIDE/SHARE DATA BASE REQUIREMENTS GROUP. 1970. Data Base Management System Requirements. New York, NY: Guide/Share; 1970 November. 120p.

HAMMER, MICHAEL. 1976. Error Detection in Data Base Systems. In: Winkler, Stanley, ed. Proceedings of the American Federation of Information Processing Societies (AFIPS) 1976 National Computer Conference (NCC): Volume 45; 1976 June 7-10; New York, NY. Montvale, NJ: AFIPS Press, 210 Summit Avenue; 1976. 795-801. LC: 55-44701.

HAMMER, MICHAEL. 1977. Self-Adaptive Automatic Data Base Design. In: Korfhage, Robert R., ed. Proceedings of the American Federation of Information Processing Societies (AFIPS) 1977 National Computer Conference (NCC): Volume 46; 1977 June 13-16; Dallas, TX. Montvale, NJ: AFIPS Press, 210 Summit Avenue; 1976. 123-129. LC: 55-44701.

HARDGRAVE, W.T. 1978. Distributed Database Technology: An Assessment. Information & Management. 1978 August; 1: 157-167.

HINOMOTO, HIROHIDE. 1976. Observations of a Firm's Information Processing with a Data Base Management System. International Journal of Computer and Information Sciences. 1976; 5(3): 277-302. ISSN: 0091-7036.

HSIAO, DAVID; HARARY, FRANK. 1970. A Formal System for Information Retrieval from Files. Communications of the ACM. 1970 February; 13(2): 67-73. ISSN: 0588-8069.

KATZAN, HARRY. 1975. Computer Data Management and Data Base Technology. New York, NY: Van Nostrand-Reinhold; 1975. 347p. ISBN: 0-442-24263-8.

KOSS, A.M.; NOONAN, J.M. 1976. A Case Study in the Use of Data Base Management. In: ACM—76: Proceedings of the Annual Conference of the Association for Computing Machinery (ACM); 1976 October 20-22; Houston, TX. New York, NY: ACM; 1976. 298-302. Available from: ACM, P.O. Box 12105, Church Street Station, New York, NY 10249.

KROENKE, DAVID M. 1977. Database Processing—Fundamentals, Modeling, Applications. Chicago, IL: Science Research Associates, Inc.; 1977. 408p. ISBN: 0-574-21100-4.

LEE, E.K.C.; LEE, E.Y.S. 1975. Development of a Data Dictionary/Directory Using a Data Base Management System. In: McEwen, Hazel E., ed. Management of Data Elements in Information Processing: Proceedings of the 2nd National Symposium on Management of Data Elements in Information Processing; 1975 October 23-24; Gaithersburg, MD. Washington, DC: National Bureau of Standards, 1976 April. 151-162. NTIS: PB 249-530.

LEONG-HONG, BELKIS; MARRON, BEATRICE A. 1977. Technical Profile of Seven Data Element Dictionary/Directory Systems. Washington, DC: National Bureau of Standards (NBS); 1977 February. 48p. (NBS Special Publication no. 500-3). CODEN: XNBSAV; LC: 76-58915.

LEONG-HONG, BELKIS; MARRON, BEATRICE A. 1978. Database Administration: Concepts, Tools, Experiences, and Problems. Washington, DC: National Bureau of Standards (NBS); 1978 March. 48p. (NBS Special Publication no. 500-28). CODEN: XNBSAV; LC: 78-606197.

LEWIS, CHARLES J. 1977. Understanding Database and Data Base. Journal of Systems Management. 1977 September; 28(9): 36-42. ISSN: 0022-4839.

LYON, JOHN K. 1976. The Database Administrator. New York, NY: A Wiley-Inter-Science Publication; 1976. 170p. ISBN: 0-471-55741-2.

MARTIN, JAMES. 1976. Principles of Data-Base Management. Englewood Cliffs, NJ: Prentice-Hall; 1976.

MARTIN, JAMES. 1977. Computer Data-Base Organization. Englewood Cliffs, NJ: Prentice-Hall; 1977. 713p. ISBN: 0-13-165423-3.

MARYANSKI, FRED J. 1978. A Survey of Developments in Distributed Data Base Management Systems. Computer. 1978 February; 11(2): 28-37. ISSN: 0018-9162.

MARYANSKI, FRED J.; FISHER, PAUL S. 1977. Rollback and Recovery in Distributed Data Base Management Systems. In: ACM—77: Proceedings of the Annual Conference of the Association for Computing Machinery (ACM); 1977 October 16-19; Seattle, WA. New York, NY: ACM; 1977. 33-38. Available from: ACM, P.O. Box 12105, Church Street Station, New York, NY 10249.

MARYANSKI, FRED J.; FISHER, PAUL S.; WALLENTINE, VIRGIL E. 1976. Evaluation of Conversion to a Back-End Data Base Management System. In: ACM—76: Proceedings of the Annual Conference of the Association for Computing Machinery (ACM); 1976 October 20-22; Houston, TX. New York, NY: ACM; 1976. 293-297. Available from: ACM, P.O. Box 12105, Church Street Station, New York, NY 10249.

MATTHEWS, J.R.; SMITH, R.J. 1978. Gauging the Impact of Change. Datamation. 1978 September; 24(9): 241-248. ISSN: 0011-6963.

MCCRACKEN, D.G. 1978. The Changing Face of Application Programming. Datamation. 1978 November; 24(11): 25-30. ISSN: 0011-6963.

MCFADDEN, FRED R.; SUVER, JAMES D. 1978. Costs and Benefits of a Data Base System. Harvard Business Review. 1978 January-February; 56(1): 131-139. ISSN: 0017-8012.

MCGEE, WILLIAM C. 1976. On User Criteria for Data Model Evaluation. ACM Transactions on Database Systems. 1976 December; 1(4): 370-387. ISSN: 0362-5915.

MCGEE, WILLIAM C. 1977. The Information Management System IMS/ VS. IBM Systems Journal. 1977; 16(2): 84-168. ISSN: 0018-8670.

NOLAN, RICHARD L. 1973. Computer Data Bases: The Future is Now. Harvard Business Review. 1973 September-October; 51(5): 98-114. ISSN: 0017-8012.

PATTERSON, ALBERT C. 1972. Data Base Hazards. Datamation. 1972 July; 18(7): 48-50. ISSN: 0011-6963.

PHISTER, M. 1976. Data Processing Technology and Economics. Revised edition. Santa Monica, CA: The Santa Monica Publishing Company; 1976. 573p. ISBN: 0-917640-01-2.

PLAGMAN, BERNARD K. 1977. Criteria for the Selection of Data Dictionary/Directory Systems. In: McEwen, Hazel E., ed. Management of Data Elements in Information Processing; 1977 September 28-30; Gaithersburg, MD. Washington, DC: National Bureau of Standards; 1978 April. 119-134. NTIS: PB 279-661.

PRYWES, NOAH S.; SMITH, DIANE P. 1972. Organization of Information. In: Cuadra, Carlos A.; Luke, Ann W., eds. Annual Review of Information Science and Technology: Volume 7. Washington, DC: American Society for Information Science; 1972. 103-158. ISBN: 0-87715-206-3; LC: 66-25096.

RAVER, N.; HUBBARD, G.U. 1977. Automated Logical Data Base Design: Concepts and Application. IBM Systems Journal. 1977; 16(3): 287-312. ISSN: 0018-8670.

ROBINSON, K.A. 1973. Database—The Ideas behind the Ideas. The Computer Journal (England). 1973; 18(1): 7-11. ISSN: 0010-4620.

ROCKE, MERLE G. 1974. The Necessity and Means of Disciplining Data Elements in a Computer Systems Environment. In: McEwen, Hazel E., ed. Management of Data Elements in Information Processing; 1974 January 24-25; Gaithersburg, MD. Washington, DC: National Bureau of Standards; 1974 April. 277-284. NTIS: COM 74-10700.

ROSS, RONALD G. 1976. Placing the DBA. Journal of Systems Management. 1976 May; 26(5): 25-33. ISSN: 0022-4839.

ROSS, RONALD G. 1978. Data Base Systems: Design, Implementation and Management. New York, NY: American Management; 1978. 229p. ISBN: 0-8144-5462-3.

SCHEUERMANN, PETER. 1978. On the Design and Evaluation of Data Bases. Computer. 1978 February; 11(2): 46-55. ISSN: 0018-9162.

SCHUSSEL, GEORGE. 1977. The Role of the Data Dictionary. Datamation. 1977 June; 23(6): 129-142. ISSN: 0011-6963.

SENKO, MICHAEL E. 1975. Information Systems; Records, Relations, Sets, Entities, and Things. Information Systems. 1975; 1(1): 3-13.

SENKO, MICHAEL E. 1977. Data Structures and Data Accessing in Data Base Systems Past, Present, and Future. IBM Systems Journal. 1977; 16(3): 208-257. ISSN: 0018-8670.

SENKO, MICHAEL E.; ALTMAN, E.B.; ASTRAHAN, M.M.; FEHDER, P.L. 1973. Data Structures and Accessing in Data-Base Systems. IBM Systems Journal. 1973; 12(1): 30-93. ISSN: 0018-8670.

SEVERANCE, DENNIS G. 1975. A Parametric Model of Alternative File Structures. Information Systems. 1975; 1(1): 51-55.

SEVERANCE, DENNIS G.; CARLIS, J.V. 1977. A Practical Approach to Selecting Record Access Paths. Computing Surveys. 1977 December; 9(4): 259-272. ISSN: 0010-4892.

SEVERANCE, DENNIS G.; DUHNE, RICARDO. 1976. A Practitioner's Guide to Addressing Algorithms. Communications of the ACM. 1976 June; 19(6): 314-326. ISSN: 0588-8069.

SHNEIDERMAN, BEN. 1973. Optimum Data Base Reorganization Points. Communications of the ACM. 1973 June; 16(6): 363-365. ISSN: 0588-8069.

SILER, KENNETH F. 1976. A Stochastic Evaluation Model for Database Organizations in Data Retrieval Systems. Communications of the ACM. 1976 February; 19(2): 84-95. ISSN: 0588-8069.

SIMONSON, WALTER E.; ALSBROOKS, WILLIAM T. 1975. A DBMS for the US Bureau of the Census. In: Kerr, Douglas S., ed. Proceedings of the International Conference on Very Large Data Bases: Volume 1; 1975 September 22-24; Framingham, MA. New York, NY: Association for Computing Machinery (ACM); 1975. 60-61. Available from: ACM, P.O. Box 12105, Church Street Station, New York, NY 10249.

STERNBERG, SEYMOUR. 1977. Position Paper on the Implementation and Use of Database Management Systems. In: ACM—77: Proceedings of the Annual Conference of the Association for Computing Machinery (ACM); 1977 October 16-19; Seattle, WA. New York, NY: ACM; 1977. 60-61. Available from: ACM, P.O. Box 12105, Church Street Station, New York, NY 10249.

TSICHRITZIS, DIONYSIOS C.; LOCHOVSKY, FREDERICK H. 1977. Data Base Management Systems. New York, NY: Academic Press; 1977. 388p. ISBN: 0-12-701740-2.

TSICHRITZIS, DIONYSIOS C.; LOCHOVSKY, FREDERICK H. 1978. Designing the Data Base. Datamation. 1978 August; 24(8): 147-151. ISSN: 0011-6963.

TEOREY, TOBY J.; OBERLANDER, LEWIS B. 1978. Network Data Base Evaluation Using Analytical Modeling. In: Ghosh, Sakti P.; Liu, Leonard Y., eds. Proceedings of the American Federation of Information Processing Societies (AFIPS) National Computer Conference: Volume 47; 1978 June 5-8; Anaheim, CA. Montvale, NJ: AFIPS Press, 210 Summit Avenue; 1978. 833-842. LC: 55-44701.

UHROWCZIK, P.P. 1973. Data Dictionary/Directories. IBM Systems Journal. 1973; (4): 332-350. ISSN: 0018-8670.

WALSH, MYLES E. 1978a. Getting Ready for IMS/VS. Datamation. 1978 December; 24(12): 109-118. ISSN: 0011-6963.

WALSH, MYLES E. 1978b. Update on Data Dictionaries. Journal of Systems Management. 1978 August; 29(8): 28-37. ISSN: 0022-4839.

WATERS, S.J. 1971. File Design Fallacies. The Computer Journal (England). 1971; 15(1): 1-4. ISSN: 0010-4620.

WIORKOWSKI, GABRIELLE K.; WIORKOWSKI, JOHN J. 1978. Does a Data Base Management System Pay Off? Datamation. 1978 April; 24(4): 109-114. ISSN: 0011-6963.

WITHINGTON, FREDERIC G. 1975. Beyond 1984: A Technology Forecast. Datamation. 1975 January; 21(1): 54-73. ISSN: 0011-6963.

WITHINGTON, FREDERIC G. 1978. IBM's Future Large Computers. Datamation. 1978 July; 24(7): 115-120. ISSN: 0011-6963.

YASAKI, EDWARD K. 1977. The Many Faces of the DBA. Datamation. 1977 May; 23(5): 75-79. ISSN: 0011-6963.

III

Applications

The application area treated in this year's *ARIST* is that of library automation. There has been a two-year hiatus since the last chapter on library automation in *ARIST*, but that does not mean that library automation was neglected; it was included in chapters that dealt with networking, databases, online systems and services, bibliographic and information processing standards, and bibliometrics. This year's chapter, entitled "Library Automation," was written by Mary Jane Pobst Reed of the Washington State Library and Hugh T. Vrooman of the Illinois State Library. It reviews the literature on computer applications in libraries for 1976-1978.

Although the authors criticize the quantity and quality of publications produced by libraries, they have cited some interesting papers, which cover a plethora of library automation subjects within the general headings of Research, Development, and Management.

The Research section treats such varied topics as: database management systems, automatic indexing, collection development formulas, networking, interlibrary loan, search keys, and virtual retrieval systems. The Development section treats hardware and software, including turnkey packages, and national efforts—e.g., the CONSER program for generating a standardized MARC-formatted database of serials labels, the work of the Network Advisory Group (NAG) of the Library of Congress, and the role of the Council on Library Resources (CLR) in designing a national bibliographic network. The Management section deals with papers on cost, service management, evaluation systems, and the problems of collecting the right data for management decisions.

Reed and Vrooman look forward to increased use of: teletext systems, packet-switched data communications, micro- and minicomputers, and videodisc storage for library applications. They expect computers to continue to be used in library operations to facilitate resource sharing, to optimize service, and to reduce costs.

7 Library Automation

MARY JANE POBST REED
Washington State Library

HUGH T. VROOMAN
Illinois State Library

INTRODUCTION

Librarians are not necessarily engaged in automation when they use computer services. Although true *automation* can perhaps exist only in flow-process industries, such as the petrochemical industry, *computer assistance* is becoming more useful to the discrete-parts industries. Libraries and their products are functionally closer to the latter group than to the former. It now seems possible to institute efficient and affordable computer assistance to handle such tasks as ordering, receipt of materials, payment, cataloging, physical processing, shelving, retrieval, searching, circulation, and even book selection and reference assistance. However, libraries are far more labor intensive than machine intensive. There also seems to be considerable fear among librarians about the increasing use of computers. Although future libraries may operate with far fewer people, library processes will still essentially be manually controlled and operated. Librarians are instituting *computer-assisted operations*, not automation. The common use of the word *automation* is an example of imprecise terminology.

The literature reflecting developments over the past few years indicates that although many major technical problems in library automation have been overcome, some remain—e.g., the accommodation of several alphabets in one database. Much of this literature only indicates how widely computers are used in libraries, as reported in such publications as the British journal *Program* and the U.S. journals *Special Libraries* and *Journal of Library Automation.*

From a review of this literature, it seems that the major topic involves the technical and political problems that are related to linking OCLC, Inc., the Research Libraries Information Network (RLIN, formerly BALLOTS), and the Washington Library Network (WLN)—the major bibliographic utilities of the United States—to form the basis of a national bibliographic network. Ancillary issues that receive attention are network governance, inter-utility cooperation, and optimization of man-machine interfaces.

Definition and Scope

This review chapter takes up library automation after a two-year hiatus. A scan of earlier *ARIST* volumes reveals that the two topics of automation and networking ran parallel from Volume 1 through Volume 10. By 1976 the topics were converging; in that year only library automation was treated (GROSCH, 1976a), and in 1977 and 1978 only networking was reviewed (PALMOUR & RODERER; TOMBERG). Now it is impossible to discuss the library use of computers without including computer networking. Of course, the computer component is only one dimension of library networking which simply reflects the profession's continuing desire in the 1970s for inter-library cooperation and resource sharing.

Unlike some previous *ARIST* articles on this topic, which were scholarly reviews, this chapter was designed primarily to indicate the state-of-the-art and to give a summary review of the literature. The type of published writings most often encountered in the library press generally cannot be included under the heading of Literature; in our survey, most of the material displaying import, style, and form was encountered outside the documents of the profession (e.g., MCQUILLAN & CERF; ROTHNIE ET AL.). Professional awareness, however, requires knowledge of the state-of-the-art; hence, the present approach was taken. Perhaps future *ARIST* schedules can accommodate both the scholarly and the status review article. With a longer time span between scholarly reviews, more and better candidate papers might be discovered.

The discussion centers on computers and associated communication technology; the politics and management of these systems are treated briefly.

Sources

In assembling this chapter, more than 1,000 items—articles, reports, monographs, government documents, and unpublished materials—were considered. Some items for which citations were found were unavailable. Included are materials that reflect the concerns of the U.S. and Canadian information profession and some pertinent tutorials. When several citations covered the same subject, the latest or most inclusive was usually reviewed on the assumption that its bibliography will lead the reader to the prior items.

Candidate citations were gathered by both manual and online literature searches. Indexes that were used include *Information Science Abstracts*, ERIC's (Educational Resources Information Center) *Resources in Education*, *Library Literature, Information News and Notes, Library and Information Science Abstracts, R & D Projects in Documentation and Librarianship, Library and Information Science Abstracts, Computing Reviews, Documentation Abstracts, Computer Abstracts, Automation Reports, Scientific and Technical Abstracts and Reports, Engineering Index*, INSPEC, COMPENDEX,

Energy Research Abstracts, and *Government Reports Announcements.* Professional library journals that report on the topic include *Program, Journal of the American Society for Information Science, Journal of Documentation, Journal of Library Automation, American Libraries, Library Journal, LJ/SLJ Hotline, Advanced Technology/Libraries* (although its reports are often inaccurate), *Drexel Library Quarterly, College & Research Libraries, Library Resources and Technical Services, Library Quarterly, On-Line Review,* and *Online.*

To keep up with technical developments, librarians should read publications whose scope lies outside disciplinary boundaries; much of the relevant literature does not appear in the professional library press. Specifically, the journals of the Institute of Electrical and Electronics Engineers (IEEE) and of the IEEE Computer Society (*Spectrum* and *Computer*), the publications of the Operations Research Society and of the Institute for Management Sciences, and the commercial publications—*Computerworld, Minicomputer News,* and *Datamation*—are more likely to keep the librarian informed about new technical developments than are those of traditional library literature.

Several series are recommended for perusal, although in general the delay in their reporting makes them more valuable as state-of-the-art pieces than as chronicles of current activity. The apparently biennial treatment by MARTIN of the national networking scene is an overview of developments and problems. The volumes that report papers from the Pittsburgh Conferences on Resource Sharing (e.g., KENT & GALVIN) contain some useful contributions. The proceedings of the American Society for Information Science (ASIS) meetings and the American Federation of Information Processing Societies (AFIPS) conferences offer some papers that are germane to the library industry. In the past year or so *Network* offered a survey of library automation in various parts of the world—a cursory treatment, much as in the former LARC series. Surveys such as *Advances in Librarianship* (VOIGT & HARRIS) and *Studies in Library Management* (HOLROYD) also contain occasional pertinent articles. Two good sources for current information on what is being done and considered come from the Library of Congress (LC)—viz., the annual report of the Librarian of Congress and *LC Information Bulletin.* The annual reports of the Council on Library Resources (CLR) and the National Commission on Libraries and Information Science (NCLIS) indicate trends at the level where policy is made.

Newsletters from the bibliographic utilities (*OCLC Newsletter, RLIN Newsletter, WLN Participant*) are useful, as are those from user networks, such as the Southeastern Library Network (SOLINET), the New England Library Network (NELINET), and AMIGOS (not an acronym).

Although many valuable tutorials were encountered, only a few are included in the bibliography. SAMUELSON ET AL. offer concise and readable guidelines for developing systems for information processing. ATHERTON & CHRISTIAN discuss the provision of online reference assistance in libraries. ATHERTON (1977) has developed for Unesco (United Nations Educational Scientific, and Cultural Organization) a handbook to aid library managers who are contemplating the use of computer systems. A good working knowledge of the theory and design of communication protocols can be obtained from an IEEE tutorial by MCQUILLAN & CERF. Another tutorial from the IEEE (ROTHNIE ET AL.) gives an overview of both relational and distributed database management systems, including query processing, reliability, and concurrency control. These are only two of the many excellent IEEE tutorials, which are part of the IEEE program for the professional development of its members and show what should be done in the library/information profession.

Increased library automation has shown the need for upgrading management capabilities in the library profession. A collection of papers from the Simmons College Institute on Quantitative Measurement and Dynamic Library Service (CHEN, 1978) furnishes an excellent tutorial on evaluating library services, demonstrating that even the least statistically sophisticated manager can practice scientific management if properly motivated.

The American Library Association (ALA) has published another edition of its bibliography on automation (WEST ET AL.), and the centennial issue of *Library Journal* included pertinent articles by CORBIN, DEGENNARO, FREEDMAN, and MARTIN (1976).

The following sections deal with the literature in research, development, and management applications. Then the future of computer applications in library operations is considered.

RESEARCH

As mentioned, much pertinent research occurs in fields that are peripheral to librarianship. For example, although a study by TELEDYNE BROWN ENGINEERING analyzed general systems and techniques for database mangement, it included several problems that face designers of library systems: identification of potential users, clustering of minicomputers, low-cost information retrieval and analysis, minicomputer-based database management systems, and data interchange among users. Librarians should be aware of such studies and should recognize transferable or analogous findings.

The application of fuzzy set theory to information science, particularly to citation retrieval, has been advocated for several years (W. JONES; RADECKI; SACHS) and is cogently challenged by ROBERTSON as being inappropriate. The librarian should be aware of this sort of controversy.

The study at MIT by LINDQUIST showed that a typical information search service (ISS) grows rapidly during its first two years; then a two-year stagnation period sets in, followed by a period of slower growth (10-12% annually). Since most ISS's are still in their initial period, we can expect stagnation soon in the entire industry unless new search services are established.

Automatic indexing has absorbed many researchers. In the United States an inconclusive comparison is reported on the effectiveness of term discrimination and term precision as automatic indexing systems (SALTON ET AL.). British studies are reviewed in *Research on Automatic Indexing, 1974-1976* (SPARCK JONES & BATES). RICHMOND discusses the possibilities of classifying documents from the British PRECIS (Preserved Context Index System) terms.

Several studies have investigated collection-development formulas and collection-overlap information on the basis of statistical data derived from computerized cataloging systems (e.g., DAVIS & SHAW and EVANS ET AL.). The latter study used OCLC archival tapes to analyze collections of the State University of New York libraries on the basis of content, components, and overlap and to use these data in making decisions about acquisitions.

Network Research

Space permits the review of only a few examples from the large body of network-oriented research. NCLIS and NBS (National Bureau of Standards) have worked together to eliminate one roadblock to a national bibliographic network (U.S. NCLIS/NBS TASK FORCE ON COMPUTER NETWORK PROTOCOL). If it is implemented, this protocol will allow disparate computer systems and system components to communicate.

Regional network design has received attention in several significant studies; most relate to interlibrary cooperation or service networks in contrast to the networks of bibliographic utilities. Service networks, as now commonly defined, are organizations that contract for the services of one or more bibliographic utilities but usually have no computer operations of their own. Hopes for a western regional service network led to various statistical surveys (e.g., D. JONES) by the Western Interstate Commission for Higher Education (WICHE). Cost and funding studies were reported in depth (MONTAGUE); retarded development at Stanford's BALLOTS (now RLIN) and the WLN computer systems resulted in decisions by many western libraries to use OCLC services, with a consequent demise of the concept of a western network.

Computer simulation was used in planning a computer-based network centered in Pittsburgh, PA (J. WILLIAMS); the model simulated the existing operations and then the planned computer-assisted operations. As the network has become operational, the model has been evaluated further. These sound studies, directed by Allen Kent at the University of Pittsburgh (of which Williams's work is a segment), have focused on design and implementation of a computer-based library resource-sharing network and the incorporation of acquisitions, cataloging, public service, interlibrary loan (ILL), and a management information system.

For more than five years William and Sandra Rouse of the University of Illinois have studied ILL activities for the Illinois State Library. A recent report (ROUSE & ROUSE, 1977b) states that if the lending library's location and call number information (sometimes available to the borrowing library through a computerized union catalog) are included with the request, faster responses result. Their nine reports are models of analysis and writing, well worth reading and emulating.

A series of reports by NELINET has investigated the potential of resource-sharing protocols based on a loan-equalizing computer system (NEW ENGLAND BOARD OF HIGHER EDUCATION, 1977; NEW ENGLAND BOARD OF HIGHER EDUCATION, 1978). A prior study of regional OCLC use

(TIGHE & LEVINE) contributed to the overall study. The feasibility study used a FORTRAN model of ILL activity to analyze market value. Results were inconclusive as to outcome of the strategy because the highest market value transaction might not be chosen often enough to justify the expense of the module in an online system. The 1978 report identified costs related to ILL in various types and sizes of libraries, surveyed regional resources, set up patterns for designing the computer system to support ILL, and began work on a lending/borrowing code. The system will provide quick information about turnaround time and lending policies of participating libraries as well as loan-leveling and request-monitoring routines.

Several authors have evaluated the effect of OCLC on user libraries—e.g., HEWITT, who surveyed 47 OCLC-user libraries in Ohio, and WHEELBARGER who studied the SOLINET region. MARKUSON investigated the system's usefulness for small libraries.

The steady stream of useful findings reported from the University of Pittsburgh, MIT, the University of Massachusetts, Purdue, and the University of Illinois is exemplified by the work of Martha Williams at the Information Retrieval Research Laboratory (IRRL) at the University of Illinois. A recent publication (WILLIAMS & MACLAURY) reports on the construction of algorithms to merge bibliographic databases with little or no resulting duplication. Somewhat related studies come from the American Institute of Physics (LERNER ET AL.), which seeks compatibility among abstracting and indexing services, and the American Chemical Society (MYERS ET AL.), which is attempting to construct interfile links for chemical-substance data in multiple files. Additional findings come from two studies of search keys for access to large bibliographic files. BOOKSTEIN & RODRIGUEZ and LEGARD & BOURNE indicate that elaborating on the usual severely truncated key will result in better retrieval—in Legard's case by increasing the 3,1,1,1 to a 4,2,2,2 key, and in Bookstein's by first reducing the file and then searching it more thoroughly.

A study that could have great impact on national library computer network developments is the simulation and gaming project of EDUCOM (EMERY ET AL.; A. JONES) to investigate the economic, political, and organizational implications of computer-to-computer networks. A useful NBS evaluation of the present situation is provided by COTTON, who discusses computer interconnection in networks from the technical, policy, and organizational viewpoints.

Another research effort with profound implications for national library networking is the study at MIT on the coupling of interactive information systems (MARCUS & REINTJES). This study postulates a virtual retrieval system, with emphasis on the requirements of a common command language, ease of use, and message interpretation and protocols in a computer network interface. Such general analyses often seem to be overlooked by workers in developmental systems for libraries.

DEVELOPMENT

Although hardware selection is time consuming in any specific application, it has been given increasingly less space in the library literature, indicating that the decisions now are fairly well specified and that the variables are well defined. A paper on the selection of a minicomputer system was given by GROSCH (1978); the concepts presented would be useful in acquiring any computer regardless of size.

A major innovation in systems structure was the introduction at OCLC of back-end as well as front-end processors to manage the rotating memory and communications traffic. An item in *COMPUTERWORLD* (1978) seems to be the only publicity beyond that given in the *OCLC Newsletter* to this important development in computer architecture. The staff of OCLC has considerable technical ability; it is unfortunate that they have not been able to produce a subject search function. This undoubtedly reflects constraints from the original design concept as a mechanism to produce catalog cards.

The MARC format, as one of the chief standards underlying computer applications and networking, continues to receive attention. A composite listing of formats for types of materials was published by LC to assist in the design of general computer programs (U.S. LIBRARY OF CONGRESS). Redefinition of the format continues to be suggested in this country (WEISBROD) and acted on in Canada (BUCHINSKI, 1976). At the University of Toronto the local and MARC formats are used together (HAJNAL ET AL.). Another ongoing contribution from IRRL is the latest compilation of summary statistics on LC's MARC database (WILLIAMS ET AL.).

The National Library of Canada (NLC), after evaluating several computer-assisted systems, has selected the Dortmunder Bibliothekssystem (DOBIS), and an in-depth analysis of DOBIS is now available. DOBIS has undergone several transformations. It originated as ELMS (Experimental Library Management System) at IBM's Los Gatos, CA, site, was expanded into the highly advertised but never purchased Library Access System 370, was translated into German at Dortmund, and, although reportedly still not operational there (ZUEST), has been transported back to Canada. Several documents on DOBIS are available from the NLC; we cite here a summary of the Canadian developments in automation (FORGET). The NLC evaluation included a summary of the characteristics of available library processing facilities (SILCOFF). Ontario, according to STIERWALT, has moved to an operating network for the province that is based on UTLAS (University of Toronto Library Automation System).

Machine-assisted authority sub-systems continue to rank high on librarians' lists of desired items; the New York Public Library's system was probably the earliest. WLN's man-machine authority system (CALK) and that of NLC (BUCHINSKI ET AL.) are in operation. LC and RLIN are exploring related problems.

Current efforts at OCLC, in addition to the hardware restructuring mentioned above, include an ILL communication system (BARRENTINE) and a serials control system (TWITCHELL & SPREHN). Predicting the arrival of serial issues is a problem that is treated by GROSCH (1976b) although it was solved with considerable elegance at the New York State Library in 1968 (PAN).

The market for turnkey computer-assisted circulation systems continues to grow and to attract new vendors. The most recent endeavors concentrate on microcomputer links between cataloging and circulation systems. The Tacoma (WA) Public Library has produced useful reports on the selection of and conversion for circulation systems (HEGARTY; LONG).

Regional online union lists of serials holdings are being developed in many areas; a typical effort is reported by CARTER. The national serials conversion (CONSER) program to provide a standardized MARC-formatted database of serials titles has come to fruition in the period under review (1976–1978); many descriptions of the effort have been published, and the treatment by WITTIG in the *Unesco Bulletin for Libraries* is a good synopsis.

One of the rare, reported library ventures into computer-assisted instruction (CAI) occurred when the Lister Hill National Center developed a CAI network to serve as many as 100 institutional users in biomedical education (WOOSTER).

The saga of planning and developing computer assistance for the libraries of the University of California continues under Salmon with another published plan, this one for 1978–1988 (UNIVERSITY OF CALIFORNIA). This analysis is pertinent to all types of libraries. The design appears sound, the recommendations seem cogent, and—more important—workable.

On a regional level, the now defunct Northeast Academic Science Information Center (NASIC) completed a project to develop tests and evaluations of computer-based information services, to market these services in the Northeast, and to produce training materials (WAX & VAUGHAN).

On the national level considerable planning has taken place. In response to its charge to outline a national information program, NCLIS indicated the significance of LC as a component of such a program (U.S. NATIONAL COMMISSION ON LIBRARIES AND INFORMATION SCIENCE). Subsequently a 1976 study funded by NCLIS analyzed the current and potential roles of LC and concluded that its current and planned bibliographic services would meet the needs of the information community (U.S. LIBRARY OF CONGRESS. NETWORK DEVELOPMENT OFFICE). In 1976 the Librarian of Congress established the Network Development Office (NDO) to act as coordinator (as recommended by the study) and to indicate LC's commitment to networking. Representatives of the information community were invited to serve on a Network Advisory Group (NAG), later reconstructed as the Network Advisory Committee (NAC). NAG identified the bibliographic component of the national network as the first segment to be undertaken, to demonstrate the viability of networking, and outlined steps in the overall project and responsibilities of various agencies (U.S. LIBRARY OF CONGRESS. NETWORK ADVISORY GROUP). Their report has served as the basis for several later efforts. The Network Technical Architecture Group (NTAG), a subcommittee of NAG, analyzed technical problems of national networking; AVRAM & HARTMANN describe NTAG's activities.

NDO has provided guidance and coordination (AVRAM, 1978a) and has monitored several reports that are essential to ongoing development. BUCH-INSKI (1978) investigated bibliographic requirements and considerations relative to the national database, listing 19 specific tasks to be accomplished. BUTLER analyzed the National Union Catalog and the Register of Additional Locations as bases for the developing national bibliographic network. DATA-FLOW SYSTEMS INCORPORATED prepared a glossary to assist the communication process; the vocabulary of library networking has been notably nonstandardized. NTAG developed general requirements for a message delivery system for the national bibliographic network, recommending that a contract be let for preparation of a detailed requirements document (NET-WORK TECHNICAL ARCHITECTURE GROUP).

Recent developments in funding have given CLR a major role in designing the national bibliographic network. Assurance that the development of the network will go forward can be found in CLR's recent announcement of the Bibliographic Services Development Program (*LC INFORMATION BULLETIN*); its purpose is to improve the mechanisms used to record and to transmit bibliographic data to users. A Management Committee and a Program Committee have been established, giving representation to CLR, LC, NCLIS, the major bibliographic utilities, and research libraries. The long-range governance and management structures remain undefined; these issues are more difficult to solve than the technical, bibliographic, economic, and legal aspects.

MANAGEMENT

For at least ten years, library managers have been warned of the profound effects of computer technology on the structure, services, and management of libraries; recent statements have come from DOUGHERTY, ROSENTHAL, H.S. WHITE, and others. Examples of a new awareness are evidenced by CAPE, CLAYTON & NISENOFF, and STANFIELD.

Welcome cost studies are beginning to appear. HITCHINGHAM and WEST & BUTLER give tutorials on evaluation, while PIERCE & TAYLOR develop a general approach to costing an automated cataloging system. Specific cost studies come from ELCHESEN, MOSLEY, and ROSS.

The California Library Authority for Systems and Services has produced a careful comparison of BALLOTS and OCLC (LEVINE & LOGAN) to assess the potential effect of either system on library operations. A follow-up study scheduled for 1979 will compare RLIN, OCLC, and WLN.

Perhaps the best reports on service management come from LANCASTER, CHEN (1976), and KIEWITT. Lancaster develops concepts of effectiveness and benefits that are pertinent to general library services, including automated environments, an approach to evaluation, and scenarios of service situations to explore and to evaluate satisfaction. In the proceedings of the 1977 NATO Advanced Study Institute, edited by LANCASTER & CLEVER-DON, the papers by Bunge, Lipetz, Helal, Leimkuhler, Oldman, and Wilson cover much the same territory as Lancaster's book but are state-of-the-art overviews. Chen, on the other hand, uses Philip Morse's theoretical predictive models to describe the operations of Harvard's Countway Library and develops additional probabilistic models. She shows that mathematical models can be easy tools for measuring library effectiveness—results can be obtained by simply inserting proper parameter values into available formulas. Kiewitt's thesis is an account of an in-depth evaluation of Indiana University's ERIC/PROBE. The project studied costs, system performance, and user performance. This description of the history and methodology of a computer retrieval system evaluation, which includes pitfalls and mistakes, should be especially valuable to those who are preparing to review computerized services. With these kinds of data, it ought to be possible to predict the performance of man-machine systems in terms of actual and stated goals.

The problem of collecting data for management decisions has always seemed to baffle librarians, who tend to collect copious but irrelevant statistics. We need to become proficient in recognizing useful data. Specification of the management information sub-system is often an afterthought if it is considered at all. The needed approach is described by BUCKLAND & TAYLOR and by HORTON; specific methods for structuring an information system are given by HAMBURG ET AL.

The collection of circulation statistics in a computer-assisted system is described by FOIL & CARTER, analysis of the statistics for collection development is covered by KRONICK & BOWDEN, and management of ILL operations is treated by ROUSE & ROUSE (1977a). The well-stated exhortation by SHIREY for data discrimination and accuracy should be read and heeded. The use of statistical reports based on spurious interpretation is a common management mistake.

A set of important studies from the University of Pittsburgh (KENT ET AL., 1979) has analyzed the use of library materials. The final report was not available for review, but judging from segments published over the past several years (e.g., BULICK ET AL.; MONTGOMERY ET AL.), the findings will constitute valuable information for managers of library collections. In fact, the various projects reported by Kent's team are consistently good and constitute perhaps the best corpus of work done in applied library research.

With the advent of bibliographic services for which user fees are charged— e.g., those from System Development Corp., Lockheed, and the *New York Times* Information Bank—considerable effort has been made to evaluate online search services. Lockheed conducted a three-year study funded by the National Science Foundation (SUMMIT & FIRSCHEIN) that investigated the public library as a link between the user and the many available machine-readable databases and evaluated the effect of user fees. The users were primarily graduate students and professionals. During the pay period, online time decreased, librarians spent more time preparing for the search, and satisfaction of patrons increased in comparison with the no-pay period. COOPER & DEWATH explored the effect of user fees on online search costs and also found that librarians spent more time preparing for the search; in addition, database connect charges decreased, and offline print costs increased. Both studies indicate that charges resulted in more carefully defined and more productive searches.

Lea Bohnert has indicated[1] that as a teacher she finds it useful to stress the commonality of the available online databases, referring to a matrix of online commands (NATIONAL FEDERATION OF ABSTRACTING AND INDEXING SERVICES). On the horizon of library resources are diverse databases that have more common features than differences.

FUTURE DIRECTIONS

Within the next year or so, the Prestel system from Britain (INFORMA-TION RETRIEVAL AND LIBRARY AUTOMATION) along with Videotex from Canada (COMPUTERDATA) will make a centralized interactive ready reference store accessible to users via telephone, television, and microprocessor interface unit. This new medium of mass communication must be considered in planning the future of libraries. Electronic mail is off again/on again with the U.S. Postal Service (KIRCHNER), and AT&T's Advanced Communications System (GANTZ) will be offering a packet-switched data communications service that can be used in library networks and services. TYMNET and IBM along with Aetna Life and COMSAT are also intent on enhancing the capability of analog and digital communications.

The increasing power of micro- and minicomputers (*COMPUTERWORLD*, 1979), the development of bubble memory, and laser/videodisc storage are changing the way we think about data processing and databases. Dedicated special-purpose devices are proliferating, and radically different publishing and storage modes will be available.

Library services should expand to provide access to nonbibliographic and numeric databases. An issue of *Drexel Library Quarterly* (H.D. WHITE) discusses numeric data files for the social sciences and points up implications for library functions. Librarians need not be statisticians, but they should be aware of the needs for various types of data and ways to satisfy those needs.

The national library network continues to evolve; OCLC is no longer the only game in town, now that RLIN has become the prestigious, exclusive network of the Association of Research Libraries. The WLN bibliographic system has been purchased and installed at the National Library of Australia. The new joint venture of RLIN and WLN in sharing databases and cooperating in development should improve services at both networks (*LJ/SLJ HOTLINE*). To many, whose concept of an online catalog has been based on the OCLC product, these West Coast developments should be welcome and may be shocking. In-house online catalogs are provided by some turnkey system vendors; CLSI's (Computer Library Services, Inc.) Libs 100 version 24 is such a system.

---

[1] Personal communication, Lea M. Bohnert, Graduate Library School, University of Rhode Island.

CONCLUSION

Our preoccupation with the deus *in* machina has existed for almost 25 years and shows no sign of abating, but it does seem to be more reasonable. Self-confidence has not been an outstanding characteristic of librarians during this time. The literature has been of little help, tending to be too esoteric or uncritical, overconfident, and insubstantial. Unfortunately, many American librarians are inadequate communicators. In contrast, British librarians generally write clearly and distinctly. This situation is disheartening and curious, especially as the librarian's life revolves around written communication.

Resource sharing, optimized services, and minimal costs are the rationales for computer services. The computer is just another tool for managing information. By using it perhaps we can perform library functions more efficiently, although nowhere does the literature offer hard evidence to support this feeling.

BIBLIOGRAPHY

ARTHUR D. LITTLE INCORPORATED. 1978. A New Governance Structure for OCLC: Principles and Recommendations. Metuchen, NJ: Scarecrow Press; 1978. 96p. ISBN: 0-8108-1146-4; LC: 78-2099.

ATHERTON, PAULINE. 1977. Handbook for Information Systems and Services. Paris, France: Unesco; 1977. 258p. ISBN: 92-3-1014579.

ATHERTON, PAULINE. 1979. Books Are for Use: Final Report of the Subject Access Project to Council on Library Resources. Syracuse, NY: Syracuse University School of Information Studies, 1978. Available from: Syracuse University School of Information Studies, 113 Euclid Ave., Syracuse, NY 13210.

ATHERTON, PAULINE; CHRISTIAN, ROGER W. 1977. Librarians and Online Services. White Plains, NY: Knowledge Industry Publications, Inc.; 1977. 124p. ISBN: 0-014236-13-X; LC: 77-25275.

AVRAM, HENRIETTE D. 1978a. U.S. Library of Congress Networking Activities. Unesco Bulletin for Libraries. 1978 March-April; 32(2): 71-80. CODEN: UNBLAB.

AVRAM, HENRIETTE D. 1978b. The National and International Network and Urban Main Libraries. Prepared for: Future of the Main Urban Library, A National Conference; 1978 October 26-27. 24p. Available from: the author, Library of Congress Network Development Office, Washington, DC 20540.

AVRAM, HENRIETTE D. 1978c. State of the Art: Toward a Nationwide Library Network. Paper prepared for: American Library Association's Library and Information Technology State of the Art Preconference Institute; 1978 June; Chicago, IL. 32p. Available from: the author.

AVRAM, HENRIETTE D.; HARTMANN, DAVID C. 1979. Objectives and Accomplishments of the Network Technical Architecture Group. Program. 1979 January; 13(1): 1-13. ISSN: 0033-0337.

BARRENTINE, JAMES K. 1977. A Computer-Based Interlibrary Loan
Communications Subsystem. Columbus, OH: Ohio College Library
Center; 1977. 56p. ERIC: ED 145861.
BOOKSTEIN, ABRAHAM; RODRIGUEZ, C.E. 1978. Performance Test
of Hybrid Access Method. Journal of Library Automation. 1978
March; 11(1): 41-46. ISSN: 0022-2232; CODEN: JLAUAY.
BUCHINSKI, EDWIN J. 1976. Mini-MARC: Implementation of a Concept.
Canadian Library Journal. 1976 April; 33(2): 167-172. ISSN: 0008-
4352.
BUCHINSKI, EDWIN J. 1978. Initial Considerations for a Nationwide
Data Base. Washington, DC: Library of Congress Network Development
Office; 1978. 57p. (Avram, H.D.; McCallum, S.H., eds. and revs.; Net-
work Planning Paper no. 3). ISSN: 0160-9742; ISBN: 0-8444-0271-0.
BUCHINSKI, EDWIN J.; NEWMAN, WILLIAM L.; DUNN, MARY JOAN.
1977. The National Library of Canada Authority Subsystem: Implica-
tions. Journal of Library Automation. 1977 March; 10(1): 28-40.
ISSN: 0022-2232; CODEN: JLAUAY.
BUCKLAND, MICHAEL K.; TAYLOR, WILLIAM D. 1976. Management
Information for Decision-Making. In: Martin, Susan K., comp. Infor-
mation * Politics: Proceedings of the 39th Annual Meeting of the Ameri-
can Society for Information Science (ASIS): Volume 13, Part I: Abstracts
of Papers, Part II: Full Papers; 1976 October 4-9; San Francisco, CA.
Washington, DC: ASIS; 1976. Part I, p24, Part II, 1-G8; microfiche;
24x reduction. ISSN: 0044-7870; ISBN: 0-87715-413-9; LC: 64-8303;
CODEN: PAISDQ.
BULICK, STEPHEN; MONTGOMERY, K. LEON; FETTERMAN, JOHN;
KENT, ALLEN. 1976. Use of Library Materials in Terms of Age.
Journal of the American Society for Information Science. 1976 May-
June; 27(3): 175-178. ISSN: 0002-8231; CODEN: AISJB6.
BUTLER, BRETT. 1978. A Nationwide Location Data Base and Service.
Washington, DC: Library of Congress; 1978. 66p. (Network Planning
Paper no. 1). ISSN: 0160-9742; ISBN: 0-8444-0268-0.
CALK, JO. 1978. On-Line Authority Control in the Washington Library
Network. In: Furuya, Natsuko Y., ed. What's in a Name? Control of
Catalogue Records through Automated Authority Files: Proceedings of
Workshops; 1977 December 8-9; Ottawa, Canada; and 1978 May 25-26;
Vancouver, Canada. Toronto, Canada: University of Toronto; 1978.
135-159. Available from: University of Toronto Library Automation
Systems, 130 St. George Street, Toronto, Ontario, Canada M581A5.
CAPE, JAMES D. 1977. Technology Impact on the Information Manage-
ment of a Government Technical Information Center. In: Fry, Bernard
M.; Shepherd, Clayton A., comps. Information Management in the
1980s: Proceedings of the 40th Annual Meeting of the American Society
for Information Science: Volume 14, Part I: Abstracts, Part II: Full
Papers; 1977 September 26-October 1; Chicago, IL. White Plains, NY:
Knowledge Industries Publications, Inc.; 1977. Part I, p43; Part II,
2-D6, microfiche, 24x reduction. ISSN: 0044-7870; ISBN: 0-914236-
12-1.
CARTER, RUTH C. 1978. Steps Toward an On-Line Union List. Journal
of Library Automation. 1978 March; 11(1): 32-40. ISSN: 0022-2240;
CODEN: JLAUAY.

CHEN, CHING-CHIH. 1976. Applications of Operations Research Models to Libraries: A Case Study of the Use of Monographs in the Francis A. Countway Library of Medicine, Harvard University. Cambridge, MA: MIT Press; 1976. 212p. ISBN: 0-262-03056-X; LC: 75-28210.

CHEN, CHING-CHIH, ed. 1978. Quantitative Measurement and Dynamic Library Service. Phoenix, AZ: Oryx Press; 1978. 290p. ISBN: 0-7201-0826-8.

CLAYTON, AUDREY; NISENOFF, NORMAN. 1977. Potential Impacts of Automation and User Fees upon Technical Libraries. Arlington, VA: Forecasting International Ltd.; 1977 June 30. 185p. NTIS: PB0271 418/6ST.

COMPUTERDATA. 1978. Canadian-Developed Videotex Offers Exciting Possibilities. Computerdata. 1978 December; 3(12): 32-33. Computerdata available from: Roy J. Whitsed Publishing, Ltd., Suite 2504, 2 Bloor St. W., Toronto, Ontario, Canada M4W 3G1.

COMPUTERWORLD. 1978. Library Net Puts Minis at Front and Back Ends. Computerworld. 1978 May 8; 12(19): 62. ISSN: 0010-4841.

COMPUTERWORLD. 1979. Intel Bubble Memory Packs 1M Bit on Chip. Computerworld. 1979 May 7; 13(19): 1. ISSN: 0010-4841.

COOPER, MICHAEL D. 1977. Input-Output Relationships in On-Line Bibliographic Searching. Journal of the American Society for Information Science. 1977 May; 28(3): 153-160. ISSN: 0002-8231; CODEN: AISJB6.

COOPER, MICHAEL D.; DEWATH, NANCY A. 1977. The Effect of User Fees on the Cost of On-Line Searching in Libraries. Journal of Library Automation. 1977 December; 10(4): 304-319. ISSN: 0022-2240; CODEN: JLAUAY.

CORBIN, JOHN B. 1976. Library Networks. Library Journal. 1976 January 1; 101(1): 203-207. ISSN: 0000-0027; ISBN: 0-8352-0892-3.

COTTON, IRA W. 1977. Computer Science and Technology; Computer Network Interconnection: Problems and Prospects. Washington, DC: National Bureau of Standards; 1977 April. 83p. (NBS Special Publication no. 500-6). CODEN: XNBSAV; USGPO: C 13:10:500-6.

COUNCIL ON LIBRARY RESOURCES. 1978. A National Periodicals Center: Technical Development Plan. Washington, DC: Council on Library Resources; 1978. 255p.

COX, CAROLYN M.; JUERGENS, BONNIE. 1977. Microform Catalogs: A Viable Alternative for Texas Libraries. Dallas, TX: AMIGOS Bibliographic Council; 1977. 113p. ERIC: ED 149739.

DATAFLOW SYSTEMS INCORPORATED. 1978. A Glossary for Library Networking. Washington, DC: Library of Congress Network Development Office; 1978. 34p. (Network Planning Paper no. 2). ISSN: 0160-9742; ISBN: 0-8444-0270-2.

DAVIS, CHARLES H.; SHAW, DEBORAH. 1979. Collection Overlap as a Function of Library Size: A Comparison of American and Canadian Public Libraries. Journal of the American Society for Information Science. January 1979; 30(1): 19-24. ISSN: 0002-8231; CODEN: AISJB6.

DEGENNARO, RICHARD. 1976. Library Automation: Changing Patterns and New Directions. Library Journal. 1976 January 1; 101(1): 175-183. ISSN: 0000-0027; ISBN: 0-8352-0892-3.

DOUGHERTY, RICHARD M. 1978. The Impact of Networking on Library Management. College and Research Libraries. 1978 January; 39(1): 15-19. ISSN: 0010-0870.

ELCHESEN, DENNIS R. 1978. Cost-Effectiveness Comparison of Manual and On-Line Retrospective Searching. Journal of the American Society for Information Science. 1978 March; 29(2): 56-66. ISSN: 0002-8231; CODEN: AISJB6.

EMERY, JAMES C.; SEGAL, RONALD; NIELSEN, NORMAN R.; ASHEN-HURST, ROBERT; BERG, SANFORD V. 1976. Simulation and Gaming Project for Inter-Institutional Computer Networking. 139p. Princeton, NJ: EDUCOM; 1976 July. NTIS: PB-259 789.

EVANS, GLYN T.; BEILBY, MARY H.; GIFFORD, ROGER. 1978. Development of a Responsive Library Acquisitions Formula. Albany, NY: State University of New York Central Administration; 1978 December. 95p. Available from: the authors, Office of Library Services, State University of New York Central Administration, State University Plaza, Albany, NY 12246.

FOIL, PATTI SUE; CARTER, BRADLEY D. 1977. Survey of Data Collecting Systems for Computer-Based Library Circulation Processes. Journal of Library Automation. 1976 September; 9(3): 222-233. ISSN: 0022-2240.

FORGET, LOUIS J.S. 1977. Automation at the National Library of Canada. Paper presented at: International Federation of Library Associations (IFLA) World Congress of Librarians; 1977 September 6-7; La Hulpe, Belgium. 50p. Available from: the author, Research and Planning Branch, National Library of Canada, Ottawa K1A 0N4 Ontario, Canada.

FORGET, LOUIS J.S.; NEWMAN, WILLIAM L. 1977. Evaluation of the DOBIS System for Use in Canada. The Canadian Journal of Information Science. 1977 May; 2(1): 61-78. ISSN: 0380-9218; CODEN: CJISDE.

FREEDMAN, MAURICE J. 1976. Processing for the People. Library Journal. 1976 January 1; 101(1): 189-197. ISSN: 0000-0027; ISBN: 0-8352-0892-3.

GANTZ, JOHN. 1978. Ma Bell's ACS Strategy. Mini-Micro Systems. 1978 September; 2(8): 38-44. Also available from: Cahner's Reprint Service, 5 South Wabash, Chicago, IL 60603.

GRAHAM, PETER S. 1977. Terminals and Printers for Library Use: Report on a Selection. Journal of Library Automation. 1977 December; 19(4): 343-357. ISSN: 0022-2240; CODEN: JLAUAY.

GROSCH, AUDREY N. 1976a. Library Automation. In: Williams, M.E., ed. Annual Review of Information Science and Technology: Volume 11. Washington, DC: American Society for Information Science; 1976. 225-266. ISBN: 0-87715-212-8; ISSN: 0066-4200; CODEN: ARISBc.

GROSCH, AUDREY N. 1976b. Serial Arrival Prediction Coding. Information Processing & Management. 1976; 12(2): 141-146.

GROSCH, AUDREY N. 1978. Selection of Minicomputer Systems for Bibliographic Applications. Paper presented at: AGARD Lecture Series no 92: Application of Inexpensive Minicomputers to Information Work; 1978 April. NTIS: AGARD-LS-92; CODEN: NGALB5.

HAJNAL, PETER I.; DE BRUIN, VALENTINA; BITEEN, DALE. 1977. MARC and CODOC: A Case Study in Dual Format Use in a University Library. Journal of Library Automation. December 1977; 10(4): 358-373. ISSN: 0022-2240; CODEN: JLAUAY.

HAMBURG, MORRIS; BOMMER, MICHAEL; CLELLAND, RICHARD; RAMIST, LEONARD; WHITFIELD, RONALD. 1976. Systems Approach to Library Management. Journal of Systems Engineering. 1976 January; 4(2): 117-129. ISSN: 0022-4820.

HAWKINS, DONALD T. 1977. Unconventional Uses of On-Line Information Retrieval Systems: On-Line Bibliometric Studies. Journal of the American Society for Information Science. January 1977; 28(1): 13-18. ISSN: 0002-8231; CODEN: AISJB6.

HEGARTY, KEVIN. 1977. Acquisition of a Computerized Circulation Control System for Tacoma Public Library. Tacoma, WA: Tacoma Public Library; 1977. 74p. Available from: the author, Tacoma Public Library, 1102 Tacoma Avenue South, Tacoma, WA 98402.

HEWITT, JOE A. 1976. The Impact of OCLC. American Libraries. May 1976; 7(5): 268-275. ISSN: 0002-9769.

HILTZ, STARR ROXANNE; TUROFF, MURRAY. 1978. The Network Nation: Human Communication via Computer. Reading, PA: Addison-Wesley Publishing Co.; 1978. 528p. ISBN: 0-201-03140X (hardbound); 0-201-03141-8 (paperback).

HITCHINGHAM, EILEEN E. 1977. Selecting Measures Applicable to Evaluation of On-Line Literature Searching. Drexel Library Quarterly. 1977 July; 13(3): 52-67. ISSN: 0012-6160; LC: 65-9911.

HOLROYD, GIDEON, ed. 1977. Studies in Library Management: Volume 4. Hamden, CT: Shoestring Press; 1977. 178p. ISBN: 0-208-01547-7.

HOUGHTON, BERNARD; CONVEY, JOHN. 1977. On-Line Information Retrieval Systems: An Introductory Manual to Principles and Practice. Hamden, CT: Linnet Books; 1977. 160p. ISBN: 0-208-01660; LC: 77-21858.

HORTON, FOREST W. 1977. Needed: A New Doctrine for Information Resources Management. In: Fry, Bernard M.; Shepherd, Clayton A., comps. Information Management in the 1980s: Proceedings of the 40th Annual Meeting of the American Society for Information Science: Volume 14, Part I: Abstracts, Part II: Full Papers; 1977 September 26-October 1; Chicago, IL. White Plains, NY: Knowledge Industries Publications, Inc.; 1977. Part I, p48; Part II, 4-A10; microfiche; 24x reduction. ISSN: 0044-7870; ISBN: 0-914236-12-1.

INFORMATION RETRIEVAL AND LIBRARY AUTOMATION. 1979. Second Online Information Meeting Report from Britain. Information Retrieval & Library Automation. 1979 January; 14(8): 1-3. ISSN: 0020-0220.

JONES, ALEXANDER M. 1977. Network Simulation Project; User Interface Manual. Princeton, NJ: EDUCOM; 1977 November. 93p. Available from: the author, EDUCOM Network Simulation Project, P.O. Box 364, Princeton, NJ 08540.

JONES, DENNIS. 1977. Library Statistical Data Base Formats and Definitions. Boulder, CO: Western Interstate Commission for Higher Education; 1977. 274p. ERIC: ED 146911.

JONES, WARREN T.   1976.   A Fuzzy Set Characterization of Interaction in Scientific Research.   Journal of the American Society for Information Science.   1976 September-October; 27(5-6): 307-310.   ISSN: 0002-8231; CODEN: AISJB6.

KENT, ALLEN; COHEN, JACOB; MONTGOMERY, K. LEON; WILLIAMS, JAMES G.; BULICK, STEPHEN; FLYNN, ROGER R.; SABOR, WILLIAM N.; MANSFIELD, UNA.   1979.   Use of Library Materials: The University of Pittsburgh Study.   New York, NY: Marcel Dekker, Inc.; 1979 April.   268p.

KENT, ALLEN; GALVIN, THOMAS J., eds.   1977.   Library Resource Sharing: Proceedings of the Conference on Resource Sharing in Libraries; 1976; Pittsburgh, PA.   New York, NY: Marcel Dekker; 1977.   356p.   ISBN: 0-8247-6605-09; LC: 77-005399.

KIEWITT, EVA L.   1979.   Evaluating Information Retrieval Systems.   Westport, CT: Greenwood Press; 1979.   168p.   ISBN: 0-313-20521-3; LC: 78-55322.

KING, DONALD W., RODERER, NANCY K.   1978.   Systems Analysis of Scientific and Technical Communication in the United States: The Electronic Alternative to Communication through Paper-Based Journals.   Rockville, MD: King Research, Inc.; 1978 May.   Available from: King Research Inc., 6000 Executive Boulevard, Rockville, MD 20852.

KIRCHNER, JAKE.   1979.   Post Office, Western Union Put ECOM on Hold.   Computerworld.   1979 May 7; 13(10): 12.   ISSN: 0010-4841.

KRONICK, DAVID A.; BOWDEN, VIRGINIA M.   1978.   Management Data for Collection Analysis and Development.   Bulletin of the Medical Library Association.   1978 October; 66(4): 407-413.   ISSN: 0025-7338.

LANCASTER, F. WILFRID.   1977.   The Measurement and Evaluation of Library Services.   Washington, DC: Information Resources Press; 1977.   395p.   ISBN: 0-87815-017-X; LC: 77-72081.

LANCASTER, F. WILFRID; CLEVERDON, CYRIL W., eds.   1977.   Evaluation and Scientific Management of Libraries and Information Centres: Proceedings of the NATO Advanced Study Institute on the Evaluation and Scientific Management of Libraries and Information Centres; 1975 August 17-29; Bristol, England.   Leyden, The Netherlands: Noordhoff; 1977.   184p.

LC INFORMATION BULLETIN.   1979.   The Bibliographic Service Development Program of the Council on Library Resources.   LC Information Bulletin.   1979 April 6; 38(14): 132-134.   ISSN: 0041-7904.

LEGARD, LAWRENCE K.; BOURNE, CHARLES P.   1976.   An Improved Title Word Search Key for Large Catalog Files.   Journal of Library Automation.   1976 December; 9(4): 318-327.   ISSN: 0022-2240; CODEN: JLAUAY.

LERNER, RITA G.; AULIANO, JOHN; FEINMAN, ROBERT; CREPS, JOHN E., JR.; DOSAMANTES, DANIEL.   1976.   Interchange of Data Bases.   New York, NY: American Institute of Physics; 1976 July.   127p.   NTIS: PB-272502/6GA.

LEVINE, JAMIE J.; LOGAN, TIMOTHY.   1977.   Online Resource Sharing: A Comparison of BALLOTS and OCLC. A Guide for Library Administrators.   Sacramento, CA: California Library Authority for Systems and Services (CLASS); 1977 June.   Available from: CLASS, 1415 Koll Circle, Suite 101, San Jose, CA 95112.

LIBRARY COMPUTER EQUIPMENT REVIEW. 1979. William Saffady, Editor-in-Chief, Westport, CT: Microform Review, Inc.; 1979. (Bi-annual; Library rate: $125.00 per year). ISSN: 0191-1295.

LINDQUIST, MATS G. 1978. The Dynamics of Information Search Services. Stockholm, Sweden: Royal Institute of Technology Library: 1978 February. 191p. (Stockholm Papers in Library and Information Science; Report TRITA-LIB-6012). Available from: System Dynamics Group, Room E40-253, Sloan School of Management, Massachusetts Institute of Technology, Cambridge, MA 02139; also available from: Swedish Council for Scientific Information and Documentation, 100 72 Stockholm, Sweden, as Report no. 732063 S. ISBN: 91-85212-32-6.

LJ/SLJ HOTLINE. 1979a. Washington Library Network and Research Libraries Group Announce Link. LJ/SLJ Hotline. 1979 April 9; 8(14): 3-4. ISSN: 0000-0078.

LJ/SLJ HOTLINE. 1979b. Conference Report: LACUNY Eyes Information Marketing. LJ/SLJ Hotline. 1979 April 23; 8(16): 5-7. ISSN: 0000-0078.

LONG, BETH. 1978. Conversion: The TacoMARC Project. Tacoma, WA: Tacoma Public Library; 1978. 133p. Available from: the author, Tacoma Public Library, 1102 Tacoma Avenue South, Tacoma, WA 98402.

MACHINE-READABLE DATA FILES CONFERENCE SECRETARIAT. 1978. Report on the Conference on Cataloging and Information Services for Machine-Readable Data Files (MRDF), 1978 March 29-31; Warrenton, VA. Arlington, VA: MRDF Conference Secretariat; 1978. 210p. Available from: Data Use and Access Laboratories, Suite 900, 1601 North Kent Street, Arlington, VA 22209.

MARCUS, RICHARD S.; REINTJES, J. FRANCIS. 1976. The Networking of Interactive Bibliographic Retrieval Systems. Cambridge, MA: Massachusetts Institute of Technology; Electronic Systems Laboratory; 1976 March. 174p. NTIS: PB-252-407.

MARKUSON, BARBARA E. 1977. Analysis of Requirements of On-Line Network Cataloging Services for Smaller Academic, Public, School and Other Libraries: A Demonstration Project Using the OCLC System. Washington, DC: U.S. Office of Education; 1977. 60p. ERIC: ED 140861.

MARTIN, SUSAN K. 1976. Tools for the Information Community. Library Journal. 1976 January 1; 101(1): 163-168. ISSN: 0000-0027; ISBN: 0-8352-0892-3.

MARTIN, SUSAN K. 1978. Library Networks, 1978-79. White Plains, NY: Knowledge Industry Publications, Inc.; 1978. 144p. ISBN: 0-914236-18-0; LC: 78-10666.

MCQUILLAN, JOHN M.; CERF, VINTON G. 1978. Tutorial: A Practical View of Computer Communications Protocols. New York, NY: Institute of Electrical and Electronics Engineers, Inc.; 1978. 258p. LC: 78-61493; IEEE no. EHO 137-0. Available from: IEEE Computer Society, 5855 Naples Plaza, Suite 301, Long Beach, CA 90803.

MONTAGUE, ELEANOR A. 1976. Cost and Funding Studies of the Proposed Western Interstate Bibliographic Network. Boulder, CO: Western Interstate Commission for Higher Education; 1972. 62p. ERIC: ED 136746.

MONTGOMERY, K. LEON; BULICK, STEPHEN; FETTERMAN, JOHN; KENT, ALLEN. 1976. Cost-Benefit Model of Library Acquisitions in

Terms of Use: Progress Report.   Journal of the American Society for Information Science.   1976 January-February; 27(1): 173-174.   ISSN: 0002-8231; CODEN: AISJB6.

MOSLEY, ISOBEL JEAN.   1977.   Cost-Effectiveness Analysis of the Automation of a Circulation System.   Journal of Library Automation.   1977 September; 10(3): 240-254.   ISSN: 0022-2240; CODEN: JLAUAY.

MYERS, DALE C.; RATHBUN, JOYCE A.; TATE, FRED A.; WEISGERBER, DAVID W.   1976.   Bridging and Interlinking the Information Resources.   Journal of Chemical Information and Computer Sciences.   1976 February; 16(1): 16-19.   ISSN: 0095-2338; CODEN: JCISD8.

NATIONAL   FEDERATION   OF   ABSTRACTING   AND   INDEXING SERVICES (NFAIS).   1977.   On-Line Command Chart: A Quick User's Guide for Bibliographic Search Systems.   Revised edition.   Philadelphia, PA: NFAIS; 1977.   Available from: NFAIS, 3401 Market Street, Philadelphia, PA 19104.

NATIONAL MICROGRAPHICS ASSOCIATION.   1976.   COM and Its Applications.   Silver Spring, MD: National Micrographics Association; 1976.   192p.   ISBN: 0-89258-043-7; LC: 76-43197.

NETWORK   TECHNICAL   ARCHITECTURE   GROUP.   1978.   Message Delivery System for the National Library and Information Service Network: General Requirements.   Washington, DC: Library of Congress Network Development Office; 1978.   35p.   (Hartmann, David C., ed; Network Planning Paper no. 4).   ISSN: 0160-9742; ISBN: 0-8444-0300-8.

NEW ENGLAND BOARD OF HIGHER EDUCATION. NEW ENGLAND LIBRARY INFORMATION NETWORK.   1977.   Demonstration and Evaluation of the Effects of Incentives on Resource Sharing Using a Computerized Interlibrary Communications System.   Wellesley, MA: New England Board of Higher Education; 1977.   70p.   ERIC: ED 148344.

NEW ENGLAND BOARD OF HIGHER EDUCATION. NEW ENGLAND LIBRARY INFORMATION NETWORK.   1978.   Implementation of a Computerized Interlibrary System to Provide Market Value Information for Resource Sharing to a Multi-Type Library Network.   Available from: New England Library Information Network, 40 Grove Street, Wellesley, MA 02181.

PALMOUR, VERNON E.; RODERER, NANCY K.   1978.   Library Resource Sharing through Networks.   In: Williams, Martha E., ed.   Annual Review of Information Science and Technology: Volume 13.   White Plains, NY: Knowledge Industry Publications, Inc.; 1978.   147-177.   ISBN: 0-914236-21-0; ISSN: 0066-4200; CODEN: ARISBc.

PAN, ELIZABETH.   1974.   New York State Library Automated Serials Control System.   Albany, NY: The State University of New York; 1974.   116p.   Available from: New York State Library, Education and Cultural Center, Albany, NY 12224.

PIERCE, ANTON R.; TAYLOR, JOE K.   1978.   A Model for Comparison of Automated Cataloging Systems.   Journal of Library Automation.   1978 March; 11(1): 6-23.   ISSN: 0022-2240; CODEN: JLAUAY.

RADECKI, TADEUSZ.   1976.   New Approach to the Problem of Information System Effectiveness Evaluation.   Information Processing & Management.   1976; 12(5): 319-326.

RICHMOND, PHYLLIS A.   1976.   Classification from PRECIS: Some Possibilities.   Journal of the American Society for Information Science.   1976 July-August; 27(4): 240-247.   ISSN: 0002-8231; CODEN: AISJB6.

ROBERTSON, STEPHEN E. 1978. On the Nature of Fuzz: A Diatribe. Journal of the American Society for Information Science. 1978 November; 29(6): 304-307. ISSN: 0002-8231; CODEN: AISJB6.

ROSENTHAL, JOSEPH A. 1978. Planning for the Catalogs: A Managerial Perspective. Journal of Library Automation. 1978 September; 11(3): 192-205. ISSN: 0022-2240; CODEN: JLAUAY.

ROSS, RYBURN M. 1977. Cost Analysis of Automation in Technical Services. In: Divilbiss, J.L., ed. The Economics of Library Automation: Proceedings of the Clinic on Library Applications of Data Processing; 1976; Urbana, IL. Champaign, IL: University of Illinois, Graduate School of Library Science; 1977. 10-27. ISBN: 0-87845-04607; LC: 77-075153.

ROTHNIE, JAMES B., JR.; BERNSTEIN, PHILIP A.; SHIPMAN, DAVID W., eds. 1978. Distributed Data-Base Management. New York, NY: Institute of Electrical and Electronics Engineers, Inc.; 1978. 260p. IEEE no.: EHO 141-2. Available from: IEEE Computer Society, 5855 Naples Plaza, Suite 301, Long Beach, CA 90803.

ROUSE, SANDRA H. 1978. Application of a Library Network Model: A Case Study of the Suburban Library System. Urbana, IL: University of Illinois Coordinated Science Laboratory; 1978. 145p. (CSL report T-74; Series report no. 9: A Mathematical Model of the Illinois Interlibrary Loan Network).

ROUSE, SANDRA H.; ROUSE, WILLIAM B. 1977a. Design of a Model-Based Online Management Information System for Interlibrary Loan Networks. In: Fry, Bernard M.; Shepherd, Clayton A., comps. Information Management in the 1980s: Proceedings of the 40th Annual Meeting of the American Society for Information Science: Volume 14, Part I: Abstracts, Part II: Full Papers; 1977 September 26-October 1; Chicago, IL. White Plains, NY: Knowledge Industry Publications, Inc.; 1977. Part I, p76; Part II, 7-G7; microfiche; 24x reduction. ISSN: 0044-7870; ISBN: 0-914236-12-1.

ROUSE, WILLIAM B.; ROUSE, SANDRA H. 1977b. Assessing the Impact of Computer Technology in the Performance of Interlibrary Loan Networks. Journal of the American Society for Information Science. 1977 March; 28(2): 79-88. ISSN: 0002-8231; CODEN: AISJB6.

SACHS, WLADIMIR M. 1976. An Approach to Associative Retrieval through the Theory of Fuzzy Sets. Journal of the American Society for Information Science. 1976 March-April; 27(2): 85-87. ISSN: 0002-8231; CODEN: AISJB6.

SALTON, GERARD; WONG, A.; YU, CLEMENT T. 1976. Automatic Indexing Using Term Discrimination. Information Processing & Management. 1976; 12(1): 43-51.

SAMUELSON, KJELL; BORKO, HAROLD; AMEY, G.X. 1977. Information Systems and Networks. Amsterdam, The Netherlands: North-Holland Publishing Co.; 1977. 148p. ISBN: 0-7204-0407-X; LC: 75-40169.

SCHOLZ, WILLIAM H. 1976. A Mathematical Model for Comparison of Bibliographic Data Bases. Journal of the American Society for Information Science. 1976 May-June; 27(3): 183-184. ISSN: 0002-8231; CODEN: AISJB6.

SHARIFY, NASSER. 1977. The Challenge of Two Centuries: Creation of Iran's Pahlavi National Library. In: The Bowker Annual of Library and

Book Trade Information, 22nd edition. New York, NY: R.R. Bowker
Co.; 1977. 417-423. ISBN: 0-8352-0967-9; ISSN: 0068-0540; LC: 55-
12434.

SHIREY, DONALD L. 1978. Management Information Systems for Large
Institutions: A Plea for More Control of Input Data. Bulletin of the
American Society for Information Science. 1978 October; 5(1): 12-13.
ISSN: 0095-4403.

SILCOFF, B. 1978. Computerized Bibliographic Centres Substudy. In:
Library Processing Facilities: Volume 2. Ottawa, Canada: National
Library of Canada; 1978 May 12. 28p. (Draft Document). Available
from: National Library of Canada, Document no. 1978-05-12.

SPARCK JONES, KAREN; BATES, R.G. 1977. Research on Automatic
Indexing 1974-1976. Cambridge, England: University of Cambridge,
Computer Laboratory; 1977. Volume I: text, 121p; Volume II: figures
and tables, 210p.

STANFIELD, JONATHAN. 1977. The Future Practice and Environment
of Information Management. In: Fry, Bernard M.; Shepherd, Clayton
A., comps. Information Management in the 1980s: Proceedings of the
40th Annual Meeting of the American Society for Information Science:
Volume 14, Part I: Abstracts; 1977 September 26-October 1; Chicago,
IL. White Plains, NY: Knowledge Industry Publications, Inc.; 1977.
Part I, p20; Part II, F-9; microfiche; 24x reduction. ISSN: 0044-7870;
ISBN: 0-914236-12-1.

STIERWALT, RALPH E. 1976. UNICAT/TELECAT: A Report on the
Development of a Union Catalog in Ontario. Ontario Library Review
(Canada). 1976 September; 60(3): 180-185. ISSN: 0030-2996.

SUMMIT, ROGER K.; FIRSCHEIN, OSCAR. 1976. Investigation of the
Public Library as a Linking Agent to Major Scientific, Educational, Social,
and Environmental Data Bases. Palo Alto, CA: Lockheed Missiles and
Space Co.; 1976. 3 volumes. (Two year interim report in 3 volumes:
Main Report, Project Evaluation, and Publicity Aspects; LMSC-D502595).
NTIS: PC E08, PB 0261858-Set.

TASK FORCE ON AMERICAN NATIONAL STANDARDS COMMITTEE
Z39, ACTIVITIES AND FUTURE DIRECTIONS. 1978. American
National Standards Committee Z39: Recommended Future Directions.
Washington, DC: National Commission on Libraries and Information
Science; 1978. 63p. LC: 78-829; USGPO: 052-003-00518-2.

TELEDYNE BROWN ENGINEERING. 1976. Study of Systems and Techniques for Data Base Management. Huntsville, AL: Teledyne Brown
Engineering; 1976. 61p. NTIS: N77-26013/IGA.

TIGHE, RUTH L.; LEVINE, JAMIE J. 1976. On-Line Shared Cataloging
in NELINET Libraries: Report of a Survey. Wellesley, MA: New England Library Information Network; 1976. 666p. (Council on Library
Resources, Washington, DC, Report no. CLR653). ERIC: ED 140773.

TOMBERG, ALEX. 1977. European Information Networks. In: Williams,
Martha E., ed. Annual Review of Information Science and Technology:
Volume 12. White Plains, NY: Knowledge Industry Publications, Inc.;
1977. 219-246. ISBN: 0-914236-11-3; ISSN: 0066-4200; CODEN:
ARISBc.

TWITCHELL, ANNE; SPREHN, MARY. 1976. Implementation of the
Ohio College Library Center's Proposed Serials Control Subsystem at the
University of South Florida Library; Some Preliminary Considerations.

Tampa, FL: University of South Florida; 1976.   37p.   ERIC: ED
124220.

TYNER, S.; STAFFORD, T.; MILLER, E.W.   1976.   UNICIRC: The Politics
in Designing an OCLC-Based Circulation System.   In: Martin, Susan K.,
comp.   Information * Politics: Proceedings of the 39th Annual Meeting
of the American Society for Information Science (ASIS): Volume 13,
Part I: Abstracts of Papers, Part II: Full Papers; 1976 October 4-9; San
Francisco, CA.   Washington, DC: ASIS; 1976.   Part I, p95; Part II, 6-E9;
microfiche; 24x reduction.   ISSN: 0044-7870; ISBN: 0-87715-4139;
LC: 64-8303; CODEN: PAISDQ.

U.S. LIBRARY OF CONGRESS.   1976.   Composite MARC Format. A
Tabular Listing of Content Designators Used in the MARC Formats.
Canadian Library Journal.   1976 April; 33(2): 67-72.   ISSN: 0008-4352.

U.S. LIBRARY OF CONGRESS. NETWORK ADVISORY GROUP. 1977.
Toward a National Library and Information Service Network.   Washington, DC: Library of Congress, Network Development Office; 1977 June.
54p.   (Avram, H.D.; Maruyama, L.S., eds.).   Available from: Library of
Congress.

U.S. LIBRARY OF CONGRESS. NETWORK DEVELOPMENT OFFICE.
1978.   The Role of the Library of Congress in the Evolving National
Network.   Washington, DC: Library of Congress; 1978.   141p.   (Final
report of a study conducted by Lawrence F. Buckland and William L.
Basinski).   ISBN: 0-8444-0269-9; USGPO: 030-000-00102.

U.S. NATIONAL COMMISSION ON LIBRARIES AND INFORMATION
SCIENCE (NCLIS).   1975.   Toward a National Program for Library and
Information Service: Goals for Action.   Washington, DC: NCLIS; 1975.
106p.   USGPO: 052-003-00086-5.

U.S. NATIONAL COMMISSION ON LIBRARY AND INFORMATION
SCIENCE (NCLIS). TASK FORCE ON THE ROLE OF THE SCHOOL
LIBRARY MEDIA PROGRAM IN THE NATIONAL PROGRAM.   1978.
Washington, DC: NCLIS; 1978.   91p.   Available from: NCLIS, 1717 K
Street, N.W., Washington, DC 20036, or from: Superintendent of Docu-
ments, Government Printing Office, Washington, DC 20402.   LC: 78-
26243; USGPO: 052-003-0062207.

U.S. NATIONAL COMMISSION ON LIBRARY AND INFORMATION
SCIENCE (NCLIS) NATIONAL BUREAU OF STANDARDS (NBS).
TASK FORCE ON COMPUTER NETWORK PROTOCOL.   1977.   A
Computer Network Protocol for Library and Information Science Appli-
cations.   Washington, DC: NCLIS; 1977.   90p.   LC: 78-9898.

UNIVERSITY OF CALIFORNIA.   1977.   A Plan for Development 1978-
1988.   Berkeley, CA: University of California; 1977 July.   224p.   ERIC:
ED 156108.

VOIGT, MELVIN J.; HARRIS, M.H., eds.   1977.   Advances in Librarianship:
Volume 7.   New York, NY: Academic Press; 1977.   348p.   ISBN: 0-12-
785007-4.

WAX, DAVID M.; VAUGHAN, PATRICIA E.   1977.   Northeast Academic
Science Information Center (NASIC) Final Report, March 1973 to
December 1976 on Grants NSF-SIS73-08366; NSF-GN-37296.   Wellesley,
MA: New England Board of Higher Education; 1977 May.   117p.   NTIS:
PB-267 758/IGA.

WEISBROD, DAVID L. 1977. NUC Reporting and MARC Redistribution: Their Functional Confluence and Its Implications for a Redefinition of the MARC Format. Journal of Library Automation. 1977 September; 10(3): 226-239. ISSN: 0022-2240; ERIC: EJ 172226.

WELLISCH, HANS H., ed. 1977. The PRECIS Index System: Principles, Applications, and Prospects: Proceedings of the International PRECIS Workshop; 1976 October 15-17; College Park, MD. New York, NY: H.W. Wilson; 1977. 211p. ISBN: 0-8242-0611-8; LC: 77-1932.

WEST, MARTHA; BUTLER, BRETT. 1977. Performance Measures in Automated Systems Management. In: Divilbiss, J.L., ed. The Economics of Library Automation: Proceedings of the Clinic on Library Applications of Data Processing; 1976; Urbana, IL. Champaign, IL: University of Illinois, Graduate School of Library Science; 1977. 48-71. ISBN: 0-87845-046-7; LC: 77-075153.

WEST, MARTHA; QUIROS, ALICE; GLUSHENOK, GEORGE, comps. 1978. Library Automation, A Bibliography 1973-77. Journal of Library Automation. 1978 December; 11(4): 339-365. ISSN: 0022-2240.

WHEELBARGER, JOHNNY J. 1977. The Effectiveness of a Computerized Library Network in Meeting the Performance Expectations of the Members in the Administration of College Libraries. 1977 August. 94p. (Ph.D. dissertation). ERIC: ED 143370.

WHITE, HERBERT S. 1977. Library Management in the Tight Budget Seventies. Bulletin of the Medical Library Association. 1977 January; 65(1): 6-12. ISSN: 0025-7338; CODEN: BMLAAG.

WHITE, HOWARD D., ed. 1977. Machine-Readable Social Science Data. Drexel Library Quarterly. 1977 January; 13(1). (Entire issue). ISSN: 0012-6160; CODEN: DRLQBK.

WILLIAMS, JAMES G. 1977. Simulation and Library Network Design. In: Fry, Bernard M.; Shepherd, Clayton A., comps. Information Management in the 1980s: Proceedings of the 40th Annual Meeting of the American Society for Information Science: Volume 14, Part II, Full Papers; 1977 September 26-October 1; Chicago, IL. White Plains, NY: Knowledge Industry Publications, Inc.; 1977. 10-A1, microfiche; 24x reduction. ISSN: 0044-7870; ISBN: 0-914236-12-1.

WILLIAMS, MARTHA E.; MACLAURY, KEITH D. 1977. A State-Wide Union Catalog Feasibility Study. Urbana, IL: University of Illinois, Coordinated Science Laboratory; 1977. 80p. ERIC: ED 148340.

WILLIAMS, MARTHA E.; BARTH, STEPHEN W.; PREECE, SCOTT E. 1979. Summary Statistics for Five Years of the MARC Database. 49p. (Submitted to Journal of Library Automation, 1979 January 23). Available from: the authors, University of Illinois, Information Retrieval Research Lab; Urbana, IL 61801.

WITTIG, G.R. 1977. CONSER (Cooperative Conversion of Serials Project): Building an On-Line International Serials Data Base. Unesco Bulletin for Libraries (France). 1977 September-October; 31(5): 305-310. (Editions in English, French, Spanish, Russian). CODEN:UNBLAB.

WOOSTER, HAROLD. 1976. An Experiment in Networking: The LHNCBC Experimental CAI Network, 1971-1975. Journal of the

American Society for Information Science.   1976 September-October;
27(5-6): 329-338.   ISSN: 0002-8231; CODEN: AISJB6.
ZUEST, PAT.   1977.   DOBIS: An Outsider's View.   Emergency Librarian.
1977 March/April; 4(4): 11-13.   ISSN: 0315-8888.

IV

The Profession

In this volume the profession is considered in terms of the increasing activity and concern about "Education and Training for Online Systems." In her review of this area Judith Wanger observes that on-the-job training has been a major contributor to the growing use of online systems. She reports that the literature is highly fragmented, reflecting the fact that education- and training-related programs, activities, and resources have attracted the interest and efforts of several types of organizations and many individuals. The central and most active source of education and training continues to be the online service organizations, although there has been increased activity by database producers and library schools. Users also continue to learn on their own and have become educators and trainers of their colleagues, working as individuals and through their online users groups and professional associations. Available data suggest that only about one-half of the online users are formally trained by online service organizations.

The roles of these various sources of education and training overlap somewhat, but, as reflected in the programs described in the literature, each is meeting one or more needs of several different target audiences: those who are potential users of online systems, those who will be the searchers, and those who already are searchers. The training approaches all tend to be labor intensive and personalized. Wanger reviews some of the important alternatives to personal instruction that are now being developed, particularly the computer-assisted instruction programs that are being designed for use on local computers.

She concludes that the tested experiences, methodologies, and principles that have been developed to date need to be consolidated into a comprehensive and cohesive body of knowledge.

8 Education and Training for Online Systems

JUDITH WANGER
Cuadra Associates, Inc.

INTRODUCTION

Education and training activities have been instrumental in the diffusion and adoption of online retrieval technology, but the magnitude of their role has not been assessed. Sketchy data indicate that on-the-job training alone— including the costs of workshops, user materials, and staff time—represents a multimillion dollar investment by those who are using online bibliographic database services. Thus, it is appropriate that this aspect of online systems and services is being recognized for the first time in its own chapter of *ARIST.*

Framework and Definitions

It is not always easy to make a clear distinction between education and training. Traditional educational objectives may require training components and vice-versa. It is more useful to think of the learning experience in terms of the degree to which the mastery of certain basic skills and a specified level of performance are to be achieved.

The area of education and training for online systems can be defined narrowly to encompass only formal workshops and courses, or more broadly to include the entire spectrum of formal and informal activities and tools associated with the learning experience. Any comprehensive review must embrace this broader definition and must include the range of programs, materials, and techniques that are available to expose potential users to the technology, to educate them to basic principles and use of the technology, to train those who will actually use the systems, and to provide for their continuing education.

Both WILLIAMS and KEENAN (1978) have adopted the broad view espoused here. Williams establishes a framework within which to review the need for and value of training, and she outlines the kinds of information that are required by each of several target audiences—from those who generate databases to those who use that information. Keenan identifies three types of formal training programs: 1) promotional activities, aimed at all potential users; 2) educational training, for students in library and information studies and for working librarians and information specialists; and 3) operational training, for searchers who will immediately be using the systems in their work.

Both authors identify several sources of education and training, including the generators of databases, the online service providers, universities, and professional associations. The central source and support for most activities and materials are the online services and the database producers. It is sometimes convenient to refer to them as one type of source—i.e., "suppliers." In other cases, it is important to refer to them separately—as online services and as database producers—to reflect the differences in their contributions and approaches.

Because data from the National Science Foundation (NSF)-sponsored "online impact study" (WANGER ET AL.) indicated that only about one-half of the respondents in this 1974-1975 survey had been formally trained by suppliers, it is important to recognize the role of users in self-instruction and as educators and trainers of their colleagues. Suppliers are reaching searchers and academicians who, in turn, frequently become educators and trainers of other potential users and of their own client groups. This cycle has greatly extended the sales and training forces of the suppliers and has contributed significantly to the growth in online system use.

Scope and Organization

Training-related literature was first reviewed in *ARIST* by MARRON & FIFE and again by MCCARN. Selected works initially reported on in those chapters are included here to characterize more completely the literature in specific areas.

Literature from 1973 was reviewed for this chapter, although this author has focused primarily on recent works. Another focus here is on education and training for use of online bibliographic reference systems; this excludes activities related specifically to technical-processing support systems, such as OCLC. As is typical of the field of education in general, considerable activity is documented only informally (e.g., newsletters, announcements, mimeographed syllabi, and notes). These sources as well as published search aids from suppliers are not usually covered by indexing and abstracting services; they are sometimes referenced in the text but are generally not included in the chapter bibliography.

In his *ARIST* chapter, MCCARN reported that very little had been written during the previous two years about online training. Strictly speaking, he was correct. What exists is fragmented and difficult to find, being represented only briefly in little-known reports and in sections of the general literature of online system use. In both the initial bibliography of online literature and its update, HAWKINS (1977; 1978) identifies a total of only 32 references from 1965 to 1977 under the heading of user education and training. This trend seems to be changing, as previous emphases on system design, evaluation, and use give way to a separate focus on how to define the search process and, therefore, how to learn it and how to teach it.

The literature in this area stems primarily from practitioners—those who are training and those who are being trained. The literature tends to be compartmentalized, primarily by the source of training or education or by the intended audience. Thus, training sources and audiences have been used as the primary organizing principles in this chapter.

GENERAL SURVEYS AND REVIEWS

For the reader who needs a state-of-the-art perspective, there are several articles and papers that together convey the full range of education, training, and learning experiences available to the potential and current user of online systems. None alone covers the full breadth of possible learning experiences, although the survey and assessment by KEENAN (1977) comes close.

Surveys

Two survey efforts, one by KEENAN (1977) and one by UNRUH, describe many training activities and programs sponsored or developed by various types of organizations. The Keenan survey, undertaken on behalf of the Commission of the European Communities—sponsors of EURONET, a planned Europe-wide telecommunications network—is the more ambitious, with its worldwide coverage of programs sponsored by online services, database producers, educational institutions, and national and international organizations. Unruh includes descriptions for selected U.S. services and producers as well as a discussion of activities being sponsored by selected online users' groups in the United States. The authors also describe some of the changes made in individual programs over the past few years.

Although the case-by-case approach (i.e., by specific organization within a particular class) in each survey is helpful, such surveys could be even more useful if the authors provided summary descriptions and statistics on their findings. For example, it would help to have summary tables that show the various components (e.g., workshops, newsletters, user aids) of full instructional programs across sources. For workshops, it would be useful to see summary tables for organizations in each group that show content, instructional staff, objectives, target audiences, duration, fees, and typical scheduling practices. This analysis would help in sorting out the roles and responsibilities that are being assumed by various groups and would be of practical value to managers, who must budget and plan for staff education and training.

The NSF-sponsored online impact study (WANGER ET AL.) still provides the only broadly based report of how users learn to use systems. These data first defined the extent to which users were learning informally—e.g., from colleagues and by self-instruction. Several other findings, including users' assessments of their learning experiences with multiple databases and multiple systems, are still of interest and need to be developed further.

Reviews

Several papers and collections of papers, as well as a tape of a panel discussion at the 1977 meeting of the AMERICAN SOCIETY FOR INFORMATION SCIENCE (ASIS), convey the flavor of debate on current issues. For example, panelists in the ASIS session identify a wide range of considerations involved in assigning roles and responsibilities to various sources of training and in developing needed programs.

Three collections of papers—ASSOCIATION OF INFORMATION AND DISSEMINATION CENTERS (ASIDIC); MACCAFFERTY; KENT & GALVIN—give various perspectives. The 1977 ASIDIC meeting, devoted entirely to "Training Methods: The 'How of Teaching,'" resulted in a summary paper of talks given by representatives of the supplier and academic communities. Although these papers may have fallen short of focusing on the "how" of teaching, they do help to formalize some important issues and problems in teaching (e.g., cost, heterogeneity of workshop attendees, and wide range of skills to be taught). The report by MacCafferty of the European Association of Scientific Information Dissemination Centers (EUSIDIC) meeting on user education contains diverse papers from database producers and users of several countries. Some are related to planned and operational online education programs. Selected papers from the 1977 Pittsburgh Conference on The On-Line Revolution in Libraries, edited by Kent & Galvin, cover several issues involved in the training and retraining of librarians and users, but they focus primarily on the adequacy of current programs and whether or not end users should be trained to do their own online searches. (Several papers from these collections are referenced individually in various sections of this chapter.)

BORGMAN provides a different type of overview, focusing on the user's point of view in what needs to be learned and why. The material is presented in the style of a manual or guide and is quite thorough. She advocates the need for and value of training and indicates what individuals can and should expect from their training.

Over the past few years, the person who has been the most vocal in identifying shortcomings in available training programs—particularly those sponsored by suppliers—is CARUSO (1978a; 1978b; 1978c). Each of her papers contains a similar assessment of the problems involved in learning to use online database services in the current mode (e.g., lack of clear objectives and too little practice time) and recommends as one solution the computer-assisted instruction (CAI) system—"TRAINER"—that is being developed at the University of Pittsburgh.

ONLINE DATABASE SERVICE SUPPLIERS

The contribution of online services and database producers to the education and training of users is extensive but is not reflected as such in the literature. Workshop schedules are frequently announced in newsletters and in a column in *ONLINE*, but some persons who have trained hundreds or thousands of users write little, if at all, for the professional literature. The reviews by UNRUH and by KEENAN (1977) confirm that, among the "supermarket" services, System Development Corp. (SDC) and Lockheed have developed the most active and comprehensive training programs. Over time, these programs have become more stable and similar. The program components include several types of training workshops: 1) regional new-user training sessions of one and a half days; 2) regional advanced-user sessions of one-half day; 3) on-site sessions tailored to user organizations' needs; and 4) multi-database sessions—i.e., the Lockheed "Update" and the SDC "Databases on Review" sessions that are given with database producers and, in the case of Lockheed, with users as co-instructors. Although multipurpose, these sessions focus on cross-file searching and on subject- or topic-oriented problem-solving. In addition, each supplier periodically announces the availability of special subject- or database-oriented workshops, sometimes given with database producers.

The fees for sessions offered by the online services vary and typically range from $25 per person for a half- or full-day session to approximately $100 per person for a multiday session. In some cases (e.g., the New York Times Information Bank), training and initial practice time are incorporated in a subscriber's start-up fee.

The economics of investing in education and training aimed at the online user have been perceived differently by database producers. Both types of suppliers associate increased use of the system with these activities, but the potential revenue is not seen in the same way. Online use is the main revenue source for most commercial online services but represents only a fraction of total revenues for database producers—less than 5%, according to KEENAN (1977).

At the time of the NSF-sponsored online impact study in 1974-1975, WANGER ET AL. reported that about 58% of the respondents in the survey learned about most of the databases from online suppliers; about 23% learned from database suppliers. In general, these data reflect the times: in 1974-1975, there was very little training with the database-producer community. The surveys by KEENAN (1977) and UNRUH suggest that the level of activity has increased but that even now only about 15% of the 70 or so bibliographic database producers are actively engaged in education- and training-related programs.

Programs sponsored by database producers vary considerably. Of nine producers, e.g., Predicasts, BIOSIS, and Chemical Abstracts Service, with some activity reported by KEENAN (1977), only four provide regularly scheduled sessions throughout the United States (and only two in Europe); three producers have only one kind of session, presumably for new users, and two have several levels of sessions (e.g., new and advanced). The workshop fees vary even more than those of the online services. About half of the suppliers in the Keenan survey did not charge for their sessions, and the other half charged around $50 per person or a flat fee of several hundred dollars.

Both types of suppliers perceive education and training as marketing tools, and the fees—variously described by some users as nominal and by others as prohibitive—are generally set to recover costs. The only actual cost figure to appear in the literature is that of BioSciences Information Service (BIOSIS). KEENAN (1977) quotes an estimate of $18 per person as the unit cost. One would need to know the basis of this figure, including the amount of online time spent during the session, to draw any conclusions or to make any meaningful comparisons among various supplier groups.

One important development in the past several years has been the joint session, which is sponsored by an online service and one or more database producers or by two database producers. These types of sessions are increasing (UNRUH; KEENAN, 1977). SDC and Lockheed initiated such joint sessions, working with their database suppliers, and joint sessions have since been introduced between Chemical Abstracts Service and BIOSIS, and between Engineering Index and the National Technical Information Service (NTIS). Others are planned for the near future.

The Online Services

An excellent presentation of objectives, content, and relationships among several components in a training program is provided by KASSEBAUM & LEITER of the National Library of Medicine (NLM). The authors trace the evolution of NLM's training program, from its eight-month course for users of the batch Medical Literature Analysis and Retrieval System (MEDLARS) and its three-week course for users of the online MEDLINE system to its present program. Although other online services and database producers may have envied the three-week course given by NLM (1971–1976), the authors report that the information load in this program was too great and that psychological and physical strain took its toll on attendees. In 1977, NLM replaced this approach with a coordinated five-level instructional program:

- Level 1: Prerequisite assignment on MEDLEARN, NLM's computer-assisted instructional program, which is available on the NLM computer on a dial-up basis from the trainees' own locations;
- Level 2: Initial five-day courses with NLM instructors, given periodically at NLM and elsewhere throughout the United States;
- Level 3: In-service (in attendees' own work environments) practicums for three to six months, with reading assignments and search exercises;
- Level 4: Advanced five-day course with NLM instructors;

- Level 5: Ongoing updates, through annual workshops, and continuing education, through specialized workshops, the
curricula for which are being developed by users.

The authors discuss the advantages they perceive in this modular approach,
which provides several entry points to meet particular users' needs. They
also describe the relationship of formal instruction to other facets of the
program, e.g., the availability of videotapes, slide/tape sets, and printed aids.

Evaluations of this program are continuing, and a change has already been
instituted in the advanced course (KASSEBAUM) to accommodate the needs
of an increasingly heterogeneous user group. In one segment of the program,
attendees will be able to focus either on advanced techniques for using the
chemically related files—e.g., RTECS (Registry of Toxic Effects of Chemical
Substances)—or for using the technical-processing files—e.g., CATLINE
(CATalog-on-Line).

No comparable elucidation of the programs of other services exists. The
start-up phase of training and education for the British Library Automated
Information Service (BLAISE) is described by GRADDON, who relates how
this new British online service is dealing with heterogeneous groups of users
and making compromises between the ideal and the practicable. In a
summary of a paper given at the 1977 ASIDIC meeting, WANGER (1977),
then at SDC, identifies the various components of the SDC Search Service
education and training program and focuses on specific challenges in teaching selected topics and developing appropriate sequencing of content.
STANLEY, of the Information Bank Service of the New York Times, discusses the need to stress training as an integral part of selling the online
service.

The first venture into computer-aided instruction for teaching the use of
online systems came from NLM. Its MEDLEARN program is described by
Eisenberg, now Kassebaum, in EISENBERG ET AL. Citing known deficiencies and limitations in the traditional modes of instruction (e.g., print, audio-
visual, and personal courses), the authors identify the strengths of the CAI
program—e.g., it overcomes computer anxiety and provides a sheltered environment to minimize the potential for confusion. In addition to its modular
design, a unique feature is that at the end of a given portion of the program,
the trainee can select a different way to have the same material presented
again. This feature is designed to overcome the limitations of any nonper-
sonalized instruction: the inability of the trainee to ask a question that leads
to the restatement of a particular instruction. An important attribute of this
paper is its articulation of several important educational principles that are
applicable to any kind of instructional approach.

Although there is no agreement on how much practice time is needed, the
literature abounds with the opinion that practice is the key to the development of searching skills. Lockheed is seeking to meet this need with its
ONTAP (Online Training and Practice) capability in the DIALOG system.
ONTAP permits searchers to compare their searches and search results to prestored "perfect" sets and to evaluate the effect of alternative formulations on

recall, precision, and cost. The full capabilities of ONTAP can be used with a one-year file of ERIC, the education database. Subsets of two chemical files are also available for practice, although exercises with prestored results are not available for comparisons. The charge for using ONTAP is $15 per hour. In a manual produced at Syracuse University, MARKEY & ATHERTON have expanded on the work of Charles Bourne and his associates, who originally designed ONTAP. They have produced a guide for the experienced searcher in using ERIC ONTAP for self-improvement.

The Database Producers

In contrast to the type of instruction provided by online services, which is aimed at teaching the use of a particular system and the principles for using a wide variety of databases on that system, the instruction provided by database producers is sharply focused on the use of a specific database. Instructional programs sponsored by database producers typically include content coverage, selection criteria, indexing and other editorial policies, and online search strategies. Database producers with a database available on more than one system face a difficult choice: whether to teach online use in a system-independent fashion or to relate the use of a database to each of the systems on which it is available. The latter approach is considered more satisfactory by users, although the issues involved have not been debated fully in the literature.

In general, tradition and lack of readiness among database producers have contributed to a cautious approach in undertaking full-scale education and training programs. ELIAS traces the educational role of BIOSIS from 1926 to 1977 and shows how changes in the organization's perception of its market-place have changed its approaches and levels of involvement in education and training activities. Initially, BIOSIS supported a fairly passive program that relied solely on printed documentation for its end users. This approach was retained as the organization's marketing efforts moved into the library community. A more active program evolved as the distribution media—print, magnetic tape, and online—and the marketing targets became more varied. Perhaps the most significant development was the establishment of a Professional Services and Education Department, which formally recognized the educational function in the organization. Although not documented, this same kind of development is evident among other database producers.

In two separate papers on the training program of the National Agricultural Library (NAL), both OLSEN and GILREATH note the need for training that resulted from the availability of a product online to a wide variety of users. Olsen's paper implies that NAL was pushed into a training mode on its agriculture database (AGRICOLA) because existing training programs and materials were inadequate. He notes that after two years of online experience with several systems, NAL realized that users were not finding citations that were known to be in the file, that intelligent people were frustrated with the systems, and that the online services' user manuals dealt with the file in too skimpy a fashion. Gilreath presents a more balanced and historically accurate view. He points out that many of the policies regarding acquisitions, selection, and indexing were documented only informally within an organization and that complete information about a given database was not readily at hand to provide to users (nor, we might add, to online services). As he puts it, the "need for information about input policies and procedures created something of a crisis among database producers, a crisis that has not wholly abated even today." Speaking as an occasional trainer on behalf of NAL, Gilreath describes the development of training workshops for AGRICOLA users. His discussions of training needs and difficulties and successful methods that he has used are particularly valuable.

Although economics and tradition may continue to restrain their activities, database producers will continue to meet pressure from users. Users' needs for database-specific training and materials are widely recognized. As both KEENAN (1978) and CARUSO (1978a) point out, there is an invisibility about an online database—its file structure and its contents. In a manual search, the eye and resourcefulness of the researcher can compensate for a lack of in-depth knowledge about the printed product. In an online search there are no comparable means of compensation that do not involve considerable time online, with its attendant increase in costs.

User and Search Aids

In the summary paper of her survey, KEENAN (1978) identifies about 20 different types of printed documentation that are available, although all types are not available from any one source. Most of these materials are prepared by the online services and database producers for various reasons. For example, a brochure of database descriptions is a sales tool for the online service, a reference tool for its users, and a promotional tool for use with the clients of these users. Major items within this list include system and database user manuals and guides and specific vocabulary aids (e.g., thesauri) prepared by the producers. These materials comprise a valuable component in the arsenal of instructionally related materials, although they are oriented more toward reference use than instructional support. According to McCarn (KEENAN, 1978), "online retrieval is both an intellectual subject and a technology. Technologies are learned through observation and use and not from written material." Nevertheless, currently available documentation has been and continues to be a major component in the instructional process. As noted earlier, about 55% of the searchers are learning to use systems through formal workshops given by suppliers. Among the approximately 45% of searchers who learned informally, most indicated that they first learned to use the system from the user's manuals (WANGER ET AL.). These data suggest the need for materials that are designed for self-instruction and informal training.

The documentation described by Keenan and others is generally not bibliographically controlled; neither are the newsletters and other announcements from online services and database producers. Thus, it is difficult for users to know what aids are available and from whom. A column in *ONLINE* is helping to remedy this problem, but the information is not always complete, and the distinction between new and old material is not always made clear.

Another part of the problem is selection; what subset of available materials should the online user have? COPPERNOLL-BLACH, in a section of a directory/guide prepared by the Chicago Online Users Group (COLUG) for new searchers in its area, identifies several major types of tools and gives some guidelines for purchasing an initial set of materials. She also includes the results of a survey of local users to evaluate about 70 different aids associated with systems and databases. Except for the basic system manuals, most of the aids were not known to most of the searchers surveyed. The survey data are too sparse to support strong recommendations for the new user, but the concept behind the survey is good and deserves further attention by users and user groups. One suspects that the problem for the user may get worse before it gets better. More and more database producers are offering database-specific manuals that duplicate, to varying degrees, the user manuals provided by the online services. It is not always clear to the user whether it is necessary to have both manuals or only one and, if the latter, which one.

A few suppliers, principally BIOSIS, Mead Data, and NLM, have developed nonprint training materials. As yet, no evaluations of these products have appeared in the literature.

LIBRARY SCHOOLS

In a challenge to schools of library and information science to accept modern technology and to prepare students to be of immediate use in jobs relating to all aspects of database processing and use, WILLIAMS states that "on-the-job training has always been needed in new fields until the education community accepted this responsibility for the field." In a 1977 survey, HARTER found that 42 of the 46 then-accredited ALA library schools that responded to his survey were providing online access to bibliographic databases for their students.

From other papers one can obtain a limited sense of how these programs are being designed, the methodologies that are being used, and the difficulties that are being encountered. WOOD, BELLARDO ET AL., and KNAPP & GAVRYCK offer detailed descriptions of programs instituted in their respective institutions for library school students. TRIOLO & REGAZZI outline the design of a continuing education institute for special librarians at the Southern Connecticut State College. Wood states that online systems were a more useful teaching tool in the information storage and retrieval course taught at Manchester Polytechnic than in the library automation course. Her report is particularly interesting for its description of the methodologies used in student evaluations of their online experiences. She used a rating scale to test views of students toward online systems and an adjectival fill-in matrix—e.g., learning to use Lockheed DIALOG is (easy) (desirable) (stimulating) (difficult) (unnecessary) (boring), etc.—to measure attitudinal changes among students. Bellardo et al. report that previous coursework at the University of Kentucky involving only demonstration and theoretical discussions was not meeting the students' professional training needs. Therefore, a separate course on Computer-Based Bibliographic Networks was developed. Students were exposed to three different systems: OCLC, MEDLINE, and DIALOG. The paper describes the three curriculum units and the attendant problems with terminals and scheduling. The authors also note the difficulties in balancing theory, readings, and hands-on practice to meet various student needs and objectives.

KNAPP & GAVRYCK and BELLARDO ET AL. discuss the use of adjunct faculty—experienced searchers from the university libraries—to teach these courses. Knapp & Gavryck describe the approach used by the State University of New York (SUNY) at Albany, which provides online system coursework during the school's intersession, when use of the library terminals is low and when the library school can piggy-back on its Bibliographic Retrieval Services, Inc. (BRS) subscription. This approach is one alternative to larger budgets or laboratory fees used by some other institutions (ATHERTON, 1977; BOURNE, 1977). Knapp & Gavryck emphasize that the intention is not to produce fully trained searchers. In this context, they discuss the major topics that are covered, the main messages that are conveyed, and the readings that are used to support classroom discussions.

Although there have been other papers from library schools (BORKO; SCOTT ET AL.; SIMPSON; TEDD & KEEN), their activities in this area—similar to the programs of suppliers—are still somewhat invisible. Curriculum objectives, syllabi, and resource materials are not being exchanged in any formal way, and it is difficult to assess the true extent to which the challenge of WILLIAMS is being met.

Major Issues

The major paper that presents some of the key issues involved in library school instruction comes from the Institute for Library Educators. In one of the position papers from this U.S. Office of Education (USOE)-funded study, MIGNON (1978a) reports on "Proposed Standards for Education in Online Searching in the Professional Librarianship Curriculum." The role and responsibility of the library school toward its students are clearly stated in two major goals: 1) consciousness raising—to ensure that all practitioners entering the profession are aware of the characteristics, value, and current limitations of online services; and 2) operator training—to provide fundamental training for those who plan to specialize in online services. The 20 faculty members deliberately used the term "training" to emphasize that technical skill is an essential ingredient in professionalism. Although we can expect some debate over the merit of these two goals, one of academia's most difficult challenges is to establish realistic competency-based indicators for operator training and to define what is meant by "the ability to execute a satisfactory search for one end user." In addition, the educators at the Institute outlined some proposed standards for faculty and instructional resources and called for voluntary periodic peer review (not certification or accreditation) of their programs.

Costs. Two related issues in the teaching of online searching in library schools concern the amount of practice time that is needed to achieve a specified level of skill and the costs of supporting the attainment of these skills. In MIGNON (1978a), it is recommended that each student have at least five hours of online time to meet the goal of providing operator training. (For the consciousness-raising objective, it is recommended that demonstrations will suffice but that it is highly desirable for all students to have one hour of hands-on time.) The budget for this first objective is $100 per student; for the second objective, $20 per student. Both figures are based on educational rates (typically $15 per hour) currently provided by the major online services.

The HARTER survey showed that an average of two and one-half hours of online time was being provided to students. In a 1976 survey of 14 library schools teaching MEDLINE in courses on health sciences librarianship, BERK & DAVIDSON report that the average was two hours. Interestingly, half of the instructors did not believe that the online time allowed was sufficient, but the range of time that they suggested was very wide—from six to 40 hours. CARUSO (1978c) reports that at least eight hours are needed to move beyond the stage at which system mechanics can hamper the intellectual functions and performance at a terminal.

The difference in cost between two and one-half hours of online time and 40 hours is considerable—about $40 vs. $600 per student. It is obvious from the training experience of the commercial suppliers that two or three hours of online exposure is too little to provide any significant level of skill in using online databases, and one must surmise that the library schools that provide very little online time either do not aspire to skill development, as a major course objective, or are sharply constrained by their budgets.

Faculty. The Institute report (MIGNON, 1978a) recommends that faculty have a level of proficiency equivalent to skills taught in the online services' advanced user training. BERK & DAVIDSON note that instructors involved in MEDLINE training had many different kinds of previous online experience— e.g., a few had no training, and several had been trained in other online systems. The need for adjunct professors becomes critical in meeting the challenge of this report, unless a significant continuing education program is launched for full-time faculty.

This reviewer did not find any consideration given by the authors cited to the ethical questions in selecting systems to be used in these courses. Because the first-learned and first-used system may well become the preferred system (WANGER ET AL.), one must ask whether or not it is possible to reconcile such considerations with the practicalities of identifying instructors and funds.

Some Alternatives

Alternative methodologies for providing students with hands-on experience are being explored or used by library schools. One alternative is hardly new: use of a locally developed system that illustrates the most important capabilities of the major retrieval systems (perhaps with its own unique features as well) but that does not emulate the protocol of any one system.

This alternative is reported on by DAVIS & GRYCZKOWSKI and by LUNDEEN. Lundeen describes the use of such a system on the University of Hawaii's Hewlett-Packard 2001 minicomputer. It is used in advanced reference courses and in the course on information storage and retrieval to teach principles of system use as well as database development. For example, the course reading list is a machine-readable file that students contribute to each year, so that they gain experience in creating records as well as in retrieving them.

A small ERIC database is also used for the retrieval component. The advantages of this approach, cited by LUNDEEN, include lowered costs (i.e., $1 per hour vs. $15 per hour for using one of the major services), and the resulting benefit of students' being able to spend more practice time online. Analogous to MEDLEARN, this training system also provides a sheltered environment for learning the basic principles of information retrieval.

Another alternative is the "emulation" system, first reported on by HEER & FOYLE. This system was a locally developed CAI program that attempted to match the protocols and features of one of the major systems. The most recent developments are the activities at the University of Pittsburgh in its NSF-supported TRAINER system and the work by Drexel University and the Franklin Institute on the IIDA (Individualized Instruction for Data Access) system; both are described in the End User section of this review because their primary objective is in training the casual user.

Although there is no question that the use of an illustrative or emulative system for teaching can provide extensive hands-on experience at relatively low cost, we do not know the extent to which this experience facilitates learning to use the "real" systems. There is a fruitful area for research here.

Needs and Evaluation

A second position paper prepared by the Institute for Library Educators reports on recommendations for better and closer working relationships among library schools and between library schools and suppliers (MIGNON, 1978b). The report makes some important recommendations for resource sharing and for the development of new resource materials, particularly workbooks that are system oriented, database oriented, and subject oriented. This need is also expressed by WOOD and by BERK & DAVIDSON; and Wood identifies the need for a "real enquiry bank," a list of real search requests, which have been found to contribute to a more satisfactory learning experience. In identifying the need for more workbooks and instructional aids, most authors have recognized the usefulness of resources that do exist (e.g., BOURNE, 1976; STOCKEY & BASENS), but their message indicates that current resources do not support adequately the total instructional process.

BERK & DAVIDSON, MIGNON (1978b), and WOOD all call for increased cooperation and resource sharing with suppliers. The educational institutions should provide educational expertise as well as a "laboratory" setting to test and to evaluate new materials and products. The "user group of online educators" that is being organized (BERGER, 1979) may help to spearhead a drive to activate these recommendations.

USERS AS EDUCATORS AND TRAINERS

Online system users who have received training from online services and database producers frequently become trainers and educators themselves. This section focuses on that role.

Online Users' Groups and Associations

A major vehicle for the development of this role has been the online users' group. BERGER (1977) describes the development of one of the first online users' groups and outlines its major objectives and programs. The need to learn more about the databases that they were searching brought this initial group together informally. Their aims were to share experiences and to promote online use in general. From reports in *ONLINE*, it seems that a major goal of the groups that have now developed in about 70 locations throughout the United States, Canada, and Europe is to manage and to support the continuing education needs of their members. These activities are also reported in newsletters. For example, the MEDLINE Users Group of the Midwest recently announced (MUG'M NEWSLETTER) a new "buddy system," in which experienced search analysts from the area were being paired with analysts in new search centers to provide initial assistance and support. The Washington, D.C. online users' group is establishing an internship program with local library schools to improve instruction in online system use (BERGER, 1979). The special guide developed by the Chicago-area group (MOORE & PYRCE) includes a directory of searchers in the area and notes the databases on which each feels competent to consult.

Within their associations, users are engaged in other promotional, education, and training-related activities, most of which are not documented. For example, a two-day workshop sponsored by the ASIS Delaware Chapter and Drexel University attracted over 150 attendees. Designed for both beginners and those with some experience, this program drew upon both the user and supplier community for its instructional support (MAZELLA).

Users as Instructors

In a less publicized role (and, unfortunately, one poorly covered in the literature), online users are acting as instructors in in-service programs. As noted by the user representatives on the panel at the ASIS 1977 meeting, the cost of sending all staff members or even new employees to formal training sessions can be prohibitive. Some limited insight into these activities is provided by HOCK and by PEARSON & BLACK. Hock's discussion of in-service training at the University of Pennsylvania is an incidental reference in his paper but is worth noting because, unlike most authors, he does not consider staff training to be much of a problem. He states that once a staff member—preferably someone who is coordinating the promotion, training, searching, and supervising—is trained, he or she can easily train others. Further, he states that although training is useful, it may not be necessary;

reading and digesting manuals, with two hours of practice, is sufficient for getting started in becoming a proficient searcher. The difficulty in learning to use online database services probably lies somewhere between the extremes presented in the literature. The various viewpoints undoubtedly reflect different, and usually unstated, assumptions about the levels of skill required.

Users as authors are also extending available system and database documentation and are contributing to the continuing education of their colleagues through a growing body of literature. Numerous tutorial and review papers on various systems and databases appear regularly in such journals as *ONLINE, ONLINE REVIEW*, and *DATABASE*.

EDUCATION AND TRAINING FOR END USERS

MCCARN provides a thorough review of the controversies surrounding the role of the intermediary in online searching and the issue of whether or not end users can and should conduct their own searches. Citing some limited evidence (e.g., SEWELL & BEVAN) that at least some end users can perform their own searches, he concludes that more work is required to develop online systems that can be used more easily by infrequent users and that online services should be made more available to all who want to use the systems. At the heart of the latter need are education and training to increase end user participation and the need for suppliers and users to provide that training and access. To a lesser or greater degree, end users *are* being trained and *are* using some online systems—e.g., the Information Bank, LEXIS, ORBIT, and DIALOG. Even in 1974-1975, the online impact study suggested that perhaps 15% of the respondent population were end users; in the more recent LINK survey, about 12% were end users.

Several projects are under way by researchers who contend that mediated searches cannot be entirely satisfactory and that online systems will not reach their true potential until end user participation increases significantly. Two NSF-supported projects are aimed primarily at the development of CAI-based systems for teaching online use to end users. One project involves the University of Pittsburgh TRAINER system, which is now being field tested with students and faculty members (CARUSO, 1978a; CARUSO & GRIFFITHS). The second project, IIDA, is being developed by Drexel University and the Franklin Institute (MEADOW & EPSTEIN; MEADOW ET AL., 1977; MEADOW ET AL., 1978). Both systems have a CAI and practice component. In addition, the IIDA system is being designed to provide a diagnostic/ assistance interface between the user and the remote host computer. The development of this diagnostic capability is requiring considerable research effort in the study of characteristics of the search process. Models of "good" searching procedures will be defined as the basis for establishing deviations in searching behavior that signal problems and the need for assistance by the user. The online "proctor" will attempt to recognize more than the obvious types of syntactic and command-use problems.

Meadow and Caruso are strong advocates for end user involvement as a supplement—not replacement—for the mediated search. MEADOW compares today's use of online systems by trained experts—the intermediaries—with the early use of computers, when programming was considered to be the sole province of the mathematician.

Although practice media and CAI systems on local computers may be required, more studies should address the broader issues of end user motivation and the relative effectiveness and acceptance of various training methodologies and media. The current research of JAHODA & BAYER may help to define some of these issues. Also, an internal study by the National Bureau of Standards (NBS) library reveals some of the motivational issues involved. BROWN reports that the NBS library was willing to try every method to interest its clients in doing their own searches, in case the demand on the library from the several thousand scientists and researchers became too great. All NBS personnel were invited to training sessions conducted by online service personnel, and a study compared those who elected to conduct their own searches with those who preferred mediated searches. The former group gave as their main reasons "convenience" or that it was "more fun." The more interesting opinions came from the latter group; some were concerned that once the word spread, they would be doing searches for their colleagues. In the view of this author, we should not be drawn into working toward a vision that characterizes end users as a homogeneous community. The short-term challenge is to make the online services more available to those end users who want to learn them and, in turn, to learn from those experiences what is needed to facilitate their use of the systems.

There seems to be less hesitancy in Europe to start that process. Reports from France (MARX), Sweden (SABSAY), and Finland (TÖRNUDD; UUTTU), describe plans—and, in Finland, operational programs—for incorporating the use of online services into university curricula for students in science and engineering. Whether these programs are intended to encourage use of terminals by end users or whether the online experience is viewed as "educational" is not always clear. In the United States there have been fewer attempts to use online searching outside of library school curricula. The NSF-supported program at the University of California at Santa Barbara is particularly worthy of note (ANTONY ET AL.). However, its objective was not to train "professional searchers" but to use online searching as a tool for helping students to become more knowledgeable information users.

The literature abounds with articles that describe promotional and educational programs for use in libraries and information centers. Articles by CRANE & PILACHOWSKI, SCHMIDT, FERGUSON, and LIPOW offer practical guidance in designing and implementing promotional programs, in giving demonstrations, and generally in educating faculty, students, and research staff to the capabilities and limitations of online searching. A multimedia aid for both education and training activities is the Mediatron system, developed at the University of London (PRATT & VICKERY). In a more recent paper (VICKERY & BATTEN), some of the self-teaching modules that have been developed for this portable multimedia "demonstrator" are described.

OVERALL ASSESSMENT OF NEEDS

The time is propitious for the researcher, theoretician, and system designer to become involved in education and training for online use. Although some needs have been expressed (BERK & DAVIDSON; MIGNON, 1978b; WOOD; CARUSO, 1978a; CARUSO, 1978b), others are embedded in the literature reviewed and require analysis and discussion.

Development of Learning Principles

The importance of adequate practice time for the novice has been noted by several authors, including MIGNON (1978a), CARUSO (1978a), and KEENAN (1978), but there is no agreement on how much time is needed (HOCK; BERK & DAVIDSON; CARUSO, 1978c). Moreover, there are no comprehensive statements on the most desirable ways to provide for this activity and the costs involved. The work of NLM (KASSEBAUM & LEITER), the experiences at the University of Pittsburgh training center, and evaluations of use of the ONTAP system of DIALOG should be studied as departure points for research and for some definitions of principles in this area.

Another area that needs study is the desirable time-phasing and spacing for the learning of multiple systems and multiple databases (BORGMAN). Data are available from the online impact study to provide a start for future studies, which are needed to respond to the criticism by CARUSO (1978a) that the system-by-system and database-by-database training approaches in use today do not provide students with basic principles that can be used to transfer knowledge to new systems and new databases. In the online impact study (WANGER ET AL.), respondents seemed to indicate that what they learned on one system was fairly easily transferred to other systems. However, the LINK survey showed that if the users subscribed to a new system that was similar to one they were already using, almost 75% would still seek training by the supplier, for at least one staff member.

A final area that needs study concerns differences in the ways that searchers perform, depending upon the way in which they were trained. From an information service manager's point of view, MOUREAU observes that "present training is mainly based on individual and solitary efforts of users by way of manuals and instructions...as well as on trial and error at the terminal." No one knows whether or not the searching procedures used by those who were "trained" in this fashion differ significantly from the procedures used by those trained in other ways. An NLM-supported project initiated by Cuadra Associates late in 1978, which focuses on differences in searching among those who were formally and informally trained, should help us to assess the relative effectiveness of various approaches. It may also point to needs that have not been identified for those who must learn, or prefer to learn, in other than formal workshops.

Development of Teaching Principles

Formal training courses and workshops, particularly for the novice, will probably continue to be important, even if resources for other modes of instruction are developed and become widely available. There is an urgent need to formalize present experiences into a set of principles to guide these instructional efforts. A limited number of findings on users' points of view toward training are available (WANGER ET AL.), but some instructional programs do not reflect any awareness of them. For example, some instructors are still giving detailed technical presentations for most of a workshop session and providing hands-on experience only at the end of that session, despite clear evidence that this approach is not desirable. One participant in the online impact study described it, uncharitably but not inaccurately, as the "worst" kind of training.

Welcome contributions in this area have been major analytic works by Atherton and by Bates. A guide, prepared by ATHERTON & JENSEN and summarized in ATHERTON & CHRISTIAN, presents a useful model for teaching and evaluating the reference interview specifically for online searching. BATES has developed a model to facilitate searching according to specific principles called "search tactics." This work should help searchers to overcome some of the decision-making problems identified by GILREATH and the "pressure points" in the 17 phases of the search-process cycle identified by STANDERA.

System Design and Evaluation

Some believe that increased online use, particularly by end users and casual users, will need to await the next generation of systems. The work of GOLDSTEIN & FORD, of SIMON & DOSZKOCS, and others already illustrates some of the issues involved in the development of more "user cordial" interfaces. Each of these efforts is susceptible to the dilemma described by MCCARN. Simpler system protocols—e.g., the menu-driven or 20-question approach system—are typically more limited in their capabilities and are also less adaptable to slower terminals. Among the alternatives for ameliorating the learning and using process are standardization of command languages (ATHERTON, 1978) and more system tutorials (MIGNON, 1978b). While we wait for developments in these areas, one principle that might be followed with currently available systems is that if a particular feature or capability of a system is difficult to teach or difficult to learn, it probably needs to be modified.

CONCLUSION

The 1970s have been important years of experimentation in education and training for online system use. Individuals in several types of organizations have been learning how to teach such use by training others and by modifying programs and materials as needed. This trial-and-error situation is not unlike the dynamic development of the online systems themselves. Over the next several years these experiences need to be consolidated into a cohesive body of education- and training-related principles that will support the improvement of all types of programs and materials.

Some professionals believe that successful searching is too narrow a goal for education and training in the use of online services. They feel that one can have good searches and yet a poor resolution of user problems, and that those who understand online systems should serve as consultants and collaborators in problem solving. It is not yet clear whether or not this is a reasonable goal for the library and information profession. However, we know that online services have changed the division of information-finding labor between the end user and the information professional, and further role changes and divisions of labor may result, with improvements in the quality and availability of education and training programs and tools.

What new directions will education and training take? One that we can be certain about is toward nonbibliographic database services. Although there is still some dispute about the extent to which librarians and information specialists should deal with such databases and the data-manipulation capabilities that they frequently provide, there is no question that the use of these services will grow, both by end users and by intermediaries. We know very little about their use and even less about the types and quality of the associated education and training programs. One would hope that the lessons from nearly ten years of experience with online bibliographic database services can be synthesized and brought to bear on the use of these new online database resources.

BIBLIOGRAPHY

ALLMEN, DIANE. 1978. Local Training for Online Searching. In: Moore, Alexandra L.; Pyrce, Sharon R., eds. Chicago Online Users Introductory Guide. Chicago, IL: Chicago Online Users Group and the Chicago Chapter of the American Society for Information Science; 1978. 7-11. Available from: Pat Fojtik, 9071 Meadow View Drive, Hickory Hills, IL 60457.

AMERICAN SOCIETY FOR INFORMATION SCIENCE (ASIS). SPECIAL INTEREST GROUP ON COMPUTERIZED RETRIEVAL SERVICES (SIG/CRS). 1977. Training for On-Line Retrieval Use: Panel Discussion Sponsored by SIG/CRS at the 39th Annual Meeting of ASIS: 1977 September 26-October 1; Chicago, IL. 2 Cassette audiotapes. Available from: Teach 'em, Inc., 625 N. Michigan Avenue, Chicago, IL 60611.

ANTONY, ARTHUR; SIVERS, ROBERT; WEISER, VIRGINIA; HODINA, ALFRED. 1978. An Online Component in an Interdisciplinary Course on Information Resources for Science and Engineering Students. Online Review (England). 1978 December; 2(4): 337-344. ISSN: 0309-314X.

ASSOCIATION OF INFORMATION AND DISSEMINATION CENTERS (ASIDIC), eds. 1977. Training Methods: The 'How' of Training: [Proceedings of] ASIDIC Spring Meeting; 1977 March 13-14; Atlanta, GA. 1977. 16p. Available from: ASIDIC, P.O. Box 8105, Athens, GA 30603.

ATHERTON, PAULINE. 1977. Training in the Classroom. In: Association of Information and Dissemination Centers (ASIDIC), eds. Training Methods: The 'How' of Training: [Proceedings of] ASIDIC Spring Meeting; 1977 March 13-14; Atlanta, GA. 1977. 9-10. Available from: ASIDIC, P.O. Box 8105, Athens, GA 30603.

ATHERTON, PAULINE. 1978. Standards for a User-System Interface Language in On-Line Retrieval Systems: The Challenge and the Responsibility. Online Review (England). 1978 March; 2(1): 57-61. ISSN: 0309-314X.

ATHERTON, PAULINE; CHRISTIAN, ROGER W. 1977. Librarians and Online Services. White Plains, NY: Knowledge Industry Publications, Inc.; 1977. 124p. ISBN: 0-914236-13-X; LC: 77-25275.

ATHERTON, PAULINE; JENSEN, BECKY. 1976. Interfaces in Computer-Based Bibliographic Searching: A Guide to Observing Pre-Search Interviews and On-Line Computer Sessions. 1976. 35p. Available from: Pauline Atherton, School of Information Studies, Syracuse University, 113 Euclid Avenue, Syracuse, NY 13210.

BATES, MARCIA J. 1978. The Testing of Information Search Tactics. In: Brenner, Everett H., comp. The Information Age in Perspective: Proceedings of the 41st Annual Meeting of the American Society for Information Science: Volume 15; 1978 November 13-17; New York, NY. White Plains, NY: Knowledge Industry Publications, Inc.; 1978. 25-27. ISSN: 0044-7870; ISBN: 0-914236-22-9; LC: 64-8303.

BELLARDO, TRUDI; KENNEDY, GAIL; TREMOULET, GRETCHEN. 1978. On-Line Bibliographic System Instruction: A Classroom Experience and Evaluation. Journal of Education for Librarianship. 1978 Summer; 19(1): 21-31. ISSN: 0022-0604.

BERGER, MARY C. 1977. Starting Up an Online Users' Group—A Case History. Online. 1977 April; 1(2): 32-37. ISSN: 0146-5422.

BERGER, MARY C. 1979. Berger Bytes. Online. 1979 January; 3(1): 77-78. (Column). ISSN: 0146-5422.

BERK, ROBERT A.; DAVIDSON, REBECCA W. 1978. MEDLINE Training within the Library School Curriculum: Quality Control and Future Trends. Bulletin of the Medical Library Association. 1978 July; 66(3): 302-308. ISSN: 0025-7338.

BORGMAN, CHRISTINE L. 1978. User Training for Online Information Retrieval Systems. In: Kent, Allen, ed. Encyclopedia of Library and Information Science. New York, NY: Marcel Dekker.

BORGMAN, CHRISTINE L.; TRAPANI, JEAN. 1975. Novice User Training on PIRETS. In: Husbands, Charles W., ed. Information Revolution: Proceedings of the 38th Annual Meeting of the American Society for Information Science: Volume 12, Part 1: Contributed Papers; 1975 October 26-30; Boston, MA. Washington, DC: ASIS; 1975. 149-150. ISBN: 0-87715-412-0; LC: 64-8303.

BORKO, HAROLD. 1978. Teaching On-Line Retrieval Systems at the University of California, Los Angeles. Information Processing & Management. 1978; 14(6): 477-480. ISSN: 0306-4573.

BOURNE, CHARLES P. 1976. DIALOG Lab Workbook. Training Exercises for the Lockheed DIALOG Information Retrieval Service. Berkeley, CA: University of California, Institute of Library Research; 1976 October. 129p. ERIC: ED 136751.

BOURNE, CHARLES P. 1977. Training in the Classroom. In: Association for Information and Dissemination Centers, eds. Training Methods: The 'How' of Training: [Proceedings of] ASIDIC Spring Meeting; 1977 March 13-15; Atlanta, GA. 1977. 11-13. Available from: ASIDIC, P.O. Box 8105, Athens, GA 30603.

BROWN, CAROLYN P. 1977. On-Line Bibliographic Retrieval Systems Use. Special Libraries. 1977 April; 68(4): 155-160. ISSN: 0038-6723.

BROWN, LORENE B.; FISHER, H. LEONARD; HARRISON, ISOM. 1976. Experiment in Information Sharing: The LLL-Atlanta University Workshops. Livermore, CA: University of California, Lawrence Livermore Laboratory; 1976 December 6. 15p. NTIS: UCID-17340.

CARUSO, D. ELAINE. 1978a. Hands On Online: Bringing It Home. Online Review (England). 1978 September; 2(3): 251-268. ISSN: 0309-314X.

CARUSO, D. ELAINE. 1978b. Online Training for Searching Online. In: Online Information: [Proceedings of the] 2nd International Online Information Meeting; 1978 December 5-7; London, England. Oxford, England: Learned Information Ltd.; 1978. 37-48. ISBN: 0-904933-15-6.

CARUSO, D. ELAINE. 1978c. Training and Retraining of Librarians and Users. In: Kent, Allen; Galvin, Thomas J., eds. The On-Line Revolution in Libraries: Proceedings of a Conference; 1977; Pittsburgh, PA. New York, NY: Marcel Dekker, Inc.; 1978. 207-228. ISBN: 0-8247-6754-3; LC: 78-15800.

CARUSO, D. ELAINE; GRIFFITHS, JOHN. 1977. A TRAINER for Online Systems. Online. 1977 October; 1(4): 28-34. ISSN: 0146-5422.

COPPERNOLL-BLACH, PENNY. 1978. How to Choose Database Guides and Thesauri. In: Moore, Alexandra L.; Pyrce, Sharon R., eds. Chicago Online Users Introductory Guide. Chicago, IL: Chicago Online Users Group and the Chicago Chapter of the American Society for Information Science; 1978. 31-35. Available from: Pat Fojtik, 9071 Meadow View Drive, Hickory Hills, IL 60457.

CRANE, NANCY B.; PILACHOWSKI, DAVID M. 1978. Introducing Online Bibliographic Service to Its Users: The Online Presentation. Online. 1978 October; 2(4): 20-29. ISSN: 0146-5422.

CVELJO, KATHERINE. 1976. On-Line Retrospective Searching as a Method in Teaching Information Sources, Services, and Research in Business, Finance, and Management. In: Information Interaction: Compendium of Presentations of the 5th Mid-Year Meeting of the American Society for Information Science (ASIS); 1976, May 20-22; Nashville, TN. Washington, DC: ASIS; 1976. 177-186.

DATABASE. 1978-. Pemberton, Jeffery K., ed. Weston, CT: Online, Inc. (Published quarterly, a magazine of database reference and review). ISSN: 0162-4105.

DAVIS, CHARLES H.; GRYCZKOWSKI, CAROLYN L. 1976. On-Line Searching in the Classroom. In: Information Interaction: Compendium of Presentations of the 5th Mid-Year Meeting of the American Society for Information Science (ASIS); 1976 May 20-22; Nashville, TN. Washington, DC: ASIS; 1976. 171-176.

EISENBERG, LAURA J.; STANDING, ROY A.; TIDBALL, CHARLES S.; LEITER, JOSEPH. 1978. *MEDLEARN*: A Computer-Assisted Instruction (CAI) Program for MEDLARS. Bulletin of the Medical Library Association. 1978 January; 66(1): 6-13. ISSN: 0025-7338.

ELIAS, ARTHUR W.   1977.   The Use of Specific Databases (BIOSIS).   In: MacCafferty, Maxine, ed.   User Education: Towards a Better Use of Information Resources: Proceedings of the European Association of Scientific Information Dissemination Centres (EUSIDIC) Conference; 1976 December 1-3; Graz, Austria.   London, England: EUSIDIC and Aslib; 1977.   53-64.   ISBN: 85142-096-6.

FERGUSON, DOUGLAS.   1977.   Marketing Online Services in the University.   Online.   1977 July; 1(3): 15-23.   ISSN: 0146-5422.

GILREATH, CHARLES L.   1977.   Effective Training: The Key to Efficient Retrieval.   Associates NAL (National Agricultural Library) Today.   New Series.   1977 October/December; 2(3/4): 22-26.   ISSN: 0364-9431; OCLC: 270-5590.

GOLDSTEIN, CHARLES M.; FORD, WILLIAM H.   1978.   The User-Cordial Interface.   Online Review (England).   1978 September; 2(3): 269-275.   ISSN: 0309-314X.

GRADDON, PAMELA H.B.   1978.   User Education from the Point of View of the Service Supplier.   In: Online Information: [Proceedings of the] 2nd International Online Information Meeting; 1978 December 5-7; London, England.   Oxford, England: Learned Information Ltd.; 1978.   75-82.   ISBN: 0-904933-15-6.

HARTER, STEPHEN P.   1977.   Instruction Provided by Library Schools in Machine-Readable Bibliographic Data Bases.   In: Fry, Bernard M.; Shepherd, Clayton A., comps.   Information Management in the 1980s: Proceedings of the 40th Annual Meeting of the American Society for Information Science: Volume 14, Part 2: Full Papers; 1977 September 26-October 1; Chicago, IL.   White Plains, NY: Knowledge Industry Publications, Inc.; 1977.   3-G10; microfiche; 24X reduction.   ISSN: 0044-7870; ISBN: 0-914236-12-1.

HAWKINS, DONALD T.   1977.   Online Information Retrieval Bibliography, 1965-1976.   Online Review (England).   1977 March; 1(1): 55p. (Supplement).   ISSN: 0309-314X.

HAWKINS, DONALD T.   1978.   Online Information Retrieval Bibliography.   Online Review (England).   1978 March; 2(1): 63-106.   ISSN: 0390-314X.

HEER, PHILIPP R.; FOYLE, JAMES K.   1974.   Multi-Media Education for On-Line Retrieval.   In: Proceedings of the 3rd Mid-Year Meeting of the American Society for Information Science (ASIS); 1974 May 16-18; Johnstown, PA.   Washington, DC: ASIS; 1974.   21-22.   Available from: ASIS, 1010 16th Street, N.W., Washington, DC 20036.

HOCK, RANDOLPH E.   1975.   Providing Access to Externally Available Bibliographic Data Bases in an Academic Library.   College & Research Libraries.   1975 May; 36(3): 208-215.   ISSN: 0010-0870.

JAHODA, GERALD; BAYER, ALAN E.   1978.   Online Searches: Characteristics of Users and Uses in One Academic and One Industrial Organization.   In: Brenner, Everett H., comp.   The Information Age in Perspective: Proceedings of the 41st Annual Meeting of the American Society for Information Science: Volume 15; 1978 November 13-17; New York, NY.   White Plains, NY: Knowledge Industry Publications, Inc.; 1978.   165-167.   ISSN: 0044-7870; ISBN: 9-914236-22-9; LC: 64-8303.

KASSEBAUM, LAURA.   1978.   New Advanced Training Curriculum.   The National Library of Medicine (NLM) Technical Bulletin.   1979 December (116): 4.   ISSN: 0146-3055.

KASSEBAUM, LAURA; LEITER, JOSEPH. 1978. Training and Continuing Education for On-Line Searching. Medical Informatics (England). 1978 September; 3(3): 165-175. ISSN: 0307-7640.

KEENAN, STELLA. 1977. The Design of Training Courses for the Users of and Specialists in Networked Information Services. 1977 November. 57p. Available from: Stella Keenan, University of Loughborough, Department of Library & Information Science, Loughborough, England.

KEENAN, STELLA. 1978. Training for On-Line: A Review and Assessment. 1978 April. 14p. Available from: Stella Keenan, University of Loughborough, Department of Library & Information Science, Loughborough, England.

KENT, ALLEN; GALVIN, THOMAS J., eds. 1978. The On-Line Revolution in Libraries: Proceedings of a Conference; 1977; Pittsburgh, PA. New York, NY: Marcel Dekker, Inc.; 1978. 303p. ISBN: 0-8247-6754-3; LC: 78-15800.

KNAPP, SARA D.; GAVRYCK, JACQUELYN A. 1978. Computer Based Reference Service—A Course Taught by Practitioners. Online. 1978 April; 2(2): 65-76. ISSN: 0146-5422.

LINK, INCORPORATED. 1978. Strategies in the Online Database Marketplace. 1978. 300p. (Privately sponsored study). For information, contact: LINK, Inc., 215 Park Avenue South, New York, NY 10003.

LIPOW, ANNE G. 1977. User Education and Publicity for On-Line Services. In: Watson, Peter G., ed. On-Line Bibliographic Services—Where We Are, Where We're Going: Proceedings of an All-Day Meeting at the Centennial Conference of the American Library Association (ALA); 1976 July 18; Chicago, IL. Chicago, IL: ALA, Reference and Adult Services Division; 1977 April. 67-71. Available from: ALA, 50 E. Huron St., Chicago, IL 60611.

LUNDEEN, GERALD. 1977. Introducing the Concepts of On-Line Boolean Searching with a Mini-Computer Based System. In: The Value of Information: Collection of Papers Presented at the 6th Mid-Year Meeting of the American Society for Information Science (ASIS); 1977 May 19-21; Syracuse, NY. Washington, DC: ASIS; 1977. 103-106. Available from: ASIS, 1010 16th St., N.W., Washington, DC 20036.

MACCAFFERTY, MAXINE, ed. 1977. User Education: Towards a Better Use of Information Resources: Proceedings of the European Association of Scientific Information Dissemination Centres (EUSIDIC); 1976 December 1-3; Graz, Austria. London, England: EUSIDIC and Aslib; 1977. 139p. ISBN: 85142-096-6.

MARKEY, KAREN; ATHERTON, PAULINE. 1978. ONTAP: Online Training and Practice Manual for ERIC Data Base Searchers. Syracuse, NY: ERIC Clearinghouse on Information Resources; 1978 June. 198p. (Based on the earlier unpublished work of Charles P. Bourne, Barbara Anderson, and Jo Robinson). Available from: Syracuse University Printing Services, 125 College Place, Syracuse, NY.

MARRON, BEATRICE; FIFE, DENNIS. 1976. Online Systems—Techniques and Services. In: Williams, Martha E., ed. Annual Review of Information Science and Technology: Volume 11. Washington, DC: American Society for Information Science; 1976. 163-210. ISSN: 0066-4200; ISBN: 0-87715-212-8; LC: 66-25096.

MARX, B. 1978. User Education and Training in French University Libraries. In: Online Information: [Proceedings of the] 2nd International

Online Information Meeting; 1978 December 5-7; London, England. Oxford, England: Learned Information Ltd.; 1978. 49-64. IBSN: 0-904933-15-6.

MAZELLA, ANGELA. 1976. On-Line Bibliographic Systems. Bulletin of the American Society for Information Science. 1976 February; 2(7): 45-46. ISSN: 0095-4403.

MCCARN, DAVIS B. 1978. Online Systems—Techniques and Services. In: Williams, Martha E., ed. Annual Review of Information Science and Technology: Volume 13. White Plains, NY: Knowledge Industry Publications, Inc.; 1978. 85-124. ISSN: 0066-4200; ISBN: 0-914236-21-0; LC: 66-25096.

MEADOW, CHARLES T. 1979. Online Searching and Computer Programming: Some Behavioral Similarities (Or. . .Why End Users Will Eventually Take Over the Terminal). Online. 1979 January; 3(1): 49-52. ISSN: 0146-5422.

MEADOW, CHARLES T.; EPSTEIN, BERNARD E. 1977. Individualized Instruction for Data Access. In: On-Line Information: [Proceedings of the] 1st International On-Line Meeting; 1977 December 13-15; London, England. Oxford, England: Learned Information Ltd.; 1977. 179-194. ISBN: 0-904933-10-5.

MEADOW, CHARLES T.; EPSTEIN, BERNARD E.; EDELMANN, JANET V.; MAHER, ANN. 1977. Individualized Instruction for Data Access (IIDA). Philadelphia, PA: Drexel University, Graduate School of Library Science; 1977 July. 162p. ERIC: ED 145826.

MEADOW, CHARLES T.; TOLIVER, DAVID E.; EDELMANN, JANET V. 1978. A Technique for Machine Assistance to Online Searchers. In: Brenner, Everett H., comp. The Information Age in Perspective: Proceedings of the 41st Annual Meeting of the American Society for Information Science: Volume 15; 1978 November 13-17; New York, NY. White Plains, NY: Knowledge Industry Publications, Inc.; 1978. 222-225. ISSN: 0044-7870; ISBN: 0-914236-22-9; LC: 64-8303.

MIGNON, EDMOND, ed. 1978a. Position Paper No. 1: Proposed Standards for Education in Online Searching in the Professional Librarianship Curriculum. 1978 June. 14p. Paper from: New Techniques in the Teaching of Online Searching: An Institute for Library Educators; 1978 March 20-24; Seattle, WA. ERIC: ED 157 553.

MIGNON, EDMOND, ed. 1978b. Position Paper No. 2: On the Relationship between Library Schools, Search Service Vendors, and Database Producers. 1978 June. 12p. Paper from: New Techniques in the Teaching of Online Searching: An Institute for Library Educators; 1978 March 20-24; Seattle, WA.

MOORE, ALEXANDRA L.; PYRCE, SHARON R. 1978. Chicago Online Users Introductory Guide. Chicago, IL: Chicago Online Users Group and the Chicago Chapter of the American Society for Information Science; 1978. 45p. Available from: Pat Fojtik, 9071 Meadow View Drive, Hickory Hills, IL 60457.

MOUREAU, MAGDELEINE L. 1978. Problems and Pitfalls in Setting Up and Operating an Online Information Service. Online Review (England). 1978 September; 2(3): 237-244. ISSN: 0390-314X.

MUG'M NEWSLETTER. 1978. Notes from the Management Office. MUG'M (MEDLINE Users Group of the Midwest) Newsletter. 1978 December; 2(6): 8. Available from: The John Crerar Library, Management Office, 35 W. 33rd Street, Chicago, IL 60616.

OLSEN, WALLACE C. 1978. AGRICOLA Training Implementation by the National Agricultural Library. International Association of Agricultural Librarians and Documentalists (IAALD) Quarterly Bulletin (The Netherlands). 1978; XXII(1-2): 1-4. ISSN: 0020-5966; OCLC: 1771-691.

ONLINE. 1977-. Pemberton, Jeffery K., ed. Weston, CT: Online, Inc. (Published quarterly). ISSN: 0146-5422.

ONLINE REVIEW. 1977-. Oxford, England: Learned Information Ltd. (Published quarterly). ISSN: 0309-314X.

PEARSON, ELLEN M.; BLACK, JOHN B. 1975. Searching the Literature On-Line at the University of Guelph. In: Marshall, Eric; Paré, Marcel (compilers). Proceedings of the 3rd Open Conference on Information Science in Canada; 1975 May 8-10; Quebec, Canada. 214-220. Available from: Canadian Association for Information Science, P.O. Box 158, Terminal Station A, Ottawa, Ontario K1N 8B2.

PRATT, GORDON; VICKERY, ALINA. 1977. The Development of Multi-Media Teaching Aids for Users of Computer-Based Information Retrieval Systems. Program: News of Computers in Libraries (England). 1977 January; 1(1): 10-15. ISSN: 0033-0337.

REES, ALAN M.; HOLIAN, LYDIA; SCHAAP, ANN. 1976. An Experiment in Teaching MEDLINE. Bulletin of the Medical Library Association. 1976 April; 64(2): 196-202. ISSN: 0025-7338.

SABSAY, P. 1977. An Attempt at Integrating Education in Information Retrieval into University Studies. In: MacCafferty, Maxine, ed. User Education: Towards a Better Use of Information Resources: Proceedings of the European Association of Scientific Information Dissemination Centres (EUSIDIC) Meeting; 1976 December 1-3; Graz, Austria. London, England: EUSIDIC and Aslib. 1977. 27-32. ISBN: 85142-096-6.

SCHMIDT, JANET A. 1977. How to Promote Online Services to the People Who Count the Most...Management...End Users. Online. 1977 January; 1(1): 32-38. ISSN: 0146-5422.

SCOTT, ALDYTH D.; SALTER, JOHN C.; SIMPSON, ALEX J. 1976. Information Searching: Methods of Teaching On-Line Techniques. Brighton, England: Brighton Polytechnic, School of Librarianship; 1976. 87p. (BLR&D Report no. 5312). Available from: British Library, Research and Development Department, Sheraton House, Great Chapel Street, London W1V 4BH England.

SEWELL, WINIFRED; BEVAN, ALICE. 1976. Nonmediated Use of MEDLINE and TOXLINE by Pathologists and Pharmacists. Bulletin of the Medical Library Association. 1976 October; 64(4): 382-391. ISSN: 0025-7338.

SIMON, RICHARD C.; DOSZKOCS, TAMAS E. 1978. Implementation of a User Interface for a Complex Numeric/Textual Data Base. In: Brenner, Everett H., comp. The Information Age in Perspective: Proceedings of the 41st Annual Meeting of the American Society for Information Science: Volume 15; 1978 November 13-17; New York, NY. White Plains, NY: Knowledge Industry Publications, Inc.; 1978. 309-313. ISSN: 0044-7870; ISBN: 0-914236-22-9; LC: 64-8303.

SIMPSON, I.S. 1976. On-Line Retrieval Using an In-House Data Base. Newcastle, England: Newcastle-upon-Tyne Polytechnic, Department of Librarianship; 1976. 71p. (BLR&D Report no. 5311). Available from: British Library, Research and Development Department, Sheraton House, Great Chapel Street, London W1V 4BH England.

STANDERA, O.R. 1978. Some Thoughts on Online Systems: The Searcher's Part and Plight. In: Brenner, Everett H., comp. The Information Age in Perspective: Proceedings of the 41st Annual Meeting of the American Society for Information Science: Volume 15; 1978 November 13-17; New York, NY. White Plains, NY: Knowledge Industry Publications, Inc.; 1978. 322-325. ISSN: 0044-7870; ISBN: 0-914236-22-9; LC: 64-8303.

STANLEY, SALLY BACHELDER. 1978. Training and Retraining: Reaction. In: Kent, Allen; Galvin, Thomas J., eds. The On-Line Revolution in Libraries: Proceedings of a Conference; 1977; Pittsburgh, PA. 229-233. New York, NY: Marcel Dekker, Inc.; 1978. ISBN: 0-8247-6754-3; LC: 78-15800.

STOCKEY, EDWARD A.; BASENS, SANDRA J. 1977. An Introduction to Data Base Searching: A Self-Instruction Manual. Philadelphia, PA: Drexel University, Graduate School of Library Science; 1977 April. 102p. Available from: Drexel University Book Store, Philadelphia, PA 19104.

TEDD, LUCY A.; KEEN, E. MICHAEL. 1978. Methods of Teaching On-Line Bibliographic Searching: Experience at the College of Librarianship, Wales. Information Processing & Management. 1978; 14(6): 453-463. ISSN: 0306-4573.

TÖRNUDD, ELIN. 1973. Scandinavian Inter-Library Cooperation in Computer-Based SDI Services and the On-Line Use of INIS for User Training. In: Lincoln, C.M., ed. Computer-Based Information Services: Practical Experience in European Libraries: Proceedings of the 5th Triennial Meeting; 1973. Loughborough, England: IATUL, University of Technology Library; 1973. 23-27.

TRIOLO, VICTOR A.; REGAZZI, JOHN J. 1978. Continuing Education in On-Line Searching. Special Libraries. 1978 May/June; 69(5/6): 189-200. ISSN: 0038-6723.

UNRUH, BETTY. 1978. User Education—The Channel for Communication. In: Online Information: [Proceedings of the] 2nd International Online Information Meeting; 1978 December 5-7; London, England. Oxford, England: Learned Information Ltd.; 1978. 65-74. IBSN: 0-904933-15-6.

UUTTU, LEENA-KAARINA. 1977. Experience of Library Instruction in Finland—With a Case Study from Helsinki University of Technology. In: NVBF Anglo-Scandinavian Seminar on Library User Education; 1976 November 2-7; Gothenberg, Sweden. 1977. 12-20. Available from: Helsinki University of Technology Library, Technical Information Service, Otaniementie 9, SF 02150 Espoo 15, Finland.

VICKERY, ALINA; BATTEN, A.M. 1978. Development of Multi-Media Teaching Packages for User Education in Online Retrieval Systems. On-line Review (England). 1978 December; 2(4): 367-374. ISSN: 0309-314X.

WANGER, JUDITH. 1977. Training in the Field. In: Training Methods: The 'How' of Training: [Proceedings of] Association for Information and Dissemination Centers (ASIDIC) Spring Meeting; 1977 March 13-15; Atlanta, GA. 1977. 3-5. Available from: ASIDIC, P.O. Box 8105, Athens, GA 30603.

WANGER, JUDITH. 1978. Some Comments on the "Training and Retraining of Librarians and Users." In: Kent, Allen; Galvin, Thomas J., eds.

The On-Line Revolution in Libraries: Proceedings of a Conference; 1977; Pittsburgh, PA.   New York, NY: Marcel Dekker, Inc.; 1978. 235-242. ISBN: 0-8247-6754-3; LC: 78-15800.

WANGER, JUDITH; CUADRA, CARLOS A.; FISHBURN, MARY.   1976. Impact of On-Line Retrieval Services: A Survey of Users, 1974-75. Santa Monica, CA: System Development Corporation (SDC); 1976 January.   307p.   NTIS: PB-268 591/5SL.   Also available from: SDC, 2500 Colorado Avenue, Santa Monica, CA 90406.

WESTMORELAND, GUY.   1977.   Training Librarians to Conduct On-line Literature Searches.   In: Watson, Peter G., ed.   On-Line Bibliographic Services—Where We Are, Where We're Going: Proceedings of an All-Day Meeting at the Centennial Conference of the American Library Association (ALA); 1976 July 18; Chicago, IL.   Chicago, IL: ALA; 1977 April. 54-59.   Available from ALA, 50 Huron Street, Chicago, IL 60611.

WILLIAMS, MARTHA E.   1977.   Education and Training for On-Line Use of Data Bases.   Journal of Library Automation.   1977 December; 10(4): 320-334.   ISSN: 0022-2240.   Also available in: MacCafferty, Maxine, ed.   User Education: Towards a Better Use of Information Resources: Proceedings of the European Association of Scientific Information Dissemination Centres (EUSIDIC) Conference; 1976 December 1-3; Graz, Austria.   London, England: Eusidic and Aslib; 1977.   5-17.   ISBN: 85142-096-6.

WOOD, F.E.   1976.   Use of On-Line Services in Teaching Librarianship and Information Studies.   Sheffield, England: University of Sheffield, Postgraduate School of Librarianship and Information Science; 1976.   66p. (BLR&D Report no. 5313).   Available from: British Library, Research and Development Department, Sheraton House, Great Chapel Street, London W1V 4BH, England.

V

Special Topics

The special topic covered in Volume 14 of *ARIST* is "Information Systems in Latin America "by Tefko Saracevic of Case Western Reserve University, Gilda Braga of the Brazilian Institute for Scientific and Technological Information, and Alvaro Quijano Solis of El Colegio de México.

Their chapter sketches the more visible activities of modern information systems in Latin America, particularly those that have been specifically established to support national development. The main limitation came from the elusiveness, scatter, and even lack of literature on the subject. The overall structure of the chapter includes subject-oriented information systems, information problems, and perceptions of the future. The subject-oriented section contains reviews of information systems in various subjects—science and technology, industry, agriculture, health, nuclear energy—and in various sectors; each subject is, in turn, further subdivided according to region or country, starting geographically from Mexico in the north and proceeding toward the south. The section on problems is devoted to the summary of most-often encountered information problems—namely, recognition of the value of information; politics; availability and accessibility of information sources; education and training of information professionals; economics; and cooperation. The section on "perceptions of the future" summarizes the most often mentioned future needs: science; appropriate technology and industry; and policy making. Finally, the conclusions focus on how these systems relate to development and some of the main issues that confront information systems in Latin America today.

9 Information Systems in Latin America

TEFKO SARACEVIC
Case Western Reserve University

GILDA MARIA BRAGA
Brazilian Institute for Scientific and
Technical Information (IBICT)

ALVARO QUIJANO SOLIS
El Colegio de México

INTRODUCTION

Purpose

By the early 1960s most Latin American countries had begun an intensive program of social and economic development, characterized, on the one hand, by the principles primarily agreed on through the United Nations (U.N.) family of agencies, the Organization of American States (OAS), and other international organizations and, on the other hand, by direct but fluctuating relationships with the industrial giant to the north, the United States. The goal of development is self-sustained social and economic growth. The strategy has included massive infusions and applications of science and technology to reduce technological gaps and to improve social conditions. Most Latin American countries established institutions (e.g., ministries, national councils for science and technology) to implement this strategy. In turn, these institutions established systems to supply scientific, technical, and related information (STI). As a rule then, information systems and activities in these areas in Latin America revolve around government support and control; development is their raison d'être, and building an information infrastructure is their function.

This chapter sketches the more visible activities in modern information systems in Latin America, particularly those systems that have been established specifically to support this development.

Scope and Limitations

The terms "sketch" and "more visible" are used deliberately above to stress the inevitable limits on the depth and scope of this chapter—inevitable because of: 1) the vastness of Latin America; 2) the size of the subject; 3) the elusiveness and chaotic state of this literature (there are few Latin American journals in librarianship and information science, and most of the literature is in the traditionally elusive papers given at conferences); and 4) restrictions on space. The bibliography includes more citations than could be mentioned in the text.

The emphasis is on the literature during 1974–1978, reports of operational systems rather than plans, and typical examples rather than comprehensive coverage (e.g., the bibliography could accommodate only about one-fourth of the items originally collected). Inevitably there may be omissions, not only because of the limitations mentioned above but also because some efforts have not been published. Many well-known systems and efforts are mentioned only in memoranda and descriptive brochures. Further, the chapter is restricted to the published literature; it is not a site visit report, such as those presented to or by U.N. agencies.

Uniqueness

This chapter is unique in several respects. The topic is being covered for the first time in *ARIST*. No other *ARIST* chapter has covered the literature from so many countries or literature that was as scattered and as elusive. This is the first chapter to cover literature that is predominantly not in the English language. The authors are from three widely separated countries. All these features have obvious advantages and disadvantages.

Organization

The chapter has five sections. The first is the Introduction. The second (and largest) contains reviews of information systems in science and technology, industry, agriculture, health, nuclear energy, and specific sectors. Each of these subjects is discussed by country or region, beginning in the north (Mexico) and proceeding south. The third section is an overview of the information problems most often mentioned. The fourth section is a similar overview of the most often elaborated perceptions of future information needs. The fifth section contains conclusions.

INFORMATION SYSTEMS IN VARIOUS SUBJECTS

The evolution of information systems in Latin America can be traced through a number of surveys and publications. A pamphlet compiled by Florence Nierman (ORGANIZATION OF AMERICAN STATES (OAS). GENERAL SECRETARIAT. PAN AMERICAN UNION) is among the first publications that specifically surveys STI systems in Latin America and provides—now for historical purposes—an excellent overview of postwar efforts. The survey by ADAMS of STI services in eight Latin American countries is probably the best and most comprehensive in the United States; its strength lies in an analysis of the broader context of these services. Adams also chronicles the involvement in assistance projects of the U.N., OAS, and other international organizations and of national agencies from the United States, Germany, France, Canada, and the United Kingdom. The assistance for STI activities was considerable, but no one source summarizes its extent or evaluates its effectiveness. ARIAS ORDOÑEZ (1978) provides a more recent summary of the scientific and technical information centers and networks in Latin America; the developments within the past decade are recounted in this exceptionally well-organized report, which ends with suggestions for specific studies of the most important problems.

Since 1964 INFORMACIÓNES FID/CLA, a newsletter of the Latin American Commission of the International Federation for Documentation (FID/CLA), has been providing news and overviews of the information activities and systems in Latin America. As such, it is a good source for an historical and current overview. FID/CLA is an energetic and key professional organization in Latin America; its general conferences provide the most important arena in which information professionals from Latin America can exchange experiences and ideas. The resulting proceedings form the most important record of achievements. FID/CLA also published a bibliography pertaining to the development of librarianship and documentation in Latin America from 1960 to 1977 (FEDERACIÓN INTERNACIONAL DE DOCUMENTACIÓN). Compiled by Victoria Galofre Neuto this is probably the most comprehensive bibliographic source on the subject.

Finally, a good but sometimes uneven and elusive set of sources for an overview of information systems in Latin America or its individual countries is found in the reports by U.N. agencies and by OAS. OAS in particular has been directly involved in many projects dealing with STI systems in Latin America, particularly through its Library Development Program and the Department of Scientific Affairs. These activities are recorded in many internal OAS memoranda and reports, but unfortunately little can be found in the open literature. A particular and historical recognition should go to Marietta Daniels Shepard, from OAS, for her pioneering efforts in promoting library and information services activities in Latin America from 1960 until her retirement in 1978. For an overview of OAS activities see ADAMS & WERDEL and SHEPARD (1974; 1975).

Science and Technology

First to emerge in many Latin American countries are national systems devoted to science and technology in general; they have been established in Argentina, Bolivia, Brazil, Chile, Colombia, Costa Rica, Cuba, Jamaica, Mexico, Peru, Uruguay, and Venezuela. The difficulties in covering the many subjects included in science and technology are obvious; however, these systems are much more than information systems. They are often national focal points for diverse pioneering information activities—e.g., development of a national information infrastructure; professional training and education; national promotion of STI; assistance to libraries; importation and adaptation or development of new methods for information processing and dissemination; adaptation or creation of standards of operations; convincing librarians and others to accept these new methods and standards; international representation; conduct of information science research. In general, these systems were established by law or decree. They are similar throughout Latin America, partly because of the powerful example from other Latin American countries and partly because of their promotion and support by Unesco (United Nations Educational, Scientific, and Cultural Organization). These STI systems have achieved unique characteristics. No counterpart systems exist in the United States. Their most important role has been not in providing information services but in creating a nucleus of competent information professionals; this nucleus is already responsible for many related developments and can be considered the crucial source of future developments.

Mexico. The National Council for Science and Technology (CONACYT) was established in 1970 by a presidential decree to encourage scientific and technical development; included was a mandate to design and to implement the National Information System for Science and Technology (SNICT). Soon thereafter CONACYT established the Center for Information Services, which became very active in many information activities and provided numerous national initiatives through the work of a small group of enthusiastic information professionals. These activities are described in several references (GOLDMAN; MEXICO. CONSEJO NACIONAL DE CIENCIA Y TECNOLOGIA, 1976a; MEXICO, CONSEJO NACIONAL DE CIENCIA Y TECNOLOGIA, 1976b; MOLINO, 1978a; MOLINO, 1978b).

The activities include:

- First steps in organizing a network of information resources comprised of the existing scientific, technical, and university libraries;
- Initiation of projects to support such a network—e.g., union lists of serials, machine-readable cataloging, and technical assistance to libraries and information centers;
- Professional development—sponsoring students, initiating education and training courses and programs; establishment of a postgraduate library and information science program at the University of Guanajuato;
- Provision of selective dissemination of information (SDI) services;
- Establishment of the Service for Coordination of Information Banks (SECOBI) as a central node in Mexico to retail online access to databases (including through vendors such as Lockheed, System Development Corp. (SDC), OCLC, Inc.); by the end of 1978, 100 terminals had been installed in Mexico; SECOBI is now trying to extend its services to Central America, and negotiations are under way with Guatemala and Costa Rica (ROMERIO); and

- Establishment of information centers in specialized subjects at various institutions around the country: Arid Zone Information Center (CIZA), Chemistry Information Center (CeMIQ), Metallurgy Information Center (CIM), and special libraries at several Regional Research and Technical Assistance Centers (CRIAT).

Another significant activity is reported at one of the oldest universities on the continent, the Autonomous National University of Mexico (UNAM); the Scientific and Humanistic Information Center (CICH) was set up in 1971 to cover a unique combination of humanities and sciences (SANDOVAL). CICH offers a wide range of bibliographic and information services (e.g., current-awareness publications and a citation index of Latin American periodicals in social sciences and economics) particularly oriented to university research in Latin America. Most of its services are supported through tapes from the Institute for Scientific Information (ISI).

Many of these developments in Mexico have been a powerful example and model for other, smaller Latin American countries. For much of Central America, Mexico also seems to serve as a principal point of contact with U.S. information activities.

Costa Rica. The National Council for Scientific and Technological Research (CONICIT) was organized in 1972. Among its charges was to develop information systems for various subjects of interest to the country (COSTA RICA). To form a national STI system CONICIT organized several sub-systems in certain subjects as part of larger regional or international information activities. So far, information sub-systems have been launched in industry, agriculture, and health.

Cuba. VALLS reports that the Cuban Academy of Sciences has established the Institute for Scientific and Technical Documentation and Information (IDICT). The Institute publishes the *Information Bulletin* and is in charge of coordinating various information centers and technical libraries and in developing a national STI system. IDICT also embarked on projects to provide computerized information retrieval services in various subjects. One subject was information science, encompassing Spanish translations of the Soviet abstracting journal *Referativnii Zhurnal,* Informatics section, to become a service for Latin America. Cuba is a member of the International Center for Scientific and Technical Information in Moscow, which evolved from co-operative information activities of socialists countries under the Council for Mutual Economic Assistance (CMEA). The Center coordinates policy and operations, particularly as they relate to national "branch" (or industrial sectoral) information systems.

Venezuela. In 1967 the National Research Council was created by law; in turn, in 1970 the Council established the National Center for Scientific and Technical Information (CONICIT) as the agency for developing and coordinating national STI activities (MENDA). CONICIT activities include: 1) preparation of national and special user bibliographies, and 2) international cooperation and initiation of the National System for Scientific and Technical

Information (SINICYT). As a part of this national system DE RODRIGUEZ & ORTEGA report on the formation of networks of information centers and libraries in: technology and industry; agriculture and cattle breeding; biomedicine; engineering and architecture; housing, building, and regional urban development; metallurgy; and socioeconomics. Services of this network include bibliographic searches, translations, document reproduction, microfilming, Telex access to other services, assistance to industry and training of information professionals. In 1978 the National System of Library and Information Services (SINASBI) was established to coordinate activities in many areas, including humanities, archives, science and technology, and informatics.

Colombia. COLCIENCIAS (nonacronym for the National Organization for Science Policy in Colombia) was started in 1970 through the support of OAS and the Colombian Institute for the Development of Higher Education (ICFES). Among its highest priorities was the development of various information activities and particularly the establishment of a national system for information (SNI). ROJAS describes in detail the initiation, objectives, and problems of COLCIENCIAS and SNI; SNI is based on the idea of a network of libraries and information centers in various subjects, including: agriculture, through the National Library of Agriculture; health, through the library of the Ministry of Health; education, through the National Center for Pedagogical Documentation; economics, through the Economic Documentation and Information Group (GIDEC); the Technical Information Service for Food Industry (SINTAL), through the Institute for Technological Research (IIT); the Technical Information Services to small and medium-sized industries (SINTEC), through the Popular Financing Corp. and others. COLCIENCIAS is also conducting educational activities for professionals and information users.

Brazil. In 1954 the Brazilian Institute for Bibliography and Documentation (IBBD) was created by law under the sponsorship of the National Research Council (CNPq) with the assistance of Unesco. In 1975 it was reorganized into the Brazilian Institute for Information in Science and Technology (IBICT). Most IBICT activities are described in brochures and some conference proceedings (ALBUQUERQUE; BRASIL. CONSELHO NACIONAL DE DESENVOLVIMENTO CIENTÍFICO E TECNOLÓGICO; BRASIL. INSTITUTO BRASILEIRO DE INFORMAÇÃO EM CIÊNCIA E TECNOLOGIA). Its main activities revolve around:

- Control of the Brazilian scientific and technical literature, published periodically as specialized bibliographies in botany, zoology, physics, chemistry, engineering, medicine, documentation, social sciences, etc.;
- Providing users with access (copies) to documents available in libraries throughout the world, via the National Union Catalog of Periodicals; and
- Literature searches in different areas of science and technology through online access to international databases.

One of IBICT's most important activities is related to recruitment, teaching, and training of personnel. Since 1955 it has been annually promoting a course in scientific documentation, which has trained more than 500 professionals from Brazil and other Latin American countries. In 1970 IBICT started a Masters degree program in information science in agreement with the Federal University of Rio de Janeiro. This program has been effective since many former students have returned to their universities or information systems and started other Masters degree programs (SARACEVIC). IBICT also promotes seminars and meetings of information specialists from different Brazilian states and Latin American countries. The Second Brazilian Conference on Information Science, held in March 1979 in Rio de Janeiro, was attended by over 800 participants, most from Brazil and others from other Latin American countries, the United States, Canada, and Europe. Some 96 papers were presented, and several panel discussions were held. Similar in size and orientation are the previously mentioned conferences of FID/CLA.

IBICT also publishes the journal, *Ciência de Informação* (*Information Science*), which is one of the most important channels for information professionals in Brazil and in Latin America. Efforts in basic research, and in information science, particularly in bibliometrics, were reported in many excellent articles.

Bolivia. In 1967 the National Center for Scientific and Technical Documentation was established by law with assistance from Unesco. In a brief note ARZADUM describes this organization and its activities; they include library and bibliographic services, reprography, creation of a national union catalog, and work toward establishment of a national information system. This effort resulted, in 1977, in the creation of the National System and Fund of Information for Development (SYFNID).

Paraguay. DE VALENZUELA reports on the information activities in Paraguay that support the creation of a National Center for Documentation, noting the relative underdevelopment of these activities. Among others, the Paraguayan Center for Sociological Studies set up the Paraguayan Center for Social Documentation in 1969 with the main objectives of assembling and preserving documents on social affairs in Paraguay and giving access to them to Paraguayan and foreign researchers. The Center also offers training courses in literature searches and publishes the journal, *Boletín del Centro Paraguayo de Documentación* (*Bulletin of the Paraguayan Documentation Center*).

Uruguay. The Center for Scientific, Technical and Economic Documentation was created in 1953 under the auspices of the Uruguain National Library; in 1973 an agreement was made with the National Council for Scientific and Technical Research (CONICYT) to enlarge the Center's activities and scope. Thus, most of the concerns with general STI activities and plans rest now with CONICYT.

DE VODANOVIC summarizes the activities of the Center, of CONICYT, and of some other information systems in Uruguay; she also proposes a plan for the development of a national information system.

Argentina. In 1958 the National Council for Scientific and Technical Research (CONICET) was established. As in other countries, information activities were given priority. CONICET, in turn, established the Center for Scientific Documentation. GIETZ describes its initial activities and proposes a national information system or a network of libraries and information centers in various subjects, including the existing information systems at the National Institute for Industrial Technology (INTI), the National Commission for Atomic Energy (CNEA), the General Directorate for Research and Development (DIGID), and the Computer Center of Engineering Faculty of Buenos Aires.

The U.S. NATIONAL ACADEMY OF SCIENCES reports on cooperation with CONICET and other organizations in the development of a Telex network between university and research libraries in Argentina to support library resource sharing, including photocopying; this network is the first of its kind in Latin America. The report also notes the development of computer-based SDI services, with the particular involvement of the Canadian Technical Information Service.

Chile. The National Center for Information and Documentation (CENID) was created in 1963 under the Council of Rectors of Chilean Universities, but in 1969, by law, it was transferred to the National Commission for Scientific and Technical Research (CONICYT). NOTAS INFORMATIVAS CENID (1976a; 1976b; 1976c; 1976d; 1977a; 1977b; 1977c) describe the various activities of CENID and of other information systems in Chile, notably those that concern health, engineering, telecommunications, sanitary engineering, and energy.

In 1969 the government of The Netherlands offered the Economic Commission for Latin America (ECLA, in Spanish CEPAL) the funds to create a documentation center to support the social and economic activities of Latin American countries. Two years later CEPAL officially approved the creation of the Latin American Center for Economic and Social Documentation (CLADES) in Santiago, Chile.

CLADES operates in a decentralized way; it processes some of the information generated in Latin America; it also promotes, coordinates, and technically supports actions leading to the creation of national centers, which will, in turn, process and disseminate socioeconomic information generated in different countries. CLADES has four basic functions: 1) technical assistance in documentation/information for creating or changing documentation/information systems; 2) in-service training of professionals through courses, meetings, and seminars; 3) studies of information problems of Latin America; and 4) dissemination of results through publications and organization of technical meetings (NOTAS SOBRE LA ECONOMÍA Y EL DESARROLLO DE AMERICA LATINA).

Industry

Industrialization is considered a key facet in development. However, its realization has been rocky, involving difficulties related to technology importation and adaptation, high capital investments, decision making on choices, and technical expertise. DEXTRE (1976), MOLINO (1978b), and

QUEVEDO deal with various factors that present problems in industrialization in Latin America and relate them to necessities for industrial information as an aid in resolving industrialization problems. With this in mind several Latin American countries established national or regional information centers specifically oriented to industry. Dextre discusses and evaluates them, particularly in Mexico, Ecuador, and Peru. In some countries the industrial information systems are part of the broader systems for science and technology reported above.

Since 1973, through its Program for Technical Information and Assistance to Industry, OAS has been very active in several projects related to: formulation of national information policies; design of national information systems; and establishment of centers for Technical Information and Assistance Service for Enterprises (SIATE), particularly oriented toward small and medium-sized firms and industries. The ORGANIZATION OF AMERICAN STATES (OAS) DEPARTMENT OF SCIENTIFIC AFFAIRS (1974; 1978) and GENERAL SECRETARIAT (1977) report that this program had worked directly with 28 and indirectly with an additional 12 information centers in 17 Latin American countries.

Mexico. Established with the help of CONACYT, the Technical Information Service (INFOTEC) is an agency that provides information and consulting services to industry (QUEVEDO). INFOTEC helps industry to identify problems and opportunities to increase efficiency and to launch new products through the use of information in any form. INFOTEC functions as a technical assistance firm for small to medium-sized industries; the assistance is centered around direct contacts with industry, including planned industrial site visits. This method follows the well-known model developed by Kjeld Klintøe of the Danish Technical Information Service; he was a U.N.-sponsored consultant to INFOTEC in 1974. INFOTEC also provides support to the Ministry of Trade and Industry in relation to the transfer of technology from foreign to Mexican firms and to foreign investments in Mexican industry.

DEXTRE (1976) considers INFOTEC activities (along with similar services in Ecuador as described below) to be the pioneering and best efforts in Latin America; she attributes their success to direct contacts with industry and to the provision of "real" information, not just a list of references. Both systems, in Mexico and Ecuador, were started and are administered largely by engineers.

Central America and the Caribbean. In 1975 OAS launched a regional project on industrial information for the countries in Central America and the Caribbean. INSTITUTO CENTROAMERICANO DE INVESTIGACION Y TECNOLOGIA INDUSTRIAL (ICAITI), located in Guatemala City, reported that by mid-1978 six countries (Costa Rica, Dominican Republic, El Salvador, Guatemala, Honduras, and Nicaragua) were cooperating on the project. Centers for Technical Information and Assistance Service for Enterprises (SIATE) have been established in the participating countries. Within great budgetary limitations these centers are trying to play an important role in technology transfer. ICAITI is also laying the groundwork for an online information network for the region.

Ecuador. The most highly developed information system in Ecuador (if not in South America) is the Industrial Information System of the Ecuadorian Center for Industrial Development (CENDES) (ADAMS; DEXTRE, 1976). Services include a current-awareness bulletin, photocopying, extensive liaison visits with industrial enterprises, and a related question-answering service. CENDES maintains a close relationship with INFOTEC in Mexico. Under the guidance of Victor D. Martínez, CENDES is a remarkably active information group, especially considering the geography and other restrictive characteristics of Ecuador.

Brazil. The Center for Technological Information (CIT) was established in 1968 as a part of the National Institute of Technology (INT) (according to a circular letter now defunct). POMPEU DAVIG & LIFCHITZ describe the industrial information activities in Brazil with particular reference to CIT. Services include publication of technical bulletins, answers to technical questions, provision of bibliographies, translations, and consultation with industrial users.

In a remarkably detailed survey POMPEU DAVIG reports on the industrial information services in São Paulo, the most industrialized state in Brazil. Richness of information activities is reflected by the many information centers devoted to particular subjects, such as wood, cellulose and paper, food technology, industrial development, aeronautics, copper, lead, nickel, zinc, and the naval sector.

Uruguay. GARGANO COVELO & VEGH VILLEGAS report on data banks for Projects of Industrial Investments, a part of the Unit of Technical Assistance for Industrial Development of the Ministry of Industry and Energy. The idea is to provide information that will be useful in industrial initiation studies, project evaluation, and project follow-up.

Agriculture

Intensive interest exists throughout Latin America for information services in agriculture, food technology, and related areas. Almost every Latin American country has established an information system in agriculture; however, here we are recounting only the most prominent efforts. In a way, agricultural information activities and professionals are a world in itself. A very active society, the Inter-American Association of Agricultural Librarians and Documentalists (AIBDA), provides a framework for professional activities and exchange of ideas. *BOLETIN INFORMATIVO DE AIBDA*, published since 1965, is an excellent source for news and descriptions of the many existing activities. The U.N. Food and Agriculture Organization (FAO) and OAS were prime initiators and sponsors of many projects dealing with the establishment of regional or national agricultural information systems. LANCASTER & MARTYN, in assessing the development of International Information Systems for Agricultural Sciences and Technology (AGRIS), also provide a penetrating analysis of the diametrically opposing attitudes toward international cooperation in agricultural information services between developing and developed countries; their diagnosis aptly describes the ambiguous relationship between the United States and Latin America in agricultural information.

Regional network. The Inter-American Institute for Agricultural Sciences (IICA) in Costa Rica, through its Inter-American Center for Agricultural Information (CIDIA), is a focus for the development of agricultural information services and centers in the Latin America and Caribbean Agricultural Information Network (AGRINTER) and on the participation in worldwide efforts by AGRIS. AGRINTER provides bibliographic and SDI services. ARBOLEDA SEPULVEDA (1975) reports on a particular concern for strengthening national agricultural information systems and resources as part of the network. CACERES RAMOS notes that because AGRINTER works through affiliates, which are government organizations, its future lies in the importance each country assigns to the activities in this subject; marketing of its services should have first priority. A very good summary of early AGRINTER activities is provided by ALVEAR; he also surveyed development of activities in agricultural information throughout Latin America.

Brazil. The extent and number of reported activities in agricultural information in Brazil exceed those from all other countries in Latin America if not the world. Several institutions and systems are involved. The National System for Agricultural Information and Documentation (SNIDA), a project initiated in 1974 and supported by FAO, is the Brazilian element of the AGRIS network. As a part of the Brazilian Enterprise for Rural Extension (EMBRATER) SNIDA collects, processes, and disseminates domestic and foreign agricultural information (CHASTINET). Chastinet also reports on the establishment in 1978, by law, of the National Library of Agriculture (BINAGRI). This library will be the central access point for documents. It is the first national library established in Latin America that is devoted to a specific subject.

Another institution involved in agricultural information activities is the Brazilian Enterprise for Agricultural Research (EMBRAPA). ACOSTA HOYOS reports on its Technical and Scientific Information System (SITCI), which covers and aids ongoing research in 41 specialized research centers throughout the country. Research topics include cotton, rice and beans, corn and soybeans, rubber, wheat, and cattle.

Nuclear Energy

The International Nuclear Information System (INIS), developed through the International Atomic Energy Agency (IAEA), is one of the more successful international efforts to surmount the political, economic, and linguistic barriers to cooperative information processing (ADAMS & WERDEL). Each country processes its own literature, sends it to INIS, and in turn receives (from INIS) tapes and secondary publications containing merged inputs from all member states. Argentina, Brazil, Chile, Mexico, and Peru are members of INIS. ZAMORA describes the use of tapes and other INIS products for information services in these countries. Cooperation on a regional level is also being considered.

Brazil. BARREIRO & MIRANDA recount the establishment and services of the Nuclear Information Center (CIN) in Brazil, particularly SDI and retrospective search services. It is difficult to obtain hard copies of documents because CIN's sets are incomplete; requests have to be sent to other Brazilian or foreign libraries. The most complete collection in Brazil (including technical reports and microforms) is at the Institute of Energy and Atomic Research (IPEN) (formerly the Institute of Atomic Energy, IEA) in São Paulo. This library has many functions that are automated and is an exemplary facility of its kind. All information professionals who are not specialists in nuclear energy at IPEN must attend intensive courses on this subject (FERRAZ & FIGUEIREDO). A combination of the holdings of CIN and IPEN could result in a national or regional library in nuclear energy for Latin America, which would solve the acute need for a complete collection on nuclear information.

Argentina. ADAMS briefly describes the information activities of the Argentine Atomic Energy Commission (CNEA), a member of INIS. CNEA has also established the Service for Technical Assistance to Industry (SATI) to provide technological information to industry in Argentina.

Health

Information on health sciences is of considerable interest in all Latin American countries. Traditionally, libraries in medical schools and research institutes have served these information needs. The Pan American Health Organization (PAHO) has played a major role in promoting and developing modern information services in health sciences and in strengthening libraries. In 1965 PAHO sought advice from the National Library of Medicine (NLM) on strengthening libraries in medical education and research in Latin America. The result was the concept of a regional medical library to serve as a backup resource for PAHO member states. Composite funding from national, international, and philanthropic organizations was arranged, and the regional medical library—BIREME—was established at the São Paulo Medical School in Brazil. The activities of BIREME, described by ADAMS, CORNING, NEGHME, and PAN AMERICAN HEALTH ORGANIZATION. REGIONAL LIBRARY OF MEDICINE (BIREME), include:

- Development of a biomedical information network in Latin America and in Brazil;
- Service as a basic resource for interlibrary loan and photocopying for this network;
- Provision of Medical Literature Analysis and Retrieval System Online (MEDLINE) services for South America through its own and contracted computer installations;
- Extensive publication of bibliographies and other documents;
- Indexing of Latin American literature included in Medical Literature Analysis and Retrieval System (MEDLARS) and the preparation and publication of the *Latin American Index Medicus* (to start in 1979);
- Operation of a cancer information program, including SDI services, and creation of a registry of Latin American specialists in oncology;

- Provision of special SDI programs on health care in Latin America in subjects such as nutrition and maternal and child care; and
- Training of information specialists and holding of seminars throughout Latin America.

BIREME has network connections with most of the medical school libraries in Latin America and with other health science libraries. In general, it is an exemplary effort in international cooperation.

In Mexico the Ministry for Health and Welfare began operation in 1978 of the Information Center for Health, which also provides MEDLINE services on the basis of a bilateral contract with NLM. A brochure describes the various services of this Center (MEXICO. SECRETARIA DE SALUBRIDAD Y ASISTENCIA).

Sectoral Systems

Several information systems have been established for specialized subjects or missions. Although some are described above, other interesting examples include:

- Information System on Hydrological Resources in São Paulo (BENTO ET AL.);
- Information Service of the Center for Economics, Law, and Management of Water in Mendoza, Argentina (SOLANES ET AL.);
- Data Base on Crystalline Structures in São Paulo (SLAETS ET AL.);
- Information and Referral Center on Sanitary Engineering and Environmental Sciences (CIRISCA) in Santiago, Chile, which cooperates with similar centers in Lima and in Buenos Aires (NOTAS INFORMATIVAS CENID, 1977a);
- Network of Socio-Economic Information (REDINSE) in Venezuela, which aims to stimulate interinstitutional cooperation at local and national levels, to centralize and to give access to information, and to organize special courses for professionals (BOLETIN INFORMATIVO DEL INSTITUTO BIBLIOTECO-LOGICO);
- Information System for Data Processing of Legislative Information (PRODASEN) in Brasilia, Brazil, which developed and is operating its own online databases and database services (CONJUNTURA ECONOMICA);
- Brazilian Enterprise for Transportation Planning (GEIPOT), which gathers information on railroad, highway, and water transportation (CONJUNTURA ECONOMICA);
- Latin American Population Documentation System (DOCPAL) of the U.N. Latin American Demographic Center (CELADE), which covers information about population in Latin America and the Caribbean (UNITED NATIONS. CENTRO LATINAMERICANO DE DEMOGRAFIA); and

- National System of Educational Documentation and Information (SISNIDE) in Peru, which is coordinated by the National Center for Educational Documentation and Information (CENDIE) (ARIAS ORDOÑEZ, 1978).

Many other information systems could be described; some are given in the bibliography.

INFORMATION PROBLEMS

All information systems share certain problems. Thus, some of the problems facing Latin American systems (e.g., economic ones) are not unique but are considerably more acute than those in the United States or other developed countries. Other problems, such as those related to general infrastructure and socioeconomic conditions, are unique to Latin America and other developing countries. These problems and/or their intensity do not seem to be well understood in general by information workers, the information industry, and government agencies dealing with STI in the United States and other developed countries. Although it is impossible to give here a thorough analysis of these problems, we categorize and briefly describe those most often mentioned in the literature.

Information and Development: Recognition

Every national or regional policy for development specifies that information resources and activities are necessary. Unesco, through its UNISIST program, has made many efforts to persuade governments to develop national policies for information and to associate provision of resources for science and technology with provision of resources for information as well. Unesco's National Information Systems (NATIS) program attempted to raise to equally high governmental policy levels programs for developing libraries and archives, coordinated with those for STI. Bolivia, Brazil, Mexico, and Venezuela have legislated specific STI policies and plans.

Still the major problem facing information systems is poor recognition of STI as a necessary ingredient in specific efforts and an associated lack of understanding of information work. DEXTRE (1977) concludes that government officers and industrial entrepreneurs tend to rely on their experience rather than to seek out information and thus do not have a real feeling for the value of information; this point was made often and can be considered valid for most countries in Latin America. ALCADE CARDOZA similarly assesses the information problems of the countries in the Andean Zone (Bolivia, Colombia, Chile, Ecuador, and Peru).

Political Situations

Internal political problems (including lack of long-term planning), typical of many developing countries, are a serious handicap for the coherent development of information systems (MOLINO, 1978b). Political and administrative changes produce opposing STI policies and can even cancel previous achievements. For example, CONACYT developed a model and plan for information services in Mexico on the basis of a long-term study that adapted to Mexican conditions the methods from the well-known Scientific Communication and Technology Transfer (SCATT) project by Russell Ackoff; several experiments and Delphi sessions were conducted (MOLINO, 1978b); however, the new presidential administration has cancelled this work, and the future of STI activities in Mexico looks bleak. ADAMS chronicled the adverse effects of political changes in Argentina and Chile.

In many countries, officials who are in charge of STI policies often come and go; this causes policy shifts at all levels. Thus, many programs have been started but were never carried out (ROBREDO).

Information Sources: Availability and Accessibility

Modern STI services, particularly those related to database searching, depend on libraries and document delivery facilities to provide documents to users. In Latin America these facilities are generally inadequate, incomplete, or not adequately connected with STI systems (TELL). For example, a study of holdings of journals published in Latin America in 550 Brazilian libraries found that only 20% of journal volumes are complete for the past five years in any of the libraries in Brazil; by comparison, the same journals were 70% complete in libraries listed in the union list of serials for the United Kingdom, the United States, and Canada (SANTOS ET AL.).

The efforts in developing STI systems were not correlated with similar efforts in developing libraries as infrastructures for document delivery, nor was the same attention given to the development of such an infrastructure as that given to STI systems. Further, the general awareness of readily available information sources is quite low, even at times among information professionals; too often their awareness is restricted to their own information systems.

Access to and distribution of information sources depend on general communication services, such as telecommunications, postal systems, etc. ROBREDO enumerates the difficulties that information networks in Latin America are facing because of problems with the reliability of these services, over which the systems have no control; he also elaborates on the technical problems in computer applications—e.g., in relation to wider adoption of standards and the constant frustrations with adaptation or development of suitable software packages. The computer facilities in many Latin American countries are fairly large, but they are underused, primarily because of software problems and the lack of suitably trained personnel.

Information Professionals: Education and Training

Not a single document discusses information systems in Latin America without mentioning the acute need for education and training of information professionals, particularly those who are competent in the modern advances in information science, computer science, and systems engineering and analysis (e.g., DE VODANOVIC; ROBREDO; SCHUR; TELL; TOMÉ). Despite the many national and international efforts in this area, too few competent professionals exist. Efforts of individual systems to train their own professionals are often in vain, unless the specialists are offered economic and professional incentives to stay within the system or profession.

TOMÉ provided statistics on the 66 library schools in 19 countries in Latin America and the Caribbean together with the information science courses they offer. She indicated that one of the important needs is to enlarge information science education and to integrate it with library school curricula; the main problem in these schools is lack of faculty. PENNA (1975b) describes the educational activities of several national, regional, and international organizations; most actively concerned with educational problems is the Latin American Association of Library and Information Science Schools (ALEBCI).

Many information scientists in Latin America received their degrees or some of their training in the United States. However, there has been no concentrated U.S. effort to assist in training and educating information scientists in Latin America or to help the educational institutions in Latin America to develop suitable information science programs and to educate the necessary faculty. However, many information scientists from the United States have been involved on an individual basis with educational efforts in Latin America, and many universities have maintained fruitful (but individual) connections with their counterparts in Latin America.

Economics

Information systems in Latin America lack adequate financial resources. However, we found no discussion in the literature pertaining to the details of their economic situation or to the economics of information in general. Thus, one cannot assess the level of financial investment in information systems in any one country or in any one system. Some figures for project support (e.g., given by OAS or other international organizations) are listed, and some overall annual budgets for some systems are mentioned, but there is not much more.

There is also no discussion of the economics of information activities, sources, and services in developed countries, such as in the United States; neither is there any discussion of the important and complicated relationships between the economics of various segments (private, government, societies) of the information industry in the United States, on the one hand, and the economics of information systems in Latin America, on the other.

Many studies and reports done by or for the United Nations and other international agencies contain numerous recommendations, but the economic aspects of these recommendations are ignored. The problem is not only a lack of economic resources but a lack of discussion about the economics of information.

Cooperation

Another issue that is not debated in the literature but is quite evident in practice is the poor cooperation among information systems in Latin America—not only from one country to another but even within the same subject, same city, or same institution with several information systems. Thus, many efforts are duplicated (e.g., in format design, software development, and acquisitions). Although touted as highly desirable, the actual degree of standardization and cooperation is low. Incompatibility is high. Resource sharing, even where possible, is infrequent, making scarce resources even scarcer. The reasons for this situation are complex. Some involve real technical difficulties, particularly in postal services and telecommunications and lack of necessary tools (e.g., up-to-date union lists); others are strongly linked to human factors, internal politics, territorial imperatives, and the like. Professional communication among information scientists (particularly through professional meetings) seems to be excellent, but cooperation in actual work and services is dismal.

PERCEPTIONS OF FUTURE INFORMATION NEEDS

What information is needed for development? This is an important question because the answers will determine the content of files and services of future information systems. Unfortunately, we found no studies (in a scientific sense) of present or future information needs in the literature for the period covered. However, several statements reflecting perceptions of information needs, based on experience, common sense, and opinion, have been recorded, particularly in reports to or by international organizations (BEVERLY; DEXTRE, 1976; ORGANIZATION OF AMERICAN STATES (OAS). GENERAL SECRETARIAT, 1977; ROMERIO; SCHLIE ET AL., 1976a; SCHLIE ET AL., 1976b; UNITED NATIONS INDUSTRIAL DEVELOPMENT ORGANIZATION). The common themes, rather than accounts of each paper, are summarized here.

There are different categories of needed information, each of which has a different role to play in development. An interesting classification is in terms of necessary knowledge:

- "Know-why" information (more scientifically oriented, readily found in the literature, and easiest to transfer);
- "Know-how" information (more technically oriented, not as readily found in literature, may need synthesis or repackaging, and harder to transfer); and
- "Show-how" information (operationally and training oriented, not found in the literature, needs to be generated or repackaged, and hardest to transfer).

Classification is most often done in terms of needs for: 1) scientific information, 2) industrial and technological information, and 3) policy and decision-making information.

Scientific Information

Scientific information, except for health sciences and agriculture, does not command much concern. When it comes to basic research, views were expressed that this is not an affordable activity; thus, the literature in this area is not of much interest. The type of science fostered in many Latin American countries is oriented toward either academics or recognition and prestige rather than toward social utility—i.e., toward solutions to the growing problems of the broader populace or of industry. Scientific priorities are questioned, and so are the scientific information and literature.

Appropriate Information for Technology and Industry

Needs in technological and industrial information attracted the most discussion by far. The perceptions here are strongly affected by: 1) individual plans and strategies of technical and industrial development, and 2) flaws and failures of previous applications of technology and industry. Failures are analyzed in relation to the importation of technology and ready made ("turnkey") factories, which often proved to be: 1) too advanced for a country (resulting in "sick industries"); 2) above the technical level of the available work force (becoming inoperable); and 3) highly capital intensive and poorly labor intensive (draining resources and not creating many jobs). Thus, the concept of appropriate technology was developed. It is becoming a pivotal point in international discussions; it is warmly embraced and promoted and has resulted in attempts to reorder priorities in development. Closely associated with and indistinguishable from this concept is appropriate information. These concepts are not well defined yet, but in general they mean technology (and associated information) that is: 1) intensive in its use of abundant resources and labor and economical in its use of scarce resources (capital and highly trained personnel); 2) small in scale, efficient, and readily replicable, maintained, and operated; and 3) compatible with the local environment. The obstacles to obtaining appropriate information are considerable. The needs are for:

- *Generation* of information materials specific to developmental problems;
- *Repackaging* of information (synthesis, translation, and scaling to the level of local use and populace, etc.);
- *Screening and evaluating* information; provision of information on technology assessment;
- Provision of information that will reduce the *dependence on technology* from developed countries (which is increasingly resented);
- Emphasizing information for *small-scale industries and technologies* and connections with small-scale industries in developed countries (a connection that generally does not now exist);
- Information for *unserved* segments of the population, particularly in rural areas; and
- Use of *unconventional channels* for distributing information.

Avenues are sought for increasing the information links among countries that are at the same stage of development (e.g., in relation to successful applications of imported technologies or about negotiations with companies in developed countries). Views are expressed (in papers cited above) that present information systems as instituted are reinforcing the dependence on developed countries and do not emphasize the development of links that will reduce dependence.

Policy and Decision-Making Information

Another area of perceived information needs also strongly expressed in all the papers mentioned is policy- and decision-making information. Needs are for information that is related to business, management, and marketing; leads, names, and addresses for contacts; industrial and technical design and operations; technoeconomic aspects; laws and regulations; licenses, patents, consultancy assessments, etc. The last area, often called negotiable information, is particularly touchy. Desires are expressed for reviews and assessments of various topics (e.g., existing technological processes) with clear presentation to permit informed choices and for information that will increase negotiating and bargaining strength (e.g., information from other developing countries on their negotiations, prices achieved, etc.).

CONCLUSIONS

Latin America is a conglomerate of 30 countries (population about 400 million) with considerable economic, social, cultural, and historical differences. It is not a homogeneous social and cultural unit any more than Europe is. Geography has favored the existence of isolated communities with defined cultures. Each country has specific developmental (industrial, technical, agricultural, and social) problems. Further, great differences can be found among various regions within each country. However, one feature that Latin American countries have defined as being common is the steady domination of their markets by imported industrialization and foreign technology, with adverse effects on national development and independence. It is this common understanding of the source of problems that is the basis for the promotion of scientific, technical, and social activities for economic and cultural integration of Latin America, or at least of activities that have some common features related to development. This promotion includes activities connected with scientific, technical, commercial, and related information that can be used in development. Thus, despite the inherent differences among Latin American countries, there are some similarities in their approach to information systems related to development. However, the stage of evolution and the achievements of such systems differ greatly from country to country and even in the same country from one region to another and from one time (or political) period to another.

Do the information systems in Latin America contribute to development, which is after all their raison d'être? This key question is impossible to answer—no relevant data or studies exist. Nevertheless, the very establishment and operation of these systems *are* development. Because these information systems were so difficult to develop, their existence is a pronounced achievement.

However, the actual state of the information systems or services is difficult to judge from the literature. Conclusions can be drawn only from personal (hence biased) experience. As is true elsewhere, evaluation of information systems and services in Latin America is not an important area of study or concern. Also the plans and designs far exceed actual accomplishments. One should not confuse an announcement of an information system or service with its existence.

Information systems and activities are often recounted in reports to the United Nations and to other international or national agencies. Many such studies are excellent, based on solid evidence; however, some are based on methods and procedures that are highly suspect. For example, some reports have been made on the basis of nothing more than a two-week trip and questionable interviews (some over the phone) or a two-day meeting pervaded by anecdotes. Reports of trips and minutes of meetings are masquerading as studies. So many U.N. and other international and national agencies have become involved recently in STI activities that the reports are proliferating and getting poorer in quality. Unfortunately, this means that even valid and reliable studies and reports, to or by such agencies, are becoming suspect. Thus, at times international and national policies are formulated, promoted, and carried out on the basis of questionable evidence and recommendations.

In many Latin American countries the information systems have reached a plateau. They were established, they opened the door for business, but their services and products are lying fallow. The systems are discovering that producing a product or offering a service is one achievement (very difficult to reach), but developing a lively market is a different one and requires different efforts. Among these efforts are: user education; promotion; marketing; dissemination and diffusion; repackaging of information; and direct user contacts with follow-up. It will be difficult to pursue these activities because they are not often a part of the education and tradition of information scientists and librarians; in addition, the use of information depends on factors over which the systems have no control, such as general education and technical training of potential users.

Machine-readable databases are rapidly entering information systems in Latin America and are causing considerable debate. Some databases are produced domestically, some are obtained through international cooperation (e.g., INIS, AGRIS), and some are purchased from developed countries for internal searching. Access to domestic or international online services is still difficult, but better telecommunications are increasing their use. U.S. online services are often used. The problems and issues are unique to each country and are quite different from those related to databases in the United States. One of the hot issues is the debate over independence vs. dependence. To what extent should efforts be expended to produce national or regional databases and thereby to reduce dependence on databases from developed countries? What databases should be imported? Should increased use be made of available online services from the United States? Doesn't this increase dependence further? Isn't such dependence contrary to development? The resolution of these and similar issues is becoming the main policy and operational issue for information systems in Latin America for the early 1980s. The issues are not only technical and operational but political and involve touchy international relations.

Information for all perceived needs described above often does not exist in a readily available form, and the present systems in Latin America are not geared to provide such information. We found little discussion of specific methods for generating appropriate information and for instituting appropriate information systems. Still these perceptions may transform the future shape of information systems in Latin America. If such a reshaping is to occur, it will require a greater commitment of resources than is presently assigned for information activities in Latin America; it will also require new channels for information dissemination, much greater cooperation, and a new type of information expertise.

BIBLIOGRAPHY

ABREU, SERGIO K.M. 1979. Projeto para um Sistema de Recuperação de Dados Metereológicos [Project for a Meteorological Data Information System]. 9p. (In Portuguese). Available from Instituto Brasileiro de Informação em Ciência e Tecnologia (IBICT). Av. General Justo 171, 20021 Rio de Janeiro, RJ. Brasil.

ACOSTA HOYOS, LUIS EDUARDO. 1976. Sistemas de Informação Técnico-Científica da EMBRAPA (SITCE) [Scientific and Technical Information Systems in EMBRAPA]. Brasilia, Brazil: Empresa Brasileira de Pesquisa Agropecuaria (EMBRAPA); 1976. 116p. (In Portuguese). Available from Instituto Brasileiro de Informação em Ciência e Tecnologia (IBICT). Av. General Justo 171, 20021 Rio de Janeiro, RJ. Brasil.

ADAMS, SCOTT. 1975. Scientific and Technical Services in Eight Latin American Countries: Development, Technical Assistance, Opportunities for Cooperation. Louisville, KY: University of Louisville, Urban Studies Center; 1975 December. 170p. NTIS: PB-253 202/6WL.

ADAMS, SCOTT; WERDEL, JUDITH A. 1976. Cooperation in Information Activities through International Organizations. In: Williams, Martha E., ed. Annual Review of Information Science and Technology: Volume 11. Washington, DC: American Society for Information Science; 1976. 303-356. ISSN: 0066-4200.

ALBUQUERQUE, CARLOS AUGUSTO. 1977. A Informação em Ciência e Tecnologia e IBICT [Information in Science and Technology and IBICT]. In: Anais do 9. Congresso Brasileiro de Biblioteconomia e Documentacao e 5. Jornada Sul-Rio-Grandense de Biblioteconomia e Documentacao; 1977; Porto Alegre, Brasil. Rio de Janeiro, Brazil: IBICT; 1977. 41-47. (In Portuguese). Available from IBICT. Av. General Justo 171, 20021 Rio de Janeiro, RJ. Brasil.

ALBUQUERQUE, MARTHA. 1977. O Subsistema de Documentação e Informações Educacionais do Instituto Nacional de Estudos Pedagógicos (INEP) [The Subsystem of Documentation and Educational Information]. In: Anais do 9. Congresso Brasileiro de Biblioteconomia e Documentação e 5. Jornada Sul-Rio-Grandense de Biblioteconomia e Documentação; 1977; Rio de Janeiro, Brasil. Porto Alegre, Brazil: IBICT; 1977. 258-267. (In Portuguese). Available from IBICT. Av. General Justo 171, 20021 Rio de Janeiro, RJ. Brasil.

ALCADE CARDOZA, XAVIER. 1974. La Información Especializada en los Paises del Grupo Andino [Specialized Information in Countries of the Andean Group]. Fichero Bibliográfico Hispanoamericano (Argentina). 1974; 13(7): 2-4. (In Spanish).

ALVEAR, ALFREDO. 1974. El AGRINTER: Sistema Interamericano de Información para las Ciencias Agrícolas [AGRINTER: Interamerican System of Information for Agricultural Sciences]. In: 4. Congreso Regional de Documentación; 1973; Bogotá, Colombia. México, D.F.: Federación Internacional de Documentación, Comisión Latino Americana; 1974. 173-188. (In Spanish). Available from IBICT. Av. General Justo 171, 20021 Rio de Janeiro, RJ. Brasil.

ANBALON CASAS, SILVIA. 1975. Antecedentes sobre la Organización de un Centro Nacional de Documentación e Información Médica en Chile [Antecedents of the Organization of a National Center of Documentation and Medical Information in Chile]. Revista Chilena de Bibliotecología y Documentación (Chile). 1975; 1(1/2): 15-16. (In Spanish).

ARBOLEDA SEPULVEDA, ORLANDO. 1975. Inventario de los Recursos Nacionales de Información y Documentación Agrícola para su Integración en el AGRINTER [Inventory of National Resources on Agricultural Information and Documentation Regarding Its Integration to the AGRINTER System]. Desarrollo Rural en las Americas (Costa Rica). 1975 September-December; 7(3): 286-304. ISSN: 0046-0028.

ARBOLEDA SEPULVEDA, ORLANDO. 1976. Acceso a la Información Agrícola: programa de acción para Mexico [Access to Agricultural Information: An Action Program for Mexico]. San Jose, Costa Rica; Instituto Interamericano de Ciencias Agrícolas (IICA); 1976. 87p. (In Spanish). Available from: IBICT. Av. General Justo 171, 20021 Rio de Janeiro, R.J. Brasil.

ARDILA SANTOS, ALVARO; JORDAN FLORES, FERNANDO. 1974. Centro de Información y Documentación de la Cámara de Representantes (CIDOC): Desarrollo, Funciones y Sistemas de Información [Information and Documentation Center of the Chamber of Representatives (CIDOC): Development, Functions and Information Systems]. In: 4. Congreso Regional de Documentación; 1973; Bogotá, Colombia. México, D.F.: Federación Internacional de la Documentación, Comisión Latino Americana; 1974. 143-149. (In Spanish). Available from IBICT. Av. General Justo 171, 20021 Rio de Janeiro, RJ. Brasil.

ARIAS ORDOÑEZ, JOSE. 1975. NATIS, Sistemas Nacionales de Información: Implementación en América Latina [National Information Systems; Implementation in Latin America]. In: Seminario Latinoamericano sobre Control y Adquisición de Material Bibliográfico; 1975; Bogotá, Colombia. Bogotã, Colombia: Unesco; 1975. 17p. (In Spanish). Available from IBICT. Av. General Justo 171, 20021 Rio de Janeiro, RJ. Brasil.

ARIAS ORDOÑEZ, JOSE. 1978. Centros y Redes de Información Científica y Tecnológica en la Comunidad Iberoamericana [Centers and Networks for Scientific and Technical Information in the Ibero American Community]. Paper presented at: Conferencia Iberoamericana sobre Información y Documentación Científica y Tecnológica, Reuniber 78; 1978 September 11-15; Madrid, Spain. 55p. Available from ICFES, Apartado Aereo 21817, Bogota, Colombia.

ARZADUM O., ELBA. 1974. El Centro Nacional de Documentación Científica y Tecnológica de Bolivia [National Center for Scientific and Technological Documentation of Bolivia]. Fichero Bibliografico Hispano-Americano (Argentina). 1974; 13(7): 20. (In Spanish).

BARREIRO, SELMA CHI; MIRANDA, ANA CHRISTINA E. 1978. O Centro de Informações Nucleares [The Nuclear Information Center]. In: Anais da 1. Reunião Brasileira de Ciência da Informação; 1975 June 15-20; Rio de Janeiro, Brasil. Rio de Janeiro, Brazil: Instituto Brasileiro de Informação em Ciência e Tecnologia (IBICT); 1978. 703-711. (In Portuguese). Available from IBICT. Av. General Justo 171, 20021 Rio de Janeiro, RJ. Brasil.

BENTO, A.A.O.; DOMINGUES, A.L.; BARTH, F.T.; SATO, H.; MONTEIRO FILHO, L.H.J.; GUERRA, M.G. 1979. SIRHI—Sistema de Informações de Recursos Hídricos [Information System in Hydrological Resources]. 1979. 15p. (In Portuguese). Available from IBICT. Av. General Justo 171, 20021 Rio de Janeiro, RJ. Brasil.

BEVERLY, JAMES E. 1977. Summary Appraisal of Technical Information Situation in Relation to Possible International Networks. Mexico, D.F.: United Nations Economic and Social Council, Economic Commission for Latin America (CEPAL); 1977 July. 89p. (CEPAL/MEX/77/14).

BEYA DE MODERNELL, MARTHA. 1974. La Enseñanza de la Documentación en el Uruguay [Teaching Documentation in Uruguay]. Boletín de la Biblioteca de la Escuela Universitaria de Bibliotecología y Ciencias Afines (Uruguay). 1973/1974; (10): 26-28. (In Spanish).

BOLETIN DE LA UNESCO PARA LAS BIBLIOTECAS. 1977. Programas de Información en la Biblioteca Nacional de Medicina en Uruguay [Information Program in the National Library of Medicine in Uruguay]. Boletín de la Unesco para las Bibliotecas (France). 1977; 31(3): 191-192. (In Spanish). ISSN: 0041-5243.

BOLETIN INFORMATIVO DE AIBDA (Asociación Interamericana de Bibliotecarios y Documentalistas Agrícolas) [Information Bulletin of AIBDA (Inter-American Association of Agricultural Librarians and Documentalists)]. 1965-. Paz de Erickson, Ana Maria, ed. Turrialba, Costa Rica: Centro Interamericano de Documentación e Información Agrícola (CIDA) (Inter-American Center for Agricultural Documentation and Information]. (In Spanish, English table of contents). ISSN: 0001-1495.

BOLETIN INFORMATIVO DEL INSTITUTO BIBLIOTECOLOGICO. 1977. Red de Información Socio-económica en Venezuela [Social Economics Information Networks in Venezuela]. Boletin Informativo del Instituto Bibliotecológico (Argentina). 1977; (45): 9-10. (In Spanish).

BRAZIL. CONSELHO NACIONAL DE DESENVOLVIMENTO CIENTÍFICO E TECNOLÓGICO (CNPq) [National Council for Scientific and Technological Development]. 1978. Ciência da Informação, Biblioteconomia e Arquivologia [Information Science, Library Science and Archives]. In: CNPq: Avaliação e Perspectivas. Brasília, Brazil: CNPq; 1978. 49-67.

(In Portuguese).   Available from IBICT. Av. General Justo 171, 20021 Rio de Janeiro, RJ. Brasil.

BRAZIL. INSTITUTO BRASILEIRO DE INFORMAÇÃO EM CIÊNCIA E TECNOLOGIA (IBICT) [Brazilian Institute for Information in Science and Technology]. 1979. Brochures on Services. Rio de Janeiro, Brazil: IBICT; 1979. Available from IBICT. Av. General Justo 171, 20021 Rio de Janeiro, RJ. Brasil.

BRAZIL. PRESIDÊNCIA DA REPÚBLICA. 1976. II. Basic Plan for Scientific and Technological Development. Rio de Janeiro, Brazil: Fundação Instituto Brasileiro de Geografia e Estatística (IBGE); 1976. 186p. Available from IBICT. Av. General Justo 171, 20021 Rio de Janeiro, RJ. Brasil.

CACERES RAMOS, HUGO. 1977. AGRINTER: Un Concepto para la Interconexión y Coparticipación Nacional, Regional y Mundial [AGRINTER: A Concept for Interconnecting and Co-participating on a National, Regional and World Wide Basis]. San José, Costa Rica: Instituto Interamericano de Ciencias Agricolas; 1977. 14p. Available from: the author; IICA-CIDIA; Turrialba, Costa Rica.

CENTRO CATALOGRAFICO CENTROAMERICANO (CCC) [Central American Cataloging Center]. 1976. Reunión de Estudio: Informe Final [Study Meeting: Final Report]; 1976 June 21-24; San Pedro de Montes de Oca, Costa Rica. San Pedro de Montes de Oca, Costa Rica: Universidad de Costa Rica; 1976. 2 volumes (discontinuous paging). (In Spanish). Available from: Efraim Rojas; Director de la Biblioteca; Universidad de Costa Rica; Ciudad Universitaria "Rodrigo Facio"; Costa Rica.

CHASTINET, YONE S. 1977. A Implantação da Rede de Coleta e Registro Bibliográfico do Sistema Nacional de Informação e Documentação Agrícola—SNIDA; uma avaliação [The Implementation of the Collection and Registry Network of the National System of Agricultural Information and Documentation]. In: Anais do 9. Congresso Brasileiro de Biblioteconomia e Documentação e 5. Jornada Sul-Rio-Grandense de Biblioteconomia e Documentação; 1977; Porto Alegre, Brasil. Porto Alegre, Brazil: IBICT; 1977. 350p. (In Portuguese). Available from IBICT. Av. General Justo 171, 20021 Rio de Janeiro, RJ. Brasil.

CHERRO DE VIEIRA, ANA MARIA. 1975. El Centro de Documentación del Instituto de Estudios Sociales [The Documentation Center of the Institute of Social Studies]. Boletín de la Biblioteca de la Escuela Universitária de Bibliotecológia y Ciencias Afines (Uruguay). 1975; 11(7): 10, 15. (In Spanish).

CONJUNTURA ECONÔMICA. 1974. Pesquisas em Documentação [Research in Documentation]. Conjuntura Econômica (Brazil). 1974; 28(1): 115-119. (In Portuguese). Available from IBICT. Av. General Justo 171, 20021 Rio de Janeiro, RJ. Brasil.

CORNING, MARY E. 1975. Biomedical Information a la Carte. In: Proceedings of the Symposium on Scientific and Engineering Secondary Information Transfer for the Developing Countries; 1975 June 23-24; Brussels, Belgium. Paris, France: International Council of Scientific Unions Abstracting Board (ICSU/AB); 1975. 10p. Available from: ICSU/AB, 17 Rue Mirabeau, 75015 Paris, France.

COSTA RICA. CONSEJO NACIONAL DE INVESTIGACIONES CIENTIFICAS Y TECNOLOGICAS (CONICIT) [National Council for Scientific and Technological Research]. 1976. Informe Anual 1975 [1975 Annual Report]. San José, Costa Rica: CONICIT; 1976. 98p. Available from CONICIT; Apartado Postal 10318; San José, Costa Rica.

DE ARAUJO, JERUSA GONCALVES. 1978. O Sistema de Informação do Instituto de Pesquisas Tecnológicas: Programa de Emergencia [The Information System of the Technological Research Institute: Emergency Program]. In: Anais da 1. Reunião Brasileiro de Ciência da Informação; 1975 June 15-20; Rio de Janeiro, Brasil. Rio de Janeiro, Brazil: Instituto Brasileiro de Informação em Ciência e Tecnologia (IBICT); 1978. 947-957. (In Portuguese). Available from IBICT. Av. General Justo 171, 20021 Rio de Janeiro, RJ. Brasil.

DE RODRIGUEZ, LOUMARY; ORTEGA, MIREYA. 1979. Situación actual de las Redes de Información en Venezuela [Situation of the Information Network in Venezuela]. 1979. 15p. Available from: IBICT. Av. General Justo 171, 20021 Rio de Janeiro, RJ. Brasil.

DE SOLANES, MARIA E.S.; DE PEÑA Y LILLO, ANA M.R.; BALMACEDA, MARIA R.C. 1979. Evaluación de un Sistema de Información en Recursos Hídricos [Evaluation of an Information System in Hydrological Resources]. 1979. 10p. (In Spanish). Available from IBICT. Av. General Justo 171, 20021 Rio de Janeiro, RJ. Brasil.

DE VALENZUELA, Z. PUCURULL. 1974. Paraguay: Plan para el Establecimiento de un Centro Nacional de Documentación [Plan for Establishment of a National Center of Documentation]. Paris, France: Unesco; 1974 August. 44p. (In Spanish). (3147/RMO.RD/DBA). Available from: Unesco, 7 Place de Fontenoy, Paris, France.

DE VODANOVIC, BETTY JOHNSON. 1977. Uruguay: Sistema Nacional de Información Científica y Técnica [Uruguay: National System for Scientific and Technical Information]. Montevideo, Uruguay: Unesco; 1977. 49p. (In Spanish). (FMR/BEP/PGI/77/134). Available from: Unesco Regional Office for Science and Technology for Latin America and the Caribbean, Montevideo, Uruguay.

DEXTRE, STELLA G. 1976. Industrial Information in Latin America. The Information Scientist (England). 1976 December; 10(4): 149-156. ISSN: 0020-0263.

DEXTRE, STELLA G. 1977. Diagnóstico para el Desarrollo de Servicios de Información Científica y Tecnológica en Panamá [Diagnosis for the Development of Technical and Scientific Information Services in Panama]. Panama: Ministerio de Planificación y Política Económica; 1977. 137p. Available from: Virginia Escala; Ministerio de Planificación; Apartado 2694; Panama 3.

FAUNCE, STEPHEN S.A. 1977. MARCAL, Manual para la Automatización de las Reglas Catalográficas para America Latina [MARCAL, Handbook for the Automation of Cataloging Rules in Latin America]. Washington, DC: Organization of American States (OAS); 1977. 131p. (Manuales del Bibliotecario, 9). ISBN: 0-875-49000-x; LC: 77-28802.

FEDERACIÓN INTERNACIONAL DE DOCUMENTACIÓN. COMISION LATINOAMERICANA (FID/CLA) [International Federation for Documentation. Commission for Latin America]. 1978. Bibliografia sobre el Planeamiento y Desarrolo de la Bibliotecologia y la Documentación en America Latina (1960-1977) [Bibliography of Planning and Development of Librarianship and Documentation in Latin America (1960-1977)]. Bogotá, Colombia: Instituto Colombiano para el Fomento de la Educación Superior (ICFES); 1978. 95p. (Compiled by Victoria Galofre Neuto). Available from ICFES, Apartado Aereo 21817, Bogota, Colombia.

FERNANDEZ, ANGEL. 1976. Estudio y Proyecto de Creación del Sistema Nacional de Información en Ciencias Agropecuarias de la Republica Argentina [Study and Project for the Creation of the National Information System in Agriculture and Cattle Breeding in Argentina]. Buenos Aires, Argentina: Universidad de Buenos Aires; 1976. 93p. (In Spanish). Available from IBICT. Av. General Justo 171, 20021 Rio de Janeiro, RJ. Brasil.

FERNANDEZ DE LA GARZA, G. 1974. La Tecnología en el Sistema Nacional de Información y Documentación de Mexico [Technology in the National Information and Documentation System in Mexico]. In: 4 Congreso Regional de Documentación; 1973; Bogota, Colombia. Mexico, D.F.: Federación Internacional de Documentación, Comision Latino Americana; 1974. 289-291. (In Spanish). Available from IBICT. Av. General Justo 171, 20021 Rio de Janeiro, RJ. Brasil.

FERRAZ, TEREZINE A.; FIGUEIREDO, REGINA CELIA. 1978. O Serviço de Disseminação Seletiva da Informação executado na Divisão de Informação do Departamento de Informação e Documentação Científicas do Instituto de Energia Atômica de Sao Paulo [Selective Dissemination of Information in the Atomic Energy Institute]. In: Anais da 1. Reunião Brasileira de Ciência da Informação; 1975 June 15-20; Rio de Janeiro, Brasil. Rio de Janeiro, Brazil: Instituto Brasileiro de Informação em Ciência e Tecnologia (IBICT); 1978. 713-723. (In Portuguese). Available from IBICT. Av. General Justo 171, 20021 Rio de Janeiro, RJ. Brasil.

FERSIVA, BERENICE; OLIVEIRA, LUIZ CARLOS. 1978. Filosofia do Sistema de Informações do Centro de Informações Tecnológicas (CIT) da Usiminas [Philosophy of the Information System of the Technological Information Center of Usiminas]. In: Anais da 1. Reunião Brasileira de Ciência da Informação; 1975 June 15-20; Rio de Janeiro, Brasil. Rio de Janeiro, Brazil: Instituto Brasileiro de Informação em Ciência e Tecnologia (IBICT); 1978. 621-631. (In Portuguese). Available from IBICT. Av. General Justo 171, 20021 Rio de Janeiro, RJ. Brasil.

FURTADO, JOÃO SALVADOR. 1978. O Sistema Estadual de Informação Científica e Tecnológica (SEICT) [State System of Scientific and Technological Information]. In: Anais da 1. Reuniao Brasileira de Ciência da Informação; 1975 June 15-20; Rio de Janeiro, Brasil. Rio de Janeiro, Brazil: Instituto Brasileiro de Informação em Ciência e Tecnologia (IBICT); 1978. 607-620. (In Portuguese). Available from IBICT. Av. General Justo 171, 20021 Rio de Janeiro, RJ. Brasil.

GARGANO COVELO, SUSANA; VEGH VILLEGAS, MARTHA. 1979. Banco de Datos de Proyectos Industriales de Inversión en el Uruguay: Metodología para su Implantación [Data Base of Inversion Industrial Projects in Uruguay]. 10p. (In Spanish). Available from IBICT. Av. General Justo 171, 20021 Rio de Janeiro, RJ. Brasil.

GIETZ, RICARDO. 1974. Bases para un Sistema Nacional de Información en Argentina [Bases for a National Information System in Argentina]. In: 4. Congreso Regional de Documentación; 1973; Bogotá, Colombia. Mexico, D.F.: Federación Internacional de Documentación, Comisión

Latino Americana; 1974. 263-270. (In Spanish). Available from IBICT. Av. General Justo 171, 20021 Rio de Janeiro, RJ. Brasil.

GOLDMAN, MYLA K. 1978. Technical Information Services in Mexico. Special Libraries. 1978 September; 69(9): 355-360. ISSN: 0038-6723.

GOMES, HAGAR ESPANHA. 1977. O Papel do IBBD no Sistema Nacional de Informação Científica e Tecnológica [The Role of IBBD (Brazilian Institute for Bibliography and Documentation) in the National System of Scientific and Technological Information]. In: Anais do 7. Congresso Brasileiro de Biblioteconomia e Documentação; 1973; Belém, Brasil. Rio de Janeiro, Brazil: Instituto Brasileiro de Informação em Ciência e Tecnologia (IBICT); 1977. 365-375. (In Portuguese). Available from IBICT. Av. General Justo 171, 20021 Rio de Janeiro, RJ. Brasil.

INFORMACIONES FID/CLA (Federación Internacional de Documentación, Comisión Latino-Americana) [Information FID/CLA (International Federation for Documentation, Commission for Latin America)]. 1964. Arias Ordonez, J.A.; De Jimenez, L.M.; De Villegas, C.L., eds. Bogota, Colombia: Instituto Colombiano para el Fomento de la Educacion Superior (ICFES). Available from: ICFES, Apartado Aereo 21817, Bogota, Colombia.

INSTITUTO CENTROAMERICANO DE INVESTIGACION Y TECNOLOGIA INDUSTRIAL (ICAITI) [Central American Research Institute for Industry]. 1978. Proyecto de Información y Asistencia Técnica a la Industria en America Central y el Caribe [Project on Information and Technical Assistance for Industry in Central America and the Caribbean]. Guatemala City, Guatemala: ICAITI; 1978. 9p. (Progress report prepared for the Organization of American States Regional Program for Scientific and Technological Development Coordination Meeting of Information and Technical Assistance Projects; 1978 June 12-16; Washington, DC). Available from: Rocío Marbán; ICAITI; Apartado Postal 1552; Guatemala City, Guatemala.

JAMAICA. NATIONAL COUNCIL ON LIBRARIES, ARCHIVES AND DOCUMENTATION SERVICES (NACOLADS). 1978. Plan for a National Documentation, Information and Library System for Jamaica. Kingston, Jamaica: NACOLADS; 1978. 81p. Available from: NACOLADS, P.O. Box 205, Kingston 10, Jamaica, W.I.

LAGE, LUCIA MARIA O. 1977. Processos de Aquisição e Disseminação de Informações no Centro de Informações Técnicas da Usiminas [Acquisition and Dissemination Process of Information in the Technical Information Center of Usiminas]. In: Anais do 7. Congresso Brasileiro de Biblioteconomia e Documentação; 1973; Belém, Brasil. Rio de Janeiro, Brazil: Instituto Brasileiro de Informação em Ciência e Tecnologia (IBICT); 1977. 6p. (In Portuguese). Available from IBICT. Av. General Justo 171, 20021 Rio de Janeiro, RJ. Brasil.

LANCASTER, F. WILFRED; MARTYN, JOHN. 1978. Assessing the Benefits and Promise of an International Information Program (AGRIS). Journal of the American Society for Information Science. 1978 November; 29(6): 282-288. ISSN: 0002-8231.

LOAIZA, HUGO T. 1977. El Sistema y Fondo Nacional de Información para el Desarrolo (SYFNID) de Bolivia [National Information System and Fund for Development (SYFNID) of Bolivia]. Actualidades, CNDCT (Centro Nacional de Documentación Científica y Tecnología) (Bolivia).

1977 October; 3(3): 1-14. (In Spanish). Available from: CNDCT, Casilla Correo 3283, La Paz, Bolivia.

MALUGANI, MARIA DOLORES. 1978a. Evolution of Latin America and Caribbean Regional Participation in AGRIS. San Jose, Costa Rica: Instituto Interamericano de Ciencias Agricolas; 1978. 22p. (GIL: AGRIS/ TC/1/INF.1). (Progress report presented at: U.N. Food and Agriculture Organization Technical Consultation of AGRIS Participating Countries; 1978 March 14-17; Rome, Italy). Available from: the author; IICA-CIDIA; Turrialba, Costa Rica.

MALUGANI, MARIA DOLORES. 1978b. AGRINTER—The Latin American and the Caribbean Information Network. Quarterly Bulletin of the International Association of Agricultural Librarians and Documentalists (IAALD). 1978; 22(1-2): 10-18. ISSN: 0020-5966.

MENDA, EDUARDO. 1974. Objetivos y Actividades del Centro Nacional de Información Científica y Técnica de Venezuela [Purposes and Activities of the National Center of Scientific and Technical Information in Venezuela]. In: 4. Congreso Regional de Documentación; 1973; Bogotá, Colombia. Mexico, D.F.: FID, Comisión Latino Americana; 1974. 293-295. (In Spanish). Available from IBICT. Av. General Justo 171, 20021 Rio de Janeiro, RJ. Brasil.

MEXICO. CONSEJO NACIONAL DE CIENCIA Y TECNOLOGIA (CONACYT) [National Council for Science and Technology]. 1976a. El Servicio Nacional de Información Científica y Tecnológica de Mexico [The National Information Service for Science and Technology in Mexico]. Mexico, D.F. CONACYT; 1976. 49p. (In Spanish; also available in English). Available from: CONACYT; Insurgentes Sur 1677; Mexico, 20, D.F.

MEXICO. CONSEJO NACIONAL DE CIENCIA Y TECNOLOGIA (CONACYT) [National Council for Science and Technology]. 1976b. Consulta a Bancos de Información (SECOBI) [Consulting the Information Data Bases (SECOBI)]. Mexico, D.F.: CONACYT; 1976. 23p. (Serie Servicios, 4). Available from: CONACYT; Insurgentes Sur 1677; Mexico, 20, D.F.

MEXICO. SECRETARIA DE SALUBRIDAD Y ASISTENCIA. SUBSECRETARIA DE PLANEACION [Ministry for Health and Public Welfare. Vice Ministry for Planning]. 1978. Centro Nacional de Información y Documentación en Salud (CENIDS) [National Center of Information and Documentation for Health]. Mexico, D.F.: Secretaría de Salubridad y Asistencia. Subsecretaria de Planeacion; 1978. 31p. (Pamphlet). Available from: CENIDS; Liverpool 54, 3er. Piso; Col. Juarez; Mexico, 7, D.F.

MOLINO, ENZO. 1978a. L'information Scientifique et Technique au Mexique [Scientific and Technical Information in Mexico]. La Revue de l'AUPELF (Canada). 1978 June; 16(1): 102-116. (In French). ISSN: 0001-2807.

MOLINO, ENZO. 1978b. Scientific and Technological Information Systems Planning Methodology: Some Considerations Derived from the Mexican Case. Mexico, D.F.: National Council for Science and Technology (CONACYT); 1978. 56p. Available from: the author; CONACYT; Insurgentes Sur 1814; 8 Piso; Mexico, 20, D.F.

NEGHME, AMADOR. 1975. Problems of Health Sciences Communications in Latin America. In: Day, Stacey B., ed. Communication of

Scientific Information.   Basel, Switzerland: S. Karger Verlag; 1975.
69-82.

NOCENTTI, MILTON A.   1977.   Metodología de un Estudio de Diagnostico
como base para la Concepción de un Sistema de Información Agrícola
[Methodology of a Diagnostic Study as a Base for the Conception of an
Agricultural Information System].   Boletin de la Biblioteca da EUBCA
(Uruguay).   1977;(13): 28-38.   (In Spanish).

NOTAS INFORMATIVAS CENID.   1976a.   Colciências: Proyecto Especial
SNI [Colciencias Special Project SNI].   Notas Informativas CENID
(Chile).   1976;(29): 4.   (In Spanish).   Available free to libraries from:
Centro Nacional de Información y Documentación, Casilla 297-V, San-
tiago, Chile.

NOTAS INFORMATIVAS CENID.   1976b.   Noticias de América Latina:
Sistema Andino de Información en Telecomunicaciones [Latin America
News: Andean System of Telecommunication Information].   Notas In-
formativas CENID (Chile).   1976;(29): 3.   (In Spanish).   Available free
to libraries from: Centro Nacional de Informacion y Documentacion,
Casilla 297-V, Santiago, Chile.

NOTAS INFORMATIVAS CENID.   1976c.   Noticias de Chile: Rol de la
Información en el Plan Nacional de Desarrolo Científico y Tecnológico
[News from Chile: Role of Information in the National Plan of Scientific
and Technological Information].   Notas Informativas CENID (Chile).
1976;(30): 1-6.   (In Spanish).   Available free to libraries from: Centro
Nacional de Informacion y Documentacion, Casilla 297-V, Santiago,
Chile.

NOTAS INFORMATIVAS CENID.   1976d.   Noticias de Chile: Información
para la Industria [News from Chile: Information for Industry].   Notas
Informativas CENID (Chile).   1976;(30): 6-7.   (In Spanish).   Available
free to libraries from: Centro Nacional de Informacion y Documentacion,
Casilla 297-V, Santiago, Chile.

NOTAS INFORMATIVAS CENID.   1977a.   Centro de Información y Refer-
encia en Ingenieria Sanitaria y Ciencias del Ambiente (CIRISCA) [Infor-
mation and Reference Center in Sanitary Engineering and Environmental
Science].   Notas Informativas CENID (Chile).   1977; (34): 5.   (In
Spanish).   Available free to libraries from: Centro Nacional de Informacion y Documentacion, Casilla 297-V, Santiago, Chile.

NOTAS INFORMATIVAS CENID.   1977b.   Colegio de Ingenieros Organiza
Servicio de Información Especializado [Engineering College Organizes
Specialized Information Service].   Notas Informativas CENID (Chile).
1977; (34): 3.   (In Spanish).   Available free to libraries from: Centro
Nacional de Informacion y Documentacion, Casilla 297-V, Santiago,
Chile.

NOTAS INFORMATIVAS CENID.   1977c.   Servício de Diseminación de
Información en Telecomunicaciones [Dissemination Information Service
in Telecommunication].   Notas Informativas CENID (Chile).   1977;
(34): 2-3.   (In Spanish).   Available free to libraries from: Centro
Nacional de Informacion y Documentacion, Casilla 297-V, Santiago,
Chile.

NOTAS SOBRE LA ECONOMÍA Y EL DESARROLLO DE AMERICA
LATINA.   1978.   Un Centro de Información para el Desarrollo: CLADES
[An Information Center for Development: CLADES].   Notas sobre la
Economia y el Desarrollo de America Latina (Chile).   1978;(268): 1-4.
(In Spanish).   ISSN: 0029-3881.

ORGANIZATION OF AMERICAN STATES (OAS). DEPARTMENT OF SCIENTIFIC AFFAIRS. 1974. Programa de Información Científica y Tecnológica de la Organización de los Estados Americanos [Programs for Scientific and Technical Information of the OAS]. Washington, DC: OAS; 1974 February. 20p. (In Spanish). Available from: OAS, 1735 I Street, N.W., Washington, DC 20006.

ORGANIZATION OF AMERICAN STATES (OAS). DEPARTMENT OF SCIENTIFIC AFFAIRS. 1978. Directorio de Instituciones y Coordinadores de los Proyectos de Información Técnica de la Organización de los Estados Americanos [Directory of Institutions and Coordinators of the Technical Information Projects of OAS]. Washington, DC: OAS; 1978 May. 18p. (In Spanish). Available from: OAS, 1735 I Street, N.W., Washington, DC 20006.

ORGANIZATION OF AMERICAN STATES (OAS). GENERAL SECRETARIAT. 1977. Report on Technical Information and Assistance Services to Business. Washington, DC: OAS; 1977 February 23. 18p. (OEA/Ser. T/I TECII/doc.2). Available from: OAS, 1735 I Street, N.W., Washington, DC 20006.

ORGANIZATION OF AMERICAN STATES (OAS). GENERAL SECRETARIAT. PAN AMERICAN UNION. 1961. Science Information in Latin America. Washington, DC: OAS; 1961. 50p. (Compiled by Florence Nierman; OAS pamphlet 016-E-6257). Available from: OAS, 1735 I Street, N.W., Washington, DC 20006.

OSPINA, HERNANDO. 1974. Red Colombiana de Información y Documentación Economica [Colombian Network of Information and Documentation in Economics]. In: 4. Congreso Regional de Documentación; 1973; Bogota, Colombia. México, D.F.: Federacion Internacional de Documentación, Comision Latino Americana; 1974. 151-158. (In Spanish). Available from IBICT. Av. General Justo 171, 20021 Rio de Janeiro, RJ. Brasil.

PAN AMERICAN HEALTH ORGANIZATION. PAN AMERICAN CENTER FOR SANITARY ENGINEERING AND ENVIRONMENTAL SCIENCES (CEPIS). INFORMATION SECTOR. 1977. Final Report of the Meeting on Consultation on Information in Sanitary Engineering and Environmental Sciences; 1977 November 14-16; Lima, Peru. Lima, Peru: CEPIS; 1977. 31p. Available from: CEPIS, Casilla Postal 4337, Lima 100, Peru.

PAN AMERICAN HEALTH ASSOCIATION. REGIONAL LIBRARY OF MEDICINE (BIREME). 1978. [Proceedings of the 10th] Meeting of the Scientific Advisory Committee, Regional Library of Medicine, Pan American Health Organization; May 1978; São Paulo, Brasil. São Paulo, Brazil: Regional Library of Medicine; 1978 May. 49p. Available from: BIREME, Rua Botucatu 862, Villa Clemeneutino, 04023 São Paulo, Brazil.

PENNA, CARLOS VICTOR. 1974. Servicios Bibliotecarios y de Información para las Zonas Rurales de America Latina [Library and Information Services for Rural Areas of Latin America]. Revista da Escola de Biblioteconomia da UFMG (Brasil). 1974; 3(2): 193-217. (In Spanish).

PENNA, CARLOS VICTOR. 1975a. Estudio Preliminar para la Organización de un Servicio Nacional de Información Educativa en el Paraguay [Preliminary Study for the Organization of a National Service for Information on Education in Paraguay]. In: 8. Congresso Brasileiro de

Biblioteconomia e Documentação; 1975; Brasilia, Brasil. 17p. (In Spanish). Available from IBICT. Av. General Justo 171, 20021 Rio de Janeiro, RJ. Brasil.

PENNA, CARLOS VICTOR. 1975b. Planeamiento de los Servicios Bibliotecarios y de Información en America Latina y el Caribe [Planning of the Library and Information Services in Latin America and Caribbean]. In: Final Report and Working Papers of the 18th Seminar on the Acquisition of Latin American Library Materials; 1973; Port-of-Spain, Trinidad and Tobago. 1975. 389-404. (In Spanish). Available from IBICT. Av. General Justo 171, 20021 Rio de Janeiro, RJ. Brasil.

PEREZ FERRERA, T. 1979. Estudio de la Información en la Industria Latinoamericana. La Creación del Centro de Bienes de Capital en Nacional Financiera, S.A. [Study of Latin American Information for Industry]. 1979. 10p. (In Spanish). Available from IBICT. Av. General Justo 171, 20021 Rio de Janeiro, RJ. Brasil.

PINHEIRO, LENA VANIA R. 1978. Sistema de Informações para a Amazônia—SIAMA [Information Systems for Amazonia]. In: Anais da 1. Reunião Brasileira de Ciência da Informação; 1975 June 15-20; Rio de Janeiro, Brasil. Rio de Janeiro, Brazil: Instituto Brasileiro de Informação em Ciência e Tecnologia (IBICT); 1978. 471-516. (In Portuguese). Available from IBICT. Av. General Justo 171, 20021 Rio de Janeiro, RJ. Brasil.

POBLACION, DINAH AGUIAR; HAMAR, ALFREDO AMÉRICO. 1974. Rede Integrada de Bibliotecas como Infra-estrutura de Sistemas de Comunicação da Informação no Brasil [Integrated Network of Libraries as Infra-Structure of Information Communication Systems in Brazil]. In: 4. Encontro de Bibliotecários Biomédicos; 1974; São Paulo, Brasil. São Paulo, Brazil: Federação Brasileira de Associações de Bibliotecários (FEBAB); 1974. 1 volume. (In Portuguese). Available from IBICT. Av. General Justo 171, 20021 Rio de Janeiro, RJ. Brasil.

POMPEU DAVIG, ANGELA. 1978. Report on the Existing Industrial Information Services in the State of São Paulo, Brasil. São Paulo, Brazil: IBICT; 1978. 33p. Available from: IBICT. Av. General Justo 171, 20021 Rio de Janeiro, RJ. Brasil.

POMPEU DAVIG, ANGELA; LIFCHITZ, ABRAHÃO. 1974. Informação Industrial no Brasil [Industrial Information in Brasil]. In: 4. Congreso Regional de Documentación; 1973; Bogota, Colombia. México, D.F.: Federación Internacional de Documentación, Comisión Latino Americana; 1974. 199-218. (In Spanish). Available from IBICT. Av. General Justo 171, 20021 Rio de Janeiro, RJ. Brasil.

QUEVEDO, JOSÉ. 1976. Meeting Importing Countries' Needs. Les Nouvelles. 1976 December; 11(4): 204-205. ISSN: 0047-4576.

ROBREDO, JAIME. 1976. Problems Involved in Setting up and Operating Information Networks in the Developing Countries. Unesco Bulletin for Libraries. 1976 September-October; 30(5): 251-254. ISSN: 0041-5243.

ROBREDO, JAIME; CHASTINET, YONE S. 1974. A Integração do Brasil ao Sistema Internacional de Informação Agrícola (AGRIS) através do Projeto PNUD/FAO/BRA/72/020 [The Integration of Brazil to the International System of Agricultural Information (AGRIS)]. Paper presented at: 4. Encontro de Bibliotecários Agrícolas; 1974; São Paulo, Brasil. 16p. (In Portuguese). Available from IBICT. Av. General Justo 171, 20021 Rio de Janeiro, RJ. Brasil.

ROCHA, FERNANDO R.A.   1978.   Programa de Información Tecnológica do Instituto de Pesquisas Tecnológicas (IPT) [Program of Technological Information of the Institute of Technological Research]. In: Anais da 1. Reunião Brasileira de Ciência da Informação; 1975 June 15-20; Rio de Janeiro, Brasil. Rio de Janeiro, Brazil: Instituto Brasileiro de Informação em Ciencia e Tecnologia (IBICT); 1978. 465-469. (In Portuguese). Available from IBICT. Av. General Justo 171, 20021 Rio de Janeiro, RJ. Brasil.

ROJAS, L.   1974.   El Sistema Nacional de Informacion de Colombia [The National Information System in Colombia]. In: 4. Congreso Regional de Documentación; 1973; Bogota, Colombia. Mexico, D.F.: Federacion Internacional de la Documentación, Comision Latino Americana; 1974. 283-284. (In Spanish). Available from: IBICT. Av. General Justo 171, 20021 Rio de Janeiro, RJ. Brasil.

ROMERIO, C.F.   1978.   A Central American Information Retrieval Network. Paris, France: Unesco; 1978 March.   22p.   (PGI/78/WS/8). Available from: Unesco, 7 Place de Fontenoy, Paris, France.

SANDOVAL, ARMANDO M.   1978.   Centro de Información Científica y Humanística: A University Information Centre in the Third World. Unesco Bulletin for Libraries.   1978 January-February; 32(1): 42-48. ISSN: 0041-5243.

SANTOS, DULCE C. DOS; LANDAU, MARIETA; CORDEIRO, ROSA INÊS DE N.; BRAGA, G.   1979.   Resultados Preliminares do Projeto de Avaliação de Periódicos em Ciência e Tecnologia [Preliminary Results of the Project on Evaluation of Journals in Science and Technology]. 1979. 7p.   (In Portuguese).   Available from IBICT. Av. General Justo 171, 20021 Rio de Janeiro, RJ. Brasil.

SARACEVIC, TEFKO.   1979.   Integrating Education in Librarianship and Information Science with Special Reference to Library Schools in Brazil and Latin America in General.   1979.   28p.   Available from: IBICT. Av. General Justo 171, 20021 Rio de Janeiro, RJ. Brasil and from the author, Case Western Reserve University, Cleveland, OH 44106.

SCHLIE, THEODORE W.; FREEMAN, JAMES E.; COYLE, VIRGINIA S. 1976a.   Report on a Conference on the Role of Scientific and Technical Information Services in the Transfer of Technology in Latin America; 1976 February 16-18; Washington, DC. Denver, CO: Denver Research Institute (DRI); 1976. 81p. Available from: DRI, University of Denver, Denver, CO 80208.

SCHLIE, THEODORE W.; KATZ, RUTH M.; COYLE, VIRGINIA. 1976b. Seminar on Industrial Information; 1976 October 1-2; Mexico, D.F. Denver, CO: Denver Research Institute (DRI); 1976. 48p. Available from: DRI, University of Denver, Denver, CO 80208.

SCHUR, HERBERT.   1977.   Colombia: Information Specialists for Development. Paris, France: Unesco; 1977. 63p. (FMR/PGI/77/277 UNDP). Available from: Unesco, 7 Place de Fontenoy, Paris, France.

SHEPARD, MARIETTA DANIELS.   1974.   Asistencia que la OEA Brinda a Latinoamerica en el Campo de la Información [OAS Assistance Given to Latin America in the Field of Information]. In: Federación Internacional de Documentación/Comisión Latinoamericana (FID/CLA), eds. 4. Congreso Regional de Documentación: La Tecnología en los Servicios de Información y Documentación; 1973 October 15-19, Bogotá, Colombia. Mexico, D.F.: FDS/CLA; 1974. 361-363.

SHEPARD, MARIETTA DANIELS. 1975. Role of the Organization of American States in the Provision of Library and Information Services for Development Purposes in Latin America: Report of the Library Development Program of the OAS. In: Final Report and Working Papers of the 18th Seminar on the Acquisition of Latin American Materials; 1973; Port-of-Spain, Trinidad and Tobago. 1975. 181-198. Available from: IBICT. Av. General Justo 171, 20021 Rio de Janeiro, RJ. Brasil.

SLAETS, JAN; LECHAT, JEAN; TREVELIN, LUIS CARLOS; MASCAREN-HAS, YVONNE P. 1979. Base de Dados Relativa a Estruturas Cristalinas [Data Base for Crystalline Structures]. 1979. 15p. (In Portuguese). Available from IBICT. Av. General Justo 171, 20021 Rio de Janeiro, RJ. Brasil.

TELL, BJORN. 1974. Venezuela: A National Scientific and Technological Information System. Paris, France: Unesco; 1974 March. 28p. (3058/RMO.RD/DBA). Available from: Unesco, 7 Place de Fontenoy, Paris, France.

TICHAUER, WERNER GUTTENTAG. 1975. Survey on the Library Situation in Bolivia. In: Final Report and Working Papers of the 18th Seminar on the Acquisition of Latin American Library Material; 1973; Port-of-Spain, Trinidad and Tobago. 1975. 363-371. Available from: IBICT. Av. General Justo 171, 20021 Rio de Janeiro, RJ. Brasil.

TOMÉ, MARTHA V. 1978. Avance en la Preparación de Bibliotecarios Especializados y de Especialistas en Información en America Latina: Análisis de la Problematica en este Proceso Educativo [Advances in Preparation of Special Librarians and Information Specialists in Latin America: Analysis of Problems in the Education Process]. Quarterly Bulletin of the International Association of Agricultural Librarians and Documentalists (IAALD). 1978 Fall-Winter; 23(3-4). (In Spanish). ISSN: 0020-5966.

U.S. NATIONAL ACADEMY OF SCIENCES (NAS). BOARD ON SCIENCE AND TECHNOLOGY FOR INTERNATIONAL DEVELOPMENT. 1976. NAS-CONICET (Argentina) Science Cooperation Program: I. The Argentine Telex Network for Scientific and Technical Information. II. Computer Based Information Services for Science and Technology. Washington, DC: NAS; 1976 August. 124p. NTIS: PB 259 991/8WL.

U.S. NATIONAL TECHNICAL INFORMATION SERVICE (NTIS). 1978. Technical Information for Development. Washington, DC: NTIS; 1978 December 28. 31p. (Annual Report of the NTIS Developing Country Staff for Fiscal Year 1978). Available from: NTIS, 425 13th Street, N.W., Suite 620, Washington, DC 20007.

UNESCO BULLETIN FOR LIBRARIES. 1976a. NATIS News: Implementation of NATIS in Venezuela. Unesco Bulletin for Libraries. 1976; 30(1): 69-70. ISSN: 0041-5243.

UNESCO BULLETIN FOR LIBRARIES. 1976b. National Systems for Agricultural Information, Argentina. Unesco Bulletin for Libraries. 1976; 30(3): 126. ISSN: 0041-5243.

UNESCO BULLETIN FOR LIBRARIES. 1977. Socio-Economic Information Network in Venezuela. Unesco Bulletin for Libraries. 1977; 31(6): 382. ISSN: 0041-5243.

UNITED NATIONS. CENTRO LATINAMERICANO DE DEMOGRAFIA (CELADE). SISTEMA DE DOCUMENTACION SOBRE POBLACION EN AMERICA LATINA (DOCPAL) [Latin American Demographic

Center (CELADE). Latin American Population Documentation System (DOCPAL]. 1978. The DOCPAL System and Its Services. In: DOCPAL Latin American Population Abstracts (Chile). 1978 June; 2(1): 2. (In Spanish; Table of Contents and summary in English). ISSN: 0378-5378.

UNITED NATIONS. INDUSTRIAL DEVELOPMENT ORGANIZATION (UNIDO). 1977. Establishment of an Industrial and Technological Bank: Report by the Executive Director of UNIDO to the Industrial Development Board, 11th Session; 1977 May 23-June 7; Vienna, Austria. Vienna, Austria: UNIDO; 1977 March 21. 15p. Available from: UNIDO, P.O. Box 837, A-1011 Vienna, Austria.

VALDES, RENATA. 1978. *RSVP:* Información Telefónica al Instante [RSVP: Instant Telephone Information]. Expansión (México). 1978 July 5; 10(244): 50-52. (Interview). Available from: Roberto Salinas, Publisher, Expansión, Homero 136; México, 5, D.F.

VALLS, JAIME. 1974. Cuba: Un Sistema de Recuperación de Datos en el Instituto de Documentación e Información Científica y Técnica (IDICT) [Cuba: A System for Data Retrieval at the Institute for Scientific and Technical Documentation and Information (IDICT)]. Paris, France: Unesco; 1974 July. 20p. (3061/RMO.RD/DBA). (In Spanish). Available from: Unesco, 7 Place de Fontenoy, Paris, France.

ZAMORA, PEDRO. 1974. INIS (International Nuclear Information System), SIDON (Sistema Internacional de Documentación Nuclear). In: Federación Internacional de Documentación/Comisión Latino Americana (FID/CLA), ed. 4. Congreso Regional de Documentación: La Tecnologia en los Servicios de Información y Documentación; 1973 October 15-19; Bogotá, Colombia. Mexico, D.F.: FID/CLA: 1974. 189-197.

Introduction to Index

Index entries have been made for names of individuals, corporate bodies, subjects and author names that have been included in the bibliography pages as well as those found in the text pages. The page numbers in the index of referring to bibliography pages are set in italics and they are listed after the page numbers relating to the text pages. Thus, the user can readily distinguish references to bibliographic materials from references to text.

Postings to acronyms are listed either under the acronym or under the fully spelled-out form depending on which form is more commonly used and known. In either case a cross reference to the alternate form is provided. Postings associated with BALLOTS, for example, are listed under BALLOTS as few people are likely to remember that BALLOTS stands for Bibliographic Automation of Large Library Operations using a Time-sharing System. In a few cases, such as the names of programs, systems and programming languages, there is no spelled-out form either because there is none or because the meaning has been changed or is no longer used.

The index is arranged on a word-by-word basis, with headings and modifiers treated as separate fields so that Cataloging, automatic systems precedes Cataloging and Indexing data bases. The sort sequence employed sorts on special characters, first, followed by alpha characters and then numeric characters. Thus, O'Neill precedes Oakman and 3M Company follows the Zs. Government organizations are listed under country name with *see* references provided from names of departments, agencies and other subdivisions.

Subject indexing is by concepts rather than by words. When authors have used different words or different forms of the same words to express the same or overlapping concepts, the terminology has been standardized. An effort was made to use the form of index entries for concepts that had previously appeared in *ARIST* indexes. Cross references have been used freely to provide broad access to subject concepts. Cross references are used for overlapping or related (but not synonymous) concepts; *see* references are used to send the reader to the accepted form of a term used in the index.

The index was prepared by Laurence Lannom. The programs for online editing of the index, page number conversions, and formatting of output were written by Scott E. Preece. The overall direction and coordination of the index were provided by Martha E. Williams. The index was generated on the DEC System 10 at the Coordinated Science Laboratory, University of Illinois. Comments and suggestions are welcomed and should be directed to the Editor.

Index*

A&I services (Abstracting and Index-
   ing services),
   cost analysis, 47
Abilock, J.G., *91*
Abreu, Sergio K.M., *269*
Abstracting and indexing services, (*see*
   A&I services)
Abstracts and abstracting,
   automatic extraction, 97
Academic libraries,
   cost analysis, 44
   unit times, 11
Academic publishing,
   page charges, 42
Access methods, (*see also* Data access)
   applications of theories and models,
   103
Accounting,
   information acquisition and use, 154
Ackerman, S.J., *143*
Acosta Hoyos, Luis Eduardo, 259, *269*
Acquisitions,
   cost analysis, 39-40
ACS (Advanced Communications
   System),
   library automation trends, 203
Aczel, J., 72, *80*
ADABAS (Adaptable Database Sys-
   tem), 175
   development, 159
Adam, Robert G., 176, *184*
Adams, Scott, 251, 259, 260, 263,
   269
Adaptable Database System, (*see*
   ADABAS)
Adeyemi, Nat M., 14, *17*
Advanced Communication System,
   (*see* ACS)

Advances in Librarianship,
   library automation literature, 195
Afanes'ev, E.V., *80*
Aggarwal, N.L., 72, *80*
Aggregation of information,
   empirical laws, 74
   information science research areas,
   69
AGRICOLA,
   user training, 226-228
Agricultural information,
   Latin America, 258-259
AGRINTER (Caribbean Agricultural
   Information Network), 259
AGRIS (International Information
   Systems for Agricultural Sciences
   and Technology),
   development, 258
   Latin American projects, 259
Ahlgren, Alice E., 41, *50*
Ahmed, Feroz, *30*
AI, (*see* Artificial intelligence)
AIBDA (Inter-American Association
   of Agricultural Librarians and
   Documentalists), 258
Aiken, Leona S., *91*
Aitchison, Thomas M., *64*
Aiyepeku, Wilson O., 15, *17*
Alais, Elliot S., *29*
Albuquerque, Carlos Augusto, 254,
   269
Albuquerque, Martha, *270*
Alcade Cardoza, Xavier, 262, *270*
ALEBCI (Latin American Association
   of Library and Information Science
   Schools), 264
Allen, M.J., *80*
Allmen, Diane, *237*

---

*Italicized page numbers refer to bibliography pages.

Alsbrooks, William T., 177, *190*
Altman, E.B., *189*
Alvear, Alfredo, *270*
Alvey, Celine H., *114*
Ambiguity,
  measures, 72
American Chemical Society,
  database research, 198
American Institute of Physics,
  abstracting and indexing services
  compatibility, 198
American National Standards
  Institute, (*see* ANSI)
American Society for Information
  Science, (*see* ASIS)
Amey, Gerald X., *31*, *212*
AMIGOS,
  library automation literature, 195
Anbalon Casas, Silvia, *270*
Anderson, C.M.B., *61*
Anderson, George A., 133, *141*
Anderson, James D., 15, *17*
Anderson, Richard C., 15, 77, *17*, *87*
Andrukovich, P.F., 75, *80*
Annual Conference of the Graduate
  Library School of the University of
  Chicago (35th-1975), 14
ANSI (American National Standards
  Institute),
  database management systems, 179
  flowcharting, 12
Antony, Arthur, 234, *237*
APL,
  computer-assisted indexing, 100
APLDEX, 100
Apollo program,
  IMS/VS development, 158
Applications programmers,
  database management systems, 172
Applied Communication Research,
  Inc.,
  information processing cost studies,
  42
Appropriate information,
  Latin America, 266

Appropriate technology,
  Latin America, 266
Apter, H., *86*
Arakelov, R.K., *87*
Arapov, M.V., 79, *80*
Arboleda Sepulveda, Orlando, 259,
  270
Architecture, computer, (*see* Computer architecture)
Ardila Santos, Alvaro, *270*
Argentina,
  Center for Scientific Documentation,
  256
  CNEA (Argentine Atomic Energy
  Commission), 256, 260
  CONICET (National Council for
  Scientific and Technical Research),
  255-256
  DIGID (General Directorate for Research and Development), 256
  information systems and services,
  255-256
  INTI (National Institute for Industrial
  Technology), 256
  nuclear energy information, 260
  political changes and information
  policy, 263
  SATI (Service for Technical
  Assistance to Industry), 260
  water resources information, 261
Argentine Atomic Energy Commission,
  (*see* Argentina, CNEA)
Arias Ordoñez, Jose, 251, 262, *270*,
  271
Arid Zone Information Center
  (Mexico), (*see* CIZA)
Arms, C.R., 15, *17*
Arms, W.Y., 15, 16, *17*
Arnovick, George N., 111, *114*
Artandi, Susan, 100, *114*
Artificial intelligence (AI),
  information retrieval, 96
Artificial languages,
  empirical properties, 75-76
Arzadum, O. Elba, 255, *271*

Asad, Syed M., *30*
Ashenhurst, Robert, *207*
Ashford, John, 47, *50*
ASIDIC (Association of Information
  and Dissemination Centers),
  1977 meeting on training, 222
ASIS (American Society for Informa-
  tion Science),
  Delaware Chapter,
  online workshop, 232
  1977 panel discussion on training,
  222
Association of Information and
  Dissemination Centers, (*see*
  ASIDIC)
Associative memory,
  computer architecture for informa-
  tion retrieval, 132-135
Astrahan, M.M., 181, *184*, *189*
AT&T,
  ACS, (*see* ACS)
Atherton, Pauline A., 41, 46, 97, 101,
  195, 226, 229, 236, *50*, *51*, *114*,
  122, *204*, *238*, *241*
Atlan, H., *80*
Attar, R., 105, *114*
Attention,
  human information processing
  related to information science,
  77
Attributes,
  data models, 161-164
Auerbach Publishers, Inc.,
  database management systems
  listings, 159
Aulbach, Louis F., 40, *51*
Auliano, John, *209*
Aurdal, Eiviand, 165, *184*
Australia,
  National Library of Australia, (*see*
  National Library of Australia)
Authority files, (*see also* Dictionaries;
  Thesauri)
  library automation, 199

Automatic extraction,
  concept vector approach, 97
Automatic indexing, (*see also* Com-
  puter-assisted indexing)
  applications of theories and models,
  99-101
  information measures, 73
  research, 196
Autonomous National University of
  Mexico (UNAM),
  Scientific and Humanistic Informa-
  tion Center (CICH), 253
Avram, Henriette D., 200, 201, *204*
Axelrod, C. Warren, 12, *17*
Axford, H. William, 10, 40, *17*, *51*
B.F. Goodrich Co.,
  IDMS, 159
Babb, E., 134, *141*
Bachman, Charles W., 159, *184*
Back-end computers,
  database management systems, 182
  OCLC, 199
Bajema, Bruce D., 47, *51*
Baker, David, 15, *17*
BALLOTS, (*see* RLIN)
Balmaceda, Maria R.C., *273*
Banerjee, Jayanta, 139, *141*
Bar-Hillel, Y., 69, *80*
Barash, H., *62*
Barboni, Edward J., *90*
Barnes, C.I., 100, *114*
Barreiro, Selma Chi, 259, *271*
Barrentine, James K., 199-200, *205*
Barth, F.T., *271*
Barth, Stephen W., *215*
Basens, Sandra J., 231, *244*
Batch processing, (*see also* Searching,
  online)
  charge estimation, 47
  sequential and tree structured files,
  103
Batcher, Kenneth E., 140, *142*
Bates, Marcia J., 236, *238*
Bates, R.G., 99, 196, *125*, *213*

Battelle-Geneva,
  library costs study, 45
Batten, A.M., 234, *244*
Baum, R.I., 139, 182, *141, 142, 184*
Baumol, W.J., *51*
Baxter, Barbara A., 10, 38, 43, *34, 63*
Bayer, Alan E., 234, *240*
Bayer, R., 75, *80, 84*
Bayesian distance,
  document clustering, 103
Becker, Curtis A., *83*
Becker, Joseph, 5, *24*
Beilby, Mary H., *207*
Belkin, N.J., 68, 71, 73, *80, 88*
Bellardo, Trudi, 228, 229, *238*
Bellassai, Marcia C., *60*
Bellomy, Fred L., 7, *21*
Bement, James H., 41, *51*
Benbasat, Izak, 171, 182, *184*
Benchmarking,
  database management system
    selection, 177
Benefeld, Alan R., *86, 121*
Bento, A.A.O., 261, *271*
Berg, John L., 170, 178, 180, *184*
Berg, Sanford O., *207*
Berger, Mary C., 231, 232, *238*
Berk, Robert A., 230, 231, 235, *238*
Bernstein, Philip A., *212*
Berra, P. Bruce, 129, 133, 134, *142, 144*
Bevan, Alice, *243*
Beverly, H.W., *55*
Beverly, James E., 265, *271*
Beya de Modernell, Martha, *271*
Bibliographic Retrieval Services, (*see* BRS)
Bibliographic Services Development
  Program, 201
Bibliographic utilities, (*see also*
  Cataloging, networks)
  network research, 197-198

Bibliometrics,
  definition, 14, 67
  system analysis and design, 14-15
BIBLIOSHARE,
  information management
    bibliography, 94
Bierman, J., *55*
Biller, Horst, 110, *115*
Billingsley, Alice, 13, *27*
BINAGRI, (*see* Brazil, BINAGRI)
Binary representations,
  information retrieval models, 98
Biological information systems,
  systems theory, 4
BioSciences Information Service, (*see*
  BIOSIS)
BIOSIS (BioSciences Information
  Service),
  user training, 224, 226
Bird, R.M., 110, *115*
BIREME (São Paulo Medical School
  regional medical library), 260-261
Birss, Edward, *186*
Biteen, Dale, *208*
Bivans, Margaret M., 41, *51*
Bjerre, Per, *119*
Blaauw, Gerrit A., 129, *142*
Black, Donald Vincent, 6, *17*
Black, John B., 232, *243*
BLAISE (British Library Automated
  Information Service),
  education and training, 225
Blake, Fay M., 12, 48, *18, 51*
Bocchino, William A., 9, 12, *18*
Bock, Rochelle, 40, *51*
Boekee, D.E., 72, *80*
Bohnert, Lea M., 203
Boland, Richard J., Jr., 9, *18*
*Boletín del Centro Paraguayo de
  Documentación*, 255
Boletín Informativo de AIBDA, 258

Bolivia,
  information systems and services,
    255
  National Center for Scientific and
    Technical Documentation, 255
  SYFNID (National System and Fund
    of Information for Development),
    255
Bommer, Michael R.W., 11, 14, *18*,
  24, *208*
Book storage,
  optimal storage by size, 13
Book use,
  cost analysis, 39-40
BOOKS,
  MARC comparison, 101
Bookstein, Abraham, 14, 15, 73, 93,
  95, 96, 104, 112, 198, *18*, *32*, *86*,
  115, *120*, *205*
Boolean logic,
  document rank ordering, 96
  fuzzy sets, 95
Borgman, Christine L., 222, 235, *238*
Borko, Harold, 3, 229, *18*, *31*, *238*,
  212
Bourgeois, Marcel, 72, *81*
Bourne, Charles P., 198, 226, 229,
  231, 208, *238*, *239*
Bowden, Virginia M., 202, *209*
Bowker Company,
  book and serial prices, 39
Boyce, Bert R., 14, *18*
Boylan, David, 175, *184*
Brachman, Ronald J., 76, *81*
Bradford's law, 14
  current research, 74
Bradford, Samuel C., 14
Braga, Gilda Maria, 15, 249-269, *18*,
  280
Brandejs, Jan Flick, 12, *18*
Braude, Robert M., 10, 40, *19*, *51*, *52*
Braunstein, Yale M., 42, 44, 49, *51*
Bray, Olin, *142*

Brazil,
  agricultural information, 259
  BINAGRI (National Library of
    Medicine), 259
  CIN (Nuclear Information Center),
    259-260
  CIT (Center for Technological Infor-
    mation), 258
  CNPq (National Research Council),
    254
  EMBRAPA (Brazilian Enterprise for
    Agricultural Research), 259
  EMBRATER (Brazilian Enterprise
    for Rural Extension), 259
  GEIPOT (Brazilian Enterprise for
    Transportation Planning), 261
  IBBD (Brazilian Institute for
    Bibliography and
    Documentation), 254
  IBICT (Brazilian Institute for
    Information in Science and
    Technology), 254-255
  industrial information
    activities, 258
  information systems and services,
    254-255
  IPEN (Institute of Energy and
    Atomic Research, *formerly* IEA
    (Institute of Atomic Energy)),
    260
  library holdings, 263
  medical information, 260-261
  nuclear energy information, 259-
    260
  PRODASER (Information System
    for Data Processing of
    Legislative Information), 261
  SITCI (Technical and Scientific
    Information System), 259
  SNIDA (National System for
    Agricultural Information and
    Documentation), 259
  water resources information, 261

Brazilian Conference of Information Science, Second (1979), 255

Brazilian Enterprise for Agricultural Research, (*see* Brazil, EMBRAPA)

Brazilian Enterprise for Rural Extension, (*see* Brazil, EMBRATER)

Brazilian Enterprise for Transportation Planning, (*see* GEIPOT)

Brazilian Institute for Bibliography and Documentation (*see* IBBD)

Brazilian Institute for Information in Science and Technology, (*see* IBICT)

Brennen, Patrick W., 15, *19*

Bres, E.S., *52*

Briner, L.L., 100, *115*

British Library, BLAISE, (*see* BLAISE)

British Library Automated Information Service, (*see* BLAISE)

Broadus, Robert N., 73, *81*

Brookes, Bertram C., 14, 68, 71, *19, 81, 115*

Brophy, Peter, 14, *19*

Brown, Carolyn P., 234, *239*

Brown, Lorene B., *239*

Brown, Maryann Kevin, *59*

Brown, Patricia L., 38, *62*

BRS (Bibliographic Retrieval Service), cost comparison study, 41

Bruce, Daniel R., 14, *19*

Bryant, Edward C., *63*

Bryce, Tim, 180, *184*

Brydon, Donald H., *64*

Bryntesson, Christer, *121*

Bubble memory, computer architecture for information retrieval, 136

Buchinski, Edwin J., 199, 201, *205*

Buckland, Michael K., 14, 202, *19, 205*

Bulick, Stephen, 15, 202, *19, 59, 205, 209, 210*

Bullen, R.H., Jr., 138, *142*

Burbulya, Yu. T., 15, *19*

Burch, John G., Jr., 13, *19*

Burks, Arthur W., *143*

Burns, Helen J., *86*

Burns, Kathleen, *26*

Buschke, Herman, *81*

Bush, J.A., *143*

Business and management information, quality indicators, 73

Butkovich, Margaret, 10, 40, *19, 51, 52*

Butler, Brett, 201, *205, 215*

Buxton, A.B., 78, *81*

Byrd, Gary D., 14, *19*

Caceres Ramos, Hugo, 259, *272*

Cahn, D.F., 96, *115*

CAI (Computer-aided instruction), library automation, 200 online retrieval training, 225, 233-234

CAIN, (*see* AGRICOLA)

California Library Authority for Systems and Services, (*see* CLASS)

Calk, Jo, 199, *205*

Calkins, Mary L., *52*

Campbell, S.G., 139, *143*

Campey, L.H., 10, *19*

Canada, Latin American information systems development, 251 National Library, (*see* National Library of Canada) Technical Information Service, Argentinan SDI system, 256

Canaday, R.H., 182, *184*

Cancelli, Anthony A., 77, *88*

Canning, Richard G., 169, 171, *184*

Cape, James D., 201, *205*

Capital Systems Group, Inc.,
   information dissemination
      innovations, 42
Capraro, Gerald T., *143*
Cardenas, Alfonso F., 165, 179,
   184
Caribbean,
   industrial information
      activities, 257
Caribbean Agricultural Information
   Network, (*see* AGRINTER)
Carlis, J.V., 165, 166, 178, 179,
   190
Carlsson, Gunnar, *124*
Carnap, R., 69, *80*
Carpenter, Mark P., 15, *29*
Carpenter, Ray L., 15, *19*
Carroll, John B., 77, *81*
Carroll, John M., *115*
Carter, Bradley D., 202, *207*
Carter, Ruth C., 200, *205*
Caruso, D. Elaine, 109, 222, 227, 230,
   233, 234, 235, *116, 239*
CASDAL (CASSM's Data Language),
   135
Cashwell, Leslie F., *24*
Casper, Cheryl A., 15, *20*
Caspi, P., *81*
Cass, J.L., *142*
CASSM (Content addressed segment
   sequential memory),
   development and organization,
      134-135
CASSM's Data Language, (*see*
   CASDAL)
Catalog cards, (*see also* Catalogs)
   production cost analysis, 40
Cataloging, (*see also* Catalog
   cards; Catalogs)
   computerized,
      collection development, 197
      costing, 201
      links to circulation systems, 200
   cost analysis, 40

Cataloging, (cont.)
   networks, (*see also* Bibliographic
      utilities)
      cost analysis, 40
Catalogs, (*see also* Catalog cards)
   relevance indicators, 73
CATLINE,
   catalog card production study, 40
Cawkell, A.E., 7, 15, 74, *20, 81, 116*
CEC, (*see* Commission of the
   European Communities)
CELADE (Latin American
   Demographic Center), 261
Cellular comparators,
   computer architecture for full text
      retrieval, 137-138
CeMIQ (Chemistry Information Center
   (Mexico)), 253
CENDES (Ecuadorian Center for
   Industrial Development), 258
CENID, (*see* Chile, CENID)
CENIDE (National Center for
   Educational Documentation and
   Information), 262
Center for Information Services
   (Mexico), (*see* Mexico, Center for
   Information Services)
Center for Scientific Documentation,
   (*see* Argentina, Center for Scientific
   Documentation)
Center for Scientific, Technical and
   Economic Documentation
   (Uruguay), 255
Center for Technological Information
   (Brazil), (*see* Brazil, CIT)
Central America,
   industrial information
      activities, 257
Central processing unit, (*see* CPU)
CEPAL, (*see* ECLA)
Cerf, Vinton G., 194, 196, *210*
Champine, George A., 179, 182, 183,
   143, 185
Chang, Hsu, 136, *143, 147, 150*

Chapanis, Alphonse, 77, *81*
Chapin, Ned, 12, *20*
Chapman, Edward A., 7, 9, 13, *20*
Charge-coupled shift register memory,
　RAP, 135
Charnes, A., *52*
Chastain, Garvin, 77, *81*
Chastinet, Yone S., 259, *272, 279*
Chemistry Information Center
　(Mexico), (*see* CeMIQ)
Chen, Ching-Chih, 14, 196, 201, 202,
　20, 28, 206
Chen, Peter Pin-Shan, 160, *185*
Chen, T.C., 136, *143, 147, 150*
Chen, W.F., *144*
Cheng, M.D., 72, *82*
Cherniavsky, V., 107, *116*
Cherro de Vieira, Ana Maria, *272*
Cheshier, Robert G., 48, *52*
Chicago Online Users Group (COLUG),
　users as educators, 232
　user aid selection, 228
Childers, Thomas, 15, *20*
Chile,
　CENID (National Center for
　　Information and Documentation),
　　256
　CONICYT (National Commission for
　　Scientific and Technical Research),
　　256
　environmental information, 261
　information systems and services,
　　256
　political changes and information
　　policy, 263
　sanitary engineering information,
　　261
Chow, D., 105, *116*
Christian, Roger W., 41, 195, 236, *51,*
　204, 238
Christopher, Martin, 45, *63*
Churchman, C. West, 8, *20*
CICH, (*see* Autonomous National
　University of Mexico, Scientific and
　Humanistic Information Center)

CICS (Customer Information and
　Control System), 169
CIDIA (Inter-American Center for
　Agricultural Information), 259
Ciência de Informação, 255
CIM (Metallurgy Information Center
　(Mexico)), 253
CIN (Brazil), (*see* Brazil, CIN)
CINCOM Systems, Inc.,
　TOTAL, (*see* TOTAL)
Circulation systems,
　automated,
　　management statistics, 202
　　turnkey systems, 200
CIRISCA (Information and Referral
　Center on Sanitary Engineering
　and Environmental Sciences), 261
CIT, (*see* Brazil, CIT)
Citation analysis, 15
　information measures, 73-74
　retrieval system design, 15
Citation networks,
　structures of scientific
　　disciplines, 78
Citation retrieval,
　fuzzy set theory, 196
CIZA (Arid Zone Information Center
　(Mexico)), 253
CLADES (Latin American Center for
　Economic and Social
　Documentation),
　foundation and activities, 256
Clark, C.V., 15, *20*
Clasquin, F.F., 39, *52*
CLASS (California Library Authority
　for Systems and Services),
　network comparisons, 201
Classification,
　current issues, 100
Clayton, Audrey, 201, *206*
Clelland, Richard C., *24, 208*
Clements, D.W.G., *52*
Cleveland, Donald B., 97, *89, 116*
Cleveland Health Science Library,
　user fees, 48

Cleverdon, C.W., 3, 201, *20*, *116*, *209*
Cliques,
  maximally connected clusters, 103
CLR (Council on Library Resources),
  library automation literature, 195
  national bibliographic network, 201
CLSI (Computer Library Services,
  Inc.), 203
Clustering,
  applications of theories and models,
    102-103
  feedback, 105
  information retrieval models, 97-98
CNEA, *(see* Argentina, CNEA)
CNPq, *(see* Brazil, CNPq)
Cobb, William J., *25*
Cockrell, Wendell, 47, *54*
CODASYL (Conference on Data
    Systems Languages),
  data manipulation and data
    definition languages, 179
  database definition, 167
  database management system
    standards, 159
Codd, E.F., 164, 181, *144*, *185*
Cognition,
  information science research
    areas, 71
Cohen, Jacob, 39, *52*, *209*
Coile, Russell G., 15, *20*, *82*
COLCIENCIAS, *(see* Colombia,
    COLCIENCIAS)
Cole, Diane Davis, *52*
Collection development,
  citation analysis, 74
  computerized cataloging, 197
  management statistics, 202
Collica, Joseph, *186*
Collier, H.R., 43, *52*
Collins, Craig, *64*
Colombia,
  COLCIENCIAS (National
    Organization for Science
    Policy in Colombia), 254

Colombia, (cont.)
  ICFES (Columbian Institute for
    the Development of Higher
    Education), 254
  information systems and services,
    254
  SNI, 254
Colombian Institute for the
    Development of Higher Education
    (see ICFES)
Colorado Academic Libraries Book
    Processing Center, 47
COLUG, *(see* Chicago Online Users
    Group)
Columbia University,
  library costs study, 44
Combined indexes,
  multiple attribute retrieval, 104
Commission of the European
    Communities (CEC),
  training survey, 221
Component design,
  system design phases, 8
Computer,
  library automation literature, 195
Computer-aided instruction, *(see*
    CAI)
Computer architecture,
  associative memories, 132
  bubble memories, 136
  definitions, 129-130
  full text retrieval, 110
  information retrieval, 129-141
  rotating associative memories, 134
  structure or directory
    processors, 138-140
  text scanning systems, 136-138
  unconventional architectures,
    132-141
  von Neumann architecture
    limitations, 130-132
Computer-assisted indexing, *(see
    also* Automatic indexing)
  experimental techniques, 100

Computer Center of Engineering
Faculty of Buenos Aires, 256
Computer Library Services, Inc.,
(see CLSI)
Computer memory, (see Memory,
computer)
Computer networks, (see Library
networks; Service networks)
Computer software, (see Software)
Computer technology,
cost analysis, 47
information processing cost
studies, 42
library automation trends, 203
Computerworld,
library automation literature, 195
Comyn, Gerard, 72, 82
CONACYT (Mexico), (see Mexico,
CONACYT)
Conference on Data Systems
Languages, (see CODASYL)
CONICET, (see Argentina, CONICET)
CONICIT (see Costa Rica, CONICIT)
CONICYT (Chile), (see Chile,
CONICYT)
CONICYT (Uruguay), (see Uruguay,
CONICYT)
CONIT (COnnector for Networked
Information Transfer), 108
COnnector for Networked
Information Transfer, (see CONIT)
Consejo Nacional de Ciencia y
Tecnologia, (see Mexico,
CONACYT)
CONSER project, 200
Constantini, L., 114
Content-addressable storage,
memory technology trends, 183
Content addressed segment
sequential memory, (see CASSM)
Conti, Dennis M., 47, 52
CONTROL 2000, 175
Convey, John, 208
Cooper, A., 32

Cooper, Michael D., 10, 13, 14, 15,
38, 41, 43, 44, 47, 48, 49, 50, 111,
112, 202, 21, 27, 52, 53, 57, 116,
206
Cooper, William S., 93, 98, 109, 18,
116
Cooperation and resource sharing,
(see also Library networks; Service
networks)
Latin America, 265
library network research, 197-198
photocopying, 40
Copeland, George P., 134, 135, 137,
144, 148
Coppernoll-Blach, Penny, 228, 239
Copyright,
library photocopying, 40
Corbin, John B., 196, 206
Cordeiro, Rosa Ines de N., 280
Corey, James F., 7, 21
Corning, Mary E., 260, 272
Cornish, I.M., 77, 82
Corporate information,
database management systems, 154
Corth, Annette, 15, 21
Cosermans, Jean, 82
Cost accounting,
technical information center, 47
Cost analysis, 37-50 (see also Cost-
benefit analysis; Costs; Economics
of information)
academic libraries, 44
acquisitions, 39
aggregate level, 45, 46
cataloging, 40
function/service level, 39-43
industrial/technical libraries, 45
information retrieval, 111-112
library automation, 201-202
online searching, 40
organization level, 43-45
production of information, 42-43
reviews of the literature, 38
structural level, 45

Cost analysis, (cont.)
  system analysis and design, 10-12
  techniques, 46-47
Cost-benefit analysis, (*see also* Cost
    analysis; Costs; Economics of
    information)
  database management system
    selection, 176
  database management systems, 156-
    157
  system analysis and design, 11-12
Costa Rica,
  CONICIT (National Council for
    Scientific and Technological
    Research), 253
  information systems and services,
    253
Costs, (*see also* Cost analysis; Cost-
    benefit analysis; Economics of
    information)
  computer memory, 131
  data conversion, 154
  database management systems, 157,
    171, 173
  interlibrary loan, 198
  libraries,
    costs increase prediction, 15
  library automation, 201-202
  online retrieval education in library
    schools, 230-231
  system analysis and design, 10-11
Cotton, Ira W., 47, 198, *53, 206*
Couger, J. Daniel, 5, *21*
Coulouris, G.F., 183, *185*
Council on Library Resources, (*see*
    CLR)
Cousins, Thomas R., 110, *116*
Cover, Thomas M., 72, *82, 86*
Cox, Carolyn M., *206*
Coyle, Virginia S., *280*
CPU (Central Processing Unit),
  von Neumann architecture, 130
Crane, Nancy B., 234, *239*
Crash recovery, (*see* Failure recovery)

Craven, Timothy C., 100, *117*
Crawford, R.G., 98, 102, *117*
Crawford, Susan G., 15, *21*
Creativity,
  information measures, 74
Creps, John E., Jr., *209*
CRIAT (Regional Research and
    Technical Assistance Centers
    (Mexico)), 253
Criminology,
  information theory extensions, 72
Croft, W.B., 93, 97, 102, 112, *117*
Crystalline structures,
  Brazilian database, 261
Cuadra Associates,
  online retrieval training study, 235
Cuadra, Carlos A., *63, 184*
Cuba,
  IDICT (Institute for Scientific and
    Technical Documentation), 253
  information systems and services,
    253
Cullinane Corp.,
  IDMS, (*see* IDMS)
Culnan, Mary J., 15, *21*
Cuozzo, D.E., 156, 157, 173, *185*
Curtice, Robert M., 161, 167, 169,
    171, 178, 180, 181, *185*
Customer Information and Control
    System, (*see* CICS)
Cveljo, Katherine, *239*
Dagaev, Katherine S., 15, *34*
Dammers, H.F., 10, *21, 53*
Daniel, Evelyn H., 11, *21*
Darling, Richard L., *57*
DASD (Direct access storage device),
  database management systems
    development, 155, 158
Data access, (*see also* Access methods)
  database management systems, 164-
    167
Data analysis,
  information theory extensions, 72

Data Base on Crystalline Structures, 261

Data conversion,
  costs, 154
  database management systems, 171

Data definition language (DDL),
  database management system components, 167

Data definitions,
  database management systems components, 167-168
  database management systems development, 158

Data dictionary/directories (DD/Ds),
  data field standardization, 171
  data quality, 178
  database management system components, 168

Data elements, (see Data fields)

Data fields,
  database management systems, 171

Data independence,
  database management system issues, 178
  database management systems, 161

Data Language/1, (see DL/1)

Data management supervision,
  database management system components, 169

Data management systems (DMS), 156
  alternatives to database management systems, 173

Data manipulation language (DML),
  database management system environment, 169-170

Data models, (see Data organization, logical)

Data organization,
  logical,
    contrasted with physical, 159-161
    database management system limitations, 177-178
    database management systems, 161-164

Data organization,
  logical (cont.)
    hierarchical, 162-163
    network, 163-164
    relational, 164
  physical, 164-167
    contrasted with logical, 159-161
    database management system limitations, 178
    record addressing, 165-166

Data storage, (see also Memory, computer)
  current research in system design, 111
  database management systems, 164-167

Data verification, (see also Quality control)
  database management, 178

Database administration, 171-172
  organizational and administrative problems, 180
  staff perspectives, 173

Database Computer (DBC),
  development and organization, 139-140

Database definition,
  data quality, 178
  database management system components, 167

Database management system (DBMS), 153-182
  applications, 177
  associative memories, 133
  back-end computers, 182
  bibliographic and non-bibliographic databases, 157-158
  commercial packages, 173-177
  components, 167-170
  database administration, 171-172
  design, 160-161
  distributed databases, 182

Database management system, (cont.)
  evolution, 180-181
  features and benefits, 155-157
  historical development, 158-159
  limitations, 177-180
  logical and physical organization
    contrasted, 159-161
  logical organization, 161-164
  memory developments, 182-183
  minicomputers, 182
  network vs. relational models, 109
  organizational and administrative
    problems, 180
  organizational impacts, 170-173
  performance and cost, 179
  physical data organization, 164-167
  proliferation, 180
  relational models, 181
  selection, 176
  staff perspectives, 172-173
  standardization, 179
  state-of-the-art and trends, 180-183
  system environment, 169-170
  vendors, 157
Database mapping,
  feature enhancement and pattern
    analysis, 96
Database producers, (see also Online
    vendors)
  cooperation with library schools, 231
  education and training, 223-224,
    226-228
Databases, (see also Database
    management system; Database pro-
    ducers; Distributed databases; Large
    databases; Meta-databases; Online
    vendors; Relational database
    models; Searching)
  bibliographic,
    merge algorithms, 198
  database management systems, 154-
    155, 157-158
  information retrieval experimental
    techniques, 109-110

Databases, (cont.)
  nonbibliographic,
    education and training, 236
  numeric,
    library service trends, 203
Dataflow Systems Inc.,
  library networking terminology, 201
Datamation,
  library automation literature, 195
DATAPRO Research Corp.,
  database management systems
    listings, 159
Date, C.J., 164, 181, 185
Datta, S., 41, 61
Davenport, R.A., 179, 182, 185
Davey, W. Patrick, 15, 19
David, A., 53
Davidson, Rebecca W., 230, 231, 235,
    238
Davies, C.C., 106, 117
Davies, E.B., 82
Davis, Charles H., 197, 231, 206, 239
Davis, Edward W., 132, 144
DBC, (see Database Computer)
DBMS, (see Database managment
    system)
DD/Ds, (see Data dictionary/
    directories)
DDL, (see Data definition language)
De Araujo, Jerusa Goncalves, 273
De Bruin, Valentina, 208
De la Vallee Poussin, Catherine, 82
De Pena y Lillo, Ana M.R., 273
De Rodriguez, Loumary, 254, 273
De Solanes, Maria E.S., 273
De Valenzuela, Z. Pucurull, 255, 273
De Vodanovic, Betty Johnson, 255,
    264, 273
DeBlasis, J.P., 180, 185
Debons, Anthony, 3, 21
DEC (Digital Equipment Corp.),
  PDP/11,
    IDMS, 159

Decision making,
  human information processing
    related to information science, 77
  information measures, 73
  information retrieval systems, 112
Decision-making information,
  Latin America, 267
Decision tables,
  system analysis and design, 12
Decision theory,
  information retrieval, 73
  Swets model of information
    retrieval, 112
DeFiore, Casper R., 133, *144*
DeGennaro, Richard, 48, 196, *53, 206*
Dehart, Florence E., 38, 43, *62*
Dei Rossi, James A., 48, *53*
DeLutis, T.G., 16, 112, *22, 117*
DeMartinis, Manlio, *144*
Demographic information,
  Latin America, 261
Design of information systems and
    services, 3-17 (*see also* Evaluation
    of information systems and services)
  bibliometrics, 14-15
  cost analysis, 10-12
  database management systems, 160-
    161, 178
  flowcharting, 12
  information retrieval experimental
    techniques, 111-113
  job description and analysis, 12-13
  online retrieval by end users, 236
  operations research and analysis,
    13-15
  physical data organization, 165-166
  principles, 8-9
  simulation, 16
  statistics, 15
  system analysis as a prelude, 7-8
  system development cycle, 5-6
  systems theory, 3
  techniques, 9-16

DeWath, Nancy A., 10, 41, 43, 112,
    202, *21, 53, 116, 206*
DeWitt, David J., 134, *144*
Dexter, M.E., *92*
Dextre, Stella G., 256, 257, 262, 265,
    273
DIALIB project,
  online searching costs, 41
  staff time, 43
  user fees, 49, 202
DIALOG, (*see* Lockheed Information
    Systems, DIALOG)
Diaries,
  staff time studies, 43, 44
Dice's coefficient,
  clustering, 98
Dictionaries, (*see also* Authority files;
    Data dictionary/directories;
    Thesauri)
  dynamic updating, 102
Diener, Edward, 77, *88*
DIGID, (*see* Argentina, DIGID)
Digital Equipment Corp., (*see* DEC)
Direct access storage device, (*see*
    DASD)
Direct comparison,
  computer architecture for full text
    retrieval, 137
Direct observation,
  staff time studies, 43
Distributed databases,
  database management systems, 178-
    179, 182
Divergence,
  information measures, 72
Divilbiss, James L., 6, 10, 11, *22*
DL/1,
  development, 158
DML, (*see* Data manipulation language)
DMS, (*see* Data management systems)
DOBIS (Dortmunder
    Bibliothekssytem),
  development and use, 199

DOCPAL (Latin American Population Documentation System), 261
Document delivery,
    Latin America, 263
Dodd, G.G., *186*
Dolby, James L., 72, *82*
Domingues, A.L., *271*
Dominick, Wayne D., 110, *116*
Donati, Robert, *117*
Donohue, Joseph C., 14, *22*
Donohue, William Anthony, 77, *82*
Dortmunder Bibliothekssystem, (*see* DOBIS)
Dosamantes, Daniel, *209*
Doszkocs, Tamas E., 96, 236, *117*, *243*
Doty, K.L., *145, 150*
Dougherty, Richard M., 201, *58, 207*
Dow, John T., *82*
Drake, Miriam A., 44, *53*
Dressen, Peter, *186*
Drexel University,
    IIDA (Individualized Instruction for Data Access), (*see* IIDA)
    online workshop, 232
Drott, M. Carl, 14, *22*
Du Bois, Daniel M., *86*
Dubovnikov, M.S., 73, *82*
Duchesne, Roderick M., 47, *53*
Dufour, Jacques, 72, *82*
Duhne, Ricardo, 166, 179, *186, 190*
Dunham, G., 107, *117, 118*
Dunn, Mary Joan, *205*
Durding, Bruce M., 77, *82*
Dyer, Charles, 6, *22*
EASYTRIEVE, 173
Eckels, Diane, 12, *22, 52, 53, 58*
ECLA (Economic Commission for Latin America, *the Spanish* CEPAL),
    CLADES foundation, 256

Economic Commission for Latin America, (*see* ECLA)
Economics of information, 10 (*see also* Cost analysis; Cost-benefit analysis; Costs)
    database management systems, 173
    Latin America, 264
    online retrieval education and training, 223-224
Ecuador,
    CENDES (Ecuadorian Center for Industrial Development), 258
    industrial information activities, 258
Edelberg, Murray, *145*
Edelmann, Janet V., *122, 242*
Edmundson, H.P., 75, *83*
Education and training, (*see also* CAI; Library schools)
    Brazil, 255
    flowcharting, 12
    Latin America, 263-264
    online retrieval systems, 109, 219-237
        definitions, 219-220
        documentation, 220-221
        end users, 233-234
        learning principles, 235
        library schools, 228-231
        locally developed and emulative systems use, 230-231
        needs assessment, 235
        surveys and reviews, 221-223
        teaching principles, 236
        user aids, 227-229
        users as educators and trainers, 232
        vendors and producers, 223-229
Education information,
    Peru, 262
Educational Resources Information System, (*see* ERIC)
EDUCOM,
    computer network study, 198
Egeth, Howard E., *89*

Ehrensberger, Michael, 171, *186*
Eisenberg, Laura J., 225, *239*
Ekaterinoslavskii, Iu. Iu., *83*
El Masri, A., 137, *145*
Elam, Joyce, 179, *186*
Elchesen, Dennis R., 12, 41, 111, 201, *22, 54, 117, 207*
Electronic mail,
  library automation trends, 203
Electronic publishing,
  cost analysis, 42
Elias, Arthur W., 226, *240*
Elliott, Roger W., 12, *23*
Ellis, Donald G., *83*
Ellis, P., 15, 78, *23, 83*
Elman, Stanley A., 41, *54*
ELMS (Experimental Library Management System),
  DOBIS development, 199
Eman, Ahmed, 135, *150*
EMBRAPA, (*see* Brazil, EMBRAPA)
EMBRATER, (*see* Brazil, EMBRATER)
Emery, James C., *207*
End users,
  database management systems, 173
  online retrieval education and training, 233-234
  system analysis and design, 9
  user interface, 108-109
Engles, Robert W., *186*
Enser, P.G.B., 102, *118*
Entity sets,
  data models, 161-164
Environmental information,
  Chile, 261
  publication patterns, 74
Environmental interface design,
  system design phases, 8
Epstein, Bernard E., 109, 233, *122, 242*
Ergodic theory,
  information theory, 72

ERIC (Educational Resources Information System),
  database,
    LIS training system, 226
    U. of Hawaii online retrieval education, 231
ERIC/PROBE,
  evaluation, 202
European Association of Scientific Information Dissemination Centers, (*see* EUSIDIC)
EUSIDIC,
  1976 meeting on user education, 222
Eustachi, Kuno, *54*
Evaluation of information systems and services, 46 (*see also* Design of information systems and services; Performance measures)
  database management system selection, 176
  information retrieval experimental techniques, 111-113
  library automation, 201-202
  public libraries, 15
  system analysis and design, 11
  system design phases, 8-9
Evans, F.J., *83*
Evans, Glyn T., 197, *207*
Evans, J.M., *185*
Experimental Library Management System, (*see* ELMS)
Fact retrieval,
  experimental techniques, 107-108
Failure recovery,
  database management systems, 168-169, 171
Fairthorne, R.A., 78, *83*
FAO (Food and Agricultural Organization),
  Brazilian agricultural information system, 259
  Latin American projects, 258
Farag, Raouf F.H., 72, *83*

Farradane, Jason, *126*
Fasana, Paul J., 5, *23*
Faulconer, Barbara A., *88*
Faunce, Stephen S.A., *273*
Fayen, Emily Gallup, 11, *27*
Feature analysis,
  human information processing
    related to information science, 77
Feature enhancement,
  database mapping, 96
Federal Republic of Germany,
  Latin American information systems
    development, 251
Federal University of Rio de Janeiro,
  information science program, 255
Federation Internationale de
  Documentation, (*see* FID)
Fee-for-service, (*see* User fees)
Feedback,
  database management systems, 168
  information retrieval, 105-106
Feeney, William, 9, *23*
Fehder, P.L., *189*
Feinman, Robert, *209*
Feldman, Jacob J., *25*
Feng, Cyril, *57*
Ferguson, Douglas, 234, *240*
Fernandez, Angel, *274*
Fernandez, de la Garza, G., *274*
Ferraz, Terezine A., 260, *274*
Fersiva, Berenice, *274*
Fetterman, John, *59*, *205*, *210*
FID (Federation Internationale de
  Documentation),
  CLA (Latin American Commission),
    Latin American information
      systems development, 251
Field addressing,
  database management systems, 166
Fielding, Derek, 47, *54*
Fields, Mary Alice S., 15, *24*
Fife, Dennis, 220, *241*
Figueiredo, Regina Celia, 260, *274*

File structures,
  clustering, 102-103
  computer architecture for
    information retrieval, 138-140
  conventional computer architecture
    limits for information retrieval,
    132
  current research in system design, 111
  information retrieval and library
    automation, 110
Finite state automata (FSA),
  computer architecture for full text
    retrieval, 138
  full text retrieval, 110
Finland,
  online retrieval by end users, 234
Finneran, Thomas R., 172, 178, *186*
Firschein, Oscar, 41, 202, *54*, *118*,
  213
Fischer, D., *51*
Fishburn, Mary, *63*, *184*
Fisher, B. Aubrey, 77, *83*
Fisher, H. Leonard, *239*
Fisher information measure,
  generalization, 72
Fisher, Paul S., 179, *188*
Fitzgerald, Ardra F., 9, 12, *23*
Fitzgerald, John M., 9, 12, *23*
Floam, Gary, 182, *186*
Florentin, J.J., *186*
Flow process analysis,
  staff time studies, 43
Flowcharting,
  system analysis and design, 12
Flowerdew, A.D.J., 38, *54*
Flynn, Roger R., *209*
Foil, Patti Sue, 202, *207*
Fong, Elizabeth, 155, 177, 180, *186*
Food and Agricultural Organization,
  (*see* FAO)
Ford, Bernard, 11, *18*
Ford, Geoffrey, *54*
Ford, Jill, *54*

Ford, William H., Jr., 107, 109, 236, *118, 240*
Forget, Louis J.S., 199, *207*
Forman, Ernest H., *83*
Forte, B., 72, *83*
Foyle, James K., 231, *240*
Fraenkel, S., 105, *114*
France,
  Latin American information systems development, 251
  online retrieval by end users, 234
Francis, D. Pitt, *54*
Franklin Institute,
  IIDA (Individualized Instruction for Data Access), (*see* IIDA)
Frederiksen, Norman, 74, *83*
Freedman, Maurice J., 196, *207*
Freeman, James E., *280*
Froberg, Gudmund, *124*
Front-end computers,
  OCLC, 199
Fry, Bernard M., *54*
Fry, James P., 154, 158, 171, *186*
FSA, (*see* Finite state automata)
Full text retrieval, (*see also* Passage retrieval)
  computer architecture, 110, 136-138
Fuller, R.H., 132, *142, 145*
Fung, H.S., 132, *151*
Funk, Mark, 14, *18*
Funk, Robert, *54*
Furniss, Mary Ann, *61*
Furtado, Joao Salvador, *274*
Fussler, Herman H., 13, *23*
Fuzzy set theory,
  information retrieval, 94-95, 196
  information theory extensions, 72
Gabidulin, E.M., 72, *83*
Galvin, Thomas J., 195, 222, *209, 241*
Gaming,
  computer networks, 198
Gantz, John, *207*
Gapen, D. Kaye, 10, 40, *28, 59*

Gargano Covelo, Susana, 258, *274*
Gates, R., *147*
Gavryck, Jacquelyn A., 228, 229, *241*
Gebhart, Friedrich, *118*
Gee, Helen Hofer, *29*
Gee, Larry G., 111, *114*
Gee, R.D., 45, *55*
Gehl, John, 67-80
GEIPOT (Brazilian Enterprise for Transportation Planning), 261
Geitz, Ricardo, 256
Gell, Marilyn Killebrew, 48, *55*
Geller, Nancy L., *23*
General Directorate for Research and Development, (*see* Argentina, DIGID)
General Electric Co.,
  IDS development, 159
General Purpose Simulation System, (*see* GPSS)
General systems theory, (*see* Systems theory)
General Theory of Bibliometrics and Other Cumulative Advantage Processes, 78-79
Gerritsen, Rob, 164, *187*
Gerson, Elihu M., 9, *26*
Gerson, Gordon M., 103, *118*
Ghosh, Jata S., 15, 78, *23, 83*
Ghosh, Sakti P., 179, *187*
Gibbons, Fred M., 175, 177, *187*
Gietz, Ricardo, *274*
Gifford, Roger, *207*
Gilbert, G. Migel, *83*
Gilchrist, Bruce, 8, *23*
Gildersleeve, Thomas R., 8, *23*
Gill, E.D., 41, *55*
Gilles, Gerard, 72, *82*
Gillespie, Constantine J., 3, *27*
Gilreath, Charles L., 226-228, 236, *240*
Glasser, Scott, *59*
Glover, Thomas W., *83*

Glushenok, George, *215*
Goddard, Haynes C., 11, *23*
Goehlert, Robert, 14, *23*
Goguen, Nancy, *186*
Gold, Steven D., 40, *55*
Goldman, Myla K., 252, *275*
Goldstein, Charles M., 109, 156, 171, 236, *118*, *187*, *240*
Goldstein, Marianne, 15, *23*
Goldstein, Robert C., 182, *184*
Goldstine, Herman H., *143*
Gomes, Hagar Espanha, *275*
Goodman, Victor, 103, *125*
Goodyear,
  STARAN, (*see* STARAN)
Gordon, Geoffrey, 16, *23*
Gore, Daniel, 11, *23*
Gosset, M., 14, *23*
Gottinger, Hans W., *83*
Gould, John D., *83*
Government documents,
  search keys, 104
GPSS (General Purpose Simulation System), 16
Graddon, Pamela H.B., 225, *240*
Graham, Peter S., *207*
Graitson, M., *118*
Gray, Robert M., 72, *83*
Greenberger, Harvey J., 12, *23*
Greenberg, Stewart, *119*
Greenblatt, Daniel L., 75, *84*
Griffith, Belver C., 14, *22*
Griffiths, John, 233, *239*
Griffiths, Jose M., 14, *19*, *81*, *115*
Grishman, Ralph, 108, *118*, *119*, *124*
Grosch, Audrey N., 13, 40, 200, *23*, *55*, *207*
Grudnitski, Gary, *19*
Gryczkowski, Carolyn L., 231, *239*
Gudes, Ehud, 171, *187*
Guerra, M.G., *271*
Haenselman, Mary, *59*
Hafner, Arthur W., 15, *24*

Hajnal, Peter I., 199, *208*
Halff, Henry M., *84*
Halperin, Michael, 15, *27*
Halstead, M., *84*
Hamar, Alfredo Americo, *279*
Hamburg, Morris, 11, 202, *24*, *208*
Hamilton, K.L., 48, *55*
Hammad, Piere, *84*
Hammer, Michael, 166, 168, 171, 178, *187*
Hansen, James V., 8, *24*
Harary, Frank, *187*
Hardgrave, W.T., 182, *187*
Harman, G.K., *84*
Harmon, Glynn, 13, *24*
Harper, D.J., 73, 93, 105, *84*, *118*
Harris, C., 78, *84*
Harris, Dale A., *84*
Harris, M.H., 195, *214*
Harrison, Isom, *239*
Harrison, R.D., *184*
Hart, Clyde W., 25
Harter, Stephen P., 15, 228, 230, *24*, *240*
Hartmann, David C., 200, *204*
Harvard,
  Countway Library,
  evaluation, 202
HARVEST,
  database structural information processing, 139
Hashing,
  record-addressing techniques, 165
Haspers, Jan H., 15, *24*
Hawgood, J., *55*
Hawkins, Donald T., 74, 94, 221, *84*, *118*, *126*, *208*, *240*
Hayes, Robert M., 5, *24*
Hayes-Roth, Barbara, *84*
Hayes-Roth, Frederick, *84*
Health information, (*see* Medical information)
Healy, Leonard D., 134, 135, *145*

Heaps, H.S., 94, *119*
Hecht, C.D., *61*
Heer, Philipp R., 231, *240*
Hegarty, Kevin, 200, *208*
Heilprin, L.B., 70, *84*
Heine, M.H., 15, *24*, *84*
Heinritz, Fred J., 12, 13
Heitger, Lester E., *24*
Helmkamp, John G., 45, 47, *55*
Henritz, Fred J., *24*
Henry, J. Shirley, 172, 178, *186*
Hensman, Sandy, 12, 15, *31*, *35*
Hepburn, G., *23*, *83*
Herlach, Gertrud, *119*
Herr, J.J., 96, *115*
Hersberger, Rodney M., 14, *31*
Herwitz, P.S., *143*
Hewitt, Joe A., 198, *208*
Hice, Gerald F., 5, *24*
Hickey, Thomas B., 104, *119*
Hierarchical data models, 162-163
Hillman Library,
  book costs study, 40
Hiltz, Starr Roxanne, *208*
Hindle, Anthony, 10, 38, 49, *19*, *25*,
  55
Hinomoto, Hirohide, 169, 177, *187*
Hirschman, Lynette, 108, *118*, *119*,
  124
Hirst, Graeme, 15, *25*
Hitchingham, Eileen E., 201, *208*
Hitt, S., *52*
Hjerppe, Roland, 111, 112, *84*, *119*
Ho, D.Y., *31*
Hobrock, Brice G., *55*
Hock, Randolph E., 232-233, 235,
  240
Hodina, Alfred, *237*
Hoglund, Lars, *123*
Holian, Lydia, *243*
Hollaar, Lee A., 129, 131, 132, 136,
  137, 138, 140, *145*, *146*
Holroyd, Gideon, 195, *208*

Honeywell,
  IDS, (*see* IDS)
Hootman, J.T., 48, *55*
Horn, John L., 77, *84*
Horton, Forest W., 202, *208*
Houghton, Bernard, *208*
Houser, Lloyd J., 15, *25*
Houston Academy of Medicine-
    Texas Medical Center,
  library costs study, 44
Hsiao, David K., 139, 182, *141*,
    142, *146*, *184*, *187*
Hsu, John H., *55*
Hubbard, G.U., *189*
Hubert, John J., 14, *25*, *84*
Huffenberger, Michael A., 153-182
Huitfeldt, Jennifer, 93-114
Hultgren, Jan, 111, *119*, *120*
Human factors,
  system analysis and design, 9
  user interface in information
    retrieval, 109
Human information processing,
  information science areas of study,
    76-77
Human memory,
  human information processing
    related to information science, 77
Humphries, K.W., *56*
Hundal, P.S., 77, *84*
Hurt, C.D., 74, *25*, *84*
Hutchinson, J.S., *146*
Hybrid access method,
  experimental access methods, 104
Hyman, Herbert H., 13, *25*
Hyperbolic distribution model,
  information science theories, 78-79
IAC, (*see* Information analysis centers)
IAEA (International Atomic Energy
    Agency),
  INIS, (*see* INIS)
Iakubovskaia, M.D., 75, *86*

IBBD (Brazilian Institute for Bibliography and Documentation), 254

IBICT (Brazilian Institute for Information in Science and Technology), 254

IBM (International Business Machines Corp.),
  CICS, (see CICS)
  DOBIS development, 199
  HARVEST, (see HARVEST)
  IMS/VS, (see IMS/VS)
  System R, (see System R)
  System 360,
  IDMS, 159

Ibragimov, I.A., *84*

ICAITI (Istituto Centroamericano de Investigacion y Tecnologia Industrial), 257

ICFES (Columbian Institute for the Development of Higher Education), 254

IDICT (Institute for Scientific and Technical Documentation (CUBA)), 253

IDMS (Integrated Data Management System), 174
  development, 159

IDS (Integrated Data Store), 174
  development, 159

IEA (Brazil), (see Brazil, IPEN)

IICA (Inter-American Institute for Agricultural Sciences), 259

IIDA (Individualized Instruction for Data Access), 109, 231, 233

ILL, (see Interlibrary loan)

Image partitioning,
  information theory extensions, 72

Impact of On-Line Retrieval Services: A Survey of Users, 1974-75, 220, 222, 223, 233, 235

IMS/VS (Information Management System/Virtual Storage), 174

IMS/VS, (cont.)
  data manipulation language, 170
  development, 158
  record-addressing techniques, 166

IMS/360,
  development, 158

Index terms,
  patterns of occurrence and probability theory, 95

Indexed addressing, (see Inverted indexes)

Indexed files, (see Inverted indexes)

Indexing, (see also Automatic indexing; Computer-assisted indexing; Index terms)
  applications of theories and models, 99-101
  current issues, 100
  probability theory, 98-99
  utility theory, 98-99

Indiana University,
  ERIC/PROBE, (see ERIC/PROBE)

Individualized Instruction for Data Access, (see IIDA)

Industrial information,
  Latin America, 256-258

Industrial/technical libraries,
  cost analysis, 45, 46

INDY,
  CASSM variants, 135

Inflation,
  library cost analysis, 10-11

Informaciónes, FID/CLA, 251

Information Services in Physics, Electrotechnology, and Control, (see INSPEC)

Informatics,
  MARK IV, (see MARK IV)

Information, (see also Information science)
  components, 73
  managing information as a resource, 153-154

Information, (cont.)
nature of information as a field of
study, 68
relation to knowledge, 71
Information analysis centers (IAC),
cost analysis, 45
Information and Referral Center on
Sanitary Engineering and Environ-
mental Sciences (Chile), (see
CIRISCA)
Information Bulletin (Cuba), 253
Information capacity (Shannon),
formula indexing, 100
Information Center for Health, (see
Mexico, Information Center for
Health)
Information decay,
information science research areas,
69
Information flow,
general theory, 79
information measures, 73
Information homomorphism,
information science research
areas, 70
Information loss,
measures, 72
Information Management System/
Virtual Storage, (see IMS/VS)
Information measures,
decision theory, 73
information science research areas,
70
information theory extensions,
72-74
reference services, 74
search length, 74
Information needs and uses,
database-specific training, 227
Latin America, 265-267
online retrieval education and
training, 235
Information Processing System
Simulator, (see IPSS)

Information production,
costs, 42-43
Information retrieval, (see also
Databases; Full text retrieval;
Passage retrieval; Searching)
computer architecture, 129-141
experimental techniques, 93-114
access methods, 103
artificial intelligence, 96
binary representation model, 98
clustering, 97-98, 102-103
databases, 109-110
design and evaluation of systems,
111-113
fact and passage retrieval, 107-108
feedback, 105-106
fuzzy set theory, 94-95
indexing, 99-101
natural language systems, 106-107
probability theory, 95-96
ranking, 106
relational approach, 98
theories and models, 94-106
user interface, 108-113
vector space models, 97
fuzzy set theory, 196
information measures, 73
mathematical foundations, 94
operations research and analysis, 14
system analysis, 7
Information Retrieval Research
Laboratory, (see University of
Illinois, Information Retrieval
Research Laboratory)
Information retrieval systems, (see also
Information retrieval)
database management systems, 156
Information science, (see also
Information)
core research areas, 68-71
aggregation of information, 69
cognition and learning, 71
decay of information, 69
form and content, 70

Information Science,
  core research areas (cont.)
    information theory, 69
    measures and performance
      criteria, 70
    modeling, 69-70
    nature of information, 68
    relating information to knowledge,
      71
    structure families, 69-70
  definition, 68
  empirical foundations, 67-80
  empirical laws, 74-78
    aggregation of information
      sources, 74
    human information processing,
      76-77
    information representation and
      semantic coding, 76
    semiotic form and information
      content, 74
  information theory extensions, 71-74
  relation to mathematical linguistics
    and statistics, 75
  theories underlying empirical laws,
    78-79
Information search services (ISS), (see
  also Online vendors; Searching)
  growth patterns, 196
Information Service of the Center for
  Economics, Law, and Management
  of Water, 261
Information services, (see also Data-
  base producers)
  online vs. print revenues, 43
  production costs, 42-43
Information Services in Physics,
  Electrotechnology, Computers and
  Control, (see INSPEC)
Information System for Data
  Processing of Legislative
  Information (Brazil), (see
  PRODASEN)

Information System on Hydrological
  Resources (Brazil), 261
Information theory (Shannon),
  ergodic theory, 72
  formal extensions, 71-74
  information science research areas,
    69
INFOTEC, (see Mexico, INFOTEC)
Inhaber, Herbert, 86
INIS (International Nuclear
  Information System),
  Latin American activities, 259-260
Input/output controllers,
  von Neumann architecture, 130
Inquiry/report module,
  database management system
    components, 169
Insolio, Cynthia, 124
INSPEC (Information Services in
  Physics, Electrotechnology,
  Computers and Control),
  SIRE system experiment, 101
Institute for Library Educators,
  library school and database supplier
    cooperation, 231
  online retrieval education
    standards, 229
Institute for Scientific and Technical
  Documentation, (see IDICT)
Institute for Scientific Information,
  (see ISI)
Institute of Atomic Energy (Brazil),
  (see Brazil, IPEN)
Institute of Energy and Atomic
  Research (Brazil), (see Brazil,
  IPEN)
Instituto Centroamericano de
  Investigacion y Tecnologia
  Industrial, (see ICAITI)
Integrated Data Management System,
  (see IDMS)
Integrated Data Store, (see IDS)

Intelligence,
  information measures, 74
Intelligence systems information
    projects,
  database management systems
    development, 158
Inter-American Association of
  Agricultural Librarians and
  Documentalists, (see AIBDA)
Inter-American Center for Agricultural
  Information, (see CIDIA)
Inter-American Institute for
  Agricultural Sciences, (see IICA)
Interface, (see User interface)
Interlibrary loan (ILL),
  management, 202
  OCLC, 199
  research, 197-198
  staff time study, 43-44
Intermediaries, (see also Searching,
    online)
  end user training and education, 233
Internal design,
  system design phases, 8
International Atomic Energy Agency,
    (see IAEA)
International Business Machines Corp.,
    (see IBM)
International Center for Scientific and
    Technical Information (Moscow),
    Cuba, 253
International Federation for
    Documentation, (see FID)
International Information Systems for
    Agricultural Sciences and
    Technology, (see AGRIS)
International Nuclear Information
    System, (see INIS)
Interviewing,
  system analysis and design, 13
Inverted indexes,
  clustered file generation, 102

Inverted indexes, (cont.)
  computer architecture for
    information retrieval, 138-140
  memory technology trends, 183
  record-addressing techniques, 165
  text files, 110
IPEN, (see Brazil, IPEN)
IPSS (Information Processing System
    Simulator),
  OCLC model, 112
IRRL, (see University of Illinois,
    Information Retrieval Research
    Laboratory)
ISI (Institute for Scientific
    Information),
  Autonomous National University of
    Mexico Scientific and Humanistic
    Information Center, 253
ISS, (see Information search services)
Ivie, E.L., 184
Jackson, Eugene B., 45, 46, 56
Jackson, Ruth L., 45, 46, 56
Jacobson, Vance, 64
Jaffe, Jack, 25
Jahnig, Frederick F., 13, 25
Jahoda, Gerald, 234, 240
Jardine, N., 120
Jensen, Becky, 236, 238
Jino, Mario, 136, 146
Job description and analysis, system
    analysis and design, 12-13
Johansson, Bo, 121
Johnson, Herbert F., 11, 25
Johnson, Kristin N., 107, 118
Johnson, T.H., 180, 185
Jones, Alexander M., 208
Jones, Dennis, 197, 208
Jones, James F., 40, 56
Jones, Warren T., 196, 120, 209
Jordan Flores, Fernando, 270
Juergens, Bonnie, 206
Jumarie, Guy, 72, 86

Jump search algorithm,
    experimental access methods, 104-
    105
Kabi, A., 45, *56*
Kain, Richard Y., 133, *141*
Kan, M.I., 15, *25*
Kannan, Krishnamurthi, 139, *142, 147*
Kantor, Paul B., 11, 14, 40, *25, 31,*
    56, 120
Kantorovich, Aharon, 77, *86*
Kaplan, Michael, *186*
Kar, Gautam, 103, *120*
Kassebaum, Laura, 224, 225, 235,
    240, 241
Katter, Robert E., 3, 5, *25*
Katz, Ruth M., *280*
Katzan, Harry, *187*
Kazakos, Dimitri S., 72, *86*
Kazlauskas, Edward John, 12, *26*
Kearney, A.T., 46, *56*
Keen, E. Michael, 229, *244*
Keen, Peter G.W., 9, *26*
Keenan, Stella, 220, 221, 223, 224,
    227, 235, *241*
Kennedy, Gail, *238*
Kennedy, Robert S., *86*
Kent, Allen, 44, 195, 197, 202, 222,
    56, 59, 205, 209, 210, 241
Kerr, Douglas S., 129, 139, *146, 147*
Kervin, John B., *86*
Keys, (*see also* Search keys)
    data models, 161-164
Khalaf, Nadim, 15, *26*
Khallaghi, M.T., 103, *126*
Khas'minskii, R.Z., *84*
Kidd, J.S., *116*
Kiewitt, Eva L., 201, 202, *209*
Kim, Chai, *86*
Kim, Soon D., *86*
King, Donald W., 3, 15, 42, 46, 47,
    26, 56, 57, 209
King, Jack B., 11, *25*

King Research, Inc.,
    copyright and photocopying study,
    40
    information processing cost studies,
    42
Kirchner, Jake, 203, *209*
Kirk, Frank G., 9, *26*
Kiss, George R., 77, *86*
Kiviat graphs, 12
Klair, Arlene, *26*
Kleijnen, Jack P.C., 38, *57*
Klement'ev, A.F., 15, *26*
Klintoe, Kjeld, 45, 257, *57*
Knapp, Sara D., 228, 229, *241*
Knowledge,
    relation to information, 71
Koch, Harvey S., *187*
Koenig, Michael E.D., 14, 100, *19,*
    120
Kolgomorov complexity,
    equivalences with Shannon
    entropy, 72
Koll, Matthew, 93, 97, *120, 122*
Korolev, E.I., 75, *80, 86*
Koss, A.M., 157, 169, 171, 177, *187*
Kountz, John, 38, 47, *57*
Kovarskaya, B.P., 15
Kraft, Donald H., 12, 14, 73, 95, 112,
    19, 23, 26, 60, 86, 115, 120
Krakowiak, S., 8, *26*
Kramer, Joseph, 45, *57*
Krasheninnikova, N.L., 15, *26*
Krentz, David M., 108, *120*
Korenke, David M., 155, 156, 167,
    178, *188*
Kroll, Michael, 15, 74, *30, 88*
Kronick, David A., 202, *209*
Krylov, Iu. K., 75, *86*
Kuch, T.D.C., 15, *26*
Kugel, Peter, *86, 121*
Kul'gavina, O.E., *87*
Kurenkova, M.G., 15, *27*

Kurtz, J.F., 156, 157, 173, *185*
La Rocco, August, *57*
Laborie, Tim, 15, *27*
Labov, W., 75, *86*
Lafreniere, Lise, *86*
Lage, Lucia Maria O., *275*
Lam, L., 103, *120*
Lancaster, F. Wilfrid, 3, 7, 9, 11, 46, 201, 258, *27*, *57*, *209*, *275*
Landau, Marieta, *280*
Langdon, Glen G. Jr., *147*
Langefors, Borje, *120*
Langley, Phyllis R., 41, *57*
Lantz, Brian E., 41, *57*
Large databases,
  database management systems, 158
Larsson, Rolf, 111, *120*, *121*
Lastovka, E.V., 15, *27*
Latin America,
  cooperation and resource sharing, 265
  information systems and services, 249-269
  agricultural information, 258-259
  economics of information, 264
  education and training, 263-264
  evolution, 250-251
  future needs, 265-267
  industrial information, 256-258
  information sources availability, 263
  medical information, 260-261
  nuclear energy information, 259-260
  policy and decision-making information, 267
  political difficulties, 262-263
  problems, 262-265
  recognition, 262
  scientific information needs, 266
  social and economic development, 249
  STI, 251-261
  technical and industrial information needs, 266-267

Latin American Association of Library and Information Science Schools, (*see* ALERCI)
Latin American Center for Econmic and Social Documentation, (*see* CLADES)
Latin American Commission (*of the* International Federation for Documentation), (*see* FID, CLA)
Latin American Demographic Center, (*see* CELADE)
Latin American Index Medicus, 260
Latin American Population Documentation System, (*see* DOCPAL)
Lawani, S.M., 15, 73, *27*, *86*
Lazorick, Gerald J., 15, *25*
LC, (*see* Library of Congress)
LC Information Bulletin,
  library automation literature, 195
LDDL (Logical data definition language), 110
LDL (Logical data language), 110
Le Ny, Jean-Francois, 76, *90*
Learmont, Carol L., *57*
Learning,
  human information processing related to information science, 77
  information science research areas, 71
Leatherbury, Maurice C., *58*
Lechat, Jean, *281*
Lee, C-J., *150*
Lee, C.Y., *147*
Lee, E.K.C., *188*
Lee, E.Y.S., *188*
Lee, S.Y., 136, *147*
Legal information,
  Brazil, 261
  passage retrieval, 107-108
Legard, Lawrence K., 198, *209*
Leguyader, H., *86*
Leilich, H-O., 134, *147*

Leimkuhler, Ferdinand F., 10, 13, 14, 44, 47, 50, *27*, *57*, *62*
Leiter, Joseph, 224, 235, *239*, *241*
Lemond, L., *87*
Leonard, Lawrence E., 40, 43, 47, *58*
Leong-Hong, Belkis, 172, 180, *188*
Lerner, Rita G., 198, *209*
Leung-Yan-Cheong, Sik K., 72, *86*
Levine, Jamie J., 198, 201, *209*, *213*
Levy, D., *62*
Lewis, Charles J., 154, 155, *188*
Libkind, A.N., *80*
Libraries, (*see also* Academic libraries; Acquisitions; Book storage; Book use; Cataloging; Collection development; Industrial/technical libraries; Interlibrary loan; Library and information center management; Library automation; Library networks; Library security systems; Public libraries; Reference services; Serials control)
  collection use studies, 202
  cost analysis, 10-11
  costs increase, 15
  flowcharting, 12
  information measures, 73-74
  Latin America, 263
  operations research and analysis, 13-14
  planning and decision-making systems, 11
  system analysis and design, 7, 9
Library Access System 370, DOBIS development, 199
Library and information center management,
  automation impacts, 201-203
  descriptive and inferential statistics, 15
  negotiation for computer services, 6
Library automation, 193-204
  current research, 196-198
  file organization, 110

Library automation, (cont.)
  future trends, 203
  hardware selection, 199
  literature sources, 194-196
  management issues, 201-203
  minicomputer applications, 47-48
  network research, 197-198
  recent developments, 199-201
  terminology, 193
Library Journal,
  user fees coverage, 48
Library networks, (*see also* Cooperation and resource sharing; Service networks)
  library automation, 197-198
  research, 197-198
Library of Congress (LC),
  library automation literature, 195
  national bibliographic network, 200-201
  Network Advisory Committee (NAC), 200
  Network Advisory Group (NAG), 200
    Network Technical Architecture Group (NTAG), 200-201
  Network Development Office (NDO), 200-201
Library schools, (*see also* Education and training)
  cooperation with database suppliers, 231
  faculty,
    online retrieval training, 230
  Latin America, 264
  online retrieval education, 228-231
Library security systems,
  cost-benefit analysis, 11
Lifchitz, Abrahão, 258, *279*
Liflyandchik, B.I., *27*
Lin, C.S., 134, *147*
Linde, Richard R., *147*
Lindford, John, 48, *58*
Lindquist, Mats G., 45, 112, 196, *58*, *121*, *210*

Line, M.B., 11, 15, *27*

Linguistic String Project,
  computer-assisted indexing, 100
  question-answering from natural
    language medical records, 108

LINK,
  database survey, 233, 235

Lipovski, G. Jack, 134, 135, *143, 144,*
    145, 147, 148, 150

Lipow, Anne G., 234, *241*

LIS, (*see* Lockheed Information
  Systems)

List merging processors,
  computer architecture for
    information retrieval, 140

Lister Hill National Center,
  CAI, 200

Liu, Jane W-S., 136, *146*

Living systems,
  systems theory, 4

Lo, D.H., *150*

Loaiza, Hugo T., *275*

Lochovsky, Frederick H., 164, 167,
    178, *190*

Lockemann, Peter, 106, *124*

Lockheed Information Systems (LIS),
  (*see also* ONTAP)
  DIALOG,
    cost comparison study, 41
    education and training, 223

Lofstrom, Mats, 111, *121*

Loftus, Elizabeth F., 77, *86*

Logan, Timothy, 40, 201, *58, 209*

Logical data definition language,
  (*see* LDDL)

Logical data language, (*see* LDL)

Logical data organization, (*see*
  Data organization, logical)

Long, Beth, 200, *210*

Lord, Kenniston W., Jr., 9, *28*

Lotka's law,
  humanities, 79

Lowenthal, Eugene, *186*

Lubans, John, Jr., *20*

Lucas, Henry C., Jr., 8, *28*

Luk, W.S., 102, *127*

Lum, V.Y., *143, 186*

Lundeen, Gerald, 231, *241*

Lunneborg, Clifford E., 74, *86*

Lupkiewicz, S., *150*

Lyders, Richard A., 12, 44, *22, 52,*
    53, 58

Lyman, Margaret, 107, *124*

Lyon, John K., 172, *188*

MacCafferty, Maxine, 222, *241*

Machine-assisted indexing, (*see*
  Computer-assisted indexing)

Machine-Readable Cataloging, (*see*
  MARC)

Machlup, Fritz, 46, *58*

MacLaury, Keith D., 198, *215*

MacLeod, Ian A., 98, 110, *117,*
    121

Madnick, S.E., *146*

MAGNUM, 176

Maher, Ann, *242*

Maier, Joan M., *58*

Mairlot, Ferdinand E., *86*

Malugani, Maria Dolores, *276*

Management information systems,
  library automation, 202

Management of libraries and
  information centers, (*see* Library
  and information center
  management)

Manchester Polytechnic,
  online retrieval education, 228

Mandlebrot, B., 75, *86*

Mansfield, Una, *209*

MARC (Machine-Readable Cataloging),
  recent developments, 199

Marchant, Maurice P., 44, *58*

Marcum, Thomas P., 11, *34*

Marcus, Richard S., 73, 108, 198, *86,*
    121, 210

Margenau, H., 68, *87*

Marin County Free Library,
  minicomputer use, 48
Marion, Robert, *186*
MARK IV, 173
Marketing of information services,
  (*see also* Promotion of information
  services)
  current research, 112
Markey, Karen, 226, *241*
Markuson, Barbara E., 198, *210*
Maron, M.E., 93, 100, *116, 121*
Marron, Beatrice A., 172, 180, 220,
  186, 188, 241
Marslen-Wilson, William D., *87*
Martin, George P., 40, *58*
Martin, James, 154, 155, 156, 160,
  161, 163, 178, 181, *188*
Martin, Susan K., 195, 196, *58, 210*
Martinez, Victor D., 258
Martyn, Bruce, 15, *28*
Martyn, John, 258, *275*
Marx, B., 234, *241*
Maryanski, Fred J., 179, 182, *188*
Mascarenhas, Yvonne P., *281*
Mason, Robert M., 45, 111, *28, 58,
  59, 121*
Massachusetts Institute of Technology,
  (*see* MIT)
Mathematical linguistics,
  relation to information science, 75
Mattaj, Alisa, 40, *59*
Matthews, J.R., 170, *188*
Mayes, J. Terry, *87*
Mazella, Angela, 232, *242*
McAllister, Paul, *17*
McCarn, Davis B., 220, 227, 233, *242*
McClure, Charles R., 14, *28*
McCracken, D.G., 169, *188*
McDonald, Dennis D., 26
McFadden, Fred R., 154, 157, 173,
  176, *188*
McGee, William C., 166, *189*
McGill, Michael J., 93-114, 97, *121,
  122*

McGrath, William E., 74, *87*
McHugh, Anita, *59*
McInroy, John Wise, 97, *121*
McKell, Lynn J., *24*
McQuillan, John M., 194, 196, *210*
McQuiston, Makala, *59*
Meadow, Charles T., 108, 109, 233,
  234, *122, 242*
Meadows, A.J., 78, *81*
Measures, (*see* Information measures;
  Performance measures)
Mediatron, 234
Medical information,
  Latin America, 260-261
  natural language processing, 107
  question-answering system, 108
Medical Literature Analysis and
  Retrieval System, (*see* MEDLARS)
MEDLARS (Medical Literature
  Analysis and Retrieval System),
  user training, 224
MEDLARS On-Line, (*see* MEDLINE)
MEDLEARN,
  benefits, 225
  NLM user training, 224
MEDLINE (MEDLARS On-Line),
  library school use, 230
  user training, 224
MEDLINE Users Group of the
  Midwest,
  users as educators, 232
Meincke, Peter P.M., 97, *122*
Mekhtiev, A.M., 78, *87*
Mellion, S.P., *87*
Memory, computer, (*see also* Data
  storage)
  cost decrease and information
  retrieval, 131
  database management systems, 169,
  182-183
  von Neumann architecture, 130
Memory, human, (*see* Human memory)
Menda, Eduardo, 253, *276*

Meta-databases,
database management, 110
Metallurgy Information Center, (see CIM)
Mexico,
Center for Information Services, 252
CONACYT (National Council for Science and Technology), 252, 263
industrial information activities, 257
Information Center for Health, 261
information systems and services, 252-253
INFOTEC, 257
cooperation with CENDES, 258
medical information, 261
political changes and information policy, 263
SECOBI (Service for Coordination of Information Banks), 252
SNICT (National Information System for Science and Technology), 252
Mick, Colin K., 37-50, 41, 42, 46, 47, 49, 54, 57, 59, 118
Microforms,
cost analysis, 39
Mignon, Edmond, 229, 231, 235, 236, 242
Military information projects,
database management systems development, 158
Mill, A., 82
Millen, J.K., 138, 142
Miller, Betty, 118
Miller, Bruce, 15, 28
Miller, David G., 86
Miller, E.W., 214
Miller, James Grier, 4, 7, 28
Miller, R.H., 57
Miller, Richard, 41, 42, 46, 47, 59
Minder, Thomas, 6, 28

Minicomputer News,
library automation literature, 195
Minicomputers,
database management systems, 175, 182
library applications, 47-48
library selection, 199
online retrieval education, 231
Minker, Jack, 94, 108, 122
Minneapolis Public Library,
user fees, 48
Minsky, Naftaly, 134, 148
Miranda, Ana Christina E., 259, 271
MIT (Massachusetts Institute of Technology),
Electronic Systems Laboratory, CONIT, (see CONIT)
libraries,
cost-benefit analysis, 11
library automation research, 198
Mitchell, R.W., 185
Modeling, (see also Simulation)
database management system selection, 177
information science research areas, 69-70
interlibrary loan, 197-198
large online systems, 112
library effectiveness, 202
Mohan, C., 109, 122
Moisse, E., 45, 59
Molino, Enzo, 252, 256, 263, 276
Moll, Joy K., 14, 29
Montague, Eleanor A., 197, 59, 210
Monteiro Filho, L.H.J., 271
Montgomery, K. Leon, 3, 12, 44, 202, 21, 28, 56, 59, 205, 209, 210
Moore, Alexandra L., 232, 242
Moravcsik, Michael J., 15, 29, 87
Morita, I.T., 10, 40, 28, 59
Morris, W.E.M., 55
Morrow, Deanna I., 12, 28

Morse, Philip M., 13, 14, *28*
Morton, Donald J., 15, *28*
Mosley, Isobel Jean, 12, 201, *28*, *211*
Moulder, Richard, 133, *148*
Moulin, Theiraut, *86*
Moureau, Magdeleine L., 235, *242*
MRI Systems Corp.,
    System 2000, (*see* System 2000)
Mukhopadhyay, Amar, 137, *148*
Multiple attribute retrieval,
    multiple and combined indexes, 104
Multiple indexes,
    multiple attribute retrieval, 104
MUMPS, 159
Murugesan, Poovanalingam, 15, *29*, *87*
Myers, Dale C., 198, *211*
NAC, (*see* Library of Congress,
    Network Advisory Committee)
NAG, (*see* Library of Congress,
    Network Advisory Group)
Nahvi, M.J., *87*
NAL, (*see* National Agricultural
    Library)
Narin, Francis, 14, 15, *17*, *29*
NASA, (*see* U.S., NASA)
NASIC (Northeast Academic Science
    Information Center),
    final report, 200
NASIS, 156
National Academy of Sciences, (*see*
    U.S., National Academy of
    Sciences)
National Aeronautics and Space
    Administration, (*see* U.S., NASA)
National Agricultural Library (NAL),
    (*see also* AGRICOLA)
    user training, 226-228
National bibliographic network,
    planning, 200-201
    protocols, 197
National Bureau of Standards, (*see*
    U.S., National Bureau of Standards)

National Center for Documentation,
    (*see* Paraguay, National Center for
    Documentation)
National Center for Educational
    Documentation and Information
    (Peru), (*see* CENIDE)
National Center for Information and
    Documentation (Chile), (*see* Chile,
    CENID)
National Center for Scientific and
    Technical Documentation (Bolivia),
    (*see* Bolivia, National Center for
    Scientific and Technical
    Documentation)
National Commission for Atomic
    Energy (Argentina), (*see* Argentina,
    CNEA)
National Commission for Scientific
    and Technical Research (Chile),
    (*see* Chile, CONICYT)
National Commission on Libraries and
    Information Science, (*see* NCLIS)
National Council for Science and
    Technology (Mexico), (*see* Mexico,
    CONACYT)
National Council for Scientific and
    Technical Research (Argentina),
    (*see* Argentina, CONICET)
National Council for Scientific and
    Technical Research (Uruguay), (*see*
    Uruguay, CORICYT)
National Council for Scientific and
    Technological Research (Costa
    Rica), (*see* Costa Rica, CONICIT)
National Council for Scientific and
    Technological Research
    (Venezuela), (*see* Venezuela,
    CONICIT)
National Information Systems pro-
    gram, (*see* NATIS)

National Institute for Industrial Technology (Argentina), (see Argentina, INTI)

National Library of Agriculture (Brazil), (see Brazil, BINAGRI)

National Library of Australia, WLN system, 203

National Library of Canada (NLC), authority system, 199
DOBIS selection, 199

National Library of Medicine (NLM), (see also MEDLARS; MEDLEARN; MEDLINE)
Latin American activities, 260-261
online retrieval education and training, 224-226
probability theory applied to retrieval, 96

National Organization for Science Policy in Columbia, (see Colombia, COLCIERCIAS)

National Research Council (Brazil), (see Brazil, CNPq)

National System and Fund of Information for Development (Bolivia), (see SYFNID)

National System for Agricultural Information and Documentation, (see Brazil, SNIDA)

National System for Scientific and Technical Information (Venezuela), (see SINICYT)

National System of Library and Information Services (Venezuela), (see SINASBI)

National System of Educational Documentation and Information, (see SISNIDE)

National Union Catalog, national bibliographic network, 201

NATIS (National Information Systems program), Latin America, 262

NATO Advanced Study Institute, 1977, 201

Natural language, semantics of data models, 110

Natural language processing, information retrieval experimental techniques, 106-107

Navathe, Shamkant, 186

NBS, (see U.S., National Bureau of Standards)

NCLIS (National Commission on Libraries and Information Science), computer network protocol, 197
library automation literature, 195
national bibliographic network, 200

NDO, (see Library of Congress, Network Development Office)

Neghme, Amador, 260, 276

Negotiation for computer services, 6

NELINET (New England Library Network), library automation literature, 195
resource-sharing protocols, 197

Nelson, Diane M., 15, 29

NEPHIS (NEsted PHrase Indexing System), 100

NEsted PHrase Indexing System, (see NEPHIS)

Netherlands, The, Latin American Center for Economic and Social Documentation (CLADES), 256

Network, library automation literature, 195

Network Advisory Committee, (see Library of Congress, Network Advisory Committee)

Network Advisory Group, (see Library of Congress, Network Advisory Group)

Network data models, 163-164

Network Development Office, (see Library of Congress, Network Development Office)

Network of Socio-Economic Information (Venezuela), (see REDINSE)

Network Technical Architecture Group, (see Library of Congress, Network Advisory Group, Network Technical Architecture Group)

Networks, (see Bibliographic utilities; Cataloging, networks; Citation networks; Library networks; National bibliographic network; Semantic networks; Service networks)

Neuhold, Erich J., 110, *115*

Neuto, Victoria Galofre, 251

New England Library Network, (see NELINET)

New York Metropolitan Reference and Research Service, user fees, 49

New York Public Library, authority system, 199

New York State Library, serials control system, 200

Newman, William L., *205, 207*

Newsbaum, J.B., *115*

Ng, F.K., *146*

Nguyen, H.B., *150*

Nguyen, Le, *150*

Nicholas, David, 14, *29*

Nielsen, Norman R., *207*

Nierman, Florence, 250

Nigan, A., 136, *143*

Nisenoff, Norman, 201, *206*

NLC, (see National Library of Canada)

NLM, (see National Library of Medicine)

Nocentti, Milton A., *277*

Nolan, Richard L., 154, 173, *189*

Nonbibliographic databases, (see Databases, nonbibliographic)

Noonan, J.M., 157, 169, 171, 177, *187*

Nord, Ake, *119*

Noreault, Terry, 93, 101, 106, *122, 124*

Northeast Academic Science Information Center, (see NASIC)

Notas Informativas CENID, 256

Notas sobre la Economia y el Desarrollo de America Latina, 256

Novikov, Iu.A., *80*

NTAG, (see Library of Congress, Network Advisory Group, Network Technical Architecture Group)

Nuclear energy information, Latin America, 259-260

Nuclear Information Center, (see Brazil, CIN)

Numeric databases, (see Databases, numeric)

Nunnally, Jum C., 77, *87*

O'Connor, John, 107, *122*

OAS (Organization of American States), agricultural information projects, 258

COLCIENCIAS support, 254

ICAITI (Instituto Centroamericano de Investigacion y Tecnologia Industrial), 257

Latin American information systems development, 251

Program for Technical Information and Assistance to Industry, 257

SIATE (Technical Information and Assistance Service for Enterprises), 257

Oberlander, Lewis B., *190*

Occurrence, (see Term occurrence)

Ochsman, Robert B., *81*

OCLC (*formerly* Ohio College Library Center),
back- and front-end processors, 199
experimental search keys, 104
impact on RLIN and WLN, 197
impact on user libraries, 198
interlibrary loan system, 199
IPSS model, 112
regional use study, 197
RLIN comparison, 40, 201
serials control system, 199
OCLC Newsletter,
library automation literature, 195
Oden, Gregg C., *87*
Oflazer, Kemal, *148*
Ohio College Library Center, (*see* OCLC)
Oldman, Christine, *63*
Oliveira, Luiz Carlos, *274*
Oliver, Ellen, 129, 133, *142*
Olsen, Harold A., 38, *59*
Olsen, Paul E., 12, 40, *29*, *59*
Olsen, Wallace C., 226, *243*
On the Relationship between Library Schools, Search Service Vendors, and Database Producers, 231
ONLINE,
user aids, 227
Online users' groups,
education and training, 232
Online vendors, (*see also* Database producers; Information search services)
cooperation with library schools, 231
education and training, 223-226
library school use, 230
Mexican services, 252
ONTAP, 225-226
Ontario,
library network, 199
Operating Systems, Inc.,
full text retrieval, 137, 138

Operations research and analysis (OR&A),
information and library system design and analysis, 13-15
Oppenheim, Charles, 15, *23*, *29*, *83*
OR&A, (*see* Operations research and analysis)
ORBIT, (*see* SDC, ORBIT)
Ordover, J. *51*
Organization of American States, (*see* OAS)
Oromaner, Mark, 15, *29*, *87*
Ortega, Mireya, 254, *273*
Ortony, Andrew, 77, *87*
Ospina, Hernando, *278*
Otis, Allen J., 135, *148*
Overlap,
computerized cataloging, 197
Owen, J.L., *60*
Ozkarahan, Esen A., 135, *148*, *149*, *150*
Pacak, Milos G., *117*, *122*
Page charges,
cost analysis, 42
PAHO (Pan American Health Organization), 260
Paice, C.D., 94, *123*
Palais, Eliot S., 15
Palmer, C.R., 48, *60*
Palmour, Vernon E., 39, *60*, *63*, *211*
Pan American Health Organization, (*see* PAHO)
Pan, Elizabeth, 200, *211*
Pansophic Systems, Inc.,
EASYTRIEVE, (*see* EASYTRIEVE)
Pao, Miranda Lee, 15, 73, *29*, *87*, *123*
Paraguay,
information systems and services, 255
National Center for Documentation, 255

Paraguayan Center for Social
  Documentation, 255
Parhami, Behrooz, 134, *149*
Parker, James L., 134, *149*
Parrish, Robert N., *81*
Passage retrieval, (*see also* Full text
  retrieval)
  experimental techniques, 107-108
Patents,
  citation networks, 78
Pathology data,
  natural language processing, 107
Pattern analysis,
  database mapping, 96
Patterson, Albert C., 171, *189*
Paull, M.C., *147*
PDP/11,
  IDMS, 159
Pearson, Charls, 72, 75, *87, 89*
Pearson, Ellen M., 232, *243*
Peng, I-F., *147*
Penland, Patrick R., *88*
Penna, Carlos Victor, 278, *279*
Perception,
  human information processing
    related to information science, 77
Perez Ferrera, T., *279*
Performance measures, (*see also*
  Evaluation of information systems
  and services; Information measures)
  information science research areas,
    70
  system analysis and design, 11
  system design and evaluation, 111
Periodicals,
  cost analysis,
    ownership vs. borrowing, 39
    replacement of paper with micro-
      form, 39
Perlmutter, Edith L., 48, *51*
Perschke, S., *114*
Persson, Olle, *123*

Peru,
  CENIDE (National Center for
    Educational Documentation and
    Information), 262
  SISNIDE (National System of
    Educational Documentation and
    Information), 262
Pettus, Clinton, 77, *88*
Phister, M., 173, *189*
Photocopying,
  resource sharing, 40
  staff time study, 43-44
Physical data organization, (*see* Data
  organization, physical)
Picard, C.F., 72, *80*
Picture-word inference,
  human information processing
    related to information science, 77
Pierce, Anton R., 12, 201, *29, 211*
Pierce, John C., 100, *123*
Pilachowski, David M., 234, *239*
Pinheiro, Lena Vania R., *279*
Pinski, Gabriel, 15, *29*
Piternick, George, 15, *29*
Pitt, William Bruce, *60*
Pittsburgh Conference on the On-Line
    Revolution in Libraries, 1977, 222
Plagman, Bernard K., *189*
Poblacion, Dinah Aguiar, *279*
Pointers,
  memory technology trends, 183
  record-addressing techniques, 165
Poisson distribution,
  information retrieval and probability
    theory, 95
Polacsek, Richard A., *26*
Policy-making information,
  Latin America, 267
Polushkiv, V.A., *88*
Polysemy,
  statistical analysis, 75
Pomerantz, James R., *89*

Pomerene, J.H., *143*
Pompeu Davig, Angela, 258, *279*
Pope, Andrew, 15, *30*
Population information, (*see*
  Demographic information)
Porat, Marc Uri, 46, *60*
Potter, Mary C., *88*
Potter, T. Robert, *61*
Powell, Ronald R., 11, 74, *30*, *88*
Pratt, Allan D., 15, *30*
Pratt, Arnold W., *117, 122*
Pratt, Gordon, 234, *60, 243*
Praunlich, Peter, 15, 74, *30, 88*
Prawat, Richard S., 77, *88*
PRECIS (PREserved Context Indexing
  System),
  document classification, 196
  role indicator assignment
    automation, 100
Preece, Scott E., *215*
PREserved Context Indexing System,
  (*see* PRECIS)
Prestel,
  library automation trends, 203
Price, Derek J. DeSolla, 14, 78, *30,
  88*
Price, Douglas S., 39, 47, 49, 50, *60*
Privacy, (*see also* Security in computer
  systems)
  database management systems, 171,
    178
Private sector,
  information services cost studies, 46
Probability theory,
  indexing, 98-99
  information retrieval, 95-96
Problem solving,
  human information processing
    related to information science, 77
PRODASEN (Information System for
  Data Processing of Legislative
  Information (Brazil)), 261
Production of information sources,
  (*see* Information production)

Program for Technical Information
  and Assistance to Industry, (*see*
  OAS, Program for Technical Infor-
  mation and Assistance to Industry)
Projects of Industrial Investment
  (Uruguay), 258
Promotion of information services,
  (*see also* Marketing of information
  services)
  online retrieval, 234
Proposed Standards for Education in
  Online Searching in the Professional
  Librarianship Curriculum, 229
Proposition 13 (California),
  effects on public information
    systems, 12
Prosser, Carolyn, *60*
Protocols,
  library networks, 197
Prywes, Noah S., 160, *189*
Public libraries,
  evaluation of service, 15
  online searching costs, 41
  online searching user fees, 202
  reference service measurement, 74
  user fees, 48-49
Publishing,
  cost analysis, 42
  online vs. print revenues, 43
Purdue University,
  library costs study, 44
Pyrce, Sharon R., 232, *242*
Quality control, (*see also* Data
  verification)
  database management systems, 171,
    178
Quantum communication theory,
  information theory, 72
Quantitatively based management
  information system, (*see*
  QUBMIS)
QUBMIS (Qualitatively based
  management information system),
  card catalog effectiveness, 40

Question-answering systems,
  medical records, 108
Questionnaire design,
  information theory extensions, 72
Quevedo, José, 257, *279*
Quiros, Alice, *215*
Radecki, Tadeusz, 14, 95, 196, *30,
  88, 123, 211*
Radhakrishnan, T., 13, *30*
Raffel, Jeffrey A., 11, *30*
Raghavan, Vijay V., 102, 103, *123,
  127*
Ramist, Leonard E., *24, 208*
Randall, G.E., *60*
Random access,
  database management systems
    development, 158
Random alarm devices,
  staff time study, 44
Rank-frequency relations,
  compared to type-token relations, 75
Ranking,
  experimental techniques, 106
  principles, 73
  probability theory and document
    ranking, 96
Raouf, Abdul, 15, *30*
RAP (Relational Associative
    Processor),
  development and organization, 135
Raper, Diane, 10, 38, 49, *25, 55*
Rastogi, Kunj B., 103, *123*
Rathbun, Joyce A., *211*
Raver, N., *189*
Record addressing,
  database management systems, 165-
    166
Recovery, (*see* Failure recovery)
REDINSE (Network of Socio-
    Economic Information
    (Venezuela)), 261
Reed, Jutta R., 39, *60*
Reed, Mary Jane Pobst, 16, 40, 193-
    204, *30, 61*

Rees, Alan M., *243*
Referativnii Zhurnal,
  Informatics section,
    Spanish translation, 253
Reference interview,
  online searching, 236
Reference services,
  measurement, 74
Regazzi, John J., 12, 14, 228, *31, 61,
  244*
Regional Research and Technical
    Assistance Centers, (*see* CRIAT)
Register of Additional Locations,
  national bibliographic network, 201
Reintjes, J. Francis, 108, 198, *121,
  210*
Relational associative processor, (*see*
  RAP)
Relational databases and models, 164
  bubble memory, 136
  CASSM and RAP, 134-135
  database management system trends,
    181
  database management systems, 175-
    176
  information retrieval, 98
  query languages, 110
Relativistic information, 72
Relevance,
  evaluation of retrieval systems, 112
Remote File Management System, (*see*
  RFMS)
Renn, Susan P., 15, *29*
Research Libraries Group, (*see* RLG)
Resnikoff, Howard L., 68, 70, *88*
Resource sharing, (*see* Cooperation
    and resource sharing)
Revill, D.H., 11, *31*
Reynolds, Rose, 38, *61, 63*
RFMS (Remote File Management
    System),
  development, 159
Richmond, Phyllis A., 196, *123, 211*
Ritchie, Maureen, 14, *29*

RLG (Research Libraries Group),
  RLIN, (*see* RLIN)
RLIN (Research Libraries Information
  Network, *formerly* BALLOTS),
  cooperation with WLN, 203
  OCLC comparison, 40, 201
  OCLC impact, 197
RLIN Newsletter,
  library automation literature, 195
Robach, C., *82*
Roberts, David C., 110, 131, 138, *123*,
  145, *149*
Robertson, Stephen E., 12, 41, 44, 50,
  73, 95, 96, 101, 196, *31*, *33*, *61*,
  63, *88*, *124*, *212*
Robinson, K.A., 164, *189*
Robredo, Jaime, 263, 264, *279*
Rocha, Fernando R.A., *280*
Rocke, Merle G., 171, *189*
Rockwell International,
  IMS/VS, (*see* IMS/VS)
Roderer, Nancy K., 46, *26*, *56*, *57*,
  209, *211*
Rodriguez, C.E., 198, *115*, *205*
Rohmer, Jean, *145*
Rojas, L., 254, *280*
Roman, W.G., *146*
Romerio, C.F., 252, 265, *280*
Rose, Lawrence L., 73, 79, *91*
Rosenberg, Arnold L., *124*
Rosenthal, Joseph A., 201, *212*
Rosing-Spiegel, Ina, *88*
Rosinski, Richard R., 77, *88*
Rosove, Perry E., 5, 7, *31*
Ross, Ronald G., 155, 172, 174, 176,
  180, *189*
Ross, Ryburn M., 201, *212*
Rotating associative memory,
  computer architecture for informa-
  tion retrieval, 134-135
Rothenberg, D.H., *31*
Rothnie, James B., Jr., 194, 196, *212*
Rouse, Sandra H., 197, 202, *212*

Rouse, William B., 14, 197, *31*, *212*
Rousseau, J., *52*
Rowat, M., *62*
Rowe, D., *61*
Royal Institute of Technology
  Library,
  3RIP system, (*see* 3RIP system)
Rubeiz, John, 15, *26*
Rubin, Rebecca Boring, 77, *89*
Rudd, Ernest, *89*
Rudolph, Jack A., 132, *149*
Rush, James E., 104, *22*, *117*, *125*
Russell, K., *52*
Ryder, J.L., *184*
Rypka, David J., *119*
Sabor, William N., *209*
Sabsay, P., 234, *243*
Sacher, Hans Joachim, *61*
Sachs, Wladimir M., 196, *212*
Sadowski, Paul J., *149*
Sager, Naomi, 106, 107, *119*, *124*
Sager, Wolfgang, 106, *124*
Salter, John C., *243*
Salton, Gerard, 11, 73, 93, 94, 97,
  101, 102, 196, *31*, *91*, *124*, *127*,
  212
Sampling,
  library collections, 15
Sampson, Gary S., 14, *31*
Sampson, J.R., *89*
Samuelson, Kjell, 10, 195, *31*, *212*
Sandoval, Armando M., 253, *280*
Sanitary engineering information,
  Chile, 261
Santos, Dulce C. dos, 263, *280*
São Paulo,
  industrial information activities, 258
São Paulo Medical School regional
  medical library, (*see* BIREME)
Saracevic, Tefko, 11, 71, 249-269,
  255, *31*, *89*, *280*
Sassone, Peter G., 45, 111, *28*, *59*,
  121

Sastri, C.C.A., 72, *83*
Satariano, William A., *31*
SATI, (*see* Argentina, SATI)
Sato, H., *271*
Savage, John E., 77, *86*
Scales, Pauline A., 15, *31*
Scardamalia, Marlene, *89*
Scatter storage,
  3RIP system, 111
Schaap, Ann, *243*
Scharer, Laura L., 9, *32*
Schema, (*see* Database definition)
Scheuermann, Peter, 160, *189*
Schindler, Steven, *186*
Schissler, L.R., *145*
Schlie, Theodore W., 265, *280*
Schmidt, Janet A., 234, *243*
Schmierer, Helen F., 100, *126*
Schneider, H.J., *124*
Schneider, Walter, 77, *89*
Schneiderman, Ben, 103
Schofield, J.L., 11, 43, *32, 62*
Scholz, William H., *212*
Schorr, Alan Edward, 15, *32*
Schueller, Charles G., *26*
Schur, Herbert, 264, *280*
Schussel, George, 168, 171, *189*
Schuster, S.A., 135, *149, 150*
Schwartz, Candy, 101, *124*
Schwartz, Jean-Jacques, *89*
Schwartz, Stephen, *124*
Schwuchow, Werner, *32, 54*
Scientific and Humanistic Information
  Center, (*see* Autonomous National
  University of Mexico, Scientific and
  Humanistic Information Center)
Scientific and technical information,
  (*see* STI)
Scott, Aldyth D., 229, *243*
Scott, Alexander, *64*
SDC (System Development
  Corporation),
  education and training, 223, 225

SDC (System Development
  Corporation), (cont.)
  ORBIT,
    cost comparison study, 41
  TDMS, (*see* TDMS)
Search aids, (*see* User aids)
Search keys, (*see also* Keys)
  experimental technology, 103-104
  research in large files, 198
Search services, (*see* Information
  search services)
Searching, (*see also* Information search
  services)
  manual,
    cost analysis, 41
    cost effectiveness, 112
  models, 233, 236
  online, (*see also* Intermediaries; On-
    line vendors)
    cost analysis, 40-42
    cost effectiveness, 112
    costs, 10
    generalized flowchart, 12
    Mexico, 252
    user fees, 202
    user interface, 108-109
    Venn diagrams, 12
    1200 baud, 42
SECOBI (Service for Coordination of
  Information Banks (Mexico)), 252
Secondary information services, (*see*
  A&I services)
Security in computer systems, (*see
  also* Privacy)
  database management systems, 171,
    178
Sedransk, Joseph, 15, *23*
Segal, Ronald, *207*
Self-reporting,
  staff time studies, 43
Semantic networks,
  structural foundations, 76
Senders, J.W., 42, *61*

Senko, Michael E., 158, 160, 167, *189*
SEQUEL, 110
Sequential addressing,
  record-addressing techniques, 165
Serials control,
  automation developments, 199-200
Service for Coordination of
    Information Banks (Mexico), (*see*
    SECOBI)
Service for Technical Assistance to
    Industry (Argentina),
    (*see* Argentina, SATI)
Service networks, (*see also*
    Cooperation and resource sharing;
    Negotiation for computer services)
  research, 197
Serviceability,
  retrieval system evaluation, 112
Sevcik, K.C., 135, *148*
Severance, Dennis G., 165, 166, 178,
    179, *186, 189, 190*
Sewell, Winifred, *243*
Shannon entropy,
  equivalences with Kolgomorov
      complexity, 72
Shannon's information theory, (*see*
    Information theory (Shannon))
Sharify, Nasser, *212*
Sharp, Geoffrey, *125*
Shaw, Deborah, 197, *206*
Shaw, William M., Jr., 16, *31, 32*
Shechkov, B.N., *90*
Shefner, Gordon J., 15, *34*
Shepard, Marietta Daniels, 251, *280,
    281*
Shera, Jesse H., *89*
Shiffrin, Richard M., 77, *89*
Shipman, David W., *212*
Shirey, D., 202, *56, 213*
Shirley, Sherrilynne, 41, *61*
Shishko, Robert, 11, *30*
Shneiderman, Ben, 104, 105, 109,
    125, 190
Shoeman, M., *52*

Shoffner, Ralph M., 47, *61*
Shoshant, Arie, *186*
Shreider, Iu.A., 79, *80*
Shwartz, Stephen P., 77, *89*
SIATE, (*see* OAS, SIATE)
Sibley, E.H., *186*
Siehler, Cynthia J., *63*
Signatures,
  hybrid access method, 104
Silcoff, B., 199, *213*
Siler, Kenneth F., 179, *190*
Simon, Julian L, 13, *23*
Simon, Richard C., 236, *243*
Simonson, Walter E., 177, *190*
Simpson, Alex J., *243*
Simpson, I.S., 229, *243*
SIMSCRIPT, 16
SIMULA, 16
Simulation, (*see also* Modeling)
  computer networks, 198
  database management system
      selection, 177
  network planning, 197
  system analysis and design, 16
SINASBI, 254
Singhania, A.K., 134, *142*
Singleton, Alan, 11, *32*
Singpurwalla, Nozer D., *83*
SINICYT (National System for
    Scientific and Technical
    Information (Venezuela)), 253
SIRE (Syracuse Information
    Retrieval Experiment),
  INSPEC experiment, 101
SISNIDE (National System of
    Educational Documentation and
    Information (Peru)), 262
SITCI, (*see* Brazil, SITCI)
Siu, M.K., *127*
Sivers, Robert, *237*
Sladek, Frea, 9, *23*
Slaets, Jan, 261, *281*
Slamecka, Vladimir, 68, 70, 71, 72,
    88, 89

Slater, Frank, *61*
SLC-II system,
  automatic indexing, 100
Slotnick, Daniel L., 134, 137, *150*
Small, Henry C., 74, *89*
SMART project,
  automatic indexing performance,
  99
Smetana, Frederick O., 41, *61*
Smith, Diane C.P., 129, 134, *147, 150*
Smith, Diane P., 160, *189*
Smith, G.C.K., 43, *62*
Smith, Gerry M., 15, 73, *32, 90*
Smith, John Myles, 129, 134, *147,
  150*
Smith, Joseph D., 104, *125*
Smith, K.C., *149, 150*
Smith, L.C., 96, *125*
Smith, R.J., 170, *188*
Smith, Sallye Wrye, 12, *32*
Smol'kov, N.A., 74, *90*
SNICT (National Information System
  for Science and Technology
  (Mexico)), 252
SNIDA, (*see* Brazil, SNIDA)
SNOP (Systematized Nomenclature of
  Pathology), 107
Soergel, Lissa, *26*
Software,
  empirical properties, 75-76
  library cost decisions, 47
Software AG,
  ADABAS, (*see* ADABAS)
Sol'c, N.A., 73, *82*
SOLINET (Southeastern Library
  Network),
  library automation literature, 195
  OCLC impact, 198
Solis, Alvaro Quijano, 249-269
Solvberg, Arne, 165, *184*
Sorum, Marilyn, 15, *28*
South America, (*see* Latin America)
Southeastern Library Network, (*see*
  SOLINET)

Southern Connecticut State College,
  online retrieval continuing education,
  228
Sowder, Calvin D., 77, *90*
Sparck Jones, Karen, 93, 99, 101, 112,
  196, *124, 125, 213*
Spectrum,
  library automation literature, 195
Spence, A. Michael, 10, 38, *32, 62*
Spencer, Carol C., 43, *62*
Sprehn, Mary, 199, *213*
St. Pierre, Paul L., 20
Staff time,
  cost analysis, 43-44
  online search costs, 41
  user fees, 49
Stafford, T., *214*
Stahl, Fred A., *187*
Stalker, George H., 72, *90*
Stamper, R., *90*
Standards and standardization,
  database management systems, 179
  flowcharting, 12
  online retrieval education in
    librarianship, 229
  user interface in information
    retrieval, 109
Standera, O.R., 236, *244*
Standford University,
  library costs study, 44
Standing, Roy A., *239*
Stanfield, Jonathan, 201, *213*
Stanley, Sally Bachelder, 225, *244*
STARAN,
  associative memory and information
    retrieval, 133
State University of New York
  (SUNY),
  libraries,
    collection analysis, 197
  online retrieval education, 229
Statistics,
  information system operations
    research and analysis, 15

Statistics, (cont.)
 relation to information science, 75
Steiner, James B., 9, *28*
Stellhorn, William H., 132, 137, 140, *146, 150*
Stellmacher, Imart, *118*
Stember, Charles Herbert, *25*
Sternberg, Seymour, 171, 177, *190*
Stevens, B.A., *125*
STI (Scientific and technical information),
 Latin America, 251-261
 Latin American needs, 266-267
Stiege, G., *147*
Stierwalt, Ralph E., *213*
Stillman, Neil, *144*
Stock, Karl Franz, 15, *32*
Stockey, Edward A., 231, *244*
Stockmeyer, Larry J., *124*
Storage hierarchy, 164
Strater, Felix R., *19*
Structural analysis of large scale systems,
 information theory extensions, 72
Structure families,
 information science research areas, 69-70
Studer, Paul A., 4, *32*
Studies in Library Management,
 library automation literature, 195
Stupkin, V.V., *90*
Stutz, Joel, 179, *186*
Su, Stanley Y.W., 129, 134, 135, *143, 144, 150, 186*
Substrings,
 search keys, 103
Sullivan, Daniel, 74, *90*
Summit, Roger K., 93, 202, *54, 118, 126, 213*
Sunneback, Jan, *121*
SUNY, (*see* State University of New York)
Suppe, F., 69, *90*

Suver, James D., 154, 157, 173, 176, *188*
Svenonius, Elaine, 100, *126*
Swanson, Don R., 14, 112, *32, 126*
Swanson, Rowena W., 3, 13, *33*
Swartwout, Donald, *186*
Sweden,
 online retrieval by end users, 234
Swets model of information retrieval, 112
SYFNID (National System and Fund of Information for Development (Bolivia)), 255
Syracuse Information Retrieval Experiment, (*see* SIRE)
Syracuse University,
 associative memory for information retrieval, 133
System analysis,
 bibliometrics, 14-15
 cost analysis, 10-12
 flowcharting, 12
 job description and analysis, 12-13
 operations research and analysis, 13-15
 prelude to system design, 7-8
 simulation, 16
 statistics, 15
 system development phases, 5-6
 techniques, 9-16
System design, (*see* Design of information systems and services)
System Development Corporation, (*see* SDC)
System development cycle, 5-6
System R, 181
System-test design,
 system design phases, 8-9
System 2000, 175
 development, 159
Systematized Nomenclature of Pathology, (*see* SNOP)

Systems analysts,
database mangement systems, 172
Systems programmers,
database management systems, 172
Systems theory,
system design, 3-5
Tacoma Public Library,
circulation system selection, 200
Tagliacozzo, Renata, 75, *90, 126*
Tague, Jean, *126*
Talavage, J., 45, 46, *62*
Tanner, P.E., *142*
Tate, Fred A., *211*
Taylor, Joe K., 12, 201, *29, 211*
Taylor, Robert, *186*
Taylor, William D., 202, *205*
TDMS (Time-Shared Data Management System), 159
Technical and Scientific Information System (EMBRAPA-Brazil), (*see* Brazil, SITCI)
Technical Information and Assistance Service for Enterprises, (*see* OAS, SIATE)
Tedd, Lucy A., 229, *244*
Teitelbaum, Henry H., *126*
Tektronix,
INDY implementation, 135
Telecommunications,
cost analysis, 47
information processing cost studies, 42
Teledyne Brown Engineering, 196
Teleprocessing (TP),
database management system components, 169
Teletext systems,
library automation trends, 203
Tell, Bjorn, 263, 264, *281*
Teorey, Toby J., *190*
Term-dependency model,
feedback, 105

Term occurrence,
information retrieval and probability theory, 95-96
Term status map,
dynamic dictionary updating, 102
Term weights, (*see* Weighting)
Tesovnik, Mary E., 38, 43, *62*
Test collections,
information retrieval experimental collections, 112-113
Text compression,
current research in system design, 111
The Online Revolution in Libraries, 1977, (*see* Pittsburgh Conference on the On-Line Revolution in Libraries, 1977)
The Systems Approach, 8
Thesauri, 75 (*see also* Authority files; Dictionaries)
computer-aided generation, 101
Thierauf, Robert J., 14, *33*
Thomas, J.J., *54*
Thomas, Pauline Ann, 12, 16, *33*
Thurber, Kenneth J., 132, *142, 150*
Tichauer, Werner Guttentag, *281*
Tidball, Charles S., *239*
Tighe, Ruth L., 198, *213*
Time-Shared Data Management System, (*see* TDMS)
Titles,
empirical properties, 78
Tobias, Audrey Silvia, 15, *33*
Toliver, David E., *122, 242*
Tomberg, Alex, *213*
Tomé, Martha V., 264, *281*
Törnudd, Elin, 234, *244*
TOTAL, 175
development, 159
Townley, Helen M., 7, *33*
TP, (*see* Teleprocessing)
TRAINER, 222, 231, 233

Training, (*see* Education and training)
Transportation information,
   Brazil, 261
Trapani, Jean, *238*
Travis, I.L., 15, 74, *33, 90*
Trefftzs, J.L., *115*
Treisman, Michell, *90*
Tremoulet, Gretchen, *238*
Tressel, George W., 38, *62*
Trevelin, Luis Carlos, *281*
Triolo, Victor A., 228, *244*
Tsichritzis, Dionysios C., 164, 167,
   178, *190*
Tu, J.C., *142*
Tuel, William G., Jr., 179, *187*
Tung, C., *143, 147, 150*
Turner, Stephen J., 14, 77, *33, 90*
Turner, William S., *24*
Turnkey systems,
   library circulation systems, 200
Turoff, Murray, *208*
Tusera, D., *145*
Tuttle, Helen Welch, 10, *33*
Twitchell, Anne, 199, *213*
Tymshare, Inc.,
   MAGNUM, (*see* MAGNUM)
Tyner, S., *214*
Type-token relations,
   compared to rank-frequency
      relations, 75
Tzeng, Oliver C.S., *90*
U.S.,
   information policy,
      pricing, 46
   Latin American information systems
      development, 251
   Library of Congress, (*see* Library of
      Congress)
   NAL, (*see* National Agricultural
      Library)
   NASA (National Aeronautics and
      Space Administration),
      NASIS, (*see* NASIS)

U.S., (cont.)
   National Academy of Sciences,
      Argentinian Telex network, 256
   National Agricultural Library, (*see*
      National Agricultural Library)
   National Bureau of Standards,
      computer network protocol, 197
      internal online retrieval use study,
         234
   National Library of Medicine, (*see*
      National Library of Medicine)
   NLM, (*see* National Library of
      Medicine)
Uhrowczik, P.P., 171, *190*
UN (United Nations),
   CELADE (Latin American Demo-
      graphic Center), (*see* CELADE)
   FAO, (*see* FAO)
   Latin American information systems
      development, 251
   Unesco, (*see* Unesco)
   UNISIST, (*see* UNISIST)
UNAM, (*see* Autonomous National
   University of Mexico)
Unesco (United Nations Educational,
   Scientific, and Cultural
   Organization),
   Brazilian information systems, 254,
      255
   Latin American information systems
      development, 252
   NATIS, (*see* NATIS)
   UNISIST, (*see* UNISIST)
Union lists,
   serials holdings automation, 200
UNISIST,
   Latin America, 262
Unit costs, (*see* Costs)
Unit times,
   academic libraries, 11
United Kingdom,
   Latin American information systems
      development, 251

United Nations, (see UN)
United Nations Educational,
  Scientific, and Cultural
  Organization, (see Unesco)
University of California,
  library automation plan, 200
University of California at Santa
  Barbara,
  online training for end users, 234
University of California, Berkeley,
  branch libraries cost analysis, 10
  library costs study, 44
University of Cambridge,
  Computer Laboratory,
  automatic indexing, 99
University of Chicago,
  Graduate Library School,
  35th Annual Conference, 14
University of Florida at Gainesville,
  CASSM, (see CASSM)
University of Hawaii,
  online retrieval education, 231
University of Illinois,
  Information Retrieval Research
    Laboratory (IRRL),
    database research, 198
University of Kentucky,
  online retrieval education, 229-230
University of London,
  Mediatron, (see Mediatron)
University of Massachusetts,
  library automation research, 198
University of Minnesota,
  microcomputer data management
    system, 40
University of Pittsburgh,
  library automation research, 198
  library costs study, 44
  library materials use studies, 202
  TRAINER, (see TRAINER)
University of Texas,
  RFMS development, 159
University of Toronto,
  MARC format use, 199

University of Toronto Library
  Automation System, (see UTLAS)
Unruh, Betty, 221, 223, 224, 244
Updating,
  database management systems, 178
Urquhart, D.J., 14, 33, 62
Uruguay,
  Center for Scientific, Technical and
    Economic Documentation, 255
  CONICYT (National Council for
    Scientific and Technical
    Research), 255
  industrial information services, 258
  information systems and services,
    255
User aids,
  online retrieval, 227-229
User fees, 48-49
  online searching, 202
  online training sessions, 223-224
User interface,
  information retrieval experimental
    techniques, 108-109
  online retrieval by end users, 236
User needs, (see Information needs
  and uses)
User training, (see Education and
  training)
USSR,
  information dynamics in scientific
    fields, 15
Utility theory,
  indexing, 98-99
UTLAS (Univeristy of Toronto
  Library Automation System),
  Ontario network, 199
Uuttu, Leena-Kaarina, 234, 244
Valdes, Renata, 282
Valian, Virginia V., 88
Vallet, C.L., 86
Valls, Jaime, 282
Van Rijsbergen, C.J., 73, 93, 95, 102,
  105, 110, 112, 84, 90, 117, 118,
  120, 125, 126

Vantine, Carol, 48, *62*
Variable linguistic rules, 75
Vasu, Ellen Storey, 15, *19*
Vaughan, Patricia E., 200, *214*
Vector space models,
  information retrieval experimental
    techniques, 97
Vegh Villegas, Martha, 258, *274*
Venezuela,
  CONICIT (National Council for
    Scientific and Technological
    Research), 253
  information systems and services,
    253-254
  Network of Socio-Economic
    Information, 261
  SINASBI (National System of
    Library and Information
    Services), 254
  SINICYT (National System for
    Scientific and Technical
    Information), 253-254
Venkatesh, K., 13, *30*
Venn diagrams,
  online searching, 12
Vernimb, Carlo, 105, *90*, *126*
Verstiggel, Jean-Claude, 76, *90*
Vickers, Peter H., *62*
Vickery, Alina, 234, *243*, *244*
Videotex,
  library automation trends, 203
Virgo, Julie A., 15, *33*
Visual attention,
  human information processing
    related to information science, 77
Visual memory,
  human information processing
    related to information science, 77
Vladutz, George E., 100, *120*
Voigt, Melvin J., 195, *214*
Vollhardt, Cilly, 45, *63*
Von Bertalanffy, Ludwig, 4, *33*

Von Neumann architecture,
  information retrieval, 130-132
Von Neumann, John, *143*
Voos, Henry, 11, 15, *33*, *34*
Vrisou Van Eck, W.F.V., *91*
Vrooman, Hugh T., 193-204
Wainwright, Jane, 47, *63*
Wald, L.D., 132, *150*
Waldhart, Thomas J., 11, *34*
Waldstein, Robert K., 101, *124*
Walker, Gregory P.M., *19*
Wallentine, Virgil E., *188*
Walsh, Myles E., 171, 174, *190*
Walter, T.P., 16, *17*
Wanger, Judith, 41, 219-237, 220,
    223, 225, 227, 230, 236, *63*, *184*,
    244
Ward, William C., 74, *83*
Washington, D.C. online users' group,
  internship program, 232
Washington Library Network, (*see*
  WLN)
Water resources information,
  Latin America, 261
Waters, D.H., *32*
Waters, S.J., *190*
Watson, J.K., *143*, *144*
Wax, David M., 200, *214*
Weeding,
  identifier method, 78
Weeks, Gerald D., *81*
Wehr, L.A., *184*
Weighting,
  applications of theories and models,
    101-102
  automatic indexing performance, 99
  relevance based, 73
Weinberg, Gerald M., 4, *34*
Weisbrod, David L., 199, *215*
Weiser, Virginia, *237*
Weisgerber, David W., *211*
Weiss, Edward C., *91*

Welch, Helen M., 10, *34*
Wellisch, Hans H., *215*
Welsh, Alan, *87*
Wender, Ruth M., 6, *34*
Werdel, Judith A., 251, 259, *269*
West Germany, (*see* Federal Republic of Germany)
West, Martha W., 10, 38, 43, 196, 201, *34, 58, 63, 215*
Western Interstate Commission for Higher Education, (*see* WICHE)
Westmoreland, Guy, *184*
Wheelbarger, Johnny J., 198, *215*
White, D. Hywell, *90*
White, G. Travis, 11, *34*
White, Herbert S., 10, 201, 203, *34, 54, 63, 215*
White, Howard D., *215*
White, Lee J., 103, *120*
Whitehead, C.M.E., 38, *54*
Whitely, Susan E., *91*
Whitfield, Ronald M., *24, 208*
WICHE (Western Interstate Commission for Higher Education), network studies, 197
Wiedekehr, Robert, *60, 63*
WIERD system, vector space models, 97
Wigington, Ronald L., 153-182
Wilde, Daniel W., *63*
Wilkin, A.P., 44, *61, 63*
Williams, Gordon, 39, *63*
Williams, James G., 16, 197, *34, 209, 215*
Williams, Martha E., 15, 68, 109, 198, 199, 220, 228, *34, 91, 126, 184, 215*
Williams, P.W., 103
Williams, Tannis Magbeth, *91*
Wills, Gordon, 45, *63*
Wilson, John H., 10, 38, 49, *34, 63*
Wilson, William H., *87*

Windsor, D.A., *91*
Wiorkowski, Gabrielle K., 157, *190*
Wiorkowski, John J., 157, *190*
Wippich, Werner, *91*
Wish, John R., 42, *64*
Wish, Mary Ann, *64*
Withington, Frederic G., 183, *190*
Wittig, G.R., 14, 200, *34, 215*
WLN (Washington Library Network), authority system, 199
compared to RLIN and OCLC, 201
cooperation with RLIN, 203
costs, 40
OCLC impact, 197
WLN Participant, library automation literature, 195
Wolfe, J.N., 45, 47, *64*
Wolfendale, Garth L., *91*
Wolthausen, John, 14, *21*
Wong, Anita, 102, *124, 269*
Wong, Patrick, *22, 117*
Wood, Barbara L., *26*
Wood, F.E., 228, 231, 235, *184*
Woodward, A.M., 15, *35*
Wooster, Harold, 139, 200, *151, 215*
Word frequencies, semantic implications, 75
Worthen, Dennis B., 15, *35*
Worthy, R.M., *142*
Wyllys, Ronald E., 3, 10, 15, *35*
Yang, C.S., *124*
Yanovskii, V.I., *35*
Yasaki, Edward K., 172, *190*
Yau, Stephen S., 132, *151*
Yormark, Beatrice, *186*
Young, Ralph, *64*
Yovits, M.C., 73, 79, *91*
Yu, Clement T., 73, 93, 98, 102, 103, 105, *91, 116, 120, 123, 126, 127, 212*
Zaaiman, R.B., 45, *64*
Zais, Harriet W., *64*

Zamora, Pedro, 259, *282*
Zeidler, H. Ch., *147*
Zimmerman, Patricia J., 8, *35*, *127*
Zipf, George K., 75, *91*
Zuest, Pat, 199, *216*

Zunde, Pranas, 67-80, 68, 70, 72, *92*
Zweben, Stuart H., 75, *92*
1200 baud,
    searching costs, 42
3RIP system, 111

Introduction to KWOC Index

The following section is a KWOC (Keyword-out-of-Context) index to *ARIST* chapters for Volumes 1 through 14. It has been produced to assist users in locating specific chapters and author names for all *ARIST* volumes to date. As is the case with KWOC indexes, it sorts on all content words and titles (a stop-word list of articles, conjunctions, and other non-content words was used) and authors. The sort word is followed by the author(s) name(s) and the full citation.

KWOC Index of *ARIST* Titles

for Volumes 1-14

Abstracting
> Keenan, Stella. Abstracting and Indexing Services in Science and Technology, *ARIST* 4, p. 273.

Activities
> Adams, Scott; Werdel, Judith A. Cooperation in Information Activities through International Organizations. *ARIST* 10, p. 303.

Adams, Scott
> Adams, Scott; Werdel, Judith A. Cooperation in Information Activities through International Organizations. *ARIST* 10, p. 303.

ADI
> Cuadra, Carlos A. Introduction to the ADI Annual Review. *ARIST* 1, p. 1.

Adkinson, Burton W.
> Berninger, Douglas E.; Adkinson, Burton W. Interaction between the Public and Private Sectors in National Information Programs. *ARIST* 13, p. 3.

Aines, Andrew A.
> Aines, Andrew A.; Day, Melvin S. National Planning of Information Services. *ARIST* 10, p. 3.

Allen, Thomas J.
> Allen, Thomas J. Information Needs and Uses. *ARIST* 4, p. 3.

Alper, Bruce H.
> Alper, Bruce H. Library Automation. *ARIST* 10, p. 199.

Alsberg, Peter A.
> Bunch, Steve R.; Alsberg, Peter A. Computer Communication Networks. *ARIST* 12, p. 183.

America
> Saracevic, Tefko; Braga, Gilda; Quijano Solis, Alvaro. Information Systems In Latin America. *ARIST* 14, p. 249.

American Institute of Physics Staff
> Techniques for Publication and Distribution of Information. *ARIST* 2, p. 339.

Analysis

> Baxendale, Phyllis.   Content Analysis, Specification, and Control. *ARIST* 1, p. 71.
>
> Fairthorne, Robert A.   Content Analysis, Specification, and Control. *ARIST* 4, p. 73.
>
> Liston, David M., Jr.; Howder, Murray L.   Subject Analysis. *ARIST* 12, p. 81.
>
> Mick, Colin K.   Cost Analysis of Information Systems and Services. *ARIST* 14, p. 37.
>
> Sharp, John R.   Content Analysis, Specification, and Control. *ARIST* 2, p. 87.
>
> Taulbee, Orrin E.   Content Analysis, Specification, and Control. *ARIST* 3, p. 105.

Announcements

> van Dam, Andries; Michener, James C.   Hardware Developments and Product Announcements. *ARIST* 2, p. 187.

Annual

> Cuadra, Carlos A.   Introduction to the ADI Annual Review. *ARIST* 1, p. 1.

Application

> Beard, Joseph J.   Information Systems Application in Law. *ARIST* 6, p. 369.

Applications

> Baruch, Jordan J.   Information System Applications. *ARIST* 1, p. 255.
>
> Blumstein, Alfred.   Information Systems Applications in the Criminal Justice System. *ARIST* 7, p. 471.
>
> Caceres, Cesar A.; Weihrer, Anna Lea; Pulliam, Robert.   Information Science Applications in Medicine. *ARIST* 6, p. 325.
>
> Levy, Richard P.; Cammarn, Maxine R.   Information Systems Applications in Medicine. *ARIST* 3, p. 397.
>
> Raben, Joseph; Widmann, R.L.   Information Systems Applications in the Humanities. *ARIST* 7, p. 439.
>
> Silberman, Harry F.; Filep, Robert T.   Information Systems Applications in Education. *ARIST* 3, p. 357.
>
> Spring, William C., Jr.   Applications in Medicine. *ARIST* 2, p. 311.
>
> Vinsonhaler, John F.; Moon, Robert D.   Information Systems Applications in Education. *ARIST* 8, p. 277.

Architectures

> Hollaar, Lee A.   Unconventional Computer Architectures for Information Retrieval. *ARIST* 14, p. 129.

ARIST Staff

> *ARIST* Staff.   New Hardware Developments. *ARIST* 1, p. 191.

Artandi, Susan

> Artandi, Susan.   Document Description and Representation. *ARIST* 5, p. 143.

Aspects
>Atherton, Pauline; Greer, Roger. Professional Aspects of Information Science and Technology. *ARIST* 3, p. 329.
>Farradane, J. Professional Aspects of Information Science and Technology. *ARIST* 6, p. 399.
>Harvey, John F. Professional Aspects of Information Science and Technology. *ARIST* 2, p. 419.
>Shera, Jesse H.; McFarland, Anne S. Professional Aspects of Information Science and Technology. *ARIST* 4, p. 439.
>Taylor, Robert S. Professional Aspects of Information Science and Technology. *ARIST* 1, p. 15.

Atherton, Pauline
>Atherton, Pauline; Greer, Roger. Professional Aspects of Information Science and Technology. *ARIST* 3, p. 329.

Automated
>Bobrow, D.G.; Fraser, J.B.; Quillian, M.R. Automated Language Processing. *ARIST* 2, p. 161.
>Damerau, Fred J. Automated Language Processing. *ARIST* 11, p. 107.
>Kay, Martin; Sparck Jones, Karen. Automated Language Processing. *ARIST* 6, p. 141.
>Montgomery, Christine A. Automated Language Processing. *ARIST* 4, p. 145.
>Salton, Gerard. Automated Language Processing. *ARIST* 3, p. 169.
>Simmons, Robert F. Automated Language Processing. *ARIST* 1, p. 137.
>Walker, Donald E. Automated Language Processing. *ARIST* 8, p. 69.

Automation
>Alper, Bruce H. Library Automation. *ARIST* 10, p. 199.
>Avram, Henriette. Library Automation. *ARIST* 6, p. 171.
>Bierman, Kenneth J. Library Automation. *ARIST* 9, p. 123.
>Black, Donald V.; Farley, Earl A. Library Automation. *ARIST* 1, p. 273.
>Griffin, Hillis L. Automation of Technical Processes in Libraries. *ARIST* 3, p. 241.
>Grosch, Audrey N. Library Automation. *ARIST* 11, p. 225.
>Kilgour, Frederick G. Library Automation. *ARIST* 4, p. 305.
>Markuson, Barbara Evans. Automation in Libraries and Information Centers. *ARIST* 2, p. 255.
>Martin, Susan K. Library Automation. *ARIST* 7, p. 243.
>Parker, Ralph H. Library Automation. *ARIST* 5, p. 193.
>Reed, Mary Jane Pobst; Vrooman, Hugh T. Library Automation. *ARIST* 14, p. 193.
>Simmons, Peter. Library Automation. *ARIST* 8, p. 167.

Avram, Henriette
>Avram, Henriette. Library Automation. *ARIST* 6, p. 171.

Awareness
   Wente, Van A.; Young, Gifford A.   Current Awareness and Dissemination. *ARIST* 5, p. 259.
Ballou, Hubbard W.
   Ballou, Hubbard W.   Microform Technology. *ARIST* 8, p. 121.
Baruch, Jordan J.
   Baruch, Jordan J.   Information System Applications. *ARIST* 1, p. 255.
Bases
   Gechman, Marvin C.   Generation and Use of Machine-Readable Bibliographic Data Bases. *ARIST* 7, p. 323.
   Luedke, James A., Jr.; Kovacs, Gabor J.; Fried, John B.   Numeric Data Bases and Systems. *ARIST* 12, p. 119.
   Schipma, Peter B.   Generation and Uses of Machine-Readable Data Bases. *ARIST* 10, p. 237.
   Stern, Barrie T.   Evaluation and Design of Bibliographic Data Bases. *ARIST* 12, p. 3.
   Wilde, Daniel U.   Generation and Use of Machine-Readable Data Bases. *ARIST* 11, p. 267.
   Williams, Martha E.   Use of Machine-Readable Data Bases. *ARIST* 9, p. 221.
Batten, William E.
   Batten, William E.   Document Description and Representation, *ARIST* 8, p. 43.
Baxendale, Phyllis
   Baxendale, Phyllis.   Content Analysis, Specification, and Control. *ARIST* 1, p. 71.
Beard, Joseph J.
   Beard, Joseph J.   Information Systems Application in Law. *ARIST* 6, p. 369.
   Beard, Joseph J.   The Copyright Issue. *ARIST* 9, p. 381.
Bearman, Toni Carbo
   Bearman, Toni Carbo.   Secondary Information Systems and Services. *ARIST* 13, p. 179.
Becker, Joseph
   Becker, Joseph; Olsen, Wallace C.   Information Networks. *ARIST* 3, p. 289.
Bennett, John L.
   Bennett, John L.   The User Interface in Interactive Systems. *ARIST* 7, p. 159.
Berninger, Douglas E.
   Berninger, Douglas E.; Adkinson, Burton W.   Interaction between the Public and Private Sectors in National Information Programs. *ARIST* 13, p. 3.

Berul, Lawrence H.
    Berul, Lawrence H.   Document Retrieval. *ARIST* 4, p. 203.
Bibliographic
    Gechman, Marvin C.   Generation and Use of Machine-Readable Biblio-
        graphic Data Bases. *ARIST* 7, p. 323.
    Park, Margaret K.   Bibliographic and Information Processing Standards.
        ARIST 12, p. 59.
    Schmierer, Helen F.   Bibliographic Standards. *ARIST* 10, p. 105.
    Stern, Barrie T.   Evaluation and Design of Bibliographic Data Bases.
        ARIST 12, p. 3.
Bibliometrics
    Narin, Francis; Moll, Joy K.   Bibliometrics. *ARIST* 12, p. 35.
Bierman, Kenneth J.
    Bierman, Kenneth J.   Library Automation. *ARIST* 9, p. 123.
Billingsley, Alice
    Leimkuhler, Ferdinand F.; Billingsley, Alice.   Library and Information
        Center Management. *ARIST* 7, p. 499
Black, Donald V.
    Black, Donald V.; Farley, Earl A.   Library Automation. *ARIST* 1, p.
        273
Blumstein, Alfred
    Blumstein, Alfred.   Information Systems Applications in the Criminal
        Justice System. *ARIST* 7, p. 471
Bobrow, D.G.
    Bobrow, D.G.; Fraser, J.B.; Quillian, M.R.   Automated Language Pro-
        cessing. *ARIST* 2, p. 161
Borko, Harold
    Borko, Harold.   Design of Information Systems and Services. *ARIST*
        2, p. 35.
Bourne, Charles P.
    Bourne, Charles P.   Evaluation of Indexing Systems. *ARIST* 1, p. 171
Braga, Gilda
    Saracevic, Tefko; Braga, Gilda; Quijano Solis, Alvaro.   Information Sys-
        tems In Latin America. *ARIST* 14, p. 249
Brandhorst, Wesley T.
    Brandhorst, Wesley T.; Eckert, Philip F.   Document Retrieval and Dis-
        semination Systems. *ARIST* 7, p. 379
Brown, Patricia L.
    Brown, Patricia L.; Jones, Shirli O.   Document Retrieval and Dissemina-
        tion in Libraries and Information Centers. *ARIST* 3, p. 263
Buckland, Michael K.
    Buckland, Michael K.   The Management of Libraries and Information
        Centers. *ARIST* 9, p. 335

Budgeting
    Wilson, John H., Jr.   Costs, Budgeting, and Economics of Information
        Processing. *ARIST* 7, p. 39
Bunch, Steve R.
    Bunch, Steve R.; Alsberg, Peter A.   Computer Communication Net-
        works. *ARIST* 12, p. 183
Butler, Brett B.
    Spigai, Francis G.; Butler, B.   Micrographics. *ARIST* 11, p. 59
Caceres, Cesar A.
    Caceres, Cesar A.; Weihrer, Anna Lea; Pulliam, Robert.   Information
        Science Applications in Medicine. *ARIST* 6, p. 325
Cammarn, Maxine R.
    Levy, Richard P.; Cammarn, Maxine R.   Information Systems Applica-
        tions in Medicine. *ARIST* 3, p. 397
Carlson, Walter M.
    Carlson, Walter M.   Privacy. *ARIST* 12, p. 279
Cartridges
    Kletter, Richard C.; Hudson, Heather.   Video Cartridges and Cassettes.
        ARIST 7, p. 197
Cassettes
    Kletter, Richard C.; Hudson, Heather.   Video Cartridges and Cassettes.
        ARIST 7, p. 197
Center
    Holm, Bart E.   Library and Information Center Management. *ARIST* 5,
        p. 353
    Leimkuhler, Ferdinand F.; Billingsley, Alice.   Library and Information
        Center Management. *ARIST* 7, p. 499
    Murdock, John; Sherrod, John.   Library and Information Center Man-
        agement. *ARIST* 11, p. 381
    Wasserman, Paul; Daniel, Evelyn.   Library and Information Center
        Management. *ARIST* 4, p. 405
Centers
    Brown, Patricia L.; Jones, Shirli O.   Document Retrieval and Dissemina-
        tion in Libraries and Information Centers. *ARIST* 3, p. 263
    Buckland, Michael K.   The Management of Libraries and Information
        Centers. *ARIST* 9, p. 335
    Markuson, Barbara Evans.   Automation in Libraries and Information
        Centers. *ARIST* 2, p. 255
    Simpson, G.S., Jr.; Flanagan, Carolyn.   Information Centers and
        Services. *ARIST* 1, p. 305
Chartrand, Robert L.
    Chartrand, Robert L.   Information Science in the Legislative Process.
        ARIST 11, p. 299

Chemical
>	Rush, James E. Handling Chemical Structure Information. *ARIST* 13, p. 209
>	Tate, F.A. Handling Chemical Compounds in Information Systems. *ARIST* 2, p. 285

Chung-Shu, Yang
>	Chung-Shu, Yang. Design and Evaluation of File Structures. *ARIST* 13, p. 125

Cleveland, Donald B.
>	Shera, Jesse H.; Cleveland, Donald B. History and Foundations of Information Science. *ARIST* 12, p. 249

Cleverdon, Cyril W.
>	Cleverdon, Cyril W. Design and Evaluation of Information Systems. *ARIST* 6, p. 41

Climenson, W. Douglas
>	Climenson, W. Douglas. File Organization and Search Techniques. *ARIST* 1, p. 107

Communication
>	Bunch, Steve R.; Alsberg, Peter A. Computer Communication Networks. *ARIST* 12, p. 183
>	Davis, Ruth M. Man-Machine Communication. *ARIST* 1, p. 221
>	Licklider, J.C.R. Man-Computer Communication. *ARIST* 3, p. 201
>	Mills, R.G. Man-Machine Communication and Problem Solving. *ARIST* 2, p. 223
>	Samuelson, Kjell. International Information Transfer and Network Communication. *ARIST* 6, p. 277

Communications
>	Dunn, Donald A. Communications Technology. *ARIST* 10, p. 165
>	Simms, Robert L., Jr.; Fuchs, Edward. Communications Technology. *ARIST* 5, p. 113

Compounds
>	Tate, F.A. Handling Chemical Compounds in Information Systems. *ARIST* 2, p. 285

Computer
>	Bunch, Steve R.; Alsberg, Peter A. Computer Communication Networks. *ARIST* 12, p. 183
>	Hollaar, Lee A. Unconventional Computer Architectures for Information Retrieval. *ARIST* 14, p. 129
>	Huskey, Harry D. Computer Technology. *ARIST* 5, p. 73
>	Licklider, J.C.R. Man-Computer Communication. *ARIST* 3, p. 201
>	Long, Philip L. Computer Technology-An Update. *ARIST* 11, p. 211
>	Terrant, Seldon W. The Computer and Publishing. *ARIST* 10, p. 273

Content
    Baxendale, Phyllis.   Content Analysis, Specification, and Control. *ARIST* 1, p. 71
    Fairthorne, Robert A.   Content Analysis, Specification, and Control. *ARIST* 4, p. 73
    Sharp, John R.   Content Analysis, Specification, and Control. *ARIST* 2, p. 87
    Taulbee, Orrin E.   Content Analysis, Specification, and Control. *ARIST* 3, p. 105
Control
    Baxendale, Phyllis.   Content Analysis, Specification, and Control. *ARIST* 1, p. 71
    Fairthorne, Robert A.   Content Analysis, Specification, and Control. *ARIST* 4, p. 73
    Sharp, John R.   Content Analysis, Specification, and Control. *ARIST* 2, p. 87
    Taulbee, Orrin E.   Content Analysis, Specification, and Control. *ARIST* 3, p. 105
Cooper, Michael D.
    Cooper, Michael D.   The Economics of Information. *ARIST* 8, p. 5
Cooperation
    Adams, Scott; Werdel, Judith A.   Cooperation in Information Activities through International Organizations. *ARIST* 10, p. 303
Copyright
    Beard, Joseph J.   The Copyright Issue. *ARIST* 9, p. 381
    Weil, Ben H.   Copyright Developments. *ARIST* 10, p. 359
Cost
    Mick, Colin K.   Cost Analysis of Information Systems and Services. *ARIST* 14, p. 37
Costs
    Wilson, John H., Jr.   Costs, Budgeting, and Economics of Information Processing. *ARIST* 7, p. 39
Crane, Diana
    Crane, Diana.   Information Needs and Uses. *ARIST* 6, p. 3
Crawford, Susan
    Crawford, Susan.   Information Needs and Uses. *ARIST* 13, p. 61
Creps, John E., Jr.
    Grattidge, Walter; Creps, John E., Jr.   Information Systems in Engineering. *ARIST* 13, p. 297
Criminal
    Blumstein, Alfred.   Information Systems Applications in the Criminal Justice System. *ARIST* 7, p. 471
Cuadra, Carlos A.
    Cuadra, Carlos A.   Introduction to the ADI Annual Review. *ARIST* 1, p. 1

Current

Wente, Van A.; Young, Gifford A.   Current Awareness and Dissemination. *ARIST* 5, p. 259

Damerau, Fred J.

Damerau, Fred J.   Automated Language Processing. *ARIST* 11, p. 107

Daniel, Evelyn

Wasserman, Paul; Daniel, Evelyn.   Library and Information Center Management. *ARIST* 4, p. 405

Data

Gechman, Marvin C.   Generation and Use of Machine-Readable Bibliographic Data Bases. *ARIST* 7, p. 323

Luedke, James A., Jr.; Kovacs, Gabor J.; Fried, John B.   Numeric Data Bases and Systems. *ARIST* 12, p. 119

Minker, Jack; Sable, Jerome. File Organization and Data Management. *ARIST* 2, p. 123

Schipma, Peter B.   Generation and Uses of Machine-Readable Data Bases. *ARIST* 10, p. 237

Stern, Barrie T.   Evaluation and Design of Bibliographic Data Bases. *ARIST* 12, p. 3

Wilde, Daniel U.   Generation and Use of Machine-Readable Data Bases. *ARIST* 11, p. 267

Williams, Martha E.   Use of Machine-Readable Data Bases. *ARIST* 9, p. 221

Database

Huffenberger, Michael A.; Wigington, Ronald L.   Database Management Systems. *ARIST* 14, p. 153

Davis, Ruth M.

Davis, Ruth M.   Man-Machine Communication. *ARIST* 1, p. 221

Day, Melvin S.

Aines, Andrew A.; Day, Melvin S.   National Planning of Information Services. *ARIST* 10, p. 3

Debons, Anthony

Debons, Anthony; Montgomery, K. Leon.   Design and Evaluation of Information Systems. *ARIST* 9, p. 25

Description

Artandi, Susan.   Document Description and Representation. *ARIST* 5, p. 143

Batten, William E.   Document Description and Representation. *ARIST* 8, p. 43

Harris, Jessica L.   Document Description and Representation. *ARIST* 9, p. 81

Richmond, Phyllis A.   Document Description and Representation. *ARIST* 7, p. 73

Vickery, Brian C.   Document Description and Representation. *ARIST* 6, p. 113

Design

    Borko, Harold.   Design of Information Systems and Services. *ARIST* 2, p. 35

    Chung-Shu, Yang.   Design and Evaluation of File Structures. *ARIST* 13, p. 125

    Cleverdon, Cyril W.   Design and Evaluation of Information Systems. *ARIST* 6, p. 41

    Debons, Anthony; Montgomery, J. Leon.   Design and Evaluation of Information Systems. *ARIST* 9, p. 25

    Katter, Robert V.   Design and Evaluation of Information Systems. *ARIST* 4, p. 31

    King, Donald W.   Design and Evaluation of Information Systems. *ARIST* 3, p. 61

    Lancaster, F. Wilfrid; Gillespie, Constantine J.   Design and Evaluation of Information Systems. *ARIST* 5, p. 33

    Stern, Barrie T.   Evaluation and Design of Bibliographic Data Bases. *ARIST* 12, p. 3

    Swanson, Rowena Weiss.   Design and Evaluation of Information Systems. *ARIST* 10, p. 43

    Wyllys, Ronald E.   System Design-Principles and Techniques. *ARIST* 14, p. 3

Developments

    ARIST Staff.   New Hardware Developments. *ARIST* 1, p. 191

    van Dam, Andries; Michener, James C.   Hardware Developments and Product Announcements. *ARIST* 2, p. 187

    Weil, Ben H.   Copyright Developments. *ARIST* 10, p. 359

Dissemination

    Brandhorst, Wesley T.; Eckert, Philip F.   Document Retrieval and Dissemination Systems. *ARIST* 7, p. 379

    Brown, Patricia L.; Jones, Shirli O.   Document Retrieval and Dissemination in Libraries and Information Centers. *ARIST* 3, p. 263

    Housman, Edward M.   Selective Dissemination of Information. *ARIST* 8, p. 221

    Landau, Herbert B.   Document Dissemination. *ARIST* 4, p. 229

    Magnino, Joseph J., Jr.   Document Retrieval and Dissemination. *ARIST* 6, p. 219

    Wente, Van A.; Young, Gifford A.   Current Awareness and Dissemination. *ARIST* 5, p. 259

Distribution

    American Institute of Physics Staff.   Techniques for Publication and Distribution of Information. *ARIST* 2, p. 339

    Doebler, Paul D.   Publication and Distribution of Information. *ARIST* 5, p. 223

    Kuney, Joseph H.   Publication and Distribution of Information. *ARIST* 3, p. 31

Document
- Artandi, Susan.   Document Description and Representation. *ARIST* 5, p. 143
- Batten, William E.   Document Description and Representation. *ARIST* 8, p. 43
- Berul, Lawrence H.   Document Retrieval. *ARIST* 4, p. 203
- Brandhorst, Wesley T.; Eckert, Philip F.   Document Retrieval and Dissemination Systems. *ARIST* 7, p. 379
- Brown, Patricia L.; Jones, Shirli O.   Document Retrieval and Dissemination in Libraries and Information Centers. *ARIST* 3, p. 263
- Harris, Jessica L.   Document Description and Representation. *ARIST* 9, p. 81
- Landau, Herbert B.   Document Dissemination. *ARIST* 4, p. 229
- Magnino, Joseph J., Jr.   Document Retrieval and Dissemination. *ARIST* 6, p. 219
- Richmond, Phyllis A.   Document Description and Representation. *ARIST* 7, p. 73
- Summit, Roger K.; Firschein, Oscar. Document Retrieval Systems and Techniques. *ARIST* 9, p. 285
- Vickery, Brian C.   Document Description and Representation. *ARIST* 6, p. 113

Doebler, Paul D.
- Doebler, Paul D.   Publication and Distribution of Information. *ARIST* 5, p. 223

Dunn, Donald A.
- Dunn, Donald A.   Communications Technology. *ARIST* 10, p. 165

Eckert, Philip F.
- Brandhorst, Wesley T.; Eckert, Philip F.   Document Retrieval and Dissemination Systems. *ARIST* 7, p. 379

Economics
- Cooper, Michael D.   The Economics of Information. *ARIST* 8, p. 5
- Hindle, Anthony; Raper, Diane.   The Economics of Information. *ARIST* 11, p. 27
- Wilson, John H., Jr.   Costs, Budgeting, and Economics of Information Processing. *ARIST* 7, p. 39

Economist's
- Spence, A. Michael.   An Economist's View of Information. *ARIST* 9, p. 57

Education
- Harmon, Glynn.   Information Science Education and Training. *ARIST* 11, p. 347
- Jahoda, Gerald.   Education for Infomation Science. *ARIST* 8, p. 321
- Silberman, Harry F.; Filep, Robert T.   Information Systems Applications in Education. *ARIST* 3, p. 357

Education (Continued)

Vinsonhaler, John F.; Moon, Robert D.   Information Systems Applications in Education. *ARIST* 8, p. 277

Wanger, Judith.   Education and Training for Online Systems. *ARIST* 14, p. 219

Empirical

Zunde, Pranas; Gehl, John.   Empirical Foundations of Information Science. *ARIST* 14, p. 67

Engineering

Grattidge, Walter; Creps, John E., Jr.   Information Systems in Engineering. *ARIST* 13, p. 297

European

Tomberg, Alex.   European Information Networks. *ARIST* 12, p. 219

Evaluation

Bourne, Charles P.   Evaluation of Indexing Systems. *ARIST* 1, p. 171

Chung-Shu, Yang.   Design and Evaluation of File Strucutres. *ARIST* 13, p. 125

Cleverdon, Cyril W.   Design and Evaluation of Information Systems. *ARIST* 6, p. 41

Debons, Anthony; Montgomery, K. Leon.   Design and Evaluation of Information Systems. *ARIST* 9, p. 25

Katter, Robert V.   Design and Evaluation of Information Systems. *ARIST* 4, p. 31

King, Donald W.   Design and Evaluation of Information Systems. *ARIST* 3, p. 61

Lancaster, F. Wilfrid; Gillespie, Constantine J.   Design and Evaluation of Information Systems. *ARIST* 5, p. 33

Rees, Alan M.   Evaluation of Information Systems and Services. *ARIST* 2, p. 63

Stern, Barrie T.   Evaluation and Design of Bibliographic Data Bases. *ARIST* 12, p. 3

Swanson, Rowena Weiss.   Design and Evaluation of Information Systems. *ARIST* 10, p. 43

Experimental

McGill, Michael J.; Huitfeldt, Jennifer.   Experimental Techniques of Information Retrieval. *ARIST* 14, p. 93

Fairthorne, Robert A.

Fairthorne, Robert A.   Content Analysis, Specification, and Control. *ARIST* 4, p. 73

Farley, Earl A.

Black, Donald V.; Farley, Earl A.   Library Automation. *ARIST* 1, p. 273

Farradane, J.
    Farradane, J.   Professional Aspects of Information Science and Technology. *ARIST* 6, p. 399
Fife, Dennis
    Marron, Beatrice; Fife, Dennis.   Online Systems-Techniques and Services. *ARIST* 11, p. 163
File
    Chung-Shu, Yang.   Design and Evaluation of File Structures. *ARIST* 13, p. 125
    Climenson, W. Douglas.   File Organization and Search Techniques. *ARIST* 1, p. 107
    Minker, Jack; Sable, Jerome.   File Organization and Data Management. *ARIST* 2, p. 123
    Senko, Michael E.   File Organization and Management Information Systems. *ARIST* 4, p. 111
Filep, Robert T.
    Silberman, Harry F.; Filep, Robert T.   Information Systems Applications in Education. *ARIST* 3, p. 357
Files
    Meadow, Charles T.; Meadow, Harriet R.   Organization, Maintenance and Search of Machine Files. *ARIST* 5, p. 169
    Shoffner, Ralph M.   Organization, Maintenance and Search of Machine Files. *ARIST* 3, p. 137
Firschein, Oscar
    Summit, Roger K.; Firschein, Oscar.   Document Retrieval Systems and Techniques. *ARIST* 9, p. 285
Flanagan, Carolyn
    Simpson, G.S., Jr.; Flanagan, Carolyn.   Information Centers and Services. *ARIST* 1, p. 305
Foundations
    Shera, Jesse H.; Cleveland, Donald B.   History and Foundations of Information Science. *ARIST* 12, p. 249
    Zunde, Pranas; Gehl, John.   Empirical Foundations of Information Science. *ARIST* 14, p. 67
Fraser, J.B.
    Bobrow, D.G.; Fraser, J.B.; Quillian, M.R.   Automated Language Processing. *ARIST* 2, p. 161
Freeman, James E.
    Freeman, James E.; Katz, Ruth M.   Information Marketing. *ARIST* 13, p. 37
Fried, John B.
    Luedke, James A., Jr.; Kovacs, Gabor J.; Fried, John B.   Numeric Data Bases and Systems. *ARIST* 12, p. 119

Fuchs, Edward
    Simms, Robert L., Jr.; Fuchs, Edward.   Communications Technology,
        ARIST 5, p. 113
Gannet, Elwood K.
    Gannet, Elwood K.   Primary Publication Systems and Services. *ARIST*
        8, p. 243
Garvey, William D.
    Lin, Nan; Garvey, William D.   Information Needs and Uses. *ARIST* 7,
        p. 5
Gechman, Marvin C.
    Gechman, Marvin C.   Generation and Use of Machine-Readable Biblio-
        graphic Data Bases. *ARIST* 7, p. 323
Gehl, John
    Zunde, Pranas; Gehl, John.   Empirical Foundations of Information
        Science. *ARIST* 14, p. 67
Generation
    Gechman, Marvin C.   Generation and Use of Machine-Readable Biblio-
        graphic Data Bases. *ARIST* 7, p. 323
    Schipma, Peter B.   Generation and Uses of Machine-Readable Data
        Bases. *ARIST* 10, p. 237
    Wilde, Daniel U.   Generation and Use of Machine-Readable Data Bases.
        ARIST 11, p. 267
Gillespie, Constantine J.
    Lancaster F. Wilfrid; Gillespie, Constantine J.   Design and Evaluation
        of Information Systems. *ARIST* 5, p. 33
Governments
    Hearle, Edward F.R.   Information Systems in State and Local Govern-
        ments. *ARIST* 5, p. 325
Grattidge, Walter
    Grattidge, Walter; Creps, John E., Jr.   Information Systems in Engi-
        neering. *ARIST* 13, p. 297
Greer, Roger
    Atherton, Pauline; Greer, Roger.   Professional Aspects of Information
        Science and Technology. *ARIST* 3, p. 329
Griffin, Hillis L.
    Griffin, Hillis L.   Automation of Technical Processes in Libraries.
        ARIST 3, p. 241
Grosch, Audrey N.
    Grosch, Audrey N.   Library Automation. *ARIST* 11, p. 225
Hammer, Donald P.
    Hammer, Donald P.   National Information Issues and Trends. *ARIST*
        2, p. 385

Handling

Rush, James E.   Handling Chemical Structure Information. *ARIST* 13, p. 209

Tate, F.A.   Handling Chemical Compounds in Information Systems. *ARIST* 2, p. 285

Hardware

ARIST Staff, New Hardware Developments. *ARIST* 1, p. 191

van Dam, Andries; Michener, James C.   Hardware Developments and Product Announcements. *ARIST* 2, p. 187

Harmon, Glynn

Harmon, Glynn.   Information Science Education and Training. *ARIST* 11, p. 347

Harris, Jessica L.

Harris, Jessica L.   Document Description and Representation. *ARIST* 9, p. 81

Harvey, John F.

Harvey, John F.   Professional Aspects of Information Science and Technology. *ARIST* 2, p. 419

Hearle, Edward F.R.

Hearle, Edward F.R.   Information Systems in State and Local Governments. *ARIST* 5, p. 325

Herner, Mary

Herner, Saul; Herner, Mary.   Information Needs and Uses in Science and Technology. *ARIST* 2, p. 1

Herner, Saul

Herner, Saul; Herner, Mary.   Information Needs and Uses in Science and Technology. *ARIST* 2, p. 1

Hersey, David F.

Hersey, David F.   Information Systems for Research in Progress. *ARIST* 13, p. 263

Hindle, Anthony

Hindle, Anthony; Raper, Diane.   The Economics of Information. *ARIST* 11, p. 27

History

Shera, Jesse H.; Cleveland, Donald B.   History and Foundations of Information Science. *ARIST* 12, p. 249

Hollaar, Lee A.

Hollaar, Lee A.   Unconventional Computer Architectures for Information Retrieval. *ARIST* 14, p. 129

Holm, Bart E.

Holm, Bart E.   Library and Information Center Management. *ARIST* 5, p. 353

Holm, Bart E. (Continued)
Holm, Bart E.   National Issues and Problems. *ARIST* 11, p. 5
Housman, Edward M.
Housman, Edward M.   Selective Dissemination of Information. *ARIST*
8, p. 221
Howder, Murray L.
Liston, David M., Jr.; Howder, Murray L.   Subject Analysis. *ARIST* 12,
p. 81
Hudson, Heather
Kletter, Richard C.; Hudson, Heather.   Video Cartridges and Cassettes.
ARIST 7, p. 197
Huffenberger, Michael A.
Huffenberger, Michael A.; Wigington, Ronald L.   Database Manage-
ment Systems. *ARIST* 14, p. 153
Huitfeldt, Jennifer
McGill, Michael J.; Huitfeldt, Jennifer.   Experimental Techniques of
Information Retrieval. *ARIST* 14, p. 93
Humanities
Raben, Joseph; Widmann, R.L.   Information Systems Applications in
the Humanities. *ARIST* 7, p. 439
Huskey, Harry D.
Huskey, Harry D.   Computer Technology. *ARIST* 5, p. 73
Indexing
Bourne, Charles P.   Evaluation of Indexing Systems. *ARIST* 1, p. 171
Keenan, Stella.   Abstracting and Indexing Services in Science and Tech-
nology. *ARIST* 4, p. 273
Information
Adams, Scott; Werdel, Judith A.   Cooperation in Information Activi-
ties through International Organizations. *ARIST* 10, p. 303
Aines, Andrew A.; Day, Melvin S.   National Planning of Information
Services. *ARIST* 10, p. 3
Allen, Thomas J.   Information Needs and Uses. *ARIST* 4, p. 3
American Institute of Physics Staff.   Techniques for Publication and
Distribution of Information. *ARIST* 2, p. 339
Atherton, Pauline; Greer, Roger.   Professional Aspects of Information
Science and Technology. *ARIST* 3, p. 329
Baruch, Jordan J.   Information System Applications. *ARIST* 1, p. 255
Beard, Joseph J.   Information Systems Application in Law. *ARIST* 6,
p. 369
Bearman, Toni Carbo.   Secondary Information Systems and Services.
ARIST 13, p. 179
Becker, Joseph; Olsen, Wallace C.   Information Networks. *ARIST* 3,
p. 289
Berninger, Douglas E.; Adkinson, Burton W.   Interaction between the
Public and Private Sectors in National Information Programs. *ARIST*
13, p. 3

Information (Continued)

Blumstein, Alfred.   Information Systems Applications in the Criminal Justice System. *ARIST* 7, p. 471

Borko, Harold.   Design of Information Systems and Services. *ARIST* 2, p. 35

Brown, Patricia L.; Jones, Shirli O.   Document Retrieval and Dissemination in Libraries and Information Centers. *ARIST* 3, p. 263

Buckland, Michael K.   The Management of Libraries and Information Centers. *ARIST* 9, p. 335

Caceres, Cesar A.; Weihrer, Anna Lea; Pulliam, Robert.   Information Science Applications in Medicine. *ARIST* 6, p. 325

Chartrand, Robert L.   Information Science in the Legislative Process. *ARIST* 11, p. 299

Cleverdon, Cyril W.   Design and Evaluation of Information Systems. *ARIST* 6, p. 41

Cooper, Michael D.   The Economics of Information. *ARIST* 8, p. 5

Crane, Diana.   Information Needs and Uses. *ARIST* 6, p. 3

Crawford, Susan.   Information Needs and Uses. *ARIST* 13, p. 61

Debons, Anthony; Montgomery, K. Leon.   Design and Evaluation of Information Systems. *ARIST* 9, p. 25

Doebler, Paul D.   Publication and Distribution of Information. *ARIST* 5, p. 223

Farradane, J.   Professional Aspects of Information Science and Technology. *ARIST* 6, p. 399

Freeman, James E.; Katz, Ruth M.   Information Marketing. *ARIST* 13, p. 37

Grattidge, Walter; Creps, John E., Jr.   Information Systems in Engineering. *ARIST* 13, p. 297

Hammer, Donald P.   National Information Issues and Trends. *ARIST* 2, p. 385

Harmon, Glynn.   Information Science Education and Training. *ARIST* 11, p. 347

Harvey, John F.   Professional Aspects of Information Science and Technology. *ARIST* 2, p. 419

Hearle, Edward F.R.   Information Systems in State and Local Governments. *ARIST* 5, p. 325

Herner, Saul; Herner, Mary.   Information Needs and Uses in Science and Technology. *ARIST* 2, p. 1

Hersey, David F.   Information Systems for Research in Progress. *ARIST* 13, p. 263

Hindle, Anthony; Raper, Diane.   The Economics of Information. *ARIST* 11, p. 27

Hollaar, Lee A.   Unconventional Computer Architectures for Information Retrieval. *ARIST* 14, p. 129

Information (Continued)

Holm, Bart E.   Library and Information Center Management. *ARIST* 5, p. 353

Housman, Edward M.   Selective Dissemination of Information. *ARIST* 8, p. 221

Jahoda, Gerald.   Education for Information Science. *ARIST* 8, p. 321

Katter, Robert V.   Design and Evaluation of Information Systems. *ARIST* 4, p. 31

King, Donald W.   Design and Evaluation of Information Systems. *ARIST* 3, p. 61

Kuney, Joseph H.   Publication and Distribution of Information. *ARIST* 3, p. 31

Lancaster, F. Wilfrid; Gillespie, Constantine J.   Design and Evaluation of Information Systems. *ARIST* 5, p. 33

Leimkuhler, Ferdinand F.; Billingsley, Alice.   Library and Information Center Management. *ARIST* 7, p. 499

Levy, Richard P.; Cammarn, Maxine R.   Information Systems Applications in Medicine. *ARIST* 3, p. 397

Lin, Nan; Garvey, William D.   Information Needs and Uses. *ARIST* 7, p. 5

Lipetz, Ben-Ami.   Information Needs and Uses. *ARIST* 5, p. 3

Lorentz, John G.   International Transfer of Information. *ARIST* 4, p. 379

Markuson, Barbara Evans.   Automation in Libraries and Information Centers. *ARIST* 2, p. 255

Martyn, John.   Information Needs and Uses. *ARIST* 9, p. 3

McGill, Michael J.; Huitfeldt, Jennifer.   Experimental Techniques of Information Retrieval. *ARIST* 14, p. 93

Menzel, Herbert.   Information Needs and Uses in Science and Technology. *ARIST* 1, p. 41

Mick, Colin K.   Cost Analysis of Information Systems and Services. *ARIST* 14, p. 37

Miller, Ronald F.; Tighe, Ruth L.   Library and Information Networks. *ARIST* 9, p. 173

Murdock, John; Sherrod, John.   Library and Information Center Management. *ARIST* 11, p. 381

Olson, Edwin E.; Shank, Russell; Olsen, Harold A.   Library and Information Networks. *ARIST* 7, p. 279

Overhage, Carl F.J.   Information Networks. *ARIST* 4, p. 339

Paisley, William J.   Information Needs and Uses. *ARIST* 3, p. 1

Park, Margaret K.   Bibliographic and Information Processing Standards. *ARIST* 12, p. 59

Parker, Edwin B.   Information and Society. *ARIST* 8, p. 345

Parkins, Phyllis V.; Kennedy, H.E.   Secondary Information Services. *ARIST* 6, p. 247

Information (Continued)

Prywes, Noah S.; Smith, Diane Pirog.   Organization of Information. *ARIST* 7, p. 103

Raben, Joseph; Widmann, R.L.   Information Systems Applications in the Humanities. *ARIST* 7, p. 439

Rees, Alan M.   Evaluation of Information Systems and Services. *ARIST* 2, p. 63

Rush, James E.   Handling Chemical Structure Information. *ARIST* 13, p. 209

Samuelson, Kjell.   International Information Transfer and Network Communication. *ARIST* 6, p. 277

Saracevic, Tefko; Braga, Gilda; Quijano Solis, Alvaro.   Information Systems In Latin America. *ARIST* 14, p. 249

Senko, Michael E.   File Organization and Management Information Systems. *ARIST* 4, p. 111

Shera, Jesse H.; Cleveland, Donald B.   History and Foundations of Information Science. *ARIST* 12, p. 249

Shera, Jesse H.; McFarland, Anne S.   Professional Aspects of Information Science and Technology. *ARIST* 4, p. 439

Sherrod, John.   National Information Issues and Trends. *ARIST* 1, p. 337

Silberman, Harry F.; Filep, Robert T.   Information Systems Applications in Education. *ARIST* 3, p. 357

Simpson, G.S., Jr.; Flanagan, Carolyn.   Information Centers and Services. *ARIST* 1, p. 305

Spence, A. Michael.   An Economist's View of Information. *ARIST* 9, p. 57

Swanson, Rowena Weiss.   Design and Evaluation of Information Systems. *ARIST* 10, p. 43

Tate, F.A.   Handling Chemical Compounds in Information Systems. *ARIST* 2, p. 285

Taylor, Robert S.   Professional Aspects of Information Science and Technology. *ARIST* 1, p. 15

Tomberg, Alex.   European Information Networks. *ARIST* 12, p. 219

Vinsonhaler, John F.; Moon, Robert D.   Information Systems Applications in Education. *ARIST* 8, p. 277

Wasserman, Paul; Daniel, Evelyn.   Library and Information Center Management. *ARIST* 4, p. 405

Weiss, Stanley D.   Management Information Systems. *ARIST* 5, p. 299

Wilson, John H., Jr.   Costs, Budgeting, and Economics of Information Processing. *ARIST* 7, p. 39

Zunde, Pranas; Gehl, John.   Empirical Foundations of Information Science. *ARIST* 14, p. 67

Interaction
> Berninger, Douglas E.; Adkinson, Burton W.   Interaction between the Public and Private Sectors in National Information Programs. *ARIST* 13, p. 3

Interactive
> Bennett, John L.   The User Interface in Interactive Systems. *ARIST* 7, p. 159

> Martin, Thomas H.   The User Interface in Interactive Systems. *ARIST* 8, p. 203

Interface
> Bennett, John L.   The User Interface in Interactive Systems. *ARIST* 7, p. 159

> Martin, Thomas H.   The User Interface in Interactive Systems. *ARIST* 8, p. 203

International
> Adams, Scott; Werdel, Judith A.   Cooperation in Information Activities through International Organizations. *ARIST* 10, p. 303

> Lorenz, John G.   International Transfer of Information. *ARIST* 4, p. 379

> Samuelson, Kjell.   International Information Transfer and Network Communication. *ARIST* 6, p. 277

Introduction
> Cuadra, Carlos A.   Introduction to the ADI Annual Review. *ARIST* 1, p. 1

Issue
> Beard, Joseph J.   The Copyright Issue. *ARIST* 9, p. 381

> Hammer, Donald P.   National Information Issues and Trends. *ARIST* 2, p. 385

> Holm, Bart E.   National Issues and Problems. *ARIST* 11, p. 5

> Sherrod, John.   National Information Issues and Trends. *ARIST* 1, p. 337

Jahoda, Gerald
> Jahoda, Gerald.   Education for Information Science. *ARIST* 8, p. 321

Jones, Shirli O.
> Brown, Patricia L.; Jones, Shirli O.   Document Retrieval and Dissemination in Libraries and Information Centers. *ARIST* 3, p. 263

Justice
> Blumstein, Alfred.   Information Systems Applications in the Criminal Justice System. *ARIST* 7, p. 471

Katter, Robert V.
> Katter, Robert V.   Design and Evaluation of Information Systems. *ARIST* 4, p. 31

Katz, Ruth M.
> Freeman, James E.; Katz, Ruth M.   Information Marketing. *ARIST* 13, p. 37

Kay, Martin
    Kay, Martin; Sparck Jones, Karen.   Automated Language Processing. *ARIST* 6, p. 141
Keenan, Stella
    Keenan, Stella.   Abstracting and Indexing Services in Science and Technology. *ARIST* 4, p. 273
Kennedy, H.E.
    Parkins, Phyllis V.; Kennedy, H.E.   Secondary Information Services. *ARIST* 6, p. 247
Kilgour, Frederick G.
    Kilgour, Frederick G.   Library Automation. *ARIST* 4, p. 305
King, Donald W.
    King, Donald W.   Design and Evaluation of Information Systems. *ARIST* 3, p. 61
Kletter, Richard C.
    Kletter, Richard C.; Hudson, Heather.   Video Cartridges and Cassettes. *ARIST* 7, p. 197
Kovacs, Gabor J.
    Luedke, James A., Jr.; Kovacs, Gabor J.; Fried, John R.   Numeric Data Bases and Systems. *ARIST* 12, p. 119
Kuney, Joseph H.
    Kuney, Joseph H.   Publication and Distribution of Information. *ARIST* 3, p. 31
Lancaster, F. Wilfrid
    Lancaster, F. Wilfrid; Gillespie, Constantine J.   Design and Evaluation of Information Systems. *ARIST* 5, p. 33
Landau, Herbert B.
    Landau, Herbert B.   Document Dissemination. *ARIST* 4, p. 229
Language
    Bobrow, D.G.; Fraser, J.B.; Quillian, M.R.   Automated Language Processing. *ARIST* 2, p. 161
    Damerau, Fred J.   Automated Language Processing. *ARIST* 11, p. 107
    Kay, Martin; Sparck Jones, Karen.   Automated Language Processing. *ARIST* 6, p. 141
    Montgomery, Christine A.   Automated Language Processing. *ARIST* 4, p. 145
    Salton, Gerard.   Automated Language Processing. *ARIST* 3, p. 169
    Simmons, Robert F.   Automated Language Processing. *ARIST* 1, p. 137
    Walker, Donald E.   Automated Language Processing. *ARIST* 8, p. 69
Latin
    Saracevic, Tefko; Braga, Gilda; Quijano Solis, Alvaro.   Information Systems In Latin America. *ARIST* 14, p. 249

Law
>   Beard, Joseph J.   Information Systems Application in Law. *ARIST* 6,
>   p. 369

Legislative
>   Chartrand, Robert L.   Information Science in the Legislative Process.
>   *ARIST* 11, p. 299

Leimkuhler, Ferdinand F.
>   Leimkuhler, Ferdinand F.; Billingsley, Alice.   Library and Information
>   Center Management. *ARIST* 7, p. 499

Levy, Richard P.
>   Levy, Richard P.; Cammarn, Maxine R.   Information Systems Applica-
>   tions in Medicine. *ARIST* 3, p. 397

Libraries
>   Brown, Patricia L.; Jones, Shirli O.   Document Retrieval and Dissemi-
>   nation in Libraries and Information Centers. *ARIST* 3, p. 263
>
>   Buckland, Michael K.   The Management of Libraries and Information
>   Centers. *ARIST* 9, p. 335
>
>   Griffin, Hillis L.   Automation of Technical Processes in Libraries.
>   *ARIST* 3, p. 241
>
>   Markuson, Barbara Evans.   Automation in Libraries and Information
>   Centers. *ARIST* 2, p. 255

Library
>   Alper, Bruce H.   Library Automation. *ARIST* 10, p. 199
>
>   Avram, Henriette.   Library Automation. *ARIST* 6, p. 171
>
>   Bierman, Kenneth J.   Library Automation. *ARIST* 9, p. 123
>
>   Black, Donald V.; Farley, Earl A.   Library Automation. *ARIST* 1, p.
>   273
>
>   Grosch, Audrey A.   Library Automation. *ARIST* 11, p. 225
>
>   Holm, Bart E.   Library and Information Center Management. *ARIST*
>   5, p. 353
>
>   Kilgour, Frederick G.   Library Automation. *ARIST* 4, p. 305
>
>   Leimkuhler, Ferdinand F.; Billingsley, Alice.   Library and Information
>   Center Management. *ARIST* 7, p. 499
>
>   Martin, Susan K.   Library Automation. *ARIST* 7, p. 243
>
>   Miller, Ronald F.; Tighe, Ruth L.   Library and Information Networks.
>   *ARIST* 9, p. 173
>
>   Murdock, John; Sherrod, John.   Library and Information Center Man-
>   agement. *ARIST* 11, p. 381
>
>   Olson, Edwin E.; Shank, Russell; Olsen, Harold A.   Library and Infor-
>   mation Networks. *ARIST* 7, p. 279
>
>   Palmour, Vernon E.; Roderer, Nancy K.   Library Resource Sharing
>   through Networks. *ARIST* 13, p. 147
>
>   Parker, Ralph H.   Library Automation. *ARIST* 5, p. 193
>
>   Pearson, Karl M., Jr.   Minicomputers in the Library. *ARIST* 10, p. 139

Library (Continued)

Reed, Mary Jane Pobst; Vrooman, Hugh T.   Library Automation. *ARIST* 14, p. 193

Simmons, Peter.   Library Automation. *ARIST* 8, p. 167

Wasserman, Paul; Daniel, Evelyn.   Library and Information Center Management. *ARIST* 4, p. 405

Licklider, J.C.R.

Licklider, J.C.R. Man-Computer Communication. *ARIST* 3, p. 201

Lin, Nan

Lin, Nan; Garvey, William D.   Information Needs and Uses. *ARIST* 7, p. 5

Lipetz, Ben-Ami

Lipetz, Ben-Ami.   Information Needs and Uses. *ARIST* 5, p. 3

Liston, David M., Jr.

Liston, David M., Jr.; Howder, Murray L.   Subject Analysis. *ARIST* 12, p. 81

Local

Hearle, Edward F.R.   Information Systems in State and Local Governments. *ARIST* 5, p. 325

Long, Philip L.

Long, Philip L.   Computer Technology-An Update. *ARIST* 11, p. 211

Lorenz, John G.

Lorenz, John G.   International Transfer of Information. *ARIST* 4, p. 379

Luedke, James A., Jr.

Luedke, James A., Jr.; Kovacs, Gabor J.; Fried, John B.   Numeric Data Bases and Systems. *ARIST* 12, p. 119

Machine

Davis, Ruth M.   Man-Machine Communication. *ARIST* 1, p. 221

Gechman, Marvin C.   Generation and Use of Machine-Readable Bibliographic Data Bases. *ARIST* 7, p. 323

Meadow, Charles T.; Meadow, Harriet R.   Organization, Maintenance and Search of Machine Files. *ARIST* 5, p. 169

Mills, R.G.   Man-Machine Communiation and Problem Solving. *ARIST* 2, p. 223

Schipma, Peter B.   Generation and Uses of Machine-Readable Data Bases. *ARIST* 10, p. 237

Shoffner, Ralph M.   Organization, Maintenance and Search of Machine Files. *ARIST* 3, p. 137

Wilde, Daniel U.   Generation and Use of Machine-Readable Data Bases. *ARIST* 11, p. 267

Williams, Martha E.   Use of Machine-Readable Data Bases. *ARIST* 9, p. 221

Magnino, Joseph J., Jr.
  Magnino, Joseph J., Jr.   Document Retrieval and Dissemination. *ARIST*
    6, p. 219
Maintenance
  Meadow, Charles T.; Meadow, Harriet R.   Organization, Maintenance
    and Search of Machine Files. *ARIST* 5, p. 169
  Shoffner, Ralph M.   Organization, Maintenance and Search of Machine
    Files. *ARIST* 3, p. 137
Man
  Davis, Ruth M.   Man-Machine Communication. *ARIST* 1, p. 221
  Licklider, J.C.R.   Man-Computer Communication. *ARIST* 3, p. 201
  Mills, R.G.   Man-Machine Communication and Problem Solving. *ARIST*
    2, p. 223
Management
  Buckland, Michael K.   The Management of Libraries and Information
    Centers. *ARIST* 9, p. 335
  Holm, Bart E.   Library and Information Center Management. *ARIST* 5,
    p. 353
  Huffenberger, Michael A.; Wigington, Ronald L.   Database Manage-
    ment Systems. *ARIST* 14, p. 153
  Leimkuhler, Ferdinand F.; Billingsley, Alice.   Library and Information
    Center Management. *ARIST* 7, p. 499
  Minker, Jack; Sable, Jerome.   File Organization and Data Management.
    ARIST 2, p. 123
  Murdock, John; Sherrod, John.   Library and Information Center Man-
    agement. *ARIST* 11, p. 381
  Senko, Michael E.   File Organization and Management Information
    Systems. *ARIST* 4, p. 111
  Wasserman, Paul; Daniel, Evelyn.   Library and Information Center
    Management. *ARIST* 4, p. 405
  Weiss, Stanley D.   Management Information Systems. *ARIST* 5, p. 299
Marketing
  Freeman, James E.; Katz, Ruth M.   Information Marketing. *ARIST* 13,
    p. 37
Markuson, Barbara Evans
  Markuson, Barbara Evans.   Automation in Libraries and Information
    Centers. *ARIST* 2, p. 255
Marron, Beatrice
  Marron, Beatrice; Fife, Dennis.   Online Systems-Techniques and
    Services. *ARIST* 11, p. 163
Martin, Susan K.
  Martin, Susan K.   Library Automation. *ARIST* 7, p. 243
Martin, Thomas H.
  Martin, Thomas H.   The User Interface in Interactive Systems. *ARIST*
    8, p. 203

Martyn, John
    Martyn, John.   Information Needs and Uses. *ARIST* 9, p. 3
McCarn, Davis B.
    McCarn, Davis Б.   Online Systems-Techniques and Services. *ARIST* 13,
        p. 85
McFarland, Anne S.
    Shera, Jesse H.; McFarland, Anne S.   Professional Aspects of Informa-
        tion Science and Technology. *ARIST* 4, p. 439
McGill, Michael J.
    McGill, Michael J.; Huitfeldt, Jennifer.   Experimental Techniques of
        Information Retrieval. *ARIST* 14, p. 93
Meadow, Charles T.
    Meadow, Charles T.; Meadow, Harriet R.   Organization, Maintenance
        and Search of Machine Files. *ARIST* 5, p. 169
Meadow, Harriet R.
    Meadow, Charles T.; Meadow, Harriet R.   Organization, Maintenance
        and Search of Machine Files. *ARIST* 5, p. 169
Medicine
    Caceres, Cesar A.; Weihrer, Anna Lea; Pulliam, Robert.   Information
        Science Applications in Medicine. *ARIST* 6, p. 325
    Levy, Richard P.; Cammarn, Maxine R.   Information Systems Applica-
        tions in Medicine. *ARIST* 3, p. 397
    Spring, William C., Jr.   Applications in Medicine. *ARIST* 2, p. 311
Menzel, Herbert
    Menzel, Herbert.   Information Needs and Uses in Science and Tech-
        nology. *ARIST* 1, p. 41
Michener, James C.
    van Dam, Andries; Michener, James C.   Hardware Developments and
        Product Announcements. *ARIST* 2, p. 187
Mick, Colin K.
    Mick, Colin K.   Cost Analysis of Information Systems and Services.
        ARIST 14, p. 37
Microfilm
    Teplitz, Arthur.   Microfilm and Reprography. *ARIST* 5, p. 87
Microform
    Ballou, Hubbard W.   Microform Technology. *ARIST* 8, p. 121
    Nelson, Carl E.   Microform Technology. *ARIST* 6, p. 77
    Veaner, Allen B.   Reprography and Microform Technology. *ARIST* 4,
        p. 175
Micrographics
    Spigai, Frances G.; Butler, Brett B.   Micrographics. *ARIST* 11, p. 59
Miller, Ronald F.
    Miller, Ronald F.; Tighe, Ruth L.   Library and Information Networks.
        ARIST 9, p. 173

Mills, R.G.
    Mills, R.G.   Man-Machine Communication and Problem Solving. *ARIST*
        2, p. 223
Minicomputers
    Pearson, Karl M., Jr.   Minicomputers in the Library. *ARIST* 10, p. 139
Minker, Jack
    Minker, Jack; Sable, Jerome.   File Organization and Data Management.
        ARIST 2, p. 123
Moll, Joy K.
    Narin, Francis; Moll, Joy K.   Bibliometrics. *ARIST* 12, p. 35
Montgomery, Christine A.
    Montgomery, Christine A.   Automated Language Processing. *ARIST* 4,
        p. 145
Montgomery, K. Leon
    Debons, Anthony; Montgomery, K. Leon.   Design and Evaluation of
        Information Systems. *ARIST* 9, p. 25
Moon, Robert D.
    Vinsonhaler, John F.; Moon, Robert D.   Information Systems Appli-
        cations in Education. *ARIST* 8, p. 277
Murdock, John
    Murdock, John; Sherrod, John.   Library and Information Center Man-
        agement. *ARIST* 11, p. 381
Narin, Francis
    Narin, Francis; Moll, Joy K.   Bibliometrics. *ARIST* 12, p. 35
National
    Aines, Andrew A.; Day, Melvin S.   National Planning of Information
        Services. *ARIST* 10, p. 3
    Berninger, Douglas E.; Adkinson, Burton W.   Interaction between the
        Public and Private Sectors in National Information Programs.
        ARIST 13, p. 3
    Hammer, Donald P.   National Information Issues and Trends. *ARIST*
        2, p. 385
    Holm, Bart E.   National Issues and Problems. *ARIST* 11, p. 5
    Sherrod, John.   National Information Issues and Trends. *ARIST* 1, p.
        337
Needs
    Allen, Thomas J.   Information Needs and Uses. *ARIST* 4, p. 3
    Crane, Diana.   Information Needs and Uses. *ARIST* 6, p. 3
    Crawford, Susan.   Information Needs and Uses. *ARIST* 13, p. 61
    Herner, Saul; Herner, Mary.   Information Needs and Uses in Science
        and Technology. *ARIST* 2, p. 1
    Lin, Nan; Garvey, William D.   Information Needs and Uses. *ARIST* 7,
        p. 5
    Lipetz, Ben-Ami.   Information Needs and Uses. *ARIST* 5, p. 3

Needs (Continued)

Martyn, John.   Information Needs and Uses. *ARIST* 9, p. 3

Menzel, Herbert.   Information Needs and Uses in Science and Technology. *ARIST* 1, p. 41

Paisley, William J.   Information Needs and Uses. *ARIST* 3, p. 1

Nelson, Carl E.

Nelson, Carl E.   Microform Technology. *ARIST* 6, p. 77

Network

Samuelson, Kjell.   International Information Transfer and Network Communication. *ARIST* 6, p. 277

Networks

Becker, Joseph; Olsen, Wallace C.   Information Networks. *ARIST* 3, p. 289

Bunch, Steve R.; Alsberg, Peter A.   Computer Communication Networks. *ARIST* 12, p. 183

Miller, Ronald F.; Tighe, Ruth L.   Library and Information Networks. *ARIST* 9, p. 173

Olson, Edwin E.; Shank, Russell; Olsen, Harold A.   Library and Information Networks. *ARIST* 7, p. 279

Overhage, Carl F. J.   Information Networks. *ARIST* 4, p. 339

Palmour, Vernon E.; Roderer, Nancy K.   Library Resource Sharing through Networks. *ARIST* 13, p. 147

Tomberg, Alex.   European Information Networks. *ARIST* 12, p. 219

New

ARIST Staff.   New Hardware Developments. *ARIST* 1, p. 191

Numeric

Luedke, James A., Jr.; Kovacs, Gabor J.; Fried, John B.   Numeric Data Bases and Systems. *ARIST* 12, p. 119

Olsen, Harold A.

Olson, Edwin E.; Shank, Russell; Olsen, Harold A.   Library and Information Networks. *ARIST* 7, p. 279

Olsen, Wallace C.

Becker, Joseph; Olsen, Wallace C.   Information Networks. *ARIST* 3, p. 289

Olson, Edwin E.

Olson, Edwin E.; Shank, Russell; Olsen, Harold A.   Library and Information Networks. *ARIST* 7, p. 279

Online

Marron, Beatrice; Fife, Dennis.   Online Systems-Techniques and Services. *ARIST* 11, p. 163

McCarn, Davis B.   Online Systems-Techniques and Services. *ARIST* 13, p. 85

Wanger, Judith.   Education and Training for Online Systems. *ARIST* 14, p. 219

Organization
> Climenson, W. Douglas.   File Organization and Search Techniques. *ARIST* 1, p. 107
>
> Meadow, Charles T.; Meadow, Harriet R.   Organization, Maintenance and Search of Machine Files. *ARIST* 5, p. 169
>
> Minker, Jack; Sable, Jerome.   File Organization and Data Management. *ARIST* 2, p. 123
>
> Prywes, Noah S.; Smith, Diane Pirog.   Organization of Information. *ARIST* 7, p. 103
>
> Senko, Michael E.   File Organization and Management Information Systems. *ARIST* 4, p. 111
>
> Shoffner, Ralph M.   Organization, Maintenance and Search of Machine Files. *ARIST* 3, p. 137

Organizations
> Adams, Scott; Werdel, Judith A.   Cooperation in Information Activities through International Organizations. *ARIST* 10, p. 303

Overhage, Carl F.J.
> Overhage, Carl F.J.   Information Networks. *ARIST* 4, p. 339

Paisley, William J.
> Paisley, William J.   Information Needs and Uses. *ARIST* 3, p. 1

Palmour, Vernon E.
> Palmour, Vernon E.; Roderer, Nancy K.   Library Resource Sharing through Networks. *ARIST* 13, p. 147

Park, Margaret K.
> Park, Margaret K.   Bibliographic and Information Processing Standards. *ARIST* 12, p. 59

Parker, Edwin B.
> Parker, Edwin B.   Information and Society. *ARIST* 8, p. 345

Parker, Ralph H.
> Parker, Ralph H.   Library Automation. *ARIST* 5, p. 193

Parkins, Phyllis V.
> Parkins, Phyllis V.; Kennedy, H.E.   Secondary Information Services. *ARIST* 6, p. 247

Pearson, Karl M., Jr.
> Pearson, Karl M., Jr.   Minicomputers in the Library. *ARIST* 10, p. 139

Planning
> Aines, Andrew A.; Day, Melvin S.   National Planning of Information Services. *ARIST* 10, p. 3

Primary
> Gannet, Elwood K.   Primary Publication Systems and Services. *ARIST* 8, p. 243

Principles
> Wyllys, Ronald E.   System Design-Principles and Techniques. *ARIST* 14, p. 3

Privacy
>   Carlson, Walter M.   Privacy. *ARIST* 12, p. 279
Private
>   Berninger, Douglas E.; Adkinson, Burton W.   Interaction between the
>   Public and Private Sectors in National Information Programs. *ARIST*
>   13, p. 3
Problem
>   Mills, R.G.   Man-Machine Communication and Problem Solving. *ARIST*
>   2, p. 223
Problems
>   Holm, Bart E.   National Issues and Problems. *ARIST* 11, p. 5
Process
>   Chartrand, Robert L.   Information Science in the Legislative Process.
>   *ARIST* 11, p. 299
Processes
>   Griffin, Hillis L.   Automation of Technical Processes in Libraries. *ARIST*
>   3, p. 241
Processing
>   Bobrow, D.G.; Fraser, J.B.; Quillian, M.R.   Automated Language Pro-
>   cessing. *ARIST* 2, p. 161
>   Damerau, Fred J.   Automated Language Processing. *ARIST* 11, p. 107
>   Kay, Martin; Sparck Jones, Karen.   Automated Language Processing.
>   *ARIST* 6, p. 141
>   Montgomery, Christine A.   Automated Language Processing. *ARIST* 4,
>   p. 145
>   Park, Margaret K.   Bibliographic and Information Processing Standards.
>   *ARIST* 12, p. 59
>   Salton, Gerard.   Automated Language Processing. *ARIST* 3, p. 169
>   Simmons, Robert F.   Automated Language Processing. *ARIST* 1, p.
>   137
>   Walker, Donald E.   Automated Language Processing. *ARIST* 8, p. 69
>   Wilson, John H., Jr.   Costs, Budgeting, and Economics of Information
>   Processing. *ARIST* 7, p. 39
Product
>   van Dam, Andries; Michener, James C.   Hardware Developments and
>   Product Announcements. *ARIST* 2, p. 187
Professional
>   Atherton, Pauline; Greer, Roger.   Professional Aspects of Information
>   Science and Technology. *ARIST* 3, p. 329
>   Farradane, J.   Professional Aspects of Information Science and Tech-
>   nology. *ARIST* 6, p. 399
>   Harvey, John F.   Professional Aspects of Information Science and
>   Technology. *ARIST* 2, p. 419

Professional (Continued)

    Shera, Jesse H.; McFarland, Anne S.   Professional Aspects of Information Science and Technology. *ARIST* 4, p. 439

    Taylor, Robert S.   Professional Aspects of Information Science and Technology. *ARIST* 1, p. 15

Programs

    Berninger, Douglas E.; Adkinson, Burton W.   Interaction between the Public and Private Sectors in National Information Programs. *ARIST* 13, p. 3

Progress

    Hersey, David F.   Information Systems for Research in Progress. *ARIST* 13, p. 263

Prywes, Noah S.

    Prywes, Noah S.; Smith, Diane Pirog.   Organization of Information. *ARIST* 7, p. 103

Public

    Berninger, Douglas E.; Adkinson, Burton W.   Interaction between the Public and Private Sectors in National Information Programs. *ARIST* 13, p. 3

Publication

    American Institute of Physics Staff.   Techniques for Publication and Distribution of Information. *ARIST* 2, p. 339

    Doebler, Paul D.   Publication and Distribution of Information. *ARIST* 5, p. 223

    Gannet, Elwood K.   Primary Publication Systems and Services. *ARIST* 8, p. 243

    Kuney, Joseph H.   Publication and Distribution of Information. *ARIST* 3, p. 31

Publishing

    Terrant, Seldon W.   The Computer and Publishing. *ARIST* 10, p. 273

Pulliam, Robert

    Caceres, Cesar A.; Weihrer, Anna Lea; Pulliam, Robert.   Information Science Applications in Medicine. *ARIST* 6, p. 325

Quijano Solis, Alvaro

    Saracevic, Tefko; Braga, Gilda; Quijano Solis, Alvaro.   Information Systems in Latin America. *ARIST* 14, p. 249

Quillian, M.R.

    Bobrow, D.G.; Fraser, J.B.; Quillian, M.R.   Automated Language Processing. *ARIST* 2, p. 161

Raben, Joseph

    Raben, Joseph; Widmann, R.L.   Information Systems Applications in the Humanities. *ARIST* 7, p. 439

Raper, Diane

    Hindle, Anthony; Raper, Diane.   The Economics of Information. *ARIST* 11, p. 27

Readable

    Gechman, Marvin C.   Generation and Use of Machine-Readable Bibliographic Data Bases. *ARIST* 7, p. 323

    Schipma, Peter B.   Generation and Uses of Machine-Readable Data Bases. *ARIST* 10, p. 237

    Wilde, Daniel U.   Generation and Use of Machine-Readable Data Bases. *ARIST* 11, p. 267

    Williams, Martha E.   Use of Machine-Readable Data Bases. *ARIST* 9, p. 221

Reed, Mary Jane Pobst

    Reed, Mary Jane Pobst; Vrooman, Hugh T.   Library Automation. *ARIST* 14, p. 193

Rees, Alan M.

    Rees, Alan M.   Evaluation of Information Systems and Services. *ARIST* 2, p. 63

Representation

    Artandi, Susan.   Document Description and Representation. *ARIST* 5, p. 143

    Batten, William E.   Document Description and Representation. *ARIST* 8, p. 43

    Harris, Jessica L.   Document Description and Representation. *ARIST* 9, p. 81

    Richmond, Phyllis A.   Document Description and Representation. *ARIST* 7, p. 73

    Vickery, Brian C.   Document Description and Representation. *ARIST* 6, p. 113

Reprography

    Teplitz, Arthur.   Microfilm and Reprography. *ARIST* 5, p. 87

    Veaner, Allen B.   Reprography and Microform Technology. *ARIST* 4, p. 175

Research

    Hersey, David F.   Information Systems for Research in Progress. *ARIST* 13, p. 263

Resource

    Palmour, Vernon E.; Roderer, Nancy K.   Library Resource Sharing through Networks. *ARIST* 13, p. 147

Retrieval

    Berul, Lawrence H.   Document Retrieval. *ARIST* 4, p. 203

    Brandhorst, Wesley T.; Eckert, Philip F.   Document Retrieval and Dissemination Systems. *ARIST* 7, p. 379

    Brown, Patricia L.; Jones, Shirli O.   Document Retrieval and Dissemination in Libraries and Information Centers. *ARIST* 3, p. 263

    Hollaar, Lee A.   Unconventional Computer Architectures for Information Retrieval. *ARIST* 14, p. 129

Retrieval (Continued)

Magnino, Joseph J., Jr.   Document Retrieval and Dissemination. *ARIST* 6, p. 219

McGill, Michael J.; Huitfeldt, Jennifer.   Experimental Techniques of Information Retrieval. *ARIST* 14, p. 93

Summit, Roger K.; Firschein, Oscar.   Document Retrieval Systems and Techniques. *ARIST* 9, p. 285

Review

Cuadra, Carlos A.   Introduction to the ADI Annual Review. *ARIST* 1, p. 1

Richmond, Phyllis A.

Richmond, Phyllis A.   Document Description and Representation. *ARIST* 7, p. 73

Roderer, Nancy K.

Palmour, Vernon E.; Roderer, Nancy K.   Library Resource Sharing through Networks. *ARIST* 13, p. 147

Rush, James E.

Rush, James E.   Handling Chemical Structure Information. *ARIST* 13, p. 209

Sable, Jerome

Minker, Jack; Sable, Jerome.   File Organization and Data Management. *ARIST* 2, p. 123

Salton, Gerard

Salton, Gerard.   Automated Language Processing. *ARIST* 3, p. 169

Samuelson, Kjell

Samuelson, Kjell.   International Information Transfer and Network Communication. *ARIST* 6, p. 277

Saracevic, Tefko

Saracevic, Tefko; Braga, Gilda; Quijano Solis, Alvaro.   Information Systems In Latin America. *ARIST* 14, p. 249

Schipma, Peter B.

Schipma, Peter B.   Generation and Uses of Machine-Readable Data Bases. *ARIST* 10, p. 237

Schmierer, Helen F.

Schmierer, Helen F.   Bibliographic Standards. *ARIST* 10, p. 105

Science

Atherton, Pauline; Greer, Roger.   Professional Aspects of Information Science and Technology. *ARIST* 3, p. 329

Caceres, Cesar A.; Weihrer, Anna Lea; Pulliam, Robert.   Information Science Applications in Medicine. *ARIST* 6, p. 325

Chartrand, Robert L.   Information Science in the Legislative Process. *ARIST* 11, p. 299

Farradane, J.   Professional Aspects of Information Science and Technology. *ARIST* 6, p. 399

Science (Continued)

> Harmon, Glynn. Information Science Education and Training. *ARIST* 11, p. 347

> Harvey, John F. Professional Aspects of Information Science and Technology. *ARIST* 2, p. 419

> Herner, Saul; Herner, Mary. Information Needs and Uses in Science and Technology. *ARIST* 2, p. 1

> Jahoda, Gerald. Education for Information Science. *ARIST* 8, p. 321

> Keenan, Stella. Abstracting and Indexing Services in Science and Technology. *ARIST* 4, p. 273

> Menzel, Herbert. Information Needs and Uses in Science and Technology. *ARIST* 1, p. 41

> Shera, Jesse H.; Cleveland, Donald B. History and Foundations of Information Science. *ARIST* 12, p. 249

> Shera, Jesse H.; McFarland, Anne S. Professional Aspects of Information Science and Technology. *ARIST* 4, p. 439

> Taylor, Robert S. Professional Aspects of Information Science and Technology. *ARIST* 1, p. 15

> Zunde, Pranas; Gehl, John. Empirical Foundations of Information Science. *ARIST* 14, p. 67

Search

> Climenson, W. Douglas. File Organization and Search Techniques. *ARIST* 1, p. 107

> Meadow, Charles T.; Meadow, Harriet R. Organization, Maintenance and Search of Machine Files. *ARIST* 5, p. 169

> Shoffner, Ralph M. Organization, Maintenance and Search of Machine Files. *ARIST* 3, p. 137

Secondary

> Bearman, Toni Carbo. Secondary Information Systems and Services. *ARIST* 13, p. 179

> Parkins, Phyllis V.; Kennedy, H.E. Secondary Information Services. *ARIST* 6, p. 247

Sectors

> Berninger, Douglas E.; Adkinson, Burton W. Interaction between the Public and Private Sectors in National Information Programs. *ARIST* 13, p. 3

Selective

> Housman, Edward M.
> Selective Dissemination of Information. *ARIST* 8, p. 221

Senko, Michael E.

> Senko, Michael E. File Organization and Management Information Systems. *ARIST* 4, p. 111

Services

> Aines, Andrew A.; Day, Melvin S. National Planning of Information Services. *ARIST* 10, p. 3

Services (Continued)

Bearman, Toni Carbo.   Secondary Information Systems and Services. *ARIST* 13, p. 179

Borko, Harold.   Design of Information Systems and Services. *ARIST* 2, p. 35

Gannet, Elwood K.   Primary Publication Systems and Services. *ARIST* 8, p. 243

Keenan, Stella.   Abstracting and Indexing Services in Science and Technology. *ARIST* 4, p. 273

Marron, Beatrice; Fife, Dennis.   Online Systems-Techniques and Services. *ARIST* 11, p. 163

McCarn, Davis B.   Online Systems-Techniques and Services. *ARIST* 13, p. 85

Mick, Colin K.   Cost Analysis of Information Systems and Services. *ARIST* 14, p. 37

Parkins, Phyllis V.; Kennedy, H.E.   Secondary Information Services. *ARIST* 6, p. 247

Rees, Alan M.   Evaluation of Information Systems and Services. *ARIST* 2, p. 63

Simpson, G.S., Jr.; Flanagan, Carolyn.   Information Centers and Services. *ARIST* 1, p. 305

Shank, Russell

Olson, Edwin E.; Shank, Russell; Olsen, Harold A.   Library and Information Networks. *ARIST* 7, p. 279

Sharing

Palmour, Vernon E.; Roderer, Nancy K.   Library Resource Sharing through Networks. *ARIST* 13, p. 147

Sharp, John R.

Sharp, John R.   Content Analysis, Specification, and Control. *ARIST* 2, p. 87

Shera, Jesse H.

Shera, Jesse H.; Cleveland, Donald B.   History and Foundations of Information Science. *ARIST* 12, p. 249

Shera, Jesse H.; McFarland, Anne S.   Professional Aspects of Information Science and Technology. *ARIST* 4, p. 439

Sherrod, John

Murdock, John; Sherrod, John.   Library and Information Center Management. *ARIST* 11, p. 381

Sherrod, John.   National Information Issues and Trends. *ARIST* 1, p. 337

Shoffner, Ralph M.

Shoffner, Ralph M.   Organization, Maintenance and Search of Machine Files. *ARIST* 3, p. 137

Silberman, Harry F.

Silberman, Harry F.; Filep, Robert T.   Information Systems Applications in Education. *ARIST* 3, p. 357

Simmons, Peter
> Simmons, Peter. Library Automation. *ARIST* 8, p. 167
Simmons, Robert F.
> Simmons, Robert F. Automated Language Processing. *ARIST* 1, p. 137
Simms, Robert L., Jr.
> Simms, Robert L., Jr.; Fuchs, Edward. Communications Technology. *ARIST* 5, p. 113
Simpson, G.S., Jr.
> Simpson, G.S., Jr.; Flanagan, Carolyn. Information Centers and Services. *ARIST* 1, p. 305
Smith, Diane Pirog
> Prywes, Noah S.; Smith, Diane Pirog. Organization of Information. *ARIST* 7, p. 103
Society
> Parker, Edwin B. Information and Society. *ARIST* 8, p. 345
Solving
> Mills, R.G. Man-Machine Communication and Problem Solving. *ARIST* 2, p. 223
Sparck Jones, Karen
> Kay, Martin; Sparck Jones, Karen. Automated Language Processing. *ARIST* 6, p. 141
Specification
> Baxendale, Phyllis. Content Analysis, Specification, and Control. *ARIST* 1, p. 71
> Fairthorne, Robert A. Content Analysis, Specification, and Control. *ARIST* 4, p. 73
> Sharp, John R. Content Analysis, Specification, and Control. *ARIST* 2, p. 87
> Taulbee, Orrin E. Content Analysis, Specification, and Control. *ARIST* 3, p. 105
Spence, A. Michael
> Spence, A. Michael. An Economist's View of Information. *ARIST* 9, p. 57
Spigai, Frances G.
> Spigai, Frances G.; Butler, Brett B. Micrographics. *ARIST* 11, p. 59
Spring, William C., Jr.
> Spring, William C., Jr. Applications in Medicine. *ARIST* 2, p. 311
Standards
> Park, Margaret K. Bibliographic and Information Processing Standards. *ARIST* 12, p. 59
> Schmierer, Helen F. Bibliographic Standards. *ARIST* 10, p. 105
State
> Hearle, Edward F.R. Information Systems in State and Local Governments. *ARIST* 5, p. 325

Stern, Barrie T.
    Stern, Barrie T.   Evaluation and Design of Bibliographic Data Bases.
        ARIST 12, p. 3
Structure
    Rush, James E.   Handling Chemical Structure Information. *ARIST* 13,
        p. 209
Structures
    Chung-Shu, Yang.   Design and Evaluation of File Structures. *ARIST*
        13, p. 125
Subject
    Liston, David M., Jr.; Howder, Murray L.   Subject Analysis. *ARIST* 12,
        p. 81
Summit, Roger K.
    Summit, Roger K.; Firschein, Oscar.   Document Retrieval Systems and
        Techniques. *ARIST* 9, p. 285
Swanson, Rowena Weiss
    Swanson, Rowena Weiss.   Design and Evaluation of Information Sys-
        tems. *ARIST* 10, p. 43
System
    Baruch, Jordan J.   Information System Applications. *ARIST* 1, p. 255
    Blumstein, Alfred.   Information Systems Applications in the Criminal
        Justice System. *ARIST* 7, p. 471
    Wyllys, Ronald E.   System Design-Principles and Techniques. *ARIST*
        14, p. 3
Systems
    Beard, Joseph J.   Information Systems Application in Law. *ARIST* 6,
        p. 369
    Bearman, Toni Carbo.   Secondary Information Systems and Services.
        ARIST 13, p. 179
    Bennett, John L.   The User Interface in Interactive Systems. *ARIST* 7,
        p. 159
    Blumstein, Alfred.   Information Systems Applications in the Criminal
        Justice System. *ARIST* 7, p. 471
    Borko, Harold.   Design of Information Systems and Services. *ARIST* 2,
        p. 35
    Bourne, Charles P.   Evaluation of Indexing Systems. *ARIST* 1, p. 171
    Brandhorst, Wesley T.; Eckert, Philip F.   Document Retrieval and Dis-
        semination Systems. *ARIST* 7, p. 379
    Cleverdon, Cyril W.   Design and Evaluation of Information Systems.
        ARIST 6, p. 41
    Debons, Anthony; Montgomery, K. Leon.   Design and Evaluation of
        Information Systems. *ARIST* 9, p. 25
    Gannet, Elwood K.   Primary Publication Systems and Services. *ARIST*
        8, p. 243
    Grattidge, Walter; Creps, John E., Jr.   Information Systems in Engineer-
        ing. *ARIST* 13, p. 297

Systems (Continued)

Hearle, Edward F.R. Information Systems in State and Local Governments. *ARIST* 5, p. 325

Hersey, David F. Information Systems for Research in Progress. *ARIST* 13, p. 263

Huffenberger, Michael A.; Wigington, Ronald L. Database Management Systems. *ARIST* 14, p. 153

Katter, Robert V. Design and Evaluation of Information Systems. *ARIST* 3, p. 31

King, Donald W. Design and Evaluation of Information Systems. *ARIST* 3, p. 61

Lancaster, F. Wilfrid; Gillespie, Constantine J. Design and Evaluation of Information Systems. *ARIST* 5, p. 33

Levy, Richard P.; Cammarn, Maxine R. Information Systems Applications in Medicine. *ARIST* 3, p. 397

Luedke, James A., Jr.; Kovacs, Gabor J.; Fried, John B. Numeric Data Bases and Systems. *ARIST* 12, p. 119

Marron, Beatrice; Fife, Dennis. Online Systems-Techniques and Services. *ARIST* 11, p. 163

Martin, Thomas H. The User Interface in Interactive Systems. *ARIST* 8, p. 203

McCarn, Davis B. Online Systems-Techniques and Services. *ARIST* 13, p. 85

Mick, Colin K. Cost Analysis of Information Systems and Services. *ARIST* 14, p. 37

Raben, Joseph; Widmann, R.L. Information Systems Applications in the Humanities. *ARIST* 7, p. 439

Rees, Alan M. Evaluation of Information Systems and Services. *ARIST* 2, p. 63

Saracevic, Tefko; Braga, Gilda; Quijano Solis, Alvaro. Information Systems In Latin America. *ARIST* 14, p. 249

Senko, Michael E. File Organization and Management Information Systems. *ARIST* 4, p. 111

Silberman, Harry F.; Filep, Robert T. Information Systems Applications in Education. *ARIST* 3, p. 357

Summit, Roger K.; Firschein, Oscar. Document Retrieval Systems and Techniques. *ARIST* 9, p. 285

Swanson, Rowena Weiss. Design and Evaluation of Information Systems. *ARIST* 10, p. 43

Tate, F.A. Handling Chemical Compounds in Information Systems. *ARIST* 2, p. 285

Vinsonhaler, John F.; Moon, Robert D. Information Systems Applications in Education. *ARIST* 8, p. 277

Wanger, Judith. Education and Training for Online Systems. *ARIST* 14, p. 219

Weiss, Stanley D. Management Information Systems. *ARIST* 5, p. 299

Tate, F.A.
> Tate, F.A. Handling Chemical Compounds in Information Systems. *ARIST* 2, p. 285

Taulbee, Orrin E.
> Taulbee, Orrin E. Content Analysis, Specification, and Control. *ARIST* 3, p. 105

Taylor, Robert S.
> Taylor, Robert S. Professional Aspects of Information Science and Technology. *ARIST* 1, p. 15

Technical
> Griffin, Hillis L. Automation of Technical Processes in Libraries. *ARIST* 3, p. 241

Techniques
> American Institute of Physics Staff. Techniques for Publication and Distribution of Information. *ARIST* 2, p. 339

> Climenson, W. Douglas. File Organization and Search Techniques. *ARIST* 1, p. 107

> Marron, Beatrice; Fife, Dennis. Online Systems-Techniques and Services. *ARIST* 11, p. 163

> McCarn, Davis B. Online Systems-Techniques and Services. *ARIST* 13, p. 85

> McGill, Michael J.; Huitfeldt, Jennifer. Experimental Techniques of Information Retrieval. *ARIST* 14, p. 93

> Summit, Roger K.; Firschein, Oscar. Document Retrieval Systems and Techniques. *ARIST* 9, p. 285

> Wyllys, Ronald E. System Design-Principles and Techniques. *ARIST* 14, p. 3

Technology
> Atherton, Pauline; Greer, Roger. Professional Aspects of Information Science and Technology. *ARIST* 3, p. 329

> Ballou, Hubbard W. Microform Technology. *ARIST* 8, p. 121

> Dunn, Donald A. Communications Technology. *ARIST* 10, p. 165

> Farradane, J. Professional Aspects of Information Science and Technology. *ARIST* 6, p. 399

> Harvey, John F. Professional Aspects of Information Science and Technology. *ARIST* 2, p. 419

> Herner, Saul; Herner, Mary. Information Needs and Uses in Science and Technology. *ARIST* 2, p. 1

> Huskey, Harry D. Computer Technology. *ARIST* 5, p. 73

> Keenan, Stella. Abstracting and Indexing Services in Science and Technology. *ARIST* 4, p. 273

> Long, Philip L. Computer Technology-An Update. *ARIST* 11, p. 211

> Menzel, Herbert. Information Needs and Uses in Science and Technology. *ARIST* 1, p. 41

> Nelson, Carl E. Microform Technology. *ARIST* 6, p. 77

Technology (Continued)

    Shera, Jesse H.; McFarland, Anne S.   Professional Aspects of Information Science and Technology. *ARIST* 4, p. 439

    Simms, Robert L., Jr.; Fuchs, Edward.   Communications Technology. *ARIST* 5, p. 113

    Taylor, Robert S.   Professional Aspects of Information Science and Technology. *ARIST* 1, p. 15

    Thompson, Charles W.N.   Technology Utilization. *ARIST* 10, p. 383

    Veaner, Allen B.   Reprography and Microform Technology. *ARIST* 4, p. 175

Teplitz, Arthur

    Teplitz, Arthur.   Microfilm and Reprography. *ARIST* 5, p. 87

Terrant, Seldon W.

    Terrant, Seldon W.   The Computer and Publishing. *ARIST* 10, p. 273

Thompson, Charles W.N.

    Thompson, Charles W.N.   Technology Utilization. *ARIST* 10, p. 383

Tighe, Ruth L.

    Miller, Ronald F.; Tighe, Ruth L.   Library and Information Networks. *ARIST* 9, p. 173

Tomberg, Alex

    Tomberg, Alex.   European Information Networks. *ARIST* 12, p. 219

Training

    Harmon, Glynn.   Information Science Education and Training. *ARIST* 11, p. 347

    Wanger, Judith.   Education and Training for Online Systems. *ARIST* 14, p. 219

Transfer

    Lorenz, John G.   International Transfer of Information. *ARIST* 4, p. 379

    Samuelson, Kjell.   International Information Transfer and Network Communication. *ARIST* 6, p. 277

Trends

    Hammer, Donald P.   National Information Issues and Trends. *ARIST* 2, p. 385

    Sherrod, John.   National Information Issues and Trends. *ARIST* 1, p. 337

Unconventional

    Hollaar, Lee A.   Unconventional Computer Architectures for Information Retrieval. *ARIST* 14, p. 129

Update

    Long, Philip L.   Computer Technology-An Update. *ARIST* 11, p. 211

Use

    Gechman, Marvin C.   Generation and Use of Machine-Readable Bibliographic Data Bases. *ARIST* 7, p. 323

    Wilde, Daniel U.   Generation and Use of Machine-Readable Data Bases. *ARIST* 11, p. 267

Use (Continued)

    Williams, Martha E.   Use of Machine-Readable Data Bases. *ARIST* 9,
        p. 221

User

    Bennett, John L.   The User Interface in Interactive Systems. *ARIST* 7,
        p. 159

    Martin, Thomas H.   The User Interface in Interactive Systems. *ARIST*
        8, p. 203

Uses

    Allen, Thomas J.   Information Needs and Uses. *ARIST* 4, p. 3

    Crane, Diana.   Information Needs and Uses. *ARIST* 6, p. 3

    Crawford, Susan.   Information Needs and Uses. *ARIST* 13, p. 61

    Herner, Saul; Herner, Mary.   Information Needs and Uses in Science
        and Technology. *ARIST* 2, p. 1

    Lin, Nan; Garvey, William D.   Information Needs and Uses. *ARIST* 7,
        p. 5

    Lipetz, Ben-Ami.   Information Needs and Uses. *ARIST* 5, p. 3

    Martyn, John.   Information Needs and Uses. *ARIST* 9, p. 3

    Menzel, Herbert.   Information Needs and Uses in Science and Tech-
        nology. *ARIST* 1, p. 41

    Paisley, William J.   Information Needs and Uses. *ARIST* 3, p. 1

    Schipma, Peter B.   Generation and Uses of Machine-Readable Data
        Bases. *ARIST* 10, p. 237

Utilization

    Thompson, Charles W.N.   Technology Utilization. *ARIST* 10, p. 383

van Dam, Andries

    van Dam, Andries; Michener, James C.   Hardware Developments and
        Product Announcements. *ARIST* 2, p. 187

Veaner, Allen B.

    Veaner, Allen B.   Reprography and Microform Technology. *ARIST* 4,
        p. 175

Vickery, Brian C.

    Vickery, Brian C.   Document Description and Representation. *ARIST*
        6, p. 113

Video

    Kletter, Richard C.; Hudson, Heather.   Video Cartridges and Cassettes.
        ARIST 7, p. 197

View

    Spence, A. Michael.   An Economist's View of Information. *ARIST* 9,
        p. 57

Vinsonhaler, John F.

    Vinsonhaler, John F.; Moon, Robert D.   Information Systems Applica-
        tions in Education. *ARIST* 8, p. 277

Vrooman, Hugh T.

    Reed, Mary Jane Pobst; Vrooman, Hugh T.   Library Automation.
        ARIST 14, p. 193

Walker, Donald E.
    Walker, Donald E.   Automated Language Processing. *ARIST* 8, p. 69
Wanger, Judith
    Wanger, Judith.   Education and Training for Online Systems. *ARIST* 14, p. 219
Wasserman, Paul
    Wasserman, Paul; Daniel, Evelyn.   Library and Information Center Management. *ARIST* 4, p. 405
Weihrer, Anna Lea
    Caceres, Cesar A.; Weihrer, Anna Lea; Pulliam, Robert.   Information Science Applications in Medicine. *ARIST* 6, p. 325
Weil, Ben H.
    Weil, Ben H.   Copyright Developments. *ARIST* 10, p. 359
Weiss, Stanley D.
    Weiss, Stanley D.   Management Information Systems. *ARIST* 5, p. 299
Wente, Van A.
    Wente, Van A.; Young, Gifford A.   Current Awareness and Dissemination. *ARIST* 5, p. 259
Werdel, Judith A.
    Adams, Scott; Werdel, Judith A.   Cooperation in Information Activities through International Organizations. *ARIST* 10, p. 303
Widmann, R.L.
    Raben, Joseph; Widmann, R.L.   Information Systems Applications in the Humanities. *ARIST* 7, p. 439
Wigington, Ronald L.
    Huffenberger, Michael A.; Wigington, Ronald L.   Database Management Systems. *ARIST* 14, p. 153
Wilde, Daniel U.
    Wilde, Daniel U.   Generation and Use of Machine-Readable Data Bases. *ARIST* 11, p. 267
Williams, Martha E.
    Williams, Martha E.   Use of Machine-Readable Data Bases. *ARIST* 9, p. 221
Wilson, John H., Jr.
    Wilson, John H., Jr.   Costs, Budgeting, and Economics of Information Processing. *ARIST* 7, p. 39
Wyllys, Ronald E.
    Wyllys, Ronald E.   System Design-Principles and Techniques. *ARIST* 14, p. 3
Young, Gifford A.
    Wente, Van A.; Young, Gifford A.   Current Awareness and Dissemination. *ARIST* 5, p. 259
Zunde, Pranas
    Zunde, Pranas; Gehl, John.   Empirical Foundations of Information Science. *ARIST* 14, p. 67